Ethical Approaches to Human Remains

Kirsty Squires · David Errickson ·
Nicholas Márquez-Grant
Editors

Ethical Approaches to Human Remains

A Global Challenge in Bioarchaeology and Forensic Anthropology

Editors
Kirsty Squires
School of Law, Policing and Forensics
Staffordshire University, Science Centre
Stoke-on-Trent, UK

Nicholas Márquez-Grant
Defence Academy of the United Kingdom
Cranfield Forensic Institute, Cranfield
University
Shrivenham, UK

David Errickson
Defence Academy of the United Kingdom
Cranfield Forensic Institute, Cranfield
University
Shrivenham, UK

ISBN 978-3-030-32925-9 ISBN 978-3-030-32926-6 (eBook)
https://doi.org/10.1007/978-3-030-32926-6

Front cover image by Eduardo Hernandez©

This Springer imprint is published by the registered company Springer Nature Switzerland AG
The registered company address is: Gewerbestrasse 11, 6330 Cham, Switzerland

Foreword by Clark Spencer Larsen

The disciplines that involve working with human remains are indebted to editors Squires, Errickson, and Márquez-Grant for their efforts in bringing together this remarkable collection of papers on the ethical challenges of working with human remains. I predict that this book will be fundamental to the ongoing discussion of building a better, more productive, and more informed understanding of the ethical treatment of human remains. The subject matter pertains especially to ethics in bioarchaeology and forensic anthropology, two complementary fields unified by a common theme—ethical issues surrounding access to and study of the remains of once-living human beings. The editors and contributors make clear that while bioarchaeology focuses primarily on the analysis of human remains from archaeological settings, forensic anthropology is primarily engaged in medico legal issues relating to individual identification and death circumstances of the recently deceased. Both fields, however, focus on the identification and study of the remains of the dead. Moreover, the content of the book is not restricted to discussions of what scientists think and do during the identification process and analysis of human remains. Rather, the book presents multiple perspectives on the remarkable complexity of ethical and other issues concerning the treatment of human remains.

The questions addressed and objectives discussed regarding the treatment of the remains of once-living people—both ancient and recent—are diverse. However, the chapters presented in this remarkable volume reveal the great distances bioarchaeologists and forensic anthropologists have come in recent years, especially in their efforts to elevate the importance of the ethical management of human remains, no matter how recent or how ancient. Indeed, it is a daunting task to compile a compendium of contributions that address such a wide range of ethical issues associated with the remains of the once-living. However, I believe that much has been achieved in the book by presenting this range of native, regional, and scientific perspectives.

I also believe that all contributors to the book would agree with me in my saying that the application of ethics to the handling and analysis of human remains has a beginning point but no end point. In this regard, ethical treatment begins from the point of discovery of the remains of deceased individuals, no matter the context.

Ethics in this regard should not start after the recovery of remains, or at some point during scientific study, or following years or even multiple decades of curation in a museum facility. Regardless of manner or origin of discovery, it is imperative that the ethical treatment of human remains is in place as a permanent behaviour. Indeed, the collection of papers provides additional and pivotal recommendations for the period of time well-preceding discovery. That is, ethics begin with formal training and preparation of students who are planning careers that will potentially involve the discovery of the remains of deceased individuals. Ethics also involves engagement with the public regarding appropriate responses to outreach (or discovery) events. Regardless, ethics can be greatly enhanced by understanding that the remains of deceased persons were once-living people. Importantly, respect for deceased individuals is engendered by a viewpoint that I share with all of my students. I emphasise at the beginning of each osteology course that we are not in the class to learn how to identify human teeth and bones, but rather to fully appreciate the remains of deceased individuals as once-living persons and to view the remains of the deceased *as though the persons the remains represent are alive today*. Of course, the remains are not alive, but the tools in hand now make it possible to reconstruct key aspects of life from the remains of deceased persons.

The high value given to *respect* is especially well articulated in the book's opening chapter by Lydia de Tienda Palop and Brais X. Currás, who focus their contribution on the perspective that dignity applies to all persons, both living *and* deceased. This compelling beginning chapter sets the tone for the entire book, reminding me of my own realisation as a student that the study of human remains in social, cultural, and behavioural context provides an avenue for viewing the remains of the deceased as a person and not as a collection of objects. By doing so, we consider ancient remains as once-living people who had meaning and purpose during their lifetimes.

I was thrilled to read the perspectives presented from different regions of the world. For example, Charlotte A. Roberts's account of how archaeological human remains has gone through a series of stages over the course of her career. In the UK and elsewhere, just several decades ago, there were relatively few trained experts in bioarchaeology or forensic anthropology, especially in proportion to other sub-disciplines in the broader fields of biological (physical) anthropology or archaeology. The remarkable growth in these areas in a number of countries is impressive, as is the availability of many more opportunities for study and training, academic and applied training, and increased infrastructure for care of the remains of deceased. These developments have established significance to bioarchaeology and forensic anthropology for understanding the human past. Simply, bioarchaeology and forensic anthropology are giving greater "voice" to the dead. On the one hand, science associated with these fields is facilitating greater understanding of the human past, and increasingly so as we strive to understand once-living people who engaged in their own cultures and societies. On the other hand, the increased breadth of the sciences involved in the analysis of past people is simultaneously promoting standards of conduct in the study and handling of the remains of past people. In fundamental ways, the increased attention to ethics pertaining to human remains is advancing the broadening understanding of appropriate treatment of our ancestors, both ancient and recent. This book does exactly that.

Clark Spencer Larsen
Department of Anthropology, Smith Laboratory
Ohio State University
Columbus, OH, USA
e-mail: Larsen.53@osu.edu

The original version of this book was revised: The Chapters 2, 6, 18, 19, 23, and Backmatter citations have been corrected. The corrections to the book is available at https://doi.org/10.1007/978-3-030-32926-6_31

Foreword by Christopher J. Knüsel

By law no one can own the dead, but does this mean that the dead should have rights similar to those accorded to the living? This volume investigates this question by looking at examples of the treatment of the dead cross-culturally and under various social circumstances. This book is as much a practical reference for the worldwide treatment of human remains in a variety of circumstances as it is a philosophical and theoretical endeavour for attributing 'respect' to the remains of the dead, a difficult to define abstraction, but one given form and definition as a result of the enquiries presented.

The maturity of a discipline can be measured in its capacity for self-reflection. This self-reflection often contributes to the creation of ethical codes of conduct and guidelines for professional practice that may then lead to disciplinary professionalisation through the adoption of standard working practices and formal systems of professional accreditation and certification. From the earliest developments of physical anthropology, by Paul Broca in the mid-nineteenth century through to Aleš Hrdlička and Franz Boas' developments in the first half of the twentieth century, what has become biological anthropology still suffers since its origin in a racial paradigm developed in an atmosphere of nationalism, colonialism, and exclusion. By contrast, approaches found in this volume reflect the coming of age of a discipline that was the domain of pioneers with broad and varied intellectual interests or inspired hobbyists in the early modern period.

Only in the opening decades of the twenty-first century could the question of the rights of the dead arise. This is due to the development and application of methods that respond to the desire to establish the personal identity of the deceased, even if only skeletonised remains or DNA survives. The ethics associated with the dead could only have arisen due to the practice of retention of such remains and their role to aid the process of restoring identity in whole or in part (the latter being the case for most bioarchaeological efforts due to the lack of a known identity or, in other words, a name). The dead act as testaments to and—when presented in a court of law—evidence of the actions of the living, whether from long ago or more recently. This question thus implies a conundrum: without the study of the dead, the dead remain unknown, so without study, the question could not be posed in the first place.

This extends to groups as well. In this volume, Fossheim (p. 71) notes: "In line with basic research ethical principles, it is the wellbeing of those now living, which forms the most central consideration …. Where there are continuities between previous populations and identifiable groups of today, knowledge of such representativeness is necessary for acting ethically and for reaching legitimate solutions". The question then becomes: if the remains of the dead are to be analysed, for how long should they be retained and, more importantly, under what circumstances is retention both permissible and justified? The claim that there is nothing to learn from the remains of the deceased is no longer in question, but the supposition that somehow all questions posed can be addressed as a result of a single, all-encompassing study is now also less conceivable due to the continued development of new methods, analytical techniques, and concepts. It is rather the manner and context of such study that draws the attention of the contributors to this volume.

Like many other origin and development scenarios known from history, the question of the rights accorded to the dead comes after a variety of protocols have been established to address new questions and circumstances, as much as from a major change in ethical principles or guiding philosophies. This book demonstrates that the rights of the deceased, if not a completely new topic, is a subject of renewed interest against the backdrop of multiple and incompletely formulated policies and statements—even more so today than in the past, due to rapid communication and dissemination fostered by the Internet and social media. This seems justification enough for this volume; its scope is broad and intellectually stimulating, as well as being of practical value.

The development of the Internet, created as it was in an atmosphere of providing information freely to all, a seemingly unquestionable virtuous endeavour, has operated for some years without close ethical scrutiny. However, the negative aspects of the Internet and globalisation have become all too evident over time. It, too, has been used to aid the trade in antiquities, as well as of human remains. The latter trade is rarely mentioned, let alone controlled by Internet venues, which begs the question of whether an ethical private commercial trade in human remains is even possible.

Scenarios by which to judge the rights of the dead in the context of what they mean for the living are explored in these pages: from discovery to field recovery, laboratory analysis, and destructive sampling to support such analyses; to dissemination of the results to survivors, including descendants, and how the dead are commemorated, displayed in museums, presented in publication, and on the Internet. The still-to-be-determined donation of an identified skeletal collection from the exhumed remains of the recent dead from crowded urban cemeteries in Lisbon (Portugal) to Simon Fraser University in Canada forms a pivotal scenario. This permits insight into the diverse historical perceptions and practical responses to the ever-increasing numbers of accumulating dead that require much more varied and more practically guided responses than entailed by an opposition between scientific and sociocultural perceptions of the dead. A recurrent theme of this volume is the distinction drawn between the 'forgotten death' and the 'present death', the long dead and the recent dead, the difference here being equivalent to those deceased in living memory and those that have passed beyond living memory.

What joins them is the desire to be remembered, and bioanthropological research provides an avenue to meet this desire.

Although there are a number of very informative treatments from the UK and USA included here, there are also those from less often considered regions of the world that aid to reveal the effects of differing political, social, and economic circumstances, as well as religious influences on attitudes to the dead and their remains. As noted by Halcrow et al. (this volume, p. 470), in Buddhism, the dominant belief in much of Southeast Asia, the body is not seen as integral to the spirit of a person, so the remains of the dead are not perceived to be sacred, but among Animists in the same region, excavating human remains is deemed to be abhorrent.

More than the social identity of the deceased, the 'cultural' milieu that governed the original funerary deposition is not clear until after analysis of the human remains and their context; these are not at all obvious upon first exposure of the remains. To arrive at a semblance of such abstract notions requires detailed recording of the grave and its context, in addition to the study of human remains, and the application of an array of scientific techniques to the depositional findspot and its contents, both human and artefactual, is fundamental to achieve this understanding. Dignity in these circumstances appears to be the antithesis of what is implied by the terms 'restful peace'. Remains displayed in a museum mean that the dead continue to influence and interact with the living, a circumstance that would appear to be a closer approximation to the notion of personal dignity of some present and many past communities. In fact, the cultural response might be more along the lines of 'how come we were forgotten and are no longer permitted to participate in the lives of our descendants', as much as attributable to a notion of a 'restful peace'.

Even if the dead are no longer recognisable as individuals, do the dead—as a whole—have inalienable rights? The dead, if not wholly lacking in agency, have reduced agency, preserved only in the memory of others, but does this exclude them from having rights? In all such questions, there is a sense of omniscience that traverses space and time. The humans of today have no map of where the dead may be found; they are often encountered surreptitiously, and this randomness means that any rights the dead may have are fragile and tenuous—and wholly in the hands of the living. In essence, this book broaches the question of what it means to be human in a social, philosophical, and juridical sense, rather than the more commonly found evolutionary sense that is often predicated on the emergence of uniquely human behaviour. Ultimately, it delves into the meaning of mortality and what that means for corporeal remains of the dead, rather than of the soul or essence of the dead individual, which is the concern of belief and religion.

The 1989 Vermillion Accord, which stipulates that relationships of mutual respect are to be encouraged between archaeological science and Indigenous communities, is not binding, even if internationally targeted. Dialogue is the recommended course of action on a case-by-case basis. In some parts of the world where there are no guidelines for the recovery of human remains, let alone legal frameworks in place to establish legal precedent, as in Zimbabwe, discussion on the matter is clearly required. Investigation of the dead permits a re-balancing of history to provide accounts that were suppressed or ignored due to political circumstances, for example of the Republican dead in the Spanish Civil War. The chapter by Renshaw demonstrates the unequal treatment accorded to the war dead due to modern conflicted sympathies and politics, as well as logistical problems created by the number and dispersed war dead on a vast geographic scale, lack of sufficient numbers of trained forensic practitioners, and the cost of exhumation and repatriation. Consensual approaches are rightly recommended throughout these chapters to come to agreements that permit research and study, for "…there is a universal mode of dealing with these issues, where to unearth and individually identify the remains is 'for the greater good' and a necessary part of justice, healing, and reconciliation" (Bennett, this volume, p. 579). There is more than one ethical stance at play in this question of the rights of the dead, but not to identify and be remembered is viewed as a 'second killing' in several contexts described in these pages. Implicit in bioarchaeology is the notion of holistic research that involves and communicates its results on the lives of the dead for the benefit of the living. Palop and Currás' (this volume, p. 32) comment provides a wonderful justification for past and future bioarchaeological enquiry: "Well-conducted archaeological practices restore dignity to the subject by reconstructing and respecting their memory". The ethical stance recommended in this volume seems to be to never forget the dead, to treat their remains with respect and dignity, but also to realise their fundamental importance for understanding the world of the living. Ultimately, the search for intellectual immortality is a search worth making.

Christopher J. Knüsel
De la Préhistoire à l'Actuel: Culture, Environnement et Anthropologie (PACEA)
Université de Bordeaux, UMR5199 PACEA
Pessac Cedex, France
e-mail: christopher.knusel@u-bordeaux.fr

Foreword by Simon Mays

The extent to which practitioners consider the ethical implications of their work, and the wider social and moral responsibilities that these entail, is a measure of the maturity of a scientific discipline. On that basis, both bioarchaeology and forensic anthropology have matured a great deal in the last 30 years. This book, with its wide-ranging consideration of ethical issues, is testament to that. I am delighted to be able to offer support for this volume by contributing a few personal thoughts on the development of ethical approaches to excavated human remains, from my perspective as an archaeologist in Britain.

By the late 1980s in Britain, we were increasingly aware that colleagues at museums in North America and Australasia were facing calls from Indigenous groups for repatriation of human remains. However, in Britain at that time, debates regarding ethical treatment of remains were muted to say the least. I even recall being advised that discussing ethical issues and human remains openly might be unwise as it could help place museum collections here at risk. Nevertheless, debates in Britain, particularly regarding the status of overseas human remains in museums, began to gather an unstoppable momentum through the late 1980s and into the 1990s. An important stimulus for this was the founding of the World Archaeological Congress (WAC), spearheaded by Prof. Peter Ucko, in the second half of the 1980s.

WAC explicitly recognised that archaeology should have a wider ethical, social, and political role, and one of its aims was to give a voice to minorities and Indigenous communities who had hitherto been marginalised in archaeology. From the start, WAC concerned itself with the question of repatriation of human remains to Indigenous groups. Initiatives such as the Vermillion Accord (1989) helped promote debates within the global archaeological community regarding the ethics of the continued holding of overseas human remains in Western museums.

In Britain, the movement towards repatriation received support at governmental level when, in 2000, the UK and Australian Prime Ministers agreed to take measures to facilitate the repatriation of remains of Australian origin held in UK museums to Aboriginal representatives. As part of this initiative, a guidance document sponsored by the UK government was produced. This gave guidelines for museums on handling claims for repatriation of human remains. The approach taken towards evaluating claims in this document was strongly influenced by the NAGPRA legislation enacted in 1990 in the USA that provided for the repatriation of remains in US museums to Native American communities.

By contrast, there was still little debate about the treatment of human remains excavated from British archaeological sites. This largely reflects the fact that there was no widespread public disquiet towards excavating and studying ancient burials, and indeed recent public opinion surveys suggest this remains the case. However, not everyone was happy. Commentating on the 'reburial issue' in 2004, Don Brothwell remarked that although it might seem absurd and unlikely, it was not beyond the bounds of possibility that modern British practitioners of Pagan beliefs might begin to press for reburial of prehistoric British remains. In the years that followed, this became a reality, as some Pagan organisations did just this. The issue was debated through the pages of archaeology magazines, online platforms, and through direct dialogue between professional archaeologists and Pagan groups.

The question of retention/display of remains in museums versus reburial continues to occupy a central role in ethical debates. This is rightly so, because our discipline depends upon the study of curated remains for its survival, and display of skeletons in museums is a vital way of engaging the public in what we do. However, as this book demonstrates, over the last ten years one of the major developments has been the broadening of debate to encompass other aspects of the treatment of human remains. In part, technological advances have driven this. The rise of biomolecular methods has resulted in an increase in requests for destructive sampling, and the tension between the generation of new knowledge using these methods and the need to keep collections intact for future researchers is at the heart of many of the ethical dilemmas that this raises. The rise of the Internet has facilitated trading in bones and other human tissue, and social media platforms provide a forum for the sharing of images of human remains online. These are areas, which raise significant ethical issues.

Human remains provide unparalleled insights into past lives. They help us to understand the ways of individuals and communities that would otherwise be forgotten. This is a powerful ethical imperative for the study of human remains. We need to be advocates for this, both among our colleagues in other areas of archaeology and to the wider public. In the past, as a profession I think we tended to shy away from debate, hoping to be left in peace to pursue our studies. Such a naïve view failed to come to terms with the wider implications of archaeological work, and so was itself arguably unethical. Building a coherent ethical framework within which to conduct our work is vital to the health of the discipline. To do so requires engagement in open debate over ethical matters. It is in that spirit that I welcome this volume.

Simon Mays
Historic England, Fort Cumberland
Portsmouth, UK
e-mail: Simon.mays@HistoricEngland.org.uk

Acknowledgements

Kirsty Squires, David Errickson, and Nicholas Márquez-Grant would like to thank a number of people for making this publication possible. Firstly, we thank Chris Wilby, Floor Oosting, and Rajan Muthu at Springer for their patience and support through the process of getting this book published. We are extremely grateful for all of the time and effort each of the individual contributors has put into our sometimes complex process, and without you this book would not have been possible. Likewise, we are very grateful for each anonymous reviewer and their significant dedication to the peer-reviewing process, their helpful comments, and suggestions which helped improve this volume. Thanks are also due to Eduardo Hernandez for producing the image on the front cover of this book.

A special thank you is to be given to Dr. Jennifer Grant. Jennifer has continually and tirelessly supported the editing process by proofreading the contributions. We are very much indebted to you.

We would also like to thank our families, our close friends, and colleagues who have unconditionally supported us day or night throughout this long process. In particular, we would like to dedicate this book to:

Kirsty Squires: To my grandfather Anthony, my mother Diane, my father Alan, Adam, Maxine, Gary, and Eduardo.

David Errickson: To Claire and my friends Carter, Martyn, G, Hill, Luke, Mark, and Tom.

Nicholas Márquez-Grant: To my mother Jennifer, my dad José, Carlos, and Izan. To Gloria.

Contents

List of Figures

List of Tables

Chapter 1
Introduction

Kirsty Squires, David Errickson and Nicholas Márquez-Grant

The rapidity of technological and cultural change in current times is forcing us to confront a myriad of moral dilemmas over issues as wide ranging as…ethics

Walker (2000, 1)

Abstract There are many complex challenges involved in the recovery/excavation, analysis, retention, and display of human remains, both in bioarchaeology and forensic anthropology. These challenges not only include the treatment of the dead, but also the opinions and feelings of the living. In the past, such considerations were not addressed until around the 1970s when professionals, particularly archaeologists, identified the need for a more structured approach to combat ethical concerns.

1.1 Ethics in Bioarchaeology and Forensic Anthropology

There are many complex challenges involved in the recovery/excavation, analysis, retention, and display of human remains, both in bioarchaeology and forensic anthropology. These challenges not only include the treatment of the dead, but also the opinions and feelings of the living. In the past, such considerations were not addressed until around the 1970s when professionals, particularly archaeologists, identified the need for a more structured approach to combat ethical concerns (Beaudry 2009). There are many definitions of what ethics are. Sellevold (2012) described ethics as a philosophy or a system of morals (what is right, what is wrong), but acknowledged that good and bad may vary between individuals and

---

K. Squires (✉)
Science Centre, Staffordshire University, Leek Road, Stoke-on-Trent ST4 2DF, UK
e-mail: Kirsty.Squires@staffs.ac.uk

D. Errickson · N. Márquez-Grant
Defence Academy of the United Kingdom, Cranfield Forensic Institute,
Cranfield University, Shrivenham SN6 8LA, UK

K. Squires et al. (eds.), *Ethical Approaches to Human Remains*,
https://doi.org/10.1007/978-3-030-32926-6_1

cultures. Further, the philosopher Kant stated that ethics is a universally desirable principal or law (Blau 2009). However, it may be difficult to set these universal principles if they are for professionals who currently practice ethically as they may not see the need for them (France 2012).

Although the dead cannot be hurt in the same way that the living can, there are many reasons why the body should be respected (Fossheim 2012). After all, the individual was once a living being, they had a status in society, they formed their own thoughts and opinions, and they made their own choices based upon their own ethical principles. Throughout history the practice of collecting and analysing skeletal remains has changed, and what was once common practice is now not. Indeed, as observed by Walker (2000, 9) "the practice of collecting human skeletal remains as war trophies and for religious purposes has deep historical roots". The bodies collected by antiquarians varied in states of preservation, some of which date back to the seventeenth century, such as Sir Hans Sloane's assemblage which included a number of human skeletons (Walker 2000), or that of Russian Tsar Peter the Great who published a Decree to obtain more human remains for his collection (Buzhilova 2011). These examples were a consequence of people's curiosity for other cultures, due to medical curiosities, colonialism, financial gain, and for political reasons (see Márquez-Grant and Fibiger 2011). In the UK, this included illicit grave robbing, for example, the notorious Burke and Hare who exhumed bodies for profit in the nineteenth century (Evans 2010). These 'practices' saw the development of legislation which attempted to regulate the treatment of human remains, although in many countries graves and bodies still fell under the umbrella of 'general heritage' or 'archaeological legislation', with no specific mention to them in such documentation (see Márquez-Grant and Fibiger 2011; Márquez-Grant et al. 2016). In Great Britain, these included the Murder Act (1752), the Anatomy Act (1832, 1984), and the Burial Act (1857). These Acts laid out provisions and punishments should these Acts be broken, for example the death penalty.

The Vermillion Accord on Human Remains was adopted at the World Archaeological Congress (WAC) in 1989 and signified an important step towards the correct treatment of human remains. This stipulated that the dead and their associated community, relatives, and guardians should be respected (WAC 1989). In addition, a year later, the Native American Graves Protection and Repatriation Act (NAGPRA 1990) became effective, establishing procedures in the discovery and recovery of Native American cultural items including human remains on particular lands. Descendants were thus granted greater input regarding the treatment of the dead. The publication of the International Council of Museums (ICOM) Code of Ethics in 2004 was highly significant as this code set the minimum standards that the public and professionals should expect of a museum service, while safeguarding invaluable heritage (Lewis 2004; ICOM 2017).

Rapidly changing views on human remains and new legislation meant that Indigenous groups were increasingly asking museums for the return of their ancestor's human remains (Payne 2012) and, perhaps, using repatriation as a 'kind of restitution for past wrongs'. As a result, in 2000, a joint declaration between the UK and Australia was established to increase efforts in the repatriation of human remains to Indigenous communities in Australia, resulting in the Guidance for the Care of Human Remains in Museums (DCMS 2005). Ethics committees were also established in museums, universities, and other institutions that held human remains in some countries (see Márquez-Grant and Fibiger 2011). Consequently, several repatriation claims were successful, including those of Saartjie 'Sarah' Baartman (1789–1815) whose body was displayed until the 1970s in the Museé de L'Homme in Paris (France) and was finally buried in South Africa in 2002 (Bredekamp 2006); the 'last' Tasmanian female, Truganini, whose body was retained due to scientific interest when she died in 1876 and it was not until 1976 that her body was repatriated, cremated, and her ashes scattered in a specific place which she had requested prior to her death (Fforde 2004); the nineteenth century 'Bushman' displayed in a museum in Spain until it was returned to Botswana in 2000 (Davies 2003); and the body of Julia Pastrana was returned from Norway to Mexico in 2013 (Márquez-Grant 2017). These repatriation claims may be substantiated by genetic, cultural, religious, and geographic links, amongst other factors, between the claimants and the deceased (Lohman and Goodnow 2006; Jenkins 2011).

As noted throughout this book, ethical considerations are not only relevant to human tissue, including skeletonised individuals, fragmented bones or human bones as part of artefacts, but all individuals whether dead or living. Therefore, it is not only bioarchaeology that should be considered, but also the related discipline of forensic anthropology in that investigations, such as age assessments, are undertaken on the living or where the relatives of the deceased are still alive. Investigations into human rights and political violations have derived from violence and warfare (Fondebrider 2012). Conflicts in wars have seen thousands of people buried in concentration camps (González-Ruibal et al. 2015), while others have resulted in the public display of human remains (Walker 2000). Some of these conflicts also saw the unnecessary physical and mental torture of the living. Similarly, we must also remember that the living may be tortured in other ways, for instance, if their relatives and/or friends have been killed they are likely to experience mental anguish, which may be compounded by forensic investigations.

The past 20 years in particular has seen a number of events that have increased public awareness and concern surrounding the treatment of human remains (Payne 2012). For example, in the late 1980s and early 1990s, Alder Hey Children's Hospital in Liverpool (UK) removed, retained, and disposed of human tissue without the consent of the deceased (before they died) or their relatives (Joy 2014). Such scandals were seen elsewhere in the UK which, in part, led to the creation of the Human Tissue Acts (2004, 2006) and the Human Tissue Authority (in 2005) to ensure the appropriate regulation of human bodies, tissues, and organs. Since the implementation of these Acts and Authority, other ethical conversations have arisen. These include discussions on the excavation, storage, and display of human remains, and sharing recorded data (see Biers, this volume; Caffell and Jakob, this volume). For example, the case of displaying Charles Byrne at the Hunterian Museum in London (UK) has been controversial as we know that his last wishes were to be buried at sea after death (Doyal and Muinzer 2011). In 2008, there was also a debate regarding the display of unwrapped Egyptian mummies at Manchester Museum (UK). The institution was required to cover all unwrapped Egyptian mummies in their exhibitions, but these were later uncovered due to public demand (Payne 2012). Likewise, the dissemination of digital data has been debated on the Digital Osteology mailing list (see Errickson and Thompson, this volume). More recently, archaeological work to remove 45,000 skeletons from St James's Gardens in London has commenced as part of the High-Speed Rail 2 (HS2) scheme; the UK's biggest ever archaeological project (Addley 2018). This burial ground was in use from 1790 to 1853 and notable people, such as Bill Richmond and Captain Matthew Flinders were buried here. The contractor and archaeologists are working with the Church of England to ensure the deceased are treated with "dignity, respect and care", though this does not alleviate the concerns of the public who do not believe the dead should be disturbed (BBC 2017). In response to the St James's excavation, members of the public protested against archaeological excavation and held a memorial service for the deceased (BBC 2017). These examples demonstrate that we must not only consider academics, professionals, the families of the dead, and the dead themselves, but also each and every person with an interest in human remains and their associated narrative.

Fossheim (2012, 9) describes human remains as a "non-renewable source of knowledge" that could be destroyed through destructive techniques and, in turn, threaten our "access to shared knowledge". With the rapid development of technology, it means we must consider the future scientific community. However, as our attitudes change, there is increasing public awareness of the educational value of human remains as well as a developing understanding, by researchers, of the needs of kin groups. For example, analysis of human remains from Lake Mungo (South Australia) has been blocked, primarily as a result of opposition to the research from an affiliated culture. Yet consideration of future generations has been maintained, and both the archaeologists and local peoples have preserved the skeletons should attitudes, beliefs, or opinions change in years to come (Payne 2012).

Despite the inception of several anthropology and archaeology organisations in the early twentieth century, such as the American Association of Physical Anthropologists (AAPA) in 1930, the American Association of Forensic Science in 1948, and the Society for American Archaeology (SAA) in 1934, ethics were not given the attention they deserved until relatively recently. Over the past 40 years these disciplines have universally acknowledged that ethics should be at the forefront of all work that involves human remains and, as a result, these organisations have incorporated ethical working practices into their individual codes of practice. In part, this can be attributed to the formation of key organisations, such as the Australian Archaeological Association in 1973, the Society of Professional Archaeologists (USA) in 1976, the World Archaeological Congress in 1986, the Chartered Institute for Archaeologists (UK) in 1982, and the British Association for Biological Anthropology and Osteoarchaeology (BABAO) in 1998. The formation of these organisations has had a profound impact on the way in which archaeologists and anthropologists conduct their work. Many of these organisations have published best practice guidelines or have, in some way, influenced governmental guidelines on the curation of human remains (e.g. in the UK, DCMS 2005; BABAO 2010a, 2019a; see also ICRC 2017). Similarly, many of these organisations (e.g. AAPA 2003; BABAO 2010b, 2019b; see also WAC 2018) have developed codes of ethics that its members are expected to follow. Greater awareness of ethical issues in archaeology and anthropology have consequently led to changes in legislation, particularly with regards to the repatriation of human remains belonging to Indigenous groups (Fforde 2004, 2014; see individual chapters in Márquez-Grant and Fibiger 2011).

In 2005, Larsen and Walker addressed bioarchaeology's responsibility and ethical standpoint on the study of ancient human remains; a question that is now all too common. Ethical considerations concerning the study, curation, display, and repatriation of human remains are the primary areas in which ethics have been addressed by bioarchaeologists, forensic anthropologists, practitioners, and museum curators. Some of these topics were discussed in Turner's (2005) edited volume, 'Biological Anthropology and Ethics', and since this publication, a number of standalone manuscripts and chapters have been produced, though these remain scattered across disciplines and journals and are, in some cases, outdated. An article by Turner et al. (2018) has recently explored the history of ethics (and ethical codes) in biological anthropology alongside current issues within this subject area, such as consent, transparency of research and associated data, and the principal of justice for the living and dead, all of which will be explored throughout the present volume. This article is particularly powerful in that it highlights the lack of high-level engagement and acknowledgement of ethics in biological anthropological research and publications (Turner et al. 2018). The discussions raised by Turner et al. (2018) are pertinent to the current climate in archaeology and anthropology, though given that this is only an article, the authors could not explore peripheral ethical concerns. More recent volumes or standalone chapters have become increasingly focused on specific research areas or issues, such as repatriation and the curation of human remains (Jenkins 2011; Giesen 2013), archaeology (Zimmerman et al. 2003; Gnecco and Lippert 2015), funerary archaeology (Parker Pearson et al. 2011; Sayer 2012), and forensic anthropology (France 2012; Passalacqua and Pilloud 2018). However, there is no comprehensive volume that brings together each of these topics, alongside emerging matters, such as digital ethics, the use of human remains on social media, the trade of human remains, and the views of Indigenous communities that are affected by those that work with human remains.

Over recent years, increasing numbers of infrastructure projects (such as the creation of motorways or rail networks), the recovery and identification of victims of genocide and war from mass graves, the significant rise in destructive sampling and associated analyses (e.g. DNA and isotope analyses), and the use of digital resources (i.e. 3D imaging, storing metadata, and social media) have raised further questions about the ethical treatment of human remains. However, these challenges are rarely tackled in the literature (APABE 2013; Williams and Atkin 2015; Márquez-Grant and Errickson 2017; Niven and Richards 2017). With this in mind, the authors felt an up to date, consolidated volume on current issues and challenges associated with human remains was both timely and necessary. This book offers a current perspective on the ethical challenges faced by bioarchaeologists, forensic anthropologists, anatomists, museum curators, commercial archaeologists and academics, and will explore areas that are rarely the focus of published works. Key ethical themes that are addressed throughout this volume include an overview of ethical concerns in bioarchaeology and forensic anthropology, the excavation, curation and display of human remains, repatriation, and new imaging techniques; alongside several invaluable case studies This book will also address current problems faced by specialists and practitioners, such as the ethics of destructive sampling, digital technology, social media, the relatives of the deceased, the trade of human remains, and the use of human taphonomic facilities. Furthermore, the book utilises case studies written by experts within the discipline who are working firsthand with communities and families associated with the human remains they study. Moreover, we hope this volume will also give Indigenous communities a voice on the subject, as all too often we only hear of ethical controversies from the perspective of scientists that work with human remains.

The main objectives of this volume are to:

- Raise awareness of current ethical problems faced by archaeologists and anthropologists that work with human remains in the field, laboratory, classroom, and museum;
- Explore ethical challenges experienced by bioarchaeologists, forensic anthropologists, archaeological practitioners, anatomists, museum curators, philosophers, and Indigenous groups that are involved in repatriation cases around the world; information that is relevant both to academics and practitioners;
- To understand how practitioners working in different contexts deal with ethical issues associated with human remains;
- Establish how ethical dilemmas can be overcome through recommendations aimed at practitioners, academics, as well as organisations and governments, and will offer considerations for their future implementation.

1.2 Current State of Play of Ethics in Bioarchaeology and Forensic Anthropology

As highlighted by Turner et al. (2018), despite the advances in ethical guidelines and principles, there is a lack of engagement with ethical issues at a higher level, particularly their consideration in publications. This is further demonstrated by a number of recently publicised cases that highlight the inadequate implementation of ethical guidelines. To add some context to the volume, these examples will be explored in the following section.

One of the greatest ethical controversies in archaeology and anthropology is ownership of the dead. In a number of countries, when dealing with recently deceased individuals in forensic cases, the coroner will take ownership of the body before it is released to the family for funerary rites (Aronson 2016; Lunn 2017). However, there can be disputes when the coroner has ordered a post mortem when either the deceased and/or their descendants hold beliefs that oppose this practice (Boglioli and Taff 1990; Burton 2012). Both Jewish and Muslim communities are against post mortems as they believe that the process desecrates the body (see AlQahtani and Adserias-Garriga, this volume; Squires et al., this volume for further details). It is also held that, if a post mortem is carried out without their consent, it breaches their human rights (Human Rights Act 1998, Article 9; Gallagher 2015). In 2015, Jewish and Muslim communities had a significant legal victory that led to the creation of a series of principles that coroners must follow where families have expressed religious objections to post mortems (Gallagher 2015). Instead, CT or MRI scans and/or blood tests are to be taken to establish the cause of death (Gallagher 2015). This review is important as it gives the family and, indeed, the deceased a voice in the treatment of the body after death. However, there are problems with the accuracy of some scanning methods, for example some parts of the body are difficult to examine (i.e. superior region of the spinal cord) and several natural causes of death, which can be identified during a post mortem, cannot be established using this technique (Bolliger and Thali 2015). In such cases invasive autopsy is necessary.

In contrast, coroners cannot claim such ownership over archaeological remains. Gatekeepers based in universities and museums are responsible for granting access to human skeletal remains (including the types of analyses and sampling that can be carried out) from archaeological sites. The implementation of ethical guidelines by such institutions, and other relevant organisations (see Bonney et al., this volume; Caffell and Jakob, this volume) aim to overcome problems associated with consent and permission to study archaeological human remains. However, this becomes more complex when dealing with individuals that belong to Indigenous groups or those that passed away in periods of conflict, where there are living relatives, or where the wishes of the deceased are known. Even though the majority of institutions practice within the law, ethical considerations are often overlooked.

In 2016, human remains from the Chaco Canyon (New Mexico, USA) site were subjected to analyses without the consent of their surviving descendants. Human remains from this site have been held in the American Museum of Natural History (New York City, USA) since the late 1890s. The museum granted researchers permission to carry out research (including destructive sampling for DNA analysis) on these remains without consulting descendants of the deceased (Balter 2017). At the time, it was believed that the remains did not belong to any living group as the museum had reached out to numerous southwestern native groups in the late 1990s to establish which group the remains belonged to, though none came forward (Balter 2017). Whilst this may have been the case, the museum would not release documentation that contained details of what it allowed researchers to examine and analyse when initially requested by interested parties. One of the main issues here is that, even though the remains may have been deemed as “culturally unidentifiable”, these remains should not have been subjected to such analyses as they were known to belong to a native group(s), many of which do not agree with destructive sampling and associated analyses (i.e. DNA and isotope analyses), as exhibited in the current Pueblo Bonito case (Balter 2017).

The problems that arise from the lack of communication between researchers and native groups has also been observed in Australia. In November 2006, the Tasmanian Aboriginal Centre demanded the repatriation of 17 Indigenous Tasmanians held by the Natural History Museum in London (UK). The museum eventually returned these human remains but, before they did, they conducted molecular analysis and generated data using digital imaging (Turnbull 2007). While this could be of value to future generations that wished to study these remains, (i.e. the study of human diversity and origins) this was known to be against the explicit wishes of the Tasmanian Aboriginal Centre (Turnbull 2007). Petrović-Šteger (2013) has clearly highlighted the complex interaction of different biological, cultural, and legal concepts that must be taken into account when museums, institutions, or researchers are involved in disputes over Aboriginal remains. Even though there are instances where researchers fail to inform or involve descendants in their work, there are some highly successful repatriation cases (e.g. Wilson 2007; Lill 2017; Watkins et al. 2017) and educational programmes (see Halcrow et al., this volume) whereby researchers actively engage with communities in scholarly activities.

What the above cases have also shown is that human remains with known identities are treated differently to those where identity is unknown. However, there are occasions where identity can be ascertained by specialist research and collaboration with descendants. The Weltmuseum in Vienna (Austria) received criticism for displaying the head of a member of the Munduruku people from Brazil. One of the main ethical concerns raised in this instance was that there was no information about the identity of this individual (Hickley 2018). Furthermore, the provenance of this head was unknown as there were no records to indicate how it arrived in Europe. Indeed, the International Council of Museums and scholars have criticised the display of the remains itself, stating that more information is needed if these remains are to be displayed (Hickley 2018). The Curator of the Museum, Claudia Augustat, remarked that "These trophy heads are objects designed for public presentation. From the point of view of the Munduruku, there is no objection to presenting them in an exhibition. I am well aware that the descendants of the group from which the head was acquired could see this differently. But the origins of the trophy head are not known" (Hickley 2018). This is problematic as the curator has acknowledged that descendants could deem this exhibition as inappropriate but there is no indication that the head will be removed from display. A similar case involving the Mütter Museum in Philadelphia (USA) occurred in 2017. Here, the skull of an Australian soldier who fought in World War I was removed from display and subsequently returned to the Australian Army in 2017 after it was identified to belong to a named casualty, who was wounded and subsequently died at Ypres (France) in September 1917 (Pacitti 2017). This case raised many ethical concerns due to the detailed description about how this individual died, which was displayed alongside the physical remains, and the ability to easily identify this person based on the information provided at the museum (Pacitti 2017). Again, descendants could have taken issue with this. Further ethical concerns have been expressed regarding the lack of consent for the retention of all human remains from World War I at this museum (Pacitti 2017). Communication and consultation with relatives and descendants must be addressed by museums in the future as this could not only tarnish the industry as a whole but will lead to significant public backlash, especially if an individual recognises their descendant in a museum display without their consent.

In 2017, the Prussian Cultural Heritage Foundation (Germany) announced that it had launched a two-year project to investigate the origins of 1,000 skulls taken from African colonies (Rwanda, Tanzania, Burundi, and East Africa). These remains were shipped to Germany in the early twentieth century by anthropologist, Felix von Luschan, who studied human development (Agence France Presse 2017). The majority of paperwork that should have accompanied the skulls has since been lost and researchers are currently using information that was written on the bones themselves as a means of identifying their origins (Agence France Presse 2017). Whilst this two-year study is important, as it attempts to identify the origins of unknown individuals, there is no consideration of whether communities from the aforementioned countries will be involved in this process. This is problematic as the analysis does not take into account those who are descendants of the deceased or those who are connected emotionally or culturally to the human remains.

Protests over "Real Bodies: The Exhibition" in Sydney (Australia) has recently captured media attention. Protestors believe that some of the plastinated bodies in this exhibition may derive from executed Chinese political prisoners that did not provide consent for their bodies to be used in such a way (Pacitti 2018). However, the chief executive of the company responsible for the exhibition has stated that the individuals from China were obtained legally. Furthermore, he claims that these individuals died from natural causes and their bodies were unclaimed by relatives (Pacitti 2018). What is of particular concern is that the identities of these individuals are unknown. Consequently, there is no proof of the bodies' identities or donor consent forms. This has raised questions as to whether New South Wales Department of Health regulations have been met as it requires international organisations to meet legal and ethical standards (Pacitti 2018). This example stresses the need for large-scale improvement on acquisition guidelines, but also the need for transparency in the acquirement process (see Jones, this volume). This is not only relevant to contemporary human remains, but also those from a historical context.

It is interesting to note the stark differences in attitudes in displaying the remains of prisoners or criminals in the past with those from the present day. Whilst the aforementioned exhibition was criticised, there has been little critical discussion around the portrayal of execution victims or cemeteries (where such individuals were buried) from the more distant past (Walsh and Williams 2018). Due to taphonomic processes human remains do not always survive in the archaeological record. At Sutton Hoo (Suffolk, UK), which is the site of a late Saxon ship burial and execution cemetery, there are no surviving skeletal remains due to the acidic sand in which they were buried. However, impressions in the soil of where these individuals were buried do survive. These marks have been preserved and are visible to museum visitors. As Walsh and Williams (2018) highlights, the ethical challenges of dealing with such evidence is complex given that no human remains are visible. Nonetheless, it is known that these individuals were executed. This raises some important questions. What makes the Sutton Hoo remains different to the remains of modern-day execution victims, whereby no relatives have claimed their bodies? Is it the fact that the plastinated bodies of the "Real Bodies" exhibition have not only been put on display, but have also been manipulated to look a certain way? Alternatively, could the reason for such differing attitudes be related to the chronological age of the remains? Finally, should we be so quick to dismiss the consent and the memory of individuals that lived in the past, just because they leave minimal traces in the archaeological record? These are questions that archaeologists, anthropologists, anatomists, and museum curators must answer when dealing with human remains and their associated burial contexts.

Ownership of the dead not only relates to physical remains of the deceased (e.g. repatriation cases) but it also extends to the memory of the dead. The use of memory for political reasons has been observed in many countries. In numerous cases, where governments or regimes have killed opposing groups, the memories of those fighting in the opposition are actively erased by failing to erect memorials or allowing families to conduct funerary rites, for example during the Spanish Civil War (see Renshaw, this volume) and in twentieth century Zimbabwe (see Silika and Squires, this volume). In some cases, the memory of the dead is used to justify military action. This was observed by the US Government who used the memory of those killed in the 9/11 terrorist attack to justify military action in the Middle East (Aronson 2016). Likewise, cultural or personal objects can have a large emotional connection to groups, especially if that is all that remains (Pickering 2015). Therefore, it could be argued that these are considered as important as the actual human remains themselves. This raises key ethical questions regarding the commemoration and remembrance of the fallen as individuals. Furthermore, living relatives must be taken into consideration, and we must think about how ethical it is to take the memory of their loved one(s) and erase it and/or use it for political means. The editors of this book recommend that greater communication with kin groups is essential as this will ensure that their needs, in terms of commemoration and remembrance of their loved one(s), are met. After all, those closest to the individual in life are most likely to understand what that person may have wanted following their death.

1.3 Structure of the Book

Previously, volumes that have addressed the ethical issues associated with working with human remains have primarily focused on specific countries, particularly the United States of America, United Kingdom, Australia, and New Zealand (Vitelli 1996; Turner 2005). There is only one book devoted to ethics in forensic anthropology (Passalacqua and Pilloud 2018) and this contains case studies from Africa, North America, South America, Asia, Europe, and Oceania. Whilst the cases included in the present volume provide an overview of ethical dilemmas encountered in a diverse range of countries, these are by no means extensive. Although other topics were considered, these examples were finally chosen as they demonstrate where ethical problems have been successfully overcome or where more needs to be done around the ethical complexities associated with the recovery and identification of human remains. Many of the points raised in these chapters can thus be applicable to other countries that face similar challenges and could inform new ethical guidelines or codes of practice. Many chapters also highlight the importance of working with local communities on both prehistoric, historic, and modern sites, as well as in a forensic setting. Finally, this volume explores how the global community can work together to increase awareness of similar and, indeed, disparate ethical considerations around the world and how we can address these in our working practices.

The book has been divided into three parts. The first section will explore ethical issues surrounding human remains particularly from a philosophical and social standpoint. This is covered by Lidia de Tienda Palop and Brais X Currás, Claire Moon, and Hallvard Fossheim. Following this, David Gareth Jones explores the growing awareness of ethical dilemmas in human anatomy. To conclude this section, Damien Huffer and Nathan Charlton explore the rise in the online trade of human remains.

The second section of this volume will address ethical dilemmas encountered in bioarchaeology and forensic anthropology, such as the excavation, analysis, curation, and display of human remains alongside challenges caused by the rise of social media, use of digital data, and creation of human taphonomy facilities. It is worth highlighting that this section is written from the perspective of practitioners based in the United Kingdom. This part is introduced by Charlotte Roberts who considers the ethical and practical challenges of working with human remains. The chapters that follow include those of Louise Loe and Sharon Clough on excavation practices, Anwen Caffell and Tina Jakob's work on the impact and management of collections particularly in a university context, Heather Bonney, Jelena Bekvalac, and Carina Phillips' on museum collections in the UK, with Trish Biers subsequently discussing the display of human remains in museums. Over the past five years there have been increased discussions around new topics within bioethics, which can be largely attributed to advancing technology. Kirsty Squires, Tom Booth, and Charlotte Roberts explore ethical issues associated with the destructive sampling and analysis of human remains. This discussion follows with chapters on social media and three-dimensional imaging by David Errickson and Tim Thompson, and Sian Smith and Cara Hirst. Nicholas Márquez-Grant and colleagues subsequently address ethical concerns in forensic anthropology, and finally the ethical considerations of creating a human taphonomic facility in the United Kingdom is addressed by Anna Williams, John Cassella, and Jamie Pringle.

The final section of this book will outline case studies and global perspectives where practitioners have faced ethical dilemmas particularly in the recovery, identification, and repatriation of human remains around the world. These selected case studies demonstrate good practice and challenges that must be addressed with the view of developing ethical practice in bioarchaeology and forensic anthropology. Unfortunately, not every country could be included, however Douglas Ubelaker and Haley Khosrowshahi provide ethical perspectives from a forensic anthropological context from the United States of America, whilst Rebekah Loveless and Brandon Linton examine the issues associated with osteological analysis and curation of Native American remains. Helen Gilmore, Amber Aranui, and Siân Halcrow then go on to tackle the repatriation of human remains in New Zealand. The ethics of conducting research on human remains in Argentina is addressed by Rocío García Mancuso and colleagues. This is followed by Siân

Halcrow and colleagues who discuss the bioarchaeology and ethical issues in Southeast Asia. A chapter on the Middle East focusing on ethical considerations of the management of the dead in forensic cases is covered by Sakher AlQahtani and Joe Adserias-Garriga. Francisca Alves Cardoso subsequently discusses the creation of identified skeletal collections for research in Portugal. A number of chapters then encompass a discussion on human remains associated with conflict, such as the Spanish Civil War by Layla Renshaw, World War casualties by Andrew Robertshaw, war graves from Russia are addressed by Tatiana Shvedchikova, the Khmer Rouge regime in Cambodia by Caroline Bennett, and victims of conflicts in Zimbabwe by Keith Silika and Kirsty Squires.

The final author contributing chapter focuses on a topic related to bioarchaeology and forensic anthropology, namely the analysis of mummified remains by Dario Piombino-Mascali and Heather Gill-Frerking. Lastly, the editors provide some concluding remarks and recommendations for future practice. Each chapter represents the opinions of the contributors and these may not necessarily align with those of the editors; however, they are intended to stimulate valuable debate.

References

Addley, E. 2018. 'Story of a Nation': HS2 Archaeological Dig Begins in UK's Biggest Excavation. *The Guardian*. 26 October. https://www.theguardian.com/science/2018/oct/26/story-of-a-nation-hs2-rail-archaeological-dig-begins-in-uks-biggest-excavation. Accessed 26 October 2018.

Advisory Panel on Archaeology of Burials in England [APABE]. 2013. *Science and the Dead: A Guideline for the Destructive Sampling of Archaeological Remains for Scientific Analysis*. Swindon: English Heritage and the Advisory Panel on Archaeology of Burials in England.

Agence France Presse. 2017. Germany to Investigate 1,000 Skulls Taken from African Colonies for 'Racial Research'. *The Guardian*. 6 October. https://www.theguardian.com/world/2017/oct/06/germany-to-investigate-1000-skulls-taken-from-african-colonies-for-racial-research. Accessed 17 May 2018.

American Association of Physical Anthropologists [AAPA]. 2003. *Code of Ethics of the American Association of Physical Anthropologists*. http://physanth.org/about/committees/ethics/aapa-code-ethics-and-other-ethics-resources/. Accessed 13 May 2018.

Anatomy Act. 1832. The Stationery Office, London.

Anatomy Act. 1984. The Stationery Office, London.

Aronson, J.D. 2016. *Who Owns the Dead? The Science and Politics of Death at Ground Zero*. Cambridge: Harvard University Press.

Balter, M. 2017. The Ethical Battle Over Ancient DNA. *Sapiens*. 30 March. https://www.sapiens.org/archaeology/chaco-canyon-nagpra/. Accessed 17 May 2018.

BBC. 2017. London Euston HS2 Exhumation Plan Prompts Memorial Service. *BBC*. 23 August. https://www.bbc.co.uk/news/uk-england-london-41020759. Accessed 26 October 2018.

Beaudry, M.C. 2009. Ethical Issues in Historical Archaeology. In *International Handbook of Historical Archaeology*, ed. D. Gaimster and T. Majewski, 17–29. New York: Springer.

Blau, S. 2009. More Than Just Bare Bones: Ethical Considerations for Forensic Anthropologists. In *Handbook of Forensic Anthropology and Archaeology*, ed. S. Blau and D.H. Ubelaker, 21–25. Walnut Creek: Left Coast Press.

Boglioli, L.R., and M.L. Taff. 1990. Religious Objection to Autopsy: An Ethical Dilemma for Medical Examiners. *American Journal of Forensic Medicine and Pathology* 11 (1): 1–8.

Bolliger, S.A., and M.J. Thali. 2015. Imaging and Virtual Autopsy: Looking Back and Forward. *Philosophical Transactions of the Royal Society of London. Series B, Biological Sciences* 370 (1674): 20140253. https://doi.org/10.1098/rstb.2014.0253.

Bredekamp, J. 2006. The Politics of Human Remains: The Case of Sarah Bartmann. In *Human Remains and Museum Practice*, ed. J. Lohman and K.J. Goodnow, 25–32. Oxford: Berghahn Books.

British Association for Biological Anthropology and Osteoarchaeology [BABAO]. 2010a. *Code of Practice: BABAO Working-Group for Ethics and Practice*. http://www.babao.org.uk/assets/Uploads/code-of-practice.pdf. Accessed 13 May 2018.

British Association for Biological Anthropology and Osteoarchaeology [BABAO]. 2010b. *Code of Ethics: BABAO Working-Group for Ethics and Practice*. http://www.babao.org.uk/assets/Uploads/code-of-ethics.pdf. Accessed 13 May 2018.

British Association of Biological Anthropology and Osteoarchaeology [BABAO]. 2019a. *Code of Practice*. https://www.babao.org.uk/assets/Uploads/BABAO-Code-of-Practice-2019.pdf. Accessed 23 November 2019.

British Association of Biological Anthropology and Osteoarchaeology [BABAO]. 2019b. *Code of Ethics*. https://www.babao.org.uk/assets/Uploads/BABAO-Code-of-Ethics-2019.pdf. Accessed 23 November 2019.

Burial Act. 1857. The Stationery Office, London.

Burton, E.C. 2012. *Religions and the Autopsy*. http://emedicine.medscape.com/article/1705993-overview. Accessed 17 May 2018.

Buzhilova, A. 2011. Russia. In *The Routledge Handbook of Archaeological Human Remains and Legislation: An International Guides to Laws and Practice in the Excavation and Treatment of Archaeological Human Remains*, ed. N. Márquez-Grant and L. Fibiger, 363–372. London: Routledge.

Davies, C. 2003. *The Return of El Negro*. Johannesburg: Penguin Books.

Department for Culture, Media and Sport [DCMS]. 2005. *Guidance for the Care of Human Remains in Museums*. London: Department for Culture, Media and Sport.

Doyal, L., and T. Muinzer. 2011. Should the Skeleton of "The Irish Giant" Be Buried at Sea? *The British Medical Journal* 343: d7597.

Evans, A. 2010. William Hare the Murderer. *International Journal of Epidemiology* 39 (5): 1190–1192.

Fforde, C. 2004. *Collecting the Dead: Archaeology and the Reburial Issues*. London: Duckworth.

Fforde, C. 2014. The Tamaki Makau-rau Accord on the Display of Human Remains and Sacred Objects. In *Encyclopaedia of Global Archaeology*, ed. C. Smith, 7209–7213. New York: Springer.

Fondebrider, L. 2012. The Application of Forensic Anthropology to the Investigation of Cases of Political Violence. In *A Companion to Forensic Anthropology*, ed. D. Dirkmaat, 639–647. Oxford: Blackwell Publishing Ltd.

Fossheim, H. 2012. Introductory Remarks. In *More Than Just Bones: Ethics and Research on Human Remains*, ed. H. Fossheim, 7–10. Oslo: The Norwegian National Research Ethics Committee.

France, D.L. 2012. Ethics in Forensic Anthropology. In *A Companion to Forensic Anthropology*, ed. D.C. Dirkmaat, 666–682. Oxford: Blackwell Publishing Ltd.

Gallagher, P. 2015. Coroners Must Send Bodies for Scans Rather than Autopsies if Religion Demands They Stay Intact, High Court Rules. *Independent*. 28 July. http://www.independent.co.uk/news/uk/home-news/coroners-must-send-bodies-for-scans-rather-than-autopsies-if-religion-demands-they-stay-intact-high-10422561.html. Accessed 17 May 2018

Giesen, M. (ed.). 2013. *Curating Human Remains: Caring for the Dead in the United Kingdom*. Woodbridge: Boydell and Brewer.

Gnecco, C., and D. Lippert (eds.). 2015. *Ethics and Archaeological Praxis*. New York: Springer.

González-Ruibal, A., X. Ayán Vila, and R. Caesar. 2015. Ethics, Archaeology and Civil Conflict: The Case of Spain. In *Ethics and the Archaeology of Violence*, ed. A. González-Ruibal and G. Moshenska, 113–136. New York: Springer.

Hickley, C. 2018. Should Museums Display Human Remains from Other Cultures? *The Art Newspaper*. 8 January. https://www.theartnewspaper.com/news/should-museums-display-human-remains-from-other-cultures. Accessed 17 May 2018.

Human Rights Act. 1998. The Stationery Office, London.

Human Tissue Act. 2004. The Stationery Office, London.

Human Tissue (Scotland) Act. 2006. The Scottish Parliament, Edinburgh.

International Committee of the Red Cross [ICRC]. 2017. *Management of Dead Bodies After Disasters: A Field Manual for First Responders*. Geneva: International Committee of the Red Cross.

International Council for Museums [ICOM]. 2017. *Code of Ethics for Museums*. Paris: International Council for Museums.

Jenkins, T. 2011. *Contesting Human Remains in Museum Collections: The Crisis of Cultural Authority*. Abingdon: Routledge.

Joy, J. 2014. Looking Death in the Face: Different Attitudes Towards Bog Bodies and Their Display with a Focus on Lindow Man. In *Regarding the Dead: Human Remains in the British Museum*, ed. A. Fletcher, D. Antoine, and J.D. Hill, 10–19. London: The British Museum.

Larsen, C.S., and P.L. Walker. 2005. The Ethics of Bioarchaeology. In *Biological Anthropology and Ethics: From Repatriation to Genetic Identity*, ed. T.R. Turner, 111–120. New York: State University of New York Press.

Lewis, G. 2004. The Role of Museums and the Professional Code of Ethics. In *Running a Museum: A Practical Handbook*, ed. P.J. Boylan, 1–16. Paris: International Council of Museums.

Lill, A. 2017. After 87 Years at the Smithsonian, Bones of Alaska Natives Returned and Reburied. *National Public Radio*. 21 October. https://www.npr.org/2017/10/21/554598592/after-87-years-at-the-smithsonian-bones-of-alaska-natives-returned-and-reburied. Accessed 17 May 2018.

Lohman, J., and K.J. Goodnow (eds.). 2006. *Human Remains and Museum Practice*. Oxford: Berghahn Books.

Lunn, M. 2017. *Essentials of Medicolegal Death Investigation*. Amsterdam: Elsevier.

Márquez-Grant, N. 2017. The Repatriation of Julia Pastrana: Scientific and Ethical Dilemas. *The Eye of the Beholder: Julia Pastrana's Long Journey Home*, ed. L. Anderson Barbata, and D. Wingate, 101–130. Seattle: Lucia | Marquand.

Márquez-Grant, N., and D. Errickson. 2017. Ethical Considerations: An Added Dimension. In *Human Remains: Another Dimension. The Application of Imaging to the Study of Human Remains*, ed. D. Errickson and T.J.U. Thompson, 193–204. London: Elsevier.

Márquez-Grant, N., and L. Fibiger (eds.). 2011. *The Routledge Handbook of Archaeological Human Remains and Legislation: An International Guides to Laws and Practice in the Excavation and Treatment of Archaeological Human Remains*. London: Routledge.

Márquez-Grant, N., H. Webster, J. Truesdell, et al. 2016. Physical Anthropology and Osteoarchaeology in Europe: History, Current Trends and Challenges. *International Journal of Osteoarchaeology* 26 (6): 1078–1088.

Murder Act. 1752. The Stationery Office, London.

Native American Graves Protection and Repatriation Act (NAGPRA). Public Law 101–601, 25 United States Code 3001 et seq., 104 Stat. 3048—Nov. 16, 1990 (1990) 101st United States Congress, Washington D.C.

Niven, K., and J.D. Richards. 2017. The Storage and Long-Term Preservation of 3D Data. In *Human Remains: Another Dimension. The Application of Imaging to the Study of Human Remains*, ed. D. Errickson and T.J.U. Thompson, 175–184. London: Elsevier.

Pacitti, E. 2017. Pathology in Perspective: Wartime Specimen Collecting and the Case of Private Hurdis' Skull. *Nursing Clio*. 13 December. https://nursingclio.org/2017/12/13/pathology-in-perspective-wartime-specimen-collecting-and-the-case-of-private-hurdis-skull/. Accessed 17 May 2018.

Pacitti, E. 2018. Real Bodies Controversy: How Australian Museums Regulate the Display of Human Remains. *The Conversation*. 29 April. https://theconversation.com/real-bodies-controversy-how-australian-museums-regulate-the-display-of-human-remains-95644. Accessed 17 May 2018.

Parker Pearson, M., T. Schadla-Hall, and G. Moshenska. 2011. Resolving the Human Remains Crisis in British Archaeology. *Papers from the Institute of Archaeology* 21: 5–9.

Passalacqua, N., and M.A. Pilloud. 2018. *Ethics and Professionalism in Forensic Anthropology*. London: Academic Press.

Payne, S. 2012. Archaeology and Human Remains. In *More Than Just Bones: Ethics and Research on Human Remains*, ed. H. Fossheim, 49–64. Oslo: The Norwegian National Research Committee.

Petrović-Šteger, M. 2013. *Claiming the Aboriginal Body in Tasmania: An Anthropological Study of Repatriation and Redress*. Ljubljana: Založba ZRC.

Pickering, M. 2015. The Big Picture: The Repatriation of Australian Indigenous Sacred Objects. *Museum Management and Curatorship* 30 (5): 427–443.

Sayer, D. 2012. *Ethics and Burial Archaeology*. London: Bristol Classical Press.

Sellevold, B. 2012. Ancient Skeletons and Ethical Dilemmas. In *More Than Just Bones: Ethics and Research on Human Remains*, ed. H. Fossheim, 139–160. Oslo: The Norwegian National Research Committee.

Turnbull, P. 2007. Scientific Theft of Remains in Colonial Australia. *Australian Indigenous Law Review* 92. http://www.austlii.edu.au/au/journals/AUIndigLawRw/2007/7.html. Accessed 17 May 2018.

Turner, T.R. (ed.) 2005. *Biological Anthropology and Ethics: From Repatriation to Genetic Identity*. New York: State University of New York Press.

Turner, T.R., J.K. Wagner, and G.S. Cabana. 2018. Ethics in Biological Anthropology. *American Journal of Physical Anthropology* 165: 939–951.

Vitelli, K.D. 1996. *Archaeological Ethics*. Oxford: AltaMira Press.

Walker, P.L. 2000. Bioarchaeological Ethics: A Historical Perspective on the Value of Human Remains. In *Biological Anthropology of the Human Skeleton*, ed. M.A. Katzenberg and S.R. Saunders, 3–40. Hoboken: Wiley.

Walsh, M., and H. Williams. 2018. Displaying the Deviant: Sutton Hoo's Sand People. In *The Public Archaeology of Death*, ed. H. Williams, B. Wills-Eve, and J. Osborne, 55–72. Sheffield: Equinox eBooks Publishing.

Watkins, J.K., S.H. Blatt, C.A. Bradbury, et al. 2017. Determining the Population Affinity of An Unprovenienced Human Skull for Repatriation. *Journal of Archaeological Science: Reports* 12: 384–394.

Williams, H., and A. Atkin. 2015. Virtually Dead: Digital Public Mortuary Archaeology. *Internet Archaeology* 40. https://doi.org/10.11141/ia.40.7.4.

Wilson, C. 2007. Ngarrindjeri Experiences of Repatriation: Engaging in an Effective Consultation Process for Returning Old People. *Indigenous Law Bulletin* 6 (29): 16.

World Archaeological Congress [WAC]. 1989. *The Vermillion Accord, Archaeological Ethics and the Treatment of the Dead: A Statement of Principles Agreed by Archaeologists and Indigenous Peoples at the World Archaeological Congress*, Vermillion, USA. http://worldarch.org/code-of-ethics/. Accessed 12 August 2018.

World Archaeology Congress [WAC]. 2018. *Code of Ethics*. http://worldarch.org/code-of-ethics/. Accessed 13 May 2018.

Zimmerman, L.J., K.D. Vitelli, and J. Hollowell-Zimmer. 2003. *Ethical Issues in Archaeology*. Oxford: AltaMira Press.

Part I
Ethical Issues Surrounding Human Remains

Chapter 2
The Dignity of the Dead: Ethical Reflections on the Archaeology of Human Remains

Lydia de Tienda Palop and Brais X. Currás

Abstract What is wrong with moving, analysing, and exhibiting an inert body of the past? Is it morally legitimate to manipulate the body or part of it that constituted the physiological essence of a subject with dignity? This chapter focuses, from a philosophical perspective, on analysing whether the notion of dignity can be applied to the human remains of a subject that no longer is. Ascribing dignity to dead bodies is problematic and needs conceptual clarifications in order to determine whether human corpses have certain moral status and should be protected or whether the notion of dignity should only be attributed to living persons. In this regard, as philosphers, we present a different notion of dignity from that used by Kant (1785) that it is commonly accepted when speaking about dignity, particularly since the Declaration of Human Rights (United Nations General Assembly 1948). In this chapter, the concepts "present dead" and "forgotten dead" are differentiated to justify that, even though the latter have not been object of special moral protection, they should be included under the concept of dignity. In addition, a notion of dignity grounded in the hermeneutical concept of understanding is presented to

Lydia de Tienda Palop—This paper falls within the Juan de la Cierva research programme IJCI-2014-19375 funded by the Ministerio de Ciencia y Competitividad of Spain.

Brais X. Currás—This paper falls within the Fundação para a Ciência e a Tecnologia postdoctoral programme (SFRH/BPD/102407/2014) and of the research project HAR2015-64632-P, "Paisajes rurales antiguos del Noroeste peninsular: formas de dominación romana y explotación de recursos (CORUS)", financed by the Ministerio de Ciencia e Innovación and directed from the Instituto de Historia (CCHS, CSIC).

The original version of this chapter was revised: Citations have been corrected. The correction to this chapter is available at https://doi.org/10.1007/978-3-030-32926-6_31

L. de Tienda Palop (✉)
Departamento de Filosofía, Universidad Complutense, Pz. Menéndez Pelayo s/n, 28040 Madrid, Spain
e-mail: lydia.tienda@uv.es

B. X. Currás
Instituto de Arqueolgoia, Universidade de Coimbra—CEAACP, R. Sobre Ribas 35, 3000-395 Coimbra, Portugal

K. Squires et al. (eds.), *Ethical Approaches to Human Remains*,
https://doi.org/10.1007/978-3-030-32926-6_2

justify the role archaeology plays in providing a particular moral status to human remains and the material elements associated to them.

2.1 Introduction

Holding that people have dignity entails admitting that human beings deserve certain moral status that must be guaranteed unconditionally. This idea—that human beings themselves have a series of rights, which prevents them from being treated as mere "things" because they are an end and not a means—is at the core of the Universal Declaration of Human Rights (United Nations General Assembly 1948). This is explicitly included in its Preamble and Article 1: "All human beings are born free and equal in dignity and rights. They are endowed with reason and conscience and should act towards one another in a spirit of brotherhood".

The concept of dignity, which entails the particular moral protection of the human being as such, implies as the Declaration of Human Rights states, a set of inalienable rights, which violation supposes an attack against the physical and mental integrity of the person, which is deemed the most serious injury that can be committed (United Nations General Assembly 1948). However, even though human rights offer us a relatively imperfect moral guide to justify public policies internationally, there is a question that falls outside their coverage and of which little has been written about: the rights of the dead. While human rights extend their protection to persons as subjects of universal rights, this applies to living human beings, but overlooks the question of what happens to human beings when they die.

The question that arises is whether or not human beings who have died have the same moral status that they have when they were alive. This raises the subsidiary questions as to whether or not human beings can be holders of post mortem rights and, if so, what kind would these be, what are the limits of the dignity of the deceased, and how would it be articulated? In order to explore this question and offer considerations that allow praxis to be guided, it is first necessary to delimit the meaning of what we understand by "being dead". Death is the biological fact that supposes the extinction of the homeostatic state inherent in living organisms (DeGrazia 2017). In short, death is a category that allows bodies to be divided into corpses and organisms, the latter of which have active metabolic functions that are perpetrated in the time lapse. The conversion of a corpse, namely the change in state or form, responds to an evolutionary process of biochemical decomposition that transmutes into another type of organism or simpler matter that are no longer the subject itself (Pinheiro 2006; Janaway et al. 2009). However, during the decomposition process, taphonomic factors (e.g. entomology, bacteria, and the general burial environment) rarely result in the complete obliteration of a body. The fact that a subject endowed with moral status may die divides the question of dignity into two differentiated levels of analysis: on the one hand, what concerns the dignity of the dead as subjects who, at a specific moment, had a life, including tangible and intangible aspects, which was not only physiological, but also biographical; on the other hand, the dignity of the dead as beings that have an entity despite being physically dead and regardless of the consideration of the individual's past life. The latter refers to the dignity of the material human remains per se as worthy of being respected for their condition of being a corpse or part of it, and not only because they belonged to a particular living individual. This distinction becomes crucial when attempting to answer ethical questions that archaeologists and anthropologists face. Therefore, this chapter will focus, from a philosophical perspective primarily, on analysing the second level of dignity mentioned—the dignity of dead bodies—which needs conceptual clarifications in order to determine whether human corpses possess a certain moral status and, therefore, are entitled to special protection or whether dignity can only be ascribed to living persons. In this regard, we will present a different notion of dignity from that used by Kant (1785), and that it is commonly accepted when speaking about dignity, particularly from the Declaration of Human Rights (United Nations General Assembly 1948), in order to justify that archaeology can play a key role in providing a particular moral status to human remains.

2.2 The Question of Human Dignity Regarding the Dead

The concept of "human dignity" that is currently assumed in the Western tradition is the result of its own history of thought. In the present day, in the wake of the Kantian tradition, when speaking of dignity in the philosophical realm, dignity refers to an autonomous capacity that characterises the human being as a subject with a will, that is, a being capable of having desires and volitions that may justify their actions. In Article 1 of the Universal Declaration of Human Rights (United Nations General Assembly 1948) it is stated that "all human beings have an inherent dignity and inalienable rights that must be respected". However, the nature of such dignity is not just a metaphysical exceptionality worthy of respect for human beings with regards to other living beings but, in spite of it being considered an ontological attribute, its definition is closely linked to the notion that the human being is a free being. The sophisticated argument that underlies dignity is articulated in relation to another concept no less complex: autonomy as developed by Kant (1785). According to Kant, human beings are worthy of unconditional respect because they are autonomous beings, capable of being governed according to their own will, and not by submission to an external will. The actions of human beings have in themselves a certain moral form, that is, they are the result of the exercise of their freedom that is substantiated in the right government of their reason, which gives them the ends to which they obey. Human beings are sovereign by virtue of that inner freedom that in turn constrains them by the moral law.

Linking dignity and freedom, and therefore autonomy, entails the consideration that only some particular living beings, namely human beings due to their moral nature, can be considered as deserving respect granted by their ineherent dignity. From this paradigm of thought, as Kant (1785) himself observed, those non-rational beings can hardly be autonomous and therefore considered ends in themselves:

> ...every rational being, exists as an end in himself and not merely as a means to be arbitrarily used by this or that will...Beings whose existence depends not on our will but on nature have, nevertheless, if they are not rational beings, only a relative value as means and are therefore called things. On the other hand, rational beings are called persons inasmuch as their nature already marks them out as ends in themselves. (Kant 1785, 1998 [Ak 4, 428])

It is true that Kant (1798) left (non-human) animals out of the group of beings with dignity because Kant believed that (non-human) animals were not rational and lack will:

> The fact that the human being can have the representation "I" raises him infinitely above all the other beings on earth. By this he is a person....that is, a being altogether different in rank and dignity from things, such as irrational animals, with which one may deal and dispose at one's discretion. (Kant 1798, 2010 [Ak 7, 127])

Following the same logical argument, the dead would also be excluded from this group, because the bodies of the dead have lost their rational essence. A dead human being is not a rational being because although their physical remains survive, their ability to reason has ceased. According to the Kantian notion laid out, it is possible to infer that while the dead being is not subject to desires and volitions in their new state, the concept of dignity cannot be applied to them. The dead individual is no longer an autonomous being, in Kantian terms this is an end in itself because they are no longer capable of giving themselves maxims of action leading to universal laws; they are simply no longer an individual because they have extinguished their active persistence.

However, Scarre (2013), who has worked extensively on these issues, provides an insight that stems from Kant's concept of dignity. In principle, it is possible to state that—for example—there is something that disgusts the human being when a human skull is used as an ashtray (Scarre 2003) or a drinking glass (Norum 2015). Apparently, there is something morally wrong in using human bones for mundane functions. Human remains do hold a certain sacredness that seems to persist beyond their mere vital status.

Scarre (2003, 2013) understands that the Kantian argument does provide a solution to the aporia mentioned around the dignity of death. Although a material body may be inert because life has abandoned it, the subject has not disappeared completely, but survives in memory. Indeed, the memories, ultimately the lived history of a subject, are part of their essence and, therefore, should be regarded as deserving respect. The damage that occurs on the memory of someone in their future is corrosive and produces an injury to the essence of the subject, even if they are no longer alive. Scarre (2003) notes that the subject is made up of tangible and intangible elements, and the latter can be the object of posthumous dignity without compromising the logic of the argument that links dignity with moral freedom. The way in which Scarre (2003) interprets Kant's notion of dignity understands that, analogous to the fact that the living being has interests, the dead would have them if they could have interests. It could be assumed that the living subject would not like to be slandered in the future, or that their memory would be vilified, but that their memory remained intact and respected in a dignified manner. Similarly, this assumption can be applied to human being's material remains. It is understandable that a human being would want their remains treated in a dignified manner and not to be used for heterogeneous purposes other than eternal rest. However, the basic problem that hinders Scarre's (2003) argument, drawn from Kant's (1785) thesis, is that dignity in itself can only be advocated for rational beings endowed with autonomy. From the Kantian (1785) thesis on the subject of dignity, it is difficult to infer an ontological property possessed by bodies when they are devoid of any rational faculty, because what gives dignity to a being is precisely the moral law that the rational being, according to their autonomous, will give to themselves. That said, autonomy is, then, the foundation of the dignity of human nature and of all rational nature. As Kant (1785, 1998, 42–43 [AK 434, 32]) states:

> In the kingdom of ends everything has either a price or a dignity. What has a price can be replaced by something else as its equivalent; what on the other hand is raised above all price and therefore admits of no equivalent has a dignity. What is related to general human inclinations and needs has a *market price*; that which, even without presupposing a need, conforms with a certain taste, that is, with a delight in the mere purposeless play of our mental powers, has a *fancy price*; but that which constitutes the condition under which alone something can be an end in itself has not merely a relative worth, that is, a price, but an inner worth, that is, *dignity*. Now, morality is the condition under which a rational being can be an end in itself, since only through this is it possible to be a lawgiving member in the kingdom of ends. Hence morality, and humanity insofar as it is capable of morality, is that which alone has dignity.

Scarre (2013, 243) recognises that Kant did not specifically deal with "the issue of archaeological disturbance of the dead" and, therefore, interprets the texts on the grounds that "humanity deserves our respect wherever we find it". Interred remains are not simply inanimate matter, like sticks and stones. They are the relics, whether whole, decayed, or the skeletal remains of human beings. To treat human remains without any regard to who they were, shows disrespect to those living persons and to humanity itself (Scarre 2013).

Conceiving that the material remains of a human body have dignity because they belonged to a rational being that *no longer is*, as Scarre's (2013) argument maintains, entails assuming certain premises, such as that the physical body belongs to a rational being, namely, it is its property. If one considers the physiological remains after death as belonging to a rational being that was and no longer is, it would be essential to trace the nature of the effective link between the physical matter that remains and the subject that no longer exist. To show that there is a link would imply understanding that the subject is not in the physical world but that it may well inhabit another, and thus all damage to their remains is detrimental to the subject that was and even to their memory. On the contrary, if it is not admitted that the subject that was does continue having a rational essence in some way even dead, a link cannot be traced between the material remains and a will belonging to the subject that was, as Scarre (2013) intends, because those remains belong to no one: the person no longer exists.

The difficulty of ascribing dignity to corpses per se is evident for the following reasons: the very concept of dignity is limited in the Kantian sense, since it is constrained by the rational faculty of a being that by virtue of this faculty is an autonomous subject. Therefore, within this theoretical framework, the moral protection given to a being is determined by their own ability of being a moral subject, capable of morally binding themselves. If the efficient link between the material remains and the subject that was is not shown in a reliable manner, it is very difficult to justify the attribution of an inner dignity to a corpse in these terms. At most, if the connection between the subject that was and the human remains cannot be proved, it is only possible to ascribe dignity to a corpse due to the symbolic capability of the human being.

2.3 The Symbolic Attitude Towards Death: Biological and Material Remains

The human being is aware of their own finitude and this configures their way of being in the world. Conscious of its physical materiality, it has a transcendental vocation, which determines its actions. The philosophical tradition has treated the issue of death as one of its major concerns, seeking the meaning and understanding of the particular being that is the human being with their finitude and their conscious desire for immortality. Surely for this reason, the human being by virtue of their overdeveloped imagination is also a symbolic being (Ortega y Gasset 2004). Human beings need ritual and sacralisation to understand themselves and this awareness of metaphysical eternity, together with their material finitude, leads them to build bridges between the physical world and the celestial. In this sense there is a clash of interests between the aims and methods of modern archaeology and the symbolic nature of the human being, which is, in itself, problematic.

Regarding the treatment of human remains we find different perspectives depending on the academic school or the country; there is no consensus about this issue within the academic community. A sociological study carried out by Rajala (2016) exploring the opinions of the archaeologists on their excavations in a pre-Roman necropolis in Italy, shows that the typical position of archaeologists is to assume death neutrally, as an object of study and, in this sense, the human remains analysed would be considered dehumanised biological material. The concerns that would arise from these positions in relation to funerary archaeology primarily relate to financing problems or with the degree of preservation of the remains rather than moral considerations of any kind. However, these results contrast with those obtained in England (Rajala 2016), where the approaches to the object of study responds to a greater tendency to humanise the remains, which leads to greater concern for the specific treatment that is given to human material.

The process of humanising biological remains raises the moral problems that archaeology and physical/biological anthropology must face. Humanising implies dignifying in the sense of providing a moral status to the object of study that transcends its mere reification and from it derives practical rules of action of respect. Consequently, the question, what is wrong with moving, analysing, and exhibiting an inert body of the past? is transformed into: is it morally lawful to manipulate the body or part of it that constituted the physiological essence of a subject with dignity?

As observed in the previous section of this chapter, following Scarre's (2013) approach, it would not be morally legitimate to treat the material remains of a subject disrespectfully because that subject as being endowed with will, following the Kantian wake, is an end in itself. Apparently, the deceased's will does not disappear because of the material fact of death, but it is possible to attend to the survival of the subject in their memory and in what we understand that their will may have been. Following this logic of respect for the will of the dead, as Scarre does, we find an added difficulty. To speak about will, which is an intangible element, opens the possibility to transcend temporality and extends the concept of dignity that guarantees the moral status to the remnant biological remains of the subject. Nevertheless, it is necessary to notice a subtelety: respecting the will of the subject does not only entail the preservation of their memory through the physical conservation of their remains, but also includes respect for their religious and cultural beliefs. The human being possesses the ability to have religious and cultural conceptions that, when they are voluntarily sustained, shape their life plans, and in this rational project that human beings are capable of designing through their will, they often include their conception of death and their transcendence (Nussbaum 1992). This will, before the act of death, is manifested not in the human remains themselves that can be actively preserved or deliberately eliminated, but in all the complexity of the ritual that accompanies the body. It is true that mortuary acts are perpetrated by relatives or human beings who survive and who have had some proximity, and we cannot always affirm with certainty that they are the result of the testamentary inheritance of a conscious will of the deceased. But what we can affirm is that those who received ritual burial were immersed in a group with certain beliefs that responded to a determined will.

In this sense, the ethical considerations related to the handling of funerary remains, which are addressed by archaeological and anthropological research, should not only deal with the bodies, but everything that surrounds/is associated with the burial: its symbolical contextualisation. The dignity of the will of a human being concerns all the materiality related to death. This includes the body and associated personal goods and clothing as well as the grave, and the objects and artefacts with a symbolic meaning that accompany the deceased that proclaim and remember their death. Death is more than the inert body. The ethical dilemmas faced by archaeologists do not focus exclusively on the biological remains of the individual but on everything that is carried along with it, and in all the elements that mark the memory of their life and the materiality of their death.

Thus, for example, the moral problem is not only to transfer, manipulate, analyse, and exhibit the remains of the person buried in a prehistoric megalithic mound, but also to open and destroy their burial. Megalithism implies a monumentalisation conceived to exhibit death (Criado 1989). The process of excavating the mound and removing all its structure subverts the will of the person, who conceived and ordered to erect that monument so that it would last and be contemplated. Alongside the body, objects such as jewellery, weapons, various utensils, ceramic pots, and plant materials are also found. These artefacts are not found in the burial by chance, but possess a strong symbolic content: the conception of transcendence in the death of the subject is ungraspable without encompassing the totality of the ritual. Especially when, in many burials, we no longer find a complete, articulated body, either because of the treatment it received as part of the funerary ritual (e.g. cremation) or because the organic remains have disintegrated as a result of decomposition.

If the archaeological investigation only considered human remains as the only one materiality susceptible to moral protection, in many cases there would be no moral crime for the desecration of the grave. This assessment could be taken into account and effectively limit the ethical protocols for the case that a body or parts of it is left in the burial, but this limitation would be inconsistent with the fact of justifying the moral status of the biological remains by their link to an intangible will. Ethical considerations must go beyond the anthropological and archaeological use of the biological remains of death (the skeleton or the mummified body), and include the use of the memory of death, and therefore of the totality of the materiality surrounding the deceased. The ethical use of the biological remains of the *factum* of death cannot be separated from the symbolic materiality that surrounds it.

Therefore, in principle, several factors can be distinguished that relate to the treatment of the material remains of death, namely the moral consideration that a cultural community, with its values, traditions, and beliefs, gives to the grave and its ancestors that therefore would have a consideration of moral respect. In this case, graves and bodies are not considered to have a universal value worthy of being respected by themselves, but what is respected is the will in the death of the subject that was previously alive, inserted in a culture that possesses those values and beliefs. This consideration—the need to respect the values and beliefs of every culture—is very different from that which considers that the human being, even when dead, must be deserving of an unconditional respect. This last statement is a universal maxim that is situated on a different plane than the culture that supports the protection of the ancestors as a basic belief. Can archaeology then continue its research without desecrating this universal moral imperative? Is this universal law a construct that cannot go beyond the limits of closed cultural systems?

The cultural aspects are particular, but the symbolic nature of the human being as an imaginative being is universal. Therefore, we can grant that regardless of the belief in which they followed, we must recognise them as having a certain symbolic vocation that, of course, covers the act of death. It can hardly leave a human being indifferent, the use of a skull as an ashtray, unless that representation as an ashtray is also invested with a symbolic halo related with the cultural meanings of the death and the uses of its remains. The symbols matter to the human being and, in fact, they conceive their life as an accumulation of artifices that overlap with the given naked nature (Ortega y Gasset 2004). Certainly, it can be argued that the decontextualisation of human remains and their use for purposes other than their peaceful rest can contravene the moral law of living human beings provided by their quality of rational and, also by virtue of their overdeveloped imagination, particularly their capability to symbolise. One may wonder whether the manipulation of human remains, used according to the purposes of the investigation, would fall within the category of utilisation similar to that of serving as a domestic utensil or would have a different status.

2.4 Forgotten Death, Present Death

Before elucidating the moral purpose that could justify archaeological and anthropological research on human remains and funerary practices, it is pertinent to make an explanatory distinction between forgotten dead and present dead as a basis for the subsequent ethical considerations that will be made in this chapter.

In principle, in archaeological research, there seems to be no special controversy with the analysis of human remains exhumed from prehistoric and historic archaeological sites. On the contrary, there are a number of publications (see below) that raise ethical issues about the treatment that is provided to the corpses that belong to the societies of the present. For instance, the exhumation, transfer, study, conservation, and exhibition of these bodies generate, in many occasions, fiery public debates and even accusations of racism and ethnocentrism that have been uttered regarding the differential treatment of the dead on the basis of their origin (Fforde 2013). Other observations have focused on the form of body preservation and exhibition (Fletcher et al. 2014; Swain 2016), while others have discussed the relevance of repatriation and reburial (Hubert 1989; several chapters in Fforde et al. 2002) and the role that research should play in these processes (McClelland and Cerezo-Román 2016). Several authors have paid attention to the problems generated by the treatment of human remains from recent conflicts (Gassiot 2008; Renshaw 2013; Brown 2016), burials from the non-distant past (Anthony 2016), or from postcolonial contexts (Pearson and Jeffs 2016). Religious feelings about death have also led to conflict between researchers and the wider community; this is especially marked in the Jewish community (Kersel and Chesson 2013; Colomer 2014). In the same way, the manipulation of the human remains and the associated material elements, such as the grave or the funerary objects in Indigenous communities, has generated a wide debate since the 1970s (Layton 1989) that survives to the present day (Martínez Aranda et al. 2014). In particular, Australian Aborigines (Richardson 1989; Parker Pearson 1999; Pardoe 2013) and Native Americans (McGuire 1989; Moore 1989; Turner 1989; Zimmerman 1989; Parker Pearson 1999; Watkins 2013) have received special attention.

Archaeologists, anthropologists, and museologists are increasingly conscious of the ethical implications that the use of the materiality of "present death" entails, namely the ethical treatment due to human remains and also to the associated funerary aspects of the recent dead. They are aware that they move in a space crossed by moral, ethical, religious, and cultural conflicts. However, the study of human remains from Antiquity does not seem to provoke many controversies. The human remains of the dead, which the researchers do not consider as belonging to anyone, those who are the ancestors of nobody, have been treated as a neutral object of study, comparable to any other archaeological object (Rajala 2016). As pointed out by Parker Pearson (1999, 171) "The dead do not care but the living most certainly do". Frequently, archaeologists must deal with the conflicts generated by their work in Indigenous communities, religious groups, or in the memory of local groups. But these issues are diluted and blurred when the object of study derives from older contexts. Human remains that are not claimed in the present and do not arouse conflict or public controversy, have not given rise to the same reflections, particularly Palaeolithic remains, tombs from the Neolithic, Bronze Age or Iron Age, and Roman burials and epitaphs, not to mention palaeoanthropological remains of the genus *Homo*.

Certainly, there is currently a growing interest in the ethical issues (Fossheim 2012) and legal issues (Márquez-Grant and Fibiger 2011) that surround the study of human remains from the past, as well as their storage and display. However, as Sellevold (2012, 144) points out, "The further back in time, the less is the chance that the remains are identifiable as direct ancestors, and the less is the ethical concern". In the same sense, Jones and Harris (1998, 262), who do address the moral issues concerning modern Indigenous groups, reject the need to think of the dead who have fallen into oblivion: "where direct descendants are not identifiable, the interests of humanity in general should take precedence, and the remains should be made available for reputable scientific research. The lack of clear associations with the living also suggests that consent to undertake scientific study is of secondary importance, since what becomes pre-eminent is enhancing the material's ability to contribute to our understanding of human development and culture". Therefore, the studies that demand the reburial of a body recovered from a burial of prehistory, Antiquity, or any other forgotten culture, are extremely scarce (e.g. Scarre 2003, 2013; Shelbourn 2015). It seems that the rights or moral statute of these ancient dead would not be recognised in a similar way to those of the recent dead; those tied with cultural bonds to social groups and living beliefs. In archaeology, there is no morally consensual requirement to preserve the symbolic and ritual conditions that accompany the body in death and that draw its funerary worldview. In fact, only when someone claims to be related to the forgotten death does conflict arise, as in the case of the Neopagans and their claim to the reburial of prehistoric human remains in Britain (Rathouse 2016). In this sense, a new variable appears in the problem, since the link established with the materiality of death seems not to be measured in time, but in terms of cultural affinity.

In light of these considerations, the distinction between the "present dead" and the "forgotten dead" must be reconverted and include the cultural rather than the temporal dimension as a criterion of demarcation. In this way, the Present Death can be conceived as that which is linked to current cultural values and, in this sense, the remains of the deceased studied belong to living cultures. Therefore, its manipulation, transfer, and exhibition would suppose the transgression of cultural values that a collective can claim as their own.

The current archaeological praxis raises ethical dilemmas based on this distinction. In this way, preserving the dignity of a body is to preserve the dignity of the particular culture under which its burial makes sense. The concept of dignity in death, which is sustained in this paradigm, would then be firmly anchored in concrete cultural principles. One can argue that if the culture that gave meaning to the burial no longer exists, no cultural principle is violated and, therefore, apparently there would be no ethical considerations involved. However, this argumentative logic leads us back to further reflections of a similar nature as those discussed in the previous section of this chapter. The moral concern of respecting the dignity of a dead person goes beyond the particular cultural values seen in the funerary tableau. To speak of ethics means to speak of universal validity and, therefore, the reflection cannot be confined to interpret particular cultural systems. The category that justifies the moral treatment of human remains and other material objects linked to funerary rites cannot rest solely on the distinction between the "living dead", namely those do matter to a particular subject—either individual or collective—and the "forgotten dead", those whose dignity rests on the possibility to have sponsors to ultimately raise voices in their defense.

The question that we face in this work is whether the dead have rights and dignity for themselves, regardless of their ideological, identity, religious, or sentimental link with the present. Should we return bodies of individuals from forgotten cultures of the past back to the earth? Should we replace their graves and their personal effects? We are not talking about the reburial of the bodies that certain communities and religious groups claim as their own, but about preserving the deceased's own right to keep their bodies according to their own beliefs, and to preserve their subjective sense of transcendence in death. For example, should we return the bodies—and their grave goods—from a Bronze Age burial to their original resting place? As Hubert (1989, 164) points out in the case of ancient Egypt, we have in-depth knowledge of the beliefs around death and the importance of not altering bodies. Should we, thus, return all the Egyptian mummies to their place of origin? The real, complex ethical problem posed lies in establishing what happens with the materiality of forgotten death: what ethical and moral principles can validate the use of the materiality of forgotten death, both in archaeological and anthropological research, and in its analysis and exhibition.

2.5 Ethical Approach to the Materiality of Forgotten Death

The number of works that have reflected and followed this line of research are scarce (Scarre 2003; Márquez-Grant and Fibiger 2011; Shelbourn 2015). The basic argument held by these authors is that the use of bodies from archaeological sites is legitimate because it serves the knowledge of history. However, Scarre (2003) does not hold the aforementioned distinction to provide human remains with moral guarantees. The author does not focus on the forgotten death or the present death, but on death itself. Scarre (2003, 238) points out that "the dead retain a moral status that places constraints on what may licitly be done to them". In this regard,

Shelbourn (2015, 144) establishes a very useful distinction between "the recently dead and the anciently dead" and raises a key question: "is archaeological research good reason to disturb the dead and their burial places?". The author (Shelbourn 2015, 144) argues that "most cultures accept that the needs of the dead must make way for the needs of the living, and the majority of exhumations occur during development or other works to meet the needs of the communities of the present. Archaeological excavation in advance of construction work is generally regarded as justified and acceptable, and may well be viewed as more respectful of the dead than excavation by cemetery clearance companies using mechanical shovels". Therefore, the manipulation of bodies would be legitimate provided certain conditions are met. This sort of research would be morally admissible if it serves the interests of the present, and as long as the research is to answer a question that cannot be answered in any other way. Nevertheless, those working with human remains should always treat them with respect and dignity.

While Shelbourn's (2015) argument opens up avenues for ethical justification, it also raises several problems. In the first place, this argument does not determine what it means to respectfully treat the remains of the death of different cultures. What one culture may deem to be worthy of respect may be a sacrilege to another; the symbolic meaning of death varies enormously from one culture to another (Bell 1997; Robben 2004). Also, we must consider that history could be seen as a form of narrative about the past imposed on subaltern groups. From these perspectives, the opening of a Neolithic tomb based on the fact that it serves historical purposes would not be sufficiently justified. As Scarre (2003, 243) points out, "those relics of humanity are being pressed into the service of a cause that is not their subjects' own" and, following this argumentative line, Scarre (2003, 243) argues that "it is fair to assume that none of the individuals that archaeologists exhume had expectations of being used as a learning resource". Regarding these assumptions, Scarre (2003, 246) concludes that "it needs to be acknowledged that there is no obvious method, and maybe no method at all, for estimating the relative moral importance of the interests of archaeologists and their audiences on the one hand, and those of the deceased subjects of their study on the other".

Scarre (2003, 247) proposes a solution to the aporia mentioned, arguing that the archaeologist uses the remains of death as a means to understand history for the benefit of knowledge, but also offers something in return to the dead because "Archaeology is one, highly effective, way of keeping in mind the reality of past lives, and so, arguably, a way of holding absurdity at bay". In this regard, Scarre (2003, 247) considers that "the revelations by archaeologists of the details of past lives are a stronger counter to Oblivion than the preservation of dead bodies intact in their graves". Although Scarre (2003, 247) notes that the archaeologist's main focus is interpreting past history rather than the willness, desires, or interests of particular individuals, it is also true that "their interpretative efforts bring back to mind patterns of living that might otherwise have been entirely forgotten".

Certainly, Scarre (2003) offers a very good solution to the problem regarding the ethical treatment of human remains through this argument. Nevertheless, he does not address all the ethical complexities associated with the issue of the ethical treatment of human remains. Although one can justify that archaeological practice can contribute to the dignification of the past, by rescuing it from oblivion and making it known in the present, the reality is that the archaeologist works are alien to what those bodies were in life. The archaeological investigation that seeks to shed light on societies of the past has not received consent to do so from the dead.

Although there is, indeed, a very clear moral differentiation between the use of death to understand the past and the desecration of a grave, the first purpose is not enough to morally justify the manipulation of the biological remains of a human being, which is illustrated by Scarre's (2003) argument. There are instances where looters remove the dead and accompanying grave goods from their burial place. Looting graves consequently results in the loss of much historical and cultural information. Information that, on the other hand, the looter does not intend to obtain, moved by a single eagerness to benefit from everything that can be recovered from the dead and that may have a value for the looter. In contrast, the researcher, the archaeologist, and the anthropologist methodically study burials using an array of well-established techniques. They seek to gather the maximum amount of information from each context studied. Their aim is to further their understanding of the dead. The body and the burial are, for the researcher, a means to understand other worlds, other cultures, and civilisations. The researcher is at the service of the dead giving meaning to their life and also to their death. However, this argument according to which the opening of a tomb can be legitimate when it is done in order to give it a historical sense clashes with the absence of a past subject that pretends in some way the attainment of that historical sense. It is unlikely that the deceased left a message, containing information about their life, to be interpreted in the future with the purpose of serving as a source of information for researchers. In reality, the researcher is responding to a question that the deceased did not formulate and is also being assigned a narrative that is not theirs.

2.6 The *Agathon* of Bioarchaeology: The Being that Understands the Being

The study of human remains provides researchers with data on diet, diseases, demographics, conflicts, and molecular data, including genetic data, which can inform us of the movement of populations (Roberts 2009; Mays 2010; Larsen 2015). Burials are also an open window to the symbolic and ritual realm of different cultures, which may be seen as one of the most elusive contexts to study in archaeology. Burials and grave goods can also inform archeologists of social structures and power relations in the past. Human remains recovered from archaeological contexts are not only a fundamental source of information but are also irreplaceable. They give the researcher answers to questions that otherwise could not be answered such as what worldview past civilisations had, what sense of transcendence, or even what moral ideas or religious systems they held.

As previously mentioned, the moral consideration of bodies does not always occupy a prominent place within research agendas of some archaeologists and anthropologists. Certainly, funerary archeology is a consolidated field of research that generates a large volume of publications (e.g. Murphy 2008; Gowland and Knüsel 2009), though these rarely address moral issues associated with working with the dead. Yet, most archaeologists deal with death in their daily work and, only in a secondary way do moral dilemmas arise. Burials are frequently opened as part of the archaeological investigation and the funerary remains are studied in specialised laboratories.

However, it should be noted that archaeological exhumations have a final purpose, which is moral, in a certain sense: understanding the original truth of human beings. Archaeology seeks to deepen knowledge and understanding and for this purpose it uses procedures that sometimes touch upon sensitive material and are therefore subject to moral discussion. Precisely because it seeks to understand causes at a primordial level, it finds ethical conflicts with the material with which it works. A drastic solution that would address this problem is to prohibit any form of anthropological analysis of human remains, which inevitably would be the end of this field of study. However, this is unlikely to happen in the near future. Another very different solution is to set limits and protocols for ethical action as a result of moral reflections.

As outlined in the previous section of this chapter, the distinction between the "forgotten death" and the "present death" offers a first and apparent explanation that those dead, who are considered deserving of moral respect, are those with whom we share a greater affinity based on cultural and chronological proximity. That is, they are closer to our current mindsets, and it is possible to find certain community bonds by sharing similar mental categories. A few bones from the Neolithic do not produce the same discomfort as a "fresh" body of the last century. This affirmation reaches its extreme in the consideration of pre-sapiens, whose dehumanisation can become absolute.

We agree with Scarre (2003, 2013) that in the discovery of the forgotten dead there is a motivation of the archaeologist for returning the dead to life in a certain way and for bringing them back to memory. Indeed, recognising that these individuals did have an entity at some point, although it was lost somewhere in time, is at the core of the research. But, in addition, the search for understanding—as already noted by the phenomenological-hermeneutic tradition initiated by Heidegger (1927, 1947) and continued by Gadamer (1992)—is always an act of opening to alterity and in the case, of the ancient dead, what was forgotten.

Therefore, archaeologists that study human remains do not pursue an exhibitionist ridicule of the being that was, but the manifestation of a finite desire to revive the memory of that individual. Well-conducted archaeological practices restore dignity to the subject by reconstructing and respecting their memory. Certainly, it could be said that the indifference to the subjects that were by forgetting the dead is one of the damaging acts that could be committed against a human being or a group of human beings that form a particular society or social group. From this point of view, there would not only be a scientific interest in carrying out archaeological research but a moral imperative of a particular nature: understanding in order to bringing back the dead in a certain way. In this sense, archaeological research cannot become pillage because it would also destroy the memory of the subject that was. On the contrary, moral recognition and an understanding attitude towards the remains, the grave, and the funerary tableau, prevents oblivion happening. Every practice that may disturb and modify the memory of the dead, this may include destroying or altering their human remains and associated funerary objects, may be harmful for the subject that was and could only be accepted when the comprehensive goal that could be achieved would be of greater benefit to preserve the worthy memory of the dead.

Yet the question of why good archaeological practice may well serve to provide a moral justification for manipulating human remains is still not sufficiently resolved. Certainly, the will of the deceased, or the lack of it, to be explained or understood can be adduced to avoid arbitrariness in the treatment of the remains of archaeological research, but this question is independent of the consideration of their dignity and their moral status as a dead being. As we have argued, dignity applies to the living because of its quality of being moral, which entails rational subjects with autonomous will, and therefore its protection and moral guarantee could hardly be extended to beings without rational will. However, a moral dimension of the human being, different from that Kant held, based on the autonomy of the will, grounded in Heideggerian roots, is still redeemable, precisely due to that rational capacity that is primordial and prior to autonomy itself: the capacity to understand. The *humanitas* can be conceived following the path of thought inaugurated by Heidegger (1927, 1947) as that opening to the being that is proper to the human being *(dasein)*, and in which takes place the event of understanding that is primarily moral because it is open to the truth of being. In this regard, Heidegger (1947, 271) argues that "if the name "ethics," in keeping with the basic meaning of the word **ἠθος,** should now, say that ethics ponders the abode of the human being, then that thinking, which thinks the truth of being as the primordial element of the human being, as one who exists, is in itself originary ethics. However, this thinking is not ethics in the first instance because it is ontology".

The subtlety that can be drawn from Heidegger's thought consists in linking the moral and the original truth of the *dasein,* which implies giving the human being new moral possibilities beyond the concept of Kantian dignity, grounded in the autonomy of the end in itself, which was outlined in the introduction of this chapter. The notion of dignity that stems from Heidegger's theory provides a new solution to the problem of ascribing moral status to the human remains because as argued by the philosopher "the human being is not the lord of beings. The human being is the shepherd of being. Human beings lose nothing in this "less"; rather, they gain in that they attain the truth of being. "They gain the essential poverty of the shepherd, whose dignity consists in being called by being itself into the preservation of being's truth" (Heidegger 1947, 260).

The event in which the being is revealed, namely the act of original understanding, as argued by Heidegger (1927, 1947) and Gadamer (1992), is the most original pure moral act that can be conceived. In this regard, Heidegger (1947, 258) points out "homelessness so understood consists of the abandonment of being by being. Homelessness is the symptom of oblivion of being. Because of it the truth of being remains unthought. The oblivion of being makes itself known indirectly through the fan that the human being always observes and handles only being". From this view, the aim of understanding can hardly be ignored as an irrefutable moral imperative because it becomes the original function of the human being insofar as the *dasein* is the being that understands the being. The event of radical understanding that is always an act of openness to reality is configured as the window to the essential. Following the logic of the argument, we can infer that this event is more primordial when the apprehension of what is understood is closer to the essence of a human being, which ultimately as a finite being is its temporality. The understanding of death, of everything that surrounds it, and of its visible remains must ultimately be conceived as a moral act, because it is an act in which the truth of being is shown. In the archaeological investigation of human remains, the truth of the being in all its magnitude is revealed, namely, being human is being-for-death and therefore everything that surrounds archaeological research must be treated with the moral respect it originally entails.

2.7 Conclusion

Through the notion of original understanding, from primarily a philosophical point of view, this chapter has laid out a different path to provide dignity and therefore moral status to human remains. Dignity should be conceived as an inner value of any being grounded in its original authenticity and not so much in its capacity to reason. The inner truth of the human being, their authenticity, which provides them with dignity, is that they are temporary beings, namely, that their inner nature is built of just time. However, the human being is aware of their own finite nature and shows a will of transcendence through different practices, such as literature, arts, and history. Their original knowledge of their inner truth and understanding that they are going to die, and their willingness to go beyond temporality, turns any practice to avoid oblivion a moral practice that gives back dignity to the human being and reminds them its original truth: that the human being is a temporary being that wishes to transcend their primary limitations. Therefore, this idea provides a philosophical basis for a revised notion of dignity that could be applied to human remains in order to establish protocols and an ethical guide based on this idea of dignity grounded in the will of transcendence and the intention to avoid oblivion that human beings essentially possess.

References

Anthony, S. 2016. Questions Raised in Excavating the Recent Dead. In *Archaeologists and the Dead Archaeologists and the Dead: Mortuary Archaeology in Contemporary Society*, ed. H. Williams and M. Giles, 21–38. Oxford: Oxford University Press.

Bell, C. 1997. *Ritual Perspectives and Dimensions*. Oxford: Oxford University Press.

Brown, M. 2016. Habeas Corpus. Contested Ownership of Casualties of the Great War. In *Archaeologists and the Dead: Mortuary Archaeology in Contemporary Society*, ed. H. Williams and M. Giles, 113–138. Oxford: Oxford University Press.

Colomer, L. 2014. The Politics of Human Remains in Managing Archaeological Medieval Jewish Burial Grounds in Europe. *Nordisk Kulturpolitisk Tidskrift* 17 (2): 168–186.

Criado, F. 1989. Megalitos, Espacio, Pensamiento. *Trabajos de Prehistoria* 46: 75–98.

DeGrazia, D. 2017. The Definition of Death. In *The Stanford Encyclopedia of Philosophy*, ed. E.N. Zalta. Stanford: Stanford University. https://plato.stanford.edu/archives/spr2017/entries/death-definition/. Accessed 19 August 2018.

Fforde, C. 2013. In Search of Others: The History and Legacy of 'Race' Collections. In *The Oxford Handbook of the Archaeology of Death and Burial*, ed. S. Tarlow and L. Nilsson Stutz, 709–731. Oxford: Oxford University Press.

Fforde, C., J. Hubert, and P. Turnbull (eds.). 2002. *The Dead and Their Possessions: Repatriation in Principle, Policy and Practice*. London: Routledge.

Fletcher, A., D. Antoine, and J.D. Hill (eds.). 2014. *Regarding the Dead: Human Remains in the British Museum*. London: The British Museum Press.

Fossheim, H. (ed.). 2012. *More Than Just Bones. Ethics and Research on Human Remains*. Oslo: The Norwegian National Research Ethics Committee.

Gadamer, H. 1992. *Verdad y método*. Salamanca: Sígueme.

Gassiot, E. 2008. Arqueología de un silencio. Arqueología forense de la Guerra Civil y del Franquismo. *Complutum* 19 (2): 119–130.

Gowland, R., and C. Knüsel (eds.). 2009. *The Social Archaeology of Funerary Remains*. Oxford: Oxbow.

Heidegger, M. 1927. *Sein und Zeit*. Tübingen: Max Niemeyer Verlag.

Heidegger, M. 1947. Letter on Humanism. English edition: McNeil W (ed) (1998) *Pathmarks*. Trans: F.A. Capuzzi. Cambridge: Cambridge University Press.

Hubert, J. 1989. A Proper Place for the Dead: A Critical Review of the 'Reburial' Issue. In *Conflict in the Archaeology of Living Traditions*, ed. E. Layton, 133–169. London: Routledge.

Janaway, R.C., S.L. Percival, and A.S. Wilson. 2009. Decomposition of Human Remains. In *Microbiology and Aging: Clinical Manifestations*, ed. S.L. Percival, 313–334. New York: Springer.

Jones, D.G., and R.J. Harris. 1998. Archaeological Human Remains. Scientific, Cultural and Ethical Considerations. *Current Anthropology* 39 (2): 253–264.

Kant, I. 1785. Grundlegung zur Metaphysik der Sitten. English edition: M.J. Gregor (1998) *Groundwork of the Metaphysics of Morals*. Cambridge: Cambridge University Press.

Kant, I. 1798. Anthropology from a Pragmatic Point of View (1798). English edition: R.B. Louden (2011). In *Anthropology, History, and Education. The Cambridge Edition of the Works of Immanuel Kant*, 227–429. Cambridge: Cambridge University Press.

Kersel, M.M., and M.S. Chesson. 2013. Looting Matters: Early Bronze Age Cemeteries of Jordan's Southeast Dead Sea Plain in the Past and Present. In *The Oxford Handbook of the Archaeology of Death and Burial*, ed. S. Tarlow and L. Nilsson Stutz, 677–694. Oxford: Oxford University Press.

Larsen, C.S. 2015. *Bioarchaeology: Interpreting Behavior from the Human Skeleton*. Cambridge: Cambridge University Press.

Layton, E. 1989. Introduction: Conflict in the Archaeology of Living Traditions. In *Conflict in the Archaeology of Living Traditions*, ed. E. Layton, 1–31. London: Routledge.

Márquez-Grant, N., and L. Fibiger (eds.). 2011. *The Routledge Handbook of Archaeological Human Remains and Legislation: An International Guide to Laws and Practice in the Excavation and Treatment of Archaeological Human Remains*. Oxford: Routledge.

Martínez Aranda, M.A., J. Bustamante García, J. López Díaz, et al. 2014. Las controversias de los "materiales culturales delicados", un debate aplazado pero necesario. *PH Investigación* 2: 1–31.

Mays, S. 2010. *The Archaeology of Human Bones*. Oxford: Routledge.

McClelland, J., and J.I. Cerezo-Román. 2016. Personhood and the Re-embodiment in Osteological Practice. In *Archaeologists and the Dead: Mortuary Archaeology in Contemporary Society*, ed. H. Williams and M. Giles, 39–67. Oxford: Oxford University Press.

McGuire, R. 1989. The Sanctity of the Grave: White Concepts and American Indian Burials. In *Conflict in the Archaeology of Living Traditions*, ed. E. Layton, 170–188. London: Routledge.

Moore, S. 1989. Federal Indian Burial Policy: Historical Anachronism or Contemporary Reality? In *Conflict in the Archaeology of Living Traditions*, ed. E. Layton, 205–215. London: Routledge.

Murphy, E.M. (ed.). 2008. *Deviant Burial in the Archaeological Record*. Oxford: Oxbow.

Norum, B. 2015. *Drink from a Real Human Skull at Borough Market this Halloween*. 9 October. https://www.standard.co.uk/go/london/bars/drink-from-a-real-human-skull-at-borough-market-this-halloween-a3086686.html. Accessed 19 August 2018.

Nussbaum, M. 1992. Human Functioning and Social Justice: Defense of Aristotelian Essentialism. *Political Theory* 20 (2): 202–246.

Ortega y Gasset, J. 2004. *Meditación de la técnica y otros ensayos*. Madrid: Alianza Editorial.

Pardoe, C. 2013. Repatriation, Reburial, and Biological Research in Australia: Rhetoric and Practice. In *The Oxford Handbook of the Archaeology of Death and Burial*, ed. S. Tarlow and L. Nilsson Stutz, 733–762. Oxford: Oxford University Press.

Parker Pearson, M. 1999. *The Archaeology of Death and Burial*. Stroud: Sutton.

Pearson, A., and B. Jeffs. 2016. Slave Trade Archaeology and the Public. The Excavation of a 'Liberated African' Graveyard on St. Helena. In *Archaeologists and the Dead: Mortuary Archaeology in Contemporary Society*, ed. H. Williams and M. Giles, 97–112. Oxford: Oxford University Press.

Pinheiro, J. 2006. Decay Process of a Cadaver. In *Forensic Anthropology and Medicine*, ed. A. Schmidt, E. Cunha, and J. Pinheiro, 85–116. New York: Humana Press.

Rajala, U. 2016. Separating the Emotions: Archaeological Mentalities in Central Italian Funerary Archaeology. In *Archaeologists and the Dead: Mortuary Archaeology in Contemporary Society*, ed. H. Williams and M. Giles, 68–96. Oxford: Oxford University Press.

Rathouse, W. 2016. Contemporary Pagans and the Study of the Ancestors. In *Archaeologists and the Dead: Mortuary Archaeology in Contemporary Society*, ed. H. Williams and M. Giles, 333–344. Oxford: Oxford University Press.

Renshaw, L. 2013. The Archaeology and Material Culture of Modern Military Death. In *The Oxford Handbook of the Archaeology of Death and Burial*, ed. S. Tarlow and L. Nilsson Stutz, 763–780. Oxford: Oxford University Press.

Richardson, L. 1989. The Acquisition, Storage and Handling of Aboriginal Skeletal Remains in Museums: an Indigenous Perspective. In *Conflict in the Archaeology of Living Traditions*, ed. E. Layton, 189–192. London: Routledge.

Robben, A.C.G.M. (ed.). 2004. *Death, Mourning and Burial. A Cross-Cultural Reader*. Malden: Blackwell.

Roberts, C.A. 2009. *Human Remains in Archaeology: A Handbook*. York: Council for British Archaeology.

Scarre, G. 2003. Archaeology and Respect for the Dead. *Journal of Applied Philosophy* 20 (3): 237–249.

Scarre, G. 2013. 'Sapient trouble-tombs'? Archaeologists' Moral Obligations to the Dead. In *The Oxford Handbook of the Archaeology of Death and Burial*, ed. S. Tarlow and L. Nilsson Stutz, 665–676. Oxford: Oxford University Press.

Sellevold, B. 2012. Ancient Skeletons and Ethical Dilemmas. In *More Than Just Bones. Ethics and Research on Human Remains*, ed. H. Fossheim, 139–163. Oslo: The Norwegian National Research Ethics Committee.

Shelbourn, C. 2015. (Preprint) Remains, Research and Respect: Some Reflections on Burial Archaeology and the Treatment of the 'Anciently Dead'. In *Heritage, Ancestry and Law. Principles, Policies and Practices in Dealing with Historical Human Remains*, ed. R. Redmond-Cooper. Builth Wells: Institute of Art and Law.

Swain, H. 2016. Museum Practice and the Display of Human Remains. In *Archaeologists and the Dead: Mortuary Archaeology in Contemporary Society*, ed. H. Williams and M. Giles, 169–183. Oxford: Oxford University Press.

Turner, E. 1989. The Souls of My Dead Brothers. In *Conflict in the Archaeology of Living Traditions*, ed. E. Layton, 193–198. London: Routledge.

United Nations General Assembly. 1948. *Universal Declaration of Human Rights*. New York: United Nations.

Watkins, J. 2013. How Ancients become Ammunition: Politics and Ethics of the Human Skeleton. In *The Oxford Handbook of the Archaeology of Death and Burial*, ed. S. Tarlow and L. Nilsson Stutz, 695–708. Oxford: Oxford University Press.

Zimmerman, L.J. 1989. Human Bones as Symbols of Power: Aboriginal American Belief Systems Toward Bones and 'Grave-Robbing' Archaeologists. In *Conflict in the Archaeology of Living Traditions*, ed. E. Layton, 216–222. London: Routledge.

Chapter 3
What Remains? Human Rights After Death

Claire Moon

Abstract This chapter is concerned with the human rights of the deceased victims of mass atrocity. It addresses these rights in the context of forensic anthropological work to establish the individual and collective identities of the victims. This work became historically and politically significant in the later decades of the twentieth century in the context of attempts to determine the numbers, identities, and cause of death of victims of state crimes and violent conflict, return their bodies to family members, and contribute evidence to legal trials for crimes such as crimes against humanity, genocide, torture, and enforced disappearance. Key amongst these efforts were attempts to recover and establish the identities of the dead who were subjected to torture and enforced disappearance in Argentina in the mid-1980s, and ongoing efforts to return human remains to families of the dead in the former-Yugoslavia following the wars of the 1990s. Our moral obligations to the dead in these contexts beg a profound and comprehensive ethical approach. With this in mind, this chapter addresses two key questions: do these dead have human rights? And if so, which specific rights do they have? This chapter puts forward some provisional lines of enquiry and argumentation for consideration. It provides resources and evidence—historical, legal, and forensic—in support of such rights, and makes several suggestions regarding which rights might be developed with respect to the dead.

This work was supported by the Wellcome Trust [grant number 205488/Z/16/Z].

C. Moon (✉)
Department of Sociology, London School of Economics and Political Science, London WC2A 2AE, UK
e-mail: c.moon@lse.ac.uk

K. Squires et al. (eds.), *Ethical Approaches to Human Remains*,
https://doi.org/10.1007/978-3-030-32926-6_3

3.1 Introduction

My contribution to this volume is expressly concerned with the rights, or human rights, of the deceased victims of mass atrocity. It concentrates on certain ethical issues arising out of the archaeology of mass violence, which means that it addresses the human rights that arise in the context of mass grave exhumations and humanitarian efforts to establish, by forensic means, the individual and collective identities of the victims. This kind of work became historically and politically significant in the later decades of the twentieth century in the context of determining the numbers, identities, and cause of death of victims of state crimes and violent conflict, returning their bodies to family members, and contributing evidence to legal trials for crimes such as crimes against humanity, genocide, torture, and enforced disappearance. Key amongst these efforts were attempts to recover and establish the identities of the deceased individuals who had been tortured and subjected to enforced disappearance in Argentina in the mid-1980s; ongoing efforts to return human remains to families of the dead in the former-Yugoslavia in the long aftermath of the wars of the 1990s; the International Criminal Tribunal for Rwanda's (ICTR) investigation into the 1994 genocide; ongoing exhumations of Spain's Civil War graves; the trial for genocide of Guatemala's former President Rios Montt in 2013; and current efforts by human rights, forensics, and family organisations to establish the numbers and identities of victims of torture, murder, and enforced disappearance perpetrated by criminal gangs and state security forces in the context of Mexico's war against organised crime.[1]

In these various contexts, our moral obligations to the dead beg a profound and comprehensive ethical approach. With this in mind, I will address two key questions that have become salient to the recovery of human remains, and to the incipient ethical demands that these dead appear to make. These questions are: do the dead have human rights? And if so, which specific rights do they have?

I outline how these questions might be addressed and advance some tentative responses to them in order to contribute to the development of ethical frameworks within which the dead are 'managed' by forensics professionals—specifically forensic anthropologists—working in humanitarian contexts. But this is not my sole aim. Since the recovery and identification of the mass victims of atrocity has historically and necessarily involved the families of the disappeared, my hope is that the arguments in this chapter might also be of use to those—too many—who are currently searching for missing relatives. Mexico is of note here. Around 200,000 people have been killed and over 40,000 disappeared since the government declared an open war against organised crime in 2006. Around 800 people a month continue to disappear (Open Society Foundations 2016). There is a widespread lack of faith in official investigations due to a profound culture of impunity,

[1]For a discussion of some relevant cases see Groen, Janaway and Márquez-Grant (2015).

and the corruption of judicial and state institutions. The failure of the state to provide even routine investigations has led to a high degree of forensic literacy amongst families of the disappeared and a faith in the ability of forensic techniques to yield invaluable information about the fate of missing family members. Some families and family organisations in Mexico have been trained, or have trained themselves, in basic forensic techniques from searching for, identifying, and exhuming grave sites, to collecting DNA and building databases of missing persons (see Schwartz-Marin and Cruz-Santiago 2016).[2] This citizen model of forensic science provocatively contests the regular centres of expertise and control of forensic techniques, and, albeit controversially, is breathing life into a more radical model of forensic action which emanates not from the state or from traditional humanitarian institutions, but instead issues from a politics of suffering, solidarity, and citizen activism. Mexico thus presents a new and progressive site of civic engagement which puts forensics techniques at the heart of citizen contestations of state power.

Forensic activity in humanitarian contexts, as the Mexican case illustrates, is distinctive. Many 'communities of interest' (Star and Greisemer 1989)—expert and non-expert—interact around the dead (Moon 2013). That is to say, the dead are not simply of concern to forensic scientists, humanitarian and human rights professionals, but to family members, communities, legal professionals, political elites, and nations. Within the humanitarian field of forensic activity, families are not simply stakeholders in, but partners to forensic investigations. I have written about these various communities of interest elsewhere (Moon 2013, 2016), so will focus here instead on developing an argument about the ethics of engaging with human remains that is addressed primarily to forensic anthropologists and family organisations who draw on forensic methods and techniques in their search for the missing.[3] As a result, my contribution to this volume is distinctive insofar as it is addressed to *both* professional forensic science practitioners *and* lay forensics organisations, which are comprised primarily of families of the missing.

With the broader implications of my argument in mind I also want to indicate at the outset a slightly different, although related, context to which this discussion is relevant: that of migration. The arguments about the human rights of the dead advanced here travel beyond the violent contexts with which I am most familiar, and are also deeply relevant to the treatment of migrant deaths at national and regional borders. Much recent attention has been concentrated on the Mexico/US

[2]For example, a coalition of family organisations formed a citizen-led forensics organisation in 2014. *Gobernanza Forense Cuidadana* put basic forensic DNA collection techniques into the hands of the families of the disappeared in order to generate a DNA database that might be used to identify the many unidentified dead. Other forensic methods deployed by families include search strategies which proceed by grids or transects.

[3]The use of 'missing' here covers both the dead and the disappeared.

border and on deaths at sea on Europe's borders where the recovery, identification, and return of those dead have assumed critical contemporary significance.[4]

These issues taken together—the dead victims of atrocity and migrant deaths at the border—demand that we begin to articulate something that, I think, is on the brink of elaboration. I would suggest that the human rights of the dead are, at the present time, begging to be established. With that in mind, this chapter will put forward some provisional lines of enquiry for consideration, including proposing arguments, providing resources and evidence, and suggestions as to how these might be taken forward to advance the human rights of the dead. My contribution will argue for a particular approach to the human rights of the dead, underpin it with empirical evidence derived from three domains—historical, legal, and forensic—and make some suggestions regarding *which rights* might be developed with respect to the dead.

3.2 Argument

I will start by reprising my two questions: do the dead have human rights? And if so, which rights do they have? These seemingly simple questions are hugely controversial and invite wildly varying responses. To date I have put them, informally, to a range of professionals and experts including international lawyers and forensic scientists.[5] I have been faced with radically polarised responses to the first of these questions, ranging from 'what a ridiculous question! Only the living can have human rights', to 'what a ridiculous question. Of *course,* the dead have human rights!'. When pushed, my interlocutors have been unable to elaborate compelling justifications for their (primarily, I think) instinctive responses, although some have ventured to articulate *which* rights the dead might have a claim to (and I return to this in the closing section of this chapter). These polarised responses demonstrate the need to address these two questions and I would argue, following Marcel Mauss ([1935] 1973, 70), that it is "generally in these ill-demarcated domains that the urgent problems lie". There is no doubt in my mind that these are, now, urgent questions.

Arguments about the *rights* of the dead have, traditionally, been conducted within the fields of law and medical ethics in relation to property rights (Smolensky 2009) and organ and tissue donation (Boddington 1998; Emson 2003; Harris 2003;

---

[4]See the Colibrí Centre (2018) in Tucson, Arizona, for its work on migrant death on the US/ Mexico border, and the Mediterranean Missing (2018) and Last Rights (2018) projects, amongst others, who work on migrant deaths on Europe's borders. The International Committee of the Red Cross (2017) also provides support to families of missing migrants.

[5]This research is the subject of a longer and ongoing study funded by the Wellcome Trust entitled 'Human rights, human remains: forensic humanitarianism and the politics of the grave' (2018–2021), led by the author of this chapter.

Savulescu 2003). Attempts to establish the *human* rights of the dead are scant, and have so far attracted philosophical *interest* but have escaped philosophical *justification*.[6] As I see it, this is at least partly because the dead are interpreted within a (generally) liberal scheme of argumentation within which they are claimed to have no *interests*.[7] This scheme of understanding does not, inevitably, accommodate different cultural interpretations of what death means. For example, some animistic beliefs maintain that 'the spirit' survives physical death and thus, within a particular cultural script, *may* be seen to be in possession of certain interests. But let us for the sake of argument agree that the dead have no interests. If that is the case, how can they possibly *benefit* from rights? I will return to interests and benefits at the end of this chapter, but at this point I simply want to suggest that we advance further with the argument by exploring it empirically rather than philosophically. This means, following Durkheim ([1895] 1982), that we approach and interpret human rights as 'social facts': as values and norms that shape (permit and constrain) human action and that can, at some level, be observed and documented. This approach requires us to eschew metaphysical or philosophical 'groundings'. It is much more prosaic. It maintains that human rights exist in the world insofar as people behave in accordance, and can be observed to behave in accordance, with the principles that human rights set out. After all, human rights are as much a practical activity as they are one of principle, and practical activity is as *constitutive* of rights as is (philosophical) *reasoning*. Such an approach would maintain that the dead have human rights insofar as people *act* as though they have rights, and would require an empirical demonstration of those actions, such as evidence of behaviour that is shaped by the idea that the dead have human rights.

An immediate and obvious problem arises. The dead cannot be rights claimers, and neither can they be bearers of responsibilities. But, I would argue, they can be rights *holders* insofar as the living behave as if they have obligations towards the dead, treat them as if they have rights, and confer rights upon them in practice. Consequently, in order to answer the question 'do the dead have human rights?' it becomes necessary to enquire into the behaviours of the living towards the dead. Specifically, it requires investigation of the histories, protocols, and practices out of which the human rights of the dead appear to be emerging, and any existing principles that appear to confer rights upon the dead.

There is no single human rights document to date that explicitly refers to the human rights of the dead. However, what I show in what follows is that there are rich resources in history, law, and forensic practice that already bestow, if at times subtly, human rights on the dead. These resources suggest that the human rights of the dead already exist both in principle and in practice. My intention is to divulge and make visible this so far subtle range of resources and practices that point to the human rights of the dead by referring to (a) important histories such as the births of modern humanitarianism and human rights; (b) legal guidelines regarding the

---

[6]For an attempt see Rosenblatt (2010).

[7]This 'liberal scheme' is the bedrock of contemporary human rights.

treatment of the dead, and (c) the regulations governing the forensic exhumation and identification of human remains. My argument is structured in three parts. The first part demonstrates how the dead were central to the histories of contemporary humanitarianism and human rights, the second part takes a look at legal codifications, specifically in International Humanitarian Law, of the 'right' treatment of the dead, and the third part investigates protocols used by forensic practitioners which govern the recovery and identification of the mass dead victims of war and atrocity.

3.3 Histories

I begin by recovering and reappraising the appearance of two important historical movements to which the dead, I think, were central: the births of contemporary humanitarianism and human rights. Both endowed the twentieth century with distinctive, enduring, complex, and often politicised moral sensibilities. The dead are rarely made visible to the instantiation of these histories, so my reprisal of them in this chapter is intended to illuminate the importance of the dead to each of these significant moral projects.

3.3.1 Humanitarianism

The history of humanitarianism is long and complex, and a full reprisal is beyond the scope of this chapter. As a result, I will focus primarily on what is relevant to my argument. This history is marked by early nineteenth century antislavery and missionary movements, through to Cold War interventions in Biafra and Cambodia, and post-Cold War humanitarian interventions in Iraq, Somalia, Rwanda, the former-Yugoslavia, and Libya (Barnett 2011). This history witnessed the appearance of the first international humanitarian organisation, the International Committee of the Red Cross (ICRC) in 1863, and the subsequent development of numerous international humanitarian organisations in the twentieth century. It is this latter history—the humanitarianism of the late nineteenth century to the present, marked by the appearance of the ICRC—that concerns us here as it bears witness to a humanitarian *type of action* that came to prominence in relation to war crimes and the crimes of state. This historical strand is crucial to this story because it also testifies to the appearance of the corpse as witness to atrocity. Here, I wish to distinguish this trajectory of humanitarianism from earlier incarnations of humanitarianism (such as movements against slavery and working conditions in industrialising England) because it brought the dead into view as a subject of humanitarian action and played a critical role in the development of ethical and legal frameworks for the treatment of the mass dead.

This specific humanitarian story was instantiated by Henry Dunant's famous commentary on the 1859 Battle of Solferino (Dunant [1862] 1959), which was the bloody and decisive battle in the struggle for Italian independence from the

Austro-Hungarian Empire. Dunant, a Swiss businessman and social campaigner, documented conditions on the battlefield and in makeshift hospitals. His account is a harrowing record of the terrible circumstances in which so many died, or were left to die due to lack of care, and includes some extraordinary passages on the dead. Solferino, he wrote, was marked by "sheer butchery… maddened with blood and fury… the soil… literally puddled with blood, and the plain littered with human remains… nothing stopped the carnage, arrested or lessened it" (Dunant [1862] 1959, 19–20). He went on: "more and more martyrs were added to the human hecatomb [sacrifice] as the firing lines ploughed the air" (Dunant [1862] 1959, 31); the "bodies of men and horses covered the battlefield; corpses were strewn over roads, ditches, ravines, thickets, and fields; the approaches of Solferino were literally thick with dead" (Dunant [1862] 1959, 41). He documented how it "took three days and three nights to bury the dead on the battlefield, but in such a wide area many bodies which lay hidden in ditches, in trenches, or concealed under bushes or mounds of earth were found only much later; they, and the dead horses, gave forth a fearful stench"; and of how "masses of greedy flies" swarmed, and "birds of prey hovered above the putrefying corpses, hoping for a feast" until finally, "the bodies were piled by the hundreds in great common graves" (Dunant [1862] 1959, 50).

Dunant's *Memory of Solferino* is not simply a battlefield memoir but is also a plea for humanitarian intervention. With the aim of preventing another Solferino, Dunant proposed setting up voluntary "relief societies for the purpose of having care given to the wounded in wartime" and advanced the idea of an "international principle, sanctioned by a Convention, inviolate in character" which, he argued, would provide a supportive and enforceable framework to underpin the work of such relief societies (Dunant [1862] 1959, 129). In 1863, one year after the publication of his memoir, Dunant organised a conference in Geneva to which sixteen countries sent representatives. A second diplomatic conference, organised by the Swiss Federal Council in 1864, involved the governments of all European countries and a number of American states. This conference drew up the 'Geneva Convention for the Amelioration of the Condition of the Wounded in Armies in the Field', otherwise known as the 1894 Geneva Convention for the protection of war victims (International Committee of the Red Cross 1894). It bound together the work of the Red Cross with new legal codes that stipulated that all war wounded were to be provided with relief regardless of nationality, that medical personnel, establishments, and volunteers engaged in relief work were to be treated with neutrality, and that a new relief agency set up for the purpose—The Red Cross—was to mark its operations by the sign of a red cross on a white background (Dunant [1862] 1959). As a result today's most well-known humanitarian agency, The Red Cross, was born.

Dunant's work provided the impetus for a significant shift in ethical enagements with battlefield suffering. It led to the eventual institutionalisation and legalisation of new codes of practice of care for the war wounded, dying, and the dead.[8] The

[8]As a result of his work Dunant was selected as the joint inaugurating recipient of the Nobel Peace Prize in 1901, along with French economist Frédéric Passy.

Red Cross holds a special place in this story as it became the central historical driver of contemporary humanitarian ideals, legal development, and forensic management of the dead, and thus provides a sharp lens onto this cluster of issues.[9] As well as generating a set of principles governing humanitarian action, the ICRC also stimulated the emergence of International Humanitarian Law (IHL), also known as the law of war or the law of armed conflict, which seeks, for humanitarian reasons, to limit the effects of armed conflict.[10] The ICRC was also a key agent in the development of the Geneva Conventions which established international legal conventions on new rights and protections of sick and wounded soldiers, prisoners of war, and civilians in and around war zones. The first Geneva Convention followed Solferino in 1864 and was later replaced by the Geneva Conventions on the war-wounded and sick of 1906, 1929, and 1949. In turn, the mandate of the ICRC stems from the four Geneva Conventions of 1949 (Forsythe 2005). During World War I, the ICRC extended its early concerns and started to address *the fate of the dead and the missing*, heralding a later twentieth century emphasis on locating and identifying the dead, missing, and disappeared.[11]

Whilst the 1864 Geneva Convention did not go so far as to stipulate guidelines for the treatment of the war dead—later Additional Protocols to the Geneva Conventions were to do that work—the Red Cross started to develop new, although ad hoc, practices ahead of later conventions prescribing such work. For example, the Battle of Mons in August 1914, an early battle of the First World War, left unexpectedly heavy British and German losses for which there was little preparation or management by their respective armies. In addition, no military unit nor government office existed to register the dead at that time. As a result, the Red Cross started to undertake some provisional death registration and management work such as compiling lists of the dead, identifying the dead, searching for graves and marking them with a cross to register their presence, as well as "bringing order to the emotional detritus of war" by returning personal effects collected from the dead to their relatives (Laqueur 2015, 460–461). It also began to move away from the practice of burying the dead where they fell. These ad hoc practices emerged prior to the development of special state bureaucracies set up for this purpose such as the War Office Casualty Branch in the United Kingdom, which was founded in 1916. These developments were typical of the way in which the Red Cross

---

[9]It is beyond the remit of this article to give a comprehensive history of the ICRC. For a good account see Forsythe (2005).

[10]The ICRC is the only institution explicitly named under International Humanitarian Law as a controlling authority, which means that it has a legal right to visit anyone captured in the context of international armed conflict, including situations of occupation, on the basis of the Geneva Conventions and their Additional Protocols (ICRC 1949a, articles 9 and 126; ICRC 1949b, articles 10 and 143, and Additional Protocol 1, article 81).

[11]Note that I am making a deliberate distinction here between 'the missing' and 'the disappeared'. 'The missing' covers those missing in action (MIA) during conflict, yet 'the disappeared' refers to those missing or killed in the context, usually, of state crimes against citizens such as during Argentina's 'Dirty War' or during Pinochet's rule of Chile from 1973 to 1990. 'Enforced disappearance' is a crime that emerged out of Latin American experiences of authoritarianism, and is now firmly lodged in the lexicon of 'crimes against humanity'.

extended its activities to cover essential work not already provided for by military or state offices, and which later led to the transformation, consolidation, and bureaucratisation of what became customary practices.[12] It is clear that the way in which the Red Cross managed the war dead at that time is a prototype of current ethical imperatives to care for the dead and their families by locating, identifying, and returning the dead to their families. These early practices also evince changing attitudes towards the war dead in the wake of Dunant's work, most specifically around the perceived need to invest the dead with dignity (for example, by not burying them where they fell in fields, ditches, and roadsides and burying them in national groups), to attend to family suffering (by returning personal effects to them), and, in the process, play a part in the restoration and maintenance of social order by locating the missing and facilitating their reinsertion back into national and familial groupings. The work of the Red Cross signified the emergence of new and particular sensibilities (ethics) and practices (in the form of new humanitarian practices and legal conventions) around the war dead. These were perhaps the inevitable companion of the amplified scale of mass death that were the consequence of new war technologies, such as aerial bombing and trench warfare, which became central to military thinking and practice in the First World War. It is no accident that the bureaucratisation of war dead management accompanied this war, given the scale of the killing. These new humanitarian sensibilities and practices around the mass war dead were, in a classic Durkheimian sense (Durkheim [1898] 1994), to form, express, and contribute to a new set of shared ideas, beliefs, and moral attitudes that served to both underpin, make, and remake society. We might interpret the practices of inserting the dead back into society through reburial in national groupings (such as the cemeteries on the Somme battlefields), or through the return of personal effects to families, as both an expression of Durkheim's 'collective consciousness', and simultaneously an instance of remaking society in the wake of mass death.

In this section I have endeavoured to make the dead visible to and within the history of modern humanitarianism, to show how the dead were central to its instantiation, and to demonstrate how they were central to the development of new moral codes that came to govern mass killing in the twentieth century.

3.3.2 Human Rights

In this section, I make a parallel argument that the dead were also central to the development of human rights in the twentieth century, and to the emergence of the legal architecture, international institutions, and new forms of politic transition with

[12]Another example included the establishment of a special Red Cross agency, which made enquiries in hospitals across London to search for missing soldiers. The search for the missing continues to form an important part of the mandate of the Red Cross today.

which human rights have become closely associated, and through which human rights have been expressed and sometimes realised.

The United Nations (UN) was created at the end of the war in October 1945 with the aim of promoting peace amongst its members (United Nations 1945). Its 1948 Universal Declaration of Human Rights (UDHR) was animated by the horrors of the Second World War, and the Holocaust in particular. The UDHR prefaces its statement of what constitutes human rights by denouncing the "barbarous acts which have outraged the conscience of mankind" (United Nations General Assembly 1948). This phrase invokes the haunting images of suffering, starvation, and death circulated by the worlds' press during liberation of the concentration camps, including photographs of piles of corpses found in camp yards, railway trucks, crowded camp morgues, and countless more human remains photographed in camp crematoria. The UDHR's relatively sparing reference to the events that brought it into being—those 'barbarous acts'—provides the springboard into its definition of human rights which are distinguished by the proposition that human dignity—the fundamental principle of the UDHR—is 'inalienable'. Human rights were the defining expression of a host of efforts to reconstruct morality in the wake of the Holocaust, which included the creation of the UN itself, war crimes trials in Nuremberg and Tokyo, a set of newly-minted crimes such as 'genocide' and 'crimes against humanity', and new legal instruments—such as the Genocide Convention in 1948—intended for their prosecution and prevention. Particular atrocities were, from that point on, constituted as heinous crimes within the broader discourse on human rights and their protection, and it was in this moment that the corpse began to bear *legal* witness to atrocities, thus opening up the arena for forensic engagement with human rights. These legal events do not mark the *first* moment within which the individual dead body came to bear witness to mass atrocity. That honour belongs, arguably and dubiously, to the Nazi investigation of the Katyn forest massacre in 1943 in which the Red Cross was involved. However, Nuremberg marks the historical moment in which mass and systematic atrocities came to be constituted as *crimes* punishable by new laws and legal institutions set up for that specific purpose, setting the scene for the corpse to play a role in such prosecutions.

The enduring message of this historic moment was that 'never again' would such atrocities go unpunished. The authority of this message seemed reconfirmed by a later clutch of institutions inspired by Nuremberg's example and similarly charged with discharging justice in atrocity's wake. Ad hoc criminal investigations initiated in Rwanda, the former-Yugoslavia, Sierra Leone, and Cambodia in the latter part of the twentieth century also seemed to confirm the Nuremberg promise that atrocities would no longer go unpunished. The International Criminal Court (ICC) was also set up in 2002. It was the first permanent international criminal tribunal that exclusively investigated atrocities in cases where national courts were either unwilling or unable to do so.

A parallel set of political developments brought human rights and the dead body into contact in new ways, turning the dead into what Laqueur (2002, 77) calls an "articulate" witness to atrocity. Political transitions across Latin America in the

1980s and 1990s and in South Africa in the mid-1990s were to bring the dead body front and centre of investigations of atrocity. The inaugurating moment of this phenomenon took place in the mid-1980s during Argentina's transition to democracy, when forensic anthropologists made the dead body attest to the terrors of Argentina's 1976–1983 military *junta* (Brennan 2018). From this point on, forensic science was put explicitly into the service of human rights investigations by making the dead speak the truth of atrocity. Forensic experts also started to pursue humanitarian objectives by returning the dead to relatives as a way of addressing family trauma and suffering, echoing the earlier humanitarian work around the dead originated by the Red Cross. Argentina, Chile, South Africa, Sierra Leone, Guatemala, and numerous others are amongst those states that have inaugurated official investigations of state crimes and war crimes, and have drawn on the 'testimonies' of the dead to investigate serious abuses of human rights. This political phenomenon has represented a move from the testimonial mode of truth to a material mode of truth, where the evidence of atrocities provided by human remains moved to occupy a prominence in investigations of the crimes of authoritarianism. The ethics and practices of this emergent 'forensic humanitarianism' (Moon 2016) has since travelled and spread widely—through an epistemic community of forensic entrepreneurs—to diverse sites such as Spain, Bosnia, Cambodia, and Rwanda. Forensic techniques have put the dead squarely at the centre of human rights investigations of atrocity, making forensics, and in particular forensic anthropology, a firm fixture of new humanitarian and human rights rationalities and practices.

There is no question that the dead were at the instantiation of the human rights enterprise. The UDHR, the codification of new crimes such as crimes against humanity and genocide, the invention of new institutions which attempted to prosecute such crimes, and the incorporation of the care of the dead into human rights investigations are all in some way *expressions of what we owe the dead*. In this sense, these measures work as memorials as well as preventive and punitive instruments. They look backwards in memory and honour of the dead as much as they look forwards in an attempt to prevent the future repetition of atrocities.

3.4 Law

Evidence of legal principles relating to the treatment of the dead is both historic and central to humanitarian activity. International Humanitarian Law (IHL) provides several rules that regulate the treatment of the dead (International Committee of the Red Cross 2005, Rules 112–117). Specifically, IHL regulates the search for, collection, treatment, return, disposal, and identification of the dead, mainly in the context of armed conflict, although these principles have been extended to the handling of the dead in the context of mass crimes of state, such as in Argentina, Chile, and South Africa.

These rules have a distinguished and established lineage. They are derived from the 1907 Hague Convention (Hague Peace Conference 1907), the 1929 and 1949 Geneva Conventions (International Committee of the Red Cross 1949a, 1949b), Additional Protocols to the Geneva Conventions of 1977 (International Committee of the Red Cross 1977), and the Rome Statute of 1998 (United Nations General Assembly 1998), which inaugurated the International Criminal Court. Strikingly, they apply the same obligations to the dead as to certain categories of the living. For instance, the obligation to search for and collect the wounded, sick, and shipwrecked "also extends to the dead". This obligation is claimed to derive from the principle of "respect for every dead" (International Committee of the Red Cross 2005, Rule 112). Specifically, the prohibition against despoiling or mutilating the dead is covered by the war crime of "committing outrages upon personal dignity" (International Committee of the Red Cross 2005, Rule 113). The practice of returning the dead and their personal effects is said to be "in keeping with the requirement of respect for family life" (International Committee of the Red Cross 2005, Rule 114). Here, IHL characterises the dead as family members, and their "right treatment" overlaps with respect for family life (International Committee of the Red Cross 2005, Rules 105 and 117). IHL also stipulates that the dead "must be disposed of in a respectful manner and their graves respected and properly maintained" (International Committee of the Red Cross 2005, Rule 115). This rule claims to reflect "a general principle of law requiring respect for the dead and their graves". There are some important details here, including requirements that the dead be buried according to rites prescribed by their religion, that they should only be cremated in exceptional circumstances, that they must be buried in individual and not collective graves, and that war graves must, where possible, be grouped according to nationality (International Committee of the Red Cross 2005). These stipulations imply a respect for the customs and beliefs of the dead held in life, for the beliefs and customs of the living members of the communities from which the deceased individual came, and, importantly, for the identities of the dead. Finally, IHL stipulates that the dead must be identified prior to their disposal (International Committee of the Red Cross 2005, Rule 116). Notably, the era of mass industrialised slaughter ushered in by the First World War also generated a new memorial practice, initially in France and Britain and is often referred to as "the tomb of the unknown solider". These memorials were dedicated to the unidentified war dead in acknowledgement of those who were not, or could not, be identified. IHL's regulating norms have underpinned the development of further norms governing how the mass dead should be managed. For instance, Interpol's 1996 General Assembly statement on disaster victim identification expresses the imperative to identify the dead, but takes it further than IHL insofar as this statement expresses this as a *right* (Interpol 1996). It states that "human beings have *the right not to lose their identities after death*" (Interpol 1996).

In sum, IHL protocols already require that the dead be treated *as if they have rights*—or at least as if they have a right to dignity—and they attempt to compel the living to act in ways that are concordant with this belief. IHL confers specific rights on the dead including the 'rights' to identification, return to families, and to proper burial. I will return to these in my conclusions. Most importantly for my argument, IHL iterates and reiterates that the dead be treated with *dignity,* and it is this principle that, I argue, turns the rights of the dead into human rights.

3.5 Forensics

There is further empirical evidence of the rights of the dead in the field of forensic practice, both insofar as these are embedded in relevant international humanitarian law (as discussed in the previous section) and in the protocols that regulate exhumation, recovery, identification, and return of human remains to families. The most important of these, the *Minnesota Protocol on the Investigation of Unlawful Death* (United Nations Office of the High Commissioner for Human Rights 2016) outlines international legal standards for the prevention and investigation of potentially unlawful deaths. It provides the most important framework governing the work of forensic anthropologists in their investigations of state crimes and war crimes. In common with IHL, the Protocol ascribes *dignity* to the dead throughout. It is woven through the Protocol's discussions of *professional ethics*, in which respecting the dignity of the dead is tied to the advancement of human rights and justice (United Nations Office of the High Commissioner for Human Rights 2016, para 42); the *codes of practice* governing the recovery of human remains, which include "respect for the dignity of the deceased" (United Nations Office of the High Commissioner for Human Rights 2016, para 90); and its regulation of *autopsy practices*, to which the Protocol states that respect and dignity of the dead are embedded within "applicable law and ethics" (United Nations Office of the High Commissioner for Human Rights 2016, para 154). The Protocol also notes that"the identification of the body or bodies" should meet "humanitarian, human rights, and other social and cultural needs" (United Nations Office of the High Commissioner for Human Rights 2016, para 115).

The ICRC also sets out a number of guides and protocols for forensic recovery and identification of the dead.[13] These protocols emphasise the *dignity* of the dead throughout. They state that "at all times" forensic practice must respect the "dignity, honour, reputation, and privacy" of the dead (International Committee of the Red Cross 2003, 131). These regulatory principles profoundly shape the practice of forensic humanitarianism. As Tidball-Binz (2012) notes, our "shared responsibility for the dead" underpins the "humanitarian need for ensuring their proper recovery, management, analysis, and identification, to protect their dignity and to prevent them [the dead] from becoming missing persons". This comment suggests that specific forensic practices—recovery and management of human remains, analysis of human remains for the purpose of establishing the cause of death, and identification—and the manner in which they are carried out *in themselves* serve to protect the dignity of the dead. At the same time, forensic humanitarian action towards the dead has not been without controversy. In the early years of the ICRC's then new forensic unit (from around 2004) "many… in the ICRC were still unfamiliar with forensics and unimpressed with the idea of humanitarian action for the dead" (Tidball-Binz 2012). That this attitude has now

[13]The main site of elaboration of these protocols is IHL (for which the ICRC is a controlling authority) as discussed in the previous section on international law (see International Committee of the Red Cross 2005, Rules 112–117). The ICRC has also produced a number of guides on best practices for the management of the dead (see for example Cordner et al 2016; International Committee of the Red Cross 2004, 2006).

changed, Tidball-Binz (2012) argues, is testimony to "results coming from the field, which proved… the… value of forensic sciences for protecting the dignity of the dead". Significant amongst these field examples, as already noted, were the exhumation and identification of the victims of Argentina's military *junta* in the mid-1980s and ongoing efforts to return human remains to families of the dead in Bosnia, amongst others. This attitude change accompanied the proliferation and institutionalisation of forensic humanitarianism historically and globally (Moon 2016).

In considering the connection between forensic practice and the dignity of the dead, the forensic practice of *identifying* deceased individuals merits special attention. Identification, as I see it, is a practice that 'reunites' the dead body with the identity of the person in life. As such, it is a practice that *restores personhood* after death. And, in cases where people have been violently and radically dehumanised through torture, beheadings, dismemberment (either prior to or after death), as is too often the case in present-day Mexico (Heinle, Ferreira and Shirk 2017), forensic identification might also be interpreted as a practice of re-humanisation after death. This sometimes entails the practical process of reassembling the person physically (bringing together body parts that may have been buried separately), reuniting the body with its identity in life and, as a consequence, facilitating the restoration of kinship ties.

The practice of forensic identification not only speaks to human rights and humanitarian concerns, but also opens out onto a broader set of social and political issues. Most crucially, it involves material and symbolic practices that 'domain' the dead, that lodge them back within social and political orders, such as back within the family, community, and nation. This is significant work. Its importance is illustrated graphically by Kristeva's (1982) essay on abjection, in which she reflects on the sight of a dead body in the morgue. She writes: "In that compelling, raw, insolent thing in the morgue's full sunlight, in that thing that no longer matches and therefore no longer signifies anything, I behold the breaking down of a world that has erased its borders" (Kristeva 1982, 4). She goes on: "The corpse, seen without God and outside of science, is the utmost of abjection. It is death infecting life" (Kristeva 1982, 4). Of course, the corpse here is actually *in place* (and this is where I would depart from Kristeva). It is in the morgue—where science is also present—an ordained transitional space within which the dead are managed, whether on their way to autopsy, identification, or 'disposal' through cremation or burial. Nevertheless, I want to pick up on some important themes that Kristeva raises in relation to how 'forensic deathwork', as I will call it, domains the dead body within three social spheres relevant to this discussion. First, by scientifically establishing identity, forensics restores personhood to 'the insolent thing'. In so doing it reconciles the dead body with the living person it once was, and in the process re-establishes kinship which permits a reunion with the family. In so doing, forensic identification also evinces humanitarian effects insofar as it facilitates the return of the body to the family and enables proper burial, which in turn may facilitate grief and mourning. Second, forensic deathwork domains the dead within law. This involves the presentation of forensic evidence within the frameworks of, for example, IHL, the Geneva Conventions, crimes against humanity, and the Genocide

Convention. Specifically, forensics experts are called upon by law to make the dead testify to political terror, endowing them with a special power as a witness to political crime, and thus they lodge the dead within the legal process. Accordingly, forensics experts play an intrinsic role in what Fleur Johns calls the 'sensory economy of law' (Johns 2017), which refers to the ways in which law evokes, circulates, and organises sensory experience. As such, forensics experts participate in law's attempts to retranslate horror, disgust, shock and trauma into justice, and in so doing, install the boundary between violence and justice. Third, forensic deathwork domains the dead within new political orders. It works on the dead bodies associated with compelling historical events—such as those killed by Argentina's military *junta*, or South Africa's apartheid regime—and yokes those bodies to new political narratives. A key example of this is the narrative of political reconciliation, which has become a popular framing for investigations of past political violence since South Africa's Truth and Reconcilliation Commission (TRC) conducted its hearings (Wilson 2001; Moon 2008).

The forensic practice of domaining the dead (within the family, within law, and within broader social and political narratives) chimes with Mary Douglas's work on pollution and taboo (Douglas [1966] 2002) insofar as it illuminates the problem of the unidentified and sometimes desecrated dead body as, in Douglas's celebrated phrase, 'matter out of place'. This concept echoes Kristeva's idea about 'death infecting life' (Kristeva 1982, 4) in relation to those dead who have yet to be lodged within the institutional and social spaces ordained for their containment. On these accounts, we can interpret forensic deathwork as the attempt to restore the dead to their 'proper' place within the social universe (family, law, and politics) and thus recover them from the state of abjection.[14]

Rather than see forensic humanitarian work as a distinctive twentieth century phenomenon as others have done (see for example Rosenblatt 2015), I would instead place it within a longer tradition of deathwork which involves various types of experts and expertise in the registration of death, establishing the cause and manner of death, handling and preparing the dead body, burying, cremating, and carrying out funeral rites. It operates within a long history of bureaucratic management of the dead that is as much bound up with the development of modern techniques of social control as it is with religious rituals and the histories of autopsy and pathology. It is, however, a distinctive form of deathwork insofar as it attempts to lodge the dead back into the familial, social, political, and historical order in the wake of atrocity, and insofar as it speaks to and within two defining moral narratives of the twentieth century—humanitarianism and human rights—which in turn provide frameworks and rationales for the practical and symbolic management of the dead.

---

[14]I am here referring to the *symbolic* power of forensic work to domain the dead. This is notwithstanding the various and often significant practical obstacles to identification such as the sometimes high numbers of bodies, co-mingled remains, and the difficulties associated with extracting DNA from cremated or preserved remains.

3.6 What Makes These 'Human' Rights?

It is clear that the human rights of the dead do not, as yet, have explicit official or legal status. However, they are implicit in the histories of humanitarianism and human rights, current international humanitarian law, and forensic practice, as highlighted in this chapter. But still the question remains: what makes these rights 'human' rights? There are a couple of central principles that recur throughout these histories, legal codes, and forensic practices that are relevant. 'Dignity' and 'respect' appear time after time. They underpin, shape, and dominate the protocols and practices governing the humanitarian treatment of the dead. These principles tell us something about the social importance of the dead, and are reflections of widespread social norms older and more pervasive than those ushered in by law and forensics.

The principle of 'dignity' is of particular interest insofar as it is absolutely central to the idea of 'the human' that is elaborated in the UDHR. The UDHR 'recognises' (that is, constitutes) "the inherent dignity of all members of the human family" (United Nations General Assembly 1948). Dignity is the core concept of human rights, and it is the single principle that defines what it is to 'be human' *both in life and,* in relation to the histories and protocols outlined, *in death*. In addition, existing legal protocols and forensic practices governing the treatment of the dead require that the dead are treated as if they have the right to dignity, and they require that the living act in ways that are concordant with this belief.[15]

3.7 Conclusions: What Remains? Residual Rights

It would be nonsensical to suggest that the dead can be fully and comprehensively invested with human rights. Most, if not virtually all, human rights are entirely irrelevant in death. So what remains of human rights after death? It could be argued that the dead, within existing principles, legal codes, and forensic practice, are *already* understood and treated as if they have at least one, *residual*, human right: the right to be treated with dignity. I use the word 'residual' here deliberately and with reference to two things: first, with reference to the dead body as what is left over, or *what remains of the human after death*; and second, with reference to *what*

[15]There are further practical aspects of exhumation and identification that dignity might shape. For example, it might translate into the use of screens around excavation sites to protect human remains from public view or the minimisation of any damage to the remains. One such measure might include, for example, avoiding the extraction of the femur to establish stature and, instead, using CT scans. This, arguably, respects the integrity (and hence dignity) of the dead by avoiding any unnecessary disarticulation of human remains.

remains of human rights after death. Dignity is already established in IHL and forensic practice as a post mortem quality of the human, and as something underpinning 'right treatment' of the dead.

Following on from this, we need to push the debate further by exploring specifically which rights the dead might 'claim', and whether the dead have a valid claim on society to protect their possession of them. We already have evidence for three specific rights that could be more explicitly articulated and consolidated upon. These are rights that are implicit in the existing histories, regulations, and practices, and recur time and again: the rights to identity, to return to families, and to proper burial. These rights might act in an entirely posthumous and rehabilitative way. That is, they might be understood to *compensate* for rights that have been stripped away in life, such as the rights to life and security, freedom from torture and inhuman treatment, the right to personhood, and the right to equal protection under law. This compensatory principle might provide the basis of the dead's claim on society to have these rights protected.

I want to reprise, finally, the issue of interests and benefits. If the dead have no interests, how can they possibly *benefit* from any rights that might be conferred on them? It seems obvious that families and society more broadly have most interest in, and might be the beneficiaries of, any rights accorded to the dead. Both potentially benefit from the restorative, rehabilitative, and social ordering imperatives inherent in addressing rights to the dead. At the same time, I would add that those facing a high risk of enforced disappearance—migrants from Central America crossing Mexico, for example, or those undertaking necessary and perilous journeys from their country of origin, such as Syria—may also have interests in the rights of the dead insofar as they and their families might be potential beneficiaries of them. The human rights of the dead—identification, return to families, and proper burial—might also provide, to them, some consolation *in life*. Overall, it seems to me that the minimum and most appropriate formulation that might be arrived at so far is as follows: the human rights OF the dead, but FOR the living.[16]

Acknowledgements I am very grateful to Kirsty Squires and Nick Márquez-Grant for their generous and thoughtful help during the writing process. I would especially like to thank Nick Márquez-Grant for his suggestions as to how the preservation of the dignity of human remains might translate further into forensic practice. I am also grateful to Ricardo Bravo (Héctor Ricardo Bravo Santillán) at the Centro de Docencia y Económicas (CIDE), Aguascalientes, México, for his comments on an earlier version of my argument, presented at CIDE in March 2018.

[16]I have derived this formulation primarily in relation to the forensic recovery and identification of the dead in the context of contemporary human rights investigations and forensic humanitarian work. At the same time I would suggest that this rights formula could potentially be applied to other cases, such as to those of unidentified human remains currently held in museums.

References

Barnett, M. 2011. *Empire of Humanity: A History of Humanitarianism*. Ithaca: Cornell University Press.

Boddington, P. 1998. Organ Donation After Death—Should I Decide or Should My Family? *Journal of Applied Philosophy* 15 (1): 69–81.

Brennan, M. 2018. *Argentina's Missing Bones: Revisiting the History of the Dirty War*. Oakland: University of California Press.

Colibrí Centre. 2018. *The Missing Migrant Project*. http://www.colibricenter.org/. Accessed 28 May 2018.

Cordner, S., R. Coninx, H. J. Kim, et al. (eds.). 2016. *Management of Dead Bodies After Disasters: A Field Manual for Responders,* 2nd ed. Geneva: International Committee of the Red Cross, International Federation of Red Cross and Red Crescent Societies, Pan American Health Organization, World Health Organization, World Health Organization Regional Office of the Americas.

Douglas, M. [1966] 2002. *Purity and Danger: An Analysis of Concepts of Pollution and Taboo*. London: Routledge.

Dunant, H. [1862] 1959. *A Memory of Solferino*. Geneva: International Committee of the Red Cross.

Durkheim, E. [1895] 1982. *The Rules of Sociological Method and Selected Texts on Sociology and Its Method*. New York: Free Press.

Durkheim, E. [1898] 1994. Social Facts. In *Readings in the Philosophy of Social Science*, ed. M. Martin and L. McIntyre, 433–440. Cambridge: MIT Press.

Emson, H.E. 2003. It Is Immoral to Require Consent for Cadaver Organ Donation. *Journal of Medical Ethics* 29 (3): 125–127.

Forsythe, D.P. 2005. *The Humanitarians: The International Committee of the Red Cross*. Cambridge: Cambridge University Press.

González Ruibal, A., and G. Moshenska (eds.). 2015. *Ethics and the Archaeology of Violence*. New York: Springer.

Groen, W.J.M., R.C. Janaway, and N. Márquez-Grant. 2015. *Forensic Archeology: A Global Perspective*. Oxford: Wiley-Blackwell.

Hague Peace Conference. 1907. Hague Convention (IV) Respecting the Laws and Customs of War on Land and Its Annex: Regulations Concerning the Laws and Customs of War on Land. In *International Peace Conference*, The Hague, 18 October 1907.

Harris, J. 2003. Organ Procurement: Dead Interests, Living Needs. *Journal of Medical Ethics* 29 (3): 130–134.

Heinle, K., O.R. Ferreira, and D. Shirk. 2017. *Drug Violence in Mexico: Data and Analysis Through 2016*. San Diego: Department of Political Science and International Relations, University of San Diego.

International Commission on Missing Persons. 2018. *Missing Migrants Program for the Mediterranean Region*. The Hague: International Commission on Missing Persons. https://www.icmp.int/wp-content/uploads/2018/01/12.1-Missing-Migrants-English.pdf. Accessed 22 August 2018.

International Committee of the Red Cross. 1894. *Geneva Convention for the Amelioration of the Condition of the Wounded in Armies in the Field, 22 August*. Geneva: International Committee of the Red Cross.

International Committee of the Red Cross. 1949a. *Geneva Convention Relative to the Protection of Civilian Persons in Time of War (Fourth Geneva Convention), 12 August*. Geneva: International Committee of the Red Cross.

International Committee of the Red Cross. 1949b. *Geneva Convention Relative to the Treatment of Prisoners of War (Third Geneva Convention), 12 August*. Geneva: International Committee of the Red Cross.

International Committee of the Red Cross. 1977. *Protocol Additional to the Geneva Conventions of 12 August 1949, and Relating to the Protection of Victims of International Armed Conflicts (Protocol I), 8 June*. Geneva: International Committee of the Red Cross.

International Committee of the Red Cross. 2003. *Progress Report: The Missing: Action to Resolve the Problem of People Unaccounted for as a Result of Armed Conflict or Internal Violence and to Assist Their Families*. Geneva: International Committee of the Red Cross.

International Committee of the Red Cross. 2004. *Operational Best Practices Regarding the Management of Human Remains and Information on the Dead by Non-Specialists*. Geneva: International Committee of the Red Cross.

International Committee of the Red Cross. 2005. *Customary International Humanitarian Law: Volume I Rules*. Cambridge: Cambridge University Press.

International Committee of the Red Cross. 2006. *The Missing: Action to Resolve the Problem of People Unaccounted for as a Result of Armed Conflict or Internal Violence and to Assist Their Families. ICRC Progress Report*. Geneva: International Committee of the Red Cross.

International Committee of the Red Cross. 2017. *Missing Migrants*. https://www.icrc.org/en/missing-migrants. Accessed 28 May 2018.

Interpol. 1996. *General Assembly on Disaster Victim Identification*, 23–29 October. Lyon: Interpol.

Johns, F. 2017. Data, Detection and the Redistribution of the Sensible in International Law. *American Journal of International Law* 111: 57–103.

Kristeva, J. 1982. *Powers of Horror: An Essay on Abjection*. New York: Columbia University Press.

Laqueur, T. 2002. The Dead Body and Human Rights. In *The Body*, ed. S.T. Sweeney and I. Hodder, 75–93. Cambridge: Cambridge University Press.

Laqueur, T. 2015. *The Work of the Dead: A Cultural History of Mortal Remains*. Princeton: Princeton University Press.

Last Rights. 2018. *Last Rights*. http://lastrights.net/. Accessed 28 May 2018.

Mauss, M. [1935] 1973. Techniques of the Body. *Economy and Society* 2 (1): 70–88.

Mediterranean Missing. 2018. *The Project*. http://www.mediterraneanmissing.eu/. Accessed 28 May 2018.

Moon, C. 2008. *Narrating Political Reconciliation: South Africa's Truth and Reconciliation Commission*. Lanham: Lexington Books.

Moon, C. 2013. Interpreters of the Dead: Forensic Knowledge, Human Remains and the Politics of the Past. *Social and Legal Studies* 22 (2): 149–169.

Moon, C. 2016. Human Rights, Human Remains: Forensic Humanitarianism and the Human Rights of the Dead. *International Social Science Journal* 65 (215–216): 49–63.

Open Society Foundations. 2016. *Undeniable Atrocities: Confronting Crimes Against Humanity in Mexico*. New York: Open Society Foundations.

Rosenblatt, A. 2010. International Forensic Investigations and the Human Rights of the Dead. *Human Rights Quarterly* 32 (4): 922–951.

Rosenblatt, A. 2015. *Digging for the Disappeared: Forensic Science After Atrocity*. Stanford: Stanford University Press.

Savulescu, J. 2003. Death, Us and Our Bodies: Personal Reflections. *Journal of Medical Ethics* 29 (3): 127–130.

Schwartz-Marin, E., and A. Cruz-Santiago. 2016. Forensic Civism: Articulating Science, DNA and Kinship in Contemporary Mexico and Colombia. *Human Remains and Violence* 2 (1): 58–74.

Smolensky, K.R. 2009. Rights of the Dead. *Hofstra Law Review* 37 (3): 763–803.

Star, S.L., and J.R. Greisemer. 1989. Institutional Ecology, 'Translations', and Boundary Objects: Amateurs and Professionals in Berkeley's Museum of Vertebrate Zoology 1907–1939. *Social Studies of Science* 19 (3): 387–420.

Tidball-Binz, M. 2012. *For Whom the Bell Tolls: The Development of Humanitarian Forensic Action*. Keynote Speech. Paper presented at Victorian Institute of Forensic Medicine, Monash University, Melbourne, Australia, 7 June 2012.

United Nations. 1945. *Charter of the United Nations*. 24 October. San Francisco: United Nations.
United Nations General Assembly. 1948. *Universal Declaration of Human Rights*. New York: United Nations.
United Nations General Assembly. 1998. *Rome Statute of the International Criminal Court (Last Amended 2010)*. New York: United Nations.
United Nations Office of the High Commissioner for Human Rights. 2016. *Minnesota Protocol on the Investigation of Potentially Unlawful Death*. New York and Geneva: United Nations.
Wilson, R. 2001. *The Politics of Truth and Reconciliation in South Africa: Legitimizing the Post-Apartheid State*. Cambridge: Cambridge University Press.

Chapter 4
Research on Human Remains: An Ethics of Representativeness

Hallvard J. Fossheim

Abstract Within the complex matrix of ethical considerations in the handling of human remains, the notion that human remains *represent,* stands out as having serious implications for research and curatorship. Representativeness reminds us of the ethical relevance of the group level of identities in the European framework, actualised not least in terms of ethnicity. In line with basic research ethical principles, it is the wellbeing of those now living, which forms the most central consideration in questions of representativeness. Where continuities exist between previous populations and identifiable groups today, knowledge of such representativeness is necessary for acting ethically and for reaching legitimate solutions.

4.1 Introduction

Ethical considerations in the European area concerning research on human remains constitute a complex web of issues, partly defined by national peculiarities of a historical and political nature (O'Donnabhain and Lozada 2014, 4–9 and relevant chapters). Among the relevant historical variables is any colonial position in a given country's past. Similarly, along a related political axis are current or recent engagements with nation building or nationalism. Cutting across such variables are the sites of ethical quandary, among which are not least excavation, curation, display, return/repatriation, and reburial. The nature of the issues at each site will, in any concrete case, be heavily shaped by the matters first mentioned—e.g., a history of nation building sets up models of us/them that strongly affect attitudes to the display of remains; a colonial past forms a backdrop to any demand for repatriation.[1]

Ethnicity is the most ethically charged notion to give impetus to and arise from these historical, political, and scientific tensions. 'Ethnicity' is a multifaceted and,

[1]For the case of the UK, the historical background with a wealth of concrete examples is provided by Fforde (2004).

H. J. Fossheim (✉)
Department of Philosophy, University of Bergen, Pb 7805 5020 Bergen, Norway
e-mail: Hallvard.Fossheim@uib.no

K. Squires et al. (eds.), *Ethical Approaches to Human Remains*,
https://doi.org/10.1007/978-3-030-32926-6_4

in many usages, fuzzy concept, sometimes overlapping with 'race' as a more or less biological notion. At other times, 'ethnicity' denotes variables primarily transferable as memes rather than genes (James 2016, especially Sect. 3). Although various disciplines of research—among them anthropology, archaeology, and medical sciences—have certainly done their part in adding to this mix, ethnicity is not a category that was created by science or has found a home only in the spheres of research (Wimmer 2013). Europe has been in the questionable position of initiating two global wars in the last century or so, both of them centrally motivated by considerations of ethnicity; the same can be said of geographically more limited conflicts (see Lipphardt 2014 for an overview of some global developments in research methods and ideologies after World War II). On a less sinister note, the map of Europe is generally a map of vaguely expressed ethnicities: collective cultural identities making each individual part of overlapping sets of shared traditions, cultural expressions, and relations to other groups. In the European area as elsewhere, ethnicity is a source of personal identity and pride as well as a constant cause of contestation. It is also a dimension of research in which archaeology constantly dips its toe and sometimes immerses itself.

It would be wholly unrealistic here to try to offer anything like a roadmap to all extant constellations of the notions and tensions just mentioned. Instead, I will provide what I hope is more useful: an analysis of representativeness as, ethically speaking, what is in play in a wide plethora of cases, combined with exploration of one case study from Norway which illustrates some of the most central challenges associated with representativeness.

Remains cannot, unlike many other human targets for research, speak for themselves. But they do *represent*. Human remains are of interest to research because they represent the individuals and groups whose remains they are. The same is true of their ethical interest: the status of human remains as something representing human individuals and groups is crucial to what makes them ethically salient. This status is what I shall call their representativeness. Part of such representativeness is quite concrete: at some time in the past, this skull was the skull of a living person, and the skull's representativeness includes its relating to that person. Perhaps more complicated and abstract is representativeness that transcends the individual that was once there by pointing to something that the individual partook in, e.g. a family, a religious tradition, or an ethnic group. Ethically speaking, these various identities, available to us through knowledge of provenance and history, are all somehow present in the human remains. Representativeness is thus an ethically relevant relation between human remains and the humans whose remains they were, where those humans must be conceived in terms of both individuals and groups.

The fact of representativeness presents us with ethical challenges. On the good side, the representing nature of human remains forms a point of departure for securing representativeness among the living, in processes where decisions are made concerning the handling of human remains. This way, we also move beyond mere descriptions of pervasive attitudes to an analysis of the *normative* considerations at the heart of those attitudes: What are the values at stake? Only by considering the normative core of the situation can we hope to be able to evaluate current conflicts and find optimal solutions for future practices.

The ethics of research on human remains belongs within the broader framework of normative research ethics. Research ethics is not primarily an academic theory in the province of philosophy, but practices and reflections that build on and revolve around a set of principles, developed and specified to provide practical help. In its most frugal form, research ethics as a general framework for relating to the world amounts to three such principles. *Respect* for the individuals and groups concerned, ensuring *good consequences* and avoiding bad ones (this is sometimes referred to in terms of beneficence), and *justice*. Varieties of these basic principles have been treated as explicitly definitive for research ethics at least since the Belmont report (National Commission for the Protection of Human Subjects of Biomedical and Behavioral Research 1979). Guidelines in research ethics, whether general or more specific, are still articulated along the outline they provide. We should thus expect any results to be traceable back to one or several of these three principles.

In what follows, I will initially (Sect. 4.2) provide information about the Sami remains from Neiden, which I take to be a paradigmatic example for illustrating the complex identities of human remains, and the sort of ethical challenges we face when making choices about the handling of such remains. Specifically, the case provides an analysis into six ways in which such human remains may be expected to represent identities that go beyond their status as mere objects. After reminding the reader of the three basic research ethical principles that any person responsible for handling human remains—and a fortiori the present argument—must recognise (Sect. 4.3), I show how issues of representativeness relate to cases where the remains belong to known individuals (Sect. 4.4). The chapter then addresses a major issue of representativeness: Should the past or the present have ethical priority? (Sect. 4.5). After thus delineating the two perspectives of representativeness (i.e. the past and the present), I face the possible objection that prioritising the present might lead to an unfortunate form of relativism and undermine claims to truth (Sect. 4.6). I conclude with a general reflection over how researchers' responsibilities are generated, partly by their co-creating of the identities they study over time (Sect. 4.7).

4.2 The Sami Remains from Neiden

Research on the Sami people in Norway provides a pertinent example of the ethical centrality of representativeness.[2] The most important collection of human bones in Norway is the Schreiner collection, which is today housed by the Institute for Basic

[2]For a still instructive overview of issues pertaining to negotiations between this ethnic group and the nation state, see Hylland Eriksen (1991, esp. 271–274).

Medicine, which is part of the University of Oslo. The original motivation behind the collection was, to a great extent, founded in the physical anthropology of the early twentieth century, and 95% of the collection stems from Kristian Emil Schreiner's period as Director of the University of Oslo's Anatomical Institute (1908–1945), the original site for the collection. Schreiner both organised excavations and participated in the trade in human remains then common between Anatomical institutes (Kyllingstad 2015).

The Schreiner collection is still in use for research (Institute of Basic Medical Sciences 2017). According to an agreement made in the 1990s, before conducting research on Sami remains belonging to the Schreiner collection, the investigator is required to ask permission from the Norwegian Sami Parliament, which has the authority to allow or deny research on this material.[3]

A recent case involving human remains from the Schreiner collection concerned 95 skeletons stemming from the Sami population of Neiden in Finnmark. The remains had been unearthed from a local graveyard in 1915 on assignment from Schreiner, against the protests of the local Sami. The Sami Parliament decided to rebury the remains. The reburial took place in 2011, although some current inhabitants of Neiden were against it because they felt the need for historically informed research to be overriding (Norwegian National Committee for the Evaluation of Research on Human Remains (SKJ) 2014). Historically informed representation is of the essence in such cases. The Neiden remains represented various values and relations on at least six related axes.

(1) The remains from Neiden represented the *Sami population* (and so it was natural and reasonable that the Sami Parliament should have the responsibility of handling the case);
(2) The Neiden remains also represented the *Skolte Sami*, a specific ethnic sub-group of the Sami that has not always been treated as at one with the greater group;
(3) In addition to this, it should go almost without saying that they represented the *local community of Neiden*;
(4) Naturally, they also represented *family lineages*;
(5) Since the Skolte Sami were traditionally inhabiting an area bordering Norway, Finland, and Russia, and at least some of the remains had been buried before the borders were formally established as they now are, there is also the ghost of *nationality* as a relevant representational dimension;
(6) Last but not least, as the Skolte Sami have traditionally been Russian Orthodox Christians, the remains have a representational value along the axis of *religion*.

The initial move for reburial was carried out by a Russian Orthodox congregation. This combination of religion and initiative was in the event a factor in the decision to rebury the remains, all on the background of ethnicity as the major category behind the story. In any concrete case, we of course also see further

[3]This procedure was first officially suggested by Lønning et al. (1998, 22 [Sect. 4]).

ethically relevant factors playing their part, such as histories of deception or force. However, these issues matter on a practical level today, mainly because representativeness makes them relevant to today's individuals or groups. In the case of Neiden, current representativeness is relevant for all the six dimensions listed.[4]

In considering how the Neiden story illustrates representativeness as a typically complex ethical issue, it also bears emphasising that the six different axes listed above are rarely entirely aligned in any single case. Each axis characteristically singles out a group or population that substantially overlaps with, without being identical to what is suggested by, those of the other axes. For instance, as ethnic determinations can come in several degrees of specification (1 and 2), these are not unproblematic even when compared to each other; and whereas any ascription of ethnicity might tend to overlap with religion (6), the two will normally not be identical; nor will any of them be identical to the dimension of nationality (5). Even a world so simple that all the circles had been concentric would still be a world with a multitude of axes of representativeness, and the challenges related to this state of affairs.

4.3 Representativeness and Research Ethics

When carrying out research on a given group, the researcher has a basic responsibility to make sure that he or she interacts with the group in a manner which is sound as far as the representativeness of the individuals involved is concerned. If we return to the three research ethical principles (outlined in the introduction of this chapter), three considerations come to the fore, which have to do with an understanding of the researcher as a responsible agent within a broader social framework. First, there is the general research ethical demand that one *respects* whoever one is doing research on. This is about acknowledging that when the research is on humans, the object of study is also a subject. It is an expression of respect for the personhood (or sometimes potential personhood) of others, which typically takes the form of an acknowledgement that those directly affected should have a say concerning the research, whether through consent or consultation.

Second, there is the general research ethical demand *not to cause undue harm*. This consideration may also be understood in terms of respect, but it often applies much more widely. We are not only autonomous, or potentially autonomous, beings. We are also vulnerable beings—beings that can get hurt, or injured, or suffer in all kinds of ways. Acknowledging that research does not take place in a vacuum means being open to the possibility that research may also have negative consequences, not only physically but on psychological, social, and political levels. Contributing to a denigratory or stigmatising misrepresentation of a given group of people is, as such, a negative consequence.

---

[4]For reminders of the relations between historical background and current practices, peruse entries including treatments of Jewish or Sami remains in Márquez-Grant and Fibiger (2011, e.g. 449–450).

Third is *justice*. Justice as a concept is both vague and ambiguous. But one obvious meaning is the fair and reasonable treatment of different groups, avoiding unreasonable favouritism of some and the mistreatment or stigmatisation of others. Judiciously understanding groups and their relations with other groups, and acting with a basis in such insight, is at the heart of justice as a research ethical consideration. These are all normative reasons expressing responsibility concerning representativeness (for a more detailed sketch of the three principles, cf. National Commission 1979, Part B).

4.4 Individuals and Representativeness

The typical case surrounding the analysis, retention, or display of human remains will bring up ethically relevant worries akin to those exemplified by the Neiden case, due to links of representativeness between a more or less limited set of remains and living groups. At one extreme end of the spectrum is a subset of cases where the human remains continue to be individualised, and can even be identified as stemming from a singled-out person. The four examples that follow are known cases that should suffice in order to indicate some of what is special about them:

- *Charles Byrne*. Against his wishes, the remains of "the Irish Giant" (eighteenth century) were procured for medical science and displayed (Greenfieldboyce 2017).
- *Sarah Baartman*. "The Hottentott Venus" died in 1815; originating in South-Western Africa, displayed in London and Paris (in the latter place also after her death and until 2002) (Parkinson 2016).
- "*El Negro*". A Tswana warrior exhumed by a French dealer a few days after his burial in 1831 and subsequently displayed in France and then Spain until 1997, his partial remains were finally reburied in Gaborone in 2000 (Westerman 2016).
- *Julia Pastrana*. Stemming from Mexico, she was presented as "the Ape Woman" on European and Russian tours; upon death, the display continued with the embalmed bodies of her and her son (Hals Gylseth and Toverud 2003). Her remains were stored with a view to medical research until buried in Mexico in 2014.

In these special situations, it can be argued that the most important and overriding representativeness involved concerns the person who was once there. A main dimension of representativeness is then one between the remains and a past individual. This is of course a relation that is always present in all cases of research on human remains, but these cases bring it to the fore.

At the same time, however, it is also important to bear in mind that no one is only an individual. The history of each of these persons presents us with an intricate web of further ways of representativeness that are sometimes potentially, sometimes obviously, ethically relevant. To mention only a couple of threads worthy of examination, Julia Pastrana was in all likelihood a Christian as well as a member of a tribe; both she and Sarah Baartman were women; Charles Byrne came from a land of relative poverty and partial subjugation.

Not unreasonably, how to deal with such cases in an ethically responsible manner must be as individualised as are the histories and backgrounds of each of these individuals. But even in such histories, which bring out and emphasise the individual in a way not typical for research, the complexities of representativeness remain. El Negro reminds us perhaps most starkly of historical perversions of representativeness, because he was individualised as a bodily presence through the display, and simultaneously obliterated as a person by the racist notions of ethnicity and race that motivated the display. Both "El Negro" and "the Hottentot Venus" similarly indicate such structures by the very names given to them.

4.5 Representativeness: Two Perspectives

In order to see the full impact and role of representativeness, we must delve deeper into the temporal perspectives it includes, because they make a practical difference to the researcher's or curator's ethical thinking and choices. Before doing this, however, we need to be clear that in most cases of contestation concerning research on human remains, ethically relevant questions generally manifest themselves on at least two different levels. On one level is the question about *what* one should do: whether we are dealing with a proposed research project on human remains in a collection, or a demand for reburial or repatriation of those remains, there is a basic question about what is the best result. Allowing the research or not? Facilitating reburial or not?

On another level, there is also the question of *how* to go about deciding what to do. This is no less an ethical question than the previous one. As indicated by the previous representativeness discussion, who is involved, who is given a say, and who is allowed to decide are ethically highly charged issues. These issues concern the process and not just the results. In this context, however, it is important to keep in mind that limitations in both knowledge and resources normally necessitate some degree of simplification. To return to the Schreiner collection as an example, most of the ancient remains are classified as either Sami or Norse, and the final say on research proposals is distributed accordingly (Lønning et al. 1998). Necessarily, the historical realities from which the material stems are more complex than what such an either/or division would seem to indicate. With a plethora of smaller and larger populations moving, interacting, and assimilating into each other through the centuries, it is utterly unlikely that the individuals whose remains are stored at the Schreiner collection thought of themselves as simply "Norse"(/Norwegian) or "Sami". If we grant for the sake of argument that they did, they certainly did not do so based on today's definitions of the two groups. Allowing even this impossible scenario, they certainly did not think of "Norse" or "Sami" as their single defining characteristic. Not all simplification means a reduction in ethical quality, however, as the legitimacy of our broad and absolute bifurcation into these two denominations does not simply rest on its ability to map onto historical or pre-historical categories.

The insight that our categories of representation are inexact might easily lead one to suppose that if proper representation were at all possible, it would consist in an infinitely more intricate and complex network of definitions and roles than what the current system allows. This thought, however, is a function of a particular perspective on the relationship between the remains and ourselves. According to this perspective, the *remains* are ultimately what is to be represented correctly. The job of posterity (us) is simply to take proper care that this is done. This perspective can be summed up as follows.

Perspective A on representativeness The people whose remains are in question are what must primarily be represented correctly.

There are ethically salient considerations that lead us in this direction of thought, and they are not completely off the mark. But this perspective cannot be the only relevant one, or even the most important one, in the sort of cases we are considering. Even if we do not consider the challenges posed by realities, such as limited knowledge and even more limited resources, there is reason to look for an alternative. For as we have found, and tried to specify for research on human remains, we have an irreducible and crucial responsibility towards the living.

What is then the alternative to Perspective A? If Perspective A sees events from the vantage point of the remains' origins, and judges our contemporary actions in light of those origins, the alternative perspective would be to see events from the vantage point of our current situation, and judge activities involving historical remains from that point of view. Our contemporary institutions are set up partly to ensure addressing and redressing mistakes, shortcomings, and injustice. Returning to the Neiden events as our example, the Sami Parliament (created through an Act by the Norwegian Parliament: Lov om Sametinget og andre samiske rettsforhold 1987) is such an institution, formed partly in recognition of past injustices carried out against the Sami people by the Norwegian state. On a practical level, the establishment marks the importance of addressing the acknowledged injustices and avoiding new ones. The appropriate approach to deciding whether, and if so how, to carry out research on a given set of remains is one that acknowledges today's people, places, and institutions. This perspective can be summed up as follows.

Perspective B on representativeness The present population is what must primarily be represented correctly.

These outlines of Perspective A and Perspective B are not solely of academic interest. The two perspectives can point in different directions as far as practical solutions go, and they do so based on a difference in the direction of the ethical considerations of each. While Perspective B places a highlight on the researcher's responsibility vis-à-vis living individuals, Perspective A focuses on the respect owed to the people whose remains are in question. The two perspectives are in practice irreducible to each other. Rarely if ever will the researcher's ethical responsibilities lie only with one of the two, but depending on the project, one or the other will tend to overshadow the alternative perspective. In some cases (partly exemplified in Sect. 4.4), where the individuals are known *as* those individuals, Perspective A should get more of a priority. In most cases, however, where the remains in question are ancient and/or individually unidentified and there are representatives among the living, we (wisely) tend to place more emphasis on Perspective B than on Perspective A, to the extent that we have to prioritise. This is partly because knowledge engenders responsibility, and so knowledge of what we might call stark individuality generates a prima facie obligation to consider the individual's wishes and perspectives qua individual. For cases where little such insight is available, the group or groups sharing central axes of identity through relations of representativeness—who were anyway always ethically relevant—come to the fore.

Ultimately, the two perspectives are not simply two directions of view—from the past looking in the direction of the present (Perspective A), or from the present looking in the direction of the past (Perspective B). Although direction of view in this sense is attendant on each perspective, that is a consequence of *priority*. The term 'perspective' denotes first and foremost what is given pride of place, what is figuratively speaking placed in the foreground, thus taking on the greatest size and most central position. Their respective functions imply that Perspective B (prioritising present populations) is inherently more ethically focused than Perspective A (prioritising past populations). Ethics serves practical thinking, with a view to acting in the world, and living people can (for better or worse) be acted upon in more thoroughgoing and affecting ways than those who are no longer living. The three research ethical principles mentioned initially—respect, good consequences, and justice—also cater to this premise, in being first and foremost concerned with subjects who are alive at the time of research. In line with this, the first principle is partly founded on a notion of autonomy. All else being equal, the living are a more central ethical concern than the dead.

There certainly is an ethical dimension to how we relate to those no longer living also, as illustrated by our ethical intuitions concerning phenomena as different as the handling of dead bodies or speaking ill of the dead. These are real issues although the individual is no longer a thinking, acting, feeling person among us. But for most scenarios, the issues are as it were shadows of the dilemmas arising when we face the living. This state of affairs is, to a great extent (although not entirely), explained by respect for the dead being a function of the fact that the dead are considered through the attribute of having been alive. The dead are not simply inanimate, but entities that used to be living. This ethically relevant fact is indicated by the very word used for the objects in question: human remains. Today's archaeological objects are the remains of what used to be living beings. Logically speaking, Perspective A to a great extent depends on the fact that Perspective B was once available for the populations and individuals now reduced to human remains. In this limited sense, at least, referring to human remains simply as "objects" can also be problematical, to the extent that this is an expression that can tend to cover up part of the remains' ethical status.

4.6 A Question of Truth

Some might perceive a threat to truthfulness in Perspective B. If the two perspectives provide somewhat different answers to the same question, and we have defined Perspective A as the historically most accurate one, does this mean that Perspective B is less reliable? And if so, how can we base our ethical stance on it?

The best way to deflate this worry is to say that the two perspectives are not meant to answer the same questions. Perspective A is meant primarily to answer questions about historical accuracy. Perspective B is intended to help find viable and fair solutions to current practical quandaries. What separates the two perspectives is thus partly a contrast between caring most of all for the past (A) and caring most of all for the present (B), partly a contrast between a primarily descriptive (A) and a more essentially normative (B) approach.

Three considerations seem to collectively resolve the reliability difficulty. First are the theoretical and practical limitations mentioned above. We normally do not know enough about details in the past and how they relate to the present to trace causal and non-causal developments sufficiently closely for a complete development of Perspective A; and even if we did possess all that knowledge, we would not have the resources to set up a process for decision-making which takes it into full account.

Second, there is the clear ethical relevance of which personal and institutional constellations are available in the present. Given the existence of a legitimate body, like the Sami Parliament in the Neiden case, it would be illegitimate and unethical to ignore that reality for some independent set of putatively more accurate computations. Many larger ethnic groups will have some representative organ, often on a national level, although its form and basis of legitimacy is something that differs from one constellation to the next. For this reason, it is impossible to frame ethical guidelines on this point for all cases, except to say that the curator and researcher have a responsibility to orient themselves concerning the existence, status, and function of such groups when relevant. This responsibility will normally extend to initiating dialogue where such relations do not already exist.

Third, as highlighted in the previous section, an overriding ethical concern and responsibility is towards the living. Respect, beneficence, and justice are all primarily directed towards protecting persons as acting and suffering beings. On this point too, the Neiden case provides ground for conferring with our ethical intuitions. The human remains represent individuals who were once there, and this fact places demands on how to treat those remains. Ethically, however, through the six dimensions spelled out earlier, the human remains also represent persons now living, and this is an irreducible part of their status. Both the individuals who were once living and the individuals who are now living are to be accorded respect, but primacy goes to the living. This is due not only to the fact that the living can be hurt in more ways than the dead, but because respect is tied to autonomy, something only the living possess. The representativeness of human remains thus provides an indication of who among the living should be taken into ethical consideration for any given case.

The original worry concerning the non-alignment of two perspectives was that acting on the basis of Perspective B could mean taking leave of truth. I have responded that the two perspectives have differing functions and indicated that the question is thus wrongly posed. A lingering worry might be that Perspective B leads to subjectivism and thus to relativism. Perspective B amounts to subjectivism, however, only if the sole criteria for being part of the group represented are subjective ones. In the Neiden case, this would amount to a status as Sami (and thus a right to vote at, run for office with, or be taken into account by the Sami Parliament) being exclusively a matter of personal tastes and opinions. In such a world, the criteria for representation on the side of those whose human remains are in question would be void of all inter-subjectively controlled criteria.

What is lacking in such a world is the establishment of Perspective A's epistemic criteria aligned with Perspective B as a control function on its ethical force. While Perspective B is the ethically salient one, such criteria provide what we might call an epistemic tempering of its claims in the form of necessary requirements. Ethics is not free-floating but supervenes on matters of fact. As exemplified by the workings of the Sami Parliament in Norway, this means that membership in the Sami caucus requires the fulfilment of objective as well as subjective criteria. The Sami Legal Act (Lov om Sametinget og andre samiske rettsforhold 1987, Sects. 2–6; cf. Sellevold 2011) thus states that voting is open to those who declare that they see themselves as Sami (subjective criterion) *and* have a further specified continuity relation to Sami language or Parliament (objective criterion). When no such relation can be agreed on, the case lacks Perspective B as an epistemic control function (for one such problematic case, see Payne 2012).

4.7 Co-creating Identities

The conclusions concerning perspectives A and B (outlined in Sect. 4.5) illustrates that, for questions of representativeness, ensuring legitimate practices requires defining who forms part of the group. Like any act of naming someone, the identification of a group is often performed to an important extent from the outside (a welcome reminder of this fact, against sometimes overly constructivist and self-determining interpretations, is Wimmer 2013). In contemporary studies, populations are normally defined by the researcher, sometimes on the basis of half-baked notions of ethnicity that combine cultural and biological factors. The ethical dimensions of relations between researchers and groups are affected by the historical dimension of those same relationships. And this is where it also becomes relevant that history is the sourcebook of prejudice. History is what makes us see groups as groups. And that history is not over, as today's actions and choices are parts of a process stretching into the future as well as the past. If history is what makes us see groups as groups, that history is an ongoing process. The research thus becomes part of a group's co-defining history. The fact that science has been a central instrument in defining and controlling groups is also what makes it pertinent to speak of a historically shaped ethical responsibility on the part of science.[5]

Research in these cases is never a disinterested mirroring of unquestionable reality. To the extent that it is not self-evident to someone whether they do belong to the group, who else belongs to the group, or what are the criteria for belonging to the group, the research actually contributes towards determining who belongs to the group and what are the criteria for doing so. It thus becomes a moot point who should represent the group in question because of one of two factors, sometimes in combination: (1) disagreement or lack of clarity about who belongs to the group, and (2) disagreement or lack of clarity about what mechanisms should be in place to ensure that the group is represented in a way that is fair to all members of the group. One might very well disagree about the latter even if there is total agreement on the former, for instance if all agree which ethnic group is represented by a set of remains, but not all agree on how to find out what the people in that group think should be done (e.g. sending out individual questionnaires? Approaching a chosen body claiming to represent the group?), or what it would take to include the group sufficiently in the process (e.g. only include their responses in a broader process? Let them have final word?).

Such questions are to a great extent about issues of *legitimacy*. Legitimacy is not simply a function of contentedness, but is co-determined by the decisions having been made in the right way with a view to due process and proper information to all parties involved (see Sect. 4.5 for further details). In cases where the group is not beforehand unambiguously defined, legitimacy therefore hinges on making the right decisions about the relevant membership or mechanisms, as indicated above. This is perhaps especially the case if the researchers bring to the table a (partial) first order determination (which individuals are included) or second order determination (what are the criteria for inclusion). Whilst the researchers are responsible for ensuring Perspective B representativeness, it would at the same time be unethical of them to simply employ their own determination of the group in question.

It can seem as if the ethical demand is to do the impossible: ensuring a fair and reasonable inclusion without unduly affecting the outcome. Again, on a more practical level, however, the closest we normally get to the ideal is demanding relevant historical knowledge on the part of the researcher or curator. They have a responsibility to be responsible, which means being knowledgeable about the situation and framework, well beyond the technicalities that inform much contemporary research. Naturally, this is not the same as avoiding all prejudice, but it is an irreducible part of reducing poor judgement and bad agency. The researcher or curator is responsible for possessing insight into the cultural and historical conditions of the living population in question. In some cases, this will also include educating oneself on who can reasonably be said to represent whom among both public and privately initiated organisations and interest groups.

---

[5]The mechanism of such a specifically historical responsibility is surprisingly elusive as seen from the vantage point of contemporary ethical theory. I pursue its details in Fossheim (2018).

4.8 Conclusion

Within the complex matrix of ethical considerations affecting archaeology and other disciplines involved in the handling of human remains, the notion that human remains *represent* stands out as having serious implications for research. Such representation reminds us of the ethical relevance of the group level of identities, in the European framework actualised not least in terms of ethnicity. In line with basic research ethical principles, it is the wellbeing of those now living, which forms the most central consideration in such questions of representativeness. Where there are continuities between previous populations and identifiable groups of today, knowledge of such representativeness is necessary for acting ethically and for reaching legitimate solutions.

Acknowledgements For their constructive comments on previous versions of this chapter, I am grateful to participants at the *Twentieth Century Histories of Knowledge About Human Variation* research group workshop, Max Planck Institute of Berlin; the *Race, Ethnicity, Ancestry, and Human Genetic Variation* NTM workshop, Oslo; the *12th World Congress of Bioethics*, Mexico City; and the *Rethinking Sami Cultures in Museums* conference, University of Oslo. Thanks to the editors of this volume for their conscientious and constructive feedback. Finally, a special thanks to Jon Kyllingstad and Ageliki Lefkaditou for their detailed and helpful comments on earlier versions of the text. The Research Council of Norway funded this research through the Cultural Conditions Underlying Social Change program (SAMKUL; project no.: 220741/F10).

References

Fforde, C. 2004. *Collecting the Dead: Archaeology and the Reburial Issue*. London: Duckworth.

Fossheim, H.J. 2018. Past Responsibility: History and the Ethics of Research on Ethnic Groups. *Studies in History and Philosophy of Science Part C: Studies in History and Philosophy of Biological and Biomedical Sciences* 73: 35–43.

Greenfieldboyce, N. 2017. The Saga of the Irish Giant's Bones Dismays Medical Ethicists. *Shots: Health News From NPR*. 13 March. https://www.npr.org/sections/health-shots/2017/03/13/514117230/the-saga-of-the-irish-giants-bones-dismays-medical-ethicists. Accessed 11 July 2018.

Hals Gylseth, C., and L.O. Toverud. 2003. *Julia Pastrana: The Tragic Story of the Victorian Ape Woman*. Stroud: Sutton.

Hylland Eriksen, T. 1991. Ethnicity Versus Nationalism. *Journal of Peace Research* 28 (3): 263–278.

Institute of Basic Medical Sciences. 2017. *Bioanthropology*. https://www.med.uio.no/imb/english/research/groups/bioanthropology/index.html. Accessed 11 July 2018.

James, M. 2016. Race. In *Stanford Encyclopedia of Philosophy*. https://plato.stanford.edu/entries/race/. Accessed 11 July 2018.

Kyllingstad, J.R. 2015. *Measuring the Master Race: Physical Anthropology in Norway 1890–1945*. Cambridge: Open Book Publishers.

Lipphardt, V. 2014. "Geographical Distribution Patterns of Various Genes": Genetic Studies of Human Variation After 1945. *Studies in History and Philosophy of Biological and Biomedical Sciences* 30: 1–12.

Lønning, I., M. Guhttor, J. Holme, et al. 1998. *Innstilling fra Utvalg for vurdering av retningslinjer for bruk og forvaltning av skjelettmateriale ved Anatomisk institutt [Proposal from the Committee for Evaluation of Guidelines for the Use and Curation of Skeletal Material at the Anatomical Institute]*. Oslo: The University of Oslo.

Lov om Sametinget og andre samiske rettsforhold (sameloven) [Sami Act]. 1987. Ministry of Local Government and Modernisation, Oslo.

Márquez-Grant, N., and L. Fibiger (eds.). 2011. *The Routledge Handbook of Archaeological Human Remains and Legislation: An International Guide to Laws and Practice in the Excavation and Treatment of Archaeological Human Remains*. New York: Routledge.

National Commission for the Protection of Human Subjects of Biomedical and Behavioral Research. 1979. *The Belmont Report*. Elkridge: Department of Health, Education, and Welfare. https://www.hhs.gov/ohrp/regulations-and-policy/belmont-report/index.html. Accessed 11 July 2018.

Norwegian National Committee for the Evaluation of Research on Human Remains. 2014. *Vedrørende utleveringskrav av skjelettmateriale fra Pasvik [Concerning Demand for Repatriation of Skeletal Material from Pasvik]*. https://www.etikkom.no/globalassets/documents/uttalelser/skjelettutvalget/skj-svarbrev-sak-2013-151-27-01-2014.pdf. Accessed 11 July 2018.

O'Donnabhain, B., and M.C. Lozada. 2014. *Archaeological Human Remains: Global Perspectives*. New York: Springer.

Parkinson. J. 2016. The Significance of Sarah Baartman. *BBC News Magazine*. 7 January. http://www.bbc.co.uk/news/magazine-35240987. Accessed 11 July 2018.

Payne, S. 2012. Archaeology and Human Remains: Handle with Care! Recent English Experiences. In *More Than Just Bones: Ethics and Research on Human Remains*, ed. H. Fossheim, 49–64. Oslo: The Norwegian National Research Ethics Committees.

Sellevold, B. 2011. Norway. In *The Routledge Handbook of Archaeological Human Remains and Legislation*, ed. N. Márquez-Grant and L. Fibiger, 317–328. New York: Routledge.

Westerman, F. 2016. The Man Stuffed and Displayed Like a Wild Animal. *BBC News Magazine*. 16 September. http://www.bbc.com/news/magazine-37344210. Accessed 11 July 2018.

Wimmer, H. 2013. *Ethnic Boundary Making: Institutions, Power, Networks*. Oxford: Oxford University Press.

Chapter 5
The Ethical Awakening of Human Anatomy: Reassessing the Past and Envisioning a More Ethical Future

David Gareth Jones

Abstract Human anatomy lives at the interface between its dependence upon high quality dead human bodies for use in teaching and research, and the need to show respect for the deceased and their families. This tension has existed throughout the 500 years of modern anatomy's development, although for many of those years the pressures to provide sufficient numbers of dead bodies obscured serious ethical deliberation. As awareness of the latter has burgeoned over recent years, attention has turned to practices such as the use of anonymous archival human material, reliance upon using unclaimed bodies as opposed to bodies specifically bequeathed for dissecting purposes, and the legitimacy of public exhibitions of dissected plastinated whole bodies. Discussion of these topics has necessitated an assessment of well-known historical incidents, including dissection as a punishment for murder, the resurrectionists (grave robbers), the dependence of iconic figures in anatomy (such as Vesalius) on the those questionable procedures, and the practice of Nazi anatomists in working closely with the authorities to obtain unclaimed bodies from ethically abhorrent sources. A dominant message to emerge from these historical episodes has been anatomists' ready acceptance of the bodies of the poor and vulnerable. As anatomists have begun to address ethical imperatives, a theme to come into increasing prominence has been the need to humanise the practice of anatomy, in an attempt to recognise the dignity of the recently deceased and their interests when alive. This provides an ethical base from which to address new challenges for human anatomists, including 3D printing of human material, the growing use of data sets freely available on the internet, and the increasing availability of donated bodies following physician assisted death.

D. G. Jones (✉)
Department of Anatomy, University of Otago, PO Box 913, Dunedin 9054, New Zealand
e-mail: gareth.jones@otago.ac.nz

K. Squires et al. (eds.), *Ethical Approaches to Human Remains*,
https://doi.org/10.1007/978-3-030-32926-6_5

5.1 Changing Ethical Standards in Anatomy

When writing about the ethical expectations of a profession, it is usually a case of the disinterested observer standing back and assessing the ethical niceties of the practices and procedures of the profession. Such an approach can be taken either when the profession has an apparently unsullied history and/or when the observer has no connections with the profession. Unfortunately, neither of these stipulations applies in the case of anatomy and certainly not when I, as the commentator, have an intimate connection with anatomy. The questionable ethical base of anatomy was all too poignantly summed up by an editorial in *The Lancet* in 1832: "It is disgusting to talk of anatomy as a science, whilst it is cultivated by means of practices which would disgrace a nation of cannibals" (Lancet 1832, 245). The events leading up to this cry of despair are well known—grave robbing undertaken largely by, and on behalf of, anatomists and medical schools (Richardson 2001), the disrespect shown by anatomists and their students for the bodies being dissected, let alone for their families, and even murders commissioned by anatomists as a means of obtaining a requisite number of bodies for medical schools (Moore 2005; Burch 2007; Jones and Whitaker 2009a). Ethical considerations of even the most basic kind were nowhere in view.

Such atrocities are far removed from the anatomy of today and yet the path between the early nineteenth century and the early twenty-first century is far from straightforward (MacDonald 2005, 2010). As a medical student in London in the late 1950s I, along with all other medical students, dissected a human body. But it was not until many years later that I thought about asking where that body had come from. Had it been bequeathed or was it unclaimed? I was a student at the period in anatomy's history when the supply of bodies in the UK was changing—from unclaimed to bequests (Richardson 2001). Of course, I was naïve and was oblivious to any ethical dimensions underlying this change. I had no interest in the source of the supply and it was not a topic of discussion with students.

The aim of this chapter is to reflect on the enormous ethical transformations that have taken place in anatomy as a profession from its earliest stages through to the present day, where it is deemed to be a mature scientific discipline. Advances in the scientific understanding of anatomy occurred many years prior to the comparable rise of ethical awareness within this discipline, a lag that led to numerous tragedies and considerable human misery. In exploring this dichotomy, the relevant ethical values required for appropriate guidance pertaining to the use of human tissue in anatomy (and by implication, its use in all related fields) will emerge.

5.1.1 Personal History of Questionable Ethical Dealings

On my arrival at the University of Otago (New Zealand) in the early 1980s as Professor of Anatomy, I had no qualms about the manner in which the Department obtained brains for neuroanatomy classes. They were obtained at post mortems and came directly to the Anatomy Department from the Pathology Department. I gave no thought to the ethical niceties of this informal trade and whether the family of the deceased had given their permission for the removal of the brain. For me the transfer of brains from one department to another was innocuous, and the notion of informed consent had not at that time entered my lexicon. Human brains had been obtained in this way for many years, and no one had raised any concerns: it was not a contentious matter and the brains were being used for good purposes. Neither had I been introduced to the concept of moral complicity. All this was to change a few years later in the light of the Cartwright Inquiry (1987–1988) in New Zealand, and the emerging debate on the role of informed consent in clinical medicine (Cartwright 1988; Jones 1989).

I also discovered that the Department of Anatomy had a very large collection of skeletal remains that once belonged to individuals from Māori and Pacific groups. They had been in storage for many years and were used in a small number of research projects in biological anthropology. The large size of this collection and its scientific and cultural significance were not generally appreciated by anyone outside the Department, and within the Department there was no serious questioning about the appropriateness of this situation. It would probably have remained that way for a few more years, except that my increasing awareness of ethical imperatives in responding to Indigenous skeletal remains (Jones and Harris 1998) led me to open discussions in 1993 with local Māori (Ngāi Tahu), informing them of the existence of this collection, inviting them to inspect it, and together aiming to seek a way forward. In further discussions over 1995–1997 the Department accepted, in principle, the Ngai Tahu Koiwi Tangata policy (Heritage New Zealand 2014), and provided a detailed inventory of the entire skeletal collection of Ngai Tahu Rohe held in the Department, including their provenance, sex, age, and year acquired. A list of unprovenanced New Zealand Polynesian remains was also supplied by the Department of Anatomy at the University of Otago. Research that had been conducted on the Köiwi Tangata remains was shared with relevant stakeholders, and subsequently led to a very positive relationship between biological anthropologists in the Department and Māori throughout New Zealand.

The Department also had a collection of preserved dissected material and organs, plus foetuses and embryos from the early part of the twentieth century. These were used to varying degrees in teaching, but by today's standards had not been obtained with appropriate consent. Decisions had to be taken on what was to be done with this material: to dispose of it, continue to use it, or leave it in storage. These were typical museum archives of anonymous human remains, specifically 'historic archival' material since its origins would have been prior to the 1960s (Department of Health 2001; Retained Organs Commission 2002).

5.1.2 Confronting Anonymous Archival Human Material

By definition, anonymous archival material has no known links to its original subject, no information is available regarding whether consent was obtained, there is no indication of the intended purpose of the tissue, and little or nothing may be known about the method of acquisition of the tissue (Jones et al. 2003). At the University of Otago, the Anatomy Museum has material dating from 1879, just three years after the foundation of the Medical School, through to the present day. While there is only limited evidence of consent for the pre-1970s material, all the more recent non-archival material has been derived from cadavers bequeathed to the anatomy department in terms of the extant Human Tissue Act (2008). In assessing the options, four possibilities emerged (Jones et al. 2003).

The first option was to dispose of the tissue through burial, or incineration, as clinical waste. Clearly, this line of action would not directly benefit any party, but it would ensure that it could not be inappropriately used in future. But would its disposal be of any positive value? It exists and hence a decision regarding its continued existence and use is unavoidable, and this is an ethical question. There is no way of side lining the ethical dimension. Disposal is not an ethically neutral resolution, since it will preclude use of the material to benefit the human community.

A second option was to use the tissue in teaching, and hence benefitting students, provided there is a focused teaching rationale with clear curricular goals, preferably now or in the foreseeable future. A third option was research focused. Like any research that involves the use of human material, justification for such work depends upon its potential scientific and/or clinical usefulness. Both these options rely upon the quality of the teaching or research, and not merely on the availability of the stored material.

This leaves a fourth possibility, that of leaving the material in storage and doing nothing with it. A rationale sometimes encountered is that it may be required for future research projects. Theoretically, this may be a compelling justification for continued storage, knowing the potential of future technological advances to transform an understanding of research questions. However, in the absence of a research question, leaving material in storage amounts to nothing better than stockpiling tissue. At best this is ethically dubious.

In summary, the potential scientific and clinical value of human tissue in storage should be taken into consideration when determining what can or cannot be done with it. But as a norm, it is preferable to use human tissue for which specific consent has been given for its use in teaching and research. Hence, the availability of archival material is always a compromise solution that should never lead to a diminution in the respect shown to the human body or its parts. Routinely, it is preferable to err on the side of altruism, and hence for consent for the use of all newly acquired human tissue (May 1985; Campbell 2009). This is unattainable for anonymous archival material, and yet even in this instance archival samples should be treated with the same care and respect as if they had been donated. This demands that those in charge of the tissue act as its custodians rather than its owners, accepting that they are responsible for safe storage of the samples, for its appropriate use, and for the quality of the research to be carried out on it. Over subsequent years, the Department of Anatomy at the University of Otago made every effort to determine whether living relatives of stored human material could be found. This proved unsuccessful, and the Department has continued to use the material for teaching and, in some instances, research.

5.2 The Emergence of a Modern Discipline: Ethical Underpinnings

These personal vignettes serve as an introduction to the far more revolutionary changes that have taken place in anatomy over the whole of its evolution as an emerging discipline, with the greatest changes covering the last 500 years. Of these the most striking, and the one with the most profound ethical ramifications, is the manner in which the bodies of the deceased have been obtained. This represents a move from the exploitation of the vulnerable and those in the lowest strata of society, to one in which donors are seen as playing an integral part in the culture of dissection-based anatomical education.

Good ethical practice is now regarded as the bequest of bodies for the specific purpose of being dissected for medical education and training and/or biomedical research, following fully informed consent on the part of the donor (Jones and Whitaker 2009a, 2012; Riederer 2016; Winkelmann 2016; Winkelmann et al. 2016). But is there any way in which one could possibly have expected that to be the norm at the start of the modern anatomical era? Vesalius's insistence in the sixteenth century on studying and dissecting the human body was a move into uncharted territory, and a move away from studying animals and relying upon the pivotal and ultimately moribund writings of Galen (AD 130–200) (Joffe 2014). The irony of Galen is that he was an experimentalist, but he did not have access to human bodies, and hence relied upon dissecting animals, and this on several occasions led to misleading interpretations. In a number of ways, he restructured the body of medical knowledge, and yet this was accompanied by a tragedy: his concepts remained unchallenged for 1300 years (Hunter 1931; Lloyd 1973; Hankinson 2008). It was during this long period that human dissection disappeared from view for one simple reason—it was not needed. The elevation of Galen's knowledge to the status of inerrancy meant there was no need to challenge it (Jones and Whitaker 2009a). The tragedy was that excessive reliance upon Galen, the experimentalist, made further experimentation redundant, a situation that continued until the fourteenth century when individuals, such as Mondino di Luzzi (AD 1276–1326), revived the practice of human dissection largely using the bodies of executed criminals (Park 1995). The drawback even here was that the major reason for undertaking dissections was to illustrate Galen's texts, not to analyse structures and advance anatomical understanding (Mavrodi and Paraskevas 2014).

The environment within which these early dissections were carried out was hostile and tended to be carried out in secret and intermittently. Few advances in anatomical understanding were being made, but gradually permission was given by a number of European universities for dissection to be undertaken. This led to significant advances by a number of key figures. Berengario da Carpi (c. AD 1479–1530) and Leonardo da Vinci (AD 1452–1519) possessed both scientific and artistic abilities and they served as a prelude to the majestic work of Andreas Vesalius (AD 1514–1564), who cast off all vestiges of the Galenic tradition, and set modern anatomy on a firm footing (Vesalius 1543). This was only possible by his assiduous dissections of human bodies, coming as they did from graveyards. But was this ethical? Undoubtedly, by contemporary standards the answer is 'no', but that would have been a non-question in the sixteenth century. In setting the groundwork for a new scientific anatomy, he acted in the only way open to him. If it had been considered unethical at the time this would have been based on the unacceptability of dissection itself, and not on the manner in which human bodies were obtained.

The reality is that knowledge of the human body cannot be acquired from reflection alone. Science is analysis and experimentation, and while ethical analysis is crucial, it cannot be undertaken in isolation of the science that gives rise to the need for this analysis in the first place. Investigations, such as those of Vesalius, have to start somewhere, and the starting point will invariably be tentative, probing where no one has previously explored, and frequently using material that no one has had access to before or has not thought of accessing. For Vesalius, the only avenue open to him of obtaining dead bodies was via grave robbing, and this in no way justified a similar practice in the eighteenth and early nineteenth centuries. The justification for Vesalius was revolutionary research; the justification 300 years later was the education of students in competing private medical schools (Cornelius 1978; Moore 2005; Burch 2007). While the education of medical students is not to be decried, there was no scientific imperative to traverse new intellectual territory.

Although Vesalius should not be judged by today's standards with their emphasis upon informed consent, neither should his manner of functioning be regarded as acceptable today (Jones 2019a). The ethical basis of anatomy in the sixteenth century bears little resemblance to the expectations of contemporary anatomists, and the transition from one to the other has been halting and fraught with debacles and scandals, as what is done to and with the dead human body has been fought over politically and professionally (Richardson 2001; MacDonald 2005, 2010; Jones 2007). This has been far from a neat, theoretical exercise, as advances have been fitfully made and then negated by unexpected backtracking and highly questionable practices, even though many of these have been in pathology departments rather than in anatomy departments (Bristol Royal Infirmary Inquiry 2001; Department of Health 2001; Walker 2001; Retained Organs Commission 2002). Nevertheless, they have all involved the use or abuse of human tissue, and the ethical implications of misdemeanours are as valid for anatomy as for any other biomedical discipline. But some things have been clear—there is a profound difference between robbing graves in an effort to obtain dead bodies, and committing murder in an effort to obtain dead bodies. Resurrectionists, no matter how one views them, were not murderers.

There is no going back to the time of Vesalius, either scientifically or ethically; our task is to learn from the past and build upon it. This is straightforward on the scientific front, since Vesalius justified his reputation as the 'Father of Modern Anatomy' (Ellis 2014), since he undoubtedly provided anatomy with a solid scientifically-based foundation. He did not achieve the same eminence ethically, and it would be erroneous to look to Vesalius or any of the other early modern anatomists for ethical guidance. They achieved remarkable advances in science on the basis of the human material available to them obtained by whatever means were open to them. Ethically, Vesalius was a man of his time and cultural climate. The same comment seems to apply to Henry Gray of *Gray's Anatomy* fame (Gray 1858). Working in the 1850s, Gray along with the illustrator, Henry Vandyke Carter, dissected bodies at St George's Hospital in London (UK), that would have come from the poor who died alone in workhouses, prisons, and hospitals (Richardson 2008a). These bodies were unclaimed, and some may have been acquired as a consequence of deception. There are no references to their origin in *Gray's Anatomy*. This was, and still is to the present day, typical of anatomy texts. On the one hand stunning illustrations of normal human anatomy grace the pages of these tomes, but on the other hand the sources of the bodies on which these illustrations were based are not mentioned anywhere (Hayes 2008; Richardson 2008b; Jones 2017).

This brief description of the origins of modern human anatomy presents a living anatomist with a conundrum. Many professions can look back with pride to the early days of their discipline, but not so with anatomy. Anatomists do not have a glittering history to reflect upon, and the stunning advances are mired in duplicity and notoriety. The contemporary challenge is to construct an ethically-based way of obtaining and utilising human bodies and body parts on the basis of fundamental principles of informed consent, beneficence, non-maleficence, justice, and the dignity of all, including the poor and disadvantaged (Jones 2019a).

5.3 The Legacy of Unclaimed Bodies

Underlying each of these developments has been a fundamental premise—the bodies were not freely donated. At the very best they were unclaimed; at the worst they were stolen. It is the latter means of acquiring the bodies of the recently deceased that has repeatedly captured the public imagination. Everyone, it seems, knows about the body snatchers; the resurrectionists of medical history (Ball 1989; Richardson 2001; Jones and Whitaker 2009a). Far less attention has been paid to the dependence of the anatomical profession on the provision of 'unclaimed bodies', that is, the bodies of those with no one to care for them following their death. The lack of anyone to bury them or at the very least arrange for their cremation has led to them being placed in the unclaimed category. In practice their relatives may be aware of the death, but are too poor to pay for a funeral (Grow and Shiffman 2017a, 2017b). In some societies, as in several US states, the bodies of vagrants and the impoverished become the responsibility of local authorities. Furthermore, legislation in these states as well as in other countries, such as Nigeria, Kenya, and Ghana, stipulates that bodies can be directly passed on to the local medical school and its anatomy department for use in medical education (Garment et al. 2007). It goes without saying that those whose bodies end up unclaimed have not been in a position to provide informed consent to what becomes of their bodies following their death. In this regard they are similar to archival human material (Kahn et al. 2017).

The notion of unclaimed bodies can be traced to the early nineteenth century in the UK, when pivotal legislation legitimising the practice of using the bodies of those with no relatives to care for them was passed as the 1832 Anatomy Act (Richardson 2001; Jones and Whitaker 2009a, b), although this was not the first time the use of unclaimed bodies had been considered. Medical historian, Ruth Richardson, in her writings has argued strongly that the original decision in the 1820s and 1830s, in the UK, to use unclaimed rather than bequeathed bodies reflected negative social attitudes towards the poor and disadvantaged. This course of action was not the sole one open to legislators at the time, since there had been some bequests of bodies, the best known of which was that of Jeremy Bentham, the English political philosopher, who died in 1832 and whose body was dissected (Richardson and Hurwitz 1987). However, the medical profession was firmly of the opinion that the preferable source of bodies for dissection was to be found in hospitals, since this was where those dying alone or whose families were too poor to provide for them at death were to be found. The inevitable result was that poverty became the sole criterion for dissection (Richardson 2001).

The Anatomy Act (1832) should have solved anatomists' ethical quibbles, since it broke the embarrassing link between capital punishment and dissection, and that between grave robbing, anatomists, and their students. This appeared to place the practice of anatomy on a higher ethical plane than previously, and yet all was still not well. The means of obtaining unclaimed bodies from hospitals following the introduction of the Anatomy Act (1832) did not produce a sufficient number for the needs of some anatomy schools, therefore, this piece of legislation had to be manipulated or ignored, and this was done repeatedly after 1832. Medical historian, Helen MacDonald, has shown that body-snatching continued long after the Anatomy Act (1832) had been passed, with bodies of the poor being surreptitiously and illegally diverted from the grave to the dissecting room (MacDonald 2010). Even the anatomy inspectors, a position established by the Anatomy Act (1832), were duped or complicit in these actions; senior anatomists expected them to be helpful to anatomy's cause by directing as many bodies as possible in their direction (Jones 2019a).

It is this desire for a ready and sufficient supply of bodies that has driven anatomists to find means of acquiring them throughout the whole era of modern anatomy. Without bodies there would have been no anatomy as we know it today. The thrust in some cases has been research into the detailed structure of the body from the macroscopic to the microscopic on the part of people such as Andreas Vesalius and John Hunter, representing as they do, epochal points in the sixteenth and nineteenth centuries respectively (Joffe 2014; Moore 2005). In other cases, it was the need to educate medical students (Richardson 2001). The argument has been a simple one: no bodies, no dissecting, no medical training (Jones and Whitaker 2012). Unfortunately, under the aegis of the unclaimed bodies mantra, deception and a cruel disregard for the feelings and concerns of families grieving the loss of a loved one have appeared in one instance after another (MacDonald 2010). All too often, the drive for an adequate supply of bodies has tended to override all other considerations. Anatomy constantly straddles the interface between legitimate commitment to high quality science and dubious ethical practices.

One might have thought that these excesses were confined to the nineteenth century, but that is far from the case. The most egregious example occurred in the mid-twentieth century during the Nazi regime, when members of the medical profession were intimately involved in experimentation on human subjects. This involvement has been well documented, with their contribution to eugenic and racist programmes, enforced sterilisation, ghettoisation, inhuman experimentation, and extermination (Seidelman 1989; Wikler and Barondes 1993; Muller-Hill 1994). Less well known was the role of anatomists to the Nazi effort, a contribution that continues to become apparent up to this day. The tragedy of anatomy over the mid-1930s to the mid-1940s in Nazi occupied territories has been documented in graphic detail by Hildebrandt (2016), from which it emerges that anatomy lost all its moral bearings during that tragic period. Some anatomists stepped away from the discipline as the horror that was overtaking it began to manifest itself (Hildebrandt 2016). Unfortunately, they were the minority, as others realised that obtaining bodies direct from the extermination camps provided them with a plentiful supply of 'high quality' material, often of relatively young people including some with congenital abnormalities that they were keen to study. Names of leading anatomists from that period stand out as paradigms of maleficence, and include Julius Halervorden, Eduard Pernkopf, Hermann Stieve, Hermann Voss, August Hirt, and Max Clara (Bazelon 2013; Hildebrandt 2016). At the very least, they claimed to have had no reason to question the use of unclaimed bodies for 'good' anatomical purposes (Lachman 1977; Seidelman 1989; Angetter 2000). Some though went as far as to work on what Hildebrandt (2016, 303) describes as the "future dead", making the deaths of living concentration camp inmates part of their research design. Hildebrandt (2016, 307) concludes: "Anatomists became the agents of evil through the convergence of their own reductionist view of human life, the National Socialists' exclusionary medical ethics, and the new 'opportunities' provided by the regime".

The extremes encountered during the Nazi regime should not be taken as the inevitable end result of the ability to use unclaimed bodies, since that would be an unfair characterisation of the moral stature of anatomists as a whole. Nevertheless, it does provide a sobering lesson, since it is a model of body acquisition that lacks ethical boundaries and constraints. The drive to obtain good quality human material emerged initially with the demise of the poor houses in the early years of the twentieth century in various countries, including the United Kingdom, Australia, and New Zealand (Jones and Fennell 1991). As the number of bodies available from this source decreased, another source opened up, namely, the vast ‘lunatic asylums’ housing long-term, mentally incapacitated patients, in one country after another. In many instances these patients had lost contact with relatives, thus at death their bodies ended up unclaimed; they were doubly disadvantaged on the grounds of their poverty and mental incapacity (Jones 2011). Consequently, they served as a major source of bodies for anatomy schools, for as long as these asylums continued to exist and for as long as anatomists’ dependence upon unclaimed bodies continued. It is significant that the transition from dependence upon use of the bodies of the poor to that of the mentally ill was a pragmatic one.

The pragmatism underlying anatomists’ willingness to utilise the bodies of the unclaimed, and therefore the bodies of those for whom no consent has been given by the deceased prior to death or the family at death, has pointed to a serious lack of ethical reflection. By legitimising unclaimed bodies as a source for dissection, and viewing it as the routine source of bodies, the profession has been exposed to moral turpitude. It has allowed anatomists to ignore the cultural inequities within societies, and has provided them with carte blanche to exploit those occupying less privileged strata than the ones they occupy. This has failed to provide them with a firm ethical foundation for addressing new and unexpected developments, such as the emergence of public plastination exhibitions of human bodies (von Hagens and Whalley 2000), 3D printing of human tissue and organs (McMenamin et al. 2014; Jones 2019b), the availability of donated bodies following medically assisted death (Wainman and Cornwall 2019), the commercialisation of human bodies and body parts (Champney et al. 2019), and dissections as seen on YouTube (Barry et al. 2016; Jones 2016b). Before discussing some of these developments, it is important to recall that the emergence of the bequest ethos heralded the start of a more ethically informed base for anatomy.

5.4 The Emergence of the Bequest Paradigm

Even though the possibility of bequests has been contemplated since the start of the nineteenth century, it failed to gain a serious hearing until the 1950s, at the earliest. Throughout the 1950s and 1960s the number of bequests gradually increased in one country after another. During the same period there was also a decrease in the number of unclaimed bodies until bequests began to displace unclaimed bodies as the norm (Jones and Fennell 1991; Dally et al. 1993; Richardson 2001; British Medical Association 2006; Jones 2007).

Since the 1990s repeated calls have been made for the use of bequeathed bodies rather than unclaimed ones, on the grounds that this is ethically superior to the use of non-consented unclaimed bodies (Jones 1994; Garment et al. 2007; Champney 2011; Jones and Whitaker 2012; Riederer and Bueno-López 2014; Riederer 2016; Kahn et al. 2017). The basis to this argument has been that the dead body has an intrinsic value that cannot be totally separated from the value ascribed to the person when alive. Consequently, we show disrespect to a person-now-dead when we dissect that person's body without their consent prior to death and/or without close friends to argue the case for them (Jones 1994). As throughout history, in most countries, it is mainly the bodies of the poor and marginalised which end up unclaimed. Accordingly, this leads to the view that the use of these bodies is a form of exploitation.

Unfortunately, the transition to the use of bequests world-wide has been a stuttering one, in spite of the fact that the International Federation of Associations of Anatomists (IFAA) in 2012 recommended that only donated bodies be used for anatomical teaching and research (Federative International Committee for Ethics and Medical Humanities of the International Federation of Associations of Anatomists 2012). Habicht et al. (2018) undertook a survey of 165 countries with medical schools to establish whether bodies used for dissection were bequeathed, unclaimed, or imported from other countries. The authors gathered information for 71 of these countries and revealed that, while 32% of these countries exclusively use bequests, unclaimed bodies remain the main source in 26% of cases, and the exclusive source in 31%. Countries that exclusively use bequeathed bodies include the United Kingdom, Austria, Denmark, France, Sweden, Australia, New Zealand, and Canada. The authors were unable to point to any one main reason for these results, but thought that a mix of religious, cultural, and folk beliefs about how the body should be treated after death lay behind them. This study is of value in pinpointing the distance that the bequest ethos has come, especially since body donation programmes exist on all continents (Habicht et al. 2018). However, it also reveals that the willingness to bequeath one's body is closely associated with views of the status of the body after death, and therefore how it is to be treated by the living. Major religio-cultural differences emerge by contrasting Muslim-majority countries with Buddhist-majority countries, with the former rejecting the bequest paradigm, and the latter accepting this paradigm (Habbal 2009; Lin et al. 2009; Subasinghe and Jones 2015; Yaqinuddin et al. 2016).

These differences should impress upon anatomists the centrality of gaining insight into the cultural setting within which they are functioning, and the importance of understanding this culture and its relevance for their interests in the science of the dead human body. There may be no simple resolution to what at first sight is an impasse for them in their pursuit for bequests, and the challenge is to find ethically acceptable alternatives. No matter which direction anatomists take when faced with this conundrum, the temptation is to take the path of least resistance, that is, resort to using unclaimed bodies, purchasing bodies from other countries, and/or largely relying on donations from subpopulations willing to donate their bodies. To avoid doing this, there needs to be serious engagement with ethical reasoning, leading to dialogue with those holding different cultural perspectives from their own scientific ones. This will involve a willingness to learn from the 'other', and to respect the 'other'. Important as dead bodies are for anatomy, it is equally important to understand where the surrounding community is coming from and what matters to them and their families. There is no room for cultural superiority.

5.5 From the Dissecting Room to Public Displays of Plastinated Human Bodies

The ethical issues troubling the anatomical profession have revolved around the manner in which dead bodies are obtained for dissection. Hence, the furore surrounding its close association with capital punishment, grave robbing, and reliance upon unclaimed bodies. Throughout all these debates little attention has been paid to the relative secrecy surrounding the dissection process itself or the exclusion of the public, although some of the early dissections were public events (Sawday 1995). In other words, modern anatomy became the exclusive province of the medical profession and health science students. All this changed in the 1990s with the first public exhibitions of dissected plastinated and dissected human bodies. These exhibitions were mounted by the originator of the plastination technique, Gunter von Hagens, and his "Body Worlds" exhibitions (Getty Images 2019). The procedure itself was developed in the 1970s and 1980s, and involves the preservation of human tissue by replacing tissue fluids with plastics, producing specimens that are dry, odourless, and durable (von Hagens 1979; von Hagens et al. 1987). Plastination is thus highly successful at replicating the original tissue and retaining the natural structure of the tissues. In brief, the decomposing dead body has been made attractive. Additionally, the tissue can be moulded whereby the arms are folded and legs are bent which gives the impression of dynamism and activity. Plastination is a procedure that has considerable attraction for anatomists for teaching and research, since plastinated human remains are far more immediate and user-friendly than the same dissected body parts preserved in formalin in bottles.

However, what has caught the public's imagination are not body parts or organs, but whole body plastinates, where the body is displayed in upright poses as if still alive. Plastinates are shown in athletic or sporting poses, playing baseball or soccer, as ballet dancers, or playing chess. The body has been dissected to reveal the intricacy of the nervous system, the respiratory and gastrointestinal systems, and blood vessels. One gains the impression that any activity can be replicated in the form of plastinates, apparently alive and in the prime of health (Jones 2016a, c). The reality of course is the opposite; not only are these plastinates dead, they have been dissected, but instead of lying horizontal on a slab in a dissecting room, they appear to be participating in the sort of activities that living people enjoy. Consequently, they have been described—misleadingly—as 'post-mortal' (Jones 2016c).

There is no doubt that it is these plastinates that constitute the crucial element in attracting around 48 million visitors of the general public in 140 cities over the past 20 years to the "Body Worlds" exhibitions. For them these constitute a way into anatomy, and have been envisaged by von Hagens as the democratisation of anatomy (Institute for Plastination 2019a; Jones and Whitaker 2009a). They are seen as being means of strengthening one's sense of health, showing the potential and limits of the body, and raising the question of the meaning of life. It is not surprising that some anatomists have been less than enthusiastic about many facets of these public displays, although there is clear division of opinion among them

(Boyde et al. 2002; Morriss-Kay 2002; Kuhnel 2004; Burr 2008). There has been considerable debate about the legitimacy of the "Body Worlds" exhibitions as education, entertainment, or an uneasy mix of both (Jones 2016c).

The commonly asked ethical questions are: Were the bodies unclaimed or bequeathed? Does this way of exhibiting human bodies constitute a threat to their dignity? Are they demeaned by being displayed rather than buried or cremated? Is their purpose educational or is it little more than morbid curiosity? (Federative International Committee for Ethics and Medical Humanities of the International Federation of Associations of Anatomists 2018).

Since the bodies displayed in the "Body Worlds" exhibitions have been donated for this purpose (Institute for Plastination 2019b), they pass the first ethical test. The same cannot be said for other exhibitions, such as "Bodies: The Exhibition", which appear to use unclaimed bodies from China and therefore raise major concerns about the source of these bodies (Mao 2018). The exhibitions are frequently criticised on the grounds that they denigrate the dead body and violate the dignity and reverence of the dead (Nahshoni 2009). However, such criticisms tend to reflect emotive responses to an unwelcome phenomenon, and overlook the source of the bodies and the extent of changes wrought by the plastination procedure (Rudolph and Perlov 2009). On the other hand, the extent to which the bodies of the deceased are employed to entertain others, possibly in exhibitionist ways, may come close to demeaning these human beings, particularly within a highly commercialised environment (Jones 2016a). This is not inevitable, although the combination of the artificial and the commercial, has the facility for exploiting them and turning the human exhibits into little more than a means of financial gain.

The core of ethical deliberation revolves around the nature of these plastinates. They are 30% human tissue and 70% plastic. Being substantially plastic they are ambivalent entities (Jones 2016a). They are more than plastic models, since they contain reminders of the original individual human person from which they were derived. This means that no two plastinates are identical, any more than two individuals are identical. The humanity of the original person is still evident even if no more than a shadow of its original self, and it is this shadow that constitutes the ethical challenge of knowing how plastinates are to be viewed. The ambivalence stemming from their partial humanness is ethically confusing, even more so when depicted as though still alive and participating in routine human activities. They have been modified to become a new entity, based on a human template but substantially artificial (Jones and Whitaker 2009b). The exhibitions claims that they are 'real' humans (von Hagens and Whalley 2000), but this is deceptive; they occupy a new category, a previously unknown category, existing somewhere between death and decay (Schulte-Sasse 2006), immortal in a physical sense, but as dead as any other corpse.

This difficulty in categorising plastinates elicits no surprise, since they do not occupy standard cultural binary categories, such as real or fake, dead or alive, bodies or persons, self or other (King et al. 2014). Visitors to exhibitions experience similar problems, as different people respond very differently to them. For some they are fascinating, intriguing, and awe inspiring; for others they are disgusting, disconcerting, or confusing. Von Hagens' proposal that they have a form of post-mortal existence on account of their ongoing physicality has moved plastination beyond technique and into metaphysical territory (Jones 2016a). They have been described as representations of real bodies (Stern 2006), or artificial representations of perfected nature. In creating entities that are immortal, and that mimic vitality, they have acquired a biological plastic existence but in doing so have lost all features of the once living individuals with no trace of the values, attitudes, or ideas that once characterised them (Jones 2016a).

These comments demonstrate the problem of isolating a single technique, namely plastination, from other approaches when studying the human body and the manner in which it is displayed. Plastination is an excellent method that complements other techniques that can be used to learn about the organisation of the human body. Provided plastination is utilised in this manner, it has a great deal to add to our understanding of the body. However, it is only when isolated from this far more encompassing context that it becomes problematic.

5.6 Emerging Ethical Conundrums

It would be very short sighted to confine our attention to the past and issues that have arisen in the history of anatomy, and that to varying extents have been satisfactorily addressed. The result has been a major increase in the ethical standing of anatomy as a scientific and human profession. Nevertheless, anatomy is never static and the need for it to continue responding to ongoing cultural and technological challenges have not ceased. It is with these thoughts in mind that two examples are raised in this section. These examples are highly pertinent since both have already entered anatomical practice in a number of anatomy schools. They serve as illustrations of the case made in this chapter, namely, that anatomy has to have an assured ethical base if it is to be capable of tackling the inevitable plethora of novel possibilities that will open up over the coming years.

5.6.1 3D Printing

In tracing the ethical dimensions of relevance to anatomy, it is tempting to look backward and conclude that all the challenges lie in the past. That would be unhelpful, since with the advent of new technologies a raft of unexpected questions is arising. One of these is bioprinting that has emerged as a major tool in regenerative medicine and industry (Gelhaus 2016; Vermeulen et al. 2017). Less extensive is the use of 3D printing in education, including anatomy education (Li et al. 2012; McMenamin et al. 2014; Lim et al. 2016; O'Reilly et al. 2016), since it has been developed more recently in the wake of the excitement generated by the clinical possibilities opened up by bioprinting. Relatively little attention has been paid to any ethical consequences of using 3D printing in teaching, since these are not immediately evident. These stem from the use of digital technology since this, in turn, brings into focus the place of consent (Jones 2019b).

3D prints of human material, such as prosections of the forearm, have enabled the production of very realistic replicas of this appendage, with small nerves and vessels clearly shown and reproducible with a high degree of accuracy (McMenamin et al. 2014). Similarly encouraging results have been obtained in a study of external cardiac anatomy (Lim et al. 2016), and of archival embryonic and foetal specimens (Young et al. 2019). Some researchers are aware of the potential ethical dilemmas in using digitised files based on data from bodies sourced from unknown anatomy schools (Smith et al. 2018; see also Smith and Hirst, this volume), and have produced 3D models from a donated body at their own institution. Others, however, have ignored these concerns and have used freely available data sets on the internet (Sander et al. 2017; Smith and Jones 2018).

Whenever data from the Internet are employed, pertinent queries include: What consent has been given by the body donor? What parts of the body are being 3D printed? What is the reason for the 3D printing? Who will use and benefit from the 3D printing? To what extent will the 3D printing be commercialised (Jones 2019b)? In approaching these questions, Jones (2019b) sought to discover how the ethical underpinning of moving from fully human material towards the part-human, part-artificial (as in plastination), and through to the totally artificial (as in 3D printing), can be mapped. What emerges is that 3D printed body parts are closer to purely artificial models than the intact body (Jones 2019b). However, one potential complicating factor is that small modifications can be made to 3D printing putting it even closer to the artificial.

The technological prospects opened up by 3D printing once again raise the role of informed consent and, in light of this, Jones (2019b) proposed that the following guidelines be implemented: (i) the provision of detailed informed consent for 3D printing as an integral part of consent for the original donation, (ii) exclude the possibility of identification of the people from whose body parts the prints were made, (iii) acknowledge that any construct, including 3D prints, is from a human donor, and that isolation from the donor as a person risks a reductionist approach to anatomy, (iv) 3D printing should only be commercialised with the express consent of the body donor, (v) in that circumstance there should be written acknowledgement and thanks for the donor's contribution, (vi) take into account possible breaches of copyright with wide-scale distribution over the internet, (vii) weigh up the comparative advantages and disadvantages of 3D printing against the use of computer simulation images, (viii) consider possible future developments in 3D printing, such as printing a head/face with its individual characteristics, and the ethical implications of these. Only experience will determine whether some of these guidelines are necessary or whether they are an overreach. But a cautious approach in the early stages of 3D development for anatomy teaching seems appropriate given the all-too-frequent ethical aberrations of the past.

5.6.2 Body Donation After Physician Assisted Death

The prolonged debates over the ethical imperative of utilising body bequests rather than unclaimed bodies appears to have been resolved, even though there remain obstacles to implementing this policy in a large number of societies (Habicht et al. 2018). However, little attention has been paid to the nature of the donations, since this is not usually of much relevance. It has been touched upon in discussions on the nature of donations when the bodies are to be plastinated and placed on public display (Jones 2016a, 2016c), and has also been raised when body donations are made by impoverished families to for-profit organisations in the USA (Grow and Shiffman 2017a, 2017b; Champney et al. 2019). In Canada, there is an increasing availability of bodies donated to anatomy programmes following physician assisted death (Wainman and Cornwall 2019). While this has been raised as an ethical issue within a specific context, there is every likelihood that it will become a far more widespread phenomenon over coming years, due to the rising availability of physician-assisted death in a growing number of countries.

On the surface this may not appear to raise any novel ethical issues since the bodies are being donated to an anatomy programme for teaching and/or research, following informed consent on the part of the donor and family. However, now is the time for ethical debate to ensure that the boundaries around donation do not become blurred. Jones (forthcoming) has proposed that a number of questions are asked: whether accepting bodies following medical assistance in dying (MAID) makes anatomists morally complicit in the manner of donors' death; whether bodies sourced in this way represent a move away from maintaining the anonymity of bodies and whether this may have repercussions on students' moral development; whether the possibility of acquiring high quality bodies in this manner serves as an inducement for individuals to donate their bodies. Not one of these is inevitable, but now is the time for ethical discernment.

Wainman and Cornwall (2019) raised a range of pertinent considerations, including the appropriateness of accepting such donations, whether a vulnerable population is capable of providing truly informed consent, the possible negative historical parallels between physician assisted dying and euthanasia, the preparedness of institutions to accept these donations, the criteria to be employed, and the transparency of their communications with potential body donors.

Since views within societies differ over the legitimacy of any form of physician assisted death, the question of moral complicity cannot be ignored, and with it the need to separate the two procedures: people must not be encouraged to undergo physician assisted death in order to make their bodies available for subsequent use in anatomy schools. Policies also need to be introduced to protect students (and staff) who object to physician assisted death and do not wish to use bodies obtained in this manner. An unexpected bonus of this procedure is that the bodies are likely to have well preserved tissue, partly because they may derive from younger individuals, and because they will arrive at a precise time and can be transferred rapidly to the anatomy school. Scientifically, bodies that possess these features are attractive and should not be discounted (Wainman and Cornwall 2019). Yet they are reminders of the many occasions in the past when these arguments have led anatomy down seriously questionable paths, in ways that fail to safeguard human dignity (Jones and Whitaker 2012).

A suggested policy has been put forward by Jones (forthcoming) to the effect that the decision to undergo physician-assisted death is made by an independent authority with no relationship to the anatomy school's need for donated bodies. Additionally, students with ethical reservations about dissecting these bodies must be provided with access to alternative bodies. Concerted ethical debate will be required for some time to ensure that this new avenue of obtaining bodies for dissection is established as an ethically judicious one.

5.7 Conclusion: Studying Human Tissue in an Impersonal Technological Environment

One of the emerging themes that is increasingly being encountered in anatomical circles is the need to humanise the practice of anatomy in the dissecting room (Štrkalj 2016). The thrust here is to personalise the dead body and help students appreciate that they are dealing with a once-living individual and not with an impersonal entity that is a mere teaching tool. In some circles, the dead body is viewed as a teacher and/or first patient (Winkelmann and Guldner 2004; Lin et al. 2009), while holding commemorations to acknowledge the gift of donated bodies has become standard practice in many medical schools (Štrkalj and Pather 2017). However, some of the technological developments, including digitisation, 3D printing, and plastination, have the potential to depersonalise the dead body. The history of anatomy should serve as a salutary warning that the attraction of obtaining sufficient quantities of dead bodies for anatomical and surgical education is a potent force in minimising ethical considerations and depersonalising the dead. Ongoing ethical vigilance is crucial.

The discussion throughout this chapter would not have been possible had it not been for the role of the Anatomical Associations over the years. The current ones in countries such as the United Kingdom, Australia, and New Zealand are exemplary for the guidelines contained in them and for the central control exercised by the Inspectors of Anatomy, and the establishment of licensed Schools of Anatomy. These have led to a system that ensures that the guidelines are implemented throughout the whole anatomical community of a particular country. This stands in striking contrast to the situation in the United States of America where, in spite of the 2006 Uniform Anatomical Gift Act (UAGA; Uniform Law Commission, The National Conference of Commissioners on Uniform State Laws 2006), the lack of central Federal control leads to an immense divergence of practice. This is most evident in the existence of for-profit organisations that stand outside the medical schools and sell body parts both nationally and internationally (Champney et al.

2019). Commercialisation of this nature has led to the phenomenon of body brokers (Grow and Shiffman 2017a, 2017b), with its numerous ethical transgressions. The existence of this trade in bodies and body parts militates against the whole ethical ethos outlined in this chapter, and is a blight upon central aspects of the anatomical profession in some parts of the world.

The commercialisation of human tissue has itself enabled the transfer of human bodies and body parts (and plastinated human material) across country borders, a practice that appears to be readily accepted by some surgical training organisations. This demonstrates all-too-clearly the need for ongoing ethical assessment, and for the Anatomical Associations to remain alert to the ongoing possibilities of serious ethical transgressions.

In their assessment of the dominant principles for proper treatment of willed body donors, Champney et al. (2019) divided them into three groups: those revolving around the donor and family, those around the donor organisations, and those around society and the country. When these three areas are considered, the ethical values that will be taken into account include detailed informed consent, respect and dignity for the donor, complete transparency on the part of every party and in every transaction, and awareness of the cultural and religious background of each society involved. Against this background the anatomical profession has a firm basis from which to tackle the host of unknowns that lie ahead within every society.

References

Anatomy Act. 1832. The Stationery Office, London.

Angetter, D.C. 2000. Anatomical Science at University of Vienna 1938–45. *Lancet* 355: 1445–1457.

Ball, H. 1989. *The Body Snatchers*. New York: Dorset Press.

Barry, D.S., F. Marzouk, K. Chulak-Oglu, et al. 2016. Anatomy Education for the YouTube Generation. *Anatomical Sciences Education* 9: 90–96.

Bazelon, E. R. 2013. The Nazi Anatomists. *Slate*. 6 November http://www.slate.com/articles/life/history/2013/11/nazi_anatomy_history_the_origins_of_conservatives_anti_abortion_claims_that.html. Accessed 25 June 2019.

Boyde, A., P. Fraher, and J.F. Morris, et al. 2002. Letter: Dissections in Display. *The Independent*, 16 March.

Bristol Royal Infirmary Inquiry. 2001. *Learning from Bristol: The Report of the Public Inquiry Into Children's Heart Surgery at the Bristol Royal Infirmary 1884–1995*. Bristol: Crown Copyright.

British Medical Association. 2006. *Human Tissue Legislation: Guidance from the BMA's Medical Ethics Department*. London: British Medical Association.

Burch, D. 2007. *Digging Up the Dead: The Life and Times of Astley Cooper, An Extraordinary Surgeon*. London: Chatto and Windus.

Burr, D.B. 2008. Congress Considering Plastination Import Ban. *American Association for Anatomy News* 17: 2–5.

Campbell, A.V. 2009. *The Body in Bioethics*. Abingdon: Routledge.

Cartwright, S.R. 1988. *The Report of the Cervical Cancer Inquiry: The Report of the Committee of Inquiry Into Allegations Concerning the Treatment of Cervical Cancer at National Women's Hospital and Into Other Related Matters*. Auckland: Government Printing Office.

Champney, T.H. 2011. A Proposal for a Policy on the Ethical Care and Use of Cadavers and Their Tissues. *Anatomical Sciences Education* 4: 49–52.

Champney, T., S. Hildebrandt, D.G. Jones, et al. 2019. BODIES R US: Ethical Views on the Commercialization of the Dead in Medical Education and Research. *Anatomical Sciences Education* 12: 317–325.

Cornelius, E.H. 1978. John Hunter as An Expert Witness. *Annals of the Royal College of Surgeons of England* 60: 412–418.

Dally, A.F., R.E. Driscoll, and H.E. Settles. 1993. The Uniform Anatomical Gift Act: What Every Clinical Anatomist Should Know. *Clinical Anatomy* 6: 247–254.

Department of Health. 2001. *Report of a Census of Organs and Tissues Retained by Pathology Services in England*. London: Her Majesty's Stationery Office.

Ellis, H. 2014. Andreas Vesalius: Father of Modern Anatomy. *British Journal of Hospital Medicine* 75 (12): 711.

Federative International Committee for Ethics and Medical Humanities (FIECM) of the International Federation of Associations of Anatomists (IFAA). 2012. *Recommendations of Good Practice for the Donation and Study of Human Bodies and Tissues for Anatomical Examination*. http://www.ifaa.net/wp-content/uploads/2017/09/IFAA-guidelines-220811.pdf. Accessed 11 July 2019.

Federative International Committee for Ethics and Medical Humanities (FIECM) of the International Federation of Associations of Anatomists (IFAA). 2018. *Ethical and Medical Humanities Perspectives on the Public Display of Plastinated Human Bodies*. www.ifaa.net/wp-content/uploads/2018/02/FICEM-on-plastination-exhibits_2018.pdf. Accessed 4 July 2019.

Garment, A., S. Lederer, N. Rogers, et al. 2007. Let the Dead Teach the Living: The Rise of Body Bequeathal in 20th-Century America. *Academic Medicine* 82: 1000–1005.

Gelhaus, P. 2016. Bioprinting. In *Encyclopedia of Global Bioethics*, ed. H. ten Have. Cham: Springer.

Getty Images. 2019. *Body Worlds*. https://www.gettyimages.co.uk/photos/body-worlds?sort=mostpopular&mediatype=photography&phrase=body%20worlds. Accessed 4 July 2019.

Gray, H. 1858. *Anatomy: Descriptive and Surgical*. London: JW Parker and Son.

Grow, B., and J. Shiffman. 2017a. In the US Market for Human Bodies, Almost Anyone Can Dissect and Sell the Dead: Part 1. *Reuters Investigates*. 24 October. https://www.reuters.com/investigates/special-report/usa-bodies-brokers/. Accessed 4 July 2019.

Grow, B., and J. Shiffman. 2017b. A Reuters Journalist Bought Human Body Parts, Then Learned a Donor's Heart-Wrenching Story: Part 2. *Reuters Investigates*. 25 October. https://www.reuters.com/investigates/special-report/usa-bodies-cody/. Accessed 4 July 2019.

Habbal, O. 2009. The State of Human Anatomy Teaching in the Medical Schools of Gulf Cooperation Council Countries: Present and Future Perspectives. *Sultan Qaboos University Medical Journal* 9: 24–31.

Habicht, J.L., C. Kiessling, and A. Winkelmann. 2018. Bodies for Anatomy Education in Medical Schools: An Overview of the Sources of Cadavers Worldwide. *Academic Medicine* 93: 1293–1300.

Hankinson, R.J. (ed.). 2008. *The Cambridge Companion to Galen*. Cambridge: Cambridge University Press.

Hayes, B. 2008. *The Anatomist*. Melbourne: Scribe.

Heritage New Zealand. 2014. *Koiwi Tangata: Human Remains*. Wellington: Heritage New Zealand, Pouhere Taonga.

Hildebrandt, S. 2016. *The Anatomy of Murder: Ethical Transgressions and Anatomical Science During the Third Reich*. New York: Berghahn.

Human Tissue Act. 2008. Parliamentary Counsel Office, Wellington.

Hunter, R.H. 1931. *A Short History of Anatomy*. London: John Bale and Sons.

Institute for Plastination. 2019a. *Mission of the Exhibition*. https://bodyworlds.com/plastination/organizations/. Accessed 4 July 2019.

Institute for Plastination. 2019b. *Body Donation*. https://bodyworlds.com/plastination/bodydonation/. Accessed 4 July 2019.

Joffe, S.N. 2014. *Andreas Vesalius: The Making, the Madman, and the Myth*. London: Authorhouse.

Jones, D.G. 1989. The New Zealand "Report of the Cervical Cancer Inquiry": Significance for Medical Education. *Medical Journal of Australia* 151: 450–456.

Jones, D.G. 1994. Use of Bequeathed and Unclaimed Bodies in the Dissecting Room. *Clinical Anatomy* 7: 102–107.

Jones, R.L. 2007. *Humanity's Mirror: 150 Years of Anatomy in Melbourne*. Victoria: Haddington Press.

Jones, D.G. 2011. The Anatomy Museum and Mental Illness: The Centrality of Informed Consent. In *Exhibiting Madness in Museums: Remembering Psychiatry Through Collection and Display*, ed. C. Coleborne and D. MacKinnon, 161–177. New York: Routledge.

Jones, D.G. 2016a. The Artificial World of Plastination: A Challenge to Religious Perspectives on the Dead Human Body. *The New Bioethics* 22 (3): 237–252.

Jones, D.G. 2016b. YouTube Anatomy Education: Sources of Ethical Perplexity. *Anatomical Sciences Education* 9 (5): 500–501.

Jones, D.G. 2016c. The Public Display of Plastinates as a Challenge to the Integrity of Anatomy. *Clinical Anatomy* 29: 46–54.

Jones, D.G. 2017. Human Anatomy: A Review of the Science, Ethics and Culture of a Discipline in Transition. In *Human Anatomy*, ed. A.K. Sisu, 3–20. Rijeka: InTech Open Science.

Jones, D.G. 2019a. The Dead Human Body: Reflections of An Anatomist. In *Healthcare Ethics, Law and Professionalism: Essays on the Works of Alastair V Campbell*, ed. V.T. Chuan, R. Huxtable, and N. Peart, 225–241. Abingdon: Routledge.

Jones, D.G. 2019b. Three-dimensional Printing in Anatomy Education: Assessing Potential Ethical Dimensions. *Anatomical Sciences Education* 12: 435–443.

Jones, D.G. forthcoming. Exploring the Policy Dimensions of Body Donation Following Medical Assistance in Dying (MAID). *Anatomical Sciences Education*.

Jones, D.G., and S. Fennell. 1991. Bequests, Cadavers and Dissections; Sketches from New Zealand History. *New Zealand Medical Journal* 104: 210–212.

Jones, D.G., and R.J. Harris. 1998. Archaeological Human Remains: Scientific, Cultural and Ethical Considerations. *Current Anthropology* 39: 253–264.

Jones, D.G., and M.I. Whitaker. 2009a. *Speaking for the Dead*, 2nd ed. Farnham: Ashgate.

Jones, D.G., and M.I. Whitaker. 2009b. Engaging with Plastination and the BodyWorlds Phenomenon: A Cultural and Intellectual Challenge for Anatomists. *Clinical Anatomy* 22: 770–776.

Jones, D.G., and M.I. Whitaker. 2012. Anatomy's Use of Unclaimed Bodies: Reasons Against Continued Dependence on an Ethically Dubious Practice. *Clinical Anatomy* 25: 246–254.

Jones, D.G., R. Gear, and K.A. Galvin. 2003. Stored Human Tissue: An Ethical Perspective on the Fate of Anonymous Archival Material. *Journal of Medical Ethics* 29: 343–347.

Kahn, P.A., T.H. Champney, and S. Hildebrandt. 2017. The Incompatibility of the Use of Unclaimed Bodies with Ethical Anatomical Education in the United States. *Anatomical Sciences Education* 10: 200–201.

King, M.R., M.I. Whitaker, and D.G. Jones. 2014. I See Dead People: Insights from the Humanities into the Nature of Plastinated Cadavers. *Journal of Medical Humanities* 35: 361–376.

Kuhnel, W. 2004. *Statement by the Anatomische Gesellschaft on the Infamous Body-World Show of Dr Gunther von Hagens*. Plexus: Newsletter of the International Federation of Associations of Anatomists, December 2004. http://an-server.pote.hu/DEPT/Plexus0412.pdf. Accessed 14 July 2019.

Lachman, E. 1977. Anatomist of Infamy: August Hirt. *Bulletin of the History of Medicine* 51: 594–602.

Lancet. 1832. Editorial. *Lancet* 19 (481): 241–246.

Li, J., L. Nie, Z. Li, et al. 2012. Maximizing Modern Distribution of Complex Anatomical Spatial Information: 3D Reconstruction and Rapid Prototype Production of Anatomical Corrosion Casts of Human Specimens. *Anatomical Sciences Education* 5: 330–339.

Lim, K.H., Z.Y. Loo, S.J. Goldie, et al. 2016. Use of 3D Printed Models in Medical Education: A Randomized Control Trial Comparing 3D Prints Versus Cadaveric Materials for Learning External Cardiac Anatomy. *Anatomical Sciences Education* 9: 213–221.

Lin, S.C., J. Hsu, and V.Y. Fan. 2009. "Silent Virtuous Teachers": Anatomical Dissection in Taiwan. *British Medical Journal* 339: b5001.

Lloyd, G. 1973. *Greek Science After Aristotle*. London: Chatto and Windus.

MacDonald, H. 2005. *Human Remains*. Melbourne: University Press Melbourne.

MacDonald, H. 2010. *Possessing the Dead*. Melbourne: University Press Melbourne.

Mao, F. 2018. 'Real Bodies' Exhibition Causes Controversy in Australia. *BBC News*. 26 April. https://www.bbc.co.uk/news/world-australia-43902524. Accessed 14 July 2019.

Mavrodi, A., and G. Paraskevas. 2014. Mondino de Luzzi: A Luminous Figure in the Darkness of the Middle Ages. *Croatian Medical Journal* 55 (1): 50–53.

May, W.F. 1985. Religious Justification for Donating Body Parts. *Hastings Center Report* 15: 38–42.

McMenamin, P.A., M.R. Quayle, C.R. McHenry, et al. 2014. The Production of Anatomical Teaching Resources Using Three-Dimensional (3D) Printing Technology. *Anatomical Sciences Education* 7: 479–486.

Moore, W. 2005. *The Knife Man: The Extraordinary Life and Times of John Hunter, Father of Modern Surgery*. London: Bantam Press.

Morriss-Kay, G. 2002. Bodyworlds: Exhibition at the Atlantis Gallery, The Old Truman Brewery, Brick Lane, London, 23 March to 29 September 2002. *Journal of Anatomy* 200 (5): 535–536.

Muller-Hill, B. 1994. Human Genetics in Nazi Germany. In *Medicine, Ethics, and the Third Reich: Historical and Contemporary Issues*, ed. J.J. Michalczyk, 27–34. Kansas City: Sheed and Ward.

Nahshoni, K. 2009. Haredim Launch Battle Against Human Body Exhibit. *Ynetnews*. 22 March. https://www.ynetnews.com/articles/0,7340,L-3690258,00.html. Accessed 14 July 2019.

O'Reilly, M.K., S. Reese, T. Herlihy, et al. 2016. Fabrication and Assessment of 3D Printed Anatomical Models of the Lower Limb for Anatomical Teaching and Femoral Vessel Access Training in Medicine. *Anatomical Sciences Education* 9: 71–79.

Park, K. 1995. The Life of the Corpse: Division and Dissection in Late Medieval Europe. *Journal of the History of Medicine and Allied Sciences* 50: 111–132.

Retained Organs Commission. 2002. *A Consultation Document on Unclaimed and Unidentifiable Organs and Tissue, a Possible Regulatory Framework*. London: National Health Service.

Richardson, R. 2001. *Death, Dissection and the Destitute*, 2nd ed. Chicago: Chicago University Press.

Richardson, R. 2008a. Historical Introduction. In *Gray's Anatomy: The Anatomical Basis of Clinical Practice*, 40th ed, ed. S. Standring, xvii–xxi. London: Elsevier.

Richardson, R. 2008b. *The Making of Mr. Gray's Anatomy*. Oxford: Oxford University Press.

Richardson, R., and B. Hurwitz. 1987. Jeremy Bentham's Self Image: An Exemplary Bequest for Dissection. *British Medical Journal* 295 (6591): 195–198.

Riederer, B.M. 2016. Body Donations Today and Tomorrow: What is Best Practice and Why? *Clinical Anatomy* 29: 11–18.

Riederer, B.M., and J. Bueno-López. 2014. Anatomy, Respect for the Body and Body Donation—A Guide for Good Practices. *European Journal of Anatomy* 18: 361–368.

Rudolph, J. N., and D. Perlov. 2009. Body Worlds: An Anatomical Exhibition of Real Human Bodies. *Summary of Ethical Review*. https://www.mos.org/sites/dev-elvis.mos.org/files/docs/press-kits/Summary%20of%202004-05%20Ethical%20Review%20%20CA%20SCI%20Center.pdf. Accessed 11 July 2019.

Sander, I.M., M.T. McGoldrick, M.N. Helms, et al. 2017. Three-Dimensional Printing of X-Ray Computed Tomography Datasets with Multiple Materials Using Open-Source Data Processing. *Anatomical Sciences Education* 10: 383–391.

Sawday, J. 1995. *The Body Emblazoned: Dissection and the Human Body in Rennaissance Culture*. London: Routledge.
Schulte-Sasse, L. 2006. Advise and Consent: On the Americanization of Body Worlds. *BioSocieties* 1: 369–384.
Seidelman, W.E. 1989. In Memoriam: Medicine's Confrontation with Evil. *Hastings Center Report* 19: 5–6.
Smith, M.L., and J.F.X. Jones. 2018. Dual-Extrusion 3D Printing of Anatomical Models for Education. *Anatomical Sciences Education* 11: 65–72.
Smith, C.F., N. Tollemache, D. Covill, et al. 2018. Take Away Body Parts! An Investigation Into the Use of 3D-Printed Anatomical Models in Undergraduate Anatomy Education. *Anatomical Sciences Education* 11: 44–53.
Stern, M. 2006. Dystopian Anxieties Versus Utopian Ideals: Medicine from Frankenstein to the Visible Human Project and Body Worlds. *Science and Culture* 15 (1): 61–84.
Štrkalj, G. 2016. *Humanistic Anatomy: A New Program for an Old Discipline*. New York: Nova Biomedical.
Štrkalj, G., and N. Pather (eds.). 2017. *Commemorations and Memorials: Exploring the Human Face of Anatomy*. Singapore: World Scientific Publishing.
Subasinghe, S.K., and D.G. Jones. 2015. Human Body Donation Programs in Sri Lanka: Buddhist Perspectives. *Anatomical Sciences Education* 8: 484–489.
Uniform Law Commission, The National Conference of Commissioners on Uniform State Laws. 2006. *Uniform Anatomical Gift Act (UAGA)*. Chicago: Uniform Law Commission.
Vermeulen, N., G. Haddow, T. Seymour, et al. 2017. 3D Bioprint Me: A Socioethical View of Bioprinting Human Organs and Tissues. *Journal of Medical Ethics* 43: 618–624.
Vesalius, A. 1543. De Humani Corporis Fabrica. *Newly Digitized 1543 Edition*. www.vesaliusfabrica.com/en/original-fabrica/the-art-of-the-fabrica/newly-digitized-1543-edition.html. Accessed 5 July 2019.
von Hagens, G. 1979. Impregnation of Soft Biological Specimens with Thermosetting Resins and Elastomeres. *Anatomical Record* 194: 247–256.
von Hagens, G., and A. Whalley (eds.). 2000. *Anatomy Art: Fascination Beneath the Surface. Catalogue on the Exhibition*. Heidelberg: Institute for Plastination.
von Hagens, G., K. Tiedemann, and W. Krit. 1987. The Current Potential of Plastination. *Anatomy and Embryology* 175: 411–421.
Wainman, B., and J. Cornwall. 2019. Body Donation After Medically Assisted Death: An Emerging Consideration for Donor Programs. *Anatomical Sciences Education* 12: 417–424.
Walker, B. 2001. *Inquiry Into the Matters Arising from the Post-mortem and Anatomical Examination Practices of the Institute of Forensic Medicine*. Sydney: The Government of the State of New South Wales.
Wikler, D., and J. Barondes. 1993. Bioethics and Anti-Bioethics in Light of Nazi Medicine: What Must We Remember? *Kennedy Institute of Ethics Journal* 3: 39–55.
Winkelmann, A. 2016. Consent and Consensus—Ethical Perspectives on Obtaining Bodies for Anatomical Dissection. *Clinical Anatomy* 29: 70–77.
Winkelmann, A., and F.H. Guldner. 2004. Cadavers as Teachers: The Dissecting Room Experience in Thailand. *British Medical Journal* 329 (7480): 1455–1457.
Winkelmann, A., A.K. Heinze, and S. Hendrix. 2016. Acknowledging Tissue Donation: Human Cadaveric Specimens in Musculoskeletal Research. *Clinical Anatomy* 29: 65–69.
Yaqinuddin, A., M.F. Ikram, M. Zafar, et al. 2016. The Integrated Clinical Anatomy Program at Alfaisal University: An Innovative Model of Teaching Clinically Applied Functional Anatomy in a Hybrid Curriculum. *Advances in Physiology Education* 40: 56–63.
Young, J.C., M.R. Quayle, J.W. Adams, et al. 2019. Three-Dimensional Printing of Archived Human Fetal Material for Teaching Purposes. *Anatomical Sciences Education* 12: 90–96.

Chapter 6
Serious Enquiries Only, Please: Ethical Issues Raised by the Online Human Remains Trade

Damien Huffer and Nathan Charlton

Abstract Today's trade in anatomical, ethnographic, and archaeological human remains makes ready use of new social media platforms such as Instagram, Facebook, Etsy and, until recently, eBay. Continuing the Colonial-era practice of collecting 'curios' or 'specimens' of natural history, today's proliferation of e-commerce and social media platforms has only expanded the reach and influence of collectors and dealers and their sense of community cohesion. In this chapter, we discuss several ethical issues underlying this trade that address what the dealer community values, how they operate, interrelate, and interact with the professional osteoarchaeological research community. We ultimately argue that participants in the trade engage with or ignore these complicating factors at their own risk, despite the ownership of human remains being legal in many jurisdictions once an individual's purchase has arrived.

6.1 Defining the Problem

There is a flourishing trade in anatomical, ethnographic, and archaeological human remains that takes advantage of new social media such as Instagram, Facebook, Etsy and, pre-2016, eBay (Vergano 2016). From the birth of e-commerce (the buying and selling of goods over the Internet) in the 1990's, through its proliferation in recent times on social media platforms, the online trade of human remains

The original version of the chapter was revised: Citations have been corrected. The correction to this chapter is available at https://doi.org/10.1007/978-3-030-32926-6_31

D. Huffer (✉)
Department of Archaeology and Classical Studies, Stockholm University, Lilla Frescativägen 7, 114 18 Stockholm, Sweden
e-mail: damien.huffer@gmail.com

N. Charlton
Department of Environmental Science and Analytical Chemistry, Stockholm University, Svante Arrhenius väg 8, Stockholm 114 18, Sweden

K. Squires et al. (eds.), *Ethical Approaches to Human Remains*,
https://doi.org/10.1007/978-3-030-32926-6_6

has today become a global phenomenon. Western markets for "tribal art" (a.k.a. "ethnographica") trace their origins to eighteenth to mid-twentieth century explorers, government officials, and missionaries visiting remote areas and peoples and collecting, trading for, or acquiring by other means, modified and unmodified human remains (Hose 1994; Legassick and Rassool 2000; Gosden and Knowles 2001; Roque 2010, 2011; Melander 2017). Separate private markets for anatomical and related medical specimens trace their origins to the eighteenth and nineteenth century whereby medical professionals sought to acquire dissection cadavers. These individuals were often affiliated with Western museums and university departments that later deaccessioned collections (Dittmar and Mitchell 2016; Nystrom 2016).

Human remains in general have been sourced, traded, and used by various groups for much of human history, but in the West this became particularly prominent from the 1800s onward (Giaimo 2017; Laskow 2017). University teaching collections are themselves being investigated with regard to their origins (Pokines et al. 2017). Today's e-commerce, however, has only expanded collectors' ability to trade and sell among themselves and source new specimens. To date, very few nations or US states have introduced restrictions on the private ownership, commercial sale, or inter-state transit of human remains (see Marsh 2016 for a summary). Most global legislation only defines what museums and universities can or cannot do with human remains and related grave goods, whether from archaeological excavations or old Colonial-era collections (Márquez-Grant and Fibiger 2011). Practitioners of the Afro-Cuban syncretic religions Santeria and Palo Mayombe, especially in the United States, have been known to purchase or even excavate skulls for ritual use (Gill, Rainwater and Adams 2009; O'Donnell 2014; Pokines 2015). At the same time, the shipment of human remains between members of the general collecting community, including allegedly authentic and rare archaeological or ethnographic specimens, are only infrequently seized by customs officers in any jurisdiction, and prosecutions remain rare (e.g. Carney 2007; Tynan 2008; U.S. Immigration and Customs Enforcement 2011; O'Donnell 2014). At the time of writing, the most expensive sales price that the authors have seen listed for any category of human remains is approximately CAD $25,500 (£14,896), reduced before eventual sale, for the alleged shrunken head of a child.[1] Skulls usually sell for less than US $1000 on social media and e-commerce platforms currently monitored by the authors, and post-cranial remains sell for even less, from tens to hundreds of dollars depending on the specimen. However, the authors have observed a wide range of variations in price between listed and final sale prices, with many transactions conducted in a de facto form of bartering facilitated through public online conversations in tandem with "direct messaging".

Despite "terms of service" allegedly prohibiting the use of most social media platforms for illicit activities, numerous studies and exposés have revealed active

[1]As of January 2018, the head in question is listed as sold, but when or to whom is unknown (Skull Store 2018). Authentic shrunken heads are highly sought after by a subset of collectors, and forgeries are common.

trafficking of a wide range of prohibited goods, from drugs (Smith 2014) and guns (Goel and Isaac 2016), to exotic animals and products derived from them (Haslett 2015; Schweig 2015). A wealth of literature exists pertaining to the use of datamining and social network analysis on new social media (Ferrara et al. 2014; Hernandez-Castro and Roberts 2015; Cavazos-Rehg et al. 2016; Moreno et al. 2016). However, exploration of the frequency and scope of the trade in cultural property of any type beyond auction house catalogues and eBay is still in its infancy. The well-connected network of human remains collectors and dealers that constitute the online market are both specialist and generalist in their focus, with wide-reaching impact on the 'enthusiasts' who, through their rhetoric, support the activities of the community (Huffer and Graham 2017). The complicated antiquities and cultural property market is frequently classified as a "grey market", but recent research is attempting to define the extent to which cultural property trafficking represents a mixture of licit and illicit items and transactions (Mackenzie and Yates 2017).

The skeletal human remains trade is itself a component of the larger "red market" (sensu Carney 2011), which involves trafficking living and dead human beings and their fresh or preserved tissues. Academic scholars and journalists interested in "red market" trafficking investigate disparate areas such as corrupt adoption agencies (Riben 2015), the illicit organ trade, sources of bodies donated to medical education and research (Wordsworth 2015), and corruption in blood donation and sale (Anand 2015). Closer to the topic at hand, there are also separate overlapping markets for 'wet' specimens from hospitals, pathology laboratories, and separate collecting communities of artefacts from abandoned asylums, antique medical equipment, and 'murderabilia' (i.e. items once owned by, or art created by, famous serial killers, whether living or dead). Discussion of the entire "red market" is outside the scope of this chapter. Furthermore, we are not focused on related ethical debates over museum repatriation or how universities assembled teaching collections in the past, but we appreciate that these are tangential topics worthy of discussion.

The private commercial trade in human skeletal remains currently exists within an uneven national and global legal framework. Due to loopholes or an absence of specific language, this renders private possession and ownership of innumerable varieties of anatomical, archaeological, or ethnographic 'specimens' legal in numerous jurisdictions once they have reached their purchaser, and despite grave desecration or cultural property legislation that would apply if the item was intercepted in transit (Seidemann 2004, 2017; Marsh 2016). While UNESCO (1970, Article 1) does not specifically address human remains, it does note that "most Indigenous communities do not accept that human remains can be regarded as "property". Within the United States, the Native American Graves Protection and Repatriation Act (NAGPRA 1990) dictates what can be done with Indigenous remains and affiliated burial objects by museums and universities, and the civil penalties incurred by individuals who disturb graves and subsequently traffic their contents. The Vermillion Accord of Human Remains, adopted in 1989 by the World Archaeological Congress (WAC 1989), is not legally binding and is more concerned with scientific research involving archaeological human remains. More country-specific legislation, such as the Human Tissue Act (2004) in England,

Wales, and Northern Ireland, is more concerned with non-osseous tissue taken from living people or cadavers obtained from morgues or autopsies and said tissue being intended for transplantation into patients in need, rather than the trade of skeletal human remains (Human Tissue Authority 2016). Many EU countries such as The Netherlands and Belgium, however, have no specific legislation regarding the possession, sale, or national or international shipment of human remains by private individuals (Márquez-Grant and Fibiger 2011). This is especially relevant in cases where it cannot be determined that either the buyer or seller were involved in grave violation on national territory.

Against this patchy and complex legal landscape, this chapter furthers discussion of ethical considerations behind how and why the private online trade in human remains operates as it does. It will provide illustrative examples of five key ethical issues, arguably ethical problems, underneath the trade that collectors and dealers have to acknowledge, circumvent, or nullify in order to participate and profit from their hobby, or for some, their stated livelihood. After delving further into the commodification of the dead and summarising data collection methods, examples are given that strongly suggest false advertising of the age or authenticity of remains for sale, customs violations, complacency in the archaeological community, authentication through science, and media complacency. Issues that do seem to ethically concern members of the collecting community are also discussed. The chapter concludes by using the examples given to query whether an ethical human remains trade is even possible and suggests what professional anthropologists can do when trafficking is encountered.

6.2 The "Exotic" Dead as Curio, Commodity, and Cultural Property

Understanding the online and offline commercial trade in human remains is, relatively speaking, a new area of research (Huxley and Finnegan 2004; Kubiczek and Mellen 2004; Huffer and Chappell 2014; Nafte 2014, 2015; Huffer and Graham 2017, 2018; Huffer et al. 2019). Collectors and dealers in this niche market have garnered their own attention in the popular press, given the esoteric and macabre nature of what they seek (Davis 2015; Gambino 2016). Individuals conduct global transactions and actively seek a variety of 'specimens'. These include allegedly authentic anatomical teaching specimens, mummies, "trophy" or "ancestral" skulls from Southeast Asian and Pacific Island cultures (e.g. the Dayak from Borneo, the Asmat from Irian Jaya, Sepik River tribes from Papua New Guinea, the Ifugao from Luzon in the Philippines, various Solomon Islands groups, and the Malekula and Ambrym cultures from Vanuatu), which are classified as "tribal art". It also includes Tibetan Buddhist artefacts made from femora or tibiae, and old or contemporary items made from human bone or teeth, such as jewellery, knife handles, and canes[2]. Artefacts that incorporate human remains expand the scope of the ethical discussion beyond the ongoing debates surrounding repatriation of cultural property in general.

As suggested above, collecting human remains from other cultures has been a human predilection even prior to the era of Western colonial expansion, but especially from the eighteenth century onward. The acquisition of skulls as war trophies is frequently observed in the historic and archaeological records (Tung 2008; Verano 2008; various chapters within Bonogofski 2011). A separate area of research concerns the analysis and repatriation of the skulls of fallen 'enemy' soldiers taken during past international conflicts, such as the First World War, Second World War, and the Vietnam War (e.g. Bass 1983; Sledzik and Ousley 1991; Weingartner 1992; Harrison 2006, 2012; Seidemann et al. 2009; Yucha et al. 2017), as well as the occasional case of Civil War-era grave robbing in the United States (Associated Press 2008; Skinner 2016). As mentioned at the beginning of this section, academic work attempting to document and quantify commercial collecting, especially outside of religious or medical contexts (Quigley 2001; Nafte 2014, 2015), is still quite rare.

Recent examples have garnered media attention due to the arguably shocking nature of the specimen being offered and the means of attempted sale. For example, Killgrove (2016) discusses a recent crowdfunding campaign run by the Viktor Wynd Museum of Curiosities, Fine Art, and Natural History in London (UK) so that they could purchase the skull of an alleged Peruvian subadult mummy. Arguably crass "rewards" were offered for various levels of donation, all allowing donors to handle human remains as they saw fit. The majority of the media exposure that this trade has received comes after a shipment has been stopped by customs in either source or demand country, on those still-rare occasions that shipments are intercepted (U.S. Immigration and Customs Enforcement 2011; O'Connor 2013; Irfan 2015; Wockner and Erviani 2016). However, only very rarely have e-commerce platforms taken action in response to exposure and public outcry (Kim 2012; Halling and Seidemann 2016). Like other categories of licit and illicit commerce facilitated by social media, today's online market for human remains is facilitated by platform developers and actively manipulated by its users, which allows remains of the dead to be exchanged for money in an allegedly safe and "hidden" virtual space.

[2]Numerous websites operated by online galleries, as well as private sellers on social media, sell items that incorporate human remains, many of which are discussed in Huffer and Chappell (2014). Some examples include: http://www.tribalartasia.com/; http://www.damaruworks.com/kapala-mala/acquiring-bone/; https://www.skullstore.ca/collections/humans?page=1.

6.3 Data Acquisition Methodology and Research Ethics

As first discussed in Huffer and Graham (2017), Instagram was thoroughly queried between November 2015 and November 2016. Additional data mining from late 2016 onwards has continued to follow many of the same hashtags, including: #humanbones, #humanskulls, #oddities, #curiosities, #realbone, and #trophyskulls, as well as re-visiting previously known accounts (Huffer et al. 2019), to document change to publicly posted content, and changes to privacy settings.

Initial data collection used Pablo Babera's 'InstaR' package (2015), however Instagram changed the way their public Application Programming Interface (API) operated in June 2016 such that only those seeking to commercialise users' data could access it in this way. A second package, written in PHP (a programming language based on C and C++) automated querying and paging through Instagram's public search page (Kapishev 2016) and enabled the current authors to continue exploring these posts, although with less rich metadata (Kapishev 2016). Data collection by automated and manual methods on Instagram continues, with more than 12,000 images (and associated text) extracted from public Instagram profiles to date (Huffer and Graham 2017, 2018). The majority of examples presented in the figures below, however, come from public Facebook accounts and the Dutch e-commerce platform Marktplaats.

Regarding data collection from Marktplaats (2018), relevant posts are screen-captured and saved by date, listed seller name or handle, and location. Collection of data on this platform began in August 2017. Data from Facebook derives from three specific groups that we have accessed and includes posts from c. 2015 through to the present day, with new data added regularly. Several new groups have emerged since our research began, including those specific to a certain geographic region (e.g. the USA and the EU), or focused on specific niche topics, such as *tsantsa* ("shrunken heads" produced by the Jivaro culture, Ecuador). A substantial degree of cross-posting occurs between the three groups actively monitored. When collecting data, a relevant post is screen-captured as it appears, labeled by date and name, and sorted by group and month. Effort is made to capture all image, text, and metadata associated with any given post, divided into separate "parts" if more than one screen shot is required to capture the entire thread legibly. If more than one post is made by the same person on the same date, they are saved as (name) 1, (name) 2, and so on.

Across platforms, users often provide means of contacting them in their posts, and other information, such as geolocation data, zip codes, and email addresses that could be used to identify them. While users may post information publicly in the hopes that prospective clients use it to arrange final sales privately, it is not the same as the original posters making information available for research. Initial Instagram research (Huffer and Graham 2017) met all requirements set out by a university ethics board (that of Carleton University, Ottawa, Ontario, Canada) (Carleton University 2014; TCPS2 2014). It was ruled that data mining publicly available social media was "research ethics exempt" with regards to research involving living human subjects. In other words, they represent public posts on social media deliberately made available to the public for purchase, or to garner appreciation of the extent of their collecting or raise interest in items that could be sold or traded if the price or exchange is right. Nevertheless, in each of the figures provided below, we have continued the practice of blacking out all usernames or other identifying information to preserve full anonymity.

With regards to the images of human remains included in the figures below, we feel it appropriate to include them to specifically illustrate our points. The dead for sale have already been "fetishised", so our discussion of the examples below cannot expand upon or negate this. Rather, the context provided calls their treatment as commodities into question. The human remains trade already displays, describes, and 'values' items allegedly removed from whatever archaeological, historic, ethnographic, or forensic context they once possessed, or with potentially fabricated provenance, ownership history, or cultural authenticity. The stories collectors and dealers attach to them can be readily embellished to increase demand and price. However, as we will demonstrate, this is only the starting point from which participants in the trade must confront or nullify the underlying ethical concerns involved.

6.4 Buyer Beware?

This section will present several examples obtained using the methods described in the previous section of this chapter. As mentioned in the introduction, the examples and topics chosen (from among many possibilities) provide visual and textual evidence illustrating how participants in the online human remains trade respond to or ignore these specific ethical issues raised by the trade's existence and their participation in or active support of it. The topics chosen do not represent a comprehensive list. It is felt that the categories selected, however, are the most suitable to begin a more detailed exploration of the ethical landscape, beyond questions of legality. Individuals seeking to participate in the trade must actively engage with these issues, or ignore them and put themselves at risk of being scammed or facing prosecution if items in transit to them are seized. The examples chosen as figures are only a few of many available within our current database, but were selected because they clearly illustrate each issue and how it is discussed, mitigated, or ignored.

6.4.1 False Advertising and Dishonest Transactions

We first turn to the topic of false advertising and implied dishonest transactions. By this, we mean a seller deliberately misleading a potential customer about the nature, source, age, or cultural authenticity of the remains being offered or knowingly defrauding each other. Collectors, dealers, and enthusiasts exist within a somewhat tight-knit community scattered around the world (mostly within Europe and North

America), and of diverse socio-economic classes and professions (Huffer and Chappell 2014; Huffer and Graham 2017). Multi-disciplinary research examining how antiquities in general are sold and the ability of forgeries to affect market demand has grown in recent years, mostly in response to an uptick in global looting, especially in conflict zones. This research is increasingly occurring simultaneously with greater public outreach by archaeologists and others who seek to raise awareness of the dangers the general antiquities trade poses to the integrity of the archaeological record (Stanish 2009; Fay 2011, 2013; Scott 2013; Brodie 2014, 2015). However, to the best of our knowledge, research specifically addressing the prevalence or effect of false advertising on antiquities markets (let alone the human remains market) does not exist. This is most likely due to the difficulty of proving intentional false advertisement, i.e. inaccurately representing the age, cultural affiliation, or materials used, including real bone vs. high-quality resin, without having the item available for expert analysis. In some areas, such as the sale of alleged Saints relics, new policy has been developed by the Vatican to address false advertising within the realm of auction house sales (Malm 2017). Global false advertising legislation also appears minimal, with protocols not specifically addressing the antiquities trade (Castendyke et al. 2008), while in the USA, legislation is only relevant at state level (Frieden and Roche 2006). More research has been conducted, however, on issues of fraud, trust, and diversification in e-commerce (Gefen 2000; Xiao and Benbasat 2011; Turban et al. 2017).

At present, only eBay and Etsy have clear terms of service and policy that, on paper, prohibit the sale (or gifting) of all categories of human remains or material save scalp hair or, on Etsy, human teeth (Etsy 2017; eBay 2018). At the time of writing this chapter, Instagram, Facebook, or Marktplaats have not followed suit, but neither have they been contacted directly by the authors to raise this issue. On Marktplaats, sellers are able to list human remains as “enkel voor studie-doeleinden” (only for study purposes), with no supporting documents or evidence required by the platform to prove that either the buyer or seller will comply, and that the buyer accepts responsibility for the “risk” involved in shipping it without supporting documentation, following payment (Fig. 6.1). In the past it was necessary to state words to this effect in order to sell human remains on eBay, with a similar lack of independent verification, until new research and public pressure caused eBay to tighten and more readily enforce its policy in 2016 (Vergano 2016). Casual assessment of a prominent Facebook group by an investigative journalist over the period 2015–2016 (Hugo 2016a) provided a general breakdown of price and quantity for several categories of human remains (e.g. bones, teeth, and organs) collated during the observation period. Huffer and Chappell (2014) and Huffer et al. (2019) provide more detail of the diversity of human remains offered on Instagram and via brick-and-mortar stores with an online presence for the period 2013–2016. All examples of items for sale, trade, or auction were obtained via the use of common search engines or manually following hashtags and handles, as opposed to automated datamining employed later (Huffer and Graham 2017, 2018). Here, Figs. 6.2 and 6.3 exemplify the tight-knit nature of the community, ready to name and shame purported scam artists and aid in resolving theft or dishonest transactions.

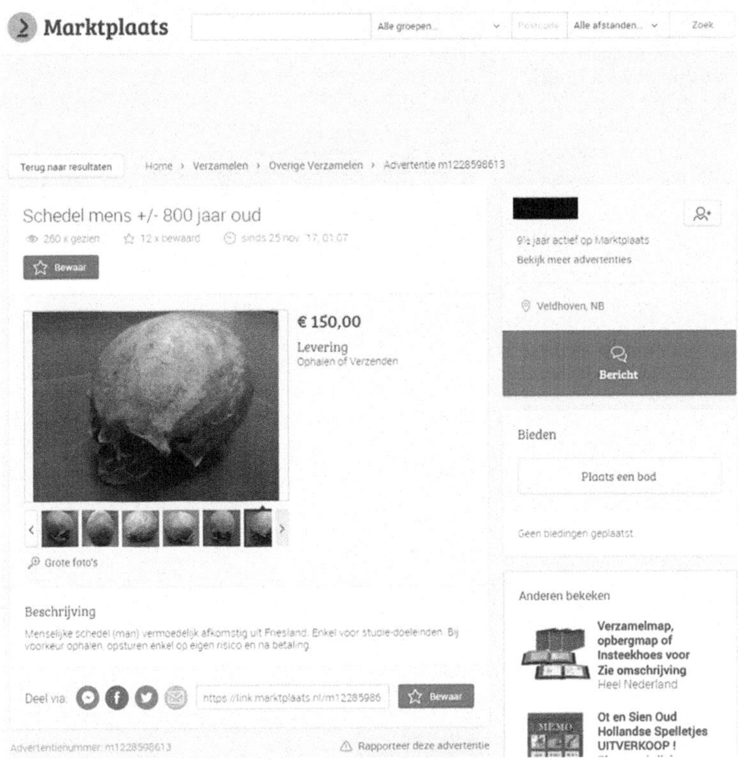

Fig. 6.1 "Human skull plus or minus 800 years old" for sale on Marktplaats.com, 25th November 2017. Text reads: "Human skull (male) presumably from Friesland. Only for study purposes. Preferably pick up, send only at your own risk and after payment."

Figures 6.4, 6.5 and 6.6a, b attest to not only the continued attempted use of eBay as a sales platform and avenue for potential fraud (Figs. 6.4a, b), but also the use of collective opinion (Figs. 6.5a and 6.6b) by community members to protect their peers against fraud from within or without.

6.4.2 *Source Country Corruption and Customs Violations*

Following on from the previous point is the related issue concerning demand for the best, most exotic, or most macabre human remains, which consequently fosters corruption within source countries or willing violation of (lax or inconsistent) customs procedures. Here, we define 'source' countries as those, usually in the developing world, from which looted or smuggled cultural property derives (Brodie 2002).

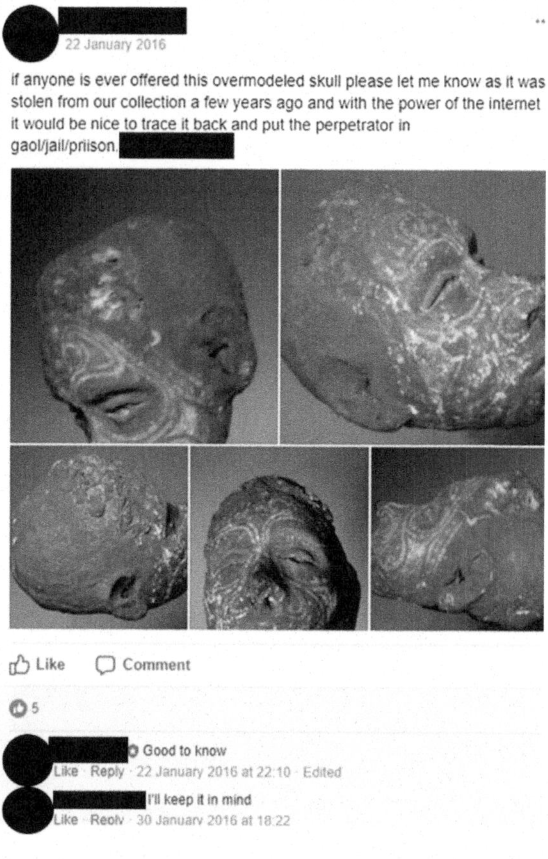

22 January 2016
if anyone is ever offered this overmodeled skull please let me know as it was stolen from our collection a few years ago and with the power of the internet it would be nice to trace it back and put the perpetrator in gaol/jail/priison.
Like
Comment
5
Good to know
Like · Reply · 22 January 2016 at 22:10 · Edited
I'll keep it in mind
Like · Reply · 30 January 2016 at 18:22

Fig. 6.2 Facebook post from a human remains collecting group; the poster requests help in tracking down a stolen specimen

We consider the fostering of corruption to refer to collectors or dealers admitting to, and sometimes discussing the logistics of, shipping, as well as examples of 'composite' pieces that incorporate real skulls with vague or unstated ownership history and provenience, suggesting the possibility of illicit export and import.

Figure 6.7 is a unique example of a 'composite' piece; a real skull sourced from somewhere in Indonesia, with decoration picked up elsewhere, made to look like an item of Asmat cultural heritage. Thus, the skull in question had to leave Indonesia by some means, even if the exact route or the number of hands it passed through is unknowable, given that the shipment was not seized in transit. Even "fake" pieces will often incorporate real human bone, but we have found that resin replicas are not in high demand by serious collectors. The remaining figures (Figs. 6.8a, 6.9, and 6.10) in this section are examples of discussions between collectors regarding

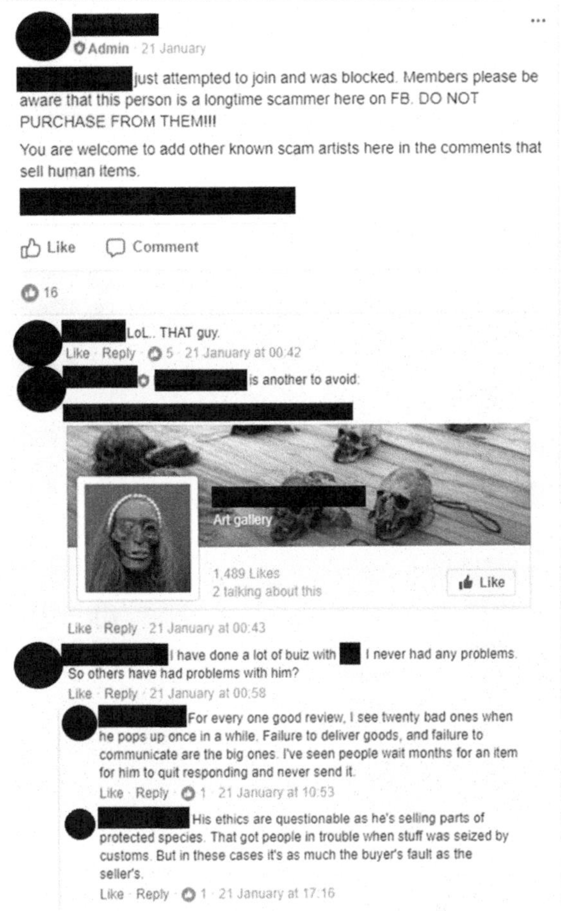

Fig. 6.3 Facebook post from a human remains collecting group; the poster identifies a suspected scam artist and warns the group about interacting with them

their experience with shipping to or from various countries, and how they have bypassed customs or used the system to their advantage. Individuals mention false declarations, relative ease of shipping, shipping freshly exhumed specimens, and the varying degree to which different country's customs officers look for or seize human remains. At the time of writing, there is no national or international publicly available information detailing the frequency of customs seizures of human remains. Nevertheless, examples such as these clearly illustrate that the risk and potential illegality of shipping or acquiring human remains is generally known, even if only sometimes openly acknowledged.

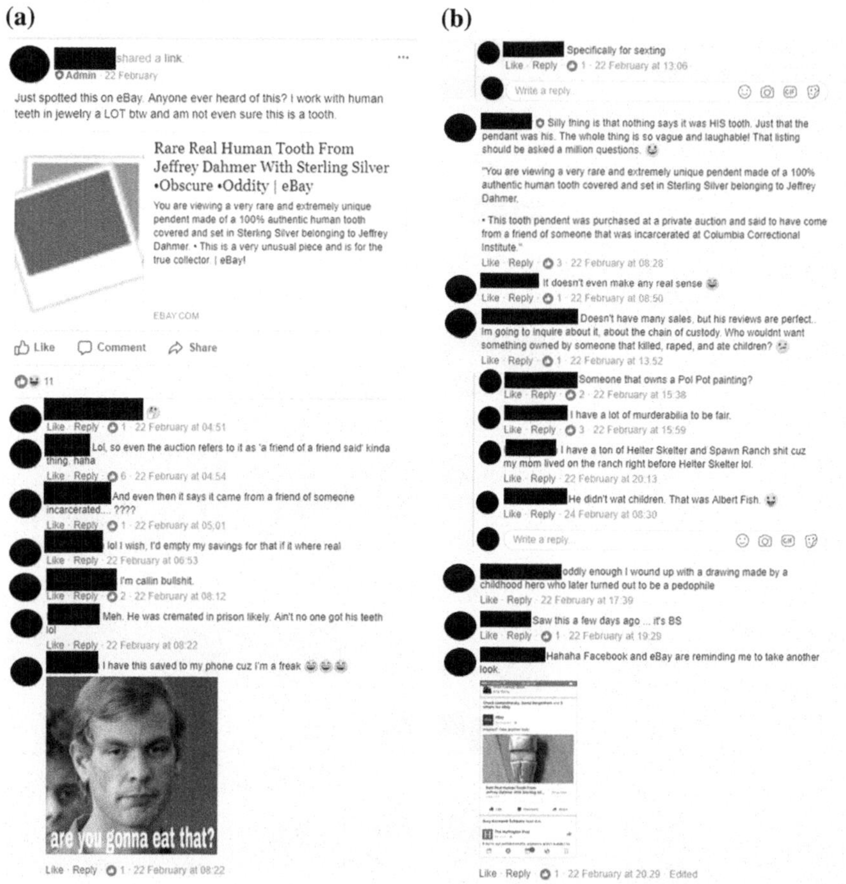

Fig. 6.4 **a**, **b** Facebook post from a human remains collecting group; an example of the attempted use of eBay to sell an alleged oddity associated with Jeffrey Dahmer, with the original poster and commenting group members expressing opinions as to its authenticity

6.4.3 Alleged Complacency by the Archaeological Community

This section provides examples that directly suggest complacency or involvement in furthering a collector's acquisitions by unidentified members of the archaeological community. Whether this occurred close to or well before the item's current owner acquired it is usually unknown. Regardless, the trade or commerce implied would be in direct violation of every professional archaeological society's code of ethics (SAA 1996; Archaeological Institute of America 1997; BABAO 2018). Figures 6.11 and 6.12 illustrate two examples in which purchases from an archaeologist (or their spouse) at some point in the past is directly stated.

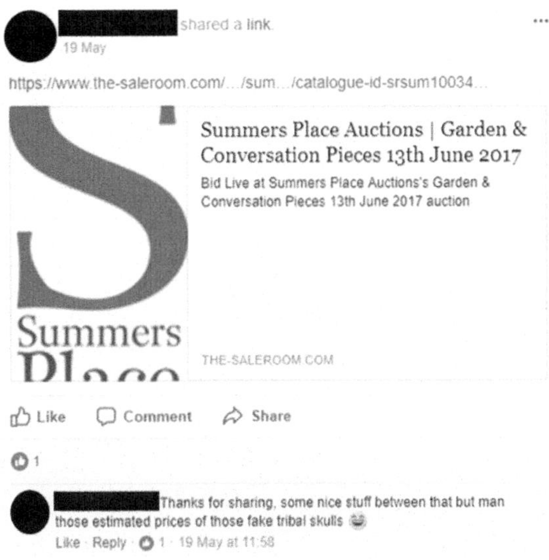

Fig. 6.5 Facebook post from a human remains collecting group; a prominent private collector questions the authenticity of the specimens offered in a forthcoming auction

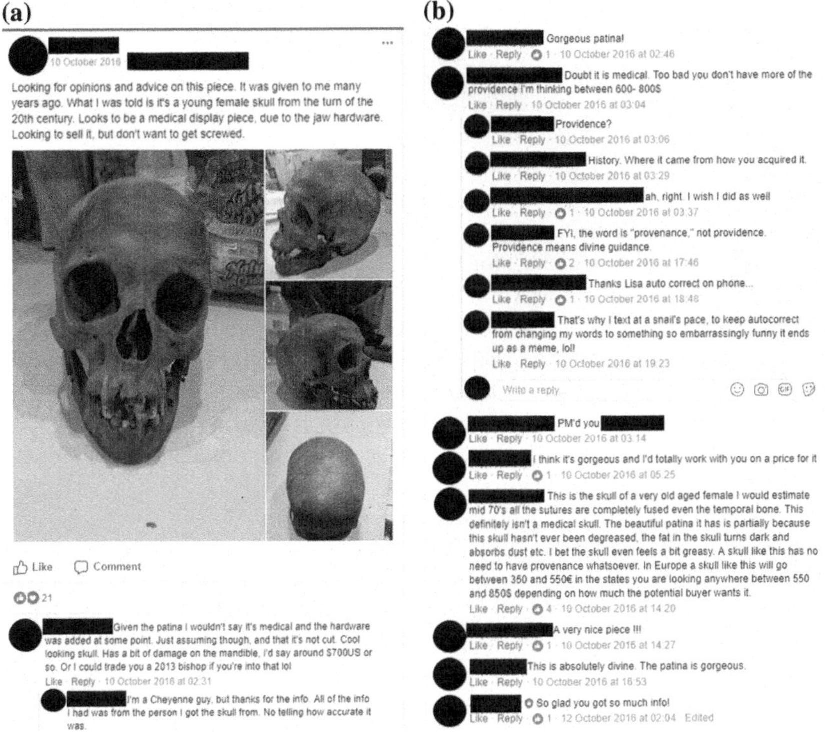

Fig. 6.6 **a**, **b** Facebook post from a human remains collecting group; group members discuss whether or not a specimen the original poster wished to sell was what it was claimed to be

Fig. 6.7 Facebook post from a human remains collecting group; the original poster describes the creation of a composite piece

14 hrs
Asmat Skull
$1,200
This is an authentically decorated Asmat skull done by me. The skull is real and Indonesian in decent. The artifacts are sourced while on my trips to papua and placed accordingly to traditional methods. Price includes shipping. Stand is not included.

Figure 6.11 is a Facebook post listing an alleged Incan skull of a “young girl” for sale, allegedly from Ecuador and purchased in the 1970s from the widow of an individual who “went on archaeological digs around the world”.

From the photographs offered, the authors (both either trained in general osteology or, in the case of Huffer, a practicing osteoarchaeologist) question the age and sex assessment provided by the seller, implying the possibility of false advertising as well. While it is always the story that sells the skeleton, Ecuador currently has state-ownership of all cultural patrimony, including excavated and still unexcavated material, with relevant legislation (e.g. Resolución Ministerial 139) as early as 1946 (Salazar 1995) and has accepted or ratified all relevant UNESCO Conventions or Protocols (UNESCO 2014). Figure 6.12 was taken from Instagram and shows two mandibles, one of which was “purchased from an archaeologist who found it on a dig years ago”. The seller appears to be based in the UK, but it is unclear where the mandibles come from or where the alleged excavation occurred. The ethical breach of practice implied by such collusion, if found to be true upon further investigation by law enforcement, would be severe (see guidelines in BABAO 2018). When already in private hands and sold through social media, however, the chance of apprehending items such as these is minimal.

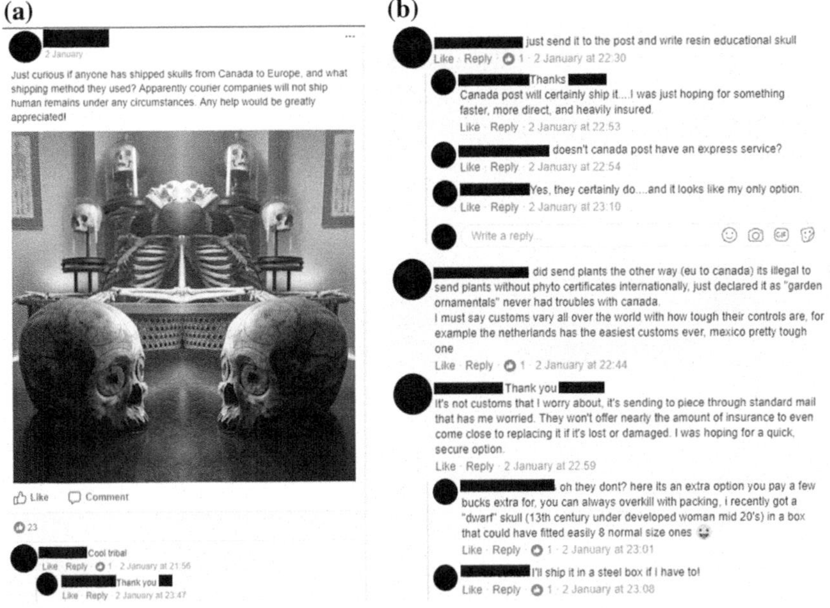

(a)
2 January
Just curious if anyone has shipped skulls from Canada to Europe, and what shipping method they used? Apparently courier companies will not ship human remains under any circumstances. Any help would be greatly appreciated!
Like Comment
23
Cool tribal
Like · Reply · 1 · 2 January at 21:56
Thank you
Like · Reply · 2 January at 23:47
(b)
just send it to the post and write resin educational skull
Like · Reply · 1 · 2 January at 22:30
Thanks
Canada post will certainly ship it....I was just hoping for something faster, more direct, and heavily insured.
Like · Reply · 2 January at 22:53
doesn't canada post have an express service?
Like · Reply · 2 January at 22:54
Yes, they certainly do....and it looks like my only option.
Like · Reply · 2 January at 23:10
Write a reply...
did send plants the other way (eu to canada) its illegal to send plants without phyto certificates internationally, just declared it as "garden ornamentals" never had troubles with canada.
I must say customs vary all over the world with how tough their controls are, for example the netherlands has the easiest customs ever, mexico pretty tough one
Like · Reply · 1 · 2 January at 22:44
Thank you
It's not customs that I worry about, it's sending to piece through standard mail that has me worried. They won't offer nearly the amount of insurance to even come close to replacing it if it's lost or damaged. I was hoping for a quick, secure option.
Like · Reply · 2 January at 22:59
oh they dont? here its an extra option you pay a few bucks extra for, you can always overkill with packing, i recently got a "dwarf" skull (13th century under developed woman mid 20's) in a box that could have fitted easily 8 normal size ones
Like · Reply · 1 · 2 January at 23:01
I'll ship it in a steel box if I have to!
Like · Reply · 1 · 2 January at 23:08

Fig. 6.8 **a**, **b** Facebook post from a human remains collecting group; the original poster and commenting group members discuss shipping methods and customs regulations

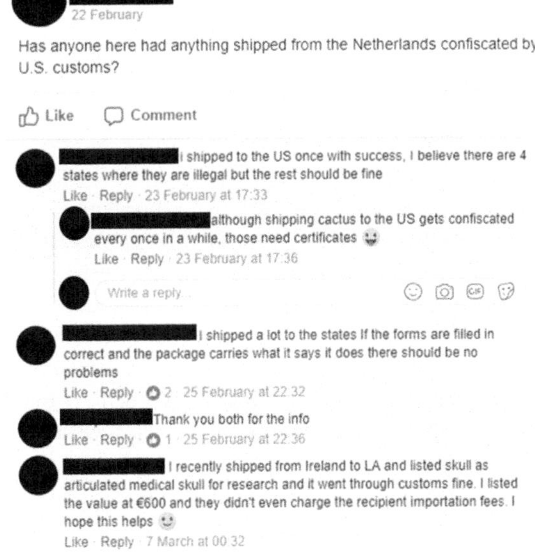

22 February
Has anyone here had anything shipped from the Netherlands confiscated by U.S. customs?
Like Comment
i shipped to the US once with success, I believe there are 4 states where they are illegal but the rest should be fine
Like · Reply · 23 February at 17:33
although shipping cactus to the US gets confiscated every once in a while, those need certificates
Like · Reply · 23 February at 17:36
Write a reply...
I shipped a lot to the states If the forms are filled in correct and the package carries what it says it does there should be no problems
Like · Reply · 2 · 25 February at 22:32
Thank you both for the info
Like · Reply · 1 · 25 February at 22:36
I recently shipped from Ireland to LA and listed skull as articulated medical skull for research and it went through customs fine. I listed the value at €600 and they didn't even charge the recipient importation fees. I hope this helps
Like · Reply · 7 March at 00:32

Fig. 6.9 Facebook post from a human remains collecting group; the original poster and commenting group members further discuss shipping methods and customs regulations

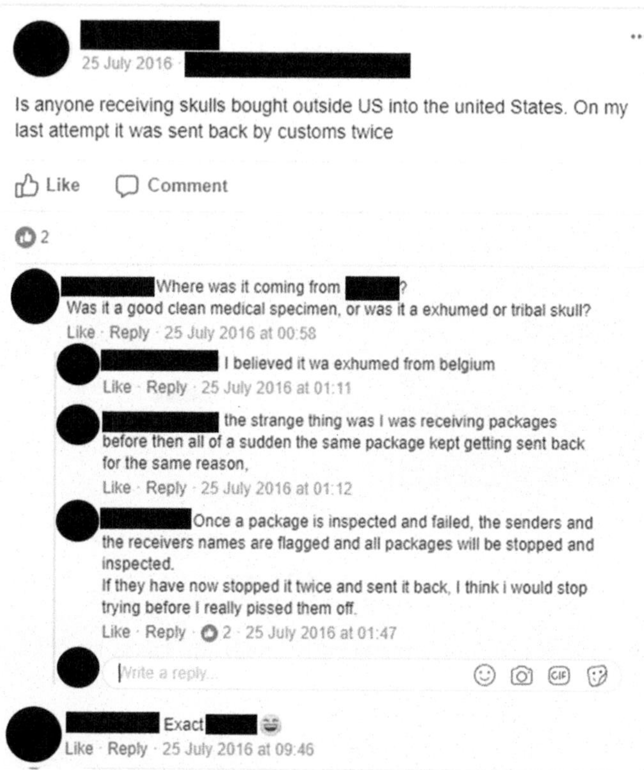

Fig. 6.10 Facebook post from a human remains collecting group; the original poster and commenting group members discuss difficulties shipping to the United States of America from Belgium

6.4.4 Authenticity and Validity Through Science

Within the antiquities trade research community, significant concern is being raised over the extent to which scientific laboratories (from C^{14} dating to DNA analysis) might contribute to the trade by 'authenticating', analysing, or conserving an item brought to them by a dealer (Caldararo 2000; Argyropoulos et al. 2011; Brodie 2011). Indeed, an international conference was held at ETH Zurich from the 16th–17th November 2017, entitled "Radiocarbon dating and protection of cultural heritage—C14 Meeting". It primarily focused on how laboratories can conduct better due diligence and more thoroughly query those who submit samples, especially individuals not affiliated with law enforcement, a university, museum, or cultural heritage management company (i.e. those most likely to be private collectors with sufficient finances). While the authors did not attend, discussion with colleagues who did attend suggests that the consensus opinion by delegates was that much greater awareness of the problem is needed, with more targeted codes of

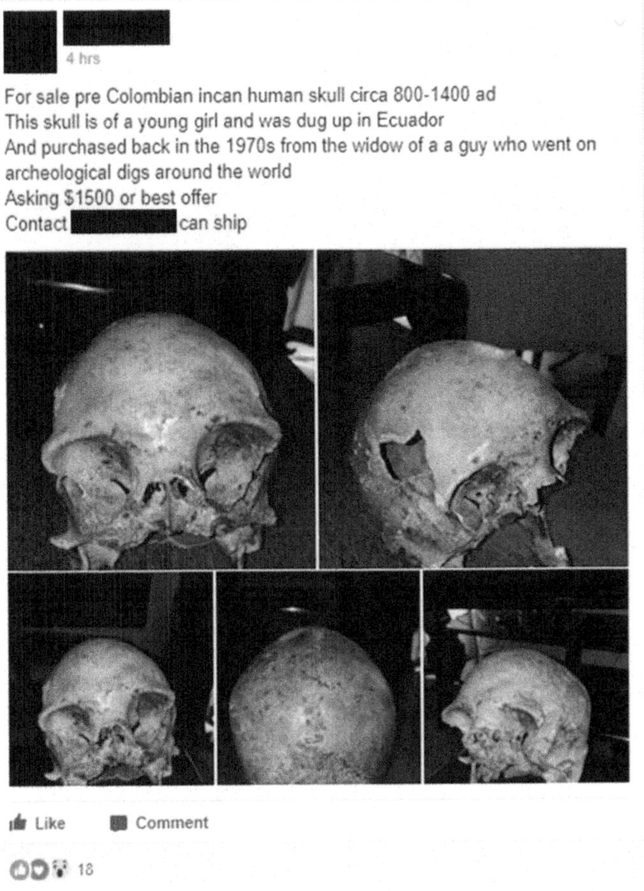

4 hrs
For sale pre Colombian incan human skull circa 800-1400 ad
This skull is of a young girl and was dug up in Ecuador
And purchased back in the 1970s from the widow of a a guy who went on archeological digs around the world
Asking $1500 or best offer
Contact can ship
Like
Comment
18

Fig. 6.11 Facebook post from a human remains collecting group; an alleged pre-Colombian Incan skull is offered for sale

conduct for laboratory staff now being developed. The conference programme is available to the public (Mödlinger 2017) and the state-of-play between AMS dating and cultural property authentication described by Huysecom et al. (2017).

While this bodes well for an eventual end to the use of legitimate archaeological science as a means to commodify or directly threaten the archaeological record, Figs. 6.13, 6.14a, b, and 6.15 show that, where the human remains trade is concerned, the problem remains. Figures 6.13 and 6.15, especially, suggest that the occasional well-established or determined collector or dealer has the financial means and contacts necessary to arrange "tests" (this is most likely to be radiocarbon dating) or purchase directly out of deaccessioned museum collections after specific analyses have been conducted. Figures 6.14a, b, on the other hand, show the proprietor of the private Embody Museum (less a museum than a private

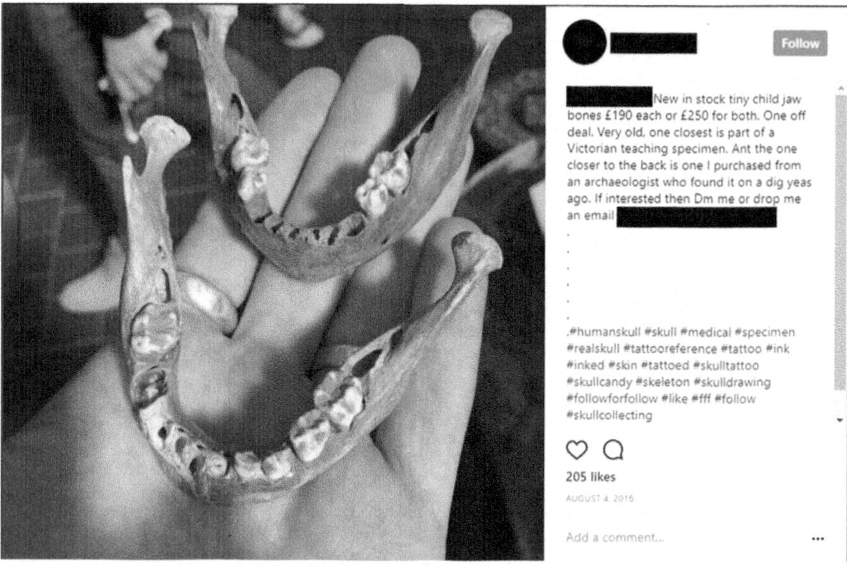

Fig. 6.12 UK based Instagram post in which two human mandibles are proffered for sale, one of which was allegedly purchased from an archaeologist

collection) which, based on the institution's Instagram and Facebook accounts, is believed to be located in Los Angeles (California, USA) (Embody Museum n.d.). The administrator(s) of the Instagram account offers advice to their followers about how to spot a fake Melanesian 'overmodeled' skull (Figs. 6.14a, b). The specific nature of this post is made to seek out anthropologists and archaeologists who will confirm which are fake remains and which are real. The thread ends when one follower begins to ask more direct questions. We have yet to encounter a post containing information on who provided the alleged analysis conducted, for what price, or what the results were, so it is possible that this information is shared only privately.

6.4.5 Media Complacency

Stepping back from the ethical concerns associated with how the human remains trade operates and how buyers and sellers negotiate with each other, this section provides examples of instances in which public mass media was arguably complacent in encouraging the fetishisation, commodification, and no-questions-asked acquisition of human remains. Figures 6.16 and 6.17 represent screen shots from two examples in which collectors and collecting is glamorised with little attention paid to legal or ethical concerns. The two examples provided were both originally downloaded from YouTube, though there are many more available online.

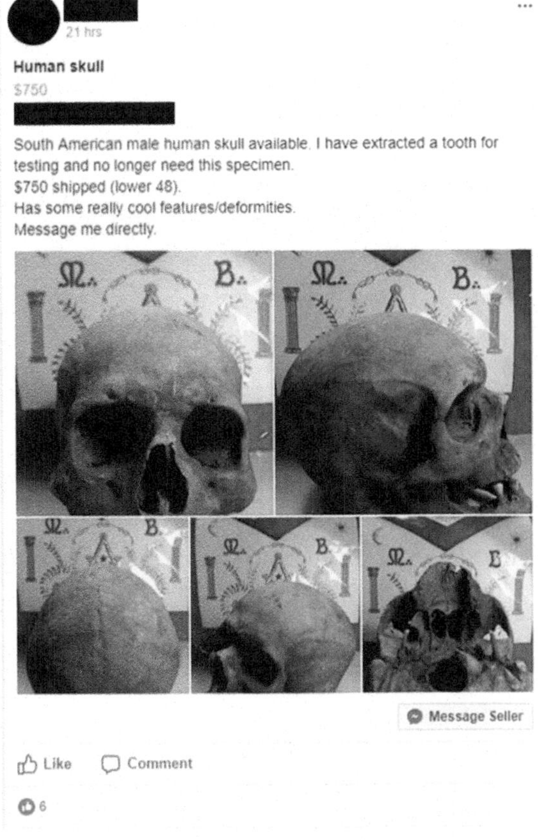

21 hrs
Human skull
$750
South American male human skull available. I have extracted a tooth for testing and no longer need this specimen.
$750 shipped (lower 48).
Has some really cool features/deformities.
Message me directly.
Message Seller
Like
Comment
6

Fig. 6.13 Facebook post from a human remains collecting group; the original poster advertises a South American male skull for sale within the United States of America. The poster states that a tooth has been removed for "testing"

Figure 6.16 illustrates a screen shot from the beginning of a video posted on the 6th April 2017 entitled "human bones collector". The original poster is identifiable by name, but it is not clear if the main person seen removing a skeleton from what appears to be a modern burial (judging from the clothing taken off the skeleton) is the same individual. Loud rap music accompanies the clip, and the looting is seen to be a team effort, with the dirty skeleton laid on the ground at the end so that posed pictures can be taken. This video was a chance discovery by the authors, but perfectly illustrates the infrequently seen process of exhuming human remains, which could subsequently enter the market, either cleaned and unmodified or modified to look like something else (e.g. a lobotomised anatomical specimen or a piece of "tribal art"). The video was reported to YouTube by the authors no more than two days after discovery, but to no effect. The existence of such videos openly hosted and shared on YouTube and other streaming media servers, to us, strongly suggests the need for guidelines to address what individuals are allowed to post or simply display on their accounts.

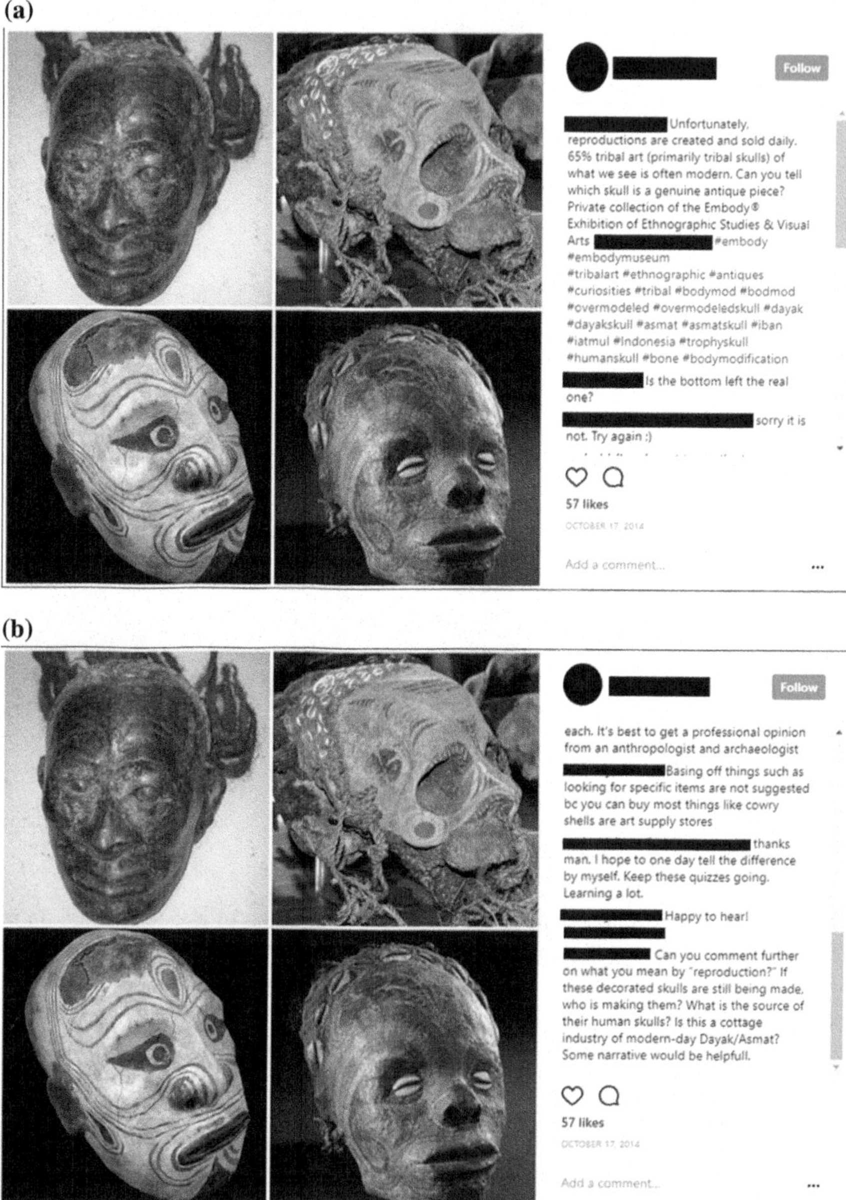

Fig. 6.14 **a**, **b** US based Instagram posts in which an individual associated with a private "museum" presents four examples of 'overmodeled' skulls from New Guinea. Followers are challenged to identify which one is an authentic c. 1800s specimen

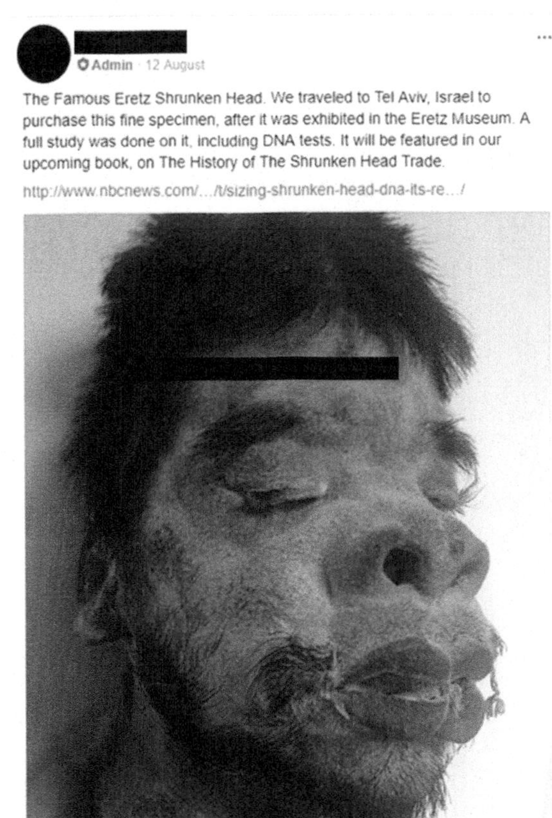

Fig. 6.15 Facebook post from a human remains collecting group; the original poster displays a *tsantsa* ("shrunken head") allegedly obtained from the Eretz Museum in Tel Aviv (Israel) after extensive scientific testing. The superimposed URL links to a webpage where prospective buyers can discuss prices and arrange confidential sale

Figure 6.17 is a striking example of more formal media complacency. Taken from a news clip entitled "The Real Relic Hunter", by *Global News* out of Toronto, it follows a reporter through the condominium and collection of the late William "Bill" Jamieson and his wife before his death on the 3rd July 2011, in the midst of shooting a mini-series about his life for History Television. Jamieson, a profligate collector of "tribal art" and "oddities" from the 1970s until his death, was a world-renowned source of ethnographica for collectors and museums alike (Bourgon 2011). In the news story mentioned above, Mr. Jamieson takes the opportunity to show off his immense collection of ethnographic artefacts and human remains, including mummies, *tsantsa* (shrunken heads), and trophy skulls. The reporter discusses how he (Mr. Jamieson, the interviewee) acquired the entire

Fig. 6.16 Screen shot of a video showing the clandestine excavation of human remains, potentially in Nagaland (India) on an unknown date and time (Jamir 2017)

Fig. 6.17 Screen shot of a video which depicts an interview with the ex-fiancée of the late William "Bill" Jamieson describing his collection, collecting practices, and the Treasure Traders show in which his collection featured before later dispersal (Global News 2012)

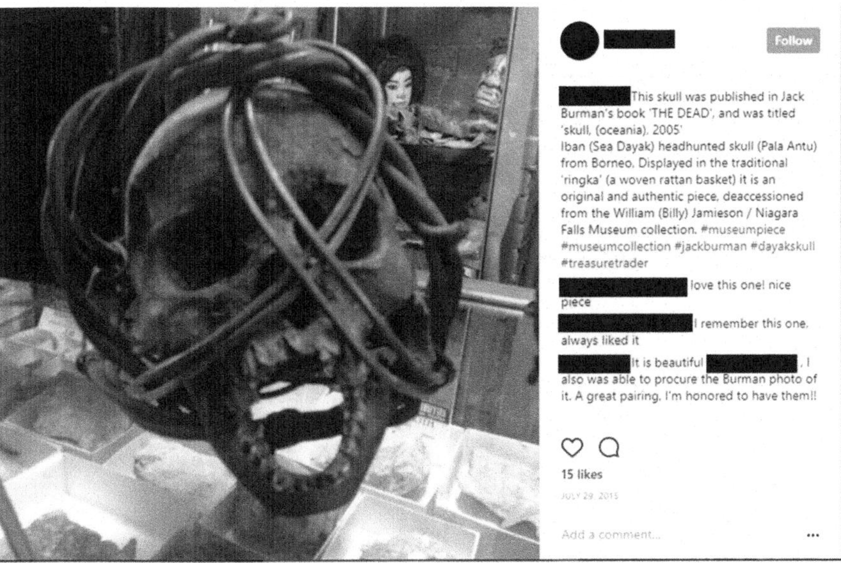

Fig. 6.18 Instagram post whereby the original poster displays an alleged Iban Dayak skull in their possession with a stated publication history noting its previous residence in the Billy Jamieson/ Niagara Falls Museum collection

collection of the Niagara Falls Museum, how and why he collects, how his fame enhanced his collecting ability and public image, and how he has sold to several notable museums and other private collectors. After his death, his collection was auctioned off to individual buyers and institutions around the world (Bourgon 2011; Global News 2012), yet it continues to entice the collecting community (Fig. 6.18). More recent journalism (e.g. Hugo 2016a, 2016b; Killgrove 2016; Kukolja 2017) is beginning to ask tough questions about how and from where collectors obtain human remains, and to address the legal and ethical complexities underpinning the trade, to which this chapter contributes. However, much remains to be done.

6.4.6 Ethical and Moral Concerns as Expressed by the Collecting Community

Though many in the human remains collecting community attempt to distance themselves from those that desecrate the resting places of the deceased, and in turn show an apparent deep reverence for the dead, how much this sentiment actually translates to community self-policing to prevent illegality remains an open-ended question. Figure 6.19 represents a plea by a group administrator for members to

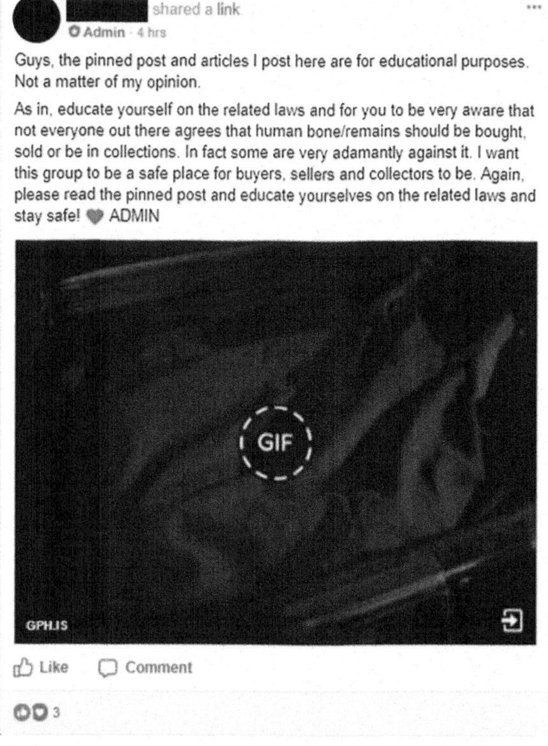

shared a link
Admin · 4 hrs
Guys, the pinned post and articles I post here are for educational purposes. Not a matter of my opinion.
As in, educate yourself on the related laws and for you to be very aware that not everyone out there agrees that human bone/remains should be bought, sold or be in collections. In fact some are very adamantly against it. I want this group to be a safe place for buyers, sellers and collectors to be. Again, please read the pinned post and educate yourselves on the related laws and stay safe! ADMIN
GIF
GPHJS
Like
Comment
3

Fig. 6.19 Facebook post from a human remains collecting group; a member of admin cautions group members to keep up to date on legislation and "stay safe"

have a good understanding of relevant laws and engage in "safe" business practices, even if this plea to stay legally "safe" (as the administrator claims to) is itself a means to drum up more business. Collectors, dealers, or their supporters sometimes present apparent concern or anger about news of cemeteries or mausoleums being vandalised or disturbed by development. Figure 6.20 illustrates a collecting group's response to a member visiting the famous Paris Catacombs, and the disrespect inherent in theft and resale from such a location.

Finally, Fig. 6.21 illustrates one individual's more whimsical use of their collection, tempered with the expressed hope that no one finds it disrespectful. It is included here specifically to demonstrate that the overall community is not entirely indifferent towards how society might perceive their unique use of or relation to the dead. Thus, while community members might express a wide range of ethical and moral opinions to justify their collecting and their relation to the dead themselves, the examples above, to us, also imply commodification fueled by substantial cognitive dissonance.

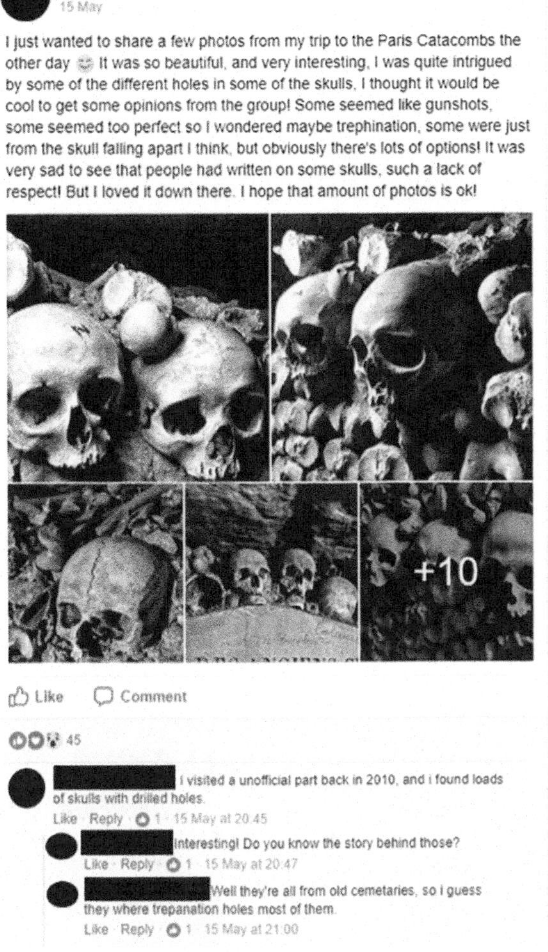

15 May
I just wanted to share a few photos from my trip to the Paris Catacombs the other day It was so beautiful, and very interesting, I was quite intrigued by some of the different holes in some of the skulls, I thought it would be cool to get some opinions from the group! Some seemed like gunshots, some seemed too perfect so I wondered maybe trephination, some were just from the skull falling apart I think, but obviously there's lots of options! It was very sad to see that people had written on some skulls, such a lack of respect! But I loved it down there. I hope that amount of photos is ok!
+10
Like
Comment
45
I visited a unofficial part back in 2010, and i found loads of skulls with drilled holes.
Like · Reply · 1 · 15 May at 20.45
Interesting! Do you know the story behind those?
Like · Reply · 1 · 15 May at 20:47
Well they're all from old cemetaries, so i guess they where trepanation holes most of them.
Like · Reply · 1 · 15 May at 21:00

Fig. 6.20 Facebook post from a human remains collecting group; the original poster describes a recent trip to the Paris Catacombs and group members comment on the disrespect inherent in vandalism and theft from such sites

6.5 Is the Human Remains Trade "Wrong"?

In this section, we use the above examples alongside the significance of the issues raised in this chapter to answer a fundamental question: Is the human remains trade (in its modern form) "wrong"? To put it another way, should the public at large be concerned with the existence of this trade and thus expend the time and energy required to pressure the key social media/e-commerce platforms to reform terms of service and better enforce use? 'Normative' ethics in the context of business practices regulates aspects of behaviour that lie beyond governmental control (Berle and Means 1932). A wide variety of unethical and/or criminal activities facilitated by social media have attracted the attention of ethicists and law enforcement (Kelly

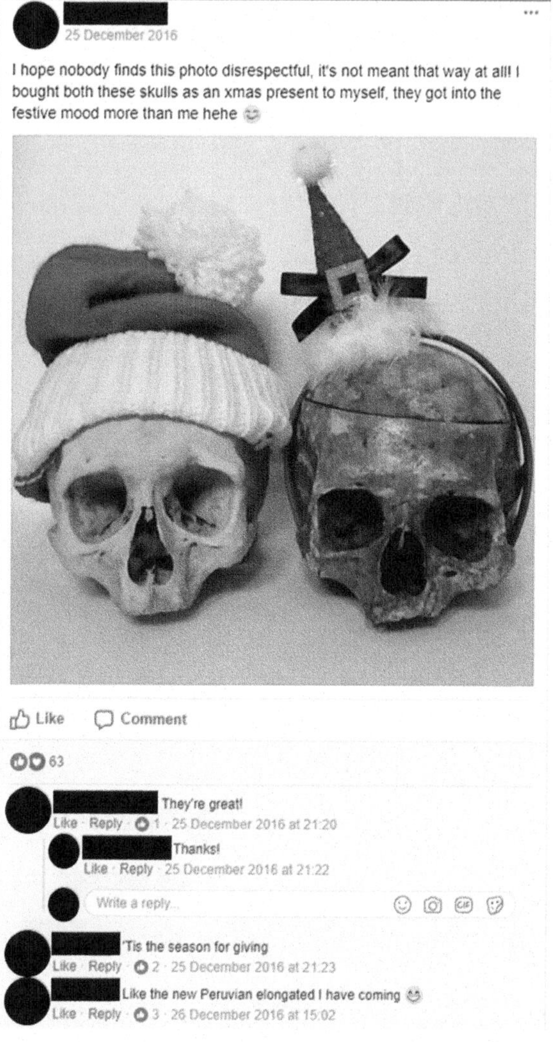

Fig. 6.21 Facebook post from a human remains collecting group; the original poster displays some uniquely decorated skulls but expresses concern that group members will find it disrespectful

2012; Vallor 2015). While the antiquities trade overall has been dismissed as a 'victimless' crime (Mackenzie 2006, 2011; Bowman Proulx 2011; Yates 2016), when material culture containing human remains is being trafficked, this is an especially difficult position to maintain.

Beyond the visceral disgust that most feel when exposed to burial looting in action by accident or via news reports (WTAE-TV 2013; Hicks 2016; Jamir 2017), or when customs seizures are reported during or after the hand-back ceremony, public awareness remains minimal. Customs seizures are a relatively rare occurrence (but see U.S. Immigration and Customs Enforcement 2011; Ramsey 2012; Cascone 2016; Daley 2018), and the majority of the trade passes under the radar and is not reported in media outlets. The human remains trade exists as its own complex ‘grey market’ (Mackenzie and Yates 2016, 2017), which combines legal and illegal transactions, and authentic and fake items. Recent research and news reports (Huffer and Chappell 2014; Kukolja 2017; Huffer et al. 2019) have begun to question the legality of selling or owning human remains with vague ownership history and provenience, as well as present substantial evidence that the collecting community acknowledges the murkier aspects of the trade itself. The extent to which relevant, verifiable, paperwork is exchanged through private direct messaging or email is unknown. Without such paperwork, determining the length of time and circumstances under which human remains have been outside their source countries, and thus whether UNESCO Conventions or state-specific cultural property legislation has been violated, is difficult. While we acknowledge that this could occur at least occasionally, especially where recent anatomical specimens are concerned, the lack of transparency and potential for criminality that e-commerce can foster should give anyone pause for concern.

The ethical dilemmas inherent in the online trafficking of cultural property have been raised at the highest levels within the discipline of archaeology, via codes of ethics that members of professional bodies, such as the Society for American Archaeology (SAA), must adhere to, as well as individual public outreach efforts through blogs and other media (SAA 1996; Barker 2000; Huffer 2009, 2011; Heritage Watch 2017). However, very little action has been taken by social media companies to curtail the ability for unethical and questionably illicit sales (of many products) to be conducted. It is this ability for small-scale collectors to readily use social media and the community it fosters to conduct clandestine sales or exchange tips about shipping or specimen conservation that can negate the ethical concerns of ‘enthusiasts’ seeking to begin collecting. High-profile collectors who have been interviewed naturally take a different approach when questioned about the underbelly of the trade. One, quoted in Davis (2015, 1), stated: “We’re respectful, we’re not making fun of it. We love this stuff, we hold it up on a pedestal”. Many would also argue that, since collectors almost exclusively seek the dead of “others”, not necessarily named individuals or their own relatives, they are doing nothing inherently wrong. The examples presented here suggest otherwise.

6.6 Conclusion: Is an Ethical Private Human Remains Trade Possible?

The examples discussed above have been included as a means of illustrating certain aspects of the human remains trade that warrant further investigation. Doing so would allow criminologists, archaeologists, and law enforcement to more effectively understand and monitor activities, and prosecute cases when seizures occur. In light of the above, we conclude by discussing whether an ethical private commercial trade is even possible.

In a 2015 article for *XO Jane* (Hunter 2015, 1), Lillith Hunter, a self-described “ethical collector of human bones and other weird stuff”, describes numerous criteria she personally uses to source the bones she buys, her take on the nature of the allegedly licit, and admittedly illicit market in 2015, and other topics. Specifically discussing her ethical stance, Hunter (2015, 1) states:

> Because of my beliefs, I only buy bones that I can touch. That's right, no Internet deals for me. You might feel like you need to ask the bones' permission to bring them home, and that's just fine. I've never held a bone that felt gross or angry to me, but I'm sure they're out there. I treat my bones with a lot of reverence and respect, and they're a really positive part of my home. Personally, I steer clear from bone fetishism or using my bones as tools. I don't flaunt skulls to guests as a status symbol or use them as seasonal decor. I'd never drink wine or serve candies out of a skull, because that's super impolite in my book. Also, you're risking the ingestion of bio-hazardous human remains or noxious chemicals. The ethics of bone collecting definitely extends into display and use, and it's something that you ought to reflect on… As a concept, it's currently at a pretty weird place in our cultural framework, where it's equal parts trendy fad and offensive horror.

It is probable that this ever-evolving trade will continue to find new avenues as social media platforms proliferate. With the exception of eBay and Etsy, no other social media platforms evaluated in this study currently attempt to restrict human remains or antiquities trading in their "terms of service" (TOS). Instagram (owned by Facebook) prefers more general statements such as: "You may not post violent, nude, partially nude, discriminatory, unlawful, infringing, hateful, pornographic or sexually suggestive photos or other content via the Service", "You are responsible for any activity that occurs through your account…" and, "You may not use the Service for any illegal or unauthorised purpose. You agree to comply with all laws, rules and regulations (for example, federal, state, local and provincial) applicable…" (Instagram 2013). The pros and cons of Instagram's current TOS, is discussed in more depth in Remsen (2016), which are then compared to Facebook and YouTube's TOS. Other smaller, or newer, subsidiary platforms are less well-thought-out, especially where "grey area" activities like cultural property commerce is involved.

In fact, we have recently encountered individuals making reference to items for sale, or their own purchases, on Facebook Marketplace, an as yet unexplored subsidiary platform on which cultural property trafficking could be readily occurring. Other much more widely used e-commerce platforms such as Craigslist sometimes continue to host advertisements seeking or selling human remains, which at times have also received media coverage (Yee 2017). Monitoring the online trade also reveals very little about activities that occur offline, so knowing its full extent and frequency in real-time is currently not possible. Recent exposes (Stevenson 2017, 1) continue to suggest "there are no international legal protections and no "obligations of ownership" for cultural property in private possession. More broadly, the legal status of these sales confers an air of legitimacy to the antiquities trade". These concerns are amplified where human remains are concerned, given the finite supply of real specimens, alleged connection to the archaeological and museum community (even if not recently), and increased reliance on open-ended new social media. Hunter (2015, 2) concludes by asking: "Is collecting bones the right thing to do? Honestly, I'm still not entirely certain. I'll probably never know, but I'll keep working on it".

As we have suggested, it does not appear that the human remains collecting community at large is giving due consideration to how participation in, or support of, their particular hobby (or for some, their stated livelihood) can foster arguably unethical or immoral behavior. The level of due diligence performed by collectors and dealers is not uniform and will likely change with increasing public exposure of (and reaction to) what lies beneath the readily-manipulatable new "face" of the trade outside of traditional auction houses or brick-and-mortar stores. The expectation of any antiquities collecting community to "self-regulate" has been readily questioned (Mackenzie 2014). Given the slow pace of change to or standardisation of legislation between countries, as well as between US states, the risk of deliberate or accidental ethical and legal breaches will continue to be the foundation on which this so-called 'victimless crime' rests.

Hunter (2015) is quoted above in an attempt to summarise, through the perspective of one current (or former) alleged collector, what engaging with or mitigating the ethical issues illustrated in Sect. 6.4 can result in (i.e. misrepresentation of an item's age, authenticity or licit origins, complacency by the media or unscrupulous archaeologists or curators, collaboration with scientific laboratories without due diligence being performed by those accepting samples, and customs violations). In other words, the "attitude" towards collecting that can manifest itself when a given collector weighs their actions, responsibilities, and limits. Given the difficulties inherent in defining the extent of the trade on and off-line, what can concerned citizens who do not collect, as well as professional anthropologists who observe human remains for sale, do in "real-time"? We do not advocate any individual putting themselves in potential danger to confront dealers selling out of premises. However, an individual browsing in a store, gallery, or flea market can make mental notes for later transcribing or take photographs and subsequently turn the information over to local law enforcement as a first step in cases where suspiciously weathered or dirty remains are encountered. More often, reporting online sales or videos to the management of the hosting platform can at least demonstrate that knowledgeable individuals are watching and oppose to social media being used for these purposes, even if no action is taken by the parent company. Most importantly, those with sufficient osteological training can reach out to local divisions of Federal agencies responsible for investigating cultural property cases. In our experience, law enforcement will readily appreciate the expertise provided in sorting out oft-times complicated cases.

References

Anand, A. 2015. Blood for Sale: India's Illegal 'Red Market'. *BBC News*. 27 January. http://www.bbc.com/news/business-30273994. Accessed 14 September 2017.

Archaeological Institute of America. 1997. *Code of Ethics*. https://www.archaeological.org/news/advocacy/130. Accessed 28 November 2017.

Argyropoulos, V., K. Polikreti, S. Simon, et al. 2011. Ethical Issues in Research and Publication of Illicit Cultural Property. *Journal of Cultural Heritage* 12: 214–219.

Associated Press. 2008. Thieves Steal Remains from Civil War-Era Graves. 67 Skeletons Secretly Exhumed After Tip-off About Looting at N.M. Cemetery. *NBC News*. 9 April. http://www.nbcnews.com/id/24022697/ns/us_news-military/t/thieves-steal-remains-civil-war-era-graves/. Accessed 10 January 2018.

Barbera, P. 2015. *'instaR: Access to Instagram API via R', v0.2.0*. https://github.com/pablobarbera/instaR/releases. Accessed 24 November 2017.

Barker, A.W. 2000. *Ethics, E-commerce, and the Future of the Past*. http://www.saa.org/portals/0/saa/publications/saabulletin/18-1/saa13.html. Accessed 24 November 2017.

Bass, W.M. 1983. The Occurrence of Japanese Trophy Skulls in the United States. *Journal of Forensic Sciences* 28: 800–803.

Berle, A.A., and G.C. Means. 1932. *The Modern Corporation and Private Property*. Piscataway: Transaction Publishers.

Bonogofski, M. (ed.). 2011. *The Bioarchaeology of the Human Head*. Tallahassee: University Press of Florida.

Bourgon, L. 2011. Bill Jamieson Was a Treasure-Hunting Rarity. *The Globe and Mail*. 29 July. https://www.theglobeandmail.com/arts/television/bill-jamieson-was-a-treasure-hunting-rarity/article4260507/. Accessed 28 November 2017.

Bowman Proulx, B.A. 2011. Drugs, Arms, and Arrowheads: Theft from Archaeological Sites and the Dangers of Fieldwork. *Journal of Contemporary Criminal Justice* 27: 500–522.

British Association for Biological Anthropology and Osteoarchaeology [BABAO]. 2018. *Ethics and Standards*. http://www.babao.org.uk/publications/ethics-and-standards/. Accessed 15 January 2018.

Brodie, N. 2002. Illicit Antiquities. In *Illicit Antiquities: The Theft of Culture and the Extinction of Archaeology*, ed. N. Brodie and K.W. Tubbs, 1–22. London: Routledge.

Brodie, N. 2011. Congenial Bedfellows? The Academy and the Antiquities Trade. *Journal of Contemporary Criminal Justice* 27: 408–437.

Brodie, N. 2014. The Internet Market in Pre-Columbian Antiquities. In *Cultural Property Crime: An Overview and Analysis of Contemporary Perspectives and Trends*, ed. J.D. Kila and M. Balcells, 237–262. Leiden: Brill.

Brodie, N. 2015. The Internet Market in Antiquities. In *Countering Illicit Traffic in Cultural Goods: The Global Challenge of Protecting the World's Heritage*, ed. F. Desmarais, 11–20. Paris: International Council of Museums.

Caldararo, N. 2000. Fake or Transitional Form? Analysis of a Purported Pre-Columbian Olmec Artifact and Comparison with Similar Published Objects from Mesoamerica. *Mexicon* 22: 58–63.

Carleton University. 2014. *Policy on the Responsible Conduct of Research*. https://carleton.ca/researchethics/wp-content/uploads/Responsible-Conduct-of-Research.pdf. Accessed 9 August 2018.

Carney, S. 2007. Inside India's Underground Trade in Human Remains. *Wired*. 27 November. https://www.wired.com/2007/11/ff-bones/. Accessed 16 January 2018.

Carney, S. 2011. *The Red Market: On the Trail of the World's Organ Brokers, Bone Thieves, Blood Farmers, and Child Traffickers*. New York: Harper Collins.

Cascone, S. 2016. Ancient Hand Returned to Egyptian Museum Thanks to Operation Mummy's Curse. *Artnet News*. 7 December. https://news.artnet.com/art-world/ancient-mummy-hand-returned-egypt-775097. Accessed 15 January 2018.

Castendyke, O., E. Dommering, A. Scheuer, et al. (eds.). 2008. *European Media Law*. Amsterdam: Kluwer Law International.

Cavazos-Rehg, P.A., M.J. Krauss, S.J. Sowles, et al. 2016. Marijuana-Related Posts on Instagram. *Prevention Science* 17: 710–720.

Daley, J. 2018. After More Than 90 Years, Looted Mummy Parts Repatriated to Egypt. *Smithsonian Magazine*. 9 January. https://www.smithsonianmag.com/smart-news/mummy-parts-repatriated-egypt-90-years-after-being-looted-180967760/. Accessed 15 January 2018.

Davis, S. 2015. Meet the Living People Who Collect Dead Human Remain. *Vice*. 13 July. http://www.vice.com/read/meet-the-living-people-who-collect-human-remains-713. Accessed 24 November 2017.

Dittmar, J.M., and P.D. Mitchell. 2016. From Cradle to Grave Via the Dissection Room: The Role of Foetal and Infant Bodies in Anatomical Education from the Late 1700s to Early 1900s. *Journal of Anatomy* 229: 713–722.

eBay. 2018. *Human Remains and Body Parts Policy*. http://pages.ebay.com/help/policies/remains.html. Accessed 30 November 2017.

Embody Museum. n.d. *Exhibition of Ethnographic Studies and Visual Arts*. https://embodymuseum.org/collection. Accessed 28 November 2017.

Etsy. 2017. *Prohibited Items Policy*. https://www.etsy.com/legal/prohibited/#Q2. Accessed 30 November 2017.

Fay, E.V. 2011. Virtual Artifacts: eBay, Antiquities, and Authenticity. *Journal of Contemporary Criminal Justice* 27: 449–464.

Fay, E.V. 2013. *Trading in Antiquities on eBay: The Changing Face of the Illicit Trade in Antiquities*. Dissertation, Keele University.

Ferrara, E., R. Interdonato, A. Tagarelli. 2014. Online Popularity and Topical Interests Through the Lens of Instagram. In *Proceedings of the 25th ACM Conference on Hypertext and Social Media*, ed. L. Ferres, G. Rossi, V. Almeida, et al. (chairs), 24–34. New York: ACM.

Frieden, J.D., and S.P. Roche. 2006. E-commerce: Legal Issues of the Online Retailer in Virginia. *Richmond Journal of Law and Technology* 13: 1–16.

Gambino, P. (ed.). 2016. *Morbid Curiosities: Collections of the Uncommon and Bizarre*. London: Laurence King Publishing.

Gefen, D. 2000. E-commerce: The Role of Familiarity and Trust. *Omega* 28: 725–737.

Giaimo, C. 2017. Stumbling on Skeletons in Old Odd Fellows Lodges. *Atlas Obscura*. 30 October. https://www.atlasobscura.com/articles/odd-fellows-found-skeletons. Accessed 16 January 2018.

Gill, J.R., C.W. Rainwater, and B.J. Adams. 2009. Santeria and Palo Mayombe: Skulls, Mercury, and Artifacts. *Journal of Forensic Sciences* 54: 1458–1462.

Global News. 2012. *Preview of Treasure Trader Premier* [video]. https://www.youtube.com/watch?v=WWIt-iYiG8A. Accessed 28 November 2017.

Goel, V., and M. Isaac. 2016. New Facebook Policy Bans Talk of Private Gun Sales, Applies to Instagram. *The New York Times*. 29 January. http://www.nytimes.com/2016/01/30/technology/facebook-gun-sales-ban.html?_r=0. Accessed 2 October 2017.

Gosden, C., and C. Knowles (eds.). 2001. *Collecting Colonialism: Material Culture and Colonial Change*. Oxford: Berg Publishers.

Halling, C.L., and R.M. Seidemann. 2016. They Sell Skulls Online? A Review of Internet Sales of Human Skulls on eBay and the Laws in Place to Restrict Sales. *Journal of Forensic Sciences* 61: 1322–1326.

Harrison, S. 2006. Skull Trophies of the Pacific War: Transgressive Objects of Remembrance. *Journal of the Royal Anthropological Institute* 12: 817–836.

Harrison, S. 2012. *Dark Trophies: Hunting and the Enemy Body in Modern War*. New York: Berghahn Books.

Haslett, C. 2015. Click to Like This: Is Instagram a Hub for Illegal Ape Deals? *Mongabay*. 10 December. http://news.mongabay.com/2015/12/click-to-like-this-is-instagram-a-hub-for-illegal-ape-deals/. Accessed 14 November 2017.

Heritage Watch. 2017. Heritage Watch. *Preserving the Past… Enriching the Future*. https://www.heritagewatchinternational.org/. Accessed 31 July 2018.

Hernandez-Castro, J. and D.L. Roberts. 2015. Automatic Detection of Potentially Illegal Online Sales of Elephant Ivory via Data Mining. *PeerJ Computer Science* 1: e10. https://doi.org/10.7717/peerj-cs.10.

Hicks, E. 2016. *Grave Robbing for Morons* [video]. https://www.youtube.com/watch?v=G-gAQuvtttk. Accessed 14 November 2017.

Hose, C. 1994. *Fifty Years of Romance and Research in Borneo*. Oxford: Oxford University Press.

Huffer, D. 2009. Conserving the Past Through Play: Educational Gaming and Anti-Looting Outreach in Cambodia. *Bulletin of the Indo-Pacific Prehistory Association* 29: 92–100.

Huffer, D. 2011. *Bringing Them Home: The Repatriation of Priceless Human Remains and Artifacts to Cambodia*. New York: Saving Antiquities For Everyone. http://savingantiquities.org/bringing-them-home-the-repatriation-of-priceless-human-remains-and-artifacts-to-cambodia/. Accessed 31 July 2018.

Huffer, D., and D. Chappell. 2014. The Mainly Nameless and Faceless Dead: An Exploratory Study of the Illicit Traffic in Archaeological and Ethnographic Human Remains. *Crime, Law and Social Change* 62: 131–153.

Huffer, D., D. Chappell, and N. Charlton et al. 2019. Bones of Contention: The Online Trade in Archaeological, Ethnographic and Anatomical Human Remains on Instagram. In *Art Crime Handbook*, ed. D. Chappell and S. Hufnagel, 527–556. London: Palgrave Macmillan Press.

Huffer, D., and S. Graham. 2017. The Insta-Dead: The Rhetoric of the Human Remains Trade on Instagram. *Internet Archaeology* 45. doi: https://doi.org/10.11141/ia.45.5.

Huffer, D., and S. Graham. 2018. Fleshing Out the Bones: Studying the Human Remains Trade with Tensorflow and Inception. *Journal of Computer Applications in Archaeology* 1: 55–63.

Hugo, K. 2016a. You Probably Don't Understand the Laws About Selling Body Parts. *BU News Service*. 1 May. http://bunewsservice.com/you-probably-dont-understand-the-laws-about-selling-body-parts/. Accessed 28 November 2017.

Hugo, K. 2016b. Human Skulls are Being Sold Online, But Is It Legal? *National Geographic*. 23 August. https://news.nationalgeographic.com/2016/08/human-skulls-sale-legal-ebay-forensics-science/. Accessed 28 November 2017.

Human Tissue Act. 2004. The Stationery Office, London.

Human Tissue Authority. 2016. *Sale of Bodies, Body Parts and Tissue*. https://www.hta.gov.uk/policies/sale-bodies-body-parts-and-tissue. Accessed 16 January 2018.

Hunter, L. 2015. *It Happened to Me: I'm an Ethical Collector of Human Bones and Other Weird Stuff*. 14 January. https://www.xojane.com/it-happened-to-me/how-to-buy-human-bones-ethically. Accessed 14 November 2017.

Huxley, A.K., and M. Finnegan. 2004. Human Remains Sold to the Highest Bidder! A Snapshot of the Buying and Selling of Human Skeletal Remains on eBay®, An Internet Auction Site. *Journal of Forensic Sciences* 49: 1–4.

Huysecom, E., I. Hajdas, M. Renold, et al. 2017. The "Enhancement" of Cultural Heritage by AMS Dating: Ethical Questions and Practical Proposals. *Radiocarbon* 59: 559–563.

Instagram. 2013. *Terms of Use*. Instagram Help Center—Privacy and Safety Center. https://help.instagram.com/478745558852511. Accessed 15 January 2018.

Irfan, A. 2015. Indonesian Government to Investigate Report on Human Skull Smuggling. *Antara News*. 18 June. http://www.antaranews.com/en/news/99239/indonesian-government-to-investigate-report-on-human-skull-smuggling. Accessed 14 November 2017.

Jamir, I. 2017. *Human Bones Collector* [video]. https://www.youtube.com/watch?v=i9TnqahuNbw. Accessed 14 November 2017.

Kapishev, R. 2016. *'instagram-php-scraper' v0.4.5*. https://github.com/postaddictme/instagram-php-scraper/releases?after=v0.4.5. Accessed 4 August 2018.

Kelly, H. 2012. Police Embrace Social Media as Crime-Fighting Tool. *CNN News*. 30 August. http://edition.cnn.com/2012/08/30/tech/social-media/fighting-crime-social-media/index.html. Accessed 30 November 2017.

Killgrove, K. 2016. Mummy Crowdfunder Leaves Archaeologists Fuming. *Forbes*. 10 October. http://www.forbes.com/sites/kristinakillgrove/2016/10/10/mummy-crowdfunder-leaves-archaeologists-fuming/#115d303f1d2d. Accessed 13 November 2017.

Kim, E. 2012. Etsy Blocks Sales of Drugs and Human Remains. *CNN Money*. 10 August. http://money.cnn.com/2012/08/10/technology/etsy-bans-drugs/index.html. Accessed 14 November 2017.

Kubiczek, P.A., and P.F. Mellen. 2004. Commentary On: Huxley AK and Finnegan M; Human Remains Sold to the Highest Bidder! A Snapshot of the Buying and Selling of Human Skeletal Remains on eBay, An Internet Auction Site. *Journal of Forensic Sciences* 49: 17–20.

Kukolja, K. 2017. Fighting Trade in Human Remains Antiquities. *The Saturday Paper*. 21 October. https://www.thesaturdaypaper.com.au/2017/10/21/fighting-trade-human-remains-antiquities/15085044005381. Accessed 14 November 2017.

Laskow, S. 2017. The Gruesome History of Making Human Skeletons. *Atlas Obscura*. 3 October. https://www.atlasobscura.com/articles/history-gruesome-skeleton-anatomists. Accessed 16 January 2018.

Legassick, M., and C. Rassool. 2000. *Skeletons in the Cupboard: South African Museums and the Trade in Human Remains 1907–1917*. Cape Town: South African Museum.

Mackenzie, S. 2006. Psychosocial Balance Sheets: Illicit Purchase Decisions in the Antiquities Market. *Current Issues in Criminal Justice* 18: 221–241.

Mackenzie, S. 2011. The Market as Criminal and Criminals in the Market: Reducing Opportunities for Organised Crime. In *Crime in the Art and Antiquities World*, ed. S. Manacorda and D. Chappell, 69–85. New York: Springer.

Mackenzie, S. 2014. Dig a Bit Deeper: Law, Regulation and the Illicit Antiquities Trade. *British Journal of Criminology* 45: 249–268.

Mackenzie, S., and D. Yates. 2016. Collectors on Illicit Collecting: Higher Loyalties and Other Techniques of Neutralization in the Unlawful Collecting of Rare and Precious Orchids and Antiquities. *Theoretical Criminology* 20: 340–357.

Mackenzie, S., and D. Yates. 2017. What Is Grey About the "Grey Market" in Antiquities? In *The Architecture of Illegal Markets: Towards an Economic Sociology of Illegality in the Economy*, ed. J. Beckert and M. Dewey, 70–87. Oxford: Oxford University Press.

Malm, S. 2017. The Vatican Bans Sales of Saints' Body Parts, Including Hair Strands and Teeth, to Stop Them Being Sold for Thousands on Online Auctions. *Daily Mail Online*. December 18. http://www.dailymail.co.uk/news/article-5191219/The-Vatican-banning-sales-relics-saints.html. Accessed 15 January 2018.

Marktplaats. 2018. *Marktplaats*. https://www.marktplaats.nl/. Accessed 4 August 2018.

Márquez-Grant, N., and L. Fibiger (eds.). 2011. *The Routledge Handbook of Archaeological Human Remains and Legislation*. London: Routledge Press.

Marsh, T. 2016. *The Law of Human Remains*. Tucson: Lawyers and Judges Publishing Company.

Melander, V. 2017. The Head-Hunters of the North and the Polynesian Shadow: Thor Heyerdahl's Skull-Collecting Act on Fatu Hiva, Marquesas Islands, 1937. *Journal of Pacific Archaeology* 8: 77–87.

Mödlinger, M. 2017. *Zurich, CH: Workshop on Connections Between AMS Dating and Looted Antiquities*. https://heritage-lost-eaa.com/2017/09/06/zurich-ch-workshop-on-connections-between-ams-dating-and-looted-antiquities/. Accessed 16 January 2018.

Moreno, M.A., A. Ton, E. Selkie, et al. 2016. Secret Society 123: Understanding the Language of Self-harm on Instagram. *Journal of Adolescent Health* 58: 78–84.

Nafte, M. 2014. *Trophies and Talismans: The Traffic of Human Remains*. Dissertation, McMaster University.

Nafte, M. 2015. Institutional Bodies: Spatial Agency and the Dead. *History and Anthropology* 26: 206–233.

Native American Graves Protection and Repatriation Act (NAGPRA). Public Law 101-601, 25 United States Code 3001 et seq., 104 Stat. 3048—Nov. 16, 1990 (1990) 101st United States Congress, Washington D.C.

Nystrom, K. (ed.). 2016. *The Bioarchaeology of Dissection and Autopsy in the United States*. London: Springer Press.

O'Connor, M. 2013. Italian Arrested 'For Smuggling Human Skulls into Asia'. *The Telegraph*. 8 November. http://www.telegraph.co.uk/news/worldnews/africaandindianocean/burundi/10436673/Italian-arrested-for-smuggling-human-skulls-into-Asia.html. Accessed 15 September 2017.

O'Donnell, J. 2014. Mexican Man Smuggled Skulls in Teddy Bears: Prosecutors. *NY Daily News*. 23 June. http://www.nydailynews.com/news/world/mexican-man-smuggled-skulls-teddy-bears-prosecutors-article-1.1840894. Accessed 16 January 2018.

Pokines, J.T. 2015. A Santeria/Palo Mayombe Ritual Cauldron Containing a Human Skull and Multiple Artifacts Recovered in Western Massachusetts, U.S.A. *Forensic Science International* 248: e1–e7.

Pokines, J.T., N. Appel, C. Pollock, et al. 2017. Anatomical Taphonomy at the Source: Alterations to a Sample of 84 Teaching Skulls at a Medical School. *Journal of Forensic Identification* 67: 600–632.

Quigley, C. 2001. *Skulls and Skeletons: Human Bone Collections and Accumulations*. London: McFarland and Company.

Ramsey, G. 2012. Peruvian Mummy's Return Points to Artifact Trafficking in LatAm. *InSight Crime*. 8 November. https://www.insightcrime.org/news/analysis/peru-artifact-trafficking-mummy-latin-america/. Accessed 15 January 2018.

Remsen, A. 2016. A Lawyer Digs into Instagram's Terms of Use. *PetaPixel*. 7 December. https://petapixel.com/2016/12/07/lawyer-digs-instagrams-terms-use/. Accessed 15 January 2018.

Riben, M. 2015. Adoption Criminality and Corruption. *The Huffington Post*. 15 March. https://www.huffingtonpost.com/mirah-riben/adoption-crimes-and-corru_b_6467540.html. Accessed 10 October 2017.

Roque, R. 2010. *Headhunting and Colonialism: Anthropology and the Circulation of Human Skulls in the Portuguese Empire, 1870–1930*. Basingstoke: Palgrave Macmillan.

Roque, R. 2011. Stories, Skulls, and Colonial Collections. *Configurations* 19: 1–23.

Salazar, E. 1995. Between Crisis and Hope: Archaeology in Ecuador. *Society for American Archaeology Bulletin* 13: 34–37.

Schweig, S.V. 2015. *Baby Animals are Being Sold into Miserable Lives…Through Instagram*. https://www.thedodo.com/baby-animals-sold-instagram-1508628620.html. Accessed 10 January 2018.

Scott, D.A. 2013. Modern Antiquities: The Looted and the Faked. *International Journal of Cultural Property* 20: 49–75.

Seidemann, R.M. 2004. Bones of Contention: A Comparative Examination of Law Governing Human Remains from Archaeological Contexts in Formerly Colonial Countries. *Louisiana Law Review* 64: 545–588.

Seidemann, R.M. 2017. The Influence of the Law on the Postmortem Narratives of Unknown Human Remains. In *Studies in Forensic Biohistory: Anthropological Perspectives*, ed. C.M. Stojanowski and W.N. Duncan, 124–142. Cambridge: Cambridge University Press.

Seidemann, R.M., C.M. Stojanowski, and F.J. Rich. 2009. The Identification of a Human Skull Recovered from an eBay Sale. *Journal of Forensic Sciences* 54: 1247–1253.

Skinner, V. 2016. Vandals Dig Up Confederate Soldier's Grave, Steal Body from VA Cemetery. *The American Mirror*. 11 January. http://www.theamericanmirror.com/vandals-dig-up-confederate-soldiers-grave-steal-body-from-va-cemetery/. Accessed 10 January 2018.

Skull Store. 2018. *Shrunken Head, Child*. https://www.skullstore.ca/collections/humans/products/shrunken-head-child. Accessed 9 August 2018.

Sledzik, P., and S. Ousley. 1991. Analysis of Six Vietnamese Trophy Skulls. *Journal of Forensic Sciences* 36: 520–530.

Smith, IV J. 2014. Here's Every Statistic You Could Want on Instagram Drug Dealers. *Observer*. 5 August. http://observer.com/2014/05/heres-every-statistic-you-could-want-on-instagram-drug-dealers/. Accessed 31 May 2018.

Society for American Archaeology [SAA]. 1996. *Principles of Archaeological Ethics*. http://www.saa.org/AbouttheSociety/PrinciplesofArchaeologicalEthics/tabid/203/Default.aspx. Accessed 28 November 2017.

Stanish, C. 2009. Forging Ahead: Or, How I Learned to Stop Worrying and Love eBay. *Archaeology* 62: 23–28.

Stevenson, A. 2017. Why Archaeological Antiquities Should not be Sold on the Open Market, Full Stop. *The Conversation*. 13 July. http://theconversation.com/why-archaeological-antiquities-should-not-be-sold-on-the-open-market-full-stop-54928. Accessed 29 November 2017.

Tri-Council Policy Statement [TCPS2]. 2014. *Ethical Conduct of Research Involving Humans*. http://www.pre.ethics.gc.ca/pdf/eng/tcps2-2014/TCPS_2_FINAL_Web.pdf. Accessed 9 August 2018.

Tung, T.A. 2008. Dismembering Bodies for Display: A Bioarchaeological Study of Trophy Heads from the Wari Site of Conchopata, Peru. *American Journal of Physical Anthropology* 136: 294–308.

Turban, E., J. Outland, D. King, et al. (eds.). 2017. *Electronic Commerce 2018: A Managerial and Social Networks Perspective*, 9th ed. Cham: Springer.

Tynan, S. 2008. *Smuggling from the Catacombs*. http://tynan.com/smuggling. Accessed 16 January 2018.

UNESCO. 1970. *Convention on the Means of Prohibiting and Preventing the Illicit Import, Export and Transfer of Ownership of Cultural Property 1970*. http://portal.unesco.org/en/ev.php-URL_ID=13039&URL_DO=DO_TOPIC&URL_SECTION=201.html. Accessed 16 January 2018.

UNESCO. 2014. *Conventions—Ecuador*. https://en.unesco.org/countries/ecuador/conventions. Accessed 30 July 2018.

U.S. Immigration and Customs Enforcement [ICE]. 2011. *ICE Returns Tribal Artifacts to Indonesian Authorities*. https://www.ice.gov/news/releases/ice-returns-tribal-artifacts-indonesian-authorities. Accessed 20 September 2017.

Vallor, S. 2015. Social Networking and Ethics. In *Stanford Encyclopedia of Philosophy*. https://plato.stanford.edu/entries/ethics-social-networking/#SocNetSerCyb. Accessed 30 November 2017.

Verano, J.W. 2008. Trophy Head-Taking and Human Sacrifice in Andean South America. In *The Handbook of South American Archaeology*, ed. H. Silverman and W.H. Isbell, 1047–1060. New York: Springer.

Vergano, D. 2016. eBay Just Nixed Its Human Skull Market. *BuzzFeed News*. 12 July. https://www.buzzfeed.com/danvergano/skull-sales?utm_term=.qarND3vxQ#.wvxqo8DkP. Accessed 30 November 2017.

Weingartner, J.J. 1992. Trophies of War: U.S. Troops and the Mutilation of Japanese War Dead, 1941–1945. *Pacific Historical Review* 61: 53–67.

Wockner, C., and K. Erviani. 2016. Police in Bali Discover Human Skull En Route to Australia. *News.com.au*. 10 June. http://www.news.com.au/national/crime/police-in-bali-discover-human-skull-en-route-to-australia/news-story/a865399a6bb885475cfe76e8c579f9c4. Accessed 14 November 2017.

Wordsworth, R. 2015. A Shortage of Legitimate Donors is Fueling the Black Market Organ Trade. *Vice*. 27 November. https://motherboard.vice.com/en_us/article/8q8ajp/the-false-choice-of-the-black-market-organ-trade. Accessed 21 November 2017.

World Archaeological Congress [WAC]. 1989. *The Vermillion Accord, Archaeological Ethics and the Treatment of the Dead: A Statement of Principles Agreed by Archaeologists and Indigenous Peoples at the World Archaeological Congress, Vermillion, USA*. http://worldarch.org/code-of-ethics/. Accessed 16 January 2018.

WTAE-TV. 2013. *Nearly 200-Year-Old Grave Dug Up* [video]. https://www.youtube.com/watch?v=n2EXUo2A72w. Accessed 14 November 2017.

Xiao, B., and I. Benbasat. 2011. Product-Related Deception in E-commerce: A Theoretical Perspective. *MIS Quarterly* 35: 169–196.

Yates, D. 2016. The Global Traffic in Looted Cultural Objects. In *Oxford Research Encyclopedia: Criminology and Criminal Justice*, ed. H.N. Pontell. Oxford: Oxford University Press. https://doi.org/10.1093/acrefore/9780190264079.013.124.

Yee, G. 2017. 'Human Skull WANTED': Why a Charleston Resident Posted This Year's Spookiest Craigslist Ad. *The Post and Courier*. 30 October. http://www.postandcourier.com/news/human-skull-wanted-why-a-charleston-resident-posted-this-year/article_94586a38-bc11-11e7-895d-67974e10b47f.html. Accessed 21 November 2017.

Yucha, J.M., J.T. Pokines, and E.J. Bartelink. 2017. A Comparative Taphonomic Analysis of 24 Trophy Skulls from Modern Forensic Cases. *Journal of Forensic Sciences* 62: 1266–1278.

Part II
Ethical Dilemmas in Bioarchaeology and Forensic Anthropology

Chapter 7
Ethical and Practical Challenges of Working with Archaeological Human Remains, with a Focus on the UK

Charlotte A. Roberts

Abstract This chapter focuses on the ethical and practical considerations concerning archaeological human remains in the UK. It first contextualises the chapter by including a personal perspective of the author's experience as a bioarchaeologist over the last 35 years in the UK. It then reflects upon the development of bioarchaeology in the UK, and its value in informing us about our past, and its rise from a "cottage industry" to a thriving area of archaeology. It then considers the guidance available for excavation, analysis, curation, and display of archaeological human remains in the UK, and makes recommendations for the future. These include having more open dialogue amongst all stakeholders, treating human remains with dignity and respect and not objectifying them, educating the public and students alike, especially in the case of destructive analyses, and debating who has the right to decide the "fate" of human remains. It further highlights areas of concern and emphasises the responsibility of all stakeholders to ensure appropriate care for our ancestors' remains. Bioarchaeologists in particular have a duty to do their best for all human remains that have been, and will be, excavated and analysed in the future, and then curated, right across the world. We also have a duty to engage all stakeholders in debates, including the public and Indigenous people.

7.1 Introduction

It is almost 40 years ago since I entered the field of bioarchaeology. I recall that no discussions took place regarding the ethical considerations that might, or should be, addressed regarding the excavation and analysis of human remains from archaeological sites, or indeed their curation and display in museums, and their use in teaching in educational establishments. This was in stark contrast to my first profession, nursing. Perhaps that was/is because bioarchaeologists work with the remains of dead humans and, in a nursing context, patients are usually alive.

C. A. Roberts (✉)
Department of Archaeology, Durham University, South Road, Durham DH1 3LE, UK
e-mail: c.a.roberts@durham.ac.uk

K. Squires et al. (eds.), *Ethical Approaches to Human Remains*,
https://doi.org/10.1007/978-3-030-32926-6_7

I personally received no mentorship on this subject matter during my undergraduate and postgraduate degrees, and there were few "qualified and authoritative" bioarchaeologists at that time who could have provided that mentorship in the UK. Furthermore, there were no guidance documents for practitioners like myself, or for professionals in commercial archaeology units or museums. This was also a time prior to the North American Native American Graves Protection and Repatriation Act (NAGPRA 1990) and other "protective" legislation for Indigenous peoples around the world (also see Rose et al. 1996). I should say though that I was party to (and keen to see) the repatriation of two skulls to Australia and New Zealand from the University of Bradford's (UK) inherited Calvin Wells Collection. There was limited media coverage for these events and not the amount that would be expected today due to the rapid development in communication systems, such as social media.

The Institute of Field Archaeologists had been founded in 1982 (now the Chartered Institute for Archaeologists, or CIfA), but there was no dedicated support for bioarchaeologists and we were "classed" as environmental archaeologists for membership purposes. I joined, but quickly realised that my expensive membership fee did not bring me any value as a bioarchaeologist. The British Association of Biological Anthropology and Osteoarchaeology (BABAO) was not founded until 1998, but did start to provide an infrastructure for practitioners that continues today. Structured training for bioarchaeologists did not commence in earnest until 1990 in the UK. Indeed, when I entered bioarchaeology, most people working in this area had not had specific training, including myself. There were extremely few bioarchaeologists in the UK working in the museum, commercial archaeology, or academic spheres, and most people were medically trained, working both in medicine and, in their "spare time", in bioarchaeology. During the 1980s museums freely opened up their doors to enable me to analyse skeletons in their collections for a large project on leprosy and tuberculosis in British skeletal remains I was involved in, and on no occasion did I complete an official "access for analysis" form. This was also a time when the destructive analysis of skeletons was not very common (although a little histological analysis was done), and biomolecular analysis (stable isotope and DNA, in particular) was not really even a twinkle in a bioarchaeologist's eye. Facilities for such analyses in archaeology were also generally unavailable and funding for bioarchaeology overall was not abundant. When visiting said museums, I was given free access and there were no rules and regulations to follow, and certainly no advice on their dos and dont's related to working with human remains under their care.

Times have changed considerably since the 1980s, and bioarchaeologists today are much better placed in terms of infrastructure. Fortunately, we have moved on, not least due to the efforts of a number of key people and organisations, including: BABAO and the working group (Margaret Clegg, Myra Giesen, Louise Loe, Rebecca Redfern (chair), and Charlotte Roberts) who produced the BABAO Ethics and Practice guidance documents (BABAO 2010a, 2010b; 2019a, 2019b), Simon Mays of Historic England who has been instrumental in the production of many guidance documents, especially those coming from APABE and English Heritage (now Historic England), the Department for Culture, Media and Sport (guidance for museums), the working group headed up by Megan Brickley and Jacqueline

McKinley that produced the first edition of the recording standards for human remains (2005, and updated by Mitchell and Brickley 2017), the Church of England (English Heritage and the Church of England 2005), Historic Scotland (2006), the Museums Galleries Scotland (2011), and the Institute of Archaeology of Ireland (2006).

We now have:

- more inclusion of bioarchaeology in university undergraduate curricula (archaeology and anthropology);
- bioarchaeology training available in many institutions at masters level, which now includes teaching on ethics;
- many bioarchaeology graduates who (should) have an awareness of ethical considerations and archaeological human remains;
- dissertation proposals focusing on human remains that normally have to be approved (and should be) in departments in universities from an ethical point of view;
- a few museums where there are specialist bioarchaeology curators, and official access forms to complete for both non-destructive and destructive analyses;
- a national organisation representing archaeology, and particularly commercial archaeologists (CIfA);
- a national organisation representing bioarchaeologists (BABAO) that has produced ethics and practice guidance documents (BABAO 2010a, 2010b; 2019a, 2019b);
- better facilities for bioarchaeological research, particularly in universities, and related funding streams, and
- a plethora of guidance documents for practitioners (archaeologists, bioarchaeologists, and museum curators) to help them with "doing the right thing" for human remains, from excavation through to analysis, including destructive analyses, along with display in museums, and their curation for future work.

This is all very well, good, and progressive, but because of the success of bioarchaeology there has become one very large "elephant in the room", the elephant being the very important issue of the ethics related to human remains that come in all "shapes and sizes". I have become increasingly concerned over the last 15 years or so about the ethics of using archaeological human remains for whatever purpose, and the need to "do the right thing".

As living people we are all individuals and have varying opinions about how human remains should be treated in archaeological contexts. On the one hand there are bioarchaeologists who feel that excavated human remains should all be curated for future research using whatever methods are chosen. On the other hand, there are those who might feel that, once analysed, the remains should be reburied. In between these extremes, there are those who believe a balance has to be struck between paying due respect to those we study while giving these once living people a voice through our analyses, but also accepting that there are times and places when their remains should be reburied or restricted from destructive analyses—and, of course, there are many opinions in between those extremes.

This chapter focuses on ethical considerations in relation to bioarchaeology in the UK. It first describes how UK bioarchaeology has "risen from the ashes" over the last 40 years and its value to archaeology. It then proceeds to discuss the good, the bad, and the ugly of the treatment of archaeological human remains, including the guidance available in relation to dealing with human remains in an ethical manner, and some of the remaining challenges. It finally makes some recommendations for the future.

7.2 Bioarchaeology in the UK: A Phoenix that Has Risen from the Ashes of the Pre-1980s

7.2.1 The Value of Bioarchaeology to Archaeology and Anthropology

It is not hard to justify the study of archaeological human remains. They are the closest we can get to our ancestors, and understanding how they lived and died is essential to understanding our past and who we are today (Roberts 2016, 2018). Bioarchaeology gives a voice to the dead; it enables the dead to tell their stories. Globally, bioarchaeology is an immensely successful sub-discipline of archaeology and of physical/biological anthropology, particularly in the UK (Roberts 2012a). It has developed into one that incorporates multidisciplinary and multi-method led contextually driven approaches to answering questions about the past. However, it is only the last two to three decades that there has been increasing recognition of its value in archaeology in the UK, and there are now many more people working in this field. In the 1980s there were probably about a dozen people (at most) working in bioarchaeology; if BABAO membership today is anything to go by (currently around 500 members in total), where the majority of members work in bioarchaeology, the increase is staggering.

The analytical methods available to bioarchaeologists are broad and some have their origin in other disciplines, such as earth sciences and genetics. Working from a macroscopic to a biomolecular approach we have the tools to advance knowledge about our past through contextually driven approaches. However, no one method has or should take precedence over another. As highlighted by Killick (2015), we have never had as many methods at our disposal as we currently have, although these techniques are not necessarily accessible to all. Furthermore, the extent to which practitioners (and curators) really understand what these methods can and cannot do is variable. There are also questions regarding whether all laboratory practices are of the highest quality and, ultimately, how robust the resultant data and research publications are (and the latter obviously relies on the quality of the review process).

The mainstay of bioarchaeological information that is collected from human remains is achieved using a "macroscopic" approach. This means recording what is observed without using more sophisticated methods of analysis. Knowledge about the various facets of bioarchaeological study, a good pair of eyes, and a magnifying glass or binocular microscope, enable us to give our ancestors a voice to be heard. We can develop biographies that tell us about their sex (biological) and gender (social construct)—see Walker and Cook (1998), their age at death, whether the shape and dimensions of their bones and teeth "fit" with what would be expected for the geographic location of their burial, and their "state" of health and well-being. Macroscopic methods of recording are relatively cheap, requiring little more than what has been described above, but also an appropriate space to do this work, relevant equipment to take measurements, "materials" to age the skeleton, and perhaps access to radiographic facilities, where needed. Macroscopic analytical methods will remain the mainstay of bioarchaeology; they are very cheap when compared to biomolecular analyses, but more importantly they provide the underlying biographical data that are essential for interpreting information that emanates from destructive analyses such as those related to isotope and DNA analyses. Of course, and a "given", contextual data from the archaeological site is essential to understand and interpret the information gathered from the skeleton (see Roberts 2018).

Anybody working as an archaeologist, but particularly as a bioarchaeologist, or people in different disciplines where archaeological human remains 'are' their focus of research, understand the immense value of bioarchaeology. Human remains provide a window into what it was to be human in past eras, and how our ancestors lived and died. Linking what we can see in the human remains, and relating this to funerary context to understand how people managed their dead, and to archaeological data that might tell us something about how people were living (e.g. housing, their diet, and work practices) we can learn much about our ancestors' worlds. Furthermore, contemporary documentary and iconographic evidence (if available) may also provide additional information that adds to our interpretations (e.g. key causes of death and which diseases were more prevalent at specific times). For example: the impact of various risk factors on health (morbidity) and death (mortality), such as the fourteenth century Black Death (deWitte 2009), whether men or women were more likely to be subject to interpersonal violence (Smith 1996) or accidental injury (Grauer and Roberts 1996), if children who were stressed due to undernutrition or disease did not grow as well as those who were not (Roberts et al. 2016), whether people with leprosy were stigmatised or not (Lunt 2013), and if height or shape as reflected in skeletal measurements (Zakrzewski 2007; Ruff et al. 2012) or variation in parts of the skeleton, such as teeth (Irish and Konigsberg 2007), varied across time and space.

Using complementary perspectives and methods from history (e.g. Rawcliffe 2013), evolutionary medicine (Nesse and Williams 1994), medical anthropology (Manderson 2016), geography (Brown et al. 2010), and biomolecular and earth sciences (see Brown and Brown 2011), amongst other disciplines, can add to our understanding of the macroscopic data we record. Of course, there are now what many would call, "more advanced cutting-edge techniques" available to archaeologists and bioarchaeologists. These can make us think more deeply about the potential questions we could answer using such analytical methods, questions that perhaps cannot be answered any other way. For example, we can apply microscopic analysis to a sample of bone or tooth to achieve a more accurate age at death for adult skeletons (e.g. Thomas et al. 2000; Robbins Schug et al. 2012), and we can use DNA analysis of a bone or tooth sample to assess the sex of a non-adult or poorly preserved adult skeleton (Cunha et al. 2000; Tierney and Bird 2015). We can also use more sophisticated non-destructive imaging techniques, such as computed tomography (CT) scanning to explore shape variation in bones (Ruff 2008) and (destructive) stable isotope analysis to answer questions about diet (Alexander et al. 2015), and diet in relation to weaning (Tsutaya and Yoneda 2015) and stress (Beaumont et al. 2015), while DNA analysis (also destructive) enables us to detect diseases that do or do not affect the skeleton, or were not affecting the bones or teeth at the time of death. This work is beginning to give us detailed information about the origin, evolution, and history of infectious diseases, such as tuberculosis (Wilbur and Stone 2012; Bos et al. 2014; Müller et al. 2014). Indeed, the value of DNA analysis is quite rightly increasingly recognised by archaeologists, bioarchaeologists, and biomolecular scientists for its worth as a piece of the jigsaw puzzle that ultimately opens a window on our past (Fernández et al. 2014; Harkins and Stone 2015; Weyrich et al. 2015; Marciniak and Perry 2017).

7.2.2 *Bioarchaeology in the 1980s and 1990s*

Bioarchaeology in the early 1980s was heavily dominated by scholars from other disciplines, primarily anatomy, dentistry, and the medical profession. However, archaeology had yet to appreciate its contribution to reconstructing the lives of our ancestors. At that time, a masters course, run by the late Don Brothwell at the Institute of Archaeology, University College London, covered human remains every alternate year (Dobney 2012), and the University of Sheffield ran a course for a few years, which was managed by the retired surgeon, Judson Chesterman (Royal College of Surgeons 2015). In its wisdom, and driven and developed by Keith Manchester and Charlotte Roberts (Roberts 2012b), the University of Bradford co-ran an MSc in Osteology, Palaeopathology and Funerary Archaeology with the University of Sheffield from 1990 to 1999. This set the stage for the development of bioarchaeology, employment of more bioarchaeologists in UK higher education and commercial archaeology, and many more masters courses in similar and related subject areas. While welcome, it has to be said that there are too many bioarchaeologists in the "system" for the jobs available, although major building projects can temporarily employ these graduates, such as the recent High Speed 2 scheme (High Speed 2 Ltd. 2018) and the Crossrail development (Crossrail 2018).

Bioarchaeological research and commercial archaeology have also developed apace, alongside bioarchaeology as a general discipline. In commercial archaeology, of great relevance to bioarchaeology and its success, was the implementation of the Planning Policy Guidance 16 (PPG16) (1990). This was developed to advise local councils in England and Wales on the treatment of archaeology in the planning process (Roberts 2018). The availability of funding pre-1990 meant that the payment for completing skeletal reports was often poor. However, since 1990, funding has greatly improved and is usually available to conduct detailed skeletal reports. Data quality has also improved (trained people and standards for recording: Brickley and McKinley 2004; Mitchell and Brickley 2017) and the resulting data are proving more useful to other bioarchaeologists for research and other commercial work. While commercial archaeology data publication remains a challenge and much can remain in "grey literature", there are outlets where those data may be made available, such as the Archaeology Data Service (n.d.), Oasis (2016), Historic Environment Records (Heritage Gateway 2012), and relevant museums (usually the closest to the excavated site). In terms of bioarchaeological research, it has only been since the 1990s that major bioarchaeological research projects have been funded by the main UK funding bodies. These include the Arts and Humanities Research Council, the Natural Environmental Research Council, and the Wellcome and Leverhulme Trusts. This welcome development has probably partly occurred because of the increasing recognition of the discipline as worthy of funding. This has occurred alongside the numbers of people increasingly applying for that funding with ambitious projects (because of more bioarchaeologists in the UK). Those little steps over the last 30–40 years have led to bigger things!

7.2.3 Working with Human Remains from Archaeological Sites

As the key component of bioarchaeology, its practitioners variously and inherently excavate, analyse, curate, and actively work with human remains. Following excavation in the commercial archaeology arena and initial analysis by a commercial bioarchaeologist, human remains may be reburied (though this is relatively rare and applied to more recent remains). They are also used in teaching and learning situations by undergraduate and postgraduate students in universities where they may be handled in laboratory situations, and used for their dissertation research (Roberts 2013). Remains may further be used in a laboratory situation for open days and other public engagement events in universities (hopefully all contained within that university environment). They can also be utilised in museum environments for outreach events and displays (see Caffell and Jakob, this volume, for further discussion on this subject). It goes without saying that qualified practitioners use human remains for their personal research within a higher education, museum, or commercial context where the remains may be curated, and they include them in grant application proposals.

During the course of their work, bioarchaeologists in all three main fields (higher education, commercial archaeology, and museums) also take images of the remains they study in the form of photographs, X-ray produced images, or of histological structures, and they may engage in sampling human remains for destructive analysis. In addition, 3D imaging is increasingly becoming "popular" for educational uses and in research (Errickson and Thompson 2017). Television programmes are also portraying archaeological skeletons for the public consumer and have been for many decades (e.g. Meet the Ancestors, To the Ends of the Earth, Secrets of the Dead, Timewatch, and Time Team). Images, whether 2D or 3D, are being rapidly transported around the world in this digital age. I do feel that we must ask ourselves whether transmitting images of human remains across the internet superhighway and on social media is acceptable (including 3D images that can be printed out at the other side of the world). Indeed, who gives us permission to do that? Some might argue that as these people are dead, anything we choose to do with them is acceptable, but is it right that their images are shared (BABAO 2019c) (see below for further discussion)?

All these "uses" have ethical implications. While the author hugely advocates public engagement and practices it in her research, and we know that archaeological human remains are very popular with the public, as seen in museum exhibitions and public surveys (e.g. Mills and Tranter 2010: 864 adults aged 18+ years in England telephone surveyed over two days in June 2009), we must still be cautious about how we, as professionals, operate. While some public surveys can be self-selective (e.g. museum displays are visited by those who choose to do so and not by those who do not), we as bioarchaeologists do need to continue to provide a mechanism whereby the public are able to appreciate the value of bioarchaeology, while showing more consideration to the remains we "use". Bioarchaeologists should also discuss issues of "consent", our inability to obtain consent from the dead for their excavation, study, publication of their biographies, curation, and display, and how we can "resolve" this inability both morally and ethically.

"Consideration" also extends to other "stakeholders", or people outside of the world of bioarchaeology who work in other fields of study and interest. These may include different artists (writers, sculptors, photographers, playwrights, and film directors), the media, politicians, geneticists, museologists, museum professionals, anthropologists, native peoples, historians of specific periods and medical, social, and art historians, all of whom make decisions about whether and how they engage with actual human remains. 'Human remains' includes samples of them and remains that may be "contested" or have troubling histories; it also includes creating images and displays of the remains themselves. For example, whether and how any of us choose to image human remains, and then display those images, is an area that is increasingly but only recently receiving attention; this should be a key focus in terms of ethics in general for the future (see Harries et al. 2018 for an excellent thought provoking overview). Finally, while it is hoped that bioarchaeology practitioners, or indeed anybody else who engages with archaeological human remains would not misuse human remains to the extent of putting them up for sale, it is clear that there are offline and online outlets that are increasingly selling both ancient and modern human remains, within and outside of the UK, and enhanced by social media (Rossington 2015; The Bone Room 2016; Human Skulls 2018).

Taken together, there should be more opportunities created for dialogue about ethical issues and human remains in their broadest sense, and particularly to discuss the uses of human remains from archaeological sites by any interested "stakeholder" [for example a recent event at The University of Edinburgh (2018)]. If we work together on this, we will ultimately be better placed to care for the "archaeological" and more recent dead. The next section considers examples of these uses and how guidance documents have helped to mitigate inappropriate use of human remains. It also considers recent developments. Nevertheless, there remain concerns about the inappropriate use of human remains.

7.3 The Treatment of Archaeological Human Remains: The Good, the Bad, and the Ugly

7.3.1 Background, Competition for "Resources, the Law, and Some Guiding Principles

In the UK the practice of bioarchaeology is, on the whole, accessible to all who wish to be involved, whether that is at a higher education level or at public outreach events. Nevertheless, not all people want to, or have the resources, to study at university, and may not come across bioarchaeology at all in their life experiences. Personally speaking, I "came across" bioarchaeology only by chance as an undergraduate student, but was never taken to museums or archaeological sites as a child where I might have viewed human remains and, to be honest, had never heard of "archaeology" before I looked for university courses! Indeed, the public today confuse archaeology with palaeontology and with anthropology, and may call bioarchaeologists forensic scientists! Providing public engagement opportunities is thus essential so that what bioarchaeologists "do" can be accurately reflected.

In other regions of the world, where excavation of human remains and the availability of necessary training to do those excavations, and then analyse the resulting human remains, may not be as readily available as in the UK, and access to education may be even less possible for a majority of people (see, for example Márquez-Grant and Fibiger 2011; Buikstra and Roberts 2012), and public engagement may be negligible. Furthermore, access to skeletal remains in those regions may not be easy, for whatever reason (e.g. poor infrastructure, and also "ownership" disputes). However, in recent years, competition for "resources" has increased between professional bioarchaeologists and their students in universities, in particular. This has been due to pressure on staff (and their students) to do high profile research with cutting edge techniques, acquire large grants from various research councils to do so, publish in "reputable" journals with high profiles, such as *Nature* and *Science*, and attract the media to their research. This has inevitably been driven by, amongst other factors, national and international league tables, for example The Complete University Guide (2018) in the UK and the Research

Excellence Framework (2017). Even within university departments, competition between staff is "fierce", as they must acquire "appropriate" resources and funding for their research. Notwithstanding this development, we should re-acquaint ourselves with laws pertaining to archaeological human remains in the UK, bearing in mind that one of the first documents produced on the law and burial archaeology for England, Wales, and Scotland was by Garrett-Frost in 1992 for the Institute of Field Archaeologists. More recently, James Logie has described the laws for Scotland in more detail (Historic Scotland 2006, Annexe A), as have Museums Galleries Scotland (2011).

In England and Wales, Scotland, and Northern Ireland, laws relating to the excavation of human remains can differ (Roberts 2018, Chap. 2). Relevant guidance documents available concern:

- human remains buried in Christian burial grounds in England since AD 597 (APABE 2017);
- human remains curated in museums and other institutions in England and Wales (DCMS 2005);
- human remains buried in Scotland (Historic Scotland 2006); and
- human remains buried in Northern Ireland (Buckley et al. 2004; Institute of Archaeologists of Ireland 2006).

Also relevant are the Human Rights Act (1988), the Human Tissue Act (2004) that covers England, Wales and Northern Ireland, the Human Tissue (Scotland) Act (2006), and the Human Tissue Authority (n.d.), which was a development out of the 2004 Act. The latter regulates human tissues and organs, and the former regulates activities related to the removal, storage, use, and disposal of human bodies, organs, and tissues from the living and deceased less than 100 years old in museums and other institutions. This all emanates from the Alder Hey Children's Hospital organs scandal (1988–1995) that involved the illegal removal, retention, and disposal of human tissues. Human rights abuse today is usually applied to the living, but archaeological human remains could be covered by Common Law regarding respectful treatment of the dead.

It is important to remember that nobody can legally own a dead body in England, Wales, and Scotland and that there is no property in a corpse. This begs the question when "stakeholders" wish to analyse skeletal remains in curated, or even "personal", collections, and/or request skeletal samples for destructive analyses: who owns the past, who decides what is appropriate, and are they in a position to decide the "fate" of any human remains? APABE (2013, 2017, 1) usefully outlines some principles that are recommended: "Human remains should always be treated with dignity and respect; burials should not be disturbed without good reason (but the demands of the modern world are such that it may be necessary to disturb burials in advance of development); human remains, and the archaeological evidence for the rites, which accompanied and commemorate their burial, are important sources of scientific information; there is a need to give particular weight to the feelings and views of living family members when known;

and there is a need for decisions to be made in the public interest, and in an accountable way". Respect for the dead is a theme that runs through other disciplines beyond bioarchaeology. For example, De Baets (2004) argues that historians should respect the dignity of the living and the dead in their studies.

While principles are recommended in this APABE (2013, 2017) guidance (note *guidance*), and there are clear legal implications relating to human remains in the UK, there are also "practice" guidance documents. These documents began to appear in the early 1990s, and are divided into excavation, analysis, curation, and display sections.

7.3.2 Guidance on Excavation

In considering that human remains have been excavated for centuries and remain a common finding in the UK, it is surprising that so very little is written about the excavation of human remains from archaeological funerary contexts, both in archaeological texts and now in online resources; at times the guidance is also quite short (e.g. Skills Passport 2018). While not being exhaustive, a scan of some of the available published literature includes Greene and Moore (2010), Mays (2010), Martin et al. (2013), and Roberts (2018). One could argue that while the basic principles of excavation apply in all archaeological contexts, dealing with human remains needs specific knowledge and skills that would not necessarily apply to archaeological finds such as pottery or plant remains. It is not even a routine inclusion in undergraduate or even specialist masters course curricula. However, the value of excavated human remains very much relies on how they are excavated and "processed" before analysis. Perhaps a landmark publication, although in desperate need of updating was that of McKinley and Roberts (1993), alongside Anderson (1993), and sections of Buckley et al. (2004; see also Institute of Archaeologists of Ireland 2006). More extensive writings have become available in the last 10 or so years (e.g. BABAO 2010b; OSSAFreelance 2005, 2012), and specific documents have appeared related to sampling: sampling strategies for large burial grounds (APABE 2015), and sampling specific skeletons for destructive analyses (APABE 2013—also see the next section of this chapter). The appearance of many of these documents is in no large part due to APABE and BABAO's efforts, and they have often reflected urgent needs for guidance as bioarchaeology as a discipline and commercial archaeology as a very viable industry have developed.

7.3.3 Guidance on Post-excavation Treatment and Analysis

Analysis of human remains has generally been driven by information in published texts (e.g. Brothwell 1981; Ubelaker 1989; Scheuer and Black 2000; Bass 2005;

White and Folkens 2005; Lewis 2007; Mays 2010; Roberts 2018) and a plethora of published journal papers in both the bioarchaeological and forensic anthropological literature. Again, while there are many avenues for securing guidance on analysing human remains, not all scholars will follow that guidance and will make decisions on how and what is recorded. The choices they make will also be dependent on the training they have or have not received.

Following NAGPRA (1990), and then the publication of Buikstra and Ubelaker (1994) and Roberts and Cox (2003), some of us in the UK were reminded that, firstly, we could not always rely on human remains being available for study, and secondly, and very importantly in relation to analysis, not all data that had been published on human remains was of good quality. This meant that our data were not necessarily comparable between sites and authors, and we needed some sort of guidance on standards for recording. Thus, in the early 2000s, a working party was set up by BABAO, and work started to create a guidance document for BABAO members. This was published in 2004 (Brickley and McKinley 2004) and updated in 2017 (Mitchell and Brickley 2017). However, it remains challenging to encourage everybody to use the same recording standards but it really is essential if we are to be able to reliably compare our data (as addressed by the Global History of Health Project (2018; Steckel et al. 2019).

When considering analysis beyond the macroscopic, and the increasing emphasis placed on destructive analyses in bioarchaeological research using biomolecular (stable isotope and DNA analysis) and histological methods, the UK has also seen some guidance emerge, particularly from APABE (2013). Various other documents and publications also consider destructive analysis, recognising the need to provide guidelines (e.g. Richards 2004, 2017; DCMS 2005; Odegaard and Cassman 2006; BABAO 2010b, 2019a, 2019b; APABE 2017). Indeed, very specific guidance is clearly provided: "All holding institutions should ensure that the scientific justification for the removal of samples from human remains are made in advance and placed on file [and there should also be]… reasons for approval given" (DCMS 2005, 21). The DCMS also addresses the need to justify where and how much of the sample is taken, and that everything related to the process should be documented, with bones and teeth being recorded fully before sampling, casts being made, and remnant samples being returned to the holding institution. Too many times people forget that the samples they analyse come from once living and breathing people like us, and this should be respected as such—the samples end up in freezers, detached from their owners, and they may or may not be analysed. If they are, the remnant samples often stay in that freezer waiting for more analysis when the scientists decide, perhaps when they receive a grant—they may also get passed onto other laboratories (with no permission from the original curating institution), and remaining samples may not get returned. There are clearly ethical implications for destructive analysis for all three key bioarchaeology sectors (commercial archaeology, museums, and universities), and the maintenance of the integrity of the skeletal collections they curate. This is especially relevant for future work of a non-destructive nature (bioarchaeologists need "intact" skeletons), and scientists will need skeletons to sample as destructive methods develop and sample sizes required will decrease again. Back to first principles, if this type of work is carried out, the human remains subject to sampling need to have their rights protected, assuming we can agree they have rights; I think they do and we have a duty of care towards them. We must also remember the guidance document (APABE 2013, and others), follow it, and spread its word beyond the UK to all sectors involved with receiving applications for analyses, and laboratories carrying out the analyses (further discussion regarding the ethics of destructive analyses can be found in Squires, Booth and Roberts, this volume).

These guidance documents on post-excavation treatment and analysis are, again, not necessarily heeded, and those leading the research may not be bioarchaeologists but rather biomolecular scientists; the research team may not even include a bioarchaeologist (see recent example: Killgrove 2018). Ethical and practical guidance may thus "fall on stony ground". However, there is increasing excellent practice in biomolecular analysis where scholars are following guidelines and thinking about ethics. Thankfully, in the last few years, there is also evidence of increasing dialogue about ethical concerns and destructive analyses from a variety of "stakeholders", and attempts to encourage scholars to attend to the very real issues related to such destructive analyses (Makarewicz et al. 2017; Morris 2017). These include competition between laboratories, the tendency for geneticists being indifferent to (macroscopic) bioarchaeological research, and the incomparable nature of data from different laboratories (Morris 2017). It is clear that this kind of research has become much more common, partly because it is potentially "more fundable" than more routine bioarchaeological research using macroscopic methods. These issues are also leading to similar behaviors in the younger generation developing their careers in biomolecular science.

Of relevance for DNA analysis is knowing whether and where DNA will survive for analysis in the body/skeleton. It is highly likely that in the early days of aDNA analysis many samples taken from human remains did not preserve DNA because nobody really knew which parts of the skeleton or parts of bones preserved DNA best –see Mundorff and Davoren (2014) on the survival of DNA in different bones, and also Hansen et al. (2017) and Sirak et al. (2017) on opposing views on the survival of DNA in the petrous portion of the temporal bone. There was also no knowledge about the possibility that X-rays might damage DNA (Frank et al. 2015; Immel et al. 2016). Furthermore, we will never know how much destructive sampling and analysis has been conducted with no resulting data because negative results have not been, and are not usually, published. Perhaps editors of journals need to take heed of this and publish those negative results so that remains are not re-sampled if they have not shown preserved DNA. Reviewers of grant applications and editors could also do better in ensuring that ethical considerations in such work are accounted for in all grant applications, and in publications; see for example the application process for BABAO grant applications where considerations of ethical issues are a mandatory part of the process (BABAO 2018). After all, the data that are produced from such DNA research becomes open access and there are serious ethical issues related to these genetic data for living people, but also for our ancestors and their deceased descendants. How this can be ethically managed is a challenge in itself (Redfern and Clegg 2017).

Related to this are the very large well-funded projects that can involve, essentially, extensive global collecting expeditions to amass large numbers (thousands) of samples from human remains into freezers across the world “in the name of science”, just like our colonial ancestors. Most samples come from human remains in museums whose curators may not have the knowledge to assess the scientific worth (or not) of such projects, or have the resources and infrastructure to assess and implement applications for access, but with promises of co-authorship in prestigious outlets and media attention, they are likely to be persuaded to part with samples. Can we say that what is happening now is any different to the nineteenth and twentieth centuries (see Gazi 2014 on museum ethics)?

7.3.4 Guidance on Curation

“If human remains are removed from curation and passed for repatriation and/or reburial then new and informative data about the past would not be possible using these new techniques. If, as we believe, the world’s population has a strong interest in its heritage, then this alone is a justification for the retention and study of human remains” (Roberts 2018, 22). I should add, however, that I do not believe that all excavated human remains should be retained for curation forever, and there can be a time and a place for reburial and repatriation. Nevertheless, if remains are curated, it has been shown that they can continue to produce new answers to questions about the past using new methods (Buikstra and Gordon 1981). Accepting that most human remains excavated in the UK are curated in museums, in commercial archaeology units, and in universities, rather than being reburied, the conditions of their curation have received much attention in recent years, and guidance has inevitably emerged. However, this was slow in coming, and started mainly in the 2000s in the UK.

A landmark finding was Caffell et al. (2001) who highlighted the damage that could be done to human remains during curation and subsequent use in a teaching situation. Considering increasing student numbers on bioarchaeology courses, it may be viewed as an inevitable effect of success, unless practices are not put in place to prevent such damage. Granted, the use of human remains in a university situation for intensive teaching is a little different to the use of human remains in a museum environment. However, it did highlight a potential problem for the UK, where the increasing undergraduate and postgraduate courses (and students) during the 2000s that focused (and focus) on bioarchaeology could compromise the integrity of skeletal collections in a university’s care.

It is not possible to see whether this research (a masters dissertation published in a conference proceedings) had a specific impact on the development of curation guidance, but some publications have further considered standards for best practice for teaching environments (Roberts 2013). Work has further shown that bioarchaeologists have tended to focus on small numbers of skeletal collections in certain regions of the UK, thus potentially damaging these collections through overuse, creating datasets that tell us much about specific populations but nothing about others that are not studied, and ignoring collections that are not known about because information is unavailable (Roberts and Mays 2011). This is in no small part due to the lack of information on most museum and university websites about what skeletal collections they curate, something the DCMS (2005) recommended should occur.

In their publication, English Heritage and the Church of England (2005, Annexe S7) considered archiving, longer-term access, and storage of human remains. This is now superseded by APABE (2017, Annexes S6 and 7). In 2005, the DCMS also published their guidance for museums, including legal requirements and curatorial practices, including the care of human remains and management of their use, as did Museums Galleries Scotland in 2011 (see also Buckley et al. 2004, 14–16 for Ireland). It has, however, been shown through subsequent research that there has been an inability and/or will to implement this guidance in most museums due to the lack of staff and resources (White 2013), and this has not been helped by the recession in the UK starting in 2008 and cuts to museum funding.

Other publications consider the experiences of caring for human remains in specific museums (Fletcher et al. 2014: British Museum; Redfern and Bekvalac 2017: Museum of London), and provide guidance on accessioning human remains, curation and managing research on them (e.g. Cassman and Odegaard 2006; Cassman et al. 2006; BABAO 2010b, 2019a, 2019b; Roberts 2018). Related to this and just as important, are the challenges of storage space for human remains in the UK (McKinley 2013) and some of the solutions (Mays 2013). Thus, there is much curation guidance available for universities, museums, and commercial archaeology units, but the wherewithal (staff and resources) to follow this guidance can be very limited, especially in provincial museums, thus compromising paying due respect to and caring for human remains they curate. It can however be argued that human remains are the most important part of any curated collections, but in the author's experience they can be the most poorly cared for.

7.3.5 *Guidance on Display*

Alongside guidance on excavation, curation, and analysis of archaeological human remains have also come recommendations on how human remains should be displayed in museums and other venues. Opinions about whether human remains should be on display, and if so how they should be displayed, vary, but surveys (again, many self-selected) indicate that the public do want to view human remains in museums (e.g. Mills and Tranter 2010). In recent feedback on a travelling exhibition co-produced by the author and a Durham University Museum colleague, "Skeleton Science" (Skeleton Science n.d.), it is also clear that visitors wish to see real skeletons rather than 3D printed ones. Indeed, one visitor stated that "we feel cheated if it is not a real skeleton".

This work has implications for museum exhibitions and "doing the right thing", but if human remains are to be used for exhibitions then they should be clearly contributing to the education of visitors, and not placed on display purely for voyeuristic purposes. Accompanying text panels that contextualise the skeleton are essential, and clear signposting to give the opportunity for visitors not to view the skeleton/skeletons/preserved body such as an Egyptian mummy. The display of human remains may provide both information about their value, but it is also important to show how they give a voice to the past and contribute to our understanding of local, national, and international histories. Some of the first such guidance on display was published by the DCMS (2005) but there are also more recent statements on how to display human remains in museums (e.g. Brooks and Rumsey 2006; Museums Galleries Scotland 2011; Antoine 2014; APABE 2017).

Clearly, the majority of exhibitions using real human remains for display in the UK do so to educate the interested public, but we should be mindful that display is not purely to generate money and visitor figures. There must be a real purpose, going forward, and guidance should be heeded and considered.

7.4 The Future of Bioarchaeology in Relation to Practice

This chapter has discussed the author's personal experience of ethics in relation to bioarchaeology, the development of bioarchaeology in the UK, and its value for understanding the past, and explored guidance on excavation, analysis, curation, and display in the UK. We now come to bioarchaeology's future.

Suffice it to say, it has a future, and a strong and bright one! We can as bioarchaeologists give voices back to our ancestors' remains, and provide stories about their past, but sometimes those voices may tell us stories that we do not necessarily want to hear. Many bioarchaeologists have strongly promoted the need to have human remains retained and curated for further research in the UK, and ethical treatment of such remains has been addressed in guidance documents in more recent times. In going forward, the following recommendations are highlighted for bioarchaeology:

- Ensure that ethical considerations are uppermost in the minds of everybody who comes into contact with human remains, from excavators to curators and all "stakeholders" in between;
- Promote much more open dialogue about human remains of whatever period of time in any part of our world to give us a chance to discuss and debate, confront where necessary, appraise, and mediate any tensions;
- Reflect more on collections of human remains that are often invisible to the public when curated, including those inappropriately collected by our ancestors often of Indigenous peoples in other parts of the world, why they exist, and on the "power" that institutions that curate human remains can be seen to have;
- Be mindful that because we cannot gain permission from the dead to excavate, analyse, curate, and display them, we must treat them with all the dignity and

respect we can apply, and train our students (and engage the public) to do the same, and think seriously about whether referring to the remains of once living humans as "samples", "materials", "specimens", and "cases" is appropriate, which can objectify the dead and is a common occurrence. Is that acceptable and would we welcome being named as such when we are dead?;
- Consider who has the right to decide the fate of any human remains—whether they are excavated, analysed, reburied, or retained for future research, or displayed, and if collections of human remains are made accessible for study, and by whom? What is proper and right?

As 40 years in bioarchaeology approaches me, I raise these questions for the younger generations coming through who are working, and will work, with archaeological human remains. Please debate these issues more. I do think that the dead have rights and should be treated differently to other archaeological finds, but even today they may be considered just as any other archaeological find, like pottery or animal bones—yes, this might seem strange, but thankfully times and opinions have and are changing, albeit slowly.

Clearly, as bioarchaeologists we all have a duty to do our best for all human remains that have been, and will be, excavated and analysed in the future, and then curated, right across the world. We also have a duty to engage all stakeholders in debates, including the public and Indigenous people.

References

Advisory Panel on the Archaeology of Burials in England [APABE]. 2013. *Science and the Dead: A Guideline for the Destructive Sampling of Archaeological Human Remains for Scientific Analysis*. Swindon: English Heritage and The Advisory Panel on Archaeology of Burials in England.

Advisory Panel on the Archaeology of Burials in England [APABE]. 2015. *Large Burial Grounds. Guidance on Sampling in Archaeological Fieldwork Projects*. Swindon: English Heritage and The Advisory Panel on Archaeology of Burials in England.

Advisory Panel on the Archaeology of Burials in England [APABE]. 2017. *Guidance for Best Practice for Treatment of Human Remains Excavated from Christian Burial Grounds in England*, 2nd ed. Swindon: English Heritage and The Advisory Panel on Archaeology of Burials in England.

Alexander, M.M., C.M. Gerrard, A. Gutiérrez, et al. 2015. Diet, Society, and Economy in Late Medieval Spain: Stable Isotope Evidence from Muslims and Christians from Gandia, Spain. *American Journal of Physical Anthropology* 156: 263–273.

Anderson. S. 1993. *Digging Up People—Guidelines for Excavation and Processing of Human Skeletal Remains*. http://www.spoilheap.co.uk/pdfs/digbone.pdf. Accessed 21 July 2018.

Antoine, D. 2014. Curating Human Remains in Museum Collections: Broader Considerations and a British Museum Perspective. In *Regarding the Dead: Human Remains in the British Museum*, ed. A. Fletcher, D. Antoine, and J.D. Hill, 3–9. London: British Museum Press.

Archaeology Data Service. n.d. http://archaeologydataservice.ac.uk/. Accessed 21 July 2018.

Bass, W.M. 2005. *Human Osteology. A Field Guide and Manual*. Columbia: Missouri Archaeological Society.

Beaumont, J., J. Montgomery, J. Buckberry, et al. 2015. Infant Mortality and Isotopic Complexity: New Approaches to Stress, Maternal Health, and Weaning. *American Journal of Physical Anthropology* 157: 441–457.

Bos, K.I., K.M. Harkins, J. Krause, et al. 2014. Pre-Columbian Mycobacterial Genomes Reveal Seals as a Source of New World Human Tuberculosis. *Nature* 514: 494–497.

Brickley, M. and J.I. McKinley (eds.). 2004. *Guidelines to the Standards for Recording Human Remains*. Southampton and Reading: IFA Paper No. 7. BABAO and IFA. https://www.babao.org.uk/assets/Uploads-to-Web/HumanremainsFINAL3.pdf.

British Association for Biological Anthropology and Osteoarchaeology [BABAO]. 2010a. *Code of Ethics*. http://www.babao.org.uk/assets/Uploads/code-of-ethics.pdf. Accessed 21 July 2018.

British Association for Biological Anthropology and Osteoarchaeology [BABAO]. 2010b. *Code of Practice*. http://www.babao.org.uk/assets/Uploads/code-of-practice.pdf. Accessed 21 July 2018.

British Association for Biological Anthropology and Osteoarchaeology [BABAO]. 2018. *Research Grants*. http://www.babao.org.uk/grants-and-prizes/research-grants/. Accessed 31 July 2018.

British Association for Biological Anthropology and Osteoarchaeology [BABAO]. 2019a. *Code of Ethics*. https://www.babao.org.uk/assets/Uploads/BABAO-Code-of-Ethics-2019.pdf. Accessed 10 November 2019.

British Association for Biological Anthropology and Osteoarchaeology [BABAO]. 2019b. *Code of Practice*. https://www.babao.org.uk/assets/Uploads/BABAO-Code-of-Practice-2019.pdf. Accessed 10 November 2019.

British Association for Biological Anthropology and Osteoarchaeology. 2019c. *BABAO Recommendations on the Ethical Issues Surrounding 2D and 3D Digital Imaging of Human Remains*. https://www.babao.org.uk/assets/Uploads/BABAO-Digital-imaging-code-2019.pdf. Accessed 10 November 2019.

Brooks, M.M., and C. Rumsey. 2006. The Body in the Museum. In *Human Remains: Guide for Museums and Academic Institutions*, ed. V. Cassman, N. Odegaard, and J. Powell, 261–289. Lanham: Altamira.

Brothwell, D. 1981. *Digging Up Bones*. London: British Museum Press.

Brown, T., and K. Brown. 2011. *Biomolecular Archaeology. An Introduction*. Chichester: Wiley-Blackwell.

Brown, T., S. McLafferty, and G. Moon (eds.). 2010. *A Companion to Health and Medical Geography*. Chichester: Wiley-Blackwell.

Buckley, L., E. Murphy, and B. Ó Donnabháin. 2004. *The Treatment of Human Remains: Technical Paper for Archaeologists*, 2nd ed. Dublin: Institute of Archaeologists of Ireland.

Buikstra, J.E., and C.C. Gordon. 1981. The Study and Restudy of Human Skeletal Series: The Importance of Long-Term Curation. *Annals of the New York Academy of Sciences* 376: 449–465.

Buikstra, J.E., and C.A. Roberts (eds.). 2012. *A Global History of Paleopathology: Pioneers and Prospects*. New York: Oxford University Press.

Buikstra, J., and D. Ubelaker (eds.). 1994. *Standards for Data Collection from Human Skeletal Remains*. Fayetteville: Arkansas Archaeological Survey.

Caffell, A., C. Roberts, and R. Janaway, et al. 2001. Pressures on Osteological Collections—The Importance of Damage Limitation. In *Human Remains: Conservation, Retrieval and Anaysis. Proceedings of a Conference Held in Williamsburg, VA, Nov 7–11th 1999*, ed. E. Williams, 187–198.. Oxford: Archaeopress.

Cassman, V., and N. Odegaard. 2006. Examination and Analysis. In *Human Remains: Guide for Museums and Academic Institutions*, ed. V. Cassman, N. Odegaard, and J. Powell, 49–75. Lanham: Altamira.

Cassman, V., N. Odegaard, and J. Powell (eds.). 2006. *Human Remains: Guide for Museums and Academic Institutions*. Lanham: Altamira Press.

Crossrail. 2018. *Uncovering a Layer Cake of London's History*. http://www.crossrail.co.uk/sustainability/archaeology/. Accessed 21 July 2018.

Cunha, E., M.-L. Fily, I. Clisson, et al. 2000. Children at the Convent: Comparing Historical Data, Morphology and DNA Extracted from Ancient Tissues for Sex Diagnosis at Santa Clara-a-Velha (Coimbra, Portugal). *Journal of Archaeological Science* 27: 949–952.

De Baets, A. 2004. A Declaration of the Responsibilities of Present Generations Toward Past Generations. *History and Theory* 43: 130–164.

Department for Culture, Media and Sport [DCMS]. 2005. *Guidance for the Care of Human Remains in Museums*. London: Department for Culture, Media and Sport.

deWitte, S. 2009. The Effect of Sex on Risk of Mortality During the Black Death in London, AD 1339–1350. *American Journal of Physical Anthropology* 139: 222–234.

Dobney, K. 2012. Don Brothwell (1933-). In *A Global History of Paleopathology: Pioneers and Prospects*, ed. J.E. Buikstra and C.A. Roberts, 22–31. New York: Oxford University Press.

English Heritage and the Church of England. 2005. *Guidance for Best Practice for the Treatment of Human Remains Excavated from Christian Burial Grounds in England*. Swindon: English Heritage and Church of England.

Errickson, D., and T.J.U. Thompson (eds.). 2017. *Human Remains: Another Dimension. The Application of Imaging to the Study of Human Remains*. London: Academic Press.

Fernández, E., A. Pérez-Pérez, and C. Gamba, et al. 2014. Ancient DNA Analysis of 8000 BC Near Eastern Farmers Supports an Early Neolithic Pioneer Maritime Colonization of Mainland Europe Through Cyprus and the Aegean Islands. *PLoS Genetics* 10 (6): e1004401. https://doi.org/10.1371/journal.pgen.1004401.

Fletcher, A., D. Antoine, and J.D. Hill (eds.). 2014. *Regarding the Dead: Human Remains in the British Museum*. London: British Museum Press.

Frank, E.M., A.Z. Mundorff, and J.M. Daveren. 2015. The Effect of Common Imaging and Hot Water Maceration on DNA Recovery from Skeletal Remains. *Forensic Science International* 257: 189–195.

Garratt-Frost, S. 1992. *The Law and Burial Archaeology*. Institute of Field Archaeologists Technical Paper 11. Birmingham: Institute of Field Archaeologists.

Gazi, A. 2014. Exhibition Ethics—An Overview of Major Issues. *Journal of Conservation and Museum Studies* 12 (1): 1–10.

Grauer, A., and C.A. Roberts. 1996. Palaeoepidemiology, Healing and Possible Treatment of Trauma in the Medieval Cemetery Population of St Helen-on-the-Walls, York, England. *American Journal of Physical Anthropology* 100 (4): 531–544.

Greene, A., and T. Moore. 2010. *Archaeology. An Introduction*. London: Routledge.

Hansen, H.B., P.B. Damgaard, A. Matgaryan, et al. 2017. Comparing Ancient DNA Preservation in Petrous Bone and Tooth Cementum. *PLoS ONE* 12: e0170940. https://doi.org/10.1371/journal.pone.0170940.

Harkins, K.M., and A.C. Stone. 2015. Ancient Pathogen Genomics: Insights into Timing and Adaptation. *Journal of Human Evolution* 79: 137–149.

Harries, J., L. Fibiger, J. Smith, et al. 2018. Exposure: The Ethics of Making, Sharing and Displaying Photographs of Human Remains. *Human Remains and Violence* 4: 3–24.

Heritage Gateway. 2012. *Historic Environments Records*. https://www.heritagegateway.org.uk/Gateway/CHR/. Accessed 21 July 2018.

High Speed 2 Ltd. 2018. *HS2*. https://www.hs2.org.uk/. Accessed 21 July 2018.

Historic Scotland. 2006. *The Treatment of Human Remains in Archaeology. Historic Scotland Operational Policy Paper 5*. Edinburgh: Historic Scotland.

Human Rights Act. 1988. The Stationery Office, London.

Human Skulls. 2018. *Human Skulls: Authentic Human Skulls for Sale*. http://www.human-skulls.com/. Accessed 21 July 2018.

Human Tissue Act. 2004. The Stationery Office, London.

Human Tissue (Scotland) Act. 2006. The Scottish Parliament, Edinburgh.

Human Tissue Authority. n.d. *Human Tissue Authority: The Regulator for Human Tissue and Organs*. http://www.hta.gov.uk. Accessed 22 July 2018.

Immel, A., A. Le Cabe, M. Bonazzi, et al. 2016. Effect of X-ray Irradiation on Ancient DNA in Sub-Fossil Bones—Guidelines for Safe X-ray Imaging. *Nature Scientific Reports* 6: 32969. https://doi.org/10.1038/srep32969.

Institute of Archaeologists of Ireland. 2006. *Code of Conduct for the Treatment of Human Remains in the Context of an Archaeological Excavation*. Dublin: Institute of Archaeologists of Ireland.

Irish, J.D., and L. Konigsberg. 2007. The Ancient Inhabitants of Jebel Moya Redux: Measures of Population Affinity Based on Dental Morphology. *International Journal of Osteoarchaeology* 17: 138–156.

Killgrove, K. 2018. International Experts Refute 'Alien' Mummy Analysis, Question Ethics and Legality. *Forbes*. 18 July. https://www.forbes.com/sites/kristinakillgrove/2018/07/18/international-experts-refute-alien-mummy-analysis-question-ethics-and-legality/#309a97003722. Accessed 31 July 2018.

Killick, D. 2015. The Awkward Adolescence of Archaeological Science. *Journal of Archaeological Science* 56: 242–247.

Lewis, M.E. 2007. *The Bioarchaeology of Children. Perspectives from Biological and Forensic Anthropology*. Cambridge: Cambridge University Press.

Lunt, D.A. 2013. The First Evidence for Leprosy in Early Mediaeval Scotland. Two Individuals from Cemeteries in St Andrews, Fife, Scotland, with Evidence for Normal Burial Treatment. *International Journal of Osteoarchaeology* 23: 310–318.

Makarewicz, C., N. Marom, and G. Bar-Oz. 2017. Ensure Equal Access to Ancient DNA. *Nature* 548: 158.

Manderson, L. (ed.). 2016. *The Routledge Handbook of Medical Anthropology*. New York: Routledge.

Marciniak, S., and G.H. Perry. 2017. Harnessing Ancient Genomes to Study the History of Adaptation. *Nature Reviews Genetics* 18 (11): 659–674.

Márquez-Grant, N., and L. Fibiger (eds.). 2011. *The Routledge Handbook of Archaeological Human Remains and Legislation*. London: Routledge.

Martin, D.L., R.P. Harrod, and V.R. Pérez. 2013. *Bioarchaeology: An Integrated Approach to Working with Human Remains*. New York: Springer.

Mays, S. 2010. *The Archaeology of Human Bones*, 2nd ed. London: Routledge.

Mays, S. 2013. Curation of Human Remains at St Peter's Church, Barton-on-Humber, England. In *Curating Human Remains: Caring for the Dead in the United Kingdom*, ed. M. Giesen, 109–121. Woodbridge: The Boydell Press.

McKinley, J.I., and C.A. Roberts. 1993. *Excavation and Post-excavation Treatment of Cremated and Inhumed Remains*. Technical Paper Number 13. Birmingham: Institute of Field Archaeologists.

McKinley, J.I. 2013. 'No Room at the Inn'...Contract Archaeology and the Storage of Human Remains. In *Curating Human Remains: Caring for the Dead in the United Kingdom*, ed. M. Giesen, 135–145. Woodbridge: The Boydell Press.

Mills, S., and V. Tranter. 2010. *Research into Issues Surrounding Human Bones in Museums*. London: Business Development Research Consultants.

Mitchell, P.D., and M. Brickley. (eds.). 2017. *Updated Guidelines to the Standards for Recording Human Remains*. Reading: Chartered Institute for Archaeologists.

Morris, A.G. 2017. Ancient DNA Comes of Age, But Still Has Some Teenage Problems. *South African Journal of Science* 113 (9/10): 1–2.

Müller, R., C.A. Roberts, and T.A. Brown. 2014. Genotyping of Ancient Mycobacterium Tuberculosis Strains Reveals Historic Genetic Diversity. *Proceedings of the Royal Society B: Biological Sciences* 281 (1781): 20133236. https://doi.org/10.1098/rspb.2013.3236.

Mundorff, A., and J.M. Davoren. 2014. Examination of DNA Yield Rates for Different Skeletal Elements at Increasing Post Mortem Intervals. *Forensic Science International: Genetics* 8: 55–63.

Museums Galleries Scotland. 2011. *Guidelines for the Care of Human Remains in Scottish Museum Collections*. Edinburgh: Museums Galleries Scotland.

Native American Graves Protection and Repatriation Act (NAGPRA). Public Law 101–601, 25 United States Code 3001 et seq., 104 Stat. 3048 – Nov. 16, 1990 (1990) 101st United States Congress, Washington, D.C.

Nesse, R.M., and G.C. Williams. 1994. *Why We Get Sick. The New Science of Darwinian Medicine*. New York: Vintage Books.

Oasis. 2016. *Oasis: Online Access to the Index of Archaeological Investigations*. https://oasis.ac.uk/pages/wiki/Main. Accessed 21 July 2018.

Odegaard, N., and V. Cassman. 2006. Treatment and Invasive Actions. In *Human Remains: Guide for Museums and Academic Institutions*, ed. V. Cassman, N. Odegaard, and J. Powell, 77–95. Lanham: Altamira Press.

OSSAFreelance. 2005. A Field Guide to the Excavation of Inhumated Human Remains. *British Archaeological Jobs and Resources Practical Guide* 14. http://www.bajr.org/BAJRGuides/14.%20Field%20Guide%20to%20the%20Excavation%20of%20Human%20Inhumated%20Remains/FieldGuidetotheExcavationofHumanInhumatedRemains.pdf. Accessed 21 July 2018.

OSSAFreelance. 2012. A Basic Overview for the Recovery of Human Remains from Sites Under Development. *British Archaeological Jobs and Resources Practical Guide* 13. http://www.bajr.org/BAJRGuides/13.%20A%20Basic%20Overview%20of%20the%20Recovery%20of%20Human%20Remains%20from%20Sites%20Under%20Development/13HumanRemainsDevelopment.pdf. Accessed 21 July 2018.

Planning Policy Guidance 16: Archaeology and Planning. 1990. The Stationery Office, London.

Rawcliffe, C. 2013. *Urban Bodies. Communal Health in Late Medieval Towns and Cities*. Woodbridge: The Boydell Press.

Redfern, R., and M. Clegg. 2017. Archaeologically Derived Human Remains in England: Legacy and Future. *World Archaeology* 49: 574–587.

Redfern, R., and J. Bekvalac. 2017. Collection Care and Management of Human Remains. In *Taphonomy of Human Remains: Forensic Analysis of the Dead and the Depositional Environment*, ed. E.M.J. Schotsman, N. Márquez-Grant, and S.L. Forbes, 369–384. Chichester: Wiley.

Research Excellence Framework. 2017. *What Is the REF*? http://www.ref.ac.uk/about/whatref/. Accessed 22 July 2018.

Richards, M. 2004. Sampling Procedures for Bone Chemistry. In *Guidelines to the Standards for Recording Human Remains*, ed. M. Brickley and J.I. McKinley, 43–45. Institute for Archaeologists Paper No. 7. Southampton and Reading: BABAO and IFA.

Richards, M. 2017. Sampling Guidelines for Bone Chemistry. In *Updated Guidelines to the Standards for Recording Human Remains*, ed. P.D. Mitchell and M. Brickley, 52–53. Reading: BABAO and CIfA.

Robbins Schug, G., E.T. Brandt, and J.R. Lukacs. 2012. Cementum Annulations, Age Estimation and Demographic Dynamics in Mid-Holocene Foragers of North Indian. *Homo* 63: 94–109.

Roberts, C.A. 2012a. History of the Development of Paleopathology in the United Kingdom (UK). In *A Global History of Paleopathology: Pioneers and Prospects*, ed. J.E. Buikstra and C.A. Roberts, 568–579. New York: Oxford University Press.

Roberts, C.A. 2012b. Keith Manchester (1938–). In *A Global History of Paleopathology: Pioneers and Prospects*, ed. J.E. Buikstra and C.A. Roberts, 56–59. New York: Oxford University Press.

Roberts, C.A. 2013. Archaeological Human Remains and Laboratories: Attaining Acceptable Standards for Curating Skeletal Remains for Teaching and Research. In *Curating Human Remains: Caring for the Dead in the United Kingdom*, ed. M. Giesen, 123–134. Woodbridge: The Boydell Press.

Roberts, C.A. 2016. Palaeopathology and Its Relevance to Understanding Health and Disease Today: The Impact of Environment on Health, Past and Present. *Anthropological Review* 79: 1–16.

Roberts, C.A. 2018. *Human Remains in Archaeology: A Handbook*, 2nd ed. York: Council for British Archaeology.

Roberts, C.A., and M. Cox. 2003. *Health and Disease in Britain: Prehistory to the Present Day*. Stroud: Sutton Publishing.

Roberts, C.A., and S. Mays. 2011. Study and Restudy of Skeletal Collections in Bioarchaeology: A Perspective on the UK and Its Implications for Future Curation of Human Remains. *International Journal of Osteoarchaeology* 21: 626–630.

Roberts, C.A., A. Caffell, K.L. Filipek-Ogden, et al. 2016. 'Til Poison Phosphorous Brought Them Death': A Potentially Occupationally-Related Disease in a Post-Medieval Skeleton from North-East England. *International Journal of Paleopathology* 13: 39–48.

Rose, J.C., T.J. Green, and V.D. Green. 1996. NAGPRA Is Forever: Osteology and the Repatriation of Skeletons. *Annual Review of Anthropology* 25: 85–103.

Rossington, B. 2015. *Human Remains Trade on eBay Selling Skulls and Spines Uncovered by the Mirror*. 31 August. https://www.mirror.co.uk/news/weird-news/human-remains-trade-ebay-selling-6354130. Accessed 21 July 2018.

Royal College of Surgeons. 2015. *Plarr's Lives of the Fellows Online: Chesterman, Judson Tyndale (1903–1987)*. http://livesonline.rcseng.ac.uk/biogs/E007155b.htm. Accessed 21 July 2018.

Ruff, C.B. 2008. Biomechanical Analyses of Archaeological Skeletons. In *Biological Anthropology of the Human Skeleton*, ed. M.A. Katzenberg and S.R. Saunders, 183–206. New York: Wiley-Liss.

Ruff, C.B., B.M. Holt, M. Niskanen, et al. 2012. Stature and Body Mass Estimation from Skeletal Remains in the European Holocene. *American Journal of Physical Anthropology* 148 (4): 601–617.

Scheuer, L., and S. Black. 2000. *Developmental Juvenile Osteology*. London: Academic Press.

Sirak, K.A., D.M. Fernandes, O. Cheronet, et al. 2017. A Minimally-Invasive Method for Sampling Human Petrous Bones from the Cranial Base for Ancient DNA Analysis. *BioTechniques* 62 (6): 283–289.

Skeleton Science. n.d. *The Skeleton Science Exhibition*. https://skeletonscience.weebly.com/. Accessed 22 July 2019.

Skills Passport. 2018. *Excavation and Lifting Skeleton*. http://www.archaeologyskills.co.uk/excavation-and-lifting-skeleton/786/. Accessed 22 July 2019.

Smith, M.O. 1996. 'Parry' Fractures and Female-Directed Interpersonal Violence: Implications from the Late Archaic Period of West Tennessee. *International Journal of Osteoarchaeology* 6: 84–91.

Steckel, R.H., C.S. Larsen, C.A. Roberts, et al. (eds.). 2019. *The Backbone of Europe: Health, Diet, Work and Violence Over Two Millennia*. Cambridge: Cambridge University Press.

The Bone Room. 2016. *The Bone Room: Natural History for Everyone*. http://www.boneroom.com/store/c1/Featured_Products.html. Accessed 21 July 2018.

The Complete University Guide. 2018. *League Tables*. https://www.thecompleteuniversityguide.co.uk/league-tables/. Accessed 22 July 2018.

The University of Edinburgh. 2018. *Dead Images: Facing the History, Ethics and Politics of European Skull Collections*. https://www.eca.ed.ac.uk/event/dead-images-facing-history-ethics-and-politics-european-skull-collections. Accessed 21 July 2018.

Thomas, C.D.L., M.S. Stein, S.A. Feik, et al. 2000. Determination of Age at Death Using Combined Morphology and Histology of the Femur. *Journal of Anatomy* 196: 463–471.

Tierney, S.N., and J.M. Bird. 2015. Molecular Sex Identification of Juvenile Skeletal Remains from an Irish Medieval Population Using Ancient DNA Analysis. *Journal of Archaeological Science* 62: 27–38.

Tsutaya, T., and M. Yoneda. 2015. Reconstruction of Breastfeeding and Weaning Practices Using Stable Isotope and Trace Element Analyses: A Review. *American Journal of Physical Anthropology* 156: 2–21.

Ubelaker, D. 1989. *Human Skeletal Remains. Excavation, Analysis and Interpretation*. Washington, D.C.: Taraxacum Press.

Walker, P.L., and D.C. Cook. 1998. Brief Communication: Gender and Sex: Vive La Difference. *American Journal of Physical Anthropology* 106: 255–259.

Weyrich, L.S., K. Dobney, and A. Cooper. 2015. Ancient DNA Analysis of Dental Calculus. *Journal of Human Evolution* 79: 119–124.

White, L. 2013. The Impact and Effectiveness of the Human Tissue Act 2004 and the Guidance for the Care of Human Remains in England. In *Curating Human Remains: Caring for the Dead in the United Kingdom*, ed. M. Giesen, 43–52. Woodbridge: The Boydell Press.

White, T.D., and P.A. Folkens. 2005. *The Human Bone Manual*. Burlington: Elsevier.

Wilbur, A.K., and A.C. Stone. 2012. Using Ancient DNA Techniques to Study Human Disease. In *A Global History of Paleopathology: Pioneers and Prospects*, ed. J.E. Buikstra and C.A. Roberts, 703–717. New York: Oxford University Press.

Zakrzewski, S.R. 2007. Population Continuity or Population Change: Formation of the Ancient Egyptian Shape. *American Journal of Physical Anthropology* 132: 501–509.

Chapter 8
Ethical Considerations in the Excavation of Burials in England: A Perspective from Developer Led Archaeology

Louise Loe and Sharon Clough

Abstract Excavating burials presents a myriad of ethical considerations involving legal constraints and regulations, religion (lay and formal), health and safety, public and academic interest, and descendants. These considerations are arguably more complex when the excavation is undertaken within the context of developer led practice in which the realities of time, cost, and methods of construction all come into play. Excavations may also become the focus of local opposition to developments or can be used as political opportunities. Drawing on the experience of two of the UK's leading archaeology practices, Oxford Archaeology and Cotswold Archaeology, this chapter discusses some of the main ethical considerations in burial excavation in England, with reference to a number of examples and 'on the ground' observations, not usually provided in the published literature. It is highlighted that, when burials are concerned, the interests of different groups are frequently discordant and require professional judgement and a pragmatic, balanced, approach in which the best solutions available at the time are found. The last 20 years has seen increasing ethical debate in the excavation of burials in England and will continue to do so. Changes in economic, political, and commercial arenas, which will directly impact on archaeology, are on the horizon and will present new ethical dilemmas for burial archaeology in the near future highlighting that a more developed ethical framework is needed.

L. Loe (✉)
Oxford Archaeology, Janus House, Osney Mead, Oxford OX2 0ES, UK
e-mail: louise.loe@oxfordarch.co.uk

S. Clough
Cotswold Archaeology, Building 11, Kemble Enterprise Park, Cirencester, Gloucestershire GL7 6BQ, UK

K. Squires et al. (eds.), *Ethical Approaches to Human Remains*,
https://doi.org/10.1007/978-3-030-32926-6_8

8.1 Introduction

Every year, thousands of burials are excavated in England, the vast majority by archaeology practices in advance of development. Comprising inhumations, cremations, and disarticulated skeletal elements, all over 100 years old, they come from contexts which range from relatively isolated prehistoric burials and small Roman cemeteries on rural sites, to large medieval and post-medieval burial grounds in urban contexts.

This chapter discusses ethical considerations in the excavation of burials, primarily in the context of developer led archaeology in England. Ethics refers to a philosophy or a system of morals which can differ from person to person and culture to culture (Sellevold 2012). It is "… the study of moral philosophy, which helps us to decide what is right and to act accordingly. Moral philosophy may be viewed as the abstract and ethics as the application—where abstract concepts become very real indeed" (Wait 2017, 2). A key factor is that ethics does not involve certainties and is never clear cut, "instead we face sometimes infinite shades of grey" (Wait 2017, 2).

The ethics of the excavation of human remains is widely discussed in a number of academic and popular publications. These consider a number of different areas, including: objections to excavation due to religious beliefs, historic grievances and perceptions of indecency (Strauss 2016), and the justifications for excavation (White and Folkens 2000; Payne 2012). According to Strauss (2016) "… depending on one's perspective, the excavation of the dead can be seen as an act of desecration or as an act in service to those who might otherwise be forgotten".

Ethical considerations involve all individuals and groups with a legitimate interest in the burials concerned (APABE 2017). In developer led practice, this can involve numerous stakeholders, including family members, descendants, local residents, developers, architects, planning authorities, curators, scientific and research communities, religious groups, and local interest groups. These individuals and groups represent a broad spectrum of value systems and religious beliefs, which are complex, multi-layered and often discordant, presenting many occasions in which ethical judgements must be made by those who excavate human remains. These situations have largely centred on concerns surrounding the extent of archaeological excavation, religious beliefs, public engagement, and the rights of descendants. They have concerned burials from all time periods, but most notably post-medieval burials (Sayer 2011, 2012; Powers et al. 2013; Wilson et al. 2013; Boyle 2015; Tarlow 2015; Renshaw and Powers 2016). Post-medieval burials invoke a heightened sensitivity and emotional response (Boyle 2015) as they may be identified by name, may have traceable living descendants, and may contain preserved soft tissue and other remains (for example, clothing). Post-medieval burials also involve a larger and broader range of stakeholders (for example, local history groups, larger religious communities, and larger scientific communities), therefore conflicts of interest are more likely. Post-medieval burials also present a particular suite of health and safety considerations, not usually encountered when excavating earlier burials, such as working in confined crypt spaces and exposure to lead dust, which require re-prioritising the way excavations are undertaken. These issues are explored in Sects. 8.3–8.6 of this chapter. These categories are broad, and it is not the aim here to present all arguments that concern them in relation to ethics and burial archaeology, but to highlight situations and considerations that the present authors believe to be especially pertinent today. Clearly, ethical considerations surrounding excavation cannot be appreciated without understanding the framework within which the work is undertaken. Therefore, a brief overview on the background to burial excavation in developer led practice in England is presented before moving on to more specific ethical issues encountered in this industry.

8.2 Background to the Excavation of Burials in Developer Led Archaeology in England

In developer led archaeology, burial excavation is undertaken in compliance with planning law. Developers are required to apply to local authorities for planning permission and, since 1990, archaeology has been a material consideration in the determination of these applications. Initially, the process was governed by Planning Policy Guidance (PPG16 1990, Note 15–16) which was introduced by the Government in 1990, to advise local authorities on archaeology within the planning process in England and Wales. Preservation in situ is an underlying principal of PPG16. Since 2012, this policy has been replaced by the National Planning Policy Framework (NPPF) (Department of Communities and Local Government 2012; Ministry of Housing, Communities and Local Government 2018), which emphasises understanding and conserving the significance of heritage assets in the context of sustainable development (Department of Communities and Local Government 2012, Sect. 12). Human remains are not given any specific consideration in this policy, that is, the policy makes no greater presumption against their disturbance than it does for any other archaeological remains (APABE 2017). The reason for this is not clear, but one suggestion is that issues surrounding the disturbance of human remains are considered to be relatively infrequent at the planning level (Harwood 2015).

Archaeological burials are excavated on a range of development type sites, ranging from large infrastructure schemes, housing and aggregates projects, to small projects, such as the re-ordering or upgrading of churches. Much of this work is undertaken on behalf of construction companies and mineral extraction companies, often in tandem with the development works. Ultimately in charge of the management of a site, these companies will employ industry standard regulations including site specific rules and codes of conduct, such as wearing high visibility clothing, hard hats, and ear and eye protectors; systems for signing on and off site;

security passes; site inductions and the use of delineated zones, such as pedestrian access points and 'no go' areas.

Site operations are dictated by rigid time scales, which on large projects, such as a housing development or road scheme, can involve several phases of programmed work. These include initial excavations for ecological conservation and access roads, demolition, a main phase of excavation, and subsequent monitoring (for example, for the installation of services), all of which will require a co-ordinated approach from different professionals, including ecologists, construction workers, engineers, and archaeologists. When some elements take more time than anticipated, the whole chain of work may be impacted, ultimately resulting in higher cost to the project funder. Thus, great pressure is placed on archaeologists to undertake their work in a timely manner. This is especially difficult in burial archaeology because it is arguably one of the most expensive and least predictable archaeological contexts to excavate, recover, analyse, and report on. Coupled with the fact that archaeology practitioners have to win their projects through a competitive tendering process, in which construction companies (or the client they are acting for) select their preferred practitioner, this time issue has created a climate in which the cost of burial excavation is a key factor, even though, ethically speaking, money and burials do not sit comfortably together. Competitive tendering and the possibility of cost cutting can risk the archaeology if it causes the excavation methodology to be compromised and/or developers are unable to cover the cost, or even go bankrupt, leaving sites partially excavated and projects stuck in limbo with the results of the excavation undocumented.

Today, and in the authors' experience, there is greater sensitivity shown in these areas than before, and roles are more clearly understood and managed more effectively. For example, construction companies recognise burials as a high-risk category, so routinely factor them into project risk assessments and contingencies in order to minimise delays and avoid bankruptcy. Careful planning, in which there is early dialogue between site managers, engineers, archaeologists, and construction workers is now fairly standard, so that expectations can be managed and unexpected discoveries, suitably mitigated (Fig. 8.1). Furthermore, from a public relations perspective, construction companies increasingly recognise the benefits of engaging with, and positively supporting, outreach opportunities presented by the archaeology.

Burial legislation is another important aspect that underpins burial excavation in developer led practice, although it does not concern ethics per se. Prior to the excavation of any human remains, a licence must be obtained from the Ministry of Justice or, for burials lying in consecrated ground, a faculty from the diocesan consistory court of the Church of England. Legalities relating to burial excavation are discussed in detail in various texts and national guidance (BABAO 2010a, 2019a; Sayer 2012; White 2013; APABE 2017). In summary, these tell us that it is unlawful to excavate buried human remains without a licence or a faculty. Secular and ecclesiastical jurisdiction provide a framework for burial excavation, which embraces the following principles:

Fig. 8.1 In 2009, during the construction of the Weymouth Relief road (Dorset), Oxford Archaeology made the discovery of a rare mass grave of vikings on Ridgeway Hill (Loe et al. 2014b). The discovery was unexpected, having not been identified by earlier surveys of the area. Early communication between the developer (Skanska Civil Engineering on behalf of Dorset County Council) and archaeologists meant that there was sufficient flexibility in the programme and working methodology to manage the discovery in a way that did not have a considerable impact on the construction timetable and yet allowed archaeologists to excavate and record the burial in the required detail and to an acceptable standard. In this case, the area in which the grave lay was fenced off and the surrounding land was cut away and developed, preserving a small island which was also levelled and developed once the excavation was complete. Image courtesy of Oxford Archaeology© (2009)

- Human remains should always be treated with dignity and respect;
- Burials should not be disturbed without good reason. However, it may be necessary to disturb burials in advance of properly authorised development;
- Human remains and the archaeological evidence around them are important sources of scientific information;
- Particular weight should be given to the feelings and views of living family members, when known;
- Decisions should be made in the public interest, and in an accountable way.

(ChurchCare 2017)

Licences issued by the Ministry of Justice typically fall under Sect. 8.25 of the 1857 Burial Act or the 1884 Disused Burial Grounds Act and the 1981 Disused Burial Grounds (Amendment) Act. When issued, Church of England faculties and Ministry of Justice burial licences set out certain conditions under which human remains may be excavated, with the primary stipulation that they are treated with decency and respect at all times, and that the works are shielded from public view during the excavation.

On large infrastructure projects, burials may be excavated under a Private Act of Parliament, which affords developers the powers to remove human remains without the need to obtain a licence or faculty. Separate legislation applies to the excavation of burials of former military personnel. For archaeologists, this primarily concerns soldiers from World War One, which are now over 100 years old, so are in the archaeological domain. Excavation is undertaken in consultation with the Commonwealth War Graves Commission and in accordance with legislation that pertains to the nationality of the personnel involved. For British military, this concerns a licence from the UK Ministry of Defence in accordance with the 1986 Protection of Military Remains Act.

8.2.1 Ethical Guidance on Burial Excavation

Walker's (2000, 19–20) global review of ethics in bioarchaeology identifies three fundamental rules that should be followed by researchers who work with archaeological human remains: (1) human remains should be treated with respect and dignity, (2) descendants should be given the authority to determine the fate of their ancestors' remains, and (3) human remains should be preserved for scientific research. In Britain, ethical guidance on the excavation of burials is set out in the British Association for Biological Anthropology and Osteoarchaeology's Code of Ethics (BABAO 2010b, 2019b), although this focuses on overarching principles and does not address practicalities. One of the main principles expressed in this document is that the excavation (and study) of human remains is a privilege and not a right (BABAO 2019b). Indeed, Roberts (2009) notes that rights are inherent, and privileges are granted on stated conditions that create responsibilities.

Guidance and advice on matters relating to burials over 100 years old in England is also provided by the Advisory Panel for Burials in England (APABE). The APABE's (2017) *'Guidance for Best Practice in the Excavation of Human Remains from Christian Burial Grounds'* is a key document, which addresses the practical aspects of excavation and the associated ethical issues, and is referred to throughout this chapter. It provides guidance on factors such as legalities, the planning framework, mitigating the impact of development on burials, and approaches to the archaeological investigation of burials. However, the document is primarily concerned with Christian burial grounds dating from the seventh century onwards.

There is currently no such similar guidance on the excavation of prehistoric burials, or burials of other faith groups, yet burials from earlier periods often pose different ethical concerns to those of more recent date. One such dilemma is whether archaeologists should excavate prehistoric burials as they have no faith or interest group to consult with or written doctrine, which could be used to inform the treatment of the human remains. In such cases, archaeologists must rely on their own current ethical framework. This is becoming an increasingly active debate involving groups, such as Druids, who claim a cultural or religious connection with burials of unknown individuals that are thousands of years old. Druids have attracted considerable media attention in recent years, primarily in relation to debates surrounding the reburial of prehistoric skeletons and their claim to the moral authority to decide their fate. This has not, so far, focused upon the actual excavation of prehistoric burials, so is not discussed further here, but needs addressing in future work.

Similarly, people of different traditions and faiths may prefer human remains to be treated in a particular way during the excavation process or may even oppose their excavation. For example, Jewish communities have objected to the excavation of medieval Jewish burial grounds in Europe, in respect of their religious law (Halacha), which stipulates that the burials of people of Jewish faith remain eternally undisturbed (Colomer 2014). Thus, among strict followers of the Halacha, excavation is considered to be "….desecration, humiliation of the dead, a form of theft, and a serious violation of Jewish law" (Colomer 2014, 175). The excavation of Jewish burials is discussed further in Sect. 8.4 of this chapter.

8.2.2 Best Practice Guidance for Excavation

A number of publications are available which provide best practice guidance on excavating burials. These include generic ones, which are not specific to faith groups or period (McKinley and Roberts 1993; Roberts 2009), whilst others are specific to Christian burials, dating from the seventh century onwards (English Heritage and the Church of England 2005; APABE 2017). The primary goals of these guidelines are to advocate decent and respectful treatment of the dead, consultation with descendants and interest groups, and maximising research potential. Thus, great emphasis is placed on careful, delicate, hand excavation, and the involvement of experts in the study of human remains (for example, osteoarchaeologists). Detailed recording, protocols for lifting and storing skeletons or bones, and strategies for sampling the soil in burial features to maximise the recovery of small bones and objects are also stressed. Excavation can take at least a day, or longer, where burials are more complex. However, in order to protect them from vandalism, theft, or damage caused by exposure to the elements, it is standard practice to excavate and recover burials in one day wherever possible.

8.3 Ethics of Excavating Burials: Practical Considerations

Whilst the principles and ethics of burial excavation are widely discussed (as discussed above), the particular ethical challenges presented by the practicalities associated with the excavation of burials in a developer led context have received less attention. Broadly speaking, these challenges concern questions relating to the extent of disturbance and the excavation and recovery of burials, and arise in a number of situations. One example is the excavation of large post-medieval burial grounds, where burials number in their thousands. When their clearance is necessitated by development, the sheer number of burials and the associated practical and logistical issues brings questions about the extent to which they should be archaeologically excavated over other methods into sharp focus. Non-archaeological clearance is usually more rapid than archaeological excavation, so is perceived to be a more affordable option for developers, but no, or limited, archaeological recording is undertaken. This point was highlighted during the clearance of St Pancras burial ground in London in 2002–2003, ahead of the construction St Pancras International station as part of the High Speed 1 rail development. The archaeological excavation and recording that was being undertaken here was perceived to be taking too long, potentially delaying the construction programme (White 2013), so the developers employed an exhumation company to recover the burials without archaeological supervision. Concerns over time and cost took precedence over the importance of the archaeological data. This prompted the Church of England, English Heritage, the Council for British Archaeology, the BABAO, the British Archaeological Trust (RESCUE), the local press, and members of the public to contest the developer's decision and as a result the archaeologists were reinstated to complete the work (Sayer 2009; White 2013).

It is argued that large burial grounds generally cannot be archaeologically excavated in their entirety because of the high cost and impracticalities of doing so. In particular, it is contended that entire archaeological excavation would impede development and could pose a considerable problem in parts of the country where development or regeneration is needed to boost the economy. Recent guidance (APABE 2015) on this problem considers intelligent sampling strategies which may involve one of the following: (1) archaeological excavation of a proportion of all burials to be impacted by a development, (2) archaeological excavation of all burials and subsequent selection of a sample for analysis, or (3) a combination of both approaches. Normally, the preferred approach is to sample at the post-excavation phase of a project (option 2), akin to that employed at the site of the Augustinian priory and hospital of St Mary Spital (London) ahead of the construction of the new Spitalfields market, London (Connell et al. 2012). Here, over 10,500 inhumations were archaeologically excavated, and 5387 skeletons were subject to detailed osteological analysis (Connell et al. 2012).

Of course, it is not necessarily always appropriate, or ethical, to archaeologically record *all* burials from a site that is being cleared. For example, when a post-medieval non-conformist burial ground in Greater Manchester was excavated ahead of redevelopment in 2012, some of the known burials were reburied without any archaeological recording, because this had been requested by the descendants (see Sect. 8.6 of this chapter for further details). On this project, archaeologists worked alongside a non-archaeological exhumation team, who removed them for immediate reburial as they were uncovered.

Burials which continue beyond the footprint of a development present further issues concerning the extent of excavation and recovery. This is especially the case in the context of densely packed cemeteries, such as urban Church of England burial grounds, where graves frequently intercut. National guidance advises against fully exposing (or 'chasing') these burials, unless they are considered to be of exceptional archaeological significance, because of the potential to encounter further burials outside the excavation area, causing unnecessary disturbance (APABE 2017). Pre-reformation Christians believed that the integrity of the corpse was essential for bodily resurrection to occur on the Day of Judgement (Richardson

2000). However, in a Christian (Church of England) context, present day religious doctrine states that the body does not need to be intact for bodily resurrection to occur (Richardson 2000). However, to some, recovering parts of skeletons and leaving the rest in situ is indecent and disrespectful. This belief can be traced back to the eighteenth to nineteenth century when there was much fear and superstition surrounding death, especially when bodies were exhumed or subjected to anatomical dissection (Richardson 2000). It is thus unsurprising that those holding such long-standing beliefs about the dead deem the partial disturbance of human remains to be unethical.

Further ethical challenges are presented by the evaluation of archaeological sites. Evaluations involve the excavation of long, narrow, trial trenches, to assess the extent of archaeological remains and to inform planning conditions and strategy for later excavation. It can be many years between evaluation and excavation, so a case can be made to leave archaeology, including burials, in situ and as undisturbed as possible, to be recovered later alongside any potential further archaeology. However, exposing human bone to the air and allowing it to dry out has a deleterious effect on its bio-chemical status, causing deterioration and dissolution of bone mineral (Huisman 2009). Deterioration can be stabilised in bone, which has been retained from the ground by keeping it cool and dry, but not if it is left in situ and covered back over; bone that has been uncovered then re-covered is found to be less well preserved than bone which has not been previously exposed (Historic England 2016). Thus, in this context, not recovering human remains during evaluations is problematical, because of the unnecessary damage this causes.

Finally, ethical issues surrounding the extent of disturbance, excavation, and recovery cannot be discussed without mentioning the use of piles, rafts or slabs, and ground beams for building foundations in burial grounds. These techniques are standard practice for non-burial archaeology, and have become the favoured approach to minimising impact on archaeology in recent years (Historic England 2015), although they are controversial in the context of human burials. The use of piles, for instance, is particularly problematical. On the one hand it can be seen that the use of piled foundations limits the extent of disturbance to a site and is considered by some to be a sensible solution where other options, such as area excavation, would entail the disturbance of larger areas, even though less invasive methods would be involved (Historic England 2015). Historic England (2015), for instance, recommends that the impact of piling upon archaeology should, under most circumstances, be limited to 2%. However, on the other hand, driven piles are extremely invasive and can cause considerable and unmitigated damage and degradation to burials, which are often destroyed without record or recovery (Fig. 8.2). Thus, licence applications involving the excavation of burials in advance of pile foundations are normally turned down by the Ministry of Justice (APABE 2017), and Historic England guidance also advises against them (Historic England 2015). Raft foundations (reinforced concrete slabs, spread out entirely or partly under the footprint of a building, also called mat foundations) are also an attractive solution, allowing for burials to remain undisturbed beneath the impact horizon of the development. Yet, the extent to which this method affects the preservation of

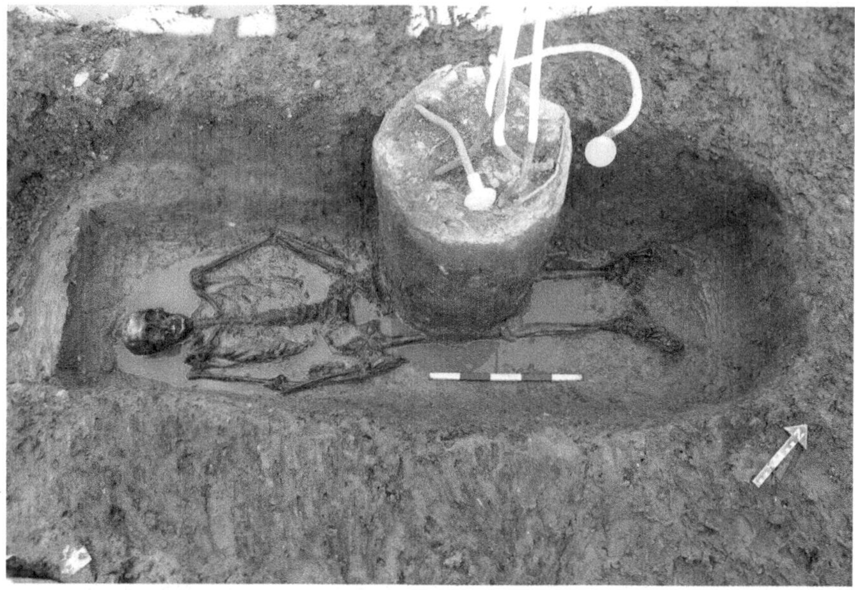

Fig. 8.2 Damage to a Roman burial caused by piling. Image courtesy of Cotswold Archaeology© (2017)

burials is currently unknown (APABE 2017). There are concerns about how the biochemistry of the substrate will affect skeletal remains and the surrounding burial environment (Historic England 2015), thus further research is needed in this area.

8.4 Religious Considerations

Religious considerations have already been discussed in the context of Christian beliefs and Christian views towards preserving the integrity of human remains (see Sect. 8.3 of this chapter). Another important factor is that, while secular law regulates rather than prevents or restricts the excavation of burials, ecclesiastical law is protective and has a presumption against disturbance (APABE 2017). As such, "the continuity in beliefs and practices surrounding post mortem disposal becomes an important ethical pressure" (Renshaw and Powers 2016, 170). For archaeologists, this often imposes practical constraints on the excavation and analysis of burials, such as requirements not to remove human remains from consecrated ground and reburial within a certain timeframe, often resulting in on site analysis (sometimes in inadequate conditions), followed by immediate re-burial. The inevitable time and space constraints that this places on the analysis of skeletons often means that only limited data capture is possible, and may mean that the research potential of burials cannot be fully realised, regardless of their archaeological and scientific significance. Similar issues have been identified in the commercial sector in the USA concerning discoveries of Native American remains on archaeological sites (see Loveless and Linton, this volume).

This situation applies to burials that are under the jurisdiction of the Church of England. The views of other faith groups, including other main world religions and pagan groups, concerning the ethics of excavation have not been written into any national guidance despite the fact that a number of burials, most notably in a non-conformist context (for example, Bashford and Sibun 2007; McCarthy et al. 2012), have now been excavated [although doctrine is covered to some extent in some research publications, for example, see Stock (1998), on Quakers]. Furthermore, the archaeological significance and appreciation of burial grounds of minority faith groups need to be articulated, so that they may be protected. As heritage assets, they are currently overlooked and poorly understood, so their protection is more difficult than other burial sites (Historic England 2018). To this end, Historic England actively commissions projects that will further our understanding of such sites, for example, on how Jewish communities' value and view historic Jewish burial grounds (Barker Langham 2015) and research into non-conformist burial grounds (Historic England 2018). Just as the views of these, and other, minority groups need to be given recognition in national guidance, so too does the archaeological value of their burial grounds and associated human remains.

Minority faiths and groups have particular requirements for the excavation of individuals buried in their cemeteries. For example, when the disused medieval burial ground at Jewbury (York) was redeveloped in the early 1980s, the project became an important lesson in reconciling the Jewish community's requirements with those of a legal, ethical, scientific, and developmental nature (Addyman 1994). A standard burial licence was issued (then by the Home Office) to York Archaeological Trust for an archaeological excavation of the cemetery on the grounds that there was no positive evidence that it was the site of a Jewish cemetery or that the "human remains found on this site [were] positively of Jewish origin" (Addyman 1994, 299). The licence imposed a strict time limit for the analysis and reburial of the skeletons in case the remains were of Jewish origin (Addyman 1994). In response to the terms of the licence, a methodology for rapid anthropological assessment of the skeletons was implemented by osteologists. However, when the excavation was underway, campaigners made a strong case against skeletal analysis and presented sufficient evidence to prove that the skeletons and the cemetery were Jewish. As a result, the Home Office responded by demanding the immediate reburial of the skeletons without anthropological analysis. York Archaeological Trust made a case for the scientific analysis of the skeletons, but this was contested by the Chief Rabbi who stated "We are convinced that the dignity shown to humans even centuries after their death can contribute more than any scientific enquiry to the advancement of human civilisation and the enhancement of the respect in which human beings hold each other" (Addyman 1994, 300).

This example not only highlights how minority faiths and groups have particular requirements for the excavation of individuals buried in their cemeteries, but how such cemeteries can be difficult to identify from records if they have fallen out of use or been put to other use. It questions the level of certainty with which burials and cemeteries should be identified as belonging to a particular group before excavation commences and what evidence is considered sufficient.

8.5 The Public and the Excavation of Burials

8.5.1 Debates and Controversies

Public feeling against the excavation of burials can be particularly strong in the context of developer led excavations. In this setting, pressure for space, coupled with the necessity to develop for economic growth, typically arouses strong public feeling against their disturbance. These often prompt debates involving the media, which are frequently motivated by religious, political, and environmental concerns. Furthermore, some have acted as stress points resulting in "the eruption of existing tensions around other grievances or differences" (Tarlow 2015, 10) while others have developed when the interests of stakeholders have not been taken into account (Wilson et al. 2013). Examples of these debates have been discussed at some length in other publications (e.g. Sayer 2012; Tarlow 2015), the majority of which are concerned with post-medieval burials. In 2008, protests were held to halt the redevelopment of a medieval and post-medieval burial ground at Bonn Square (Oxford), because it involved the loss of green space. Similarly, local inhabitants and businesses in Jericho (Oxford) strongly opposed the clearance of the Radcliffe Hospital burial ground in 2013, because it was felt that the new development would have a detrimental impact on the historic character of the area (Maclean 2013). In addition, locals held peaceful protests in opposition to the redevelopment of the non-conformist burial ground in Greater Manchester by a large supermarket chain (see Sect. 8.3 of this chapter for further details). In this case, the knowledge that infant burials would be disturbed caused great concern amongst the local community who, during the excavation, left soft toys and flowers next to the entrance of the site. In this example, it was children, the most vulnerable members of the community, who had instilled a sense of duty and care amongst the living.

A sense of duty and care was also the prevailing feeling surrounding the excavation of 250 Australian and British soldiers from mass graves in Fromelles (Northern France), but on an international scale (Scully and Woodward 2013). The soldiers fought and died in the battle of Fromelles (1916) and shortly after death were buried by Germans behind enemy lines (Loe et al. 2014a). The graves remained undetected until the early 2000s, when aerial photographs, followed by geophysical survey and the digging of test pits, drew attention to them (Pollard et al. 2008). Following a campaign by amateur historians, families, and supporters, the Australian and British governments agreed to fund the excavation of the soldiers and the construction of a new Commonwealth War Graves Commission cemetery close to the recovery site, so that they could be reburied in individual graves with a headstone, to commemorate them by name, wherever possible. Genetic identity was determined using DNA, historical, artefactual, and anthropological evidence (Loe et al. 2014a). The excavation was controversial with some questioning the need to exhume and identify soldiers who died a long time ago (for example, Stanley 2014), whilst others argued that it was our duty to honour these men by giving them a dignified burial (Summers 2010; Renshaw 2017). Others used the excavation as an opportunity to criticise the then Australian prime minister, Kevin Rudd, in the media (see Sayer 2012). In addition, Oxford Archaeology was accused of being "… unaware of the significant impact of [the] project on people's lives" (Sayer 2012, 91), in not publicly disclosing information about the excavation. That was not the case and reflects a lack of understanding of the complexities of excavating human remains from a recent military conflict. Oxford Archaeology (and all participants on the project) was acutely aware of the wide range of individuals affected by this project and non-disclosure of information was in fact the client's decision. Given the fact that some soldiers were likely to be Australian meant that the project was completely governed by Australian military regulations as well as British. The excavation was conducted under intense media scrutiny which, coupled with the aforementioned issues, brought the ethical treatment of the dead and their surviving family members into sharp focus (Cox and Jones 2014). This involved maintaining absolute objectivity and a disconnection from the aforementioned issues. It was also imperative that Oxford Archaeology remained focused on achieving the aims of the project within the tight timescale imposed by the client as well as treating the dead with the utmost care and respect.

8.5.2 Public Engagement

There is pressure from some members of the public who wish to be allowed to view the excavation of human remains. However, it is generally accepted that visiting or viewing developer led burial excavations is impractical and sometimes inappropriate for the general public, because of considerations relating to health and safety, security, time constraints, decency, and respect. Nonetheless, lack of information, involvement, and regular communication can cause public suspicion, unease, or even mistrust (Sayer 2011, 2012). For example, some have challenged the legal condition (Burial Act 1857) to screen burial excavations from public view. This piece of legislation was implemented to protect the public from unexpectantly encountering human remains in the context of grave digging. However, it is argued that in the context of today's archaeology projects, this practice creates the sense that there is something to hide (Sayer 2012). It may even sensationalise the discovery of human remains by creating a separate space accessible only to a select group (Sayer 2012). Yet these arguments all too often focus on the living and ignore the decent treatment and respect of the dead.

Practicalities and public inclusion on burial excavations need to be finely balanced. It is important to consider that not everyone wants to view the excavation of burials and that it could be deemed unethical for everyone to view human remains. Balance was achieved during excavations of the post Roman (fifth to seventh century) burial ground at Hinkley Point Nuclear Power station (Somerset), where high security completely excluded the possibility of site visits for the public, but information was shared through a programme of outreach talks, displays, YouTube videos, and a website (South West Heritage 2013). In other examples, feelings of exclusion were dispelled when archaeologists delivered talks to the general public about excavations at a post-medieval burial ground in Greater Manchester (discussed further in Sect. 8.5.1 of this chapter), and in London, public engagement involving historical research on burials excavated at Bedlam proved highly successful (Cross Rail 2018).

Issues surrounding public engagement on burial excavations were crystallised in the Fromelles project. In keeping with policies of the Australian and British armies and of the Commonwealth War Graves Commission, no images or footage of human remains from the mass graves have been allowed to enter the public domain. That is, soldiers who fought and died in World War One are treated in the same manner as current day military fatalities. The highly sensitive nature of the project and the fact that human remains had to be protected from DNA contamination meant that members of the public were not allowed to visit the graves whilst they were being excavated, but they could obtain information at an on-site visitors' facility. Here, they could gain a limited view of the operation from a long-distance viewing window. However, these measures created feelings of exclusion, especially among families who, in donating their own DNA to the project, felt they had the right to see the excavation (Layla Renshaw, pers. comm.). In this project, feelings of exclusion were magnified because of its association with a highly emotive event, the excavation seen by some as an opportunity to raise the public profile of the Battle of Fromelles (Renshaw 2017).

8.5.3 *Excavating the Famous Dead*

Excavations involving the recovery and identification of known individuals who are of great public interest have received considerable attention in recent years. Examples include searches for King Alfred (Albert and Tucker 2014), King Harold (Farmer 2014) and, most notably, Richard III (BBC 2012). In such projects, considerable media and public interest weigh heavily on the approach to excavation and post-excavation, even when the notable person may not be Royal, or have any known place of burial. For example, the re-development of Dorchester Prison (Dorset) created a media flurry as it was the known execution site of Elizabeth Martha Brown (c. 1811–1819—9th August 1856), née Clark, who was the last woman to be hanged in public in Dorset. She was executed outside Dorchester Prison after being convicted of the murder of her second husband, John Brown.

A 16 year old Thomas Hardy witnessed the event and he is said to have based the hanging of Tess (in the eponymous novel) on his experience of watching Brown's death. This ordinary woman, due to her deathly influence, has been the subject of much research (Thorne 2000). Her actual burial place is unknown, because executed felons were not given marked graves or buried in coffins with name plates. However, this did not stop the Hardy Society weighing in on the debate, and Julian Fellowes (President of the Hardy Society and Baron Fellowes of West Stafford) is quoted as "wishing the remains to be moved and reburied in West Stafford church (which was the inspiration for the church where Angel Clare marries Tess in Hardy's novel)" (Stretton 2017). Such was Martha Brown's influence on Hardy's plot narrative, that locals have a strong sense of ownership of her remains (which have yet to be and, in fact, may never be, identified). Martha Brown is also regarded as a heroine, the abused wife who killed her husband with an axe in an act of self-defence (Curtis 2016). Both of her children died without issue, so there are unlikely to be any direct living descendants, precluding the application of DNA analysis to identify her remains. Despite the fact that Martha's burial location is unknown and there are no known living descendants, the public continue to petition for exhumation and reburial of Martha's suspected remains.

Where exhumation of the famous dead is necessitated by development (as was the case with the skeleton reputed to be Martha Brown), all aspects of the archaeologists' work will be publicly scrutinised more than usual. Thus, there is the temptation to afford this category of burial greater attention in terms of its ethical treatment. This is entirely inappropriate, as this should be the benchmark for all burial excavations. Other ethical issues relating to the excavation of the famous dead include questions relating to whether this is justified for those not threatened by development. Some have argued that, because of the advances in molecular science (e.g. DNA analysis), now is a good time to be undertaking this work, while others have maintained that, unless burials are threatened, they should not be disturbed (History Extra 2015). Other questions include whether it is right to employ excavation to inform projects looking for famous burials, especially when the association is tenuous. This potentially results in unnecessary disturbance (and hence damage) to burials if analyses show that they are not the individual of interest, or firm evidence is not found. This was recently the case in Scotland where a lead coffin was opened in the hope of finding the Scottish Clan Chief Simon Fraser. Instead, the poorly preserved skeleton of a female was identified (Press Association 2018). Although renovation of the mausoleum was being undertaken in this instance, and the coffin may have been examined as part of this, the possibility of a famous individual ensured interference. In addition, as the case of Martha Brown demonstrates, local interest can create a public sense of ownership of famous burials; thus, there is a wider group of stakeholders involved in these excavations, with differing views to contend with, than there might otherwise be.

8.6 Descendants

Generally speaking, it is universally acknowledged that decisions regarding the treatment of deceased individuals of known personal identity lie with living close family members (Walker 2000). Tracing living relatives so that they can have input into the fate of their ancestors poses particular ethical issues. The current legal system in England requires excavations, which are likely to encounter burials that have living descendants (i.e. burials less than 100 years old) to be advertised in the local newspaper and at the site before the work commences. This was successfully implemented on the project at the non-conformist burial ground in Greater Manchester (as discussed in Sect. 8.3 of this chapter). Nonetheless, as highlighted in national guidance (APABE 2017), even when this legal requirement does not apply, it is ethical to consider the interests of living relatives of all burials, including those over 100 years old. However, the names of those recovered are often not known prior to the excavation of a burial ground and when they are found during excavation, tracing relatives can be a very detailed, time consuming, and costly process because the number of generations that descendants span is often very large. Additionally, descendants can be unaware that they have a distant relative buried in a particular place, so will often not respond to any adverts or information posted publicly, which they might have done had they known.

In a recent case, a descendant accidentally came across an image of their great, great grandfather in an archaeological publication where the skeleton had been identified by name. The descendant had not been traced at the time of excavation, nor had they known about the burial (and subsequent exhumation) of their relative until years after the excavation. Had there been awareness of the descendant, the image may not have been shown in the publication or the identity of the skeleton may not have been disclosed.

The often-extensive primary and secondary documentary sources (for example, burial registers, fee books, and local histories) associated with post-medieval burials can present exciting opportunities for public engagement; they can inspire enquiry into the past and they feed into the popularity of ancestry research. Ancestry research means that there is much greater activity than ever before in identifying the burial places of ancestors. This highlights important ethical considerations in the handling of data.

Some of the aforementioned issues around tracing relatives were encountered in the Fromelles project, which involved a dedicated media campaign and outreach programme to trace living relatives. The purpose of this campaign was to ask descendants to donate DNA samples to help identify the excavated soldiers who had died in the Battle of Fromelles (1916). Some of the traced relatives did not know they were related to a soldier from the battle before they had been contacted or had accepted a long time ago that their relative was killed there, so were not looking for them (Stanley 2014).

Tracing relatives therefore presents clear ethical and practical difficulties when named individuals are found during the excavation of a post-medieval burial ground. When relatives are not traced, is it ethically correct to show images and share information associated with named burials when there is the potential that they may be identified as someone's relative in the future? This question should be considered through wide and open debate and addressed in a balanced way in which reasonable efforts are made to trace relatives and personal data is handled sensitively.

8.7 Conclusion

The fast pace of development, legislation, health and safety, religious requirements, and scientific and community interest mean that excavating burials in a developer led context presents a myriad of ethical considerations. Those discussed here concern the extent of excavation and recovery, public engagement and concern, the interests of minority faith groups, and the interests of descendants. In circumstances like these, ethical concerns do not always agree well, presenting issues that are not easily resolved, or may remain unresolved (APABE 2017). Thus, complete recovery of skeletons or assemblages may not always be achievable when they lie partially outside the extent of an excavation or where numbers are so high that the cost to excavate is unrealistic. Similarly, religious requirements to retain human remains on consecrated ground can mean difficult decisions must be made about maximising their scientific value. These and other decisions require moral reasoning to justify why one of the principles or rules of autonomy, non-maleficence, beneficence, and justice has been chosen (Thompson 2001). Further, they require: "…archaeologists [to] exercise professional judgement in their practical responses …and be willing to be held accountable for their judgements" (APABE 2017, 4). It is currently recommended that, where post-medieval burials of known individuals are concerned, decisions should involve their descendants (when known), and for other burials, decisions should involve current secular attitudes to the dead, such as secular concepts of ethics and Christian theology, though these can sometimes conflict with one another (APABE 2017).

The ethical considerations in burial excavation discussed here are the main ones that are encountered today but this is not a static picture; there are a number of changes, either on the horizon or already taking place, in archaeology, which will no doubt impact on burial excavation and arouse new debate in the future. For example, large infrastructure projects involving the excavation of the largest cemeteries yet encountered in this country (for example, HS2) are currently underway, funding cuts are forcing museums to stop receiving archives (including human remains), and planning heritage officer jobs in local authorities are under threat due to reduced budgets. In addition, recent government measures aimed to stimulate house building, threatens to drastically reduce the scope and depth of archaeological desk-based investigations, which are required before development takes place. For example, under the Housing and Planning Act (2016), permission for the development of brownfield sites is, in principle, issued without robust archaeological assessments being carried out, thereby putting potentially important archaeological sites at risk of damage and destruction during development (Council for British Archaeology 2016). Precisely what the implications of these changes are for burial archaeology is uncertain, but they are likely to bring questions relating to the extent of excavation, recovery, retention, and other such factors into even sharper focus. Therefore, it is clear that a more developed ethical framework for burial excavation is needed. For example, this should include ethical codes and guidance for burial archaeology that address issues concerning information associated with named burials (e.g. how they are stored and accessibility), social media and media, burials of all periods, and all faith and interest groups. Additionally, it is essential that archaeologists develop and maintain an open dialogue about burial archaeology and the ethical issues with all stakeholders, including the Church and other faith groups, developers/construction companies, planning authorities, descendants, and local communities, among others. Ethical aspects of burial archaeology should be debated and discussed among everyone through professional forums, education in schools, outreach, and other similar activities. Ethical debate has had an increasingly high profile in burial excavation over the last two decades and will continue to do so in the decades to come.

Acknowledgements This contribution was supported by Oxford Archaeology and Cotswold Archaeology. We would like to thank the editors for inviting us to contribute to this volume. Special thanks goes to several individuals who read earlier versions of this chapter and provided constructive comments for which we are hugely grateful.

References

Addyman, P.V. 1994. Circumstances of Excavation and Research. In *The Jewish Burial Ground at Jewbury. The Archaeology of York. Volume 12: The Medieval Cemeteries*, ed. J.M. Lilley, G. Stroud, D.R. Brothwell et al., 298–300. York: Council for British Archaeology.

Advisory Panel on the Archaeology of Burials in England [APABE]. 2015. *Large Burial Grounds: Guidance on Sampling in Archaeological Fieldwork Projects*. Swindon: Historic England and The Advisory Panel on Archaeology of Burials in England.

Advisory Panel on the Archaeology of Burials in England [APABE]. 2017. *Guidance for Best Practice for Treatment of Human Remains Excavated from Christian Burial Grounds in England*, 2nd ed. Swindon: Historic England and The Advisory Panel on Archaeology of Burials in England.

Albert, E., and K. Tucker. 2014. *In Search of Alfred the Great: The King, the Grave, the Legend*. Stroud: Amberley Publishing.

Barker Langham. 2015. *Jewish Burial Grounds: Understanding Values*. London: Barker Langham.

Bashford, L., and L. Sibun. 2007. Excavations at the Quaker Burial Ground, Kingston-upon-Thames, London. *Post-Medieval Archaeology* 41: 100–154.

BBC. 2012. Richard III Dig: 'Strong Chance' Bones Belong to King. *BBC News*. 12 September. http://www.bbc.co.uk/news/uk-england-leicestershire-19561018. Accessed 7 May 2018.

Boyle, A. 2015. Approaches to Post-Medieval Burial in England: Past and Present. In *The Archaeology of Death in Post-medieval Europe*, ed. S. Tarlow, 39–60. Warsaw/Berlin: De Gruyter.

British Association for Biological Anthropology and Osteoarchaeology [BABAO]. 2010a. *Code of Practice*. http://www.babao.org.uk/assets/Uploads/code-of-practice.pdf. Accessed 24 July 2018.

British Association for Biological Anthropology and Osteoarchaeology [BABAO]. 2010b. *Code of Ethics*. http://www.babao.org.uk/assets/Uploads/code-of-ethics.pdf. Accessed 24 July 2018.

British Association for Biological Anthropology and Osteoarchaeology [BABAO]. 2019a. *Code of Practice*. https://www.babao.org.uk/assets/Uploads/BABAO-Code-of-Practice-2019.pdf. Accessed 04 October 2019.

British Association for Biological Anthropology and Osteoarchaeology [BABAO]. 2019b. *Code of Ethics*. https://www.babao.org.uk/assets/Uploads/BABAO-Code-of-Ethics-2019.pdf. Accessed 04 October 2019.

Burial Act. 1857. The Stationery Office, London.

Churchcare. 2017. *Human Remains*. http://www.churchcare.co.uk/cathedrals/getting-advice/human-remains. Accessed 1 March 2018.

Colomer, L. 2014. The Politics of Human Remains in Managing Archaeological Medieval Jewish Burial Grounds in Europe. *Nordisk Kulturpolitisk Tidsskrift* 17 (2): 168–186.

Connell, B., A. Gray Jones, R. Redfern, et al. 2012. *A Bioarchaeological Study of Medieval Burials on the Site of St Mary Spital: Excavations at Spitalfields Market, London E1, 1991–2007*. London: Museum of London Archaeology.

Council for British Archaeology. 2016. *CBA Response to New Neighbourhood Planning and Infrastructure Bill Announcement*. http://new.archaeologyuk.org/cba-response-to-new-neighbourhood-planning-and-infrastructure-bill-announcement. Accessed 24 July 2018.

Cox, M., and P. Jones. 2014. Ethical Considerations in the Use of DNA as a Contribution Toward the Determination of Identification in Historic Cases: Considerations from the Western Front. *New Genetics and Society* 33 (4): 295–312.

Cross Rail. 2018. *Bedlam Burial Ground Register*. http://www.crossrail.co.uk/sustainability/archaeology/bedlam-burial-ground-register. Accessed 30 April 2018.

Curtis, J. 2016. Remains of the Hanged Woman Who Inspired Thomas Hardy to Write Tess of the D'Urbervilles to be Saved from Property Developer's Diggers. *Daily Mail*. 27 May. http://www.dailymail.co.uk/news/article-3612610/Remains-hanged-woman-inspired-Thomas-Hardy-write-Tess-D-Urbervilles-saved-property-developer-s-diggers.html#ixzz5Ds0qDXAT. Accessed 30 April 2018.

Department of Communities and Local Government. 2012. *National Planning Policy Framework*. https://www.gov.uk/government/publications/national-planning-policy-framework–2. Accessed 20 October 2018.

Disused Burial Grounds Act. 1884. The Stationery Office, London.

Disused Burial Grounds (Amendment) Act. 1981. The Stationery Office, London.

English Heritage and the Church of England. 2005. *Guidance for Best Practice for Treatment of Human Remains Excavated from Christian Burial Grounds*. Swindon: English Heritage.

Farmer, B. 2014. Richard III Archaeologists Now Search for King Harold—To See if He Survived Battle of Hastings. *Telegraph*. 12 October. https://www.telegraph.co.uk/history/11157181/Richard-III-archaeologists-now-search-for-King-Harold-to-see-if-he-survived-Battle-of-Hastings.html. Accessed 30 April 2018.

Harwood, R. 2015. *Archaeology and Human Remains*. http://www.publiclawtoday.co.uk/local-government/planning/318-planning-articles/26094-archaeology-and-human-remains. Accessed 25 April 2018.

Historic England. 2015. *Piling and Archaeology: Guidelines and Best Practice*. Swindon: Historic England.

Historic England. 2016. *Preserving Archaeological Remains: Decision-Taking for Sites Under Development*. Swindon: Historic England.

Historic England. 2018. *Understanding and Protecting Historic Burial Grounds of Minority Faith Groups*. https://historicengland.org.uk/research/current/discover-and-understand/faith-and-commemoration/understanding-burial-grounds/. Accessed 24 July 2018.

History Extra. 2015. *Following the Success of the Richard III Excavation, Is It Time to Dig Up Other Famous Skeletons*? https://www.historyextra.com/period/tudor/following-the-success-of-the-richard-iii-excavation-is-it-time-to-dig-up-other-famous-skeletons/. Accessed 30 April 2018.

Housing and Planning Act. 2016. The Stationery Office, London.

Huisman, H. (ed.). 2009. *Degradation of Archaeological Remains*. Den Haag: Sdu Uitgevers.

Loe, L., C. Barker, K. Brady, et al. 2014a. Remember Me to All. *The Archaeological Recovery and Identification of Soldiers Who Fought and Died in the Battle of Fromelles 1916*. Oxford: Oxford Archaeology.

Loe, L., A. Boyle, H. Webb, et al. 2014b. *'Given to the Ground'. A Viking Age Mass Grave on Ridgeway Hill, Weymouth*. Dorset Natural History and Archaeological Society Monograph Series, Vol. 22. Dorset: Dorset History and Archaeological Society.

Maclean, R. 2013. Freuds Anger at University Building Project. *The Oxford Student*. 2 May. https://www.oxfordstudent.com/2013/05/02/freuds-anger-at-university-building-project/. Accessed 27 October 2018.

McCarthy, R., S. Clough, A. Boyle, et al. 2012. The Baptist Chapel Burial Ground, Littlemore, Oxford. *Post Medieval Archaeology* 46: 281–290.

McKinley, J.I., and C.A. Roberts. 1993. *Excavation and Post-excavation Treatment of Cremated and Inhumed Remains. Technical Paper Number 13*. Birmingham: Institute of Field Archaeologists.

Ministry of Housing, Communities and Local Government. 2018. *National Planning Policy Framework*. https://www.gov.uk/government/publications/national-planning-policy-framework–2. Accessed 20 October 2018.

Payne, S. 2012. Archaeology and Human Remains: Handle With Care! Recent English Experiences. In *More Than Just Bones: Research and Human Remains*, ed. H. Fossheim, 49–64. Oslo: The Norwegian National Research Committee.

Planning Policy Guidance (PPG16) Note 15–16. 1990. The Stationery Office, London.

Pollard, T., O. Lelong, G. MacKinnon, et al. 2008. *Pheasant Wood Fromelles. Data Structure Report*. Unpublished GUARD Report. Glasgow: University of Glasgow.

Powers, N., A.S. Wilson, J. Montgomery, et al. 2013. 'No Certain Proof but the Coffin Lid'. Exploring the Commercial and Academic Need for a High Level Research Framework to Safeguard the Future of the Post-Medieval Burial Resource. In *Archaeology, the Public and the Recent Past*, ed. C. Dalglish, 125–144. Woodbridge: The Boydell Press.

Press Association. 2018. Headless Body is Not C18th Scottish Clan Chief, Says Experts. *The Guardian*. 19 January. https://www.theguardian.com/science/2018/jan/19/headless-body-is-not-scottish-clan-chief-simon-fraser-experts. Accessed 30 April 2018.

Protection of Military Remains Act. 1986. The Stationery Office, London.

Renshaw, L. 2017. Anzac Anxieties: Rupture, Continuity and Authenticity in the Commemoration of Australian War Dead at Fromelles. *Journal of War and Culture Studies* 10 (4): 324–339.

Renshaw, L., and N. Powers. 2016. The Archaeology of Post-Medieval Death and Burial. *Post Medieval Archaeology* 50 (1): 159–177.

Richardson, R. 2000. *Death, Dissection and the Destitute*. Chicago: University of Chicago Press.

Roberts, C.A. 2009. *Human Remains in Archaeology*. York: Council for British Archaeology.

Sayer, D. 2009. Is There a Crisis Facing British Burial Archaeology? *Antiquity* 83 (319): 199–205.

Sayer, D. 2011. Bowls, Bobbins and Bones: Resolving the Human Remains Crisis in British Archaeology, a Response. *Papers from the Institute of Archaeology* 21: 10–14.

Sayer, D. 2012. *Ethics and Burial Archaeology*. London: Bloomsbury Publishing.

Scully, J.L., and R. Woodward. 2013. Naming the Unknown of Fromelles: DNA Profiling, Ethics and the Identification of First World War Bodies. *Journal of War and Culture Studies* 5 (1): 59–72.

Sellevold, B. 2012. Ancient Skeletons and Ethical Dilemmas. In *More Than Just Bones: Research and Human Remains*, ed. H. Fossheim, 139–160. Oslo: The Norwegian National Research Committee.

South West Heritage. 2013. *Archaeology at Hinkley Point—Find Out About Archaeology at Hinkley Point*. https://archaeologyathinkleypoint.wordpress.com/. Accessed 30 April 2018.

Stanley, P. 2014. Book Review: The Lost Legions of Fromelles. *The Conversation*. 17 July. https://theconversation.com/book-review-the-lost-legions-of-fromelles-28095. Accessed 4 April 2018.

Stock, G. 1998. Quaker Burial: Doctrine and Practice. In *Grave Concerns, Death and Burial in England 1700–1850*, ed. M. Cox, 129–143. York: Council for British Archaeology.

Strauss, M. 2016. When Is It Okay to Dig Up the Dead? *National Geographic*. https://news.nationalgeographic.com/2016/04/160407-archaeology-religion-repatriation-bones-skeletons/?user.testname=none. Accessed 1 October 2018.

Stretton, R. 2017. Campaigners Including Julian Fellowes have Called for the Remains of Martha Brown and Other Bodies Buried at Dorchester Prison to be Exhumed and Reburied Before Development of the Site. *Worcester News*. 18 May. http://www.worcesternews.co.uk/news/15292152.Campaigners_fight_for_legacy_of__one_of_Dorchester_s_most_historic_figures_/. Accessed 30 April 2018.

Summers, J. 2010. *Remembering Fromelles. A New Cemetery for a New Century*. Maidenhead: Commonwealth War Graves Commission.

Tarlow, S. 2015. Introduction: Death and Burial in Post-Medieval Europe. In *The Archaeology of Death in Post-Medieval Europe*, ed. S. Tarlow, 1–18. Warsaw/Berlin: De Gruyter.

Thompson, T. 2001. Legal and Ethical Considerations of Forensic Anthropological Research. *Science and Justice* 41 (4): 261–270.

Thorne, N. 2000. *In Search of Martha Brown: The True Story of the Mysterious Woman Thomas Hardy Saw Hanged*. Plymouth: Dashwood Press.

Wait, G. 2017. *CIfA Professional Paper: An Introduction to Professional Ethics*. Reading: Chartered Institute for Archaeologists.

Walker, P.L. 2000. Bioarchaeological Ethics: A Historical Perspective on the Value of Human Remains. In *Biological Anthropology of the Human Skeleton*, ed. M.A. Katzenberg and S.R. Saunders, 3–39. New York: Wiley-Liss.

White, B. 2013. The United Kingdom. In *The Routledge Handbook of Archaeological Human Remains and Legislation*, ed. N. Márquez-Grant and L. Fibiger, 479–491. London: Routledge.

White, T.D., and P.A. Folkens. 2000. *Human Osteology*, 2nd ed. San Diego: Academic Press.

Wilson, A., N. Powers, J. Montgomery, et al. 2013. 'Men that are Gone….Come Like Shadows, so Depart'. Research Practice and Sampling Strategies for Enhancing Our Understanding of Post-Medieval Human Remains. In *Archaeology, the Public and the Recent Past*, ed. C. Dalglish, 145–161. Woodbridge: The Boydell Press.

Chapter 9
'The Dead Teach the Living': Ethical Considerations Concerning the Management of Collections of Human Remains in Universities

Anwen Caffell and Tina Jakob

Abstract This chapter discusses ethical implications that arise from teaching with collections of human remains. Despite focusing on UK universities, many recommendations are also applicable to teaching in non-UK institutions, although it has to be acknowledged that ethical issues are variable across cultural and geographic borders and evolve through time. This chapter has arisen out of the need to provide a solid grounding for advancing research, through training future generations of human bioarchaeologists to deal with the realities of working with human remains in archaeological and related contexts. This is achieved through scrutinising current university teaching practices involving human remains, stressing the importance of using real human remains, supplemented with the use of casts and images, in teaching. The need for ethics training at all levels of teaching and research in universities and other institutions is also highlighted. In addition to evaluating 'traditional' teaching with human remains, this chapter covers ethical aspects of using digital and social media and aims to assist university staff to develop their own ethical guidelines and policies, including those related to public outreach and other forms of recruitment. It is important that such policies are developed, and that particular care is taken to make these specific to ethical issues surrounding human remains.

'The Dead Teach the Living'—This title was inspired by Charlotte Roberts (2013) who drew our attention to the motto of the Paleopathology Association (n.d.): *Mortui viventes docent.*

A. Caffell (✉) · T. Jakob
Department of Archaeology, Durham University, South Road, Durham DH1 3LE, UK
e-mail: a.c.caffell@durham.ac.uk

K. Squires et al. (eds.), *Ethical Approaches to Human Remains*,
https://doi.org/10.1007/978-3-030-32926-6_9

9.1 Why This Chapter is Timely

Universities fulfil several main functions: they provide education for students and act as foci for research, innovation, and public engagement (Boulton and Lucas 2008). There are more than 50 British universities that teach undergraduate degree programmes in archaeology, anthropology, forensic archaeology/anthropology, Egyptology, and palaeoanthropology. Any degree programme in archaeology is likely to involve teaching on human remains, even at the most basic level, without necessarily providing laboratory-based practical education. Currently, more than 15 of these universities also provide specialist masters courses focusing on human bioarchaeology, including programmes that have emerged relatively recently specialising in biomolecular techniques (e.g. the analysis of stable isotopes and trace elements, ancient DNA, and proteomics). Although the focus of this chapter will be on the UK, there are a large number of courses worldwide—in Europe, North and South America, Africa, Asia, Australia, and New Zealand (Márquez-Grant and Fibiger 2011)—where aspects of human bioarchaeology are taught and collections of human remains are curated. Many of these countries will have their own specific circumstances surrounding the care and handling of human remains that are linked to their historical and cultural evolution, particularly concerning issues of excavation, study, and repatriation of the remains of Indigenous peoples in North America, Australia, and New Zealand (Beck and Teague 2001; Currie and McBride 2001; Westaway and Burns 2001; Byrne 2003; Roberts 2009, 34–37; Mayes 2010; Giesen and White 2013; Gilmore et al. 2013).

Many authors have explored the value of human remains for research and advancing understanding of the human condition when justifying the excavation, study, and retention of collections of human remains, citing the developments of new research questions and new methodologies as reasons why collections of human remains should be retained (Buikstra and Gordon 1981). They have typically also stressed the importance of engaging with communities and disseminating and explaining the results of their findings to the wider public as part of this process (for example, Walker 2000; Hunt 2001; Roberts 2009, 21–22; Sayer 2010; White et al. 2012, 357–378; DeWitte 2015). While there has been focus on education in the sense of what we learn from studying human remains, few have explicitly considered the valuable role that human remains fulfil in educating future bioarchaeologists. However, education is cited as a reason to support the retention of human remains by public organisations, such as the British Association for Biological Anthropology and Osteoarchaeology (BABAO 2019a), the Department of Culture, Media and Sport (DCMS 2005), and by the Society for American Archaeology (SAA 1984). Roberts (2009, 28–29) has cited teaching as an important role that collections of human remains fulfil, and goes on to explore this in more detail in a later publication (Roberts 2013). White et al. (2012, 5–7, 25–27) discuss the importance of using real human remains in teaching human bioarchaeology and outline effective methods for teaching and learning. These authors also note the impact that the lack of access to education in palaeontology for Indigenous scholars has had for the development of this field within some Asian and African countries (White et al. 2012, 374). If we are to continue to learn from collections of human remains then it is vital to ensure that people are trained to a high standard to enable them to develop and carry out such research.

This chapter will outline the importance of studying human remains from archaeological contexts and evaluate why it is necessary that real human remains, not only casts, are used for teaching. Some of these recommendations will also be applicable for teaching in anthropological and forensic science programmes. It will consider the types of teaching that universities undertake that include human remains, and suggest how teaching can be delivered following ethical practices. We will also examine why it is important that students are taught about ethics in relation to the study of human remains, both for their own immediate studies and in terms of the wider benefit to the practice of human bioarchaeology as a scholarly field. Universities have a duty to educate students about ethics in relation to human remains, but it is also important that students see good ethical practice being implemented. As curators of skeletal collections, the duty of universities, and by extent laboratory managers and programme directors, to curate those collections ethically and sensitively will be considered in relation to research access policies, particularly when evaluating requests for destructive sampling of human remains. This extends to managing archives of associated materials, such as datasets and radiographs.

While the aim of this chapter is to address the topics outlined above, the authors recognise that ethical considerations in teaching bioarchaeology are an evolving field and it is acknowledged that there will be room for improvement as ethical practices develop. Practices and opinions change through time, and vary by culture, religious beliefs, and background (Walker 2000; Roberts 2009, 17–21; White et al. 2012, 357; Giesen and White 2013), and consequently what is considered acceptable in one time or place may not be considered so in another. It is also important to note, that this chapter has been written from the perspective of archaeological practice in the United Kingdom. Therefore, the recommendations made will be most suited to similar cultural situations, and sensitivity is necessary when evaluating which recommendations can be applied to different settings (Giesen and White 2013). It is difficult to establish consistent standards of ethical practice that are acceptable across different cultures (Giesen and White 2013), but the suggestions we make here should at least provide a starting point for discussion and collaboration.

9.2 The Need for Ethical Education in the Study of Human Remains in Archaeology and Bioarchaeology

Human remains are an important source of information on life in the past that should be central to archaeological interpretations (Buikstra and Gordon 1981; Grauer 1995; Walker 2000; Hunt 2001; Larsen 2002). Analysis of human remains can also be central to forensic cases, where the evidence may be presented as testimony in court and the outcome can impact directly on modern lives (White et al. 2012, 358–361; İşcan and Steyn 2013). It is therefore imperative that universities teach students about human remains and instil ethical standards. At the most obvious level, this involves training students who wish to specialise in human bioarchaeology, particularly through intensive masters-level courses that aim to prepare students to work as specialists in commercial archaeology, forensic anthropology, or to go on to study at doctoral level.

However, even if students have no intention of specialising in human bioarchaeology following their undergraduate studies, archaeologists must know how to deal appropriately with human remains, and understand the information that can be gained from studying the physical remains of past populations. Field archaeologists will invariably encounter human skeletons during watching briefs and excavations, and must be familiar with the correct legal procedures as well as understand the practicalities of how to uncover, record, lift, transport, wash, package, and store the remains (Janaway et al. 2001; Roberts 2009, 22–27, 73–102; BABAO 2019a; Sayer 2010; Parker Pearson et al. 2013). Archaeologists should be able to differentiate animal from human remains, and be aware of the basic anatomy of the human skeleton to enable them to accurately interpret the position and orientation of human remains in situ. These skills are also necessary to recover all the bones, including the small bones of the hands and feet, and associated tissues such as ossified cartilage or pathological structures such as kidney and gall bladder stones (Roberts 2009, 74–77). Excavators should be aware of which parts of the skeleton provide the most information on age and sex, recognise the presence of major pathological lesions, and understand the value of differential diagnosis in order to appreciate why recovering all bones and fragments is important. Ideally, they should also not mistake pathological woven bone or dental calculus deposits for soil and avoid removing these during cleaning. Archaeologists must appreciate the importance of employing a fully-trained human bioarchaeologist during excavation, as well as for the analysis of the skeletons to maximise the information gained (Mays et al. 2004; Roberts 2009, 74). Ultimately, they must value the contribution that human remains can make to the interpretation and understanding of the site, in order that the information obtained during their analysis is integrated in full with the other archaeological findings, and not just relegated to an appendix (Roberts 2009). Archaeologists conducting academic research must understand the limitations of bioarchaeological methods when drawing on the data obtained from human skeletal remains if they are not to misinterpret these data. The role of universities in teaching human remains therefore extends beyond training specialists.

9.3 Why Universities Need Collections of Human Remains for Teaching

"The most important single resource for the osteologist is a collection of skeletal remains" (White et al. 2012, 6). Therefore, in order to fulfil their duty, universities require skeletal collections to be able to teach students about human remains. These should encompass collections of 'articulated' skeletons from inhumation burials, as well as sets of disarticulated bone elements (White et al. 2012). It is imperative that students learn about normal human skeletal anatomy, and while this can be taught, at least to a basic level, using plastic models and casts, these cannot replicate the range of normal anatomical variation that occurs in the human skeleton or capture the finer details of texture and shape that are important when learning normal anatomy (Fig. 9.1; Janaway et al. 2001; Roberts 2009, 29, 2013; White et al. 2012, 25–27). Furthermore, they cannot reproduce the myriad ways in which archaeological human remains can break or become damaged in the ground due to taphonomic factors (Figs. 9.2 and 9.3). Anyone working with archaeological human remains will be well aware that skeletons are frequently incomplete, and their bones may be fragmented and/or show erosion of surface details (Brickley 2004, 2017; McKinley 2004, 2017; White et al. 2012, 6–7). Archaeologists also have to deal with fragmented cremated bone, where the cremation process may have caused the bone to warp and/or shrink (Wahl 1982; Mayne Correia 1997; McKinley 2000, 406). A detailed understanding of anatomy is essential if cremated bone fragments are to be identified successfully. Learning with fragmented and cremated remains also means the students learn normal anatomy more thoroughly, as it forces them to learn tiny details of shape and texture they would otherwise have overlooked when looking at a complete bone. Frequently students might think they have learned a bone thoroughly, only to find that when they are given a small fragment of it they cannot picture what that part of the bone looks like in order to be confident in their identification. They might realise that they rely on the distal end of the radius to determine side, for example, so when they have a fragment of the proximal end alone they are unable to side it. Disarticulated bones are also frequently encountered in archaeological contexts, especially from medieval and post-medieval cemeteries due to the disturbance of earlier burials to make space for later interments (Gilchrist and Sloane 2005, 180, 195–196; Roberts 2009, 51; Sayer 2011, 202), or in prehistoric contexts such as Neolithic chambered tombs reflecting the funerary rituals practiced at the time (Ray 1999, 20–24; Roberts 2009, 43). These should not be ignored, since they hold valuable information about people in the past.

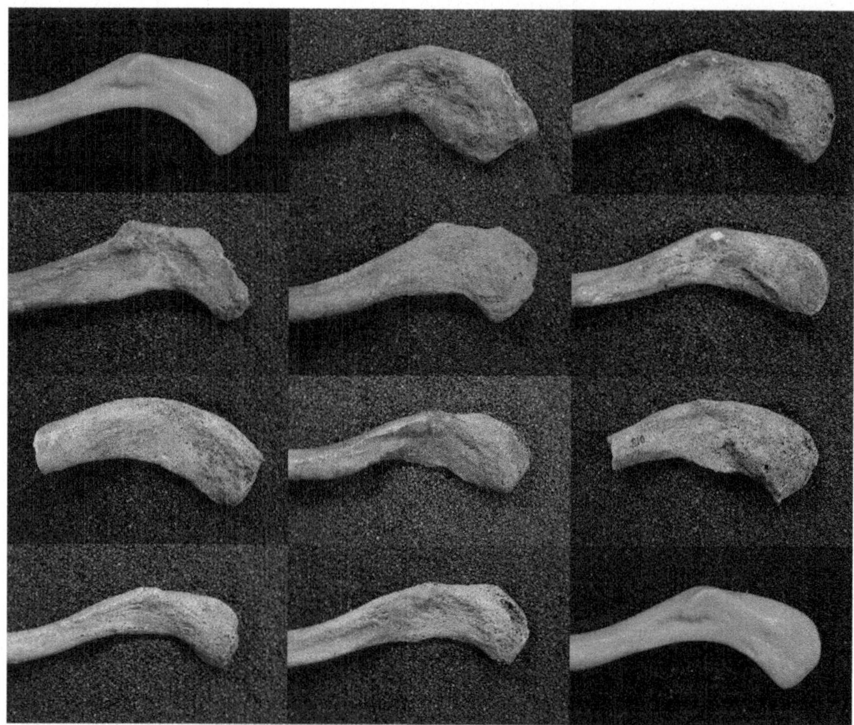

Fig. 9.1 Inferior view of the lateral clavicle, showing the range of variation in the expression of anatomical features in ten archaeological clavicles compared to two plastic clavicles (top left and bottom right). Students who learned anatomy using plastic skeletons alone would find it difficult to appreciate what was normal variation. Photograph by Anwen Caffell©

When learning about pathological conditions that can affect the skeleton, it is essential that students are able to see various expressions and stages of these pathological lesions alongside the normal appearance of the bones (Roberts 2013). For example, students need to become familiar with the early manifestations of common conditions such as joint degeneration, which can be subtle and if missed will impact on the interpretation of the population. Teaching pathology can and should be supported with the use of photographs, three-dimensional images (3D; for example, Errickson and Thompson 2017; Errickson et al. 2017; Wilson et al. 2017), and replicas of pathological bones (Fig. 9.4). Until recently the only sources of the latter were casts, for example, Bone Clones (2018) and France Casting (2015), but recent developments in three-dimensional printing (for example, Errickson et al. 2017) promise a new source of pathological bone models. Not only do such materials expand the educational experience of students beyond the limits of the physical collections of human remains curated by the university at which they are studying, their use can also help protect the physical remains from unnecessary handling and the damage that may cause (Caffell et al. 2001; Janaway et al. 2001).

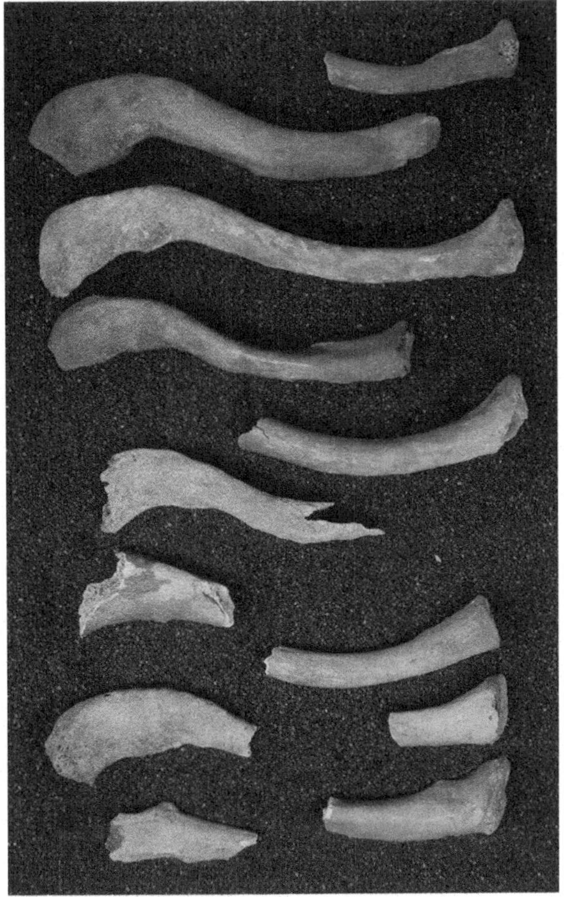

Fig. 9.2 Archaeological clavicles showing range of variation in size, shape, surface preservation, and amount of fragmentation. Real human remains may break in many different ways, and it is essential that students are able to identify and side bone fragments. Photograph by Anwen Caffell©

Where these materials form a viable substitute for real remains, it is recommended that they are used.

However, while photographs are a valuable resource, they are two-dimensional and the bone or tooth cannot be rotated and viewed from all angles. To address this issue, interactive three-dimensional imaging techniques have been developed by resources such as Digitised Diseases (n.d.) and applications such as Dactyl (Anthronomics 2018). Such techniques allow images to be rotated on screens, but they still lack the physicality of handling a three-dimensional element, and their success at capturing fine surface detail is varied. Furthermore, it should be noted that when viewed on a screen these images are technically still in two dimensions. Although 3D casts or prints allow a replica bone to be handled, at present the weight and texture may not closely mimic the original pathological bone. For example, someone handling a real bone with osteoporosis will get a sense of the fragility and lightness of the bone, which may be missing when handling a cast or 3D print due to the more solid and heavier nature of the materials of which it is

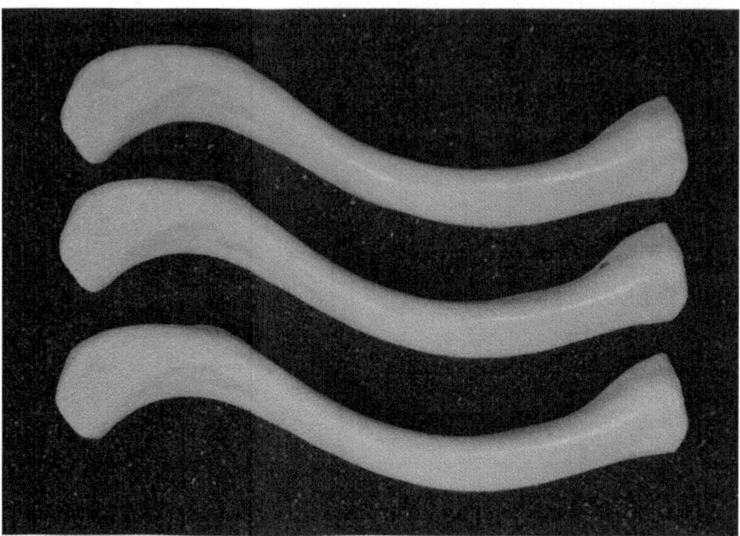

Fig. 9.3 Three clavicles from three plastic skeletons, each of which is identical and complete. Students who study plastic material alone would not learn the different ways in which bone can fragment, or how to recognise parts of bone elements when they are damaged post mortem. Photograph by Anwen Caffell©

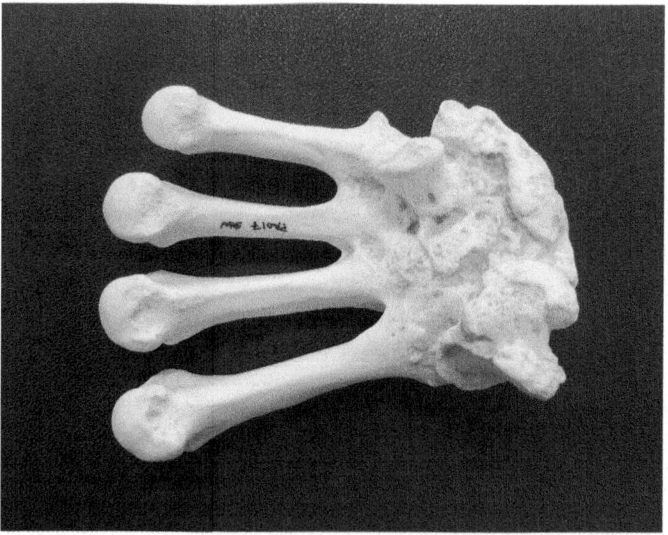

Fig. 9.4 Cast of hand with septic arthritis produced by France Casting (2017). Casts of unusual pathological conditions can provide a valuable supplement to teaching with real human remains. Photograph by Tina Jakob©

composed. Fine surface detail, including variations in colour, can be crucial when diagnosing pathological conditions such as the presence of woven new bone, but these are, at present, often not replicated adequately in casts or 3D prints. As noted by White et al. (2012, 367), "no cast, no image, no measurement, no description can adequately record the information potential held by an original bone". Therefore, the only way to be truly prepared to deal with the real-life situation presented by archaeological human remains is to learn and practice with real human bone, under the guidance of experienced bioarchaeologists. For these reasons universities must maintain collections of human skeletal remains to ensure that students receive an optimal education.

9.4 Curating Collections of Skeletal Remains

Universities are responsible for curating collections of skeletal remains from archaeological sites, many of which may be sizeable and of some regional, national, or even international significance. For example, skeletal remains identified as prisoners captured after the Battle of Dunbar who died following imprisonment in Durham have informed on health in seventeenth century Scotland, and the resulting research into the survivors has developed links with their descendants in North America (Gerrard et al. 2018). Human remains recovered from the rural graveyard of the Church of St Michael and St Lawrence (Fewston, North Yorkshire, UK) have contributed to our understanding of eighteenth to nineteenth century pauper apprentices, and the adverse health consequences that they experienced (Caffell and Holst 2017; Gowland et al. 2017, 2018). Among the skeletal collections curated at the University of Bradford, skeletons from a mass grave associated with the Battle of Towton (North Yorkshire) have informed us on medieval warfare (Fiorato et al. 2000), and skeletons excavated from the medieval Hospital of St James and St Mary Magdalene (Chichester, UK) have provided insight into the palaeopathology of leprosy (Magilton et al. 2008); the existing and likely future contributions made by students to the analysis of this population are acknowledged by Lee and Magilton (2008, 263).

It is therefore important that universities ensure collections are curated appropriately, and that any conservation guidelines regarding the conditions in which those remains are kept are followed to ensure the remains are protected from damage (Roberts 2009, 29; for a review of various guidelines that have been issued see Giesen 2013; see also Biers, this volume). This includes keeping collections in suitable stores, within appropriate climatic conditions: an ambient temperature of 18 °C (range 10–25 °C) and an ambient relative humidity of 50–55%, with limited fluctuations in both (Janaway et al. 2001; DCMS 2005; Roberts 2009, 97–98). However, most of these guidelines do not consider the impact of these factors on the preservation of ancient DNA (Simpson 2017; BABAO 2019a), which is becoming an increasing concern with the rapidly expanding applications of biomolecular techniques. It also means ensuring human remains are packed appropriately within archival-quality bags and boxes of adequate size, using acid-free tissue or bubble-wrap as protection for fragile remains, with each bag clearly labelled (Janaway et al. 2001). However, as noted by Janaway et al. (2001, 202), human remains risk becoming a 'Cinderella material', meaning that resources are not directed towards curating them adequately, with time and money instead spent on caring for other archaeological materials. This observation could be even more applicable in universities due to a lack of funding and appropriate training compared to museums, where collections are managed by curators familiar with developments in storage, packaging, and conservation (Janaway et al. 2001; Giesen et al. 2013). Ideally, the condition of a collection curated by a university should be documented prior to or at the time of its arrival, and use of the collection and its condition should be monitored (Roberts 2009, 97; Giesen et al. 2013). The latter can be achieved through systematically recording which skeletons and bone elements are used for teaching each year, including as examples laid out on benches for laboratory classes, and as skeletons the students lay out during classes and in their independent study time. Maintaining a 'sign-out' system to record when skeletons are removed from storerooms, the purpose of removal, and its duration, can also assist with this process (Fig. 9.5). These records should be kept for future reference.

Universities must consider the source of their collections to ensure that they are acquired on an ethically sound and legal basis (DCMS 2005; Roberts 2009, 29). Many collections in Britain, especially recently, will derive from archaeological excavations conducted by commercial units (Roberts 2013, 124; Swain 2013, 25), for example, the collections currently curated by the Department of Archaeology at

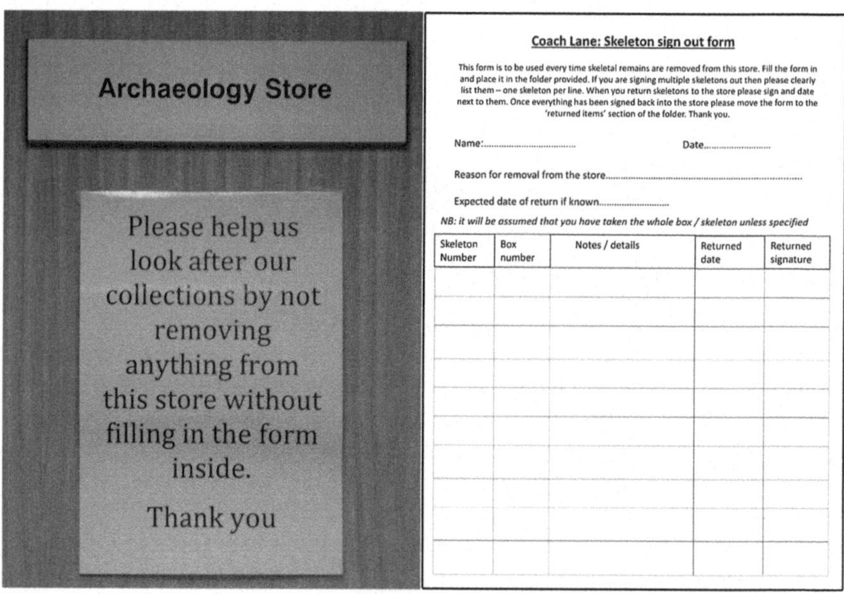

Coach Lane: Skeleton sign out form

This form is to be used every time skeletal remains are removed from this store. Fill the form in and place it in the folder provided. If you are signing multiple skeletons out then please clearly list them – one skeleton per line. When you return skeletons to the store please sign and date next to them. Once everything has been signed back into the store please move the form to the 'returned items' section of the folder. Thank you.

Name:.................................... Date..........................

Reason for removal from the store..

Expected date of return if known............................

NB: it will be assumed that you have taken the whole box / skeleton unless specified

Skeleton Number	Box number	Notes / details	Returned date	Returned signature

Fig. 9.5 Notice on human remains storage room in the Department of Archaeology, Durham University (left), reminding those using the collections to complete the sign out forms (right). Photograph by Tina Jakob©

Durham University include Fishergate House (York), excavated by Field Archaeology Specialists (Holst 2005), and Coach Lane (North Shields), excavated by Pre-Construct Archaeology (Proctor et al. 2016). The terms of the burial licence must be correct to ensure that the remains are legally retained. Those managing collections within universities should maintain a good relationship with the archaeological units that supply the collections, consulting on potential research that may be conducted (particularly when it concerns destructive sampling), inviting their participation, and committing to keeping them informed of any outputs. Where appropriate, archaeological units should be invited to contribute to publications arising from such research.

We need to bear in mind that collections of archaeological human remains are not just composed of the skeletons themselves (Giesen et al. 2013). Universities also have a duty to curate associated documents, such as site records, plans of the excavation, skeletal recording forms, any skeletal reports that have been written, and any publications that have arisen. An archive of photographic material may contain photographs taken in situ during excavation, as well as photographs taken during the initial skeletal assessment and analysis, and any photographs taken by students or staff during research. For most collections acquired in recent years, photographs are likely to be digital, but older collections may have physical photographs as well. Radiographs are another source of information, and again could be digital or plain film; these also need curating in an appropriate manner. As scanning and 3D printing techniques develop, it is likely that curation of 3D images and scans, along with 3D prints, becomes an increasing requirement. Data sets gathered for research, particularly by students, should form part of the collection, and any raw data collected during dissertation research projects should be submitted in electronic form to be easily incorporated into a collection's archive. Thought should be given to the format in which such data is submitted (Archaeology Data Service Guidelines 2015), and any electronic archives should be curated to ensure they are not lost through obsolescence, as technological advances can mean files become unreadable (UK Data Service 2018). When destructive sampling is undertaken, it is recommended that any unused samples should be returned and kept. These might include samples of bone, sectioned teeth, small enamel or calculus fragments, and histological thin-section slides. A database of research carried out on all collections of human remains curated by the university should be maintained, particularly with reference to destructive sampling to monitor the level of sampling permitted for the collections curated. Records of collection management and use also need to be maintained, and all of these records enhance the value of the collection for teaching and research (Giesen et al. 2013).

Universities have a responsibility to ensure that all human remains are treated in an ethical manner while also preserving teaching collections for the benefit of future generations, and should develop their own ethical guidance documents that are appropriate for their collection curation and teaching needs (discussed in more detail below: Sect. 9.6). Resources are also required, in the form of money and staff time, in order to curate collections to the recommended standards (Roberts 2013).

9.5 Teaching Ethics

Students need to be educated about ethics in a theoretical sense, so they develop an understanding of the complex issues surrounding the excavation, analysis, display, repatriation, and reburial of human remains, and develop an appreciation and respect for other cultural viewpoints, opinions, and beliefs (Walker 2000; DCMS 2005; White et al. 2012, 357). The value of dialogue in reaching positive, mutually beneficial solutions where there are conflicting requirements should be promoted, as advocated by Walker (2000). He and his colleagues worked closely with the Chumash Indians of Southern California to develop an ossuary that met the spiritual needs of the tribe, safeguarded the security of the remains, and ensured that osteological research could continue with tribal collaboration and under their supervision (Walker 2000, 29–30). This was achieved through involving, rather than excluding, the Chumash: listening to, understanding, and respecting their concerns, finding common ground within their existing religious beliefs, and building trust. Importantly, the results of bioarchaeological analyses were used to benefit the tribe themselves, and so the Chumash came to value and appreciate the information gained from bioarchaeological analyses. In turn, the researchers benefited from continued access to the remains and insights into the culture they would have lacked otherwise (Walker 2000). However, Walker (2000) does recognise that it is not always easy to develop such a relationship, and several examples of problematic community projects are described by Boutin et al. (2017, 194).

Students need to understand that the study of human remains is a privilege and not a right (Roberts 2009, 17), and they should be provided with activities and assessments that allow them to demonstrate they are developing an appropriate awareness and understanding of ethical issues. These could include preparing for student-led seminars where the arguments for and against the excavation, retention, study, display, or reburial of human remains are discussed, or writing essays evaluating whether these activities are justified. At more advanced levels, they need to learn how to consider ethical issues, which they can apply to their own research. This is particularly important in relation to preparing dissertation research designs that are usually required before any actual research can be undertaken. At Durham University, MSc Human Bioarchaeology and Palaeopathology and MSc Bioarchaeology students complete a research design that includes a section on ethical considerations as part of their module on Research and Study Skills in Archaeological Science. This provides a 'dry run' and aims to instil ethical awareness in advance of putting together the research proposal for their dissertation. As part of this proposal, they complete a departmental ethics and data protection form that must be reviewed and approved by the Departmental Ethics Peer Review Group, and in exceptional cases by the Faculty's Ethics Sub-Committee, before commencing their research (Durham University 2015).

9.6 Ethical Teaching

In general, university staff and mentors should ensure that all students are treated in a fair and objective manner. They should avoid conflicts of interest when dealing with students, give due acknowledgement to students' contributions in publications, and not let personal or professional differences with colleagues affect a student's opportunities of collaboration (AAPA 2003; BABAO 2019b).

Teaching in universities extends from first year undergraduate modules to specialist masters degrees (White et al. 2012, 5). What is appropriate for each level will vary. For introductory first year modules, the learning outcomes of the classes may be perfectly achievable through using plastic model skeletons for many of the activities. If students are simply learning the basic structure of the human skeleton then these will suffice, and it is recommended that where models can reasonably be substituted for real human remains they should be (BABAO 2019a). However, for students that take more specialised undergraduate modules in their second and third years, and certainly for masters students, they will need to see and handle real human remains in order to learn and appreciate the intrinsic variation within the human skeleton (White et al. 2012, 25–27).

University teaching itself takes different forms (Entwistle et al. 2002; Laurillard 2002; Biggs 2011; Henderson et al. 2017; Krahn and Bowlby 2017). Lectures provide the framework of the subject and introduce students to methods and theoretical concepts that they must understand. Seminars and tutorials are student-led, and provide the opportunity for them to present and discuss topics they have researched. Finally, practical work is an essential component when learning about human remains. Practical work can be divided into taught laboratory sessions, and the hours of independent practical study that students are expected to undertake on masters-level courses. It is only through the latter that they can familiarise themselves sufficiently with human remains to become 'masters' in their chosen subject.

Each of these teaching environments has its own particular concerns surrounding the ethical treatment of human remains. However, there are also overarching ethical practices that encompass all forms of teaching, both conscious and subconscious. Each university should have an 'ethics policy' specifically tailored towards human remains that at least should be available on an internal computer network, but ideally should be published on public-facing Departmental web pages (DCMS 2005; Roberts 2009, 100). This document should outline the ways in which any physical remains they curate will be stored, transported, handled, displayed/viewed, and accessed for research. Ideally, it should encompass digital materials, including lecture presentations made available to students, and provide clear guidance on appropriate use of social media in relation to human remains. While general guidelines on the appropriate and inappropriate uses of social media within a university context are emerging, for both staff (Harvard University 2014; Durham University 2019c; University of Western Australia 2017a), and students (Swansea

University 2014; University of Edinburgh 2015; University of Western Australia 2017b), to the authors' knowledge no guidelines specific to human remains within universities yet exist. This is particularly relevant in our age of increased use of social media where students could potentially post images of, and 'selfies' with, human remains since many expect to maintain a constant social media presence. Such an example of taking inappropriate 'selfies' with human remains and posting them on the internet occurred at the University of Wolverhampton (UK) resulting in disciplinary action against the students concerned and potential damage to the University's reputation (Express and Star 2011). The act of taking 'selfies' with human remains in a museum exhibition has already been taken for granted by some visitors and has led to negative comments when they were notified that this behaviour was unethical (Redfern and Clegg 2017). Instances such as these raise the question whether mobile phones should be banned from the laboratory. However, students argue that they benefit from being allowed to take photographs of bones for their own private study, and they will likely need to take photographs of bones for their dissertation research. It would be more beneficial to educate students on acceptable ethical practices relating to photographs and the use of social media. Any ethics policy document also needs to define appropriate and inappropriate behaviour with regards to the handling of, and attitudes towards, human remains (DCMS 2005; White et al. 2012, 358; Roberts 2013). Roberts (2009, 96) makes the important point that retention of collections of human remains "allows for an educational use of the remains in teaching, as long as ethical guidelines are provided to those both teaching and being taught". Staff and students have a duty to comply with these ethical guidelines and departments should review such documents on a regular basis to ensure they are fit for purpose.

Any education on human remains must aim to instil ethical working practices, attitudes, and behaviours within the next generation of bioarchaeologists. To achieve this, lecturers must actively teach students about ethical considerations surrounding human remains, so students learn about what is acceptable and what is not appropriate. Teaching on ethical working practices should begin with the first lecture and first practical session, with explicit instructions concerning what is viewed to be appropriate behaviour and attitudes (DCMS 2005; BABAO 2019a). Students should be required to read their Departmental ethics guidelines and sign a declaration that they have read them. Any consequences for not following these guidelines should be stated clearly. However, in reality, many university archaeology and anthropology departments in the UK and abroad have no ethical guidance policy or only use general ethical guidelines, for example the Codes of Ethics and Practice developed by professional organisations, such as the American Association of Physical Anthropologists (AAPA 2003) and BABAO (2019a, 2019b; Baker 2018, pers. comm. Binder 2018, pers. comm. Newman 2018, pers. comm. Santos 2018, pers. comm.). In addition, even in cases of gross violation of ethics protocols, for example students hiding bones from the teaching collection for their own personal study, in the current 'age of the student', laboratory managers and course directors have little leverage to enforce such codes (Newman 2018, pers. comm.).

Academics also have a duty to ensure their own behaviour and attitudes conform to ethical standards, as students absorb and reflect what is modelled for them by their lecturers. Subconsciously, they will be emulating their lecturers in order to appear 'more academic'. It is important that lecturers pay attention to the language they use when discussing human remains, to avoid objectifying and dehumanising them, even unintentionally. For example, the use of the word 'specimen' is almost ubiquitous, probably derived from the medical literature. No doubt people start using this term to refer to human remains in an attempt to sound objective and scientific, and it becomes assimilated as 'normal'. However, we argue that it is dehumanising to refer to the remains of a once-living person as a 'specimen'. It reduces them to a 'curiosity in a cabinet', something less-than human, and effectively strips them of any rights to ethical treatment that each person should have. Instead, it is recommended that the word 'specimen' is replaced by 'individuals', 'skeletons', 'bones', or 'elements', whichever is appropriate in the circumstances; 'samples' may be appropriate when discussing small parts of a bone or tooth that have been removed for further, frequently destructive, analysis. This type of change in language can feel unnatural when everyone else is using inappropriate terminology in teaching and publications, but once the connotations have been considered the use of the old word should start to jar, and the new terms become accepted; soon the new words will become the new normal, similar to the way that 'humankind' replaced 'mankind' in the 1980s.

To a lesser extent, abbreviations, particularly during spoken and formal written communication, can also contribute towards the dehumanising of skeletal remains. There is a difference between referring to 'the vertebrae' or 'the verts', and the 'tibia and fibula' or the 'tib and fib'; the casualness of the latter implies less respect, and this in turn feeds into an overall attitude that is less respectful towards human remains. However, there is a place for abbreviations of bone names in tables or personal notes, where space or efficiency demands it. Similarly, lecturers should avoid making jokes about human remains as this contributes towards creating a subconscious environment of disrespect. These requirements of behaviour and language should extend to any Ph.D. students working as laboratory demonstrators or tutors. Maintaining a respectful environment and working culture is an ongoing process and the responsibility of all, and students educated in such an environment will likely continue to act and work in the same way.

Equally important to the tone of language used during lectures and practical sessions is the sensitive use of images. Images obviously form a part of lecture slides, but they may also support practical sessions. Sensationalism of pathological conditions through the use of deliberately shocking images should be avoided, and any images relating to living individuals should be appropriately anonymised. Image attribution is also important. Lecturers are typically required by their institutions to make their lecture notes available to students, and students increasingly expect these will take the form of copies of the lecture slides including the images. With the use of the Internet becoming ever more frequent, the risk that copies of lectures end up shared on the web without the awareness or permission of the lecturer increases, especially on slide sharing websites. Ideally, Higher Education Institutions should provide clear guidance for students governing the appropriate use and sharing of lecture slides made available to them. Durham University (2019a, 2019b) has regulations governing the recording of lectures, which includes the explicit statement that such recordings may not be made available to others or published in any form, including on the Internet. However, this regulation is restricted to recordings of lectures and does not extend to other course materials. In contrast, more stringent regulations are in place at the University of California, Berkeley (2012, 19–20), which prohibits the sharing of lecture notes or other course materials for commercial benefit, and provides additional specific guidance concerning the recording or sharing of course notes (University of California, Berkeley 2018): "…class notes and recordings are based on the intellectual effort of the instructor, who has an interest in protecting this effort and ensuring the accuracy of any public representation of his or her work. Prior approval of the instructor is required for the recording of course notes and the sharing of course notes and other class materials beyond the students enrolled in the course". Similar statements have been included in course syllabus at Kennesaw State University (Fig. 9.6; Brown 2018, pers. comm.).

A necessary aspect of student-led seminars should be learning how to present and discuss topics relating to human remains in an ethical manner, thereby practicing using respectful language and creating slides using appropriate images. Lecturers should provide feedback on ethical aspects of presentations, and be

> "Some lecture slides, notes, or exercises used in this course may be the property of the textbook publisher or other third parties. All other course material, including but not limited to slides developed by the instructor(s), the syllabus, assignments, course notes, course recordings (whether audio or video) and examinations or quizzes are the property of the University or of the individual instructor who developed them. Students are free to use this material for study and learning, and for discussion with others, including those who may not be in this class, unless the instructor imposes more stringent requirements. Republishing or redistributing this material, including uploading it to web sites or linking to it through services like iTunes, violates the rights of the copyright holder and is prohibited. There are civil and criminal penalties for copyright violation. **Publishing or redistributing this material in a way that might give others an unfair advantage in this or future courses may subject you to penalties for academic misconduct.**"

Fig. 9.6 Text included in course documents at Kennesaw State University (Georgia, USA) advising students not to share lecture slides or course materials online. Photograph courtesy of Bob Brown (2018)

prepared to correct any inappropriate language or attitudes. This can be done in a constructive manner, as with any other feedback given to students.

Ethical treatment of human remains in practical sessions is equally important. Ideally, any practical work involving human remains should take place in a secure, dedicated laboratory, the purpose of which is clearly signposted (Roberts 2009, 103). A laboratory protocol should exist governing activities and setting out the expected procedures to follow, with the aim of ensuring a professional and respectful working environment. Maintaining order is essential, as it contributes towards the professional environment, but also for the sake of both ethical curation and ease of teaching. If a disarticulated bone or isolated tooth is not returned to its storage location it might then be difficult to find it again, especially when the remains are not labelled (White et al. 2012, 8). Teaching collections are placed under intensive pressure from handling during practical sessions, during independent study, and student research projects, and it is therefore important that adequate resources (time, money, and a dedicated collection curator) are made available to protect and maintain these collections. Research into the impact of handling on a teaching collection demonstrated that those skeletons used most intensively suffered the most damage in terms of both loss of elements and fragmentation of bones, suggesting that monitoring and managing the level of use would help distribute the pressure more evenly (Caffell et al. 2001). Also, this study highlighted the difficulty of establishing the amount of use through time experienced by skeletal collections, and individual skeletons within it, due to a lack of consistent internal documentation of use for teaching and research.

Attention should be paid to the human remains' physical environment to ensure the bones and teeth are as protected as they can be from any damage. Laboratory bench surfaces should be padded with suitable material to minimise damage to fragile bones. Bubble-wrap is a readily available material, but becomes easily damaged and needs to be replaced frequently. Plastazote foam is an alternative, but can become rucked or ripped. A more permanent, but expensive solution may involve purchasing durable, gently-padded bench-toppers which can be wiped clean (Fig. 9.7). An extra layer of bubble-wrap can always be used to help protect particularly fragile bones. Skeletal material made available for students to study in the laboratory should be stored in such a way as to provide ease of access combined with protection for the bones. Bags, boxes, or drawers should be large enough to accommodate the bones even if the material is not packed efficiently, since, despite training, students may be less careful than experienced individuals. Fragile bones in particular should be protected with bubble-wrap or acid-free tissue paper.

Boxes and bags should be clearly labelled, and any packaging material that is no longer fit for purpose as a result of wear-and-tear should be replaced on a regular basis. Bones risk being lost from bags that are ripped or that will not seal properly, and damaged boxes may not adequately protect the bones within. Faded or illegible writing on bags will mean that the provenance of the bone is lost. Monitoring and maintenance/replacement of packaging is an ongoing activity, since it will degrade

Fig. 9.7 Example of dedicated human remains laboratory with durable gently-padded bench toppers installed. These help to protect the bones and can be easily cleaned (Department of Archaeology, Durham University). Photograph by Tina Jakob©

with use. When selecting human remains for laboratory classes there should be a system to keep track of where the material came from so it can be returned to the correct place. This avoids relying on memory alone, and prevents potential confusion later. It is recommended that bones are marked neatly and legibly with site code and skeleton/context number to ensure that if they are misplaced, the bones can be returned once found (Caffell et al. 2001, 195; Janaway et al. 2001, 204). Although this process can be time-consuming, it is particularly important for a teaching collection where many students may be using the collection at the same time; for example, Redfern and Bekvalac (2013) note that collections used for teaching at the Museum of London are marked on a routine basis. However, it is recognised that this practice may not be acceptable to some cultures, and some

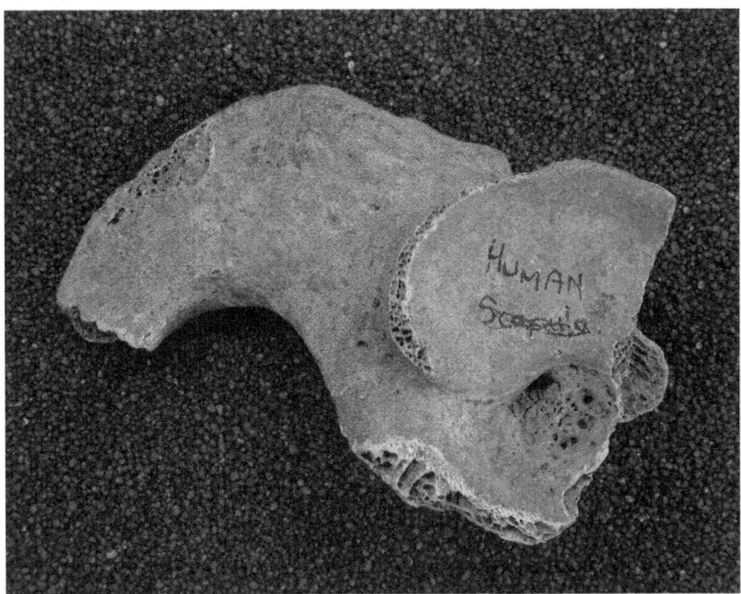

Fig. 9.8 Human ischium inappropriately, and incorrectly, marked as a human scapula. Note that marking on a joint surface is generally not advised as this is an area which frequently needs to be inspected for pathological changes. Photograph by Anwen Caffell©

methods of marking may affect the integrity of the bone (DCMS 2005; BABAO 2019a; see Bonney, Bekvalac and Phillips, this volume). Any other marking of bone surfaces should be avoided. Human remains that have been in teaching collections for a long time may have been drawn or written on inappropriately, whether prior to their inclusion in the teaching collection or during their use as teaching materials (Fig. 9.8), and the advice of a conservator may be required to remove such markings if possible. For example, an individual had used a black ballpoint pen to scratch a pentagram onto the frontal bone of a cranium which meant that whenever it was used during teaching it gave the impression that this was tolerable, to the discomfort of the academic staff. In this instance, a trained conservator was able to remove the marks, thus ensuring the cranium could be used without suggesting such behaviour was acceptable.

Good handling practices for human remains should be actively taught and reinforced through demonstration and leading by example, both on the part of lecturers and laboratory demonstrators. Laboratory coats should be worn in the laboratory when handling human remains (Roberts 2009, 104), and these should be buttoned up to avoid bone fragments being caught on loose clothing, a particular risk with wool garments. Some institutions require the use of gloves when handling human remains, but Roberts (2009, 104) makes the point that direct handling of bones without the barrier created by gloves is essential when learning anatomy: learning to identify bones and bone fragments is a tactile process as well as a visual one. Gloves may be provided should students feel they would like to wear them. Bones should always be handled over padded benches ensuring that if they are dropped it minimises the risk of damage. Careful handling should be encouraged, particularly for fragile bones, such as those from the face, that may be easily broken (Roberts 2009). Students need their attention drawn to good practice, such as ensuring bones are not placed too close to the edges of the bench where they might be knocked off, or the use of skull-rings to prevent crania from rolling away (Roberts 2009). Reconstruction of bones should be avoided unless conducted in consultation with a trained conservator and for a specific justified purpose, since bones can easily become damaged through the use of inappropriate materials such as Blu-Tack™, masking tape, and many household adhesives (Caffell et al. 2001; Roberts 2013). Any such conservation interventions should be documented (BABAO 2019a).

Students should be trained to be aware that they have a responsibility to contribute towards maintaining order and keeping laboratory spaces clean and tidy. If students have been working in private study, then it is their responsibility to return the study material they have been using to the correct place, ensuring it is packed appropriately and protected from damage. Packing of material used during laboratory classes should be monitored, especially in the first laboratory sessions, and students that are packing material inappropriately should be advised accordingly. Some students may struggle with fitting the remains back into the space available as they lack spatial awareness; others may simply be careless. The former may need guidance in how to pack the remains appropriately, while the latter may require educating on the consequences of poor curation practices. Human remains should always be packed with the heavier long bones such as the femora and tibiae at the bottom of the box with lighter, more fragile bones on top (Janaway et al. 2001). Sweeping the bench and checking the contents of the dustpan after use should become a habit, as aside from leaving the laboratory ready for use, this will ensure that any small tooth or bone fragments are not overlooked. Inappropriate behaviour within the laboratory should be corrected in a constructive manner. The aim is to instil in students the necessity of adhering to a code of practice, for example that provided by BABAO (2019a), and to ensure they understand that this becomes their personal responsibility. When students move on to conduct research in other institutions the hope is they will take these practices with them and act in an appropriate manner.

While the use of a dedicated human bone laboratory for teaching is ideal, it is recognised that this may not always be possible in practice. If any teaching on human remains occurs in a non-dedicated laboratory space, then this needs to be made clear with a sign on the door when such teaching is in progress (Fig. 9.9; Durham University 2015). Some form of easily stored padding needs to be placed on the benches for the duration of the class if they are not already padded. If human remains need to be transported from their dedicated storage space, then they must be concealed from view, either in boxes or on padded trays that are covered with a cloth or sheet of bubble-wrap. It is good practice to keep a record of material that is removed from storage for classes elsewhere via a 'sign out' form. This form should

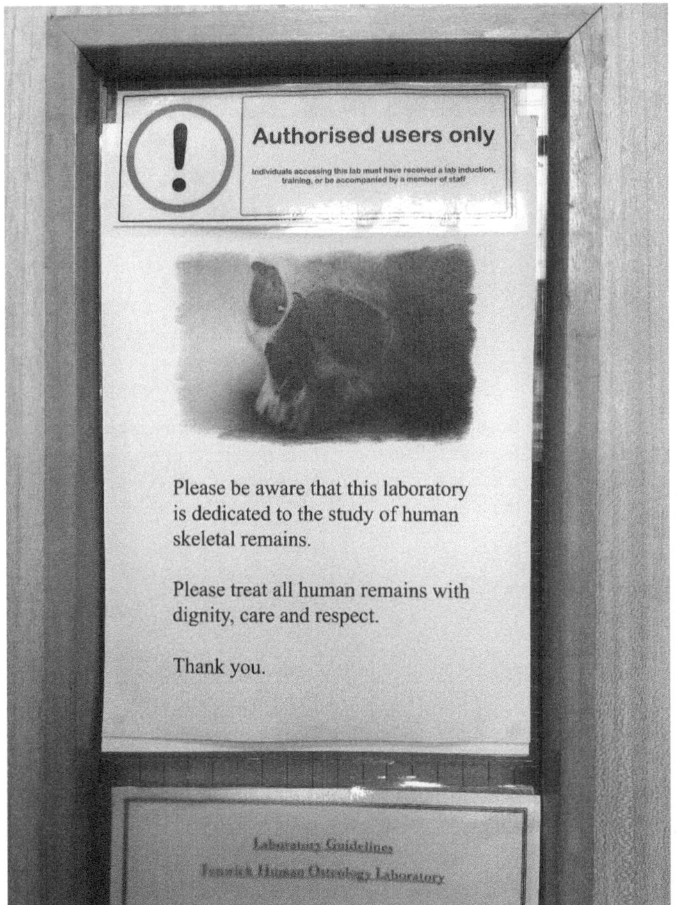

Fig. 9.9 Sign on door used to indicate that the room is used for human remains teaching (Department of Archaeology, Durham University). Photograph by Anwen Caffell©

log the details of the material removed, such as what it is, site code, and skeleton number, as well as who is responsible for the remains, the date it was removed, and eventually returned (Fig. 9.10). These data should be kept to form part of the collection archive (Caffell et al. 2001; Janaway et al. 2001).

It can be argued that any casts of skeletal material and plastic models should also be extended similar ethical treatment to that advocated for human remains. If casts and models were not treated in a similar manner to human remains then this might erode the way in which human remains themselves were treated.

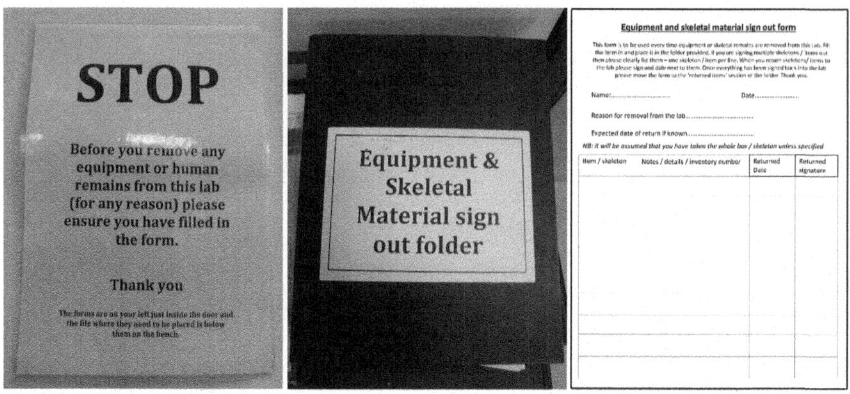

Fig. 9.10 Sign out system in place, with reminders that the sign out forms must be completed before material is removed from the laboratory. These documents provide a record allowing the location of materials to be tracked both currently and retrospectively (Department of Archaeology, Durham University). Photograph by Tina Jakob©

9.7 Research

Aside from teaching, the other main activity associated with human remains curated by universities is research. This may be in the form of internal research conducted by that institution's staff or students, or external research by visiting academics. Regardless of who is conducting the research, any research involving human remains must be of value to modern people in order to justify it (Walker 2000, 13). All researchers have an ethical duty to publish the results of research conducted on human remains, and to communicate their results to the wider public (BABAO 2019b). Managing research access to the collections of human remains curated by universities is an important aspect of curation (BABAO 2019a).

Internal research by students can include studies of skeletal collections for undergraduate or masters dissertations, or for Ph.D. theses. All students, regardless of the level of their studies, need to consider the ethical implications of their research, and complete ethics forms that are reviewed by an ethics panel prior to receiving approval for their research topic. By the time students are ready to think about their dissertations, they should have been taught about ethical issues surrounding human remains. Any students who apply for access to collections curated by other institutions (museums, other universities, and archaeological units) should be supported in their access applications. This will include reviewing any completed access application forms prior to submission to ensure they are completed correctly and with adequate detail, as students will need to learn how to do this. It is likely that this will also involve writing letters of support for the student, to verify that their research is appropriately supervised. Students visiting other institutions should be reminded to uphold the ethical standards of behaviour they have been taught, which by the time they reach their dissertation research should be second nature.

Visiting academics may include academic staff from other institutions, post-doctoral researchers, and students. The latter are typically doctoral students, although some masters students do conduct research outside their home institution; undergraduate students rarely access skeletal collections elsewhere, away from the direct instruction of their supervisors (APABE 2013, 16). It is important that universities curating skeletal remains manage access to these collections (Roberts 2013), and it is therefore recommended that they use an 'access request form' similar to that provided by the Advisory Panel on the Archaeology of Burials in England (APABE 2013, 17) or Roberts (2009, 99) to enable collection managers to determine whether access should be granted. The information requested should include:

- the name and position of the person applying for access, along with their affiliation;
- the name and contact details of the person supervising the work (if a student), or in overall charge of the project (if conducting research for a larger project);
- the title and outline of the research project;
- the purpose of the research, i.e. whether part of a student project (and if so, what level), or whether part of a research project (and if so, details of supporting grant);
- specification of the skeletal collection, and skeletons if applicable, for which access is requested;
- details of any associated documentation for which access is requested;
- details of any equipment for which access is requested; or state whether equipment required is supplied by the researcher;
- details of types of analysis that will be conducted (macroscopic, radiographic, photographic, destructive sampling);
- if the project involves destructive sampling, then further detail must be supplied about what will be sampled, and how;
- how research will be disseminated (whether the data and results will be published, whether the research will form part of public outreach programmes);
- duration of visit and preferred dates;
- a list of conditions to which the applicant agrees to adhere, provided access is granted.

Those managing human skeletal collections have a duty to evaluate all requests in an impartial manner, including such points as whether the applicant has the appropriate credentials/supervision, and whether the proposed research will make a genuine contribution to knowledge, balanced against other proposed research, and existing research that has already been undertaken on that collection. Particular care needs to be paid to access requests that involve destructive sampling, something that is becoming increasingly frequent and which requires careful management (Redfern and Bekvalac 2013; see Squires, Booth and Roberts, this volume). The guidelines prepared by APABE (2013) provide an invaluable resource to aid collection managers in their decisions. Requests should be evaluated by a qualified individual or a panel/committee, which should request clarification on the methods or changes to the research design if necessary (Roberts 2009, 98; Redfern and Bekvalac 2013). The panel must: establish that the research questions are relevant and can only be answered through destructive analysis, consider the impact of destructive sampling on the collection in terms of its future use for teaching and research, and ensure that any proposed destructive sampling adheres to established guidelines (DCMS 2005; BABAO 2019a; APABE 2013). Redfern and Bekvalac (2013) provide an example of how implementing such guidelines works in practice within a museum context. This includes requesting that an adequate record of the remains is made prior to sampling, including detailed photographs that are well-exposed and in focus; that Tyvek™ labels detailing the samples taken are placed in the bag and taped to the inside of the storage box in which the remains are housed, noting the name of the researcher, the sampled element, and date; and that a detailed list of what was sampled be provided. Consideration should be given as to the fate of material such as histological slides, and unused samples or parts of samples. These should be returned to the original institution following completion of the research project, so they can be curated alongside the collection from which they derived (Redfern and Bekvalac 2013; Biers, volume; Bonney, Bekvalac and Phillips, this volume). Copies of any publications arising from the research conducted should be deposited with the institution(s) that manage the skeletal collections used, to form part of the documentary material archived (Redfern and Bekvalac 2013; BABAO 2019a).

9.8 Promotional Activities

Universities need to recruit students for their courses, and prospective students want to find and investigate the courses available, so they can choose the one best suited to their requirements. Consequently, universities must advertise the courses they run, and provide information on their structure and scope. Advertising traditionally takes the form of posters and flyers, but increasingly short videos on social media, such as YouTube, are also used to attract potential students. The printed prospectus has largely been replaced by online webpages as a source of further information. It is important that any form of advertising for courses involving the study of human remains emphasises the educational aspect of the course, and does not sensationalise human remains or promote a 'ghoulish' interest in human remains; the latter should be actively discouraged. The information provided should be factual, and any use of images or film footage should show human remains in a sensitive and respectful manner, promoting their educational purpose. Williams and Atkin (2015) provide a discussion of the appropriate use of digital media in relation to human remains, although this is not specifically aimed at universities.

Open Days are another useful means by which universities can provide information for potential students on the courses they run. These need to be conducted in a similar fashion to laboratory practical sessions. Visitors should be notified of the presence of human remains, and provided with the option of not entering the laboratory space in which they are displayed. Any display of human remains during Open Days must be sensitive and in context, and the person delivering the Open Day material must use appropriate language and behaviour when speaking of, or handling, human remains. Course directors also have an ethical duty to inform students of their job prospects prior to enrolling on a course. However, this is often in direct conflict with the desires of university management to maximise the number of students taking each course. The field of human bioarchaeology is highly competitive and opportunities are limited (Roberts 2009, 222–223): there are few jobs specialising in human osteology in the commercial field and secure long-term academic positions are scarce. Many students will not end up working in their field of study. However, they may end up working in related fields, or find that the skills they learn are transferable to other areas, such as government, commerce, and industry.

9.9 Outreach Activities and Community Archaeology

Public outreach and community engagement are important aspects of the purpose of universities, which have a duty to inform the wider public of academic activities and research findings (Boulton and Lucas 2008), and many authors have stressed the importance of public education related to human bioarchaeology (for example, Hunt 2001; White et al. 2012, 372–373; Boutin et al. 2017). It is an essential part of developing good relationships with communities, and in attracting and maintaining support for research. Dialogue with communities has a positive impact on research outcomes too, as listening to local knowledge and experiences can inform and strengthen research findings. The relationship has the potential to be mutually beneficial. As previously mentioned, within a North American context, Walker (2000, 29–30) detailed the constructive relationship developed with the Chumash Indians of Southern California, which resulted not only in the development of mutually acceptable curation and research practices but that also enriched the scientific research conducted. In the UK, close collaboration with direct descendants of individuals excavated from the graveyard at Fewston, and the local community, enabled the development of the Fewston Assemblage Project. The community secured Heritage Lottery Funding that enabled extensive further research and drove the project forward, allowing the professional organisations involved (JB Archaeology,[1] York Osteoarchaeology,[2] Durham University,[3] and the University of

[1]http://www.jbasarchaeology.co.uk/.

[2]http://www.yorkosteoarch.co.uk/index.php.

[3]https://www.dur.ac.uk/archaeology/.

York[4]) to work alongside volunteers researching their local history. The outcome was much richer for all concerned (Washburn Heritage Centre 2016; Alexander et al. 2017). In contrast, as explored by Sayer (2010), research conducted in a secretive manner, following the removal of human remains and artefacts with little or no explanation, and with no effort to engage with the community affected is damaging for both public and scientific communities. Sayer (2010, 17) advocates "inclusion, openness and accountability" when archaeologists deal with the remains of the dead.

Outreach should also go beyond the involvement of communities in specific archaeological excavations or research projects, and take the form of more general public education (DCMS 2005). The recent creation of the role of 'Outreach Officer' (introduced in September 2017) on the BABAO Board of Trustees attests to the importance this organisation places on developing and supporting public education. The aim is to participate in increased numbers of outreach events, such as the British Science Festival, London Anthropology Day, the Manchester Science Festival, and the York Festival of Ideas, and thereby engage with more people from different backgrounds. By supporting BABAO in these activities, for example through the loan of casts and other teaching materials, universities are indirectly participating in these events.

Within the context of universities, outreach activities may be conducted by university staff or postgraduate students, and both should adhere to standards governing acceptable behaviour and ethical treatment of human remains (as outlined above). It is recommended that what is appropriate for display or handling during an outreach event should be considered, and casts, models, 3D images, and photographs should be used in preference to actual human remains, particularly those taking place away from university premises, unless a case can be made for the contrary (DCMS 2005). Before taking materials for outreach activities, the person organising the activity should check the material is not required for another purpose, for example a taught laboratory session, at the same time. All materials used for outreach should be signed out from the laboratory, and it should be clear who is responsible for that material while it is away from the Department. Care should be taken to transport these items safely and return them promptly, as they may be required for teaching, independent study, or research.

9.10 Conclusion

Teaching the next generation of bioarchaeologists is essential if research into human skeletal remains is to continue. While the latter is frequently cited as a justification for retaining human remains, the former is often neglected or taken for

[4]https://www.york.ac.uk/archaeology/.

granted. If we do not train scholars, then we will have no meaningful research, thereby relinquishing the benefits gained from such research and simultaneously losing support for the curation of human skeletal collections. As outlined in this chapter, it is imperative that students are educated in the theory and practice of the ethics of working with human remains in order that they can conduct research ethically, care for collections appropriately, collaborate with and promote sensitive and open dialogue with communities, and ultimately teach the following generation in their turn. They must be aware of the complex, ever-changing field of ethics and contribute towards its development, actively engaging with public concerns as they evolve.

Acknowledgements We would like to thank the editors for inviting us to contribute to this volume, and for their helpful comments on the text. We are grateful to Nicholas Syrotiuk (Data Research Manager) and Colin Hopkins (Infrastructure Architect, Durham University) for their helpful suggestions regarding long-term digital data curation; Bob Brown, Kennesaw State University, Georgia, USA, for allowing us to include his material on sharing lecture notes and slides; and Steve Robertson (Archaeological Science Technician, Durham University) for drawing our attention to a recent undergraduate dissertation on how storage conditions affect DNA degradation. Brenda Baker (Arizona State University, Tempe, USA), Michaela Binder (Österreichisches Archäologisches Institut und Österreichische Akademie der Wissenschaften, Wien, Österreich), Sophie Newman (University of Sheffield, Sheffield, UK), and Ana Luisa Santos (Universidade de Coimbra, Coimbra, Portugal) are thanked for their discussions on ethical guidelines used in their respective laboratories.

References

Advisory Panel on the Archaeology of Burials in England [APABE]. 2013. *Science and the Dead: A Guideline for the Destructive Sampling of Archaeological Human Remains for Scientific Analysis*. Swindon: English Heritage.

Alexander, M., J. Austick, J. Buglass, et al. 2017. *The Fewston Assemblage: Churchyard Secrets Revealed*. Washburn: Washburn Heritage Centre.

American Association of Physical Anthropologists [AAPA]. 2003. *Code of Ethics of the American Association of Physical Anthropologists*. http://physanth.org/about/position-statements/aapa-code-ethics-sexual-harrassment/. Accessed 28 June 2018.

Anthronomics. 2018. *Dactyl*. http://anthronomics.com/. Accessed 20 July 2018.

Archaeology Data Service. 2015. *Guidelines for Depositors*. http://archaeologydataservice.ac.uk/advice/guidelinesForDepositors.xhtml. Accessed 13 June 2018.

Beck, L., and L. Teague. 2001. Reburial Laws in Action: Case Studies from Arizona. In *Human Remains: Conservation, Retrieval and Analysis. Proceedings of a Conference Held in Williamsburg, VA, Nov 7–11th 1999*, ed. E. Williams, 5–10. Oxford: Archaeopress.

Biggs, J.B. 2011. *Teaching for Quality Learning at University: What the Student Does*. Maidenhead: McGraw-Hill Education.

Bone Clones Inc. 2018. *Osteological Reproductions*. https://boneclones.com/. Accessed 13 June 2018.

Boulton, G., and C. Lucas. 2008. *What Are Universities For?* Amsterdam: Leuven League of European Research Universities.

Boutin, A.T., M. Long, R.A. Dinarte, et al. 2017. Building a Better Bioarchaeology Through Community Collaboration. *Bioarchaeology International* 1 (3–4): 191–204.

Brickley, M. 2004. Compiling a Skeletal Inventory: Articulated Inhumed Bone. In *Guidelines to the Standards for Recording Human Remains.* IFA Paper No. 7, ed. M. Brickley and J.I. McKinley, 6–7. Southampton and Reading: BABAO and IFA.

Brickley, M. 2017. Compiling a Skeletal Inventory: Articulated Inhumed Bone. In *Updated Guidelines to the Standards for Recording Human Remains*, ed. P.D. Mitchell and M. Brickley, 7–9. Reading: CIfA.

British Association for Biological Anthropology and Osteoarchaeology [BABAO]. 2019a. *Code of Practice.* https://www.babao.org.uk/assets/Uploads/BABAO-Code-of-Practice-2019.pdf. Accessed 3 October 2019.

British Association for Biological Anthropology and Osteoarchaeology [BABAO]. 2019b. *Code of Ethics.* https://www.babao.org.uk/assets/Uploads/BABAO-Code-of-Ethics-2019.pdf. Accessed 3 October 2019.

Buikstra, J.E., and C.C. Gordon. 1981. The Study and Restudy of Human Skeletal Series: The Importance of Long-Term Curation. *Annals of the New York Academy of Sciences* 376: 449–465.

Byrne, D. 2003. The Ethos of Return: Erasure and Reinstatement of Aboriginal Visibility in the Australian Historical Landscape. *Historical Archaeology* 37 (1): 73–86.

Caffell, A., and M. Holst. 2017. *Osteological Analysis: The Church of St. Michael and St. Lawrence, Fewston, North Yorkshire.* Unpublished Osteological Report 1017. York: York Osteoarchaeology.

Caffell, A., C. Roberts, R. Janaway, et al. 2001. Pressures on Osteological Collections—The Importance of Damage Limitation. In *Human Remains: Conservation, Retrieval and Analysis. Proceedings of a Conference held in Williamsburg, VA, Nov 7–11th 1999*, ed. E. Williams, 187–198. Oxford: Archaeopress.

Currie, D., and K. McBride. 2001. Respect for the Ancestors: New Approaches for the Recovery and Analysis of Native American Burials. In *Human Remains: Conservation, Retrieval and Analysis. Proceedings of a Conference Held in Williamsburg, VA, Nov 7–11th 1999*, ed. E. Williams, 61–68. Oxford: Archaeopress.

Department for Culture, Media and Sport [DCMS]. 2005. *Guidance for the Care of Human Remains in Museums.* London: Department for Culture, Media and Sport.

DeWitte, S.N. 2015. Bioarchaeology and the Ethics of Research Using Human Skeletal Remains. *History Compass* 13 (1): 10–19.

Digitised Diseases. n.d. *Digitised Diseases.* http://www.digitiseddiseases.org. Accessed 16 June 2018.

Durham University. 2015. *Department of Archaeology Ethical Policy.* https://www.dur.ac.uk/archaeology/aboutus/ethics/. Accessed 28 June 2018.

Durham University. 2019a. *Encore Lecture Capture Technology Guidance for Students.* https://www.dur.ac.uk/encore/guidanceforstudents/. Accessed 3 October 2019

Durham University. 2019b. *Department of Archaeology Undergraduate Handbook 2019-2020.* Unpublished.

Durham University. 2019c. *Personal Internet Presence and the Use of Social Media.* https://www.dur.ac.uk/resources/hr/policies/PersonalInternetPresenceandtheuseofSocialMediaV2.0.pdf. Accessed 3 October 2019.

Entwistle, N., V. McCune, and J. Hounsell. 2002. Approaches to Studying and Perceptions of University Teaching-Learning Environments: Concepts, Measures and Preliminary Findings. *Occasional Report* 1: 1–19.

Errickson, D., and T. Thompson (eds.). 2017. *Human Remains: Another Dimension. The Application of Imaging to the Study of Human Remains*. London: Academic Press.

Errickson, D., I. Grueso, S.J. Griffith, et al. 2017. Towards a Best Practice for the Use of Active Non-contact Surface Scanning to Record Human Skeletal Remains from Archaeological Contexts. *International Journal of Osteoarchaeology* 27: 650–661.

Express and Star. 2011. *University Students in Skull Prank.* https://www.expressandstar.com/news/2011/03/30/university-students-in-skull-prank/. Accessed 14 June 2018.

Fiorato, V., A. Boylston, and C. Knüsel (eds.). 2000. *Blood Red Roses: The Archaeology of a Mass Grave from the Battle of Towton AD 1461*. Oxford: Oxbow Books.
France Casting. 2015. http://www.francecasts.com/. Accessed 13 June 2018.
France Casting. 2017. http://www.francecasts.com/casts/humans/pathology_and_anomolies/. Accessed 3 October 2019.
Gerrard, C., P. Graves, A. Millard, et al. 2018. *Lost Lives, New Voices: Unlocking the Stories of the Scottish Soldiers at the Battle of Dunbar 1650*. Oxford: Oxbow Books.
Giesen, M. 2013. Introduction: Human Remains Curation in the United Kingdom. In *Curating Human Remains: Caring for the Dead in the United Kingdom*, ed. M. Giesen, 1–11. Woodbridge: The Boydell Press.
Giesen, M., K. McCarrison, and V. Park. 2013. Dead and Forgotten? Some Observations on Human Remains Documentation in the UK. In *Curating Human Remains: Caring for the Dead in the United Kingdom*, ed. M. Giesen, 53–64. Woodbridge: The Boydell Press.
Giesen, M., and L. White. 2013. International Perspectives Towards Human Remains Curation. In *Curating Human Remains: Caring for the Dead in the United Kingdom*, ed. M. Giesen, 13–23. Woodbridge: The Boydell Press.
Gilchrist, R., and B. Sloane. 2005. *Requiem: The Medieval Monastic Cemetery in Britain*. London: Museum of London Archaeology Service.
Gilmore, H., C. Schafer, and S. Halcrow. 2013. Tapu and the Invention of the "Death Taboo": An Analysis of the Transformation of a Polynesian Cultural Concept. *Journal of Social Archaeology* 13 (3): 331–349.
Gowland, R.L., A. Caffell, M. Alexander, et al. 2017. Indentured: Bioarchaeological Evidence for Pauper Apprentices in Nineteenth Century Yorkshire, England. In *Abstracts of the 86th Annual Meeting of the American Association of Physical Anthropologists, New Orleans, Louisiana, USA, 19–22 April 2017.*
Gowland, R.L., A. Caffell, S. Newman, et al. 2018. Broken Childhoods: Rural and Urban Non-adult Health During the Industrial Revolution in Northern England (Eighteenth–Nineteenth Centuries). *Bioarchaeology International* 2 (1): 44–62.
Grauer, A. (ed.). 1995. *Bodies of Evidence: Reconstructing History Through Skeletal Analysis*. New York: Wiley-Liss.
Harvard University. 2014. *Guidelines for Using Social Media*. http://hwpi.harvard.edu/files/provost/files/social_media_guidelines_vers_2_0_eff_081814.pdf. Accessed 29 June 2018.
Henderson, M., N. Selwyn, and R. Aston. 2017. What Works and Why? Student Perceptions of 'Useful' Digital Technology in University Teaching and Learning. *Studies in Higher Education* 42 (8): 1567–1579.
Holst, M.R. 2005. *Fishergate House Artefacts and Environmental Evidence: The Human Bone*. Archaeological Planning Consultancy Ltd. Unpublished Manuscript on File in the Fenwick Human Bone Laboratory. Durham: Department of Archaeology, Durham University.
Hunt, D.R. 2001. The Value of Human Remains for Research and Education. In *Human Remains: Conservation, Retrieval and Analysis. Proceedings of a Conference Held in Williamsburg, VA, Nov 7–11th 1999*, ed. E. Williams, 129–134. Oxford: Archaeopress.
İşcan, M.Y., and M. Steyn. 2013. *The Human Skeleton in Forensic Medicine*, 3rd ed. Springfield: CC Thomas.
Janaway, R., A. Wilson, A. Caffell, et al. 2001. Human Skeletal Collections: The Responsibilities of Project Managers, Physical Anthropologists, Conservators and the Need for Standardized Condition Assessments. In *Human Remains: Conservation, Retrieval and Analysis. Proceedings of a Conference Held in Williamsburg, VA, Nov 7–11th 1999*, ed. E. Williams, 199–208. Oxford: Archaeopress.
Krahn, H., and J.W. Bowlby. 2017. Good Teaching and Satisfied University Graduates. *Canadian Journal of Higher Education* 27 (2/3): 157–179.
Larsen, C.S. 2002. Bioarchaeology: The Lives and Lifestyles of Past People. *Journal of Archaeological Research* 10 (2): 119–166.
Laurillard, D. 2002. *Rethinking University Teaching: A Conversational Framework for the Effective use of Learning Technologies*. Abingdon: Routledge.

Lee, F., and J. Magilton. 2008. Discussion. In *'Lepers Outside the Gate': Excavations at the Cemetery of the Hospital of St James and St Mary Magdalene, Chichester, 1986–87 and 1993.* Chichester Excavations 10, CBA Research Report 158, ed. J. Magilton, F. Lee and A. Boylston, 263–269. York: Council for British Archaeology.

Magilton, J., F. Lee, and A. Boylston (eds.). 2008. *'Lepers Outside the Gate': Excavations at the Cemetery of the Hospital of St James and St Mary Magdalene, Chichester, 1986–87 and 1993.* Chichester Excavations 10, CBA Research Report 158. York: Council for British Archaeology.

Márquez-Grant, N., and L. Fibiger (eds.). 2011. *The Routledge Handbook of Archaeological Human Remains and Legislation: An International Guide to Laws and Practice in the Excavation and Treatment of Human Remains.* Abingdon: Routledge.

Mayes, A. 2010. Shades of Gray: Skeletal Analysis and the Repatriation Process. *American Indian Culture and Research Journal* 34 (1): 25–39.

Mayne Correia, P.M. 1997. Fire Modification of Bone: A Review of the Literature. In *Forensic Taphonomy: The Postmortem Fate of Human Remains*, ed. W.D. Haglund and M.H. Sorg, 275–293. Boca Raton: CRC Press.

Mays, S., M. Brickley, and N. Dodwell. 2004. *Human Bones from Archaeological Sites: Guidelines for Producing Assessment Documents and Analytical Reports*. English Heritage, Swindon: Centre for Archaeology Guidelines.

McKinley, J.I. 2000. The Analysis of Cremated Bone. In *Human Osteology in Archaeology and Forensic Science*, ed. M. Cox and S. Mays, 403–421. Cambridge: Cambridge University Press.

McKinley, J.I. 2004. Compiling Skeletal Inventory: Disarticulated and Co-mingled Remains. In *Guidelines to the Standards for Recording Human Remains*, IFA Paper No. 7, ed. M. Brickley and J.I. McKinley, 14–17. Southampton and Reading: BABAO and IFA.

McKinley J.I., and M. Smith. 2017. Compiling a Skeletal Inventory: Disarticulated and Co-Mingled Remains. In *Updated Guidelines to the Standards for Recording Human Remains*, ed. P.D. Mitchell and M. Brickley, 20–24. Reading: CIfA.

Paleopathology Association. n.d. https://paleopathology-association.wildapricot.org/. Accessed 13 June 2018.

Parker Pearson, M., M. Pitts, and D. Sayer. 2013. Changes in Policy for Excavating Human Remains in England and Wales. In *Curating Human Remains: Caring for the Dead in the United Kingdom*, ed. M. Giesen, 147–157. Woodbridge: The Boydell Press.

Proctor, J., M. Gaimster, and J.Y. Langthorne. 2016. *A Quaker Burial Ground at North Shields: Excavations at Coach Lane, Tyne and Wear*. Oxford: Oxbow Books.

Ray, K. 1999. From Remote Times to the Bronze Age: c. 500,000 BC to c. 600 BC. In *Death in England: An Illustrated History*, ed. P.C. Jupp and C. Gittings, 11–39. Manchester: Manchester University Press.

Redfern, R., and J. Bekvalac. 2013. The Museum of London: An Overview of Policies and Practice. In *Curating Human Remains: Caring for the Dead in the United Kingdom*, ed. M. Giesen, 87–98. Woodbridge: The Boydell Press.

Redfern, R., and M. Clegg. 2017. Archaeologically Derived Human Remains in England: Legacy and Future. *World Archaeology* 49: 1–14.

Roberts, C.A. 2009. *Human Remains in Archaeology: A Handbook*. York: Council for British Archaeology.

Roberts, C. 2013. Archaeological Human Remains and Laboratories: Attaining Acceptable Standards for Curating Skeletal Remains for Teaching and Research. In *Curating Human Remains: Caring for the Dead in the United Kingdom*, ed. M. Giesen, 123–134. Woodbridge: The Boydell Press.

Sayer, D. 2010. *Ethics and Burial Archaeology*. London: Duckworth.

Sayer, D. 2011. The Organization of Post-Medieval Churchyards, Cemeteries and Grave Plots: Variation and Religious Identify as Seen in Protestant Burial Grounds. In *The Archaeology of Post-Medieval Religion*, ed. C. King and D. Sayer, 199–214. Woodbridge: The Society for Church Archaeology and The Society for Post-Medieval Archaeology.

Simpson, J. 2017. *DNA Degradation: A Study of Environmental Factors Contributing to the Decay of DNA Within Bone*. Dissertation, Durham University.

Society for American Archaeology [SAA]. 1984. Resolution. *American Antiquity* 49: 215–216.

Swain, H. 2013. Dealings with the Dead: A Personal Consideration of the Ongoing Human Remains Debate. In *Curating Human Remains: Caring for the Dead in the United Kingdom*, ed. M. Giesen, 25–29. Woodbridge: The Boydell Press.

Swansea University. 2014. *Social Media Guidelines for Students*. https://www.swansea.ac.uk/media/Social%20media%20guidelines%20April%2014.pdf/. Accessed 29 June 2018.

UK Data Service. 2018. *Data Storage*. https://www.ukdataservice.ac.uk/manage-data/store/storage. Accessed 13 June 2018.

University of California, Berkeley. 2012. *Berkeley Campus Code of Student Conduct*. http://sa.berkeley.edu/sites/default/files/UCB-Code-of-Conduct-new%20Jan2012.pdf. Accessed 22 June 2018.

University of California, Berkeley. 2018. *Berkeley Academic Guide 2018–19: Classroom Note-Taking and Recording Policy*. http://guide.berkeley.edu/academic-policies/#otherpoliciestext. Accessed 22 June 2018.

University of Edinburgh. 2015. *Social Media Guidance for Students*. https://www.ed.ac.uk/website-programme/training-support/guidelines/social-media. Accessed 29 June 2018.

University of Western Australia. 2017a. *University Policy on Social Media*. http://www.hr.uwa.edu.au/policies/policies/conduct/social-media. Accessed 29 June 2018.

University of Western Australia. 2017b. *Social Media Guidelines*. http://www.student.uwa.edu.au/learning/it/social-media-guidelines. Accessed 29 June 2018.

Wahl, J. 1982. Leichenbranduntersuchungen. Ein Überblick über die Bearbeitungs-und Aussagemöglichkeiten von Brandgräben. *Prähistorische Zeitschrift* 57: 2–125.

Walker, P.L. 2000. Bioarcheological Ethics: A Historical Perspective on the Value of Human Remains. In *Biological Anthropology of the Human Skeleton*, ed. M.A. Katzenberg and S.R. Saunders, 3–39. New York: Wiley-Liss.

Washburn Heritage Centre. 2016. *Churchyard Secrets*. http://www.washburnvalley.org/churchyard-secrets. Accessed 13 June 2018.

Westaway, M., and A. Burns. 2001. Investigation, Documentation and Repatriation of Aboriginal Skeletal Remains: Case Studies from the Goolum Goolum Aboriginal Co-operative Community Boundary, Victoria, Australia. In *Human Remains: Conservation, Retrieval and Analysis. Proceedings of a Conference held in Williamsburg, VA, Nov 7–11th 1999*, ed. E. Williams, 1–4. Oxford: Archaeopress.

White, T.D., M.T. Black, and P.A. Folkens. 2012. *Human Osteology*, 3rd ed. Amsterdam: Academic Press.

Williams, H., and A. Atkin. 2015. Virtually Dead: Digital Public Mortuary Archaeology. *Internet Archaeology* 40. doi: https://doi.org/10.11141/ia.40.7.4.

Wilson, A.S., A.D. Holland, and T. Sparrow. 2017. Laser Scanning of Skeletal Pathological Conditions. In *Human Remains: Another Dimension. The Application of Imaging to the Study of Human Remains*, ed. D. Errickson and T. Thompson, 123–134. London: Academic Press.

Chapter 10
Human Remains in Museum Collections in the United Kingdom

Heather Bonney, Jelena Bekvalac and Carina Phillips

Abstract Human remains collections can be found in museums, university departments, and even private collections across the UK. These collections pose many ethical challenges in their management and care, many unique to human remains, which can differ according to the type of holding institution, nature of the collection, and the way in which it is used or studied. These collections are often associated with legacies of poor ethical standards, particularly in terms of early collecting practices. This chapter will explore these factors and the challenges they pose. In the modern context of fluid socio-political and cultural change, museums and other holding institutions are faced with ever-changing external influences and must be able to respond in a dynamic and transparent way. This chapter will also discuss the ethical care and curation of human remains collections in UK museums and other repositories, with a focus on collections acquired and/or curated in England where reference to legislation concerning the care and management of collections is required. Finally, it will explore the concept of harm to communities, public and to science, that can be caused by a lack of transparency and poor decision and policy making with regard to human remains collections.

10.1 Introduction

Human remains hold a unique status within UK museum collections, which places particular responsibility on those who care for them. The reasons for this are numerous and complex. This chapter will examine the nature and ethical impli-

H. Bonney (✉)
Natural History Museum, Cromwell Road, London SW7 5BD, UK
e-mail: h.bonney@nhm.ac.uk

J. Bekvalac
Centre for Human Bioarchaeology, Museum of London, 150 London Wall, London EC2Y 5HN, UK

C. Phillips
Royal College of Surgeons of England, 35-43 Lincoln's Inn Fields, London WC2A 3PE, UK

K. Squires et al. (eds.), *Ethical Approaches to Human Remains*,
https://doi.org/10.1007/978-3-030-32926-6_10

cations of different types of human remains collection, and the types of institution that may hold them. It will also discuss relevant legislation and guidance and how this applies to the different activities that may involve collections of human material.

10.2 Types of Human Remains Collections

Human remains collections can be diverse in origin and nature. They include anatomical and biomedical collections, originating from or held in medical schools and research institutions, archaeological collections from excavations in the UK and further afield, and others are made up of remains collected world-wide during exploration and the colonial era, which may also include artefacts or objects partly or wholly comprising human material. Some collections may include all of these, such as those at the Royal College of Surgeons (RCS) of England and the Natural History Museum, both located in London. Each type of collection presents its own challenges and considerations in terms of its management and the ethical considerations can differ widely.

10.2.1 Medical Collections

Medical collections comprise of specimens of human tissue collected by medical staff or medical institutions to aid teaching and research in the anatomy, physiology, and pathology of the human body. They sometimes also include comparative specimens of animal tissue and objects relating to medical treatment. Anatomical collections comprise of parts of a human body, which have been prepared and preserved to demonstrate specific structures within the body, such as hands that have been prosected to demonstrate the tendons. Whereas pathology specimens are those which have been preserved and prepared because they are 'abnormal' and differ from the expected structure. These can include examples of trauma and developmental malformations, as well as disease. Historically, these types of specimens were described as 'morbid anatomy', e.g. Matthew Baillie, a pioneer in systematic pathology (Ellis 2011), entitled his important work "The Morbid Anatomy of the Most Important Parts of the Human Body in 1793" (Baillie 1793). Perhaps because of the use of 'morbid anatomy', the term 'anatomical collections' is sometimes used interchangeably with medical collections, and can misleadingly include pathology collections. Both anatomical and pathological collections can include skeletal material and preserved soft tissue, either dried or preserved in fluid. Some institutions also care for histological specimens, comprising of smaller specimens or samples of human tissue, which may have been prepared and mounted onto microscope slides, or stored as blocks of tissue preserved in wax. These micro-specimens are found in various medical institutions, including universities and museums, and are often associated with the larger (macroscopic) pathology specimen from which they may have been removed and retained to support teaching of pathological diagnosis.

Medical collections have a long history. Advances in fluid preservation techniques in the seventeenth century together with an increase in the dissection of human bodies in the eighteenth century, enabled individuals to create large medical specimen collections to support study and research (Alberti 2011; Mitchell et al. 2011). Today, surviving historical collections tend to be used for public display more often than in medical teaching, although larger historical collections are often still associated with medical institutions or universities (e.g. John Hunter's collection, displayed in the Hunterian Museum at the Royal College of Surgeons in London, UK).

Up until the mid-twentieth century, curators of museums were still actively adding to anatomical and pathological collections. Many medical institutions had dedicated staff preparing and preserving new specimens whilst a number of companies in the UK, such as Adam Rouilly, sold human skeletons as anatomical teaching aids. The preparation of new anatomical specimens has decreased in volume; however, they do continue to be prepared for the support of anatomical teaching alongside already developed collections. Many anatomy departments have collections of bones and specimens preserved in fluid, which they use in conjunction with cadavers to teach anatomy. Individuals donating their body to medical education have the option to consent to parts of their body being retained indefinitely. A small number of medical schools have museums which act as study and teaching spaces, though these are only open to medical and health trainees and professionals, e.g. the Anatomy and Pathology Museum at the RCS (London) and the Gordon Pathology Museum at King's College London. As many of the specimens in these collections are less than 100 years old they fall within the scope of the Human Tissue Act (2004) (see Sect. 10.4.1 for further details).

Both historical and modern medical collections can include named individuals (e.g. the Hunterian Museum at the RCS). Historical collectors and medics such as John Hunter, may have recorded the patient name in their notes alongside specimen information. For named individuals that died over 100 years ago, the same ethical considerations as described for archaeological remains (see Sect. 10.2.2 below) should take place. Ethical consideration surrounding the public display of these remains is also important and is discussed further in Sect. 10.7 of this chapter. More recent collections may have records, which provide details of the individual, the tissue itself, e.g. records associated with pathological tissue, or records of consent from a donor. For individuals whose date of death is within the last 100 years, all associated patient data should be held securely and confidentially in accordance with the Human Tissue Act (2004).

Public museums holding medical collections are often managed by individuals with experience of working with human remains in a museum setting and should be familiar with museum collections standards (see Sect. 10.5 below). In contrast, collections housed within medical institutions are regularly cared for by a single medical or health professional, who take on the responsibility in addition to their primary role. In some instances, a 'collection' could comprise of a single skeleton or several disarticulated teaching skeletons. However, they often include fluid preserved specimens, which require specialist conservation/maintenance (Moore 1999; Simmons 2014). It can be a challenge for individuals in this situation to know how best to care for these collections with limited resources. Section 10.5 of this chapter should act as a guide for documentation standards. However, it is also advised to contact individuals working at museums that hold similar collections for advice.

10.2.2 Archaeological Collections

Here we refer to archaeological collections as those that have been excavated/exhumed in a controlled or uncontrolled (such as unexpected discovery during building works) manner either within the UK or elsewhere. The dates of excavation/exhumation usually vary from the nineteenth century up to the present day, and the records and documentation associated with such collections vary accordingly in terms of their detail and scope. The date of the remains themselves range from thousands of years BP through to the twentieth century. These collections are largely osteological, although some do contain individuals with preserved soft tissue, particularly those which have come from post-medieval crypt contexts. In some ways, these collections are less ethically complex than the other types of collection discussed in this chapter, as the circumstances of their collection/excavation are generally known, many are from within the UK so those caring for them are more familiar with the legal background, and the public have become accustomed to the excavation of historic burials and reasons for doing so through popular programming, such as Time Team, or news coverage of large cemetery excavations, for example those being excavated as part of the Crossrail project. It should be considered that for the most part, none of the individuals in these collections will have given consent for their exhumation or for their remains to be retained in a collection. Some archaeological collections may comprise of named or identified individuals, which raise particular ethical considerations with regards to their care and access. These concerns will be addressed in the following section.

10.2.3 Named Individuals

Akin to medical collections (see above), there are archaeologically derived collections of curated human skeletal remains in museums and universities where the identity of individuals is known from the presence of associated biographical information. These details are predominantly revealed by coffin (depositum) plates from the burial and most typically occur in post-medieval period burials. Coffin plates are an invaluable source as they provide the means to identify specific details about the associated individual, including their name, dates of birth and death, and age at death. However, the legibility of coffin plates does vary in accordance with their condition, which is dependent upon a number of factors, including type of metal used and the burial environment, which can affect the clarity and ability to read all of the details (Cowie et al. 2008; Miles et al. 2008; Henderson et al. 2013). Yet for the majority of archaeological human skeletal remains there is no associated evidence that provides biographical information. Thus, it is not possible to know the names of all individuals recovered from exhumations.

Skeletal collections, where such biographical information is available for individuals, are generally referred to as 'Identified Skeletal Collections' or 'Known/Named Individuals' (Henderson and Cardoso 2018). Two of the most well-known identified skeletal collections in the UK are those from Christ Church Spitalfields (London) and St Bride's Church (Fleet Street, London). There are also a number of identified collections from overseas with significant collections in the USA and South Africa, and the important European collection from Coimbra in Portugal (see Cardoso, this volume). When biographical details are present, they provide a means for accessing and investigating documentary sources with a more personal focus for learning about the named individual. Documentary information, including Parish registers, registers of birth and death, marriage, death certificates, trade directories, tax returns, and wills, ultimately provide a personal insight into their life. This enables researchers to build a fuller picture of their life history, as well as potentially identifying friends and associates, family connections, and constructing their family trees. When details of marital status are recorded, it is possible to extrapolate information about the ages, and patterns, of marriage amongst males and females. Evidence pertaining to their offspring gives valuable details of child birth, numbers of births, and infant mortality. A number of the Parish records include information about the place where a person was living at the time of their death. These addresses allow researchers to locate their domicile and business residences. Consequently, individuals can then be marked on historical maps of the respective time period, placing them in a geographical context. Occupations and businesses are more typically listed for males, and with some occupations this enables further research using Trade Directories, which were generally comprised annually as a list of the trade/occupation of individuals with an associated address and records of Guilds (also known as Livery Companies). The Guilds were comprised of skilled craftsmen, such as carpenters, bakers, and weavers, who formed trade associations as collective members of the same trade establishing a means for the public to have assurance that they were fully qualified in their trade (Palfreyman 2010). Multiple listings of occupations for an individual provide another way of learning about their individual life course, their place in society, contribution to business and community, and the commercial landscape over time, which may have warranted the need for an alternative occupation. If an individual changed their occupation a number of times, it is valuable having the knowledge of the time period in which this happened as it allows the researcher to check key dates against historical events such as warfare, social, and political upheaval that could have caused a person's circumstances to change. As with so many aspects of archaeological and historical research, these documentary sources are singularly valuable resources but do have limitations, particularly biases and imperfections, such as variance and errors in spellings (of names), they are not always complete, and volumes may be damaged due to the path of time. Therefore, each of these shortcomings should be considered when using these resources in research.

Within the extensive archaeological collections of human skeletal remains curated by the Centre for Human Bioarchaeology (CHB) at the Museum of London there are a small number of excavated cemetery sites, which have known named individuals. Apart from one medieval (fourteenth century) individual from the excavation of St Mary Graces as part of the Royal Mint Excavations (MIN86) in London, in close proximity to the Tower of London, the other individuals are all within the post medieval period from the eighteenth and nineteenth century. The five post-medieval London sites currently curated with known named individuals include Bow Baptists, Bethnal Green, Chelsea Old Church, St Benet Sherehog/No 1 Poultry, and St Marylebone Church, all of which were associated with coffin plates which displayed biographical information, but these only make up a small percentage (3%) of the c. 20,000 skeletal remains curated. Research based upon them has produced fascinating insights into the individuals lives and life stories as well as providing a more nuanced understanding of the times and places in which they lived and worked (Cowie et al. 2008; Miles et al. 2008; Henderson et al. 2013).

The CHB also assists St Bride's Church (Fleet Street, London) with curation and research access to the important identified skeletal collection of 227 individuals retained in the church. The individuals were found when the crypts, which had been sealed in 1853, were rediscovered while the church was being archaeologically excavated by Professor Grimes after it had been bombed in World War II, causing devastating destruction to the church building but remarkably not the iconic spire (Redpath 1959; Morgan 1973). The skeletal remains of the individuals retained in the St Bride's crypt are not all of the individuals that would have been interred in the crypt space, and only belong to those individuals who were found to be skeletal upon discovery in the 1950s; those with any surviving soft tissue that were deemed to be well-preserved were reburied within a vault within the precinct of the church (Morgan 1973; Milne 1997). The decision to retain the skeletal remains of the aforementioned individuals at a time when the field of osteoarchaeology did not exist, was forward thinking in that these archaeologists were aware of the significance of these individuals and the information that could be gleaned from them in the future.

Funding in the 1980s from The Leverhulme Trust enabled the skeletal remains to be re-boxed, catalogued, and analysed, which subsequently produced valuable paper-based records of the individuals, and publications highlighting the intrinsic significance of the collection (Scheuer and Bowman 1994; Scheuer 1998). With funding from the Society of Antiquaries and City of London Archaeological Trust (CoLAT), these skeletal remains were analysed and recorded on to the Wellcome Osteological Research Database, an Oracle platform database which was created by Brian Connell and Dr Peter Rauxloh. The database is a bespoke osteological database in response to the extensive number of skeletal remains excavated from the St Mary Spital site (1998–2001) and allows users to record and capture the vast amount of information for the skeletal remains from this, and previous, excavations (Connell and Rauxloh 2003). All of the skeletal remains from this site were analysed and recorded following standard osteological methods and guidelines (Buikstra and Ubelaker 1994; Brickley and McKinley 2004). The St Bride's crypt individuals were also recorded on the database. This was a valuable addition as it enabled a direct comparison with the records for the individuals excavated from St Bride's Lower Churchyard in the 1990's which formed part of the curated collections at the Museum of London. The St Bride's collection has been accessed for research over the years for non-metrics (Berry and Berry 1967), forensics (Gapert et al. 2009a, 2009b), the application of digital radiography (Bekvalac 2012), and a case study on one of the male individuals with a severe form of kyphoscoliosis for the Index of Care (Conlogue et al. 2016). Since 2008, the CHB has assisted St Bride's Church with requests for research access to the collection to ensure that research proposals are justified and methodologically sound. There has been a steady increase in studies on the collection for masters and PhD research within a variety of fields, including health, metrics, and environmental impact, producing interesting resultant data and research publications (van Schaik et al. 2017).

The skeletal remains in the St Bride's crypt collection are contemporary to the world-renowned Christ Church Spitalfields identified collection, curated at the Natural History Museum, London. These are significant research collections that have been key to several studies within the field of forensics, patterns of health and growth, and development (Humphrey 1998; King et al. 2005). When the excavation of the crypt took place at the end of the 1990s, the archaeological processes employed were unique and the resultant data produced ground breaking publications in style and approach as they conveyed details of the lives of this particular group of individuals (Molleson et al. 1993; Reeve and Adams 1993; Cox 1996).

Named individuals within an archaeological collection has raised discussions within the museums and institutions curating such identified individuals about whether they should be treated in a different manner to those where such details are not known (e.g. at the Curating Human Remains in the UK Conference; Royal Albert Memorial Museum and Art Gallery 2016). From a curatorial perspective of overall care, the treatment of all curated human remains would be the same, and appropriate practices followed to retain them with respect and dignity (DCMS 2005; Giesen 2013; APABE 2017). Particular consideration should be given to the display of these individuals as part of an exhibition, and of the potential for descendants to become aware of the remains of ancestors curated in an institution through the process of a public display. Interestingly, this occurred during the Wellcome Skeletons: London's Buried Bones exhibition in 2008 when a distant relative of Milborough Maxwell, one of the females excavated from Chelsea Old Church in 2000, realised after visiting and enjoying the exhibition that she was indeed a relative. The relative contacted staff at the CHB and was very interested in the information that was obtained from osteological and stable isotope analyses, the latter of which revealed the intriguing inference of a Caribbean signature. The relative was very generous in providing further information about Milborough Maxwell, which was particularly useful because, up until that time, it had not been possible to find out anything more than her name from her coffin plate, and that her coffin had been richly decorated and lined. The Maxwell's descendent did not want to rebury her remains and was happy for her skeletal remains to remain in the collection at the Museum of London. Biographical, historical, or osteological research which may lead to publications containing details of identified individuals should also be given careful consideration, particularly if there may be any implications for living descendants. If a relative contacts a museum about an individual in a collection, processes and protocols should be followed to establish the family connection, and for ongoing liaison in respect to either continued retention of the remains or eventual reburial (DCMS 2005; APABE 2017).

10.2.4 Ethnographic Collections

There is a distinct sub-set of human remains collections, which in some cases overlap with archaeological collections, but which have a specific ethical background, which is important to be aware of. These remains may not have been part of planned archaeological excavations but were instead collected by various travellers in the eighteenth and nineteenth centuries, which included explorers, ship's surgeons, naturalists, missionaries, and even leisure travellers. Some were collected as 'curios', destined for auction houses, and subsequently residing in private collections (although ultimately, many of these have been transferred to museum collections as a result of bequests), while others were collected as examples of specific ethnographic practices, which were sent to museums for anthropological study. Some may even have been collected as war or conflict 'trophies', or as the result of judicial or extra-judicial executions, such as two skulls from the Battle of Shella donated to Liverpool Museum in 1891 (Hill 2016). Many were collected as 'scientific' specimens to form collections, which were studied by scholars working in physical anthropology but largely focused on eugenics, in the late nineteenth century/early twentieth century, to investigate 'racial typologies' (Marks 1995; Caspari 2003; Relethford 2010). Some of this work was later used to justify slavery and other human rights atrocities such as the Holocaust (Comas 1961). The ways in which some of these remains were acquired and used may be regarded as inappropriate, illegal, or unethical by modern standards, and they may be the subject of requests to return to their originating communities. The history of these collections in particular demonstrates why documented ethical standards and guidance are crucial to the care of human remains, and why all human remains should be treated with the utmost dignity and respect.

10.3 Institutions in Which Human Remains Collections are Held

A wide variety of institutions hold collections of human remains, all of which may be governed by different sets of regulations, guidelines, or professional standards (see Sect. 10.4 below). Institutions caring for human remains collections include museums (which may have a focus on cultures, natural history, science, and archaeology e.g. the British Museum, and/or art e.g. the Victoria and Albert Museum, both located in London), universities (including a diverse range of disciplines such as medical schools, biology, archaeology, or forensic science departments), commercial archaeology units, local authority museums and archives, academic institutions such as the Royal Academies or Royal Colleges, private collections held by individuals, and even schools. Some institutions will have established policies and procedures, and dedicated specialist staff for managing the collections, and others may have neither. Unlike publicly funded museums, universities do not have a fundamental or legal obligation to make their collections available to the wider scientific community, though it could be argued that they should have an ethical obligation to do so. The frequency and degree to which a collection is accessed and utilised will, to a point, dictate the level of resourcing allocated by the curating institution.

10.4 Regulations and Guidance

There is a wide variety of guidance relating to the care and curation of human remains, which may or may not be applicable to different types of collection and/or institution. The legislation and guidance relating to human remains collections is outlined and discussed below.

10.4.1 Legislation

One of the most important pieces of legislation applicable to human remains collections in England, Wales, and Northern Ireland is the Human Tissue Act (2004), which came into force in 2006 following an investigation into the removal and retention of organs without consent at Alder Hey Children's Hospital in Liverpool and Bristol Royal Infirmary (Woodhead 2013). The Human Tissue Authority (HTA), a non-departmental public body of the Department of Health, was established to regulate activities relating to the removal, storage, use, and disposal of human tissue from living individuals, and those who died less than 100 years ago. The Human Tissue Act (2004, Sect. 53) refers to "relevant material", which is defined as "material, other than gametes, which consists of or includes human cells…". A detailed but not exhaustive list of relevant material falling under the scope of the Act can be found on the website of the HTA (Human Tissue Authority 2017a). It should be noted that, if a collection includes human tissue of unknown age, then the earliest known acquisition date, or a written statement from an objective and independent expert stating there is good reason to believe the material is more than 100 years is acceptable. Given the poor standard of documentation associated with many historical collections, this is a reasonable compromise to mitigate against the unjustified disposal of thousands of remains in collections where there is no documentary proof of their age.

The Human Tissue Act (2004) only covers England, Wales, and Northern Ireland. Scotland has separate legislation (Human Tissue Act (Scotland) 2006) and is therefore not regulated by the HTA and instead is regulated by Scottish Ministers. However, according to the Human Tissue Authority (2017b), "while provisions of the Human Tissue (Scotland) Act 2006 are based on authorisation rather than consent, these are essentially both expressions of the same principle". This chapter focuses on the Human Tissue Act (2004) and its regulators, the Human Tissue Authority unless stated otherwise (e.g. see Sect. 10.7 below). For further information on the Human Tissue (Scotland) Act (2006) and how it affects museums see Museum Galleries Scotland (2011).

The Human Tissue Act (2004) regulates activity involving human remains that are less than 100 years old. Institutions require a Human Tissue Authority licence where this activity falls within a number of 'scheduled purposes', which include (but are not limited to) anatomical examination, transplantation, public display, research in connection with the disorders or functioning of the human body, and education or training relating to human health (Human Tissue Act 2004, Sect. 1). Notably, human remains that date within the last 100 years but pre-date 2006 can be stored and used for teaching of subjects, such as archaeology and forensic science without a licence, as this is not a scheduled purpose. However, care must be taken in such scenarios that the material is not used for demonstration or display at events such as public open days or external tours, which would be considered public display. In order to obtain a licence, establishments are assessed against the Human Tissue Authority's core standards, which cover areas such as consent, governance, quality systems, traceability, and premises (Human Tissue Authority 2017c). Broadly, an institution needs to demonstrate that it has the appropriate consents for the relevant material it holds, including secure record keeping of that consent; that there is a suitable governance framework, including assessment of risk and systems to deal with adverse events; that it can fully trace all relevant material from receipt and its whereabouts; that the premises where relevant material is stored or used is appropriate, safe, clean, and secure (Human Tissue Authority 2017c). As part of the licensing, a staff member is appointed as a 'Designated Individual', and they have the primary legal duty to ensure suitable practices are carried out, that the conditions of the licence are complied with, and that the other persons working under the licence are suitable. The Designated Individual may also be supported in their role by one or more 'Person(s) Designated' who is able to direct in relation to licensable activities. The HTA ensures compliance with standards by carrying out inspections of licensed establishments.

The fundamental underlying principle of the Human Tissue Act is that of consent (Human Tissue Authority 2017d). Under the Act, appropriate and valid consent must be obtained from the individual or their nominated representative for the removal, storage, or use of their tissue for scheduled purposes (Human Tissue Authority 2017b). What constitutes 'appropriate' and 'valid' consent varies according to the circumstances, and there are a number of exceptions, including activities relating to coroners and police, imported tissue, use of tissue from the living for research where it is ethically approved and non-identifiable to the researcher, and of 'existing holdings' (Human Tissue Authority 2017e). However, this area of regulation is complex, and the Human Tissue Authority Codes of Practice provide comprehensive guidance which should be consulted (the seven Codes of Practice covering different sectors and licensable activities are available on the Human Tissue Authority website, Human Tissue Authority 2017e).

Many human remains collections include material that is regarded by the Human Tissue Act (2004) as 'existing holdings'; that is, relevant material from an individual who died less than 100 years ago, but which entered a collection prior to the date of the Act coming into force in 2006. The requirements of the Act are not retrospective, so existing holdings can continue to be used for the scheduled purpose for which they were already held (e.g. public display and medical training), provided the institution is appropriately licensed (Human Tissue Authority 2017c). Although it is not necessary to retrospectively obtain consent (and in most cases, would be impossible to achieve), the human tissue must be used within the boundaries of the consent that is known. For example, the anatomy and pathology collections at the Royal College of Surgeons of England were primarily collected in the 1950s and used for the training of surgeons. The anatomy specimens which were collected at this time were prepared from the bodies of individuals who specifically consented to their bodies being used to support medical education. Therefore, human tissue from these donors can only be used to support medical training and education and cannot be used for other scheduled purposes, such as public display. Consequently, today these specimens are stored and used within the Anatomy and Pathology Museum at the RCS, which is not open to the general public, but can be accessed by medical, health, and relevant scientific trainees and professionals who need to study the human body. Tissue within the pathology collection at the RCS however, was donated by medics, such as pathologists and surgeons, with no information on the individual the tissue originated from, and the nature of consent is unknown. An application to the Human Tissue Authority could therefore be made for this tissue to be used for a scheduled purpose such as public display. At the RCS, a small number of pathology specimens have been displayed in the publicly accessible Hunterian Museum under a public display licence, although the majority of the pathology collection is still stored and used within the non-public Anatomy and Pathology Museum because it is important material for supporting education. As with all human tissue, consideration of the ethics of public display is vital and needs to be carefully considered before displaying any human remains (see Sect. 10.7 below).

Another example of an area where the consent provisions of the Human Tissue Act (2004) do not apply is that of imported tissue. Human tissue may be imported into the UK for various reasons, including research tissue banking and public display (e.g. the Body Worlds exhibitions by Gunther von Hagens). However, the Human Tissue Authority (2017c, 6) states that "where human tissue is imported, importers should endeavour to ensure that it is sourced from a country that has an appropriate ethical and legal framework". The Code of Practice for Public Display (Human Tissue Authority 2017f, 4) also specifies that "the country of origin should have a legal and ethical framework, which includes consent and protects the interests of the deceased and their families".

Public display represents a tiny fraction of the activities regulated by the Human Tissue Authority. At the time of writing, more than 800 organisations are licensed by the Human Tissue Authority, and only 17 of these for public display (Human Tissue Authority 2017g). There has been some criticism of how museums in particular are regulated by the Human Tissue Authority. White (2013) discusses the results of a survey (White 2011) which assessed the impact and effectiveness of the Human Tissue Act in the management of museum collections. The survey focused on two areas of the legislation, Sect. 47, the right to deaccession human remains that were less than 1000 years old (discussed below) and the licencing requirement for the public display for human remains (relevant material) less than 100 years old (White 2011, 2013). The results indicated that the licensing requirement may not have been sufficiently publicised, with some museums being unaware of the requirement, and highlighted concerns in the sector over licence fees (White 2013). Since this survey, the Human Tissue Authority has consulted with organisations holding licences and has improved its codes of practice and guidance to help increase understanding of how the Human Tissue Act and Human Tissue Authority regulations affect the sector. A comparison of the licence fees for 2018–2019 (Human Tissue Authority 2017h) with those for 2011–2012 (White 2013) suggests that the Human Tissue Authority have also attempted to address concerns over licence fees within the museum sector. Significantly, the fee for establishments holding fewer than 20 items has been removed (recorded as £1000 in 2011–2012 by White 2013) and the annual cost of a public display licence has been reduced from £2100 in 2011–2012 (White 2013) to £1225 for 2018–2019 (Human Tissue Authority 2017h). However, an application fee, payable by an establishment requesting a licence for the first time, has increased from £1600 in 2012 (White 2013) to £3100 (Human Tissue Authority 2017h). As White (2013) suggests, this could be a prohibiting factor for museums yet to apply for a licence, but considering the removal of a fee for a public display licence for a museum with fewer than 20 items this is likely to affect a smaller number of establishments than before. The consultation with museums and the reduction in annual licence fees suggests the Human Tissue Authority has recognised that the museum sector is different to many of the other sectors that are responsible for human remains.

Notably in Scotland, the regulation of the public display differs, here a supplementary order (Scottish Statutory Instrument 2006 No. 328) to the Human Tissue (Scotland) Act (2006), names specific museums and stipulates the person(s) responsible for these museums (e.g. Trustees or Universities) exempting them from the necessity of obtaining a licence for public display. Provided the appropriate authorisation is given (a similar concept to consent in England, Wales, and Northern Ireland), these museums can publicly display human remains that are less than 100 years old. Museums that are not listed in the order, must apply to Scottish Ministers for a licence for public display.

The British Museum Act (1963) applies to the British Museum, London, and the Natural History Museum, London. Section 5 (Disposal) of this Act is directly relevant to the care of human remains collections, which prohibits the disposal of 'any object' vested in the Trustees, unless under very specific circumstances, for instance if it is a duplicate, 'unfit to be retained' and can be disposed of without detriment to research, or if it is "useless to the purposes of the Museum" due to damage, physical deterioration, or infestation by pests (1963, Sect. 5). This Act meant that it was not possible for either of these museums to deaccession human remains, even for the purposes of repatriation to communities of origin. The Human Tissue Act (2004) made this possible when it was brought into force in 2006, which empowers the Trustees' of both museums to deaccession human remains which are less than 1000 years old if they believe it is appropriate to do so.

When making decisions about the care of human remains collections, an important consideration is whether they were legitimately acquired. It is unlawful to remove or disturb human remains in England without legal authority (Burial Act 1857). There are a number of secular and ecclesiastical laws, which form the framework for the exhumation of human remains depending on the nature of their burial place and the future use of the land (APABE 2017). In general, land that is consecrated falls under ecclesiastical law (with the exception of disused burial grounds, see below), and other land under secular law, in which case permission must be sought from the Ministry of Justice, by application for authority to excavate human remains for archaeological purposes (APABE 2017). Should the application be approved, a licence will be issued by the Secretary of State, and this licence will normally be subject to a number of conditions, which require respectful treatment of the remains and may include Health and Safety measures, screening of the site from the public, and whether scientific analysis is to be carried out (APABE 2017). The licence is issued for a fixed period of time, requires renewal, and stipulates a date of archive deposition.

Exhumation of human remains from consecrated ground will generally require a faculty, issued by the consistory court. The law of the Church of England assumes that remains should lie undisturbed and should not be exhumed other than in exceptional cases (APABE 2017). Unlike secular law, church law also does not consider older remains as having less protection than those from more recent burials. A faculty issued by the consistory court is for a fixed time period and will generally include instructions and timescales for storage and reburial. It will usually assume that reburial is to occur, unlike secular licences, which, since 2012, can include provision for permanent deposition in a repository such as a museum.

In addition to exhumation licences and faculties, there may be other documentation required for due diligence in accepting collections if the remains have been removed from cathedral grounds, scheduled monuments, disused burial grounds, or from land subject to compulsory purchase. The relevant laws that should be consulted are the Disused Burial Grounds Act (1884), Town and Country Planning (Churches, Places of Religious Worship and Burial Grounds) Regulations (1950), Ancient Monuments and Archaeological Areas Act (1979), Disused Burial Grounds (Amendment) Act (1981), and Care of Cathedrals Measure (2011).

10.4.2 Guidance and Best Practice

In addition to legal requirements, a number of organisations have issued ethical guidelines or 'best practice' documents. These may or may not be a requirement for different individuals or institutions depending on their membership or accreditation status with the publishing organisation.

The Museum Ethnographers Group (MEG) devised Guidelines on the Management of Human Remains, which were adopted in 1991 (MEG 1991) and revised/republished in 1994. These professional guidelines were among the first created by a UK museum association (Giesen 2013), and specifically address the differences of collections depending on the nature in which they were acquired and how this should influence their care. The guidelines do not specifically address ethical issues but do provide guidelines for areas of consideration for curators when caring for and making decisions concerning human remains.

The Department for Culture, Media and Sport (DCMS) introduced the 'Guidance for the Care of Human Remains in Museum Collections' in 2005 (DCMS 2005). In 2011, National Museums Scotland published 'Guidance of the Care of Human Remains in Scottish Museums' (National Museums Scotland 2011). Both documents cover a variety of topics including museum procedures such as acquisition and loans, in addition to repatriation. Furthermore, some of the guidance is applicable to human remains collections regardless of the type of institution they are housed in.

A number of other organisations in the UK have published guidelines for working with and caring for human remains collections, primarily aimed at archaeologists. These include the Advisory Panel on the Archaeology of Burials in England (APABE 2017), English Heritage (Mays et al. 2004), British Association of Biological Anthropology and Osteoarchaeology (BABAO 2010a, 2010b), and the Chartered Institute for Archaeologists (Brickley and McKinley 2004; Mitchell and Brickley 2017).

The establishment of the Advisory Panel on the Archaeology of Christian Burials in England (APACBE) in 2005 was in response to the document 'Guidance for the Care of Human Remains in Museums' issued by the Department for Culture,

Media and Sport (DCMS 2005) to provide guidance and advice to professionals whose work encompassed working with archaeological burials. In the form of the title and function of APACBE, the focus was initially Christian burials. However, it became evident that advice was required not just for Christian burials but all archaeological burials that may be encountered. This led to a consultation in 2009 by the Church of England, English Heritage (now Historic England), and Ministry of Justice, who have the legal responsibilities for archaeological burials in England. In 2010, APACBE became the Advisory Panel on the Archaeology of Burials in England (APABE) to reflect that its advisory capacity covered all archaeologically derived burials. The aim of APABE (2010) remained to offer support with the objective "to foster a consistent approach to ethical, legal, scientific, archaeological and other issues surrounding the treatment of archaeological burials".

The panel forming APABE are drawn from individuals working in museums, the fields of archaeology and osteology, with representatives from the Church of England, Historic England, and Ministry of Justice, which hold the statutory responsibilities for burials in England. The panel is able to offer advice, support, and guidance for individual casework and with matters or issues relating to the interpretation of guidance documents for those working with human remains.

Arts Council England administers an Accreditation Scheme for museums, which sets national standards for the key areas of collections management (Arts Council 2018). These standards define good practice and encourage development within organisations as a means of raising standards across the sector. Although accreditation applies to the many types of collections within museums, there are specific benefits in relation to human remains. Museums, which are accredited by the Arts Council and hold a Human Tissue Authority licence, are exempt from completing a number of sections (relating to loans, condition checking and conservation, audit, policies and procedures, premises, and risk assessment) on regular Human Tissue Authority licence public display compliance updates as these are demonstrated as part of the accreditation process.

10.5 Collections Management

The management of human remains collections involves numerous procedures and processes, all of which will require complex ethical decision making depending on the process and the nature of the remains involved. Although many of these procedures may at first glance seem museum specific, in reality they may be carried out at any institution holding remains, and existing guidance and best practice should be applicable to most organisations with little modification required. Human remains have a unique status within museum collections, and any institution holding them should consider whether it would be appropriate to have a Human Remains Policy in place, covering, at a minimum, the basic principles of what they hold, why they are held, access, governance, and disposal. The Spectrum standards published by the Collections Trust (2017) set out collections management standards and procedures which are made available online. Meeting the Spectrum standard for nine primary procedures (object entry, acquisition and accessioning, location and movement control, inventory, cataloguing, object exit, loans in, loans out, and documentation planning) is compulsory for museums seeking Arts Council Accreditation (Collections Trust 2017).

10.5.1 Acquisition

One of the overriding principles of the care of human remains collections is that of due diligence. This refers primarily to provenance checks of material that is either being acquired or brought into an institution on loan. Material should only be acquired or borrowed if it is legally and ethically sound.

The key legal requirements relevant to the acquisition or borrowing of human remains are: Human Tissue Authority licensing and consent requirements, appropriate exhumation licence/faculty/pastoral measure, and export licence for country of origin if imported (also bearing in mind that if they have been culturally modified, they may be considered cultural objects). Ethically, an institution should consider a number of factors, including: the circumstances of the remains' collection, the country of origin (are they likely to be, or have they already been, subject to a request for return?), the purpose of acquisition, and whether there will be limitations on use (e.g. poor condition may limit research, but may be of use for teaching). If the remains are less than 100 years old but not being used for a scheduled purpose, they will require differential treatment to other parts of a collection to ensure there is no breach of the Human Tissue Act (2004).

Human Tissue Authority licenced relevant material held under a public display licence can only be loaned to another licenced establishment. Anatomical specimens used in medical training can be approved by the Designated Individual for movement to unlicensed premises for storage or use for an authorised purpose provided it falls within the consent given. All loans, regardless of the age or nature of the material, should have a written and signed agreement covering the use of any material and resulting data/images if relevant, and should have detailed records and be tracked.

10.5.2 Documentation

Good documentation is vital for both collections managers/curators and users of the collection, and is a fundamental principle of collections management. It is the foundation of any work involving a collection, such as locating material, answering queries, selecting material for exhibitions or public engagement, monitoring sensitive or Human Tissue Authority relevant material, and continuity/preservation of knowledge with staff changes. Human remains collections will have varying levels of documentation associated with them, depending on their context. Some collections will also have documentation that has not been associated with them, but which can be found by conducting archival research. This can be an extensive and time-consuming exercise, and should be prioritised for remains that are under active study or for due diligence where they are to be displayed, sampled, or loaned.

Arts Council Accreditation requires museums to comply with the Spectrum standard for documentation for the nine primary procedures, which were outlined above (Collections Trust 2017). Any institution caring for human remains collections should consider what level of documentation is appropriate for their collections, and what is required in order to enable ethical decision making regarding any request for the use of those remains. Where no documentation appears to be associated with the remains, consideration should be given to declining requests until archival provenancing can be undertaken, to ensure that there are no significant ethical issues with their background. If remains are poorly provenanced or documented, their appropriateness for inclusion in any proposed project should also be considered.

10.5.3 Storage and Access

A number of guidelines refer to human remains being kept in secure storage with restricted access (MEG 1994; DCMS 2005). Storage should have suitable environmental parameters to protect against deterioration of remains, particularly large variations in temperature and humidity, and the area should be regularly monitored (DCMS 2005). Ideally, human remains should be stored separately from other types of collection, although this may not always be possible in smaller organisations. Individuals that do not form part of a commingled assemblage should be stored in individual boxes as far as possible, and inert packing materials should be used. Foams that off-gas (emit volatile compounds) should be avoided. Where practical, bones should be numbered individually on the bone, over a barrier layer of reversible conservation adhesive, such as Paraloid, so that the numbers can be removed later if required (BABAO 2010a). Although this may not sound ethical, where collections are regularly used for research or teaching, this enables the tracking of individuals, and makes it possible to reconcile individuals should accidental mixing of elements occur. The labelling of bags/boxes/labels that can also be disassociated from the remains, and from each other, does not prevent this. Additionally, consideration should be given to facilitating visits from source communities and lineal descendants of identified individuals.

10.6 Digitisation (Use of Images/Scans/Digital Collections)

Digitisation is increasingly becoming a priority activity for many institutions holding human remains, because it increases access to collections and aids collections management, via a digital archive available for viewing without physically handling remains. Imaging can involve photography, 2D radiography, or 3D scanning including computed tomography (CT), laser, and photogrammetric scanning. Many museums are also advocating 'open data' models with licensing systems that enable distribution and sharing of images and scans.

Whilst the open sharing of images and data for the purposes of scientific research is a laudable pursuit, the sensitive nature of many human remains collections means that a conscious ethical decision-making process should be employed for each individual use of images and/or data, which renders a fully inclusive 'open data' model largely unmanageable. It may be appropriate to use a scan for research purposes when anonymised for example, but not in a commercial education software application. Some institutions in the UK have made selective datasets, including images or scans, available. These projects include Digitised Diseases, the result of a collaboration between the University of Bradford, Museum of London Archaeology, and the Royal College of Surgeons of England (Wilson 2014), or the London Human Remains Digitisation Project by the Natural History Museum in London (Natural History Museum 2017). The beliefs of source cultures regarding images of the dead should be considered and consultation with communities should also be undertaken when acquiring and/or using images, particularly if the remains are under claim for return to their country of origin, or have already been returned.

The production and display of images do not fall under the scope of the Human Tissue Act (2004). However, the Human Tissue Authority Codes of Practice (Human Tissue Authority 2017e) require a licensed establishment to have suitable practices in place to ensure that remains of the deceased are treated with dignity and respect at all times and to prevent the misuse of images.

10.7 Display

Human remains within museum collections come in many guises, and the display of human remains may be incorporated in a multitude of ways within the contextual and narrative framework of museum galleries. Within British museums, the public have for many years been accustomed to seeing skeletal, mummified, and pathological collections. In the eighteenth and nineteenth century, it was not an uncommon practice for anatomists to display their pathological collections and human skeletal remains in a museum style to which visitors could view them (Chaplin 2005; Alberti 2007; Mitchell et al. 2011). The display of human remains is an area full of complexities and mixed emotions, with a combination of a long-held fascination for people but also particular roles in past societies and cultures. The many mediums now available for displaying human remains has added to the contention of the discussion around display and what is or is not acceptable, and what may be deemed to be acceptable in Britain and Europe may not be in other parts of the world (Roberts 2009). This is something which has become much more pertinent in recent years, notably with overseas Indigenous communities having a more powerful voice, and the need to acknowledge their cultural beliefs, and regulations brought in with the Human Tissue Act (2004). With display, there can often be a blurred line between art and science which may lead to legal controversy (Lewis 2015) and strong public responses as seen from the Gunther von Hagen's Body World exhibitions (Tuffs 2003; Collier 2010). With the advent of digital platforms and social media, there are now ever more avenues and forums in which to 'display' human remains, all of which bring with them exponential challenges. Yet despite these challenges, care and respect for the deceased must be at the centre of our work. Debate and discussion should continue as a means to highlight concerns around display on digital platforms, and for the development of best practice for managing such displays.

The display of human remains in museums may be included within gallery spaces as part of permanent displays and on a temporary basis for exhibitions (see Biers, this volume). In recent years, the ethics of displaying human remains has been a focus of debates and discussions within the sector. Consequently, museums have carried out independent in-house surveys to gauge visitors' feelings about human remains being on display, and also larger scale surveys, such as the one undertaken by Mills and Tranter (2010) which explored public opinion relating to human remains and the issues raised in light of museums having them within their collections. The survey did not make a distinction between isolated skeletal elements or more complete remains, such as articulated skeletons, referring only to 'human bones'. Although this may not seem significant, this aspect of the presentation of human remains can have a marked effect on the perceptions and responses of the viewer. Individual skeletal elements, although part of a person, may not evoke the same response as more complete or articulated remains which are more obviously human in appearance. It is important that factors such as this are taken into account when posing questions regarding human remains, so responses are not subject to assumptions and can be interpreted with the correct context. The overall public consensus from the Mills and Tranter (2010) survey indicated that the display and inclusion of human remains within British museums was something that was not an unexpected feature. The authors found that "Overall the majority (91%) 'agree', albeit at differing levels, that museums should be allowed to display human bones" and 87% agreed with the statement, that displaying human burials and bones is considered by most to 'help the public understand how people have lived in the past'" (Mills and Tranter 2010, 7).

In light of the many debates and issues raised relating to human remains, it is integral to remember that these are the remains of people, and it is our duty to respect and diligently care for them within museums. It is imperative for there to be consideration of the context in which human remains are shown, for example why have they been included and what has been selected, what they are adding to the narrative, how they are displayed, their location in the gallery/exhibition, and sensitivity to those visiting museums. The presence of signage in strategic locations to forewarn visitors that human remains are on display is a good practice to follow. Similarly, an advance warning notification located at the entrance of the museum would allow visitors to make a choice as to whether they wish to see the remains or not. When the first 'Skeletons: London's Buried Bones' exhibition was opened at the Wellcome Collection in 2008, there were signs at key points before entering the space that warned visitors that real human skeletal remains were on display within the exhibition (Redfern and Bekvalac 2013). Such signage was also clearly visible for the more recent touring 'Skeletons: Our Buried Bones' exhibitions at The Hunterian in Glasgow, MShed in Bristol, and Leeds City Museum. At the Museum of London, when the Centre for Human Bioarchaeology is involved in outreach events that will feature skeletal remains, signs are displayed prior to visitors reaching the area where human remains are on display. This alerts them that human remains are being used in outreach activities and allows visitors to make an informed decision as to whether they want to go into the area of the activity.

Following on from the DCMS (2005) report, and the subsequent development and implementation of guidelines and individual museum polices, there has been a concerted move by museums in acknowledging the importance of including human remains in relevant displays and the mindfulness of their placement. A good example of this was seen in the 'Doctors, Dissection and Resurrection Men' exhibition at the Museum of London (October 2012–April 2013), which, although clearly from the title and associated exhibition information, contained human remains, a great deal of thought and deliberation went into the design and planning of the space and placement of the human remains (Bekvalac 2015). A particular focus of the discussion and review was the inclusion and placement of an articulated and mounted skeleton of a child. Aware that this could be very emotive for visitors to the exhibition, it was paramount for careful thought and discussion as to where the child was to be placed within the exhibition space, and a decision was taken to create a special location for the child and to use a screen to shield the remains from open view. This gave visitors the option to enter this space or not.

Institutions should sensitively deal with access to human remains on display, particularly if there are collections from native or Indigenous communities, with the cultural beliefs of the source community used as the guiding principle for what is acceptable. The Museum of London collections are all archaeologically derived from sites that have undergone development within the London area and fortunately have associated contextual documentary records. Other museums and institutions have collections derived from a number of sources, which can be more problematical, as discussed in Sects. 10.5.1 and 10.5.2 of this chapter. Museums often face challenges from legacies of the past with ongoing work in the present, such as the work around repatriation requests from Indigenous communities. These challenges range from working with the political and social constructs of a different era, to the availability and legibility of source documentation, or the manner of collection of remains which may be ethically and/or legally unacceptable not just in the present but also at the time of collection. Present day repatriation requests from Indigenous communities are complex, and work on these is complicated further when dealing with a range of these issues. Since the publication of the DCMS (2005) report, museums have produced their own guidelines based on their collections of human remains, including the display of human remains within these collections (Museum of London 2011; British Museum 2013; Natural History Museum 2014). These standards and guidelines have assisted museums and institutions to think more in terms about best curatorial practice and the complex ethical issues associated with human remains and the retention of them.

10.8 Destructive Sampling

Destructive sampling is an area of collections care that has seen an exponential increase in recent years, particularly in relation to the developments in the field of ancient DNA and other genomic research. There are a number of areas of destructive sampling that require careful ethical scrutiny, such as DNA analysis of named individuals, in addition to the standard considerations given to the use of human remains in projects that do not involve a destructive element (APABE 2017).

Assessments should be undertaken of any previous destructive sampling of human remains. These should encompass what the samples were taken for and, whether the analysis was successful. If the remains have previously undergone a particular type of analysis, it may influence the success of a sampling request, for example the preservation of the remains should be a priority. Likewise, it may be ethically unacceptable to allow re-sampling for the same type of analysis if strong justification is not given, such as advancing techniques and significant time having elapsed since the previous sampling. It should be considered whether the request will significantly reduce the amount of material available to future researchers wanting to undertake a different form of analysis, be it non-destructive or destructive. In general, sampling should avoid areas that are morphologically important or form anatomical landmarks. If a tooth or morphologically important area is to be sampled, then it would be advisable to only allow this where the antimere is present and comparable. Surface moulds should be taken of any teeth that will be damaged by sampling, and remains should be fully photographically documented before and after sampling. If a particular collection has not been previously sampled and the chances of successful analysis are in question, then it would be advisable to run a preliminary study comprising a subsample of the collection before removing further samples. Museums should request the return of unused residues and extracts, so that these can be curated and used for future analyses without further damaging the remains. Any destructive sampling application process should be fair, transparent, and unbiased.

DNA analysis of remains from identified individuals, and from those dating within the last 100 years requires special consideration. Ancient DNA analysis has the ability to provide highly sensitive personal information about the individual being sampled, their ancestors, and potentially living descendants. The Human Tissue Authority does not cover DNA analysis of 'existing holdings', and so the questions relating to such analysis are ethical rather than legal. Curators should be aware of the Medical Research Council (2014) 'Human Tissue and Biological Samples for Use in Research: Operational and Ethical Guidelines'. This document covers issues of consent where medical information about living individuals may be discovered or put into the public domain by the publication of ancestral data. DNA is not specifically covered in the guidelines but it directs the reader to a number of other relevant sources. There are particular ethical implications with depositing genomic data in the public domain, which should be carefully considered by both researchers and curators. Further discussion of this subject can be found in Biers (this volume).

Destructive sampling of remains which are subject to a claim for return to their community of origin or to lineal descendants is a complex and sensitive issue. Many Indigenous communities are understandably opposed to the sampling of remains. Institutions should be aware that sampling of remains that are under claim without the consent of the source community may be considered deeply harmful. This is particularly the case where such sampling is for scientific research purposes. In some cases, it may be determined that sampling could be beneficial in determining the provenance of a specimen where this is unclear. This may take the form of stable isotope analysis, or perhaps radiocarbon dating where it is thought that remains may be more than 1000 years old and therefore outside the scope of the Human Tissue Act (2004). Again, many communities may still be strongly opposed to such sampling and an institution should discuss the benefits and drawbacks of the analysis (and implications of not undertaking the work) with the claimants. Consent and/or collaboration with the community should be considered as appropriate.

10.9 Conclusion

Museums and institutions, both nationally and internationally, have large-scale holdings of human remains, with the majority of British collections in museums and universities being derived from archaeological interventions. Prior to the development of the discipline of archaeology and the establishment of professional archaeological field units in the latter half of the twentieth century, collections of human remains were acquired through antiquaries and Victorian collectors, via practices that are largely regarded as unethical today. When caring for and working with collections, there is an overriding responsibility to consider the ethical context of our work, and whether it is appropriate. The major principle on which this assessment should be based is that of harm. Will the process or work being undertaken cause harm to the public, to the community from which the remains originate, or to science (either by reputational damage to the field of study, or physical damage to the remains themselves, which may have negative implications for future research)? Work on more recent remains with traceable descendants carries a particular risk of potential harm to the living and should be subject to more rigorous scrutiny. Those who curate collections from various cultures are also responsible for maintaining awareness of a wider view of beliefs regarding what constitutes harm as this differs significantly between cultural groups. Whilst Christian and agnostic backgrounds do not recognise the concept of harm to the dead (in Christian theology, although physical remains should be treated with respect and reverence, it is the fate of the soul, not the physical remains, which matters; APABE 2017), other cultures do and this can have a significant and distressing impact on the living.

In Britain, the formation of commercial archaeological units and the development of planning guidance has seen the establishment of formulated processes and consultation in light of the potential of disturbing human remains. This subsequently leads to the excavation, recovery, removal, and retention or reburial of remains (Roberts 2009), which enables the continuing development and expansion of such collections in an ethical and transparent manner. In 2003, the DCMS Working Group on Human Remains published a key report which encouraged institutions to be more transparent in providing details of the holdings of human remains within their collections (DCMS 2003). Since the publication of this document, there has been a greater degree of openness and, with the development of online platforms, museums are now able to share information online and keep it regularly updated.

In addition to the transparent sharing of information about holdings, all institutions should be encouraged, where appropriate, to have a policy relating to the storage and use of their human remains collections, to develop written procedures, and to make these available externally on request. They may also want to consider establishing consultation or advisory panels, whether internal or external, formal or informal, to consider ethics and policy when making decisions relating to processes such as display, destructive sampling, deaccessioning, or research projects. Resourcing in the cultural sector is a significant issue and it is recognised that many institutions may not have specialist curators for human collections. Advisory panels may be of particular benefit where this is the case.

The ethical considerations for the care of human remains collections will remain complex and ever changing, influenced by ongoing social and political change. Institutions should continue to engage in clear and transparent discussion and maintain flexibility in their approach to the development of best practice in relation to the ethical care of human remains.

References

Advisory Panel on the Archaeology of Burials in England [APABE]. 2010. *Advisory Panel on the Archaeology of Burials in England (APABE)*. http://www.archaeologyuk.org/apabe/. Accessed 27 August 2018.

Advisory Panel on the Archaeology of Burials in England [APABE]. 2017. *Guidance for Best Practice for the Treatment of Human Remains Excavated from Christian Burial Grounds in England*, 2nd ed. London: Advisory Panel on the Archaeology of Burials in England.

Alberti, S. 2007. The Museum Effect: Visiting Collections of Anatomy and Natural History in Victorian Britain. In *Science in the Marketplace: Nineteenth-Century Sites and Experiences*, ed. A. Fyfe and B. Lightman, 371–404. Chicago: University of Chicago Press.

Alberti, S.J.M. 2011. *Morbid Curiosities. Medical Museums in Nineteenth-Century Britain.* Oxford: Oxford University Press.

Ancient Monuments and Archaeological Areas Act. 1979. The Stationery Office, London.

Arts Council. 2018. *About Accreditation.* https://www.artscouncil.org.uk/accreditation-scheme/about-accreditation. Accessed 27 August 2018.

Baillie, M. 1793. *The Morbid Anatomy of the Most Important Parts of the Human Body.* London: Johnson.

Bekvalac, J. 2012. Implementation of Preliminary Digital Radiographic Examination in the Confines of the Crypt of St Bride's Church, Fleet Street, London. In *Proceedings of the Twelfth Annual Conference of the British Association for Biological Anthropology and Osteoarchaeology*, ed. P.D. Mitchell and J. Buckberry, 111–118. Oxford: British Archaeological Reports.

Bekvalac, J. 2015. The Display of Archaeological Human Skeletal Remains in Museums. In *Heritage, Ancestry and Law: Principles, Policies and Practices in Dealing with Historical Human Remains*, ed. R. Redmond-Cooper, 114–121. Builth Wells: Institute of Art and Law.

Berry, A.C., and R.J. Berry. 1967. Epigenetic Variation in the Human Cranium. *Journal of Anatomy* 101: 361–379.

Brickley, M., and J. McKinley (eds.). 2004. *Guidelines to the Standards for Recording Human Remains.* Institute of Field Archaeologists Paper Number 7. Reading and Southampton: IFA and BABAO.

British Association of Biological Anthropology and Osteoarchaeology [BABAO]. 2010a. *Code of Ethics.* http://babao.org.uk/assets/Uploads/code-of-ethics.pdf. Accessed 29 May 2018.

British Association of Biological Anthropology and Osteoarchaeology [BABAO]. 2010b. *Code of Practice.* http://www.babao.org.uk/assets/Uploads/code-of-practice.pdf. Accessed 29 May 2018.

British Museum Act. 1963. The Stationery Office, London.

British Museum. 2013. *British Museum Policy: Human Remains in the Collection.* https://www.britishmuseum.org/pdf/Human%20Remains%20policy%20July%202013%20FINAL.pdf. Accessed 23 August 2018.

Buikstra, J., and D. Ubelaker (eds.). 1994. *Standards for Data Collection from Human Skeletal Remains.* Fayetteville: Arkansas Archaeological Survey.

Burial Act. 1857. The Stationery Office, London.

Care of Cathedrals Measure. 2011. The Stationery Office, London.

Caspari, R. 2003. From Types to Populations: A Century of Race, Physical Anthropology, and the American Anthropological Association. *American Anthropologist* 105: 65–76.

Chaplin, S. 2005. John Hunter and the Anatomy of a Museum. *History Today* 55 (2): 19–25.

Collections Trust. 2017. *Spectrum.* https://collectionstrust.org.uk/spectrum/. Accessed 29 May 2018.

Collier, R. 2010. Cadaver Shows Stir Controversy. *Canadian Medical Association Journal* 182 (14): E687–E688.

Comas, J. 1961. "Scientific" Racism Again? *Current Anthropology* 2: 303–340.

Conlogue, G., M. Viner, R. Beckett, et al. 2016. A Post-mortem Evaluation of the Degree of Mobility in an Individual with Severe Kyphoscoliosis Using Direct Digital Radiography (DDR) and Multi-detector Computed Tomography (MDCT). In *New Developments in the Bioarchaeology of Care: Further Case Studies and Extended Theory*, ed. L. Tilley and A. Schrenk, 153–173. New York: Springer.

Connell, B., and P. Rauxloh. 2003. *A Rapid Method for Recording Human Skeletal Data.* London: Museum of London.

Cowie, R., T. Kausmally, and J. Bekvalac. 2008. *Late 17th- to 19th-Century Burial and Earlier Occupation at All Saints, Chelsea Old Church, Royal Borough of Kensington and Chelsea.* London: Museum of London Archaeology Services.

Cox, M. 1996. *Life and Death in Spitalfields 1700 to 1850*. York: Council for British Archaeology.

Department for Culture, Media and Sport [DCMS]. 2003. *The Report of the Working Group on Human Remains*. London: Department for Culture, Media and Sport.

Department for Culture, Media and Sport [DCMS]. 2005. *Guidance for the Care of Human Remains in Museums*. London: Department for Culture, Media and Sport.

Disused Burial Grounds Act. 1884. The Stationery Office, London.

Disused Burial Grounds (Amendment) Act. 1981. The Stationery Office, London.

Ellis, H. 2011. Matthew Baillie: Pioneer of Systematic Pathology. *British Journal of Hospital Medicine* 72 (10): 594.

Gapert, R., S. Black, and J. Last. 2009a. Sex Determination from the Foramen Magnum: Discriminant Function Analysis in an Eighteenth and Nineteenth Century British Sample. *International Journal of Legal Medicine* 123: 25–33.

Gapert, R., S. Black, and J. Last. 2009b. Sex Determination from the Occipital Condyle: Discriminant Function Analysis in an Eighteenth and Nineteenth Century British Sample. *American Journal of Physical Anthropology* 138: 384–394.

Giesen, M. 2013. Introduction: Human Remains in the United Kingdom. In *Curating Human Remains: Caring for the Dead in the United Kingdom*, ed. M. Giesen, 1–11. Woodbridge: The Boydell Press.

Henderson, C.Y., and F.A. Cardoso (eds.). 2018. *Identified Skeletal Collections: The Testing Ground of Anthropology*? Oxford: Archaeopress.

Henderson, M., A. Miles, D. Walker, et al. 2013. *'He Being Dead Yet Speaketh': Excavations at Three Post-Medieval Burial Grounds in Tower Hamlets, East London, 2004–2010*. London: Museum of London Archaeology.

Hill, K. 2016. Souvenirs: Narrating Overseas Violence in the Late Nineteenth Century. In *Britain and the Narration of Travel in the Nineteenth Century*, ed. K. Hill, 175–186. London: Routledge.

Human Tissue Act. 2004. The Stationery Office, London.

Human Tissue (Scotland) Act. 2006. The Scottish Parliament, Edinburgh.

Human Tissue Authority. 2017a. *Relevant Material Under the Human Tissue Act 2004*. https://www.hta.gov.uk/policies/relevant-material-under-human-tissue-act-2004. Accessed 27 August 2018.

Human Tissue Authority. 2017b. *Human Tissue Act*. https://www.hta.gov.uk/policies/human-tissue-act-2004. Accessed 27 August 2018.

Human Tissue Authority. 2017c. *Code of Practice A: Guiding Principles and the Fundamental Principle of Consent*. London: Human Tissue Authority.

Human Tissue Authority. 2017d. *Code of Practice C: Anatomical Examination. Code of Practice and Standards*. London: Human Tissue Authority.

Human Tissue Authority. 2017e. *HTA Codes of Practice and Standards*. https://www.hta.gov.uk/hta-codes-practice-and-standards-0. Accessed 27 August 2018.

Human Tissue Authority. 2017f. *Code of Practice D: Public Display. Code of Practice and Standards*. London: Human Tissue Authority.

Human Tissue Authority. 2017g. *Find an Establishment*. https://www.hta.gov.uk/establishments. Accessed 27 August 2018.

Human Tissue Authority. 2017h. *HTA Licence Fees 2018/19*. https://www.hta.gov.uk/sites/default/files/Fees/tables2018-19_0.pdf. Accessed 27 August 2018.

Humphrey, L.T. 1998. Growth Patterns in the Modern Human Skeleton. *American Journal of Physical Anthropology* 105: 57–72.

King, T., L.T. Humphrey, and S. Hillson. 2005. Linear Enamel Hypoplasias as Indicators of Systemic Physiological Stress: Evidence from Two Known Age-at-Death and Sex Populations from Post Medieval London. *American Journal of Physical Anthropology* 128: 547–559.

Lewis, T. 2015. Human Remains as 'Artistic Expression' and the Common Law Offence of Outraging Public Decency: 'Human Earrings', Human Rights and R.V. Gibson Revisited. In *Heritage, Ancestry and Law: Principles, Policies and Practices in dealing with Historical Human Remains*, ed. R. Redmond-Cooper, 60–82. Builth Wells: Institute of Art and Law.

Marks, J. 1995. *Human Biodiversity: Genes, Race, and History*. New York: Aldine de Gruyter.

Mays, S., M. Brickely, and N. Dodwell. 2004. *Human Bones from Archaeological Sites: Guidelines for Producing Assessment Documents and Analytical Reports*. Swindon: English Heritage.

Medical Research Council. 2014. *MRCS Ethics Series: Human Tissue and Biological Samples for Use in Research: Operational and Ethical Guidelines*. Swindon and London: Medical Research Council.

Miles, A., W. White, and D. Tankard. 2008. *Burial at the Site of the Parish Church of St Benet Sherehog Before and After the Great Fire: Excavations at 1 Poultry*. London: Museum of London Archaeology.

Mills, S., and V. Tranter. 2010. *Research Into Issues Surrounding Human Bones in Museums*. London: Business Development Research Consultants.

Milne, G. 1997. *St. Bride's Church London: Archaeological Research 1952–60 and 1992–5*. London: English Heritage.

Mitchell, P.D., C. Boston, A.T. Chamberlain, et al. 2011. The Study of Anatomy in England from 1700 to the Early 20th Century. *Journal of Anatomy* 219: 91–99.

Mitchell, P.D., and M. Brickley. 2017. *Updated Guidelines to the Standards for Recording Human Remains*. Reading: Chartered Institute for Archaeologists.

Molleson, T., M. Cox, A.H. Waldron, et al. 1993. *The Spitalfields Project. Volume 2: The Anthropology—The Middling Sort*. York: Council for British Archaeology.

Moore, S. 1999. Fluid Preservation. In *Care and Conservation of Natural History Collections*, ed. D. Carter and A. Walker, 92–132. Oxford: Butterworth Heinemann.

Morgan, D. 1973. *Phoenix of Fleet Street: 2000 Years of St Bride's*. London: Charles Knight.

Museum Ethnographers Group [MEG]. 1991. *Museum Ethnographers' Group Guidelines on Management of Human Remains*. Bawburgh: Museum Ethnographers Group.

Museum Ethnographers Group [MEG]. 1994. Professional Guidelines Concerning The Storage, Display, Interpretation and Return of Human Remains in Ethnographical Collections in United Kingdom Museums. *Journal of Museum Ethnography* 6: 22–24.

Museum of London. 2011. *Policy for the Care of Human Remains in Museum of London Collections*. London: Museum of London.

Museums Galleries Scotland. 2011. *Guidelines for the Care of Human Remains in Scottish Museum Collections*. Edinburgh: Museums Galleries Scotland.

Natural History Museum. 2014. *Human Remains Policy*. London: Natural History Museum.

Natural History Museum. 2017. *London Human Remains Collection*. http://www.nhm.ac.uk/our-science/collections/palaeontology-collections/london-human-remains-collection.html. Accessed 23 August 2018.

Palfreyman, D. 2010. *London Livery Companies: History, Law and Customs*. Southend-on-Sea: Oracle.

Redfern, R.C., and J. Bekvalac. 2013. The Museum of London: An Overview of Policies and Practice. In *Curating Human Remains: Caring for the Dead in Great Britain*, ed. M. Giesen, 87–98. Woodbridge: The Boydell Press.

Redpath, W. 1959. *Fleet Street's Church Restored, 1940–1957: A Survey of Seventeen Eventful Years*, 2nd ed. London: Guild of St. Bride on Behalf of the Rector and Churchwardens.

Reeve, J., and M. Adams. 1993. *The Spitalfields Project. Volume 1: The Archaeology—Across the Styx*. York: Council for British Archaeology.

Relethford, J. 2010. Race and Conflicts Within the Profession of Physical Anthropology During the 1950s and 1960s. In *Histories of American Physical Anthropology in the Twentieth Century*, ed. M.A. Little and K.R. Kennedy, 207–219. Lanham: Lexington Books.

Roberts, C.A. 2009. *Human Remains in Archaeology: A Handbook*. York: Council for British Archaeology.

Royal Albert Memorial Museum and Art Gallery. 2016. *World Cultures: Curating Human Remains in the UK Conference*. http://rammworldcultures.org.uk/curating-human-remains-uk-conference/. Accessed 29 May 2018.

Scheuer, J.L. 1998. Age at Death and Cause of Death of the People Buried at St. Bride's Church, Fleet Street. In *Grave Concerns: Death and Burial in England 1700–1850*, ed. M. Cox, 100–111. York: Council for British Archaeology.

Scheuer, J.L., and J.E. Bowman. 1994. The Health of the Novelist and Printer Samuel Richardson (1689–1761): A Correlation of Documentary and Skeletal Evidence. *Journal of the Royal Society of Medicine* 87: 352–355.

Simmons, J.E. 2014. *Fluid Preservation. A Comprehensive Guide*. Lanham: Rowman and Littlefield.

Town and Country Planning (Churches, Places of Religious Worship and Burial Grounds) Regulations. 1950. The Stationery Office, London.

Tuffs, A. 2003. Von Hagens Faces Investigation Over Use of Bodies Without Consent. *British Medical Journal* 327: 1068.

van Schaik, K., R. Eisenberg, J. Bekvalac, et al. 2017. The Radiologist in the Crypt: Burden of Disease in the Past and Its Modern Relevance. *Academic Radiology* 24 (10): 1305–1311.

White, E. 2011. *Giving Up the Dead: The Impact and Effectiveness of the Human Tissue Act and the Guidance for the Care of Human Remains in English Museums*. Dissertation, Newcastle University.

White, E. 2013. The Human Tissue Act and The Guidance. In *Curating Human Remains: Caring for the Dead in the United Kingdom*, ed. M. Giesen, 43–52. Woodbridge: The Boydell Press.

Wilson, A.S. 2014. Digitised Diseases: Preserving Precious Remains. *Journal of the British Archaeological Association* 136: 36–41.

Woodhead, C. 2013. Care Custody and Display. In *Curating Human Remains: Caring for the Dead in the United Kingdom*, ed. M. Giesen, 31–41. Woodbridge: The Boydell Press.

Chapter 11
Rethinking Purpose, Protocol, and Popularity in Displaying the Dead in Museums

Trish Biers

Abstract Since the 1990s, debate about the display of human remains and objects made from human materials has seen a significant increase in the published literature that includes regulatory codes, ethical guidelines, declarations of community protest, and professional statements of support, both for and against displaying the dead. This chapter presents an overview of some of these debates in the wider framework of decolonising display and the purpose for, and popularity of, showing human remains in museums. A review of the ethical guidelines available to museums, professionals, and descendant communities is presented, followed by a discussion of best practice for displaying the dead for public view.

11.1 Introduction

The concentration of this chapter is to discuss the ethical considerations directly related to displaying the dead for public view. While the focus here is the display of human remains[1] in institutions, it is intrinsically linked with wider issues of curation and repatriation, which are featured in this volume. Ethical dilemmas arise because descendant communities, scientists and researchers, curators, and the public have different ethical concerns, though there is some overlap between groups with consensus that human remains should be treated with respect and dignity (Fforde et al. 2002; DCMS 2005; Lohman and Goodnow 2006; Brooks and Rumsey 2006; Cassman et al. 2007; Sadongei and Cash Cash 2007; Jenkins 2011;

[1]The term human remains is used to mean the bodies, and parts of bodies, of once living people from the species *Homo sapiens* (defined as individuals who fall within the range of anatomical forms known today and in the recent past). This includes osteological material (whole or part skeletons, individual bones or fragments of bone and teeth), soft tissue including organs and skin, embryos, and slide preparations of human tissue (DCMS 2005).

T. Biers (✉)
Duckworth Laboratory, Department of Archaeology, University of Cambridge, Cambridge CB2 3DZ, UK
e-mail: tmb40@cam.ac.uk

K. Squires et al. (eds.), *Ethical Approaches to Human Remains*,
https://doi.org/10.1007/978-3-030-32926-6_11

Clegg et al. 2013; Giesen 2013; Fletcher et al. 2014; Gazi 2014; Marselis 2016; Swain 2016; Human Tissue Authority 2017a; Overholtzer and Argueta 2017).

Attitudes towards death, the deceased individual, and treatment of human remains is remarkably different across populations and has been throughout time (Metcalf and Huntingdon 1991; Parker Pearson 1999). Many cultures regarded human remains as intrinsic social actors, and as a nexus between the living and the dead. For example, in the fifteenth and sixteenth centuries in Peru, the deceased Inka nobility were regularly consulted by the living, and paraded through Cusco during seasonal times of the year (Biers 2013). In Europe, the rise of Christianity prioritised sight as a means of accessing the holy dead body through relics comprising of skeletal and mummified fragments of saints. To see the dead was to feel the emotive rapture and it was persuasive (Binski 1996). Some communities such as the Toraja of South Sulawesi, attribute the body with continued agency and identity despite their death, and this can be seen in the practice of dressing and grooming the dead before burial (Tarlow 2009). The integrity of the body is consequently of the utmost importance, when the body is manipulated, removed, and 'sold off', it can cause great distress for the living. The potent symbolic value of human remains can be used to represent multiple belief systems and offer control over one's biological patrimony which is why it is not surprising that issues surrounding the treatment and use of human remains pose some of "the most vexing ethical dilemmas skeletal biologists face" (Walker 2008, 15).

How we view death is deeply embedded in our culture. Our exposure to it, our triumph over it, or our avoidance of it, can dictate how we view it in mortal flesh behind a glass case. Though we are familiar with the process of decay in the natural world, there is something preternatural when decay is suspended in a human body. The physical form can be transformed into another entity such as a taboo, an ancestor, a political tool, or biomatter, all dependent on our own personal beliefs and ideals. The body is "malleable" as a collection of biological processes, it is fundamentally created by its social context (Robb 2009, 28). This is where the debate lies in deliberating concepts of personhood and the objectification of the dead when they are on display in a museum or gallery because we put them into another context, with interpretation that is restricted (Alberti et al. 2009).

11.1.1 What Is the Purpose of Displaying the Dead?

There is a long tradition of displaying bodies and body parts in museums, especially in Europe and Britain. After the Enlightenment (1685–1815), dead bodies could be presented as part of scientific, ethnographic, archaeological, or medical exhibitions (Brooks and Rumsey 2006; Adams 2009; Swain 2016). Museums were filled with spoils of conquest, bought or looted during colonial expansions, and bartered or gifted during expeditions by wealthy explorers. Understanding the motivations and circumstances that contributed to bringing human remains into museums is an important aspect of the history of collections acquisition (Bennett 1995; Stallybrass and White 1986; Wilson 2015).

Human remains are consistently displayed in museums, and in Britain the public expect to see such displays (Kilmister 2004; Mills and Tranter 2010; Clegg et al. 2013). The *Scoping Survey of Historic Human Remains in English Museums,* undertaken on behalf of the Ministerial Working Group on Human Remains in February 2003, found that human remains were housed in roughly 132 museums and universities with 67.4% having some or all of their human remains collections on permanent display (Weeks and Bott 2003). Only seven institutions reported having all of their collections on public long-term display while 21% of institutions had human remains on temporary display (for less than one year) (Weeks and Bott 2003). The display of human remains for medical and/or teaching purposes was also noted, for example at the Wellcome Museum of Anatomy and Pathology at the Royal College of Surgeons in London (UK), with no public access allowed but biomedical students and researchers could seek special permission to see the collections.

The majority of work on human remains in the United Kingdom is uncontroversial and has wide popular and academic support (Swain 2002; APABE 2017). Research into human remains and their context are an important source of direct evidence about the past, including past demography and mortality, mortuary treatment, adaptation and genetics, and history and evolution of disease (Walker 2008). Some of this information can be lost, however, when only parts of bodies are on display, as these are curated more like objects rather than people, such as amputated limbs as war relics (Rees Leahy 2008). Dismantling the body changes the narrative. This then, can determine how much or how little context accompanies a display, which is essential and often expected by the public. On the other hand, anatomical and medical museums whose specimens span upwards of 200 years of medical history, explicitly show body parts as wet specimens usually as a single entity existing on their own. Heads, faces, flesh, and hair are vividly presented bringing us closer to the realities of past afflictions and the physicality of death.

11.1.2 Public Views

> Described as "fascinating, intriguing, and inspiring," by NBC, "absolutely extraordinary," by NPR and "a must see" by FOX TV, Mummies of the World instils a sense of curiosity and wonder in each and every visitor. Having been visited by over 1.6 million people nationwide, Mummies of the World: The Exhibition is one of the most popular museum exhibitions traveling North America. (Exhibitions Intl, LLC. April 2017)

There is little debate that, in general, exhibitions that feature displays of human remains are popular with the public (Swain 2002; Lohman and Goodnow 2006; Brooks and Rumsey 2006; Jenkins 2011; Clegg et al. 2013; Marselis 2016; Swain 2016; Overholtzer and Argueta 2017). Attendance tripled at the San Diego Museum of Man during their 'Mysteries of the Mummies' exhibition between 1998 and 1999 (Biers 2000). Travelling exhibitions such as the above mentioned 'Mummies of the

World: The Exhibition' and Gunther von Hagen's controversial 'Body Worlds' have had millions of viewers on an international stage (Barbian and Berndt 2001; Wholley 2001; Barilan 2006; Exhibition Intl, LLC 2017).

The Mütter Museum in Philadelphia (USA) is a medical history museum associated with The College of Physicians of Philadelphia that has a significant collection of anatomical and pathological specimens, antique medical instruments, and wax models. One of the highlights of the collection is the Hyrtl Skull Collection composing of 139 human skulls from Viennese anatomist Joseph Hyrtl (1810–1894). His research focused on debunking claims of phrenologists and that racial differences were the cause of anatomical traits, concentrating on the variation in the 'Caucasian population of Europe' (The Mütter Museum 2018). What is especially unique about this collection is that there is known age, place of origin, and cause of death of each person, and sometimes occupation. While visiting, the author overheard several visitors express surprise that these details were known about each person and then tried to find a skull reflective of their own age or job. One child, probably between eight and ten years of age, proclaimed, "Dad, he's the same age as you!" The visitors appeared fascinated with this display and several of them lingered, peering into the glass reading every label[2] and according to the Curator Anna Dhody, "it is one of the visitor favourites in the Museum". Sledzik and Barbian (2001, 227) have suggested that displaying human remains can be beneficial for visitors as "the seeing" of human remains "offers them [museum visitors] knowledge of themselves".

Currently on display in the 'Objects of Wonder' exhibition at the National Museum of Natural History (NMNH), Smithsonian Institution in Washington D.C., are the mortal remains of Robert Kennicott, a nineteenth century naturalist and collector for the Smithsonian Institution (Fig. 11.1). After an investigation of his skeletal remains to determine the cause of his death, in 2001, Kennicott's family donated his body to the Smithsonian to advance scientific research on the effects of mercury-based dental fillings and to test the accuracy of facial reconstruction software (Bruwelheide et al. 2017). Grover Krantz was a physical anthropologist who actively involved himself in Bigfoot/Sasquatch research and is also on display, along with his dog Clyde, in the 'Q? rius' science education centre, an area geared towards families, at the National Museum of Natural History, Smithsonian Institution. They are without question a highlight for children who visit the centre.[3] Patterson (2007, 69) notes that children have demonstrated they are curious about challenging content, asking questions about cause of death, how faces are reconstructed, and how bog mummies are made. Conversations about these topics allows children to "express their concerns and to hear about a variety of viewpoints on the topic" (Patterson 2007, 70).

---

[2]The Mütter Museum is currently relabelling these skulls to be more modern in context, aligning with visitor enquiries and ethics of the collection (on their website).

[3]During her employment at the NMNH, the author spoke at length to museum educators and archivists about the display of Professor Krantz and his dog.

Fig. 11.1 Robert Kennicott's display in the 'Objects of Wonder' exhibition at the National Museum of Natural History, Smithsonian Institution (Washington D.C., USA). Photograph by Trish Biers (2017)

Despite a general tendency in Britain to support the display of human remains, (there have been several successful exhibitions curated by the Museum of London; mentioned in this volume) there are some human bodies that seem more contentious than others. In 2001, a survey in Britain asked respondents which types of human remains they would least like to see in a museum. Two of the most common responses were "a baby's skeleton" and "a medically preserved baby" (Brooks and Rumsey 2006, 283). Children remains in general are more likely to cause emotional responses when on display (Sledzik and Barbian 2001; Brooks and Rumsey 2006; Alberti et al. 2009). Visitors want to know how they died and how they came to be in a museum. Deeper still, is the underlying awareness that the collection of such bodies was likely due to social disparities and the medical exploitation of the poor, the disfigured, and minorities "because the public recognizes that differential treatment experienced in life continues after death" (Wilson 2015, 31).

11.1.3 Collaborative Communication: Decolonising Display

European institutions displaying the material cultures of Africa, Asia, Oceania, and the Americas have long been associated with the formation of controlled territories (Wintle 2013). As a consequence, descendant communities attest to the unequal status that exists both for remains and descendant populations. Ethical differences in conduct towards human remains are institutional as much as they are cultural, and while the ethical dimensions regarding the treatment of human remains are universally acknowledged, appropriate ethical behaviours in the academic or museum institution do not always exist cross-culturally (Sadongei and Cash Cash 2007). The Native American Graves Protection and Repatriation Act (NAGPRA), 25 U.S.C. 3001–3013, 43 CFR Part 10 was passed on the 16th November 1990 in the United States of America (1990), to resolve the disposition of Native American cultural patrimony and human remains under the control of Federally funded museums. This has acted as a catalyst for the momentum of the decolonisation movement in museums, particularly in the last few years as more museums are addressing the history and legacy of colonial collecting practices in their own institutions. Essentially, decolonisation can be broadly defined as the process of reversing colonialism in institutions by sharing authority and inviting representatives of descendant communities to engage in museum practice[4] (Smith 2005; Wintle 2013; Colwell 2017a).

In the United Kingdom, it has been 'formally' recognised that human remains acquired between 100 and 200 years ago from Indigenous peoples in colonial circumstances were obtained under unacceptable conditions, and where there was a very uneven divide of power (DCMS 2005). The Museums Association (2015, s2.3) Code of Ethics: Additional Guidance requires museums to respect the interests of originating communities and that the display of human remains can "cause distress to certain individuals or groups". Discussion and debate about the ethics of displaying human remains in museums and galleries in Britain are an extension of the wider debate to decolonise museums through repatriation claims of descendant communities including Australia, New Zealand, the Pacific region, and North America (Alberti et al. 2009; Feikert 2009; Giesen 2013; Joy 2014). As commented on earlier, human remains are fairly accepted in the United Kingdom. Colwell (2017b) notes that claims for Egyptian mummies, Viking bodies, and bog mummies do not have the same socio-political potency for the British and European public.

As archaeology in North America grew into a thriving discipline, so did the growth of museum collections containing Native American remains. Where 'white cemeteries' were reinterred, tribal cemeteries were emptied into museum or university storage (Colwell 2017b). Prior to NAGPRA in 1990, Native American remains were on display in several institutions then subsequently removed from view after the legislation went into effect. In their critique of how little involvement Indigenous populations have had in how ethical treatment protocols can and should be developed, Sadongei and Cash Cash (2007, 100) state that "we are confident that the ethical practices rooted in the social sciences are resilient enough to accommodate the value systems of Indigenous communities".

In 2007, the United Nations Declaration on the Rights of Indigenous Peoples (UNDRIP) was adopted by The General Assembly and published in 2008. This declaration gives Indigenous peoples the right to the repatriation of their human

[4]The annual conference theme for the Museum Ethnographers Group (MEG) in April 2018 was '*Decolonising the Museum in Practice*'. This event was held at the Pitt Rivers Museum in Oxford (UK).

remains but makes no reference to museums or display (United Nations 2008, Article 12.1). However, UNDRIP does support the potential for collections collaboration in Article 13 and 15. These state that Indigenous peoples have the right to revitalise and transmit to future generations their histories, languages, oral traditions, and philosophies thus encouraging active participation in museum interpretation (United Nations 2008, Article 13.1). Furthermore, Indigenous peoples have the right to the dignity and diversity of their cultures, traditions, histories, and aspirations, which shall be appropriately reflected in education and public information, which is directly aligned with the underlying mission of museums as public institutions (United Nations 2008, Article 15.1).

The display of the corpse is often cited as a reinforcement of colonial and institutional authority by Indigenous activists because of the traditional focus on human classification and "the ability of Europeans to obtain control over uncharted worlds" (Smith 2005, 424). However, what if the source community is the authority and they support the display of their ancestors? In their collaboration with descendant communities in Central Mexico, Overholtzer and Argueta (2017) discuss the criticisms that have been faced by the Xaltocan museum, an institution that has no policies against the display of human remains, was established and is run by community members, has no colonial past as an institution, and has no standing with North American or European curators. The 'collaborative exhibit', features skeletal remains and elaborate on the active role played by the dead in Mexican culture (as requested by the descendant community). The authors go on to discuss that, though there has been "*no* criticism in Mexico regarding the museum", their project has been criticised and censored by North American academics for its emphasis on showing human remains which, according to the Society for American Archaeology, do not take into account a diverse cultural audience, which may find offense in imagery of human remains (Overholtzer and Argueta 2017; Society for American Archaeology 2018). Overholtzer and Argueta (2017) state that in the decolonisation process of heritage, some collaborative partnerships with Indigenous communities necessitate communing with the dead, and that it would be more useful to have nuanced policies regarding their display rather than blanket policies prohibiting display.

In conversation with Dr. Guido Lombardi (2018, pers. comm.), a medical doctor and archaeologist in Lima (Perú) and an active member in the World Mummy Congress, he advocates the local community role in choices of how human remains are treated:

> Human remains are always attractive, and here, because their visibility was part of our heritage, there's less trouble as to debate if showing them is unethical. Mummies, as you know, were in many instances, part of the living though in a liminal state…surprisingly, some museums here are pulling human remains out of display because of some degree of foreign pressure…we can handle human remains our way, honouring our ancestors appropriately both by studying them, storing them the best we can, and whenever the chance occurs, by displaying them contextually. In Perú, local archaeologists and museum professionals have the concept of "Museos de Sitio" and that the goal for moving archaeological material is to bring it back to the source, which is closest to the descendants of local ancient 'cultures' who are local professionals."

According to Nilsson Stutz (2016, 268), in her comparison between Scandinavian and North American museum exhibitions, European museums display human burials with "pride and confidence", and the display of the ancient dead and death are virtually without controversy. In North America, most museums do not display human remains from archaeological contexts due to Indigenous advocacy and post-colonial critiques, and possible offense to descendant communities. However, Nilsson Stutz (2016) notes that the opposite is true when the remains are more modern or medical in nature. Gunther Von Hagen's exhibition Body Worlds was wildly successful in the United States but when it was shown in Sweden there was socio-political debate in the media about the ethics of the display (Nilsson Stutz 2016). In contrast, Sledzik and Barbian (2001, 229–230) report that, in their experience, visits by descendants of human remains held at the National Museum of Health and Medicine in Maryland (USA) can be constructive and "mutually supportive" and note that "families take great pride that their relative is part of this unique collection". Lohman and Goodnow (2006, 10) suggests that there is "a growing awareness that what may be appropriate for one museum is not necessarily appropriate elsewhere" leaving the argument to display the dead or not down to curators, communities, and context.

11.2 Ethical Decision Making: From Guidelines to Protocol

Human remains may be viewed differently in different localities, regions, or countries (BABAO 2010a, 4). In this light, local sensitivities and historical context are important when making decisions about whether to display human remains. The 'Code of Ethics' for the British Association of Biological Anthropology and Osteoarchaeology (2010a, 4–5) recommends that "biological remains should only be…viewed for legitimate purposes", and "consultation with and permission from the curating institution or relevant stakeholder" though it is vague on specifics. In the British Museum publication, 'Regarding the Dead: Human Remains in the British Museum', the decision to display remains over 100 years old should "balance the public benefits of display… against…known feelings of a community which has cultural continuity with the remains…and for whom the remains have cultural importance" (Antoine 2014, 7).

Ethical decision making about displaying the dead is open to interpretation due to diverse beliefs, cultural politics, and traditions of care (Brooks and Rumsey 2006; Lohman and Goodnow 2006; Cassman et al. 2007; Fossheim 2012; Sellevold 2012; Giesen and White 2013; White 2013). Guidance in ethical codes tends to focus on general principles rather than specific practice with the bulk of the documentation about curation, repatriation, and claims rather than display per se (BABAO 2010b; Brooks and Rumsey 2006). Consequently, these guidelines give local museum professionals, some with country-specific frameworks, responsibility of assessing the degree of sensitivity of the human remains to be displayed while trying to navigate the interests and beliefs of descendant communities (Brooks and Rumsey 2006; Giesen and White 2013; Swain 2016; Overholtzer and Argueta 2017). Giesen and White (2013, 20) state that, "no universal approach can be established as one community's methods may not be appropriate for another".

11.2.1 International Accords

In 1989, the World Archaeological Congress (WAC) adopted the 'Vermillion Accord on Human Remains' as a model for international ethics issues and respect for the dead, the living descendants, and scientific research (WAC 1989). More specifically for displaying the dead, the WAC 'Tamaki Makau-rau Accord on the Display of Human Remains and Sacred Objects', adopted in 2006, builds upon the principles of respect adopted by the Vermillion Accord. It states that: "display means the presentation in any media or form of human remains and sacred objects, whether on a single occasion or on an ongoing basis, including conference presentations or publications" (WAC 2006). According to the Tamaki Makau-rau Accord any organisation considering displaying human remains or those institutions that already were doing so should take account of the following principles:

- Permission should be obtained from the affected community or communities;
- Should permission be refused, that decision is final and should be respected;
- Should permission be granted, any conditions to which that permission is subject should be complied with in full;
- All display should be culturally appropriate;
- Permission can be withdrawn or amended at any stage and such decisions should be respected;
- Regular consultation with the affected community should ensure that the display remains culturally appropriate.

The International Council of Museums (ICOM) produced the 'Code of Ethics and Standards for Museum Practice' in 2006 and recently updated it in 2017. This document underlines the need for an international code of ethics for the conservation and display of human remains. The ICOM (2017) contribution concentrates on collections acquisition, storage and care, research, and display, highlighting professional practice and standards for museums and their staff. Throughout the code, emphasis is placed on the "interests and beliefs of members of the community, ethnic or religious groups from which the [human remains] originated, where these are known" (ICOM 2017, Article 2.5). Guidelines 4.1–4.5 of the code relate specifically to displaying the dead and what to consider ahead of exhibition preparation (ICOM 2017, 25):

4.1. Displays, Exhibitions, and Special Activities

- Displays and temporary exhibitions, physical or electronic, should be in accordance with the stated mission, policy, and purpose of the museum. They should not compromise either the quality or the proper care and conservation of the collections.

4.2. Interpretation of Exhibitions

- Museums should ensure that the information they present in displays and exhibitions is well-founded, accurate, and gives appropriate consideration to represented groups or beliefs.

4.3. Exhibition of Sensitive Materials

- Human remains and materials of sacred significance must be displayed in a manner consistent with professional standards and, where known, taking into account the interests and beliefs of members of the community, ethnic or religious groups from whom the objects originated. They must be presented with great tact and respect for the feelings of human dignity held by all peoples.

4.4. Removal from Public Display

- Requests for removal from public display of human remains or material of sacred significance from the originating communities must be addressed expeditiously with respect and sensitivity. Requests for the return of such material should be addressed similarly. Museum policies should clearly define the process for responding to such requests.

4.5. Display of Unprovenanced Material

- Museums should avoid displaying or otherwise using material of questionable origin or lacking provenance. They should be aware that such displays or usage can be seen to condone and contribute to the illicit trade in cultural property.

The Native American Graves Protection and Repatriation Act (NAGPRA 1990) promotes Indigenous visibility and ethical discourse around collections of human remains in North America, however, formally, it does not comment on, condone, or condemn the display of human remains. Informally, NAGPRA has significant influence over how museums in North America curate exhibitions with no North American remains on display unless by express permission of the tribe. This has carried weight internationally for other Indigenous communities with several museums no longer displaying the remains of people from the Torres Strait and Solomon Islands, Greenland, Australia, and New Zealand[5] (Jenkins 2011).

11.2.2 British Regulations

In the United Kingdom, there are nationally recognised documents for ethical standards and the display of human remains for public view. These are the Human Tissue Authority's (2017a) 'Code of Practice (D) Display' and the Department of Culture, Media and Sport's (DCMS 2005) 'Guidance for the Care of Human Remains in Museums'. These publications reflect an amalgamation of previous resources including adaptations from the Museum Ethnographers Group (MEG 1994, 2003) 'Professional Guidelines Concerning The Storage, Display, Interpretation And Return Of Human Remains In Ethnographical Collections In United Kingdom Museums', from the DCMS (2003) report 'The Report of the Working Group on Human Remains', from the Museums and Galleries Commission (2000) guidelines 'Restitution and Repatriation', and the World Archaeological Congress (WAC 1989) 'The Vermillion Accord'. Scotland has its own Human Tissue (Scotland) Act (2006), where subsection 6A deals specifically with the control of human remains on public display and Museums Galleries Scotland (2011) have produced 'Guidelines for the Care of Human Remains in Scottish Museum Collections' to address issues surrounding the display of human bodies. The National Museum of Ireland also has a policy on human remains that comments on ethics and display of the dead (National Museum of Ireland 2006).

11.2.3 The Human Tissue Authority in Britain

Museum professionals in the United Kingdom regularly refer to the numerous hospital organ retention scandals that were uncovered in the 1990s that resulted in the passage of the Human Tissue Act of 2004. The Human Tissue Act (2004) does not define public display, however it does state that human remains should be treated with appropriate respect and dignity. In 2005, the Human Tissue Authority was created by Parliament, whose remit is defined in the Human Tissue Act (Human Tissue Act 2004, Sect. 14) and regulates the public display of human remains as part of its Code of Practice (D) Public Display (Human Tissue Authority 2017a), one of seven Codes of Practice that give guidance to professionals working with human remains (Table 11.1).

[5]The author discussed this at length with the Division Head of Anthropology, Dr. Laurie Burgess, at the National Museum of Natural History, Smithsonian Institution (Washington D.C., USA).

Table 11.1 Codes of Practice of the Human Tissue Authority (2017b), which were published in April 2017 and the last major review of the documents since 2009

Code	Code details
Code A	Guiding principles and the fundamental principle of consent
Code B	Post-mortem examination
Code C	Anatomical examination
Code D	Public display
Code E	Research
Code F	Donation of solid organs and tissue for transplantation
Code G	Donation of allogenic bone marrow and peripheral blood stems cells for transplantation

The Human Tissue Authority (2017a) considers public display to be an "exhibition or display in which the body of a person, or relevant material which has come from the body of a person, is used for the purpose of being exposed to view by the public". The Human Tissue Authority Code of Practice (D) Public Display emphasises that bodies of the deceased, body parts, or other human specimens should be treated with respect in an environment that is secure, that the dignity of the deceased should be maintained at all times whilst they are on display, and that their display is in line with the consent given. For human remains that are imported, it means that the country of origin should have a legal and ethical framework which includes consent and protects the interests of the deceased and their families (Human Tissue Authority 2017a).

The Human Tissue Act (2004) makes consent a legal requirement for the storage and display of human material where it is less than 100 years since the person's death. This then requires the museum or holding institution to be licensed by the Human Tissue Authority for public display (Human Tissue Act 2004, Sect. 1(1)). Institutions in the public display sector that are licensed include national museums with permanent collections, pathology and medical museums, small specialist museums that feature temporary exhibitions, and human health foundations (Human Tissue Authority 2017a). The legal requirements of the Human Tissue Act and the guiding principles in the Human Tissue Authority Code D do not apply to bodies (or relevant material) where the person died before the first of September 2006 when the Human Tissue Act Regulations came into effect (though a license to store remains would still be required). Furthermore, the guidance does not apply to whole bodies or parts of bodies that are historical human remains, or human remains incorporated into artefacts, which are more than 100 years old (Human Tissue Authority 2017a). The display of archaeological remains, therefore, does not require a public display license, which is interesting considering they are, after all, still human remains. One of the ultimate goals of HTA licensing of institutions that display human remains is the assurance to the public that bodies or tissue from the deceased are handled with care, treated with respect, and that dignity applies to both the viewed and the viewer (Human Tissue Authority 2017a), but museum professionals have been critical from the start of the Human Tissue Authority licensing scheme and overall lack of communication between sectors (Steel 2006).

11.2.4 Department of Culture, Media, and Sport (DCMS)

Ethical issues raised by the display of human remains acknowledges their unique status within museum collections and the important responsibilities placed on those who curate and exhibit them (Brooks and Rumsey 2006; Cassman et al. 2007; Redfern and Bekvalac 2013; Fletcher et al. 2014). To facilitate best practice for the treatment of human remains in the United Kingdom and in response to repatriation claims abroad, the Department of Culture, Media, and Sport (DCMS 2005) drafted the 'Guidance for the Care of Human Remains in Museums', which "should be read by anyone involved in the display of human material" (Human Tissue Authority 2017a). This document provides guidance for museums and other institutions in England, Wales, and Northern Ireland that hold human remains in permanent collections. The guidance brings together best practice advice relating to collections acquisition and access, repatriation, conservation, de-accessioning, display, educational use, loans, research, and storage (DCMS 2005).

In the UK especially, visitor surveys show that the majority of museum visitors are comfortable with and often expect to see human remains, as part of museum displays (see also Mills and Tranter 2010). According to the DCMS (2005, 20) guidelines, there are many compelling reasons for using human remains in displays including, "to educate medical practitioners, to educate people in science and history, to explain burial practices, to bring people into physical contact with past people, and to encourage reflection". In Sect. 2.7 of the DCMS Guidelines (2005, 20)—titled 'Public Display'—it is acknowledged that museums have a choice as to whether they display remains and/or images of the deceased in their exhibitions, and that, "careful thought should be put into the reasons for, and circumstances of, the display of human remains". Human remains should be displayed only if the institution believes that it makes a material contribution to a "particular interpretation" which could not be equally effective in a different way. "Sufficient explanatory material" should also be made available indicating perhaps more text within an exhibition explaining why human remains are being shown as part of the narrative (DCMS 2005, 20). The display itself should be secure and reflective of storage protocols with monitored environments and in a specially partitioned part of a gallery. The importance here being that visitors should have a *choice* if they want to view human remains or not (Gill-Robinson 2004)

While the DCMS (2005) guidelines are "just a guidance" with museums having no obligation to implement them (White 2013, 50), they can provide supplemental architecture for museum policies about collections of human remains. The guidelines recommend implementing appropriate practice for dealing with the display of human remains as part of an overall policy on human remains in their care and make this public, for example on their institution's website. Both the Natural History Museum in London and the Museum of London have collections of British human remains on their websites, which are not often on display, with informative text about the excavations, historic background, and photographs of pathologies. The Pitt Rivers Museum in Oxford (UK) has a guide to human remains in the museum on their website, alongside a link to the catalogue database, a history of the Shrunken Head (*tsantas*) in the collection, hyperlinks to further resources, and photographs of remains as PDF files (Pitt Rivers Museum 2018). There is a description for potential visitors of what to expect on display (see quote below) and some mention of the imperialistic strategy of collecting. This approach provides visitors with the necessary tools to make an informed decision as to whether a visit is appropriate for them.

> The collections include human remains acquired to show some aspect of culture: the remembrance of the dead (e.g. hair bracelets and brooches), modification of the body to conform to standards of beauty (e.g. skulls showing evidence of head-binding), the treatment of illness and injury (e.g. skulls showing trepanning), and religious practices (e.g. skull bowls from Tibet, used in tantric Buddhist rituals to make sacrificial offerings to protective deities).... (Pitt Rivers Museum 2018)

The Wellcome Trust (WT), a leading institution for biomedical and medical humanities research in the UK, is home to the Wellcome Collection which holds over 500 human remains and objects made with human tissues in their collections. They have their 'policy on the care of human remains in museums and galleries' online and is supportive of the "strong educational value and high level of public interest in displays featuring human remains" (Wellcome Trust 2005, Sect. 4.1). It explicitly states compliance with the DCMS (2005) guidelines and its role as the founding framework for the WT's own policy, which is transparent in their acknowledgement of sensitivities of both source communities and potential audiences when deciding to display human remains. Institutional collections such as the Duckworth Laboratory at the University of Cambridge (UK) also incorporate the DCMS (2005) guidelines into their 'Policy on the Curation and Conservation of Human Remains' (Mirazón-Lahr 2011).

Before the Human Tissue Act (2004) and DCMS (2005) guidelines were implemented in England, Wales, and Northern Ireland, public display of the dead was not covered by statute and, as such, there were no restrictions on the display of human remains or material of human origin (Human Tissue Authority 2017a). The Museum Ethnographers Group (MEG) adopted professional guidelines in 1991 concerning the storage, display, interpretation, and return of human remains in ethnographic collections in the United Kingdom. These 18 directives were later published in 1994 as the 'Guidelines on Management of Human Remains' (MEG 1994). Three of these directives refer to the display of human remains and place emphasis on the role of the curator, specifically that curators should take a proactive rather than a reactive position about the display of human remains. Existing displays should undergo evaluation to consider whether the current practice of display of human remains is likely to cause offence to actual or cultural descendants (MEG 1994, Sect. 3.1). Curators should inform themselves of the concerns of Indigenous peoples and where practicable should seek their involvement through consultation (MEG 1994, Sect. 3.2). Curators should be aware of the likely public effects of exhibitions as they often carry authority, thus it is crucial to evaluate whether an exhibition is reinforcing cultural stereotypes or broadening an understanding of a particular group of people in a way which is relevant to the present day (MEG 1994, Sect. 3.3). Notwithstanding the regional placement of the framework in the UK, the section on 'Display and Interpretation' in the MEG's (1994) 'Guidelines on Management of Human Remains' can easily extend into the ethical narrative of a global network of museums and institutions that house and display human remains. Unfortunately, there is almost no practical training for putting such a narrative in place, aside from conference workshops, which can be expensive and have limited attendance due to the lack of support for museum professionals.

11.3 Public Engagement and Display

The display of human material and public engagement with human remains in the areas of medicine and the humanities are becoming increasingly popular (Human Tissue Authority 2017a). As the interest of the public grows, museums are finding new roles for their collections, and exploring novel ways of engaging with the public. Specialty events featuring guest speakers, cocktails, film screenings, and tactile activities are selling out in UK museums, providing revenue for the museum, and merriment with an 'educational and morbid twist' for the visitor. These events have their own ethical considerations such as the possible exploitation of the dead for profit, and dignity in death. In the author's experience, curators have forbidden photography, and politely reminded guests about the sensitive nature of some of the medical specimens on display (though this does not stop people from trying to take photographs, which is problematic).

Handling sessions at museums or at special events are a good way in which the public may learn about archaeological remains and skeletal biology such as Anthropology Day in London or the Cambridge Science Festival. However, direct contact by the public may entail a greater risk of offending religious and other sensitivities than is the case in a more controlled environment such that those contemplating organising handling sessions should "weigh carefully" the potential benefits against the risks involved (DCMS 2005, Sect. 2.8). Visitors need to be informed as to the differences between real human remains and casts when skeletal components are on view so that they can decide for themselves and their children what they want to engage with (APABE 2017).

The Human Tissue Authority (2017a) seeks to ensure that all those engaged in activities that involve the public display of human material are aware of the statutory and regulatory requirements, as well as the guiding principles of consent and dignity, which should underpin the conduct of these activities. Public display may mean many things, and the Human Tissue Authority Code of Practice includes examples, which illustrate situations that are, or are not, considered to be display to the public. In broad terms, it should be taken to mean "events that are open to the public, whether by ticket sale or free access, regardless of the location and purpose of the venue and whether temporary or permanent" (Human Tissue Authority 2017a). For staff and volunteers, this will include ensuring that there is a clear policy on the behaviours, actions, and attitudes demonstrated by staff and visitors, whether directed at the exhibits that might be considered to disregard the dignity of the deceased (Human Tissue Authority 2017a). The photography of human remains for educational and general museum use will be acceptable in most cases, although in considering any photography, views of cultural communities and genealogical descendants should be considered where known (DCMS 2005).

Societies have evolved complex ways of dealing with the physical and emotional consequences of death, and these can mimic a spectrum of differing levels of acceptability in relation to the display of human remains (Hallam et al. 2005; Brooks and Rumsey 2006). The dichotomy between scientific value and the decolonisation of collections requires ethical guidelines that promote transparency of the acquisition and research of collections, protect cultural heritage, and support the needs of all interested parties, i.e. descendant communities, researchers, and the public. A direct effect of the Human Tissue Act (2004) is that institutions had to create inventories of their holdings of human remains and whether or not these remains were under or over 100 years old, forcing institutions to review their collections and procedures. In her analysis of the impact and effectiveness of the Human Tissue Act (2004) and the DCMS (2005) guidance for museums, White (2013, 50) suggests that there will be an "ongoing learning process…as those with an interest in the fate of human remains change or expand…the publication of the Guidance has undoubtedly helped to foster new relationships built upon respect, openness, and cooperation that would not otherwise have been possible".

11.4 Discussion

Burial practice and the commemoration of the dead transform and adjust, sometimes over relatively short periods of time (Hallam and Hockey 2001). These shifts can reveal themselves via the range of different attitudes visitors bring to viewing a dead human body in a museum. It could be argued that museums are playing an important role in introducing visitors, especially young people, to the reality of human mortality (Patterson 2007). Archaeologist Parker Pearson (1999, 183) suggests that "…death is treated as a medical failure and is hidden from society at large… Archaeology is the only medium by which many people will ever see or touch the remains of dead bodies". Pathology museum collections are also part of a 'confronting death' narrative in that they can provide a direct comparison with archaeological remains about disease and the human body in pre-modern treatment regimes. Pathology collections are especially important because they give visitors the chance to view the effects of diseases that have been eradicated, their historical significance, and their influence on modern medicine. Perhaps, one of the main reasons displays of human remains are incredibly popular amongst the public is due to a reflection of the deeper nature to which we examine our own bodies, our own illnesses, and contemplate our own deaths, thus peeking into the past on the reality of death of other people.

Though not all institutions find the display of human remains problematic, historically in Western museums, temporal or geographic distance enabled objectification of dead bodies and body parts. Bodies become “nonbodies” and were regarded as objects, divorced from contextual frameworks, whether artistic, historical, scientific, or medical (Hallam and Hockey 2001, 4–5). Museums have a choice as to whether they want to display human remains. However, simply removing human remains from display does not always pacify the issue as museums are often attacked for not displaying more of their collections (both objects and human remains) (Brooks and Rumsey 2006; see also Manchester Museum 2008a, 2008b). How do we as museum professionals, descendant communities, bioarchaeologists, anthropologists, historians, and scientists, ensure the well-being of human remains that are on display for the public? Through focusing on the practical elements of display, we can endeavour to address the socially ethical questions that we are faced with.

11.5 Ethical Practice in Display

Using Marstine’s (2011, 10) new museum ethics *paradigm shift*, which is characterised by “social responsibility, radical transparency, and shared guardianship of heritage”, and the previously discussed ethical guidelines for the United Kingdom and abroad, a series of agendas are presented here to help institutions with human remains on display or those that are considering it for future exhibitions.

11.5.1 Community Agenda

The Museums Association (2015, Sect. 2.3) suggests that museums should be “proactive” and to consult with existing descendant communities when displaying human remains. The creation of Advisory Panels and the use of focus groups are an inclusive way to hear multiple views about the display of human remains and for the distillation of themes for a potential exhibition. Members should represent a diverse background, taking into account practical and/or personal knowledge, ensuring alternative views as constructive contributions, and encouraging open reflection on ethical considerations (Marstine 2011). The Museum of Archaeology and Anthropology (MAA) at the University of Cambridge used focus groups[6] during the planning phase of the exhibition, ‘Hide and Seek: looking for children in the past’ (2016–2017). The potential display of a locally excavated skeleton of an Anglo-Saxon female aged 12–15 years old was discussed at length due to concerns

[6]The focus group included theologians, archaeologists, educators, museum professionals, community leaders, and the general public.

over the display of a 'young person' (see Sect. 11.1.2 of this chapter), deemed appropriate to display, and eventually became one of the highlights of the exhibition particularly among young audiences with no negative feedback (Harknett 2017).

11.5.2 Gallery Agenda

Public notices, or warnings, are becoming standard practice in museums informing visitors that human remains are on display in their galleries, thus giving them a choice in how they plan their visit (Brooks and Rumsey 2006; Museums Association 2015, Sect. 2.3; Swain 2016; Tatham 2016). The Human Tissue Authority (2017a) suggests that any display featuring material of human origin should not disregard the dignity of the deceased and make visitors aware they will come across human remains, whose display may provoke an emotional or ethical response, particularly in the very young. A notice about what type of content will be presented in an exhibit that is potentially challenging benefits adults who can then decide if it is age appropriate for the child they are with (Patterson 2007). One comment in the visitor feedback from the MAA Childhood exhibition stated, "design of wall allowing the choice to view the child's skeleton, or not, was great. It offers respect for the deceased and the visitor" (Harknett 2017). Where applicable, displaying the remains with their grave goods or in a recreated traditional context provides more context into the social intimacies and intricacies of human burial practices and is well-received by visitors (Biers 2001; Harknett 2018).

11.5.3 Interpretive Agenda

In addition to the physical manifestation of the display of human remains, cultural context, supporting text, and interpretation need to be considered equally. Barbian and Berndt (2001) argue that carefully developed labelling using accessible language is important to make the display of human remains into an educational experience. Marstine (2011, 14) exemplifies how communicative strategies in exhibitions could encourage conversation and critical thinking, "A transparent wall text might tell us that an artefact is of unknown provenance; a radically transparent wall text would additionally engage the ethical issue of exhibiting works of unknown provenance". In a previous exhibition evaluation reported on by the author (Biers 2001), it was found that 75% of visitors were 'Roamers' and 25% were 'Readers' which led to the editing of museum labels so that the first three lines of text were highly informative, while the latter half of the text was more supplemental in nature. Years of museum experience has led to the consensus that visitors want to know 'what is it?', 'where is it from?', 'how old is it?', and 'how did it get in the museum?' In displaying human remains, the questions can be more multifarious such as whether the wishes and intentions of the deceased are being met, can this information be known, and the ethos of why they are being displayed. The concept of consent and the ability to make an informed decision is a key aspect of the Human Tissue Act (2004), however, applying consent to the ancient dead is much more complex (Alberti et al. 2009; Tarlow 2009; Jones and Whitaker 2013; Woodhead 2013; Wilson 2015; Knott 2018). Pro-active museum texts could discuss the consent issue and ancient remains by posing scenarios or questions to visitors. The Museums Association (2015, Sect. 2.3) states that human remains should only be displayed if "the museum believes that they make a material contribution to a particular interpretation".

11.5.4 Front-of-House Agenda

Once an exhibition is successfully opened, it is the Front-of-House staff and volunteers that face the public daily and engage with viewers who may have an emotive response to seeing human remains on display. Staff and volunteers should be given a choice to work in these galleries and for those that choose to do so, should have training in the ethical issues that are inherent to displaying the dead. Training can provide museum staff and volunteers with an informed front, answering visitor questions respectfully and be assuring with the public who may want to engage in ethical debate. In 2015, the Museum of Archaeology and Anthropology in Cambridge had a training session for their Front-of-House staff by an osteoarchaeologist who covered topics such as excavating burials, current legislation for display, and treatment of the dead along with answering questions and concerns that listeners had[7].

11.5.5 Evaluation Agenda

Communication is fundamental between curators with their expertise and museum educators who have first-hand knowledge of the visitor experience. Together, they can collaborate on formal evaluations of gallery displays that feature human remains, because if we are not evaluating how the public experience these displays then why display the dead at all? Where Gunther von Hagen's Body Worlds exhibition is often described as shocking by anatomical associations (IFAA 2018), gallery evaluations show the content is extremely popular (Barilan 2006). Tatham (2016) advocates that where time and funds permit, both *formative* (before the

[7]The training session was presented by the author in relation to the *Hide and Seek: Looking for Children in the Past* exhibition, as well as the permanent Cambridge gallery display of a Roman skeleton in a sarcophagus.

interpretation is created) and *summative* (after the interpretation has been installed) evaluations should be conducted. Focus groups are useful for formative interpretations of exhibit content and educators can track how visitors respond to the display (Harknett 2017). Evaluations are useful tools that promote visibility, or identify a lack thereof, and can pinpoint curatorial, educational, or ethical targets.

This series of agendas, or protocol, are non-culturally specific and can be used as a template for displaying the dead regardless of the size of the holding institution. Where the beliefs about the dead body can vary regionally, the way museums approach displaying the body does not necessarily have to.

11.6 Conclusion

Open negotiations on how the dead are displayed in museums and galleries are crucial to descendant community collaboration, exhibition design, collections research, and public access. Acknowledging historical practices stemming from colonial determination should not be shrouded but revealed through transparent communication serving as a 'jumping off point' to active dialogue about cultural sensitivity and important directions such as decolonisation. Although human remains on display have an appeal for many museum-going audiences, they are in fact undeniably popular, they can be a source of great distress for some, and institutions that continue to display human remains must address this through community feedback (pre-exhibition focus groups), considerate exhibition design (conscientious display), meaningful interpretation (both emic and etic), and evaluation (surveys of the public).

Acknowledgements The author would like to thank Erica Jones, David Hunt, Chris Dudar, Eric Hollinger, Bill Billeck, Laurie Burgess, Erin Guthrie, Kristin Macak, Janine Hinton, and Meredith Luze of the National Museum of Natural History in Washington D.C., Jelena Bekvalac and Rebecca Redfern from the Museum of London, Sarah-Jane Harknett and Jody Joy at the Museum of Archaeology and Anthropology in Cambridge, Rose Tyson previously at the San Diego Museum of Man, Guido Lombardi, Marta Mirazón-Lahr, Catherine Kneale, the University of Maryland College Park Anth221 summer forensic students, and especially Dave Lloyd. Thank you to Kirsty Squires, David Errickson, and Nicholas Márquez-Grant for including me in this volume, giving me feedback on the content, and patiently allowing me to complete this research.

References

Adams, E. 2009. Defining and Displaying the Human Body: Collectors and Classics During the British Enlightenment. *Hermathena* 187: 65–97.

Advisory Panel on Archaeology of Burials in England [APABE]. 2017. *Guidelines for Best Practice for the Treatment of Human Remains Excavated from Christian Burial Grounds in England*, 2nd ed. Swindon: Advisory Panel on Archaeology of Burials in England.

Alberti, S., R. Drew, P. Bienkowski, et al. 2009. Should We Display the Dead? *Museum and Society* 7: 133–149.

Antoine, D. 2014. Curating Human Remains in Museum Collections: Broader Considerations and a British Museum Perspective. In *Regarding the Dead: Human Remains in the British Museum*, ed. A. Fletcher, D. Antoine, and J.D. Hill, 3–9. London: The British Museum Press.

Barbian, L., and L. Berndt. 2001. When Your Insides Are Out: Museum Visitor Perceptions of Displays of Human Anatomy. In *Human Remains: Conservation, Retrieval, and Analysis: Proceedings of a Conference Held in Williamsburg, VA, Nov 7–11th 1999*, ed. E. Williams, 257–266. Oxford: Archaeopress.

Barilan, Y.M. 2006. Bodyworlds and The Ethics of Using Human Remains: A Preliminary Discussion. *Bioethics* 20 (5): 233–247.

Bennett, T. 1995. *The Birth of the Museum: History, Theory, Politics*. Oxon: Routledge.

Biers, T.M. 2000. *Mysteries of the Mummies: Educating the Public About Human Remains*. Poster Presented for the 27th Annual Meeting of the Paleopathology Association, San Antonio, Texas, USA, 11–12 April 2000.

Biers, T.M. 2001. *The Educational Value of Using Human Skeletal Remains and Mummies in Museum Exhibits*. Co-chairs of Panel Presentation at the Annual Meeting of the Southwestern Anthropological Association, San Diego, California, USA, 11–13 April 2001.

Biers, T.M. 2013. *Investigating the Relationship Between Labour and Gender, Material Culture, and Identity at an Inka Period Cemetery: A Regional Analysis of Provincial Burials from Lima, Peru*. Dissertation, University of Cambridge.

Binski, P. 1996. *Medieval Death*. Ritual and Representation: British Museum Press, London.

British Association of Biological Anthropology and Osteoarchaeology [BABAO]. 2010a. *Code of Ethics. Working-Group for Ethics and Practice*. http://www.babao.org.uk/assets/Uploads/code-of-ethics.pdf. Accessed 18 August 2017.

British Association of Biological Anthropology and Osteoarchaeology [BABAO]. 2010b. *Code of Practice. Working-Group for Ethics and Practice*. http://www.babao.org.uk/assets/Uploads/code-of-practice.pdf. Accessed 18 August 2017.

Brooks, M.M., and C. Rumsey. 2006. The Body in the Museum. In *Human Remains: Guide for Museums and Academic Institutions*, ed. V. Cassman, N. Odegaard, and J. Powell, 261–289. Walnut Creek: AltaMira Press.

Bruwelheide, K.S., S.S. Schlachtmeyer, D.W. Owsley, et al. 2017. Unearthing Robert Kennicott: Naturalist, Explorer, Smithsonian Scientist. In *Studies in Forensic Biohistory: Anthropological Perspectives*, ed. C.M. Stojanowski and W.N. Duncan, 92–123. Cambridge: Cambridge University Press.

Cassman, V., N. Odegaard, and J. Powell. 2007. Introduction: Dealing with the Dead. In *Human Remains: Guide for Museums and Academic Institutions*, ed. V. Cassman, N. Odegaard, and J. Powell, 1–3. Walnut Creek: AltaMira Press.

Clegg, M., R. Redfern, J. Bekvalak, et al. 2013. *Global Ancestors: Understanding the Shared Humanity of Our Ancestors*. Oxford: Oxbow Books.

Colwell, C. 2017a. *Plundered Skulls and Stolen Spirits: Inside the Fight to Reclaim Native America's Culture*. Chicago: University of Chicago Press.

Colwell, C. 2017b. The Long Ethical Arc of Displaying Human Remains. *Atlas Obscura*. 16 November. https://www.atlasobscura.com/articles/displaying-native-american-remains. Accessed 30 July 2018.

Department for Culture, Media and Sport [DCMS]. 2003. *Working Group on Human Remains Report*. London: Department for Culture, Media and Sport.

Department for Culture, Media and Sport [DCMS]. 2005. *Guidance for the Care of Human Remains in Museums*. London: Department for Culture, Media and Sport.

Exhibitions Intl, LLC. 2017. *Press Release for Mummies of the World Exhibition: The Exhibition to Open at Union Station*. 19 April. http://www.unionstation.org/news/mummies-world-exhibition-open-union-station. Accessed 31 July 2018.

Feikert, C. 2009. *Repatriation of Historic Human Remains: United Kingdom*. https://www.loc.gov/law/help/repatriation-human-remains/united-kingdom.php. Accessed 30 July 2018.

Fforde, C., J. Hubert, and P. Turnbull. 2002. *The Dead and Their Possessions: Repatriation in Principle, Policy and Practice*. Routledge: London.

Fletcher, A., D. Antoine, and J.D. Hill (eds.). 2014. *Regarding the Dead: Human Remains in the British Museum*. London: The British Museum Press.

Fossheim, H. 2012. *More Than Just Bones: Ethics and Research on Human Remains*. Oslo: The Norwegian National Research Ethics Committee.

Gazi, A. 2014. Exhibition Ethics—An Overview of Major Issues. *Journal of Conservation and Museum Studies* 12 (1): 1–10.

Giesen, M. (ed.). 2013. *Curating Human Remains: Caring for the Dead in the United Kingdom*. Woodbridge: The Boydell Press.

Giesen, M., and L. White. 2013. International Perspectives Towards Human Remains Curation. In *Curating Human Remains: Caring for the Dead in the United Kingdom*, ed. M. Giesen, 13–24. Woodbridge: The Boydell Press.

Gill-Robinson, H. 2004. Bog Bodies on Display. *Journal of Wetland Archaeology* 4 (1): 111–116.

Hallam, E., and J. Hockey. 2001. *Death, Memory and Material Culture*. Oxford: Berg.

Hallam, E., J. Hockey, and G. Howarth. 2005. *Beyond the Body: Death and Social Identity*. London: Routledge.

Harknett, S.J. 2017. *Evaluation of the Exhibition 'Hide and Seek: Looking for Children in the Past' 2016–2017*. Cambridge: Museum of Archaeology and Anthropology, University of Cambridge.

Harknett, S.J. 2018. *How We Located the Most Visited Object in Our Museum*. Connecting Collections Blog: University of Cambridge Museums (UCM). https://www.museums.cam.ac.uk/blog/2018/04/13/how-we-located-the-most-visited-object-in-our-museums/. Accessed 10 November 2019.

Human Tissue Act. 2004. The Stationery Office, London.

Human Tissue (Scotland) Act. 2006. The Scottish Parliament, Edinburgh.

Human Tissue Authority [HTA]. 2017a. *Code of Practice and Standards, D Public Display*. https://www.hta.gov.uk/regulated-sectors/public-display. Accessed 6 August 2018.

Human Tissue Authority [HTA]. 2017b. *HTA Codes of Practice and Standards*. https://www.hta.gov.uk/hta-codes-practice-and-standards-0. Accessed 15 August 2018.

International Council for Museums [ICOM]. 2017. *Code of Ethics for Museums*. Paris: International Council for Museums.

International Federation of Associations of Anatomists [IFAA]. 2018. *Ethical and Medical Humanities Perspectives on the Public Display of Plastinated Human Bodies*. www.ifaa.net/wp-content/uploads/2018/02/FICEM-on-plastination-exhibits_2018.pdf. Accessed 15 August 2018.

Jenkins, T. 2011. *Contesting Human Remains in Museum Collections: The Crisis of Cultural Authority*. New York: Taylor and Francis.

Jones, D.G., and M.I. Whitaker. 2013. The Contested Realm of Displaying Dead Bodies. *Journal of Medical Ethics* 39 (10): 652–653.

Joy, J. 2014. Looking Death in the Face: Different Attitudes Towards the Bog Bodies and Their Display with a Focus on Lindow Man. In *Regarding the Dead: Human Remains in the British Museum*, ed. A. Fletcher, D. Antoine, and J.D. Hill, 10–19. London: The British Museum Press.

Kilmister, H. 2004. Visitor Perceptions of Human Remains and Their Wider Relevance to Natural History. *NatSCA News* 3: 18–21.

Knott, J. 2018. Hunterian to Consider Release of "Irish Giant" Skeleton. *Museums Association News*. 20 June. https://www.museumsassociation.org/museums-journal/news/20062018-hunterian-to-consider-release-of-irish-giant-skeleton. Accessed 8 August 2018.

Lohman, J., and K. Goodnow (eds.). 2006. *Human Remains and Museum Practice*. London and Paris: Museum of London and United Nations Educational, Scientific and Cultural Organisation.

Manchester Museum. 2008a. *Policy Document for the Strategic Development of The Manchester Museum: Policy on Human Remains*. http://www.museum.manchester.ac.uk/aboutus/reportspolicies/fileuploadmax10mb,120796,en.pdf. Accessed 25 March 2018.

Manchester Museum. 2008b. *Official Statement from the Manchester Museum About the Temporary Covering Up of the Unwrapped Mummies in the Ancient Egypt Gallery*. http://www.museum.manchester.ac.uk/aboutus/pressreleases/pressreleasesarchive/. Accessed 25 March 2018.

Marselis, R. 2016. On Not Showing Scalps: Human Remains and Multisited Debate at the National Museum of Denmark. *Museum Anthropology* 39 (1): 20–34.

Marstine, J. 2011. The Contingent Nature of the New Museum Ethics. In *The Routledge Companion to Museum Ethics: Redefining Ethics for the Twenty-First-Century Museum*, ed. J. Marstine, 3–25. London: Routledge.

Metcalf, P., and R. Huntington. 1991. *Celebrations of Death: The Anthropology of Mortuary Ritual*. New York: Cambridge University Press.

Mills, S., and V. Tranter. 2010. *Research into Issues Surrounding Human Bones in Museums*. London: Business Development Research Consultants.

Mirazón-Lahr, M. 2011. *Policy on the Curation and Conservation of Human Remains*. Cambridge: Duckworth Laboratory, University of Cambridge.

Museums and Galleries Commission. 2000. *Restitution and Repatriation: Guidelines for Good Practice*. London: Museums and Galleries Commission.

Museums Association. 2015. *Code of Ethics: Additional Guidance*. https://www.museumsassociation.org/download?id=1173810. Accessed 8 August 2018.

Museums Ethnographers Group [MEG]. 1994. *Professional Guidelines Concerning the Storage, Display, Interpretation and Return of Human Remains in Ethnographical Collections in the United Kingdom*. Aberdeen: Museum Ethnographers Group.

Museum Ethnographers Group [MEG]. 2003. Guidance Notes on Ethical Approaches in Museum Ethnography. *Journal of Museum Ethnography* 15. www.museumethnographersgroup.org.uk/en/resources/343-meg-publications.html. Accessed 22 July 2018.

Museum Galleries Scotland. 2011. *Guidelines for the Care of Human Remains in Scottish Museum Collections*. https://www.museumsgalleriesscotland.org.uk/media/1089/guidelines-for-the-care-of-human-remains-in-scottish-museum-collections.pdf. Accessed 31 July 2018.

National Museum of Ireland. 2006. *Policy on Human Remains*. https://www.museum.ie/NationalMuseumIreland/media/Corporate-Information/Policies%20and%20Guidelines/Policy-Human-Remains-Final.pdf. Accessed 31 July 2018.

Native American Graves Protection and Repatriation Act (NAGPRA). Public Law 101-601, 25 United States Code 3001 et seq., 104 Stat. 3048–Nov. 16, 1990 (1990) 101st United States Congress, Washington, D.C.

Nilsson Stutz, L. 2016. To Gaze Upon the Dead: The Exhibition of Human Remains as Cultural Practice and Political Practice in Scandinavia and the USA. In *Archaeologists and the Dead: Mortuary Archaeology in Contemporary Society*, ed. H. Williams and M. Giles, 268–292. Oxford: Oxford University Press.

Overholtzer, L., and J.R. Argueta. 2017. Letting Skeletons Out of the Closet: The Ethics of Displaying Ancient Mexican Human Remains. *International Journal Heritage Studies* 24: 508–530.

Parker Pearson, M. 1999. *The Archaeology of Death and Burial*. Stroud: Sutton.

Patterson, A.R. 2007. "Dad Look, She's Sleeping": Parent-Child Conversations About Human Remains. *Visitor Studies* 10: 55–72.

Pitt Rivers Museum. 2018. *Pitt Rivers Museum*. https://www.prm.ox.ac.uk/. Accessed 1 March 2018.

Redfern, R., and J. Bekvalac. 2013. The Museum of London: An Overview of Policies and Practice. In *Curating Human Remains, Caring for the Dead in Great Britain*, ed. M. Giesen, 87–98. Woodbridge: The Boydell Press.

Rees Leahy, H. 2008. Under the Skin. *Museum Practice* 43: 36–40.

Robb, J. 2009. Assembling Bodies: Art, Science and Imagination. In *Exhibition Catalogue. Cambridge: Museum of Archaeology and Anthropology*, ed. A. Herle, M. Elliot, R. Empson, 28–29. Cambridge: University of Cambridge.

Sadongei, A., and P. Cash Cash. 2007. Indigenous Value Orientations in the Care of Human Remains. In *Human Remains: Guide for Museums and Academic Institutions*, ed. V. Cassman, N. Odegaard, and J. Powell, 97–101. Lanham: Altamira Press.

Sellevold, B.J. 2012. Ancient Skeletons and Ethical Dilemmas. In *More Than Just Bones: Ethics and Research on Human Remains*, ed. H. Fossheim, 139–160. Oslo: The Norwegian National Research Ethics Committees.

Sledzik, P.S., and L.T. Barbian. 2001. From Privates to Presidents: Past and Present Memoirs from the Anatomical Collections of the National Museum of Health and Medicine. In *Human Remains: Conservation, Retrieval and Analysis*, ed. E. Williams, 227–234. Oxford: Archaeopress.

Smith, C. 2005. Decolonising the Museum: The National Museum of the American Indian in Washington, DC. *Antiquity* 79: 424–439.

Society for American Archaeology [SAA]. 2018. *Editorial Policy, Information for Authors, and Style Guide for American Antiquity, Latin American Antiquity, and Advances in Archaeological Practice*. Cambridge: Cambridge University Press.

Stallybrass, P., and A. White. 1986. *The Politics and Poetics of Transgression*. London: Methuen.

Steel, P. 2006. Introduction of Human Remains Licence Leads to Confusion. *Museums Journal* 106 (9): 6.

Swain, H. 2002. The Ethics of Displaying Human Remains from British Archaeological Sites. *Public Archaeology* 2: 95–100.

Swain, H. 2016. Museum Practice and the Display of Human Remains. In *Archaeologists and the Dead: Mortuary Archaeology in Contemporary Society*, ed. H. Williams and M. Giles, 169–183. Oxford: Oxford University Press.

Tarlow, S. 2009. The Dead Body and the Law in Modern Britain. In *Exhibition Catalogue,* ed. A. Herle M. Elliot, R. Empson, 26–27. Cambridge: Museum of Archaeology and Anthropology, University of Cambridge.

Tatham, S. 2016. Displaying the Dead: The English Heritage Experience. In *Archaeologists and the Dead: Mortuary Archaeology in Contemporary Society*, ed. H. Williams and M. Giles, 184–203. Oxford: Oxford University Press.

The Mütter Museum. 2018. *Exhibitions: Hyrtl Skull Collection*. http://muttermuseum.org/exhibitions/hyrtl-skull-collection/. Accessed 31 July 2018.

United Nations. 2008. *Declaration on the Rights of Indigenous Peoples*. 61/295 Resolution Adopted by the General Assembly. Sixty-first Session, Supplement No. 53 (A/61/53), Part One, Chap. II, Sect. A. New York.

Walker, P.L. 2008. Bioarchaeological Ethics: A Historical Perspective on the Value of Human Remains. In *Biological Anthropology of the Human Skeleton*, 2nd ed, ed. M.A. Katzenberg and S.R. Saunders, 3–40. New York: Wiley Liss.

Weeks, J., and V. Bott. 2003. *Scoping Survey of Historic Human Remains in English Museums Undertaken on Behalf of the Ministerial Working Group on Human Remains*. London: Department for Culture, Media and Sport.

Wellcome Trust. 2005. *Policy on the Care of Human Remains in Museums and Galleries*. https://wellcome.ac.uk/funding/managing-grant/full-wellcome-trust-policy-care-human-remains-museums-and-galleries. Accessed 31 July 2018.

White, L. 2013. The Impact and Effectiveness of the Human Tissue Act 2004 and the Guidance for the Care of Human Remains in Museums in England. In *Curating Human Remains: Caring for the Dead in the United Kingdom*, ed. M. Giesen, 43–52. Woodbridge: The Boydell Press.

Wholley, A.L. 2001. Attraction of the Macabre: Issues Relating to Human Soft Tissue Collections in Museums. In *Human Remains: Conservation, Retrieval and Analysis. Proceedings of a Conference held in Williamsburg, VA, Nov 7–11th 1999*, ed. E. Williams, 275–281. Oxford: Archaeopress.

Wilson, E.K. 2015. The Collection and Exhibition of a Fetal and Child Skeletal Series. *Museum Anthropology* 38 (1): 15–27.

Wintle, C. 2013. Decolonising the Museum: The Case of the Imperial and Commonwealth Institutes. *Museum and Society* 11 (2): 185–201.

Woodhead, C. 2013. Care, Custody and Display of Human Remains: Legal and Ethical Obligations. In *Curating Human Remains: Caring for the Dead in the United Kingdom*, ed. M. Giesen, 31–42. Woodbridge: The Boydell Press.

World Archaeological Congress [WAC]. 1989. The Vermillion Accord. In *Archaeological Ethics and the Treatment of the Dead: A Statement of Principles Agreed by Archaeologists and Indigenous Peoples at the World Archaeological Congress, Vermillion, USA*. http://worldarch.org/code-of-ethics/. Accessed 12 August 2018.

World Archaeological Congress [WAC]. 2006. *The Tamaki Makau-rau Accord on the Display of Human Remains and Sacred Objects*. http://worldarch.org/code-of-ethics/. Accessed 31 July 2018.

Chapter 12
The Ethics of Sampling Human Skeletal Remains for Destructive Analyses

Kirsty Squires, Thomas Booth and Charlotte A. Roberts

Abstract The rise of more sophisticated forms of analysis has allowed bioarchaeologists to address and answer a wide range of questions regarding past diets, health, mobility, population history, kinship, and taphonomy. However, all of these techniques, e.g. DNA analysis, radiocarbon dating, isotope analysis, and histological analysis require destructive sampling of human remains, which raises ethical issues pertaining to preservation and survival as well as cultural concerns of both past and contemporary societies regarding the post mortem treatment of the dead. This chapter will explore the validity of conducting destructive sampling for the purpose of academic research. It will explore how curators, bioarchaeologists, and archaeologists currently deal with ethical issues surrounding destructive sampling and associated analyses, including the curation of skeletal remains for research purposes, access enquiries, and matters of consent. It is recommended that bioarchaeologists, archaeologists, and curators ensure ethics are at the core of all work carried out when working with human remains. It is thus proposed that these methods should be reserved for focused research questions as opposed to exploratory studies. It is also recommended that researchers and curators receive adequate training in procedures related to destructive sampling as a means of controlling the number of times samples can be taken from bones and teeth which will, in turn, preserve skeletal remains for future generations to study using even more advanced techniques. Following an introduction to the subject matter, this chapter will explore ethics and human remains, technical analyses applied to archaeological human remains, religious and cultural beliefs, and finally makes recommendations for best practice when conducting destructive sampling.

K. Squires (✉)
Staffordshire University, Science Centre, Leek Road, Stoke-on-Trent ST4 2DF, UK
e-mail: Kirsty.Squires@staffs.ac.uk

T. Booth
The Francis Crick Institute, 1 Midland Road, London NW1 1ST, UK

C. A. Roberts
Department of Archaeology, Durham University, South Road, Durham DH1 3LE, UK

K. Squires et al. (eds.), *Ethical Approaches to Human Remains*,
https://doi.org/10.1007/978-3-030-32926-6_12

12.1 Introduction

Traditional methods of analysing skeletal remains can provide a wealth of information about ancient individuals, for example their biological age at death, biological sex, stature, and longstanding pathological conditions that leave lesions on bones and teeth (see relevant chapters in Brickley and McKinley 2004 and Mitchell and Brickley 2017). Whilst these techniques are undoubtedly useful in providing baseline information, they do have limitations with respect to our understanding of the lives of past populations. Over the past 30 years, new methods of analysis that can be destructive to the integrity of archaeological human remains have become widely employed in archaeology and anthropology as a means of answering questions concerning dietary habits, ancestry, migratory patterns, diagnosis of disease, and the evolution of pathogens, chronology, taphonomic processes, and other characteristics relating to both unburned and burned human remains that cannot be answered by traditional, macroscopic analyses or contextual evidence alone (e.g. Fitch et al. 2010; Bos et al. 2011; Preus et al. 2011; Müller et al. 2014; Nauman et al. 2014; Weyrich et al. 2017). These methods have undoubtedly started to revolutionise our understanding of the past, particularly the evolution and history of disease (Harkins and Stone 2015). Yet, despite the increased application of these methods, ethical issues associated with destructive analyses are addressed in only a limited number of publications (Jones and Harris 1998; Elders et al. 2009; APABE 2013; Lynnerup 2013; Antoine and Ambers 2014; Roberts 2016).

This chapter will address the ethics of sampling human remains for destructive analyses primarily from a UK perspective, though examples from other countries will be addressed as a means of highlighting key issues associated with the destructive analysis of human remains. It will examine the ethical implications of using destructive methods in academic research in light of religious and cultural beliefs, matters of ownership of human remains held in curating institutions, and the validity of destructive techniques. The necessity to preserve human remains for future generations and new analytical methods will also be explored. The conclusion makes recommendations for good practice when sampling human remains for destructive analyses. It is hoped that this chapter will encourage greater discussion and debate around the use of destructive analyses, and how we can encourage researchers, curators, and archaeologists to address ethical issues pertaining to destructive sampling in their daily work. We hope that people working with human remains in other countries with less infrastructure and guidance than the UK (from bioarchaeologists to museum curators) will find this chapter useful for developing their own policies and practices.

12.2 Ethical Considerations

Ethical considerations pertaining to the destructive sampling of human remains can be divided into two main strands. The first is concerned with the preservation of skeletal integrity for future curation, display, and analyses. The second relates to cultural concerns of past and contemporary societies regarding the post mortem treatment of human remains, including bone, teeth, and other tissues.

Ethical issues surrounding destructive analyses remain at the forefront of academics working in universities, including those that supervise student theses which use these methods, and many institutions have implemented in-house ethics policies with reference to the use of archaeological human remains in research and teaching (e.g. see Roberts 2013; Durham University 2017a, 2017b; Staffordshire University 2018). Additionally, in a number of UK universities, at least, individuals undertaking projects that use (and sample) human remains (faculty as well as both undergraduate and graduate students) have to complete ethics forms and acquire approval for the work required prior to the commencement of a project. However, the extent to which universities produce and implement institutional level ethical policies is currently unknown. Similarly, some museums have guidelines that apply to those accessing human remains for destructive analyses, a point that will be returned to at a later stage of this chapter (e.g. see Museum of London n.d.; Natural History Museum n.d.; British Museum 2017).

Yet, despite the importance of ethics within this context, researchers often fail to discuss the ethical implications of their work in publications. Indeed, ethical considerations in relation to research involving the destructive analysis of human remains may not be a priority. Some researchers conduct destructive analyses with no clear research aims or questions, which can result in exploratory destruction of human remains for the purpose of potentially pinpointing a unique discovery and publishing it in a high-profile journal. An excellent example of this has been highlighted by Wilbur et al. (2009) who identified a case whereby samples were taken from a skeleton for the purpose of detecting TB using aDNA, despite the fact that the skeletal remains did not manifest adequate indication of this pathology. Wilbur et al. (2009) also emphasise that valid research questions and justification for conducting destructive sampling of human remains is essential. Nevertheless, organisations such as the British Association for Biological Anthropology and Osteoarchaeology's (BABAO) have developed a Code of Ethics (BABAO 2010a) and a Code of Practice (BABAO 2010b) which outline the standards and ethical principles expected of its members' work (BABAO 2018a). Although these codes have recently been updated, there is still only one point devoted to ethical considerations surrounding destructive sampling (BABAO 2010a, 2019). However, the Code of Practice (BABAO 2010b, 16) does address ethical considerations and recommendations when undertaking destructive sampling, and in the BABAO grant application process applicants have to address ethical implications of their research in the application form (BABAO 2018b). Many of the points raised in this document relating to destructive analyses are closely aligned with the guidelines and protocols that are implemented by museums, not only in the UK, but around the world (Smithsonian National Museum of Natural History n.d.; WAC 1989; DCMS 2005; APABE 2013, 2017; Human Remains Working Group 2013). One of the fundamental points raised in each of these documents is that destructive sampling should only be conducted if traditional analyses cannot answer the proposed research questions. In 2017, a widely reported study by Hedenstierna-Jonson et al. (2017) involved aDNA analysis to confirm the presence of a female "Viking warrior" in a richly furnished grave from Birka (Sweden), despite the fact that osteological analyses had generated the same finding. One might think that there is a risk that in the future all individuals interred with weapons from both the Viking period and early Anglo-Saxon period in England, might be subjected to the same analyses to pinpoint the exact number of females afforded these grave provisions. However, we know that there is evidence to show that traditional adult sex estimation methods employed by bioarchaeologists have a high success rate, typically ranging from 70 to 100% (Djuric et al. 2007; Bidmos et al. 2010; Krishan et al. 2016). This demonstrates that, provided there is sufficient osteological evidence, it is unnecessary to conduct destructive sampling to estimate the sex of adult remains. Curators of skeletal remains must therefore be aware of this when approached by researchers to carry out this type of research. This further highlights the fact that we need to be more responsible and selective in the techniques we employ in our research. Indeed, the Human Remains Working Group (2013) based in Germany, identify that it is the responsibility of curators to establish whether destructive analyses are justified based on the research questions posed by the researcher, although it is unknown the extent to which curators follow these guidelines.

As outlined by APABE (2013), it is essential that adequate recording (i.e. skeletal inventory forms and reports) of skeletal remains is carried out by osteoarchaeologists prior to conducting destructive sampling. This is important as it ensures that researchers conducting destructive analysis employ a specific justifiable sampling strategy that makes most efficient use of the human remains available and assures that the provenance of particular bones and skeletons is reliable. The presence of this documentation also allows for accurate recording of the sampling that has taken place which can be integrated within existing systems. Such documentation should be mandatory and referred to by curators of human remains and samplers/laboratories that are conducting destructive sampling as it will inform them of the completeness and condition of the remains following their recovery from archaeological sites. Museum guidelines and protocols also emphasise that the smallest amount of bone or tooth should only be used in analyses (Smithsonian National Museum of Natural History n.d.; WAC 1989; DCMS 2005; APABE 2013, 2017; Human Remains Working Group 2013). The BABAO guidelines for sampling recommend destructive sampling should avoid 'diagnostic' areas, by which it means morphologically-significant areas of the skeleton as well as those with palaeopathological and taphonomic modifications (Richards 2004, 2017). In some instances, museums will have guidelines stipulating that sampling can only take place from a bone or tooth if the antimere (opposite side) is present. Applying these guidelines can be complicated when dealing with incomplete human skeletons or single human bones where traditional macroscopic osteological methods can produce little biological information with any certainty. On the one hand, destructive sampling in these cases will result in the loss of a greater proportion of the surviving skeleton but, on the other, only methods which involve destructive sampling are often capable of providing detailed or, in some cases, any information about the individual. The amount of bone or tooth required, and the capacity to be able to record the bone or tooth before it is sampled, has to be weighed against the amount of extra information that could be acquired through destructive techniques.

Recent research has demonstrated that certain destructive analyses, such as stable isotope analysis and radiocarbon dating, can also be applied successfully to cremated bone (Olsen and Thrane 2013; Harvig et al. 2014), something not thought possible until recently. Non-destructive osteological analyses of cremated human bones can produce more information than had been previously assumed, but the fragmentary and often incomplete nature of cremation burials means that destructive techniques are often vital for obtaining the maximum amount of information and, as a result, the case for destructive analysis will have to be weighed against the potential of the surviving remains. Destructive sampling applications to those who curate skeletal remains are often considered alongside the possibility that new, or developments in old, analytical techniques may be able to provide the same or more information with similar or less-destructive techniques. However, these considerations have to be balanced against the possibility that techniques are unlikely to advance if they cannot be tested and refined using samples of bones and teeth from archaeological human remains.

Destructive sampling of teeth, where there are fewer morphologically non-significant areas, may require further deliberation. Some museums require that teeth are accurately imaged or cast before they are destructively sampled (Heather Bonney 2017, pers. comm.). This is particularly true for certain types of stable isotope analysis (discussed below in Sect. 12.4.2 of this chapter) which necessarily target particular aspects of the tooth. The pertinence of these issues may vary depending on the context. They may apply less often to the analysis of single loose teeth, where biomolecular analysis can potentially address a much broader range of questions than the analysis of morphology alone. Similarly, asymmetrical patterns of wear/abrasion notwithstanding, the presence of antimeres may also lessen the impact of destructive sampling of teeth.

12.3 Ethics of Sampling Human Remains from Museum Collections

Where such methods are to be implemented in research, some museums and other curating institutions, such as universities or commercial archaeology companies, will ask researchers who wish to access human remains to submit a research proposal, including their methodology, detailing how remains are going to be sampled and analysed, and the rationale for employing such techniques (e.g. see Museum of London n.d.; Natural History Museum n.d.; Redfern and Bekvalac 2013; Durham University 2017a, 2017b; British Museum 2017; Staffordshire University 2018). Requests for destructive analyses are approved (or rejected) by curators of collections and, if established, an ethics (or similar) board/committee. In many cases, destructive sampling agreements include provisions to image bones before they are sampled in order to mitigate the information lost by sampling. In most cases, this takes the form of standardised photographs, but methods of preserving the morphology of the bone in anticipation of destructive sampling are becoming more sophisticated, for instance the use of micro-computed tomography (micro-CT), which preserves a detailed, high-resolution three-dimensional image of the bone and, importantly, its internal structures (Franklin et al. 2016). However, these advanced imaging methods can be prohibitively expensive and/or unavailable to the majority of museums or curating institutions, or indeed researchers accessing the skeletal remains.

These processes are not practiced universally and many organisations do not request any of the above information from researchers. There is also a tendency for larger institutions in cities, particularly with osteology curators, to have access procedures and forms to complete while these may be absent in smaller provincial museums. The presence of such procedures is often related to the availability of staff and resources, and relative knowledge of archaeological human remains and their potential for research, alongside an understanding of what is an acceptable request. Human remains curators with specialist training are usually rare in curatorial organisations. Furthermore, destructive sampling requests submitted by researchers often necessarily include scientific explanations that some curators may be unfamiliar with, even those with some training in the analysis of ancient human remains. This has significant ramifications for the quality of the curatorial environment, and the care of remains, including whether they are subject to conservation, and the ultimate preservation of collections of human remains for the future. It also throws up questions about the ethical awareness and conduct of researchers and curators alike.

In 2013, the Museums Association conducted a survey into staff cuts and the replacement of highly skilled staff with volunteers. In this survey, it was identified that 47% of museums experienced an increase in the number of interns and volunteers and 37% of museums had faced staff cuts over a 12-month period (Museums Association 2013). This is particularly problematic when museums hold human remains. Volunteers do not have the same degree of training, knowledge, and skill set as qualified museum workers who generally have greater understanding and experience of the ethical challenges of curating assemblages of human remains, though in some instances curators have little knowledge of their human remains collections. A study by Edwards (2013) illustrated that, due to staff cuts, curators had to take on further responsibilities for collections or management. Indeed, this may include the curation of human remains, which they have limited experience of. Neither museum workers nor volunteers normally have the knowledge, say, of a qualified master's student who might have focused on archaeological human remains in their studies. Specialist archaeological human remains curators are very rare (e.g. at the Museum of London, the British Museum, and the Natural History Museum).

Unfortunately, local authorities have made significant cuts to museum funding in recent years. The increasing trend to replace experienced staff with volunteers within the museum sector is somewhat concerning. It is clear that volunteers, alongside workers in organisations that do not formally request an application form from researchers for research projects that involve destructive analyses, need training in the ethics of curating archaeological human remains as well as protocols that should be implemented when researchers want to sample collections. This would require funding from local councils, the Museums Association, charities such as the National Lottery Heritage Fund, or even organisations representing researchers who want access to archaeological human remains for destructive analysis. On a similar line, museums are facing a storage crisis. Archaeological excavations regularly lead to the recovery of human remains. Due to the storage crisis, some museums can no longer accept human remains for storage (Edwards 2013; McKinley 2013). This subject has been addressed in further detail elsewhere in this volume.

12.4 Methodological Advances and Human Remains

The following section will explore ethical issues associated with techniques that involve destructive sampling and analysis of human remains. There is particular emphasis on the use of DNA analysis given the many issues associated with this method. However, isotope analysis, radiocarbon dating, and analyses of internal bone microstructure will also be explored from an ethical standpoint. These are by no means the only destructive methods, but they are the ones that are most widely used in the study of human remains.

12.4.1 Ancient DNA and Proteomics

Since its discovery in 1985, deoxyribonucleic acid (DNA) fingerprinting has been widely adopted by forensic anthropologists in the identification of human remains from individual burials, mass graves, and mass disasters. Analysis of DNA extracted from archaeological human bones (ancient or aDNA) has been used to identify the sex of individuals, particularly for juvenile skeletons where traditional osteological methods cannot be employed (Stone et al. 1996; Tierney and Bird 2015), diseases (Papagrigorakis et al. 2006; Schuenemann et al. 2013), ancestry (Casas et al. 2006; Haak et al. 2015), and kinship (Haak et al. 2008; Deguilloux et al. 2014), and its use is becoming much more frequent in bioarchaeology.

Consequently, there has been some discussion and debate about the ethical issues pertaining to destructive sampling of remains for these purposes (Kaestle and Horsburgh 2002; Kaestle and Smith 2005; Hagelberg 2013; Sirak et al. 2017). Recent major advances in DNA sequencing technology (Next Generation Sequencing—NGS) has meant that aDNA researchers are now able to analyse whole genome (or genome-wide) information from ancient individuals, rather than small but informative sections of the genome (e.g. mitochondrial DNA; Li and Durbin 2011). Whole genome data does not represent all of an ancient individual's genetic information, but a distribution of DNA sequences obtained from across their genome. The number of ancient human sequences obtained using NGS is variable depending on preservation but often number in the hundreds of thousands or even millions. The ability to examine whole genome data from an ancient human skeleton provides biological information on that individual and their ancestors, thus profiling people and populations whose physical remains may not have survived in the archaeological record. Recent studies of prehistoric palaeogenomes have produced groundbreaking new insights into extinct hominins, patterns of inbreeding with modern human populations, and prehistoric population movements (Green et al. 2006; Meyer et al. 2012; Allentoft et al. 2015; Haak et al. 2015; Fu et al. 2016).

The amount of information that can be garnered from palaeogenomic analysis provides a particular quandary for evaluating the ethics of destructive sampling. This is because it can provide a level of biological information about individuals and populations that far surpasses what can be gained from the assessment of skeletal morphology alone. However, the kinds of questions these two types of data can be used to address currently overlap, but only slightly, for instance in the estimation of biological sex and ancestry (Skoglund et al. 2013). This situation is complicated by unpredictable variation in the preservation of DNA in ancient skeletons, meaning that it is difficult to know before sampling how much information is likely to be obtained from a particular individual. Whilst certain measures of bone degradation correlate with DNA preservation and are potentially useful for pre-screening, many of the sampling methods involved are more or equally as destructive as DNA sampling (Haynes et al. 2002; Ottoni et al. 2009). However, in the majority of ancient bones (c. 75%, David Reich 2018, pers. comm.) particularly from temperate environments, and where aDNA is preserved well in skeletal elements, there is usually sufficient DNA present to answer the research questions posed, depending on the available resources (e.g. targeted in-solution Capture Arrays—see below: Gamba et al. 2014; Haak et al. 2015; Fu et al. 2016). In addition, previous concerns about modern DNA contamination have now been mitigated by bioinformatic analyses which can authenticate ancient DNA sequences, meaning that whilst modern DNA contamination remains an issue and attempts to reduce risks are important, it is not the pervasive problem it was once feared to be in the early years of aDNA analyses (Yang and Watt 2005; Key et al. 2017; Llamas et al. 2017).

DNA sampling is amongst the least destructive methods of analysis since it only requires 50–100 mg of bone powder, which is less than that usually needed for analyses such as radiocarbon dating or stable isotope analysis. However, one of the initial problems encountered with NGS when applied to ancient bones and teeth was that the majority of DNA sequences were bacterial (over 90% in most cases; Gamba et al. 2014). This problem was mostly resolved by the discovery that specific denser parts of the petrous portion of the temporal bone were resistant to bacterial invasion and DNA degradation (Pinhasi et al. 2015). Endogenous ancient DNA yields from petrous bone samples are still variable and can still be zero, but they are consistently several fold higher than yields retrieved from other bones (Gamba et al. 2014). More recent experiments have identified that tooth cementum can sometimes contain DNA of a quality comparable to petrous bones and this material is now the second-best choice for ancient DNA researchers if the petrous bone sample analysis fails or is unavailable (Hansen et al. 2017).

Initial sampling strategies for the temporal bone and tooth cementum were very destructive and did not seem to consider any ethical concerns related to sampling archaeological human remains (Damgaard et al. 2015; Pinhasi et al. 2015). An understandable lack of knowledge amongst museum professionals and bioarchaeologists regarding the accelerating development of ancient DNA research may have also hampered attempts to properly appraise sampling applications from non-archaeologists, i.e. biomolecular scientists. However, the area surrounding the otic capsule (the bony outer wall of the inner ear in the temporal bone that surrounds the inner ear structures) was quickly recognised as the part of the petrous portion of the temporal bone that was most likely to yield the best quality DNA (Pinhasi et al. 2015). Early sampling techniques included sand-blasting most of the temporal bone away or cutting it in half to expose the desirable parts. Similarly, the initial method of sampling tooth cementum involved the destruction of almost the entire tooth (Damgaard et al. 2015). These highly destructive methods were initially necessary in order to define precisely the best sources of DNA, but through interactions with archaeologists, bioarchaeologists, and curators, ancient DNA researchers have begun to realise the pertinence of developing less-destructive means of taking bone powder samples. Thus, sampling methods are becoming more precise and less destructive, although it is unclear how far these minimally-destructive methods have been adopted (Sirak et al. 2017). There is still a requirement for custodians of human remains to be alert and assertive when dealing with ancient DNA researchers, explaining the ethical argument for minimal destructive sampling and putting formal agreements in place to ensure that guidelines on destructive sampling are adhered to.

This situation may be complicated further, both regarding the ethics of destructive sampling and aDNA analysis more generally, by the significant legacy value of both the samples and the resulting data. The sampling and associated laboratory work produces bone powder, DNA extracts, and DNA libraries (extracts that have been amplified and indexed for sequencing). In some cases, bone powder and DNA extracts have the potential to be used for future analyses. For example, aDNA libraries can be perpetually sequenced to produce data, although the amount of new information that can be acquired with each new sequencing run is limited by preservation. Targeted amplification of particular predefined DNA sequences using in-solution Capture Arrays can enrich a DNA library for pre-defined informative parts of the genome, and ensure that sequencing is more efficient, but this comes at a cost of parts of the unselected regions of the genome, potentially limiting the legacy potential of capture libraries.

In line with APABE (2013) guidelines, researchers have the responsibility to return all samples to the original curating institution so they can be stored with the rest of the sampled skeleton. Most biomolecular researchers would agree on the requirement for returning remnants of the physical sample such as bone powder, but opinion tends to be more ambivalent regarding molecular products produced through laboratory work, such as DNA extracts or collagen in the case of radiocarbon dating and stable isotope analysis. In particular, ancient DNA libraries may be a tricky problem in this regard. This is because they are mostly composed of synthetic DNA sequences with negligible quantities of the original DNA extract. Laboratories invest significant time, labour, and resources into making these products and they are often essential for fulfilling rigorous scientific demands for replication as well as contributing to internal standards of calibration and quality control. However, there has been a tendency amongst some researchers and laboratories to assume ownership of molecular products, resulting in samples being retained and/or passed on to other research groups without the knowledge and consent of the institutions that hold their parent collections (Callaway 2017; Makarewicz et al. 2017; Redfern and Clegg 2017). These cases have damaged the reputation and moral authority of biomolecular researchers, and certain larger museums (including the Natural History Museum (London), Museum of London, and the National Museum of Wales) now have standard destructive sampling agreements which specifically include molecular products.

However, there is still an outstanding ethical discussion to be had about whether museums in all cases are the most appropriate place for the storage of molecular products. The ideal situation would be that *all* samples taken from human remains would be returned to respective curators to be kept with their collections. Nevertheless, in reality few institutions have the resources and expertise to store and curate molecular products adequately, and in a way which facilitates scientific ethical demands on efficient replication of results. In this sense there may be an ethical case to answer regarding whether museums have the most appropriate facilities to store these remains without significant investment in facilities and staff training. Biomolecular researchers often feel that the scientific demands on replication mean that these products need to be close to hand to allow for an efficient response if their work is challenged. Clearly at the very least there is an ethical requirement for researchers to be transparent about molecular products, instruct custodians of their legacy value, and come to an agreement relating to how and where they should be used, stored, and shared. The best results for all parties tend to emerge from true collaboration and transparency between researchers, archaeologists, and museum professionals, as it ensures the interests of all involved are appreciated and respected, including the sampled human remains of once living people (Holst 2017; Redfern and Clegg 2017).

Raw ancient DNA sequence data are often stored on publicly-available databases once they have been published, facilitating future reanalysis, and data mining. The availability of this information has ethical implications, particularly when dealing with data from the remains of the recently dead, in assuming consent for their DNA to be accessible in perpetuity. Most of the human palaeogenomes generated so far come from prehistoric human remains where ethical concerns related to past beliefs are more difficult to resolve. However, as studies of aDNA begin to move into historical periods, where an individual's desires regarding the post mortem fate of their body may be more tangible, researchers will have to begin addressing ethical issues around consent. Interpreting individual consent through a prism of past values inferred from the historical record, whilst also considering modern cultural concerns, is very challenging. Concerns about the consent of the dead will need to be weighed against what we are likely to learn about certain individuals and populations and how those analyses are likely to benefit living populations.

The legacy of aDNA data touches on the final ethical concern in terms of its application to living populations. This has been a particularly high-profile issue in the analysis of DNA from Native American and Australian ancient remains, where projects have been generated without consulting Indigenous groups who may have a stake in the outcome and associated research questions that do not align with the interests or concerns of local Indigenous communities. This kind of approach can often be regarded as a new form of scientific colonialism without dialogue or inclusion of relevant Indigenous groups (TallBear 2013). In Europe, recent results from analyses of prehistoric genomes have comparatively little political and ethical ramifications for living populations. However, aDNA studies will inevitably begin expanding into the more recent European past, investigating past populations and individuals where findings, particularly those linked to health and disease, may have greater implications for living individuals and populations. Therefore, aDNA researchers will have to begin to appreciate and incorporate ethical considerations in future studies.

The analysis of human bone samples for pathogenic bacteria has not benefited as much from new NGS techniques so far, mostly because of the difficulties in identifying pathogenic DNA sequences amongst the abundant bacterial and human data obtained using NGS methods. Yet, the ability to properly recognise ancient DNA sequences using NGS data has helped neutralise authentication problems associated with studies of ancient pathogenic bacteria (Roberts and Ingham 2008). The case for destructive sampling of human bones for pathogenic DNA is now strengthened provided appropriate authentication methods are used. There are still problems with the interpretation of the presence of pathogenic bacteria in ancient human remains, because it is difficult to know whether particular bacteria were pathogenic to humans in the distant past. A study of *Yersinia pestis* bacterial ancient DNA in Bronze Age European remains looked at specific genes that are known to affect the transmissibility of the disease in an attempt to circumvent this problem, and this kind of approach may represent a way forward for assessing whether bacteria found in ancient human remains were actively infecting the individual (Valtueña et al. 2017). However, a better way of addressing population-level exposure to particular diseases may be through the analysis of human genetic markers associated with disease resistance (Barnes et al. 2011). Whilst these new developments significantly reduce the possibility of false positives in the search for pathogenic bacteria, the complexities of the survival of DNA and picking out sequences associated with pathogenic bacteria may mean that false negatives are still likely to occur. Specific studies of pathogenic bacteria have focused on sampling bone from active lesions where pathogens might be expected to have been more abundant, increasing the chances of detecting related ancient sequences (Donoghue and Spigelman 2006). However, whilst intuitive, the idea that pathogenic bacterial DNA sequences are more likely to survive in and around active lesions has not been proven, and sampling from lesions has produced negative results (von Hunnius et al. 2007). Therefore, when sampling ancient bones for pathogen DNA, there is a requirement for discussions around the impact of destructive sampling, particularly on diagnostic lesions and the probable return from the aDNA analysis.

In contrast, there has been little discourse concerning the use of other techniques that require destructive sampling of bone and teeth. The analysis of dental calculus (or mineralised plaque) is a relatively new technique which can be used for dietary reconstruction (Buckley et al. 2014), exploration of health and disease (Warinner et al. 2014; Weyrich et al. 2015), and potentially population affinity (Eisenhofer et al. 2017). These insights can be accessed due to the presence of organic matter (DNA and ancient proteins) preserved in the calculus. Most of the DNA recovered from calculus is bacterial and can provide information on ancient oral microbiomes and pathogens. Dental calculus can sometimes retain a small level of host DNA, meaning that it can provide a method of investigating ancient human genomes at a very shallow level without having to sample bone directly (Ozga et al. 2016). Proteins found in ancient calculus can be linked to specific foodstuffs and host immune response, which is applicable to reconstructions of ancient diet and disease (Warinner et al. 2014, 2015). The extent to which this type of study may be regarded as destructive to the ancient human skeleton is arguable given that the calculus can be scraped from the teeth without affecting teeth or bones, and therefore can be regarded as non-destructive to the skeleton itself. There is, indeed, the argument that calculus sampling is more likely to be allowed by curators because this material adheres to most archaeological teeth and the process is less destructive than sampling bone and teeth directly. Dental calculus is not included as 'relevant material' under the Human Tissue Act (2004), but the presence of host human DNA in certain samples may raise questions about whether it should be classed as a category of human remains, akin to kidney or urinary stones. However, given that ancient human DNA has also been recovered from cave sediments, it may be questionable whether the presence of ancient human DNA is an appropriate qualifier for classification as human remains (Slon et al. 2017).

The analysis of ancient proteins extracted from archaeological and fossil bones is an emergent field in biomolecular archaeology that, as of yet, has generated few applications to the study of human remains, but has potentially lucrative applications to the study of ancient disease through monitoring protein expression

(Cappellini et al. 2014). In addition, recent analysis of peptides extracted from tooth enamel using minimally destructive methods has shown how they can be used to estimate biological sex, providing potentially a more reliable method than osteological analysis of the skeleton, particularly for juvenile individuals (Stewart et al. 2017). Similarly, studies of ancient proteins in faunal remains have suggested that they may provide a method for assessing the biological age of individuals (Procopio et al. 2018).

12.4.2 Stable Isotope Analysis

Stable isotope analysis of human remains has become a popular and lucrative method for reconstructing palaeodiet (Privat et al. 2002) and past mobility patterns (Price et al. 2002, 2006). Isotope analysis is also becoming increasingly popular in the field of forensic human identification as a means of establishing the geographical life history of individuals who were victims of crime or fatalities in mass disasters (Fraser and Meier-Augenstein 2007). Palaeodietary reconstruction tends to focus on carbon (^{13}C) and nitrogen (^{15}N) from collagen in bone or tooth dentine (Ambrose and DeNiro 1986). Studies of mobility predominantly look at strontium (^{87}Sr/^{86}Sr) and oxygen (^{18}O) in tooth enamel, although new research continues to identify further stable isotopes that may have complementary interpretive potential (Evans et al. 2006; Katzenberg 2008). To conduct carbon and nitrogen stable isotope analysis, 0.5 g of bone is needed, and to carry out strontium and oxygen analysis, 50 mg of dental enamel is required and often results in the destruction of the dental crown (APABE 2013). Whilst this may not seem like a significant quantity, the bone samples are larger than those needed for aDNA analysis and taking samples from enamel can lead to the destruction of skeletal elements. The ethical implications of this will be explored in the following section of this chapter.

Carbon and nitrogen analysis is mostly focused on the origin of an individual's dietary protein, but may have broader applications to studies of physiology and health (Reitsema 2013). Enrichment of ^{15}N reflects trophic level, translating into the relative position of an organism on the food chain, whereas enrichment of ^{13}C is mostly related to whether the protein originated from a marine or terrestrial environment. These two values are often interpreted together to infer likely sources of dietary protein. In the main, these figures are most useful for identifying variable diets in individuals and populations, as well as distinguishing and potentially quantifying the extent to which an individual acquired protein from marine or terrestrial sources (Richards et al. 2003). They may also provide some impression about the extent of protein that was obtained from animal or plant sources (Richards et al. 2000). However, other factors may have an influence and can either confound or add to interpretations. For instance, consumption of high levels of freshwater fish can enrich nitrogen without producing a corresponding enrichment of carbon (Nehlich et al. 2010). Babies that were being breastfed show enriched nitrogen due to them having a trophic level above the individual from whom they were feeding

(Fuller et al. 2006). Environmental changes can also influence absolute stable isotope values (Stevens and Hedges 2004; Lee-Thorp 2008). Each of these influential variables means that stable isotope analysis has a broad range of interpretive potential, but also several possible confounding factors.

The number of years of an individual's life represented by analyses of bulk collagen can depend on the sampled element, specifically the rate at which these elements remodel and possibly also whether they were affected by pathologies (Katzenberg and Lovell 1999). Tooth dentine is laid down at different stages of childhood and is not remodeled, therefore stable isotope analysis will reflect a childhood signature. By contrast, analysis of stable isotope analysis of a bone from a more active part of the skeleton that was subject to frequent activity-related remodeling will provide a signature of diet in the years before the individual's death. Whether the bone sampled remodels quickly or slowly may also affect the interpretation of results, as the longer a bone takes to remodel, the more likely it is that the result will reflect a composite signature, amalgamating temporal dietary variability into an averaged signature that may not be directly indicative of that individual's diet at any specific point in their lifetime (Jørkov et al. 2009; Olsen et al. 2014).

In addition, ethical considerations concerning this type of analysis should focus on whether methods would be able to address specific research questions confidently, in spite of potential confounding variables so far as to be able to justify the destruction of skeletal material. The development of single amino acid and single compound stable isotope analysis allows for the analysis of stable isotopes in compounds which originate from a particular food source and is helping to remove some of the ambiguities associated with this method (Fogel and Tuross 2003; Styring et al. 2010). Any leftover collagen can potentially be reused for other analyses such as radiocarbon dating, removing the need to resample. This highlights the importance of transparency with curating institutions regarding leftover materials.

The methodological basis of stable isotope analysis of ancient skeletons to investigate past mobility is that different mineralised tissues take on stable isotopic signatures of underlying geology through individual consumption of food and drinking water (Price et al. 2002; Evans et al. 2006). Different geologies have different strontium isotopic compositions based on their age and radiogenic properties. Sea spray can produce specific coastal signatures. Lighter oxygen isotopes evaporate more quickly than heavier ones, therefore areas with higher levels of rainfall will have higher relative proportions of the lighter oxygen isotopes (Budd et al. 2004). These analyses are performed on tooth enamel because it is resistant to diagenetic processes that can alter the stable isotope signatures (Wang and Cerling 1994; Lee-Thorp 2008). In addition, as teeth form in a regular way during childhood, the stable isotopes represent a childhood signature that can be compared to the geological signature of where the skeleton was found in order to infer whether the individual was likely to have grown up locally. Therefore, combining strontium and oxygen stable isotope analyses can, in the first instance be used to identify non-locals (Price et al. 2002; Evans et al. 2006, 2010; Pollard et al. 2011).

As with dietary stable isotope analysis, confounding factors and aspects of interpretation can affect the ethical case for this kind of analysis (Montgomery 2010). For instance, oxygen isotopes can also be affected by the consumption of boiled water or weaning (Brettell et al. 2012; Montgomery et al. 2013). It can be difficult in studies with small samples to distinguish genuine outliers from natural variability or statistical noise. Sampling of large numbers of individuals to produce isoscapes is helping to mitigate these problems (Pellegrini et al. 2016). The development of isoscapes involves the alteration of a relatively large number of skeletons, but each stable isotope project produces data that contributes to these isoscapes and cumulatively improves interpretations of stable isotope data more generally.

The use of stable isotope analysis to provide a likely origin for a specific individual can be less secure, as large and sometimes quite diverse geographical regions can produce similar isotopic signatures, and certain locations can lie at an interface between diverse geologies (Montgomery 2010). Indeed, most studies of mobility using stable isotopes routinely highlight the caveats associated with assigning specific regional origins of individuals. Inference of likely origins of non-local individuals is usually achieved through a probabilistic approach based on historical context and geography (Chenery et al. 2010; Hughes et al. 2014; Neil et al. 2016; Parker Pearson et al. 2016; Pellegrini et al. 2016). In certain circumstances, this may be used as an exclusive method of assessing whether an individual is likely to have originated from a particular place. There is an ethical case for researchers to lay out the methodological and interpretative limitations that will affect the ability to address particular research questions and, to weigh the importance of the questions that can be addressed against the impact on the skeletal collections.

Until relatively recently, these stable isotope studies have been focused on the ‘bulk’ analysis of mineralised tissues, which comes with potential problems of mixed signatures (as discussed above). However, more recently studies have begun to focus on incremental isotope analysis which use knowledge of the standard growth of tooth enamel and dentine during childhood and serial-sampling of teeth to track higher-resolution changes over an individual’s life covered by the period of growth (Britton et al. 2009; Montgomery et al. 2013; Britton et al. 2015). This kind of analysis has provided an insight into weaning, mobility in childhood, and periods of physiological stress including possibly starvation (Beaumont et al. 2013). The focus of these methods on quite limited time periods helps to nullify some of the potential problems of mixed signatures. Incremental stable isotope analysis is potentially slightly more destructive than bulk analysis, as it requires several samples to be taken from a single tooth, but the resolution of information and interpretive potential of the method is significantly improved (Britton et al. 2009; Beaumont et al. 2013). This highlights the complexities of measuring up the case for destructive analysis; indeed, it is clear that it does lead to innovations in methods that may not otherwise have been possible. Often, the payoff from destructive sampling is implicit in what the results can then be used to say, but there is an ethical case for researchers to outline focused research questions and rationalise why certain methods have been chosen over others before sampling takes place in order to justify the scale of destructive sampling (Makarewicz and Sealy 2015). Indeed, there is the argument for limiting the number of isotope studies given the sheer quantity of data we currently have from such research. We must therefore ask ourselves what further analyses will contribute to our knowledge of diet, mobility, weaning, and physiological stress.

12.4.3 Radiocarbon Dating

Radiocarbon dating is one of the oldest techniques applied to archaeological remains to acquire an absolute calendrical age range, and "remains the most widely employed method of inferring chronometric age for organic materials from the late Pleistocene and Holocene" (Taylor 2009, 863). This is most commonly utilised when there is little, if any, contextual material evidence to date remains or when dealing with fossil assemblages (Wild et al. 2005). Radiocarbon dating can now be used to produce precise chronologies for sites and contexts through modelling using Bayesian statistical techniques in software such as OxCal (Ramsey 2009; Bayliss 2015). Articulated human remains can be particularly important in these instances; in most cases they must represent the remains of individuals that were buried soon after they died, and therefore provide an accurate date for the formation of a specific deposit. The pertinence of human remains in constructing these precise chronologies will depend on their stratigraphic position and associations. Therefore, in these instances the case for sampling must be weighed against not only what information radiocarbon dating will reveal about the individual specifically, but also how far the date will contribute towards a precise chronological model of a site (Bayliss 2015). The value of a particular skeleton can be assessed in advance in programmes like OxCal using stratigraphic information from a site. The importance of human remains to these models can then be weighed against the potential impact of destructive sampling. Collagen extracted from an archaeological bone can be used for both radiocarbon and stable isotope analysis, which is why there is an imperative for researchers to attempt to, as far as possible, make maximum use of single samples and make curators aware of any remnant material. There may be some discussions to be had in these cases whether most museums include appropriate facilities or space to store leftover materials, but transparency regarding the existence of leftover material is still required in the first instance.

Early methods of radiocarbon dating (radiometric dating) required large samples of bone, often entire long bones. The advent of radiocarbon dating by Accelerator Mass Spectrometry (AMS) reduced the amount of bone powder required substantially, whilst also making date ranges more precise (Bowman 1990; Taylor 2001). Currently 0.5–1.0 g of bone or tooth (1.0–3.0 g for cremated bone) is sufficient for most radiocarbon dating laboratories. Radiocarbon dating can only succeed in samples where collagen is preserved to a particular standard. There is currently no way to non-destructively prescreen bone for collagen preservation associated with radiocarbon dating, although certain methods are less-destructive (%Nitrogen) than radiocarbon dating itself (Brock et al. 2010). Radiocarbon laboratories provide guidance on the skeletal elements (usually those containing high proportions of cortical bone structures, such as long bones, e.g. ORAU 2018) that are most likely to succeed, ensuring that any destructive sampling of human remains has the best chance of being successful. When most of the skeleton is present, the ability to sample long bones means that there is usually plenty of scope to sample bones minimally and avoid morphologically-significant areas, although in situations where less of the skeleton is present, this will depend on the representation of particular skeletal elements. Beyond ensuring the sampling of bones that are more likely to contain preserved collagen, controlling for possible failure is more difficult as the factors which dictate whether a bone will fail are not well understood (Brock et al. 2010). Future research may begin to systematically identify the variability associated with lower success rates for radiocarbon dating. This knowledge can then be factored into ethical considerations for sampling human remains.

Radiocarbon dating has long been a standardised technique utilised by archaeologists in the UK and there are several laboratories that offer commercial dating. As with other forms of testing, there is a requirement for specific research questions to be laid out and considerations as to how far sampling human remains for radiocarbon dating will answer these questions. Up until recently these questions tended to be quite straightforward as the primary focus was on acquiring an absolute date for a particular site or feature. There are some limitations on the precision of dates depending on where the radiocarbon determination falls on the calibration curve, with determinations corresponding with plateaus producing very broad dates (Ramsey 2009). The ability to anticipate these kinds of problems will depend on how much is known about the general date of the bone. However, most archaeologists and researchers are usually well aware of limits on interpretations linked to the calibration curve and take them into consideration when choosing samples for dating. The development of chronological modelling software like OxCal provides the opportunity to address a much more varied and refined research questions that require multiple samples across sites and contexts (Bayliss 2015).

Recent developments facilitating radiocarbon dating of cremated bone have further enhanced the amount of useful information that can be extracted from this category of human remains (Lanting et al. 2001). The process involves AMS dating of the carbon in the carbonate (in the inorganic phase of bone), rather than the collagen, which is lost during cremation. However, results have to be treated with caution, as the exchange of carbon between the bone and fuel during burning means that the bone carbonate takes on the signature of the fuel (Snoeck et al. 2014). This is largely inconsequential if the fuel was composed of short-lived species, but if internal wood of longer-lived species such as oak are used, it can produce an 'old-wood' effect in the bone, making the cremated bones look older than they actually are. Examining the types of wood represented in the ash associated with cremated bone deposits can help to assess whether a cremated bone is likely to have been affected by old wood fuel. Thus, the ethical case for sampling cremated bone must be considered in terms of how reliably the research question can be addressed using radiocarbon dating.

There is a case for resampling certain human skeletons that have been radiocarbon dated in the past where modern methods would provide more precise dates. The ability to combine two radiocarbon dates on the same material in order to refine their range consequently provides more information (Ward and Wilson 1978). However, it is common in certain quarters to completely disregard old radiocarbon dates with large associated errors which sometimes make any new dates less precise when combined. The case for repeat radiocarbon dating of human remains has to consider the impact on collections against the new information that would be provided and whether future developments may be able to achieve this balance more effectively.

12.4.4 Analysis of Internal Bone Microstructure

Histological analysis of thin-sections of bone and teeth has been employed since the 1970s to estimate age at death and to explore metabolism, growth, and health and disease (Stout and Teitelbaum 1976; Miszkiewicz and Mahoney 2017) as well as to gain a better understanding of the conditions surrounding burnt and unburnt bone and taphonomic processes in the burial environment which can, in turn, inform researchers of past funerary practices (Herrmann 1977; Turner-Walker and Jans 2008; Squires et al. 2011; Booth et al. 2015; Squires 2015). A wealth of methods can be employed to analyse chemical and structural changes to bone, particularly the loss of bone collagen and alteration to hydroxyapatite; these techniques have been successfully employed to investigate burning patterns and diagenetic modifications in forensic, archaeological, and fossil bone (Hedges et al. 1995; Hedges 2002; Nielsen-Marsh et al. 2007; Smith et al. 2007; Thompson et al. 2009; Squires et al. 2011; Dal Sasso et al. 2016; Carroll et al. 2017; Thompson et al. 2017; Dal Sasso et al. 2018; Carroll 2019). The wealth of information these techniques can provide about the lives of individuals in the past and the identity of individuals who have perished as a result of criminal activity are invaluable.

The sampling process that allows researchers to examine the microscopic structure of bone can be particularly destructive. In the first instance, sections of bone, between two to three centimeters in length and one centimeter wide must be obtained otherwise the sample will be too small (Cho 2012; APABE 2013). If the bone is not fragmented in the first instance (i.e. this is often the case with cremated bone), sections of bone are cut using a small rotary blade saw. These bone sections may then have to be embedded in epoxy resin as this will enhance the integrity of the sample (Booth 2016). Microtomes are normally used to cut thin-sections of bone. The rotary blade runs at a slow speed and allows the user to cut sections, typically, between 50 and 100 μm (Cho 2012). If sections are cut any thinner, there is the risk that they will disintegrate, and if the samples are thicker than 100 μm, the samples will not be translucent enough for examination under a microscope. Despite the impregnation of bone samples in resin, certain friable samples are still susceptible to fragmentation when cut using the microtome, particularly burned bone (Squires et al. 2011). However, most unburnt archaeological bone fragments are robust enough to be cut on a saw microtome, often without having to be embedded (Booth 2016). In instances where the bone does fragment during cutting, further undamaged samples must be obtained for the researcher to successfully mount on glass slides prior to examination. It is preferable that the bone fragment is not embedded in resin, as it may then be reused for other analyses. As with all other techniques, there is an ethical obligation to return all leftover materials, particularly if they can be used for further analyses. In instances where fragile samples are the focus of an investigation, researchers must have a strong rationale for conducting histological analysis as they run the risk of causing extensive damage to human remains if they are unable to obtain pristine samples for examination. Other methods of microscopic examination, such as Scanning Electron Microscopy, require the similar production of bone sections (Turner-Walker and Syversen 2002). Methods of analysing structural and chemical change in bones require quantities of bone powder (Squires et al. 2011).

Recent research has identified non-destructive means of obtaining diagenetic information from bones, most notably Raman spectroscopy (Halcrow et al. 2014; Dal Sasso et al. 2018) and micro-CT (Booth et al. 2016), but neither of these techniques are capable of capturing the full spectrum of diagenetic changes a bone may undergo, and destructive methods of analysis are still required. Therefore, each case for destructive sampling will have to be considered on its own terms, incorporating the same factors discussed above for other techniques, with the potential of new information balanced against the overall impact to the skeleton, both aesthetically and in terms of future research. In the vast majority of cases, ethical considerations associated with destructive sampling for histological, chemical, or structural analysis are not addressed in publications. In the UK, applying for permission to conduct destructive sampling from museums is usually thought to be sufficient. However, applications to sample human remains do not consider the complex ethical issues around destructive method sampling, unless museums ask the applicant to do so.

12.5 Religious and Cultural Beliefs, and Destructive Sampling

Ethical concerns regarding the study of archaeological human remains have been raised by Indigenous and religious groups for many years (National Park Service n.d.; Lynnerup 2013). Some research has been carried out to establish how the public feel about storing human remains in museums, not only on display, but also for their use in future research (Mills and Tranter 2010). On the whole, the general public are in favour of the study of human remains, although there is evidence to suggest that individuals belonging to a faith group are less likely to be in favour of research conducted on human remains than those of no religion. English Heritage, now Historic England, commissioned a study in 2009 which identified that 14% of 855 survey respondents, whose religion was important to them, did not agree with human remains being stored in museums (Mills and Tranter 2010). This compares with 4% of individuals who did not belong to a religious group holding the same view (Mills and Tranter 2010). However, what constitutes "research" on human remains is vague in many of the questionnaires distributed in these types of studies and there is no mention of destructive analyses, which suggests non-transparency of research, i.e. what it actually entails. This raises the question regarding the public perception of scientists conducting destructive sampling as part of their research or, indeed, whether the public know this is carried out. Yet, there is evidence from surveys completed by the public to indicate that religious groups would be against these forms of analyses (Mills and Tranter 2010; Sayer 2010).

In relation to this, attitudes of religious groups towards post mortem examinations also need addressing as they may be helpful in informing practitioners of the potential ethical challenges they may face when conducting destructive sampling of both archaeological and modern human remains; this is because this process is disruptive to the "natural" form of the body. Post mortems are carried out when the cause of death is unknown or following an unexpected death, which may be violent and/or sudden. Some religions are opposed to post mortems, including Islam, members of the Jewish faith, and some Christian groups, as it desecrates the human body (Rispler-Chaim 1993). In the Islamic faith, it is believed that the dead may feel pain (Sheikh 1998); the Prophet Muhammad stated that "to break the bone of a dead person is like breaking the bone of a living person" (Sheikh 1998, 166; see also AlQahtani and Adserias-Garriga, this volume). Furthermore, the removal of any body part is forbidden in Islam (Rispler-Chaim 1993). Under traditional Jewish law (Halacha) there is a general prohibition against post mortems because they disfigure the body and it is believed that God created Man in His own image and that this is retained in death (Goodman et al. 2011). Thus, the body must be treated with dignity, honour, and respect (Goodman et al. 2011; see also AlQahtani and Adserias-Garriga, this volume). However, non-invasive means of determining the cause of death are becoming necessary due to the opposition of post mortems by some religious groups. Virtopsies, or virtual autopsies, involve the use of MRI and CT scanners to take images of the body to establish the cause of death (Thali et al. 2007; Roberts et al. 2012). Bearing all this in mind, care must be taken when projecting the views of the present onto the past and in acknowledging that the precise views about the integrity of the body after death may have varied between different groups and individuals, as well as through time. Nonetheless, these modern beliefs potentially hold ramifications for destructive sampling in archaeological research and, indeed, in some forensic contexts.

Researchers that intend to conduct destructive sampling of human remains from sites where individuals belonging to the aforementioned faith groups were interred should not only make formal requests to analyse these remains, but should raise any conflicts of interest in regard to religious beliefs and the techniques that are being used to analyse human remains in any publications that result from such work. For example, there are instances where researchers have conducted destructive sampling on human remains from archaeological Christian and Islamic burials without addressing religious beliefs and ethical issues pertaining to the destructive nature of their analyses (Pereira et al. 2006; Matheson et al. 2009; Gomes et al. 2015; Gleize et al. 2016; Salazar-García et al. 2016). While some of these papers (i.e. Matheson et al. 2009) declare that permission was granted from the relevant authorities to analyse remains, they do not consider ideological beliefs or whether these were considered when they decided to use destructive analyses in their research. However, it is of course difficult to know what questions are asked by curators of applicants who wish to conduct destructive analyses on remains they curate, and what discussions take place "behind closed doors". Furthermore, journal editors, pressed for space, are unlikely to allow a full dialogue about the ethical implications of the research to be published as part of the paper (although this should be done in an ideal world).

Needless to say, human remains from more recent historical times may be linked to surviving descendants and thus ethical concerns are more likely to be taken into account in these instances (Jones and Harris 1998). Regardless of the age of remains, ideological and associated ethical issues surrounding destructive analyses must be addressed by researchers (and curators). All human remains represent once living people regardless of their date of death. It is clear that greater discourse between archaeologists and bioarchaeologists/forensic anthropologists is needed with religious groups to ensure they are conducting destructive analyses in an ethical manner, while simultaneously respecting ideological beliefs of the dead and their communities, if this information is known to researchers. Additionally, ethical consideration pertaining to the beliefs of Indigenous groups is also needed. Such concerns have been successfully addressed in the United States of America by the foundation of a Repatriation Committee (see Ubelaker and Khosrowshahi, this volume, for further details). Destructive analyses are typically deemed taboo by Native Americans. However, there are cases where the Repatriation Committee has accepted requests by researchers to conduct destructive sampling of human remains (Colwell-Chanthaphonh 2010).

Over recent years, concerns relating to the consent for, and ownership of, samples have been raised (O'Rourke et al. 2005; Tarlow 2006; Henderson 2007; APABE 2013). This is particularly pertinent when scientists wish to carry out aDNA analysis of remains that belonged to members of Indigenous groups, either recently deceased individuals, recently excavated human remains, or older human bones curated in a variety of institutions (Jones and Harris 1998; O'Rourke et al. 2005; Walsh-Haney and Lieberman 2005). The consent process requires an open dialogue between archaeologists, anthropologists, museum curators, and, most importantly, representatives from Indigenous groups (Colwell 2017). This has been successfully achieved in a number of instances in the United States of America (O'Rourke et al. 2005; Malhi et al. 2007). One of the most famous and longest-running examples of this, which ended with what was regarded to be a mostly positive outcome on all sides, was that of Kennewick Man, a 9000 year old human skeleton that was recovered from the banks of the Columbus River (USA) in 1996. There were various contentious components of the post-excavation history of these remains, not least spurious claims from the anthropological analysis of the remains that Kennewick Man had European ancestry (Kaestle and Smith 2005). Collaboration between geneticists, archaeologists, and relevant Indigenous groups eventually facilitated whole genome analysis of Kennewick Man, which proved that he was most closely related to modern day Native American populations (Rasmussen et al. 2015). The bones were then returned to the relevant tribes for reburial. Thus, issues around the practical and ideological aspects of the ethics of sampling can be overcome when there is proactive dialogue between all stakeholders.

There are not only issues regarding the consent of exhuming, analysing, and storing ancient human remains, but also sampling from modern populations. In a report produced by the National Research Council (1997), ethical considerations concerning human genetic variation research was explored with a focus on living participants. This report highlights that ethical protocols must be adhered to when sampling *all* human remains, regardless of their ancestral and cultural affinities. The report states that "consent alone cannot justify research on populations that will not be able to benefit from it because such research violates basic principles of social justice and equality" (National Research Council 1997, 59). This point further emphasises the need for a strong rationale behind studies that propose destructive analyses of human remains.

12.6 Conclusion and Recommendations

Over the past two decades, there has been an exponential rise in the use of destructive analyses in bioarchaeology. These methods continue to develop at a rapid rate, meaning researchers are taking increasing numbers of samples. Indeed, in some cases, these samples may be being stored illegally (i.e. researchers not following curating institution guidelines and returning samples to museums) for future analyses using newly developed techniques without consent. This situation is balanced somewhat by improvements in the efficiency in methods of analysis, meaning that the amount of samples required is progressively decreasing, and samples can be reused. However, this should not be a reason for complacency and every effort should be made to ensure that all destructive sampling of human remains includes provision for maintaining morphological integrity of the remains, and thus their future use in research. As mentioned in the introduction of this chapter, we need to be confident that the methods employed are based on sound, highly focused research questions which will, in turn, add to our body of knowledge of people in the past, rather than forming part of a vague list of exploratory studies. Ethics should always be at the core of any research carried out.

The following recommendations have been made to improve the ethical awareness of destructive sampling in the UK (though many of these may be followed in other countries):

- Curators and researchers must follow the DCMS (2005) and the English Heritage and Advisory Panel on the Archaeology of Burials in England guidelines at all times (APABE 2013, 2017);
- Detailed osteological reports should be produced prior to destructive sampling taking place;
- Those working in museums should ensure that all researchers submit detailed applications outlining their research rationale, an ethical framework within which they intend to work, and the extent of any destructive sampling;
- Ideally, a centralised ethics committee that governs destructive sampling of human remains should be implemented in the museum and commercial sectors, and in universities. This committee should work closely with BABAO to inform best practice;
- All applications for destructive analyses should be uploaded onto a universal database;
- Museums should keep records of all destructive analyses conducted on their skeletal collections, although unfortunately this is not currently the case as museums rarely have the resources or the staff to do so;
- Researchers should be more aware of ethical issues associated with their work. It is therefore recommended that researchers explicitly address the ethics of their research in future publications, e.g. consideration of religious groups, extent of destructive sampling, any prior sampling of the remains, and validity of the methodology used (see Wilbur et al. 2009);
- All remnants of samples that have been taken from skeletal remains should be returned to the respective curating institution and should be stored with the rest of the skeleton(s) from which the sample(s) derived, with any reports or associated publications;
- Researchers need to be transparent with museums and other curating institutions about molecular products before sampling is undertaken, and come to a mutually agreeable understanding of what should happen to them once the results have been published.

Ideally, the above recommendations (and those outlined by the DCMS 2005 and APABE 2013) would be mandatory as opposed to suggested guidelines. The lack of enforced codes of practice and ethics is likely to lead to poor professional practice as researchers and institutions may choose to ignore these principles. In any case, it is clear that greater dialogue is essential between archaeologists, bioarchaeologists, forensic anthropologists, curators, and Indigenous and religious groups if we are to ensure ethical practices are carried out when undertaking destructive sampling and analysis. Indeed, training and guidance on these matters should be introduced at undergraduate and postgraduate level for all those enrolled on courses that deal with human remains and museum studies. Further training and awareness is also needed in museums and the commercial sector. It should be remembered that "Human remains are not just another artifact; they have potency. They are charged with political, evidentiary, and emotional meaning…." (Cassman et al. 2006, 1). They should be treated with respect and dignity because they represent once living people.

Acknowledgements The authors would like to thank Siân Halcrow (University of Otago) for her insight into the use of destructive sampling of human remains belonging to Indigenous groups. Thanks are also due to Emily Carroll (Bournemouth University) for sharing chapters of her unpublished Ph.D. thesis.

References

Advisory Panel on Archaeology of Burials in England [APABE]. 2013. *Science and the Dead: A Guideline for the Destructive Sampling of Archaeological Remains for Scientific Analysis.* Swindon: English Heritage and The Advisory Panel on Archaeology of Burials in England.

Advisory Panel on Archaeology of Burials in England [APABE]. 2017. *Guidelines for Best Practice for the Treatment of Human Remains Excavated from Christian Burial Grounds in England*, 2nd ed. Swindon: Advisory Panel on Archaeology of Burials in England.

Allentoft, M.E., M. Sikora, K.G. Sjögren, et al. 2015. Population Genomics of Bronze Age Eurasia. *Nature* 522 (7555): 167–172.

Ambrose, S.H., and M.J. DeNiro. 1986. Reconstruction of African Human Diet Using Bone Collagen Carbon and Nitrogen Isotope Ratios. *Nature* 319 (6051): 321–324.

Antoine, D., and J. Ambers. 2014. The Scientific Analysis of Human Remains from the British Museum Collection. Research Potential and Examples from the Nile Valley. In *Regarding the Dead: Human Remains in the British Museum*, ed. A. Fletcher, D. Antoine, and J.D. Hill, 20–30. London: The British Museum Press.

Barnes, I., A. Duda, O.G. Pybus, et al. 2011. Ancient Urbanization Predicts Genetic Resistance to Tuberculosis. *Evolution* 65 (3): 842–848.

Bayliss, A. 2015. Quality in Bayesian Chronological Models in Archaeology. *World Archaeology* 47 (4): 677–700.

Beaumont, J., A. Gledhill, J. Lee-Thorp, et al. 2013. Childhood Diet: A Closer Examination of the Evidence from Dental Tissues using Stable Isotope Analysis of Incremental Human Dentine. *Archaeometry* 55 (2): 277–295.

Bidmos, M.A., V.E. Gibbon, and G. Štrkalj. 2010. Recent Advances in Sex Identification of Human Skeletal Remains in South Africa. *South African Journal of Science* 106 (11/12): 1–6.

Booth, T.J. 2016. An Investigation into the Relationship Between Funerary Treatment and Bacterial Bioerosion in European Archaeological Human Bone. *Archaeometry* 58 (3): 484–499.

Booth, T.J., A.T. Chamberlain, and M. Parker Pearson. 2015. Mummification in Bronze Age Britain. *Antiquity* 89 (347): 1155–1173.

Booth, T., R.C. Redfern, and R.L. Gowland. 2016. Immaculate Conceptions: Micro-CT Analysis of Diagenesis in Romano-British Infant Skeletons. *Journal of Archaeological Science* 74: 124–134.

Bos, K.I., V.J. Schuenemann, G.B. Golding, et al. 2011. A Draft Genome of Yersinia Pestis from Victims of the Black Death. *Nature* 478: 506–510.

Bowman, S. 1990. *Radiocarbon Dating.* Berkeley: University of California Press.

Brettell, R., J. Montgomery, and J. Evans. 2012. Brewing and Stewing: The Effect of Culturally Mediated Behaviour on the Oxygen Isotope Composition of Ingested Fluids and the

Implications for Human Provenance Studies. *Journal of Analytical Atomic Spectrometry* 27 (5): 778–785.
Brickley, M., and J.I. McKinley (eds.). 2004. *Guidelines to the Standards for Recording Human Remains*. IFA Paper No. 7. Southampton and Reading: BABAO and IFA.
British Museum. 2017. *Human Remains*. http://www.britishmuseum.org/about_us/management/human_remains.aspx. Accessed 21 July 2018.
British Association for Biological Anthropology and Osteoarchaeology [BABAO]. 2010a. *Code of Ethics: BABAO Working-Group for Ethics and Practice*. http://www.babao.org.uk/assets/Uploads/code-of-ethics.pdf. Accessed 21 July 2018.
British Association for Biological Anthropology and Osteoarchaeology [BABAO]. 2010b. *Code of Practice: BABAO Working-Group for Ethics and Practice*. http://www.babao.org.uk/assets/Uploads/code-of-practice.pdf. Accessed 21 July 2018.
British Association for Biological Anthropology and Osteoarchaeology [BABAO]. 2018a. *Ethics and Standards*. http://www.babao.org.uk/publications/ethics-and-standards/. Accessed 8 May 2018.
British Association for Biological Anthropology and Osteoarchaeology [BABAO]. 2018b. *BABAO Research Project Grants*. http://www.babao.org.uk/grants-and-prizes/research-grants/. Accessed 8 May 2018.
British Association for Biological Anthropology and Osteoarchaeology [BABAO]. 2019. *BABAO Code of Ethics*. https://www.babao.org.uk/assets/Uploads/BABAO-Code-of-Ethics-2019.pdf. Accessed 18 November 2019.
Britton, K., B.T. Fuller, T. Tütken, et al. 2015. Oxygen Isotope Analysis of Human Bone Phosphate Evidences Weaning Age in Archaeological Populations. *American Journal of Physical Anthropology* 157 (2): 226–241.
Britton, K., V. Grimes, J. Dau, et al. 2009. Reconstructing Faunal Migrations Using Intra-Tooth Sampling and Strontium and Oxygen Isotope Analyses: A Case Study of Modern Caribou (*Rangifer tarandus granti*). *Journal of Archaeological Science* 36 (5): 1163–1172.
Brock, F., T. Higham, P. Ditchfield, et al. 2010. Current Pretreatment Methods for AMS Radiocarbon Dating at the Oxford Radiocarbon Accelerator Unit (ORAU). *Radiocarbon* 52 (1): 103–112.
Buckley, S., D. Usai, T. Jakob, et al. 2014. Dental Calculus Reveals Unique Insights into Food Items, Cooking and Plant Processing in Prehistoric Central Sudan. *PLoS ONE* 9 (7): 1–10.
Budd, P., A. Millard, C. Chenery, et al. 2004. Investigating Population Movement by Stable Isotope Analysis: A Report from Britain. *Antiquity* 78 (299): 127–141.
Callaway, E. 2017. Stop Hoarding Ancient Bones, Plead Archaeologists. *Nature*. 11 August. https://doi.org/10.1038/nature.2017.22445.
Cappellini, E., M.J. Collins, and M.T. Gilbert. 2014. Biochemistry. Unlocking Ancient Protein Palimpsests. *Science* 343 (6177): 1320–1322.
Carroll, E. 2019. *Transition of Cremation Practices in Late Iron Age and Roman South-East Britain*. Dissertation, University of Reading.
Carroll, E., G. Müldner, M. Lewis, et al. 2017. *Ashes to Ashes: A New Approach to the Analysis of Burnt Human Remains*. Paper presented at the 19th Annual Conference of the British Association for Biological Anthropology and Osteoarchaeology (BABAO). Liverpool John Moores University, Liverpool, 8–10 September 2017.
Casas, M.J., E. Hagelberg, R. Fregel, et al. 2006. Human Mitochondrial DNA Diversity in an Archaeological Site in *al-Andalus*: Genetic Impact of Migrants from North Africa in Medieval Spain. *American Journal of Physical Anthropology* 131: 539–551.
Cassman, V., N. Odegaard, and J. Powell. 2006. Introduction. Dealing with the Dead. In *Human Remains: Guide for Museums and Academic Institutions*, ed. V. Cassman, N. Odegaard, and J. Powell, 1–3. Lanham: Altamira Press.
Chenery, C., G. Müldner, J. Evans, et al. 2010. Strontium and Stable Isotope Evidence for Diet and Mobility in Roman Gloucester, UK. *Journal of Archaeological Science* 37 (1): 150–163.

Cho, H. 2012. The Histology Laboratory and Principles of Microscope Instrumentation. In *Bone Histology: An Anthropological Perspective*, ed. C. Crowder and S. Stout, 341–360. Boca Raton: CRC Press.

Colwell, C. 2017. *Plundered Skulls and Stolen Spirits: Inside the Fight to Reclaim Native America's Culture*. Chicago: The University of Chicago.

Colwell-Chanthaphonh, C. 2010. Remains Unknown: Repatriating Culturally Unaffiliated Human Remains. *Anthropology News* 51 (3): 4–8.

Dal Sasso, G., I. Angelini, L. Maritan, et al. 2018. Raman Hyperspectral Imaging as an Effective and Highly Informative Tool to Study the Diagenetic Alteration of Fossil Bones. *Talanta* 179: 167–176.

Dal Sasso, G., M. Lebon, I. Angelini, et al. 2016. Bone Diagenesis Variability Among Multiple Burial Phases at Al Khiday (Sudan) Investigated by ATR-FTIR Spectroscopy. *Palaeogeography, Palaeoclimatology, Palaeoecology* 463: 168–179.

Damgaard, P.B., A. Margaryan, H. Schroeder, et al. 2015. Improving Access to Endogenous DNA in Ancient Bones and Teeth. *Scientific Reports* 5: 11184.

Deguilloux, M.F., M.H. Pemonge, F. Medisco, et al. 2014. Ancient DNA and Kinship Analysis of Human Remains Deposited in Merovingian Necropolis Sarcophagi (Jau Dignac et Loirac, France, 7th–8th Century AD). *Journal of Archaeological Science* 41: 399–405.

Department for Culture, Media and Sport [DCMS]. 2005. *Guidance for the Care of Human Remains in Museums*. London: Department for Culture, Media and Sport,

Djuric, M., D. Dunjic, D. Djonic, et al. 2007. Identification of Victims from Two Mass-Graves in Serbia. A Critical Evaluation of Classical Markers of Identity. *Forensic Science International* 172: 125–129.

Donoghue, H.D., and M. Spigelman. 2006. Pathogenic Microbial Ancient DNA: A Problem or an Opportunity? *Proceedings of Biological Science* 273 (1587): 641–642.

Durham University. 2017a. *The Fenwick Human Osteology Laboratory*. https://www.dur.ac.uk/archaeology/facilities_services/fhol/. Accessed 21 July 2018.

Durham University. 2017b. *Ethical Policy*. https://www.dur.ac.uk/archaeology/aboutus/ethics/. Accessed 21 July 2018.

Edwards, R. 2013. *Archaeological Archives and Museums 2012*. http://socmusarch.org.uk/socmusarch/gailmark/wordpress/wp-content/uploads/2016/07/Archaeological-archives-and-museums-2012.pdf. Accessed 21 July 2018.

Eisenhofer, R., A. Anderson, K. Dobney, et al. 2017. Ancient Microbial DNA in Dental Calculus: A New Method for Studying Rapid Human Migration Events. *Journal of Island and Coastal Archaeology* 0: 1–14.

Elders, J., L. Humphrey, S. Mays, et al. 2009. *Sampling Human Remains for Ancient DNA Analysis*. APABE Supplementary Guidance Note 1. http://www.archaeologyuk.org/apabe/pdf/apabe_supplementary_guidance_note_adna_analysis.pdf. Accessed 21 July 2018.

Evans, J.A., C.A. Chenery, and A.P. Fitzpatrick. 2006. Bronze Age Childhood Migration of Individuals Near Stonehenge, Revealed by Strontium and Oxygen Isotope Tooth Enamel Analysis. *Archaeometry* 48 (2): 309–321.

Evans, J.A., J. Montgomery, G. Wildman, et al. 2010. Spatial Variations in Biosphere $^{87}Sr/^{86}Sr$ in Britain. *Journal of the Geological Society of London* 167 (1): 1–4.

Fitch, A., A. Grauer, and L. Augustine. 2010. Lead Isotope Ratios: Tracking the Migration of European-Americans to Grafton, Illinois in the 19th century. *International Journal of Osteoarchaeology* 22: 301–319.

Fogel, M.L., and N. Tuross. 2003. Extending the Limits of Paleodietary Studies of Humans with Compound Specific Carbon Isotope Analysis of Amino Acids. *Journal of Archaeological Science* 30 (5): 535–545.

Franklin, D., L. Swift, and A. Flavel. 2016. 'Virtual Anthropology' and Radiographic Imaging in the Forensic Medical Sciences. *Egyptian Journal of Forensic Sciences* 6: 31–43.

Fraser, I., and W. Meier-Augenstein. 2007. Stable ^{2}H Isotope Analysis of Modern-Day Human Hair and Nails Can Aid Forensic Human Identification. *Rapid Communications in Mass Spectrometry* 21 (20): 3279–3285.

Fu, Q., C. Posth, M. Hajdinjak, et al. 2016. The Genetic History of Ice Age Europe. *Nature* 534 (7606): 200–205.

Fuller, B.T., J.L. Fuller, D.A. Harris, et al. 2006. Detection of Breastfeeding and Weaning in Modern Human Infants with Carbon and Nitrogen Stable Isotope Ratios. *American Journal of Physical Anthropology* 129 (2): 279–293.

Gamba, C., E.R. Jones, M.D. Teasdale, et al. 2014. Genome Flux and Stasis in a Five Millennium Transect of European Prehistory. *Nature Communications* 5: 5257. https://doi.org/10.1038/ncomms6257.

Gleize, Y., F. Mandisco, M.-H. Pemonge, et al. 2016. Early Medieval Muslim Graves in France: First Archaeological, Anthropological and Palaeogenomic Evidence. *PLoS One* 11 (2): e0148583. https://doi.org/10.1371/journal.pone.0148583.

Gomes, C., C. Magaña-Loarte, E. Dorado-Fernández, et al. 2015. Study of Medieval Critical Samples—A Genetic Approach to the Study of the Mudejar Community. *Forensic Science International Genetics Supplement Series* 5: e193–e195.

Goodman, N.R., J.L. Goodman, and W.I. Hofman. 2011. Autopsy: Traditional Jewish Laws and Customs "Halacha". *American Journal of Forensic Medicine and Pathology* 32 (3): 300–303.

Green, R.E., J. Krause, S.E. Ptak, et al. 2006. Analysis of One Million Base Pairs of Neanderthal DNA. *Nature* 444: 330–336.

Haak, W., G. Brandt, H.N. de Jong, et al. 2008. Ancient DNA, Strontium Isotopes, and Osteological Analyses Shed Light on Social and Kinship Organization of the Later Stone Age. *Proceedings of the National Academy of Sciences of the United States of America* 105 (47): 18226–18231.

Haak, W., I. Lazaridis, N. Patterson, et al. 2015. Massive Migration from the Steppe was a Source for Indo-European Languages in Europe. *Nature* 522 (7555): 207–211.

Hagelberg, E. 2013. Analysis of DNA from Bone: Benefits Versus Losses. In *More Than Just Bones: Ethics and Research on Human Remains*, ed. H.J. Fossheim, 95–112. Oslo: Norwegian National Research Ethics Committee.

Halcrow, S.E., J. Rooney, N. Beavan, et al. 2014. Assessing Raman Spectroscopy as a Prescreening Tool for the Selection of Archaeological Bone for Stable Isotopic Analysis. *PLoS ONE* 9 (7): e98462. https://doi.org/10.1371/journal.pone.0098462.

Hansen, H.B., P.B. Damgaard, A. Matgaryan, et al. 2017. Comparing Ancient DNA Preservation in Petrous Bone and Tooth Cementum. *PLoS ONE* 12: e0170940. https://doi.org/10.1371/journal.pone.0170940.

Harkins, K.M., and A.C. Stone. 2015. Ancient Pathogen Genomics: Insights into Timing and Adaptation. *Journal of Human Evolution* 79: 137–149.

Harvig, L., K.M. Frei, T.D. Price, et al. 2014. Strontium Isotope Signals in Cremated Petrous Portions as Indicator for Childhood Origin. *PLoS One* 9 (7): e101603. https://doi.org/10.1371/journal.pone.0101603.

Haynes, S., J.B. Searle, A. Bretman, et al. 2002. Bone Preservation and Ancient DNA: The Application of Screening Methods for Predicting DNA Survival. *Journal of Archaeological Science* 29 (6): 585–592.

Hedenstierna-Jonson, C., A. Kjellström, R. Zachrisson, et al. 2017. A Female Viking Warrior Confirmed by Genomics. *American Journal of Physical Anthropology* 164 (4): 853–860.

Hedges, R.E. 2002. Bone Diagenesis: An Overview of Processes. *Archaeometry* 44 (3): 319–328.

Hedges, R.E., A.R. Millard, and A.W.G. Pike. 1995. Measurements and Relationships of Diagenetic Alteration of Bone from Three Archaeological Sites. *Journal of Archaeological Science* 22 (2): 201–209.

Henderson, M. 2007. Museum Surrenders Vital Clues to Human Evolution. *The Times*. 12 May.

Herrmann, B. 1977. On Histological Investigations of Cremated Human Remains. *Journal of Human Evolution* 6: 101–103.

Holst, M. 2017. Response to the Paper by Redfern and Clegg by Malin Holst. *World Archaeology* 49 (5): 588–593.

Hughes, S.S., A.R. Millard, S.J. Lucy, et al. 2014. Anglo-Saxon Origins Investigated by Isotopic Analysis of Burials from Berinsfield, Oxfordshire, UK. *Journal of Archaeological Science* 42: 81–92.

Human Remains Working Group. 2013. *Recommendations for the Care of Human Remains in Museums and Collections*. Berlin: German Museums Association.

Human Tissue Act. 2004. The Stationery Office, London.

Jones, D.G., and R.J. Harris. 1998. Archaeological Human Remains: Scientific, Cultural, and Ethical Considerations. *Current Anthropology* 39 (2): 253–264.

Jørkov, M.L.S., J. Heinemeier, and N. Lynnerup. 2009. The Petrous Bone—A New Sampling Site for Identifying Early Dietary Patterns in Stable Isotopic Studies. *American Journal of Physical Anthropology* 138 (2): 199–209.

Katzenberg, M.A. 2008. Stable Isotope Analysis: A Tool for Studying Past Diet, Demography, and Life History. In *Biological Anthropology of the Human Skeleton*, 2nd ed, ed. M.A. Katzenberg and S.R. Saunders, 411–441. Hoboken: Wiley.

Katzenberg, M.A., and N.C. Lovell. 1999. Stable Isotope Variation in Pathological Bone. *International Journal Osteoarchaeology* 9 (5): 316–324.

Kaestle, F.A., and K.A. Horsburgh. 2002. Ancient DNA in Anthropology: Methods, Applications, and Ethics. *American Journal of Physical Anthropology* 119 (S35): 92–130.

Kaestle, F.A., and D.G. Smith. 2005. Working with Ancient DNA: NAGPRA, Kennewick Man and Other Ancient Peoples. In *Biological Anthropology and Ethics: From Repatriation to Genetic Identity*, ed. T.R. Turner, 241–262. Albany: State University of New York Press.

Key, F.M., C. Posth, J. Krause, et al. 2017. Mining Metagenomic Data Sets for Ancient DNA: Recommended Protocols for Authentication. *Trends in Genetics* 33 (8): 508–520.

Krishan, K., P.M. Chatterjee, T. Kanchan, et al. 2016. A Review of Sex Estimation Techniques During Examination of Skeletal Remains in Forensic Anthropology Casework. *Forensic Science International* 165: e1–e8.

Lanting, J.N., A.T. Aerts-Bijma, and J. van der Plicht. 2001. Dating of Cremated Bones. *Radiocarbon* 43 (2A): 249–254.

Lee-Thorp, J.A. 2008. On Isotopes and Old Bones. *Archaeometry* 50 (6): 925–950.

Li, H., and R. Durbin. 2011. Inference of Human Population History from Individual Whole-Genome Sequences. *Nature* 475 (7357): 493–496.

Llamas, B., G. Valverde, L. Fehren-Schmitz, et al. 2017. From the Field to the Laboratory: Controlling DNA Contamination in Human Ancient DNA Research in the High-Throughput Sequencing Era. *STAR: Science and Technology of Archaeological Research* 3 (1): 1–14.

Lynnerup, N. 2013. The Ethics of Destructive Bone Analyses (with Examples from Denmark and Greenland). In *More Than Just Bones: Ethics and Research on Human Remains*, ed. H. J. Fossheim, 81–94. Oslo: Norwegian National Research Ethics Committee.

Makarewicz, C., N. Marom, and G. Bar-Oz. 2017. Ensure Equal Access to Ancient DNA. *Nature* 548: 158.

Makarewicz, C.A., and J. Sealy. 2015. Dietary Reconstruction, Mobility, and the Analysis of Ancient Skeletal Tissues: Expanding the Prospects of Stable Isotope Research in Archaeology. *Journal of Archaeological Science* 56: 146–158.

Malhi, R.S., B.M. Kemp, J.A. Eshleman, et al. 2007. Mitochondrial Haplogroup M Discovered in Prehistoric North Americans. *Journal of Archaeological Science* 34: 642–648.

Matheson, C.D., K.K. Vernon, A. Lahti, et al. 2009. Molecular Exploration of the First-Century Tomb of the Shroud in Akeldama, Jerusalem. *PLoS One* 4 (12): e8319. https://doi.org/10.1371/journal.pone.0008319.

McKinley, J.I. 2013. 'No Room at the Inn' … Contract Archaeology and the Storage of Human Remains. In *Curating Human Remains: Caring for the Dead in the United Kingdom*, ed. M. Giesen, 135–145. Woodbridge: The Boydell Press.

Meyer, M., M. Kircher, M.T. Gansauge, et al. 2012. A High-Coverage Genome Sequence from an Archaic Denisovan Individual. *Science* 338 (6104): 222–226.

Mills, S., and V. Tranter. 2010. *Research into Issues Surrounding Human Bones in Museums*. London: Business Development Research Consultants.

Miszkiewicz, J.J., and P. Mahoney. 2017. Human Bone and Dental Histology in an Archaeological Context. In *Human Remains: Another Dimension. The Application of Imaging to the Study of Human Remains*, ed. D. Errickson and T. Thompson, 29–43. London: Academic Press.

Mitchell, P.D., and M. Brickley (eds). 2017. *Updated Guidelines to the Standards for Recording Human Remains*. Reading: Chartered Institute for Archaeologists.

Montgomery, J. 2010. Passports from the Past: Investigating Human Dispersals Using Strontium Isotope Analysis of Tooth Enamel. *Annals of Human Biology* 37 (3): 325–346.

Montgomery, J., J. Beaumont, M. Jay, et al. 2013. Strategic and Sporadic Marine Consumption at the Onset of the Neolithic: Increasing Temporal Resolution in the Isotope Evidence. *Antiquity* 87 (338): 1060–1072.

Müller, R., C.A. Roberts, and T.A. Brown. 2014. Genotyping of Ancient Mycobacterium Tuberculosis Strains Reveals Historic Genetic Diversity. *Proceedings of Biological Science* 281 (1781): 1–8.

Museum of London. n.d. *Centre for Human Bioarchaeology*. https://www.museumoflondon.org.uk/collections/other-collection-databases-and-libraries/centre-human-bioarchaeology. Accessed 21 July 2018.

Museums Association. 2013. *Cuts Survey 2013: Paid Jobs Lost to Volunteers*. http://www.museumsassociation.org/news/30092013-cuts-survey-2013-paid-jobs-in-museums-lost-to-volunteers. Accessed 21 July 2018.

National Park Service. n.d. *National NAGPRA: Law, Regulations, and Guidance*. https://www.nps.gov/nagpra/mandates/INDEX.HTM. Accessed 21 July 2018.

National Research Council. 1997. *Evaluating Human Genetic Diversity*. Washington, D.C.: National Academic Press.

Natural History Museum. n.d. *Human Comparative Collection*. http://www.nhm.ac.uk/our-science/collections/palaeontology-collections/human-comparative-collection.html. Accessed 21 July 2018.

Nauman, E., T.D. Price, and M.P. Richards. 2014. Changes in Dietary Practices and Social Organization During the Pivotal Late Iron Age Period in Norway (AD 550-1030): Isotope Analyses of Merovingian and Viking age Human Remains. *American Journal of Physical Anthropology* 155: 322–331.

Nehlich, O., D. Borić, S. Stefanović, et al. 2010. Sulphur Isotope Evidence for Freshwater Fish Consumption: A Case Study from the Danube Gorges, SE Europe. *Journal of Archaeological Science* 37 (5): 1131–1139.

Neil, S., J. Evans, J. Montgomery, et al. 2016. Isotopic Evidence for Residential Mobility of Farming Communities During the Transition to Agriculture in Britain. *Royal Society Open Science* 3 (1): 150522. https://doi.org/10.1098/rsos.150522.

Nielsen-Marsh, C.M., C.I. Smith, M.M.E. Jans, et al. 2007. Bone Diagenesis in the European Holocene II: Taphonomic and Environmental Considerations. *Journal of Archaeological Science* 34 (9): 1523–1531.

O'Rourke, D.H., M.G. Hayes, and S.W. Carlyle. 2005. The Consent Process and aDNA Research: Contrasting Approaches in North America. In *Biological Anthropology and Ethics: From Repatriation to Genetic Identity*, ed. T.R. Turner, 231–240. Albany: State University of New York Press.

Olsen, J., and H. Thrane. 2013. 'Old Wood' Effect in Radiocarbon Dating of Prehistoric Cremated Bones? *Journal of Archaeological Science* 40: 30–34.

Olsen, K.C., C.D. White, F.J. Longstaffe, et al. 2014. Intraskeletal Isotopic Compositions ($\delta^{13}C$, $\delta^{15}N$) of Bone Collagen: Nonpathological and Pathological Variation. *American Journal of Physical Anthropology* 153 (4): 598–604.

Ottoni, C., H.E. Koon, M.J. Collins, et al. 2009. Preservation of Ancient DNA in Thermally Damaged Archaeological Bone. *Science of Nature* 96 (2): 267–278.

Oxford Radiocarbon Accelerator Unit [ORAU]. 2018. *Sample Selection and Identification*. https://c14.arch.ox.ac.uk/selection.html. Accessed 21 July 2018.

Ozga, A.T., M.A. Nieves-Colón, T.P. Honap, et al. 2016. Successful Enrichment and Recovery of Whole Mitochondrial Genomes from Ancient Human Dental Calculus. *American Journal of Physical Anthropology* 160: 220–228.

Papagrigorakis, M.J., C. Yapijakis, P.N. Synodinos, et al. 2006. DNA Examination of Ancient Dental Pulp Incriminates Typhoid Fever as a Probable Cause of the Plague of Athens. *International Journal of Infectious Diseases* 10 (3): 206–214.

Parker Pearson, M., A. Chamberlain, M. Jay, et al. 2016. Bell Beaker People in Britain: Migration, Mobility and Diet. *Antiquity* 90 (351): 620–637.

Pellegrini, M., J. Pouncett, M. Jay, et al. 2016. Tooth Enamel Oxygen "Isoscapes" Show a High Degree of Human Mobility in Prehistoric Britain. *Scientific Reports* 6 (34986): 1–9.

Pereira, L., A.C. Morales, A. Goios, et al. 2006. The Islamization of Iberian Peninsula: A Demographic Shift or a Cultural Change? Search for an Answer Using Extant and Ancient DNA from Mértola (Southeast Portugal). *International Congress Series* 1288: 828–830.

Pinhasi, R., D. Fernandes, K. Sirak, et al. 2015. Optimal Ancient DNA Yields from the Inner Ear Part of the Human Petrous Bone. *PLoS One* 10 (6): e0129102. https://doi.org/10.1371/journal.pone.0129102.

Pollard, A.M., M. Pellegrini, and J.A. Lee-Thorp. 2011. Some Observations on the Conversion of Dental Enamel $\delta^{18}O_p$ values to $\delta^{18}O_w$ to Determine Human Mobility. *American Journal of Physical Anthropology* 145 (3): 499–504.

Preus, H.R., O.J. Marvik, K.A. Selvig, et al. 2011. Ancient Bacterial DNA (aDNA) in Dental Calculus from Archaeological Human Remains. *Journal of Archaeological Science* 38: 1827–1831.

Price, T.D., J.H. Burton, and R.A. Bentley. 2002. The Characterization of Biologically Available Strontium Isotope Ratios for the Study of Prehistoric Migration. *Archaeometry* 44 (1): 117–135.

Privat, K.L., T.C. O'Connell, and M.P. Richards. 2002. Stable Isotope Analysis of Human and Faunal Remains from the Anglo-Saxon Cemetery at Berinsfield, Oxfordshire: Dietary and Social Implications. *Journal of Archaeological Science* 29 (7): 779–790.

Procopio, N., A.T. Chamberlain, and M. Buckley. 2018. Exploring Biological and Geological Age-Related Changes Through Variations in Intra- and Inter-Tooth Proteomes of Ancient Dentine. *Journal of Proteome Research* 17 (3): 1000–1013.

Ramsey, C.B. 2009. Bayesian Analysis of Radiocarbon Dates. *Radiocarbon* 51 (1): 337–360.

Rasmussen, M., M. Sikora, A. Albrechtsen, et al. 2015. The Ancestry and Affiliations of Kennewick Man. *Nature* 523 (7561): 455–458.

Redfern, R., and J. Bekvalac. 2013. The Museum of London: An Overview of Policies and Practice. In Curating Human Remains. Caring for the Dead in the United Kingdom, ed. M. Giesen, 87–98. Woodbridge: The Boydell Press.

Redfern, R., and M. Clegg. 2017. Archaeologically Derived Human Remains in England: Legacy and Future. *World Archaeology* 49 (5): 1–14.

Reitsema, L.J. 2013. Beyond Diet Reconstruction: Stable Isotope Applications to Human Physiology, Health, and Nutrition. *American Journal of Human Biology* 25 (4): 445–456.

Richards, M. 2004. Sampling Procedures for Bone Chemistry. In *Guidelines to the Standards for Recording Human Remains*, ed. M. Brickley, J.I. McKinley, 43–45. IFA Paper No. 7. Southampton and Reading: BABAO and IFA.

Richards, M. 2017. Sampling Guidelines for Bone Chemistry. In *Updated Guidelines to the Standards for Recording Human Remains*, ed. P.D. Mitchell, M. Brickley, 52–53. Reading: CIfA.

Richards, M.P., R.E.M. Hedges, R. Jacobi, et al. 2000. FOCUS: Gough's Cave and Sun Hole Cave Human Stable Isotope Values Indicate a High Animal Protein Diet in the British Upper Palaeolithic. *Journal of Archaeological Science* 27 (1): 1–3.

Richards, M.P., R.J. Schulting, and R.E. Hedges. 2003. Archaeology: Sharp Shift in Diet at Onset of Neolithic. *Nature* 425 (6956): 366.

Rispler-Chaim, V. 1993. The Ethics of Post-Mortem Examinations in Contemporary Islam. *Journal of Medical Ethics* 19: 164–168.

Roberts, C.A. 2013. Archaeological Human Remains and Laboratories: Attaining Acceptable Standards for Curating Skeletal Remains for Teaching and Research. In *Curating Human Remains. Caring for the Dead in the United Kingdom*, ed. M. Giesen and V. Park, 123–134. Woodbridge: The Boydell Press.

Roberts, C.A. 2016. Palaeopathology and Its Relevance to Understanding Health and Disease Today: The Impact of Environment on Health, Past and Present. *Anthropology Review* 79: 1–16.

Roberts, C., and S. Ingham. 2008. Using Ancient DNA Analysis in Palaeopathology: A Critical Analysis of Published Papers, with Recommendations for Future Work. *International Journal of Osteoarchaeology* 18 (6): 600–613.

Roberts, I.S.D., R.E. Bernamore, E.W. Benbow, et al. 2012. Post-Mortem Imaging as an Alternative to Autopsy in the Diagnosis of Adult Deaths: A Validation Study. *Lancet* 379: 136–142.

Salazar-García, D.C., A. Romero, P. García-Borja, et al. 2016. A Combined Dietary Approach Using Isotope and Dental Buccal-Microwear Analysis of Human Remains from the Neolithic, Roman and Medieval Periods from the Archaeological Site of Tossal de les Basses (Alicante, Spain). *Journal of Archaeological Science Reports* 6: 610–619.

Sayer, D. 2010. *Ethics and Burial Archaeology*. London: Bristol Classical Press.

Schuenemann, V.J., P. Singh, T.A. Mendum, et al. 2013. Genome-Wide Comparison of Medieval and Modern Mycobacterium Leprae. *Science* 341: 179–183.

Sheikh, A. 1998. Death and Dying—A Muslim Perspective. *Journal of the Royal Society of Medicine* 91: 138–140.

Sirak, K., M. Novak, and O. Cheronet. 2017. A Minimally-Invasive Method for Sampling Human Petrous Bones from the Cranial Base for Ancient DNA Analysis. *BioTechniques* 62 (6): 283–289.

Skoglund, P., J. Storå, A. Götherström, et al. 2013. Accurate Sex Identification of Ancient Human Remains Using DNA Shotgun Sequencing. *Journal of Archaeological Science* 40 (12): 4477–4482.

Slon, V., C. Hopfe, C.L. Weiß, et al. 2017. Neandertal and Denisovan DNA from Pleistocene Sediments. *Science* 356 (6338): 605–608.

Smith, C.I., C.M. Nielsen-Marsh, M.M.E. Jans, et al. 2007. Bone Diagenesis in the European Holocene I: Patterns and Mechanisms. *Journal of Archaeological Science* 34 (9): 1485–1493.

Smithsonian National Museum of Natural History. n.d. *Anthropology Sampling Review Committee*. http://anthropology.si.edu/cm/sampling.htm. Accessed 21 July 2018.

Snoeck, C., F. Brock, and R.J. Schulting. 2014. Carbon Exchanges Between Bone Apatite and Fuels During Cremation: Impact on Radiocarbon Dates. *Radiocarbon* 56 (2): 591–602.

Squires, K.E. 2015. The Use of Microscopic Techniques in Cremation Studies: A New Approach to Understanding the Social Identity of Cremation Practicing Groups from Early Anglo-Saxon England. In *The Archaeology of Cremation: Burned Human Remains in Funerary Studies*, ed. T.J.U. Thompson, 151–172. Oxford: Oxbow Books.

Squires, K.E., T.J.U. Thompson, M. Islam, et al. 2011. The Application of Histomorphometry and Fourier Transform Infrared Spectroscopy to the Analysis of Early Anglo-Saxon Burned Bone. *Journal of Archaeological Science* 38 (9): 2399–2409.

Staffordshire University. 2018. *Research Ethics*. https://www.staffs.ac.uk/research/opportunities-for-academics/research-governance/research-ethics. Accessed 10 November 2019.

Stevens, R.E., and R.E. Hedges. 2004. Carbon and Nitrogen Stable Isotope Analysis of Northwest European Horse Bone and Tooth Collagen, 40,000 BP-Present: Palaeoclimatic Interpretations. *Quaternary Science Reviews* 23 (7–8): 977–991.

Stewart, N.A., R.F. Gerlach, R.L. Gowland, et al. 2017. Sex Determination of Human Remains from Peptides in Tooth Enamel. *Proceedings of the National Academy Sciences of the United States of America* 114 (52): 13649–13654.

Stone, A.C., G.R. Milner, S. Pääbo, et al. 1996. Sex Determination of Ancient Human Skeletons Using DNA. *American Journal of Physical Anthropology* 99: 231–238.

Stout, S.D., and S.L. Teitelbaum. 1976. Histomorphometric Determination of Formation Rates of Archaeological Bone. *Calcified Tissue Research* 21: 163–169.

Styring, A.K., J.C. Sealy, and R.P. Evershed. 2010. Resolving the Bulk δ^{15}N Values of Ancient Human and Animal Bone Collagen via Compound-Specific Nitrogen Isotope Analysis of Constituent Amino Acids. *Geochimica et Cosmochimica Acta* 74 (1): 241–251.

TallBear, K. 2013. *Native American DNA: Tribal Belonging and the False Promise of Genetic Science*. Minnesota: University of Minnesota Press.

Tarlow, S. 2006. Archaeological Ethics and the People of the Past. In *The Ethics of Archaeology: Philosophical Perspectives on Archaeological Practice*, ed. C. Scarre and G. Scarre, 181–198. Cambridge: Cambridge University Press.

Taylor, R.E. 2001. Radiocarbon Dating. In *Handbook of Archaeological Sciences*, ed. D.R. Brothwell and A.M. Pollard, 23–34. Chichester: Wiley.

Taylor, R.E. 2009. Radiocarbon Dating. In *Encyclopedia of Palaeoclimatology and Ancient Environments*, ed. V. Gornitz, 863–868. Dordrecht: Springer.

Thali, M.J., C. Jackowski, L. Oesterhelweg, et al. 2007. VIRTOPSY—The Swiss Virtual Autopsy Approach. *Journal of Legal Medicine* 9: 100–104.

Thompson, T.J.U., M. Gauthier, and M. Islam. 2009. The Application of a New Method of Fourier Transform Infrared Spectroscopy to the Analysis of Burned Bone. *Journal of Archaeological Science* 36 (3): 910–914.

Thompson, T.J.U., D. Gonçalves, K.E. Squires, et al. 2017. Thermal Alteration to the Body. In *Taphonomy of Human Remains: Forensic Analysis of the Dead and the Depositional Environment*, ed. E.M.J. Schotsman, N. Márquez-Grant, and S.L. Forbes, 318–334. Chichester: Wiley.

Tierney, S.N., and J.M. Bird. 2015. Molecular Sex Identification of Juvenile Skeletal Remains from an Irish Medieval Population Using Ancient DNA Analysis. *Journal of Archaeological Science* 62: 27–38.

Turner-Walker, G., and M. Jans. 2008. Reconstructing Taphonomic Histories Using Histological Analysis. *Palaeogeography, Palaeoclimatology, Palaeoecology* 266 (3–4): 227–235.

Turner-Walker, G., and U. Syversen. 2002. Quantifying Histological Changes in Archaeological Bones Using BSE-SEM Image Analysis. *Archaeometry* 44 (3): 461–468.

Valtueña, A.A., A. Mittnik, F.M. Key, et al. 2017. The Stone Age Plague and Its Persistence in Eurasia. *Current Biology* 27 (23): 3683–3691.

Von Hunnius, T.E., D. Yang, B. Eng, et al. 2007. Digging Deeper into the Limits of Ancient DNA Research on Syphilis. *Journal of Archaeological Science* 34: 2091–2100.

Walsh-Haney, H., and L.S. Lieberman. 2005. Ethical Concerns in Forensic Anthropology. In *Biological Anthropology and Ethics: From Repatriation to Genetic Identity*, ed. T.R. Turner, 121–131. Albany: State University of New York.

Wang, Y., and T.E. Cerling. 1994. A Model of Fossil Tooth and Bone Diagenesis: Implications for Paleodiet Reconstruction from Stable Isotopes. *Palaeogeography, Palaeoclimatology, Palaeoecology* 107 (3–4): 281–289.

Ward, G.K., and S.R. Wilson. 1978. Procedures for Comparing and Combining Radiocarbon Age Determinations: A Critique. *Archaeometry* 20 (1): 19–31.

Warinner, C., J.F.M. Rodrigues, R. Vyas, et al. 2014. Pathogens and Host Immunity in the Ancient Human Oral Cavity. *Nature Genetics* 46 (4): 336–344.

Warinner, C., C. Speller, M.J. Collins, et al. 2015. Ancient Human Microbiomes. *Journal of Human Evolution* 79: 125–136.

Weyrich, L.S., K. Dobney, and A. Cooper. 2015. Ancient DNA Analysis of Dental Calculus. *Journal of Human Evolution* 79: 119–124.

Weyrich, L.S., S. Duchene, J. Soubrier, et al. 2017. Neanderthal Behaviour, Diet and Disease Inferred from Ancient DNA in Dental Calculus. *Nature* 544: 357–361.

Wilbur, A.K., A.S. Bouwman, A.C. Stone, et al. 2009. Deficiencies and Challenges in the Study of Ancient Tuberculosis DNA. *Journal of Archaeological Science* 36 (9): 1990–1997.

Wild, E.M., M. Teschler-Nicola, W. Kutschera, et al. 2005. Direct Dating of Early Upper Palaeolithic Human Remains from Mladec. *Nature* 435 (7040): 332–335.

World Archaeological Congress [WAC]. 1989. *The Vermillion Accord, Archaeological Ethics and the Treatment of the Dead: A Statement of Principles Agreed by Archaeologists and Indigenous Peoples at the World Archaeological Congress, Vermillion, USA*. http://worldarch.org/code-of-ethics/. Accessed 5 August 2018.

Yang, D.Y., and K. Watt. 2005. Contamination Controls When Preparing Archaeological Remains for Ancient DNA Analysis. *Journal of Archaeological Science* 32 (3): 331–336.

Chapter 13
Sharing Is Not Always Caring: Social Media and the Dead

David Errickson and Tim J. U. Thompson

Abstract People around the world are connected by the touch of a button through the medium of social media. These outward facing platforms have encouraged those working in science, including disciplines with human remains, to share their research with the wider public. However, because technology is rapidly evolving, it is challenging for good practice guidance to keep up. As a result, a number of ethical concerns have been raised resulting from social media's ubiquity. Such concerns include whether human remains should be shared and displayed online, and all arguments seem to point towards justification and contextualisation. Furthermore, the rapid technological development of other imaging devices, such as three-dimensional documentation, has added to this discussion. This chapter addresses some of these conversations, using recent news media examples, in an attempt to drive forward further conversations. This chapter does not aim to solve the issues discussed, but does recommended guidance for the future.

13.1 Introduction

It seems that technology is increasingly at the centre of everything we do. Younger generations engage so readily with technology and the digital environment that it is being progressively incorporated into university level learning, teaching, and engagement (Bailey-Ross et al. 2017). This increase has been echoed over the past 15 years with a rise in the uptake and predominance of social media. For example, a number of platforms have been launched such as Facebook in 2004 (and its Messenger app in 2011), Twitter in 2006, Instagram in 2010, and Snapchat in 2011.

D. Errickson (✉)
Cranfield Forensic Institute, Defence Academy of the United Kingdom, Cranfield University, Shrivenham SN6 8LA, UK
e-mail: david.errickson@cranfield.ac.uk

T. J. U. Thompson
School of Health and Life Science, Teesside University, Borough Road, Middlesbrough TS1 3BX, UK

K. Squires et al. (eds.), *Ethical Approaches to Human Remains*,
https://doi.org/10.1007/978-3-030-32926-6_13

These public facing fora are predicted to have a combined global revenue of upwards of 39 billion euros in 2019 (Statista 2018). They are also expected to continually increase in their popularity, and to become more and more accessible to all worldwide.

With the increasing use of social media in large areas of our lives, students, academics, professionals, and the public alike have taken to these platforms to share their personal and professional experiences through the medium of images, videos, and micro-blogging. The positive impact in the discipline can be seen: It has encouraged academics to share their data with the wider public who would not normally see the research that is undertaken within an institution, it has allowed individuals to interact with professionals within a museum setting, and it has helped set up a larger network of engaging, cross-disciplinary conversations at the touch of a button (see the Digi-Osteo Mailing[1] List, for example).

As with social media, the discipline has similarly witnessed a large uptake in the use of other technology to record and share information. This is demonstrated by the availability of three-dimensional (3D) documentation equipment and more recently its concurring fabrication methodologies of 3D printing. These techniques are easy to use, affordable (some are in the form of apps for tablets), and available to the wider public. As a result, these types of technologies have been used to combine the humanities both within and beyond academia (Bailey-Ross et al. 2017), and are increasingly associated with the analysis of human remains both in bioarchaeology and forensic anthropology (Errickson and Thompson 2017).

13.2 Why We Need This Chapter

Scarre and Scarre (2006) asks whether archaeologists have a privileged status in dealing with the remains of the past. The authors believe that we do, and it should be noted that, although this chapter attempts to raise some discussion points for future deliberation, these considerations are set within a moveable boundary; there are academics with diverging views on this matter. Despite this seeming fluidity, it is worth considering that ethical behaviour is concerned with the critical appraisal of human conduct (Scarre and Scarre 2006) and the boundaries that concern this have been argued to be rigid (Thompson 2001). If this is the case, determining the ethicality of behaviour with regard to displaying human remains should be relatively straightforward.

Media coverage (including social media) has the power to access more people and is arguably more influential than museums (Calugay 2015). Therefore, academics and professionals should lead by example when engaging with these public forms of communication and outreach. It is our experience and belief that most of

[1]The Digital Osteology (Digi-Osteo) mailing list was created in February 2015 by Alison Atkin and David Errickson. The JISCMAIL email service was used as a means of encouraging cross-disciplinary communication on ethical considerations in our digital work.

those working with human remains are aligned to the 1989 Vermillion Accord (or code of ethics for their specific profession and country) and accept the ethical obligation to treat human remains with respect and dignity (WAC 1989). However, we also believe that there are a number of individuals who feel that they are working within these ethical boundaries, but do not. Further still, there are small numbers of individuals who simply do not attempt to work within them—even if they are aware of them. It has also been suggested that there are some, the 'average lay person', who may not be aware of any ethical issues that relate to human remains at all (Calugay 2015).

Oftentimes, focusing on the legality of using human remains is easier (Thompson 2001, 2003). Thus, Redfern and Clegg (2017) suggest that with the increasing use of digital media, institutions will have to re-work policies and procedures that concern issues, such as copyright, in regard to image ownership. However, a bigger issue is that there is currently a distinct lack of guidance for using digital technology in bioarchaeology—especially where ethical considerations are concerned (Atkin 2015). In disciplines associated with human remains, there has also been a clear paradigm shift towards the use of technology in recording, visualising, and analysing 3D digital bioarchaeological data (Hassett 2018). This is largely attributable to the reduction in price of the technical equipment needed and therefore an increase in accessibility. There are a number of benefits for using digital data such as improving education, protecting remains from degradation through physical handling, and to present evidence within the courtroom when the actual human remains are not present (for a more advanced discussion on the use of digital data please refer to Errickson and Thompson 2017). This in turn has led to the creation of a number of self-described, sub-disciplines, such as *Virtual Anthropology* (Weber 2014). Within *Virtual Anthropology*, Weber (2014) states that the implementation of new technology such as three-dimensional (3D) imaging has been useful in six categories that directly relate to bioarchaeology and anthropology: digitising, exposing, comparing, reconstructing, materialising, and sharing (see Smith and Hirst, this volume).

Nonetheless, and similar to the use of social media, there are currently no legislative guidelines with regards to the use of human remains and 3D imaging. Some groups of professionals are working towards digital guidelines, however it is only in the past few years where these issues have been raised and grappled with (for example the Skeletons, Stories, and Social Bodies Conference in 2017 at the University of Southampton (UK), and the World Archaeology Congress 8 in Kyoto (Japan) in 2016). As a result, the key aims of this chapter are to: (1) explore and reflect on the key issues surrounding the display of digitised human remains on social media, and (2) recommend future considerations concerning the display of human remains, social media, and imaging technologies. As the authors of this chapter are both from within the forensic archaeological and anthropological context, the emphasis of this chapter is on bioarchaeology and forensic anthropology. To support our arguments and illustrate our point, some anonymised examples will be used throughout this chapter. Note that all personal communication has been approved for use. It is worth highlighting that the purpose of this chapter is to inform those who use images of human remains on social media platforms, and not to assign blame.

13.3 The Digital Afterlife

Harries et al. (2018) state that images have both a therapeutic and non-therapeutic value. There is almost an expectation by the general public and students alike for the use of images to display human remains when discussing death and burial, such as using an image to demonstrate a particular point in a university lecture. This expectation can be placed into the non-therapeutic category as it incorporates the use of images as an aid to teaching, illustrative lectures, and published papers. Moreover, the use in a museum setting could also be absorbed into this category. This expectation goes hand in hand with the digital generation we live in today. We carry the capability to immediately image and share what we see with anyone and everyone at any given time. But, because everything is so instantaneous, often an action is undertaken before there is time to process the consequence.

The authors of this chapter both work with human remains in archaeological and anthropological contexts. We have both assisted the police, educated students, and undertaken research all of which involved the handling of human remains. There is an understanding that without access and study of human remains our biological profiling methods would be inaccurate, the future generation of students would have limited experience, and that our current knowledge of the body would be limited. Thus, there is certainly a need to work with human remains to expand our knowledge and because of the sensitive nature of the discipline, we are mindful of both living individuals and the dead. There are some instances (certainly in education), where human remains may not be available for teaching and images are best suited as an alternative. However, it could be argued that the use of human remains through examination, physical display, or through the medium of image could be construed as putting the remains back to work in the form of another life.

A thought that comes to mind is: are we exploiting the dead by putting them to work because of this increased expectation? Surely, any bioarchaeology and forensic anthropology student expects to be able to study using human remains? But this 'new life' may not be what the now-deceased individual wanted. If we think about Charles Byrne and how he wanted to be buried at sea (Doyal and Muinzer 2011), are we being disrespectful by restricting his last wishes? Does the notion of self-determinism extend after death? The American Academy of Forensic Sciences (AAFS) states that forensic anthropologists shall not demonstrate disrespect to the dead, or their family members, or otherwise betray confidence placed in them by the public (American Academy of Forensic Sciences 2018). Similarly, the British Association for Biological Anthropology and Osteoarchaeology (BABAO 2010) states that it is a privilege to work with human remains. Of course, we may not know what the last wishes of the individual were and therefore we may fall back to any cultural affiliation that may be left, but in some cases the province may be unknown. Perhaps we could ask how different this new afterlife is in comparison to the unfortunate dead that were being buried to fertilise rice fields or coconut groves, or occasionally, sacrificial (bone) offerings to Neak Ta (guardian spirits) during the 1980s in Cambodia (Zucker 2013; see Bennett, this volume).

Öhman and Luciano (2018) suggest that a digital afterlife in some forms may lead to prolonged grief for surviving kin and therefore we must consider others. For example, individuals who have died in recent wars still have surviving family members. Yet, there are some companies who exploit death by enabling the living to become virtually immortal in the form of an avatar (Ternime 2018). These digital profiles allow others to access our memories and thoughts when we are dead, but this is a decision we can make in the present. In the present, the living person can make the decision to live on in this digital format, however this is not always up to the individual and therefore, deceased individuals (or family members) may not have had this choice. Can we assume that because we want someone's memory to live on, that the dead would also want this?

13.4 Selfie or Selfish?

According to Redfern and Clegg (2017) the only negative feedback gained from a temporary exhibition about gladiatorial combat at the Museum of London (London, UK) in 2015 (Museum of London 2015) was that the visitors "were upset because they were asked not to take selfies with the human remains and to delete the images". The authors ask, is it ok to take a selfie with human remains in the image, and if it is, when is it not acceptable?

For example, in 2014 and 2017, several newspapers reported on people taking selfies at the concentration and extermination camps at Auschwitz-Birkenau (Poland) and then posting them onto social media platforms (Dewey 2014; Drewett 2017). In these images there were no human remains, only the image of the location itself. As a result, a large debate ensued online, with the main focus on whether the art of 'selfie taking' is acceptable or not at these sensitive locations (Dewey 2014). The argument against this act focused on the respect for the dead and whether those individuals taking the photographs understand the contextual historical connotations that are associated with these sites.

It could be argued that because of the progression in technology, and being in the digital age, we may just be seeing a new form of documentation. Social media allows us to share information instantly to those around the world, and in this format it is a useful way of capturing and sharing our lives. Therefore, the act of sharing could be an innocent way of allowing us to relive our adventures, experiences, and thoughts with others, and being able to post immediately online enables the act of sharing one very specific moment in time that has affected the photographer in an emotional way. For example, a photograph at Auschwitz-Birkenau could be shared because of the connection the individual had with the site of interest, and this method of documentation is a way for them to express their feelings in a seemingly innocent action.

On the other hand, this example cannot be directly compared with dealing with human remains, but more with the association of cultural atrocities. However, there are other examples that may be more specific to our discipline. For example, on Tripadvisor's Choeung Ek Killing Fields 'attraction' page, there are a number of individuals who have taken selfies with the human remains (Tripadvisor 2018). Furthermore, what about the individual who surfed on a paddle board through Paris' Catacombs (Killgrove 2016)? Although some newspapers are insensitive, (this could be due to the writer not understanding the sensitive nature of human remains) (Holmes 2016), there are further examples of 'academic' social media selfies in archaeological and academic contexts where human remains are visible, but the context is not present.

These examples may include human remains that are unrecognisable (or at least to the lay public), and therefore the art of selfie taking could be down to a matter of consent. However, there are also examples of where the individual is known, or are from a contemporary context. For example, in 2015 a teen posted a selfie to Facebook which showed their dead grandfather in the background resulting in the individual being 'slammed' by others on social media (James 2015). Another example from 2017 showed a professor and graduate students posing for a selfie with two severed heads which were to be used for medical research (Mullick 2018), but in this example there are actual medical codes of conduct that should have been followed.

Displays of human remains in museums are one of the most effective tools at attracting visitors (Walker 2000). Akin to a museum display, images depicting human remains in such an environment should be done in a 'respectful manner'. It is understood that the display of bones is useful for helping to create a link with our own body and our morality (Harries et al. 2018). Likewise, they can also memorialise the individual while visually raising the awareness of contemporary violence (Auchter 2018). Therefore, if the image is displayed in a respectful manner, then perhaps the outcry will be less likely.

Similarly, does it only matter if the 'object' being photographed is human remains as opposed to a representation of the dead? For example, the remains at Pompeii (Italy) are the representative shell of what once was. Furthermore, there are a number of individuals who were not found after the numerous battles in the World Wars. Yet, there are memorials that represent these individuals, such as the British Memorial to the Missing (Soissons, France) and the Thiepval Memorial to the Missing (Somme Battlefields, France). Perhaps there is a difference between posing with death and documenting it. For example, a photograph of a war memorial seems respectful as a means of recording it, but once we pose with the memorial, the boundaries become stretched.

There are instances where there must be an all-round understanding where it may be inappropriate to take and share images of the dead. In these examples, ground rules have been laid out and respect of these wishes should be granted without exception. For example, in some anatomical museums there is often an embargo on photographing their contents. These institutions include the Wellcome Museum of Anatomy and Pathology (Royal College of Surgeons, London) and St Barts Hospital (London). Interestingly, The Hunterian (2018) Anatomy Museum (Glasgow, Scotland) states that "visitors are welcome to take photographs and that they hope the visitor will share them on their social networks", however photography in the anatomy museum is not permitted. Yet, an Internet search of any museum's anatomy exhibition will bring up images of the anatomical 'specimens' online. In some displays, this restriction of photography is not always a universal view. For example, when the touring Body Worlds exhibition was on display at Newcastle-upon-Tyne (England) in 2014, it forbade any photographs to be taken. Yet, the permanent Body Worlds exhibition in Amsterdam (The Netherlands) does not have this photographic restriction in place.

13.5 Why Put These Pictures in the Public Domain in the First Place?

An interesting question is, do the public even need to be protected from the dead? (Sayer 2010). Is it actually acceptable to share photographs of a skeleton on social media? (Atkin and Errickson 2016). A key question to address is why people feel the need to put such images on social media and, by doing so, it has sparked this debate. As before, context is key—both with the period in history that the remains derive from and the intent of the display. Academics for example, may feel that such images represent the field in which they work. The images here are used not to represent a deceased person, but a field of study. In the eyes of the academic, they are anonymous remains. Interestingly, there is often a subtle aspect of these debates, which surrounds not the legitimacy of showing such images, but rather the legitimacy of those who can show such images. Academics and those working in osteology are 'permitted' to show such images as they are objective experts. The conversation is different with students, who many argue show disrespect by displaying such images on social media; that they are not taking the privilege of studying human remains seriously enough. For example, an article in the Express and Star (2011) stated that three forensic students held "lewd poses" alongside human remains and took photographs, which were later posted to social media. But, if these students had just taken a photograph with the remains, would there have been such uproar?

This harks back to the question posed earlier (in Sect. 13.2 of this chapter) by Scarre and Scarre (2006) regarding the privilege of archaeologists. Yet there is often less discussion surrounding the reasons why students display such images on social media, when compared to academic staff, and as a result, assumption about intent are made. It is worth highlighting that generational factors can be influential here—the relationship between millennials and their engagement with social media differs from that of Generation X or the Baby Boomers. Social media is not about frivolous communication per se, but rather is a mechanism for recording one's experience and sharing that with others—who may, in turn, have similar experiences to share. Thus, the displaying of images of human remains on social media draws one into a community of people with similar experiences. The contradiction with the assumption that it is all about frivolous showing off is striking. Clearly, there is a hierarchy of permissible display at play on social media oriented around the context of the remains and social media, and one which is maintained by both academia and the public. Yet, the question we must keep asking of those who display images in this way is: is it necessary to post a picture of an individual's skeleton on social media, is there a wider purpose, or is it being done as a moment of infinite jest of most excellent fancy?

13.6 Social Media and Trading

A greater issue that has been influenced by social media concerns the increasingly different ways in which human remains are traded. Although this is not the intention of this chapter (see Huffer and Charlton, this volume), attention should be brought to it in this context. Although eBay and a number of other selling platforms now try and regulate such trade, it is not difficult to find examples of human remains that are being sold online (eBay 2018). For example, there are no regulations in place on outward facing platforms such as Instagram, and although it is not illegal in some parts of the world, it is certainly not acceptable.

Potentially, there is a similar argument to trading as there is to posting an image of a human skeleton online. What if the individual undertaking the action does not understand that they may be doing something misguided? Here we must consider whether they have had permission to sell human remains, but this is also where one's view of oneself is pushed upon the individuals of the past and some individuals justify their actions as they are content with the same happening to their body. For example, the following are excerpts from a conversation with an individual who was selling human remains in the UK.

Anon	I will only sell medical teaching or things that have come from museums……I do feel uncomfortable with anything outside of that.
DE/Author	…Do they just give you them?
Anon	Very often get them from auctions of surplus school equipment.
DE	Do you mind if I ask how would you feel about being sold on?
Anon	Personally I believe once you're dead you're dead. If I felt like someone could get some benefit from what I leave behind I would be rather proud. A lot like how I would feel if I wrote a book and someone took my ideas and learnt from it and went forward……If a medical student used my skull or, if an artist drew my skull or someone just had me sitting on a shelf and their son or daughter asked a question about me that led to some knowledge whether that be

> medical or about how people lived in my time or even if someone just understood that's what's under the skin. I would feel much more content than thinking my family had to struggle to pay to dispose of me or I took up space in a graveyard to grow a tree. Or a house a homeless person. In regards to money changing hands for my remains I would have no problem at all with it.

The seller was very aware of the laws in both the UK and internationally. Furthermore, there was acknowledgement that the incorporation of a provenance law to the UK would be beneficial to control/restrict this type of selling from happening (Horwood 2015). Although one point did occur during the conversation —the seller is assuming that because they are comfortable with the trade of their own body, those in the past were equally comfortable too. We must be very careful not to overlay our own biases on those around us. Those in the past may not have wanted this—especially those who have cultural and religious tendencies. Likewise, the same could apply today. Indeed, the very question itself may not have even existed. Still, since we do not allow the trade of present human lives, why should we allow the trade of past lives?

13.7 Higher Education

As discussed previously, we live in a digital world and are therefore encouraged to use technology and digital resources in an academic setting. At Teesside University (Middlesbrough, UK) every new first year university student will now be given an iPad loaded with apps ready for use in the learning environment. This is part of the Future Facing Learning initiative established by the University, designed, in part, to allow students to learn using the digital environment that they are used to. With regards to human remains, there are a number of online resources that can help compliment teaching through this approach, such as the Anthronomics (2016) and Digitised Diseases (2016) packages. Other apps can permit the creation of 3D models, such as Scann 3D (2018) and Trnio (2018). But a question we would like to tease out is: should a restriction on mobile phones in the laboratory be implemented to ban photographs if digital resources are an appropriate tool to teach? If students are provided with technology, there is an expectation to be able to use it. But, as discussed above, in this process we risk the mismanagement of human remains in the form of digital data (see Smith and Hirst, this volume). A question to consider is, how often do we encourage students to read the latest ethical guidelines, and how do we ensure that our students have understood them and their implications?

In an educational setting (such as a university), it is good practice to inform the students at the outset that respect for the human remains that they are working with should be undertaken at all times (see Caffell and Jakob, this volume). This is reiterated by the British Association for Biological Anthropology and Osteoarchaeology (BABAO 2010, 1) who state that human remains must be treated with respect… and it is a privilege and not a right to work with human remains. As a result, some universities only use casts of human remains to teach undergraduates, while some academic institutions have even started to utilise 3D data.

13.8 The Rise of 3D Imaging

This chapter has discussed the use of 2D images on social media, however we are now experiencing a paradigm shift with the influx of affordable new technology. As a result, there are a host of 3D documentation techniques that are being applied within bioarchaeology. For the most part this rise in digital recording includes laser scanning, structured light scanning, and photogrammetry (Errickson and Thompson 2017).

These techniques have a large advantage over traditional documentation methods as they enable the documentation of its target in a three-dimensional format. Similarly, they reduce invasiveness and physical handling, and encourage statistical exploration through methods such as geometric morphometrics and volumetric studies (Errickson 2017). Additionally, because this data can be stored in a digital format, this information can be shared as a file with other individuals around the world (Hassett 2018) or stored within an online repository (Lee and Tibbo 2007). But, similar to that of social media, there is limited guidance in relation to 3D imaging technologies, and the question should be asked, do the same ethical boundaries apply with the additional dimension. That is, if we should not display photographs of human remains online, should we upload the 3D data of human remains?

Márquez-Grant and Errickson (2017) highlighted many of these ethical considerations surrounding the 3D debate while highlighting the advantages of placing 3D images of human remains online. For example, 3D images can be much more engaging for the general public, and these images increase the understanding of the information displayed (for example, how the elbow articulates and moves). However, and as discussed, human remains that are shared online must have their contemporary contextual information alongside them. For example, as part of the Mary Rose project, a 3D skull of a male who died on board the Mary Rose was placed online (The Mary Rose 2018). This example did contain some contextual information with regards to who the person was, although more explanation of identification techniques could also be included. However, if this information was omitted, why show the image in the first place?

Mostly, the 3D digital data that is placed online is either part of a dedicated website which was part of a focused project (e.g. Digitised Diseases 2016), or on online community forums (such as Sketchfab 2018). It would appear (however it should be noted that it is not always the case), that dedicated websites, such as Digitised Diseases (2016), include further contextual information about human remains, which are conveyed in an educational way and therefore justify the placement of such images online. Some of those that are placed and shared on online community forums do not include further information. Again, the authors would argue, why place the human remains online if there is not a reason to do so?

3D data can be printed out into a physical object. Often, these representations are accurate in comparison to the original, and this technique is becoming more widely available. For example, between 2009 and 2016, fused deposition modelling and 3D printing patents expired meaning that this fabrication technology become much more accessible to everyone. Perhaps there is a fine line between sharing the digital version of human remains and allowing the viewers to download them as a printable format. However, there are some projects, such as Digitised Diseases (2016), that restrict their data from being used in this way as they do not allow the data to be downloaded. Yet, if this was enabled, individuals would be able to download the data and potentially change the dataset or print it. In this sense, everyone could have a copy of Richard III's skull (although it should be noted that the displayed 3D skeleton of Richard III was intentionally printed in white to make it clear that it was not the actual skeleton) (Levitt 2016).

Having the actual data gives the user the opportunity to manipulate it. This is now being exploited as we find the human remains of past people being used in ways that is not ethical. These manipulated data sets are then shared with others for printing within their own homes, or worse yet, sold for profit. Some examples the authors have come across include, a 3D printed vertebrae candle holder, and a femur that was manipulated into a bracelet. Here the authors see some parallels with that of trading actual human remains. Yet a key problem is, if there were guidelines, how could these actions be regulated? Further still, even if academics and professionals no longer made their data available, the ease of acquiring the scanning and printing technologies means that they could create their own dataset anyway. For example, photogrammetry is an imaging method where the user takes photographs of an object and then using free open-source online software, can create a 3D model of the object. Therefore, the user can record human remains that are displayed within a museum and, at home, turn them into 3D models. This cannot be stopped, unless further restriction in museums is undertaken. However, this brings the argument full circle. Why should we stop anyone taking photographs of their experiences and where do we draw the line?

13.9 Conclusion

Perhaps there are two areas we must consider when sharing information. This is justification and permission. Justification is important to the wider contextualisation of the act. For example, what is the reason behind doing it? This question is ultimately our individual responsibility. Indeed, using images as aides to our words helps understanding, but a selfie without context does not. Furthermore, is the act of a selfie disrespectful to human remains? Likewise, we must not only consider whether sharing data loses our exclusive control over the content, but whether the permissions of those groups associated to the human remains are also agreed upon. Do the relatives want their loved one posted online and are there any biological features that might make that individual identifiable?

The authors note it is important to approach the act of sharing human remains on social media with nuance and flexibility (one with considerations to bear in mind). Williams and Atkin (2015, 5) describe this conflict:

> This has led to a range of odd double standards; we passionately debate how we display human remains in museums with sensitivity and respect for past communities and contemporary stakeholders, yet millions of images and incalculable quantities of writing about human bodies and mortuary contexts from both the distant and recent past are freely available online.

Yet, Harries et al. (2018, 10) argue that:

> Images of human remains are like human remains in their likeness and the ethical considerations which inform the display of 'real' human remains should likewise inform the display of human remains……we must be similarly considerate of public sentiment and the views of communities and genealogical descendants when thinking about circulating and showing an image of that body.

There is not necessarily a right or wrong answer to the discussions addressed in this chapter, other than the fact that context is crucial, but it is clear that the argument centres upon justification and permission. To consider this, we as professionals within our respective disciplines do need to see an increase in collaboration across the wider scope of our own subject. There must be an improved effort to combat the misuse of images, but we must also listen to each other's opinions rather than stating our one-sided biased approach.

13.10 Recommendations

The following list includes a number of recommendations for future consideration:

- Permission to use an image should be sought when seeking to publish an image of human remains on social media. Naturally this is quite complicated when the remains are from the past, but issues including the right to self-determination, 'ownership', and cultural responsibility need to be considered;
- Respect must be demonstrated to the individual in the image. This includes, for example, the manner in which a photograph is taken, whether the remains are anonymised, and whether other (living) people are also in the photograph;
- What is the justification for posting the images. This is different to the justification for taking the image in the first place, but we do need to interrogate why the image needs to be posted publicly on social media;
- Education is key. The issues that we have raised here all rely on an understanding and appreciation of the implications of handling the dead. There is no

point in having an array of codes of ethics and practice if fellow academics, students, and members of the public are not aware of them or do not understand why they are needed. We must do more to engage in public debate in this area, and encourage others to read our guidance documents.

References

Atkin, A. 2015. *Digging Up the Digital Dead: Best Practice for Future(istic) Osteoarchaeology*. https://deathsplaining.wordpress.com/2015/10/02/digging-up-the-digital-dead-best-practice-for-futureistic-osteoarchaeology/. Accessed 20 July 2018.

Atkin, A., and D. Errickson. 2016. *Do Androids Dream of Ethical Leaps?* http://ethics.americananthro.org/do-androids-dream-of-ethical-leaps/. Accessed 20 July 2018.

American Academy of Forensic Sciences. 2018. *Bylaws*. https://www.aafs.org/wp-content/uploads/MASTER-BYLAWS.pdf. Accessed 18 February 2018.

Anthronomics. 2016. *Anthronomics*. http://anthronomics.com/. Accessed 1 August 2018.

Auchter, J. 2018. Displaying Dead Bodies: Bones and Human Biomatter Post-Genocide. *Human Remains and Violence* 4 (1): 41–55.

Bailey-Ross, C., S. Gray, J. Ashby, et al. 2017. Engaging the Museum Space: Mobilizing Visitor Engagement with Digital Content Creation. *Digital Scholarship in the Humanities* 32 (4): 689–708.

British Association for Biological Anthropology and Osteoarchaeology [BABAO]. 2010. *Code of Ethics*. http://www.babao.org.uk/index.php/publications/ethics-and-standards/. Accessed 20 July 2018.

Calugay, S. 2015. Bodies in Museums: The Moral Standing and Display of the Dead. *The Post Hole* 46: 15–27.

Dewey, C. 2014. The Other Side of the Infamous "Auschwitz selfie". *The Washington Post*. 22 July. https://www.washingtonpost.com/news/the-intersect/wp/2014/07/22/the-other-side-of-the-infamous-auschwitz-selfie/?noredirect=on&utm_term=.8a073b56c682. Accessed 27 June 2018.

Digitised Diseases. 2016. *Digitised Diseases*. http://www.digitiseddiseases.org/mrn.php?mrn=xx. Accessed 4 June 2016.

Doyal, L., and T. Muinzer. 2011. Should the Skeleton of "The Irish Giant" be Buried at Sea? *British Medical Journal* 343: 1290–1292.

Drewett, Z. 2017. British Tourists Slammed for Taking Smiling Selfies at Auschwitz. *Metro*. 28 November. https://metro.co.uk/2017/11/28/is-it-ever-okay-to-pose-for-selfies-at-auschwitz-7114547/. Accessed 28 June 2018.

eBay. 2018. *Human Remains and Body Parts Policy*. https://pages.ebay.co.uk/help/policies/remains.html. Accessed 12 August 2018.

Errickson, D. 2017. Shedding Light on Skeletal Remains: The Use of Structured Light Scanning for 3D Archiving. In *Human Remains: Another Dimension. The Application of Imaging to the Study of Human Remains*, ed. D. Errickson and T. Thompson, 93–102. London: Academic Press.

Errickson, D., and T. Thompson (eds.). 2017. *Human Remains: Another Dimension. The Application of Imaging to the Study of Human Remains*. London: Academic Press.

Express and Star. 2011. University Students in Skull Prank. *Express and Star*. 30 March. https://www.expressandstar.com/news/2011/03/30/university-students-in-skull-prank/. Accessed 27 June 2018.

Harries, J., L. Fibiger, J. Smith, et al. 2018. Exposure: The Ethics of Making, Sharing and Displaying Photographs of Human Remains. *Human Remains and Violence* 4 (1): 3–24.

Hassett, B.R. 2018. Which Bone to Pick: Creation, Curation, and Dissemination of Online 3D Digital Bioarchaeological Data. *Archaeologies* 1–19. https://doi.org/10.1007/s11759-018-9344-z.

Holmes, S. 2016. Real-Life 'Indiana Jane' Adventurer Becomes the First Person to SURF Past the Six Million Skeletons in Paris's Catacombs. *Daily Mail.* 30 October. http://www.dailymail.co.uk/news/article-3887496/Real-life-Indiana-Jane-adventurer-person-SURF-past-six-million-skeletons-Paris-s-catacombs.html Accessed 21 July 2018.

Horwood, R. 2015. *Authenticity, Provenance, and Working with Museums.* BCLJ/JATIP Annual Symposium, DePaul University, Chicago, USA, 6 April 2015.

James, A. 2015. Saudi Teen Selfie with Dead Grandfather Goes Viral; Boy Gets Slammed on Social Media. *International Business Times.* 1 July. https://www.ibtimes.co.in/saudi-teens-selfie-dead-grandfather-goes-viral-boy-gets-slammed-social-media-637751. Accessed 25 July 2018.

Killgrove, K. 2016. October Was Apparently Unethical Use of Human Skeletons Month. *Forbes.* 1 November. https://www.forbes.com/sites/kristinakillgrove/2016/11/01/october-was-apparently-unethical-use-of-human-skeletons-month/#421248f825be. Accessed 25 July 2018.

Lee, C.A., and H.R. Tibbo. 2007. Digital Curation and Trusted Repositories: Steps Towards Success. *Journal of Digital Information* 8 (2). https://journals.tdl.org/jodi/index.php/jodi/article/view/229/183. Accessed 4 August 2018.

Levitt, S. 2016. *Displaying Replica Bones and Skeletons.* http://www.honour.org.uk/displaying-replica-bones-and-skeletons/. Accessed 1 August 2018.

Márquez-Grant, N., and D. Errickson. 2017. Ethical Considerations: Another Dimension. In *Human Remains: Another Dimension. The Application of Imaging to the Study of Human Remains*, ed. D. Errickson and T. Thompson, 193–204. London: Academic Press.

Mullick, S. 2018. 'Severed Heads Not Donated to Yale for Study,' Claim Authorities After Grotesque Selfie Goes Viral. *International Business Times.* 6 February. https://www.ibtimes.co.in/severed-heads-not-donated-yale-study-claim-authorities-after-grotesque-selfie-goes-viral-759568. Accessed 25 July 2018.

Museum of London. 2015. *"Looking for Londoners" Glory and Gore*, 31 July–1 Nov [exhibition].

Öhman, C., and F. Luciano. 2018. An Ethical Framework for the Digital Afterlife Industry. *Nature Human Behaviour* 2: 318–320.

Redfern, R., and M. Clegg. 2017. Archaeologically Derived Human Remains in England: Legacy and Future. *World Archaeology* 49 (5): 574–587.

Sayer, D. 2010. Who's Afraid of the Dead? Archaeology, Modernity and the Death Taboo. *World Archaeology* 42 (3): 481–491.

Scann 3D. 2018. https://www.scann3d.com.au/. Accessed 9 August 2018.

Scarre, C., and G. Scarre. 2006. Introduction. In *The Ethics of Archaeology: Philosophical Perspectives on Archaeological Practice*, ed. C. Scarre and G. Scarre, 1–14. Cambridge: Cambridge University Press.

Sketchfab. 2018. *Sketchfab.* https://sketchfab.com/. Accessed 12 August 2018.

Statista. 2018. *Global Revenue from Social Media from 2013 to 2019 (in billion euros).* https://www.statista.com/statistics/562397/worldwide-revenue-from-social-media/. Accessed 25 June 2018.

Ternime. 2018. *Eternime.* http://eterni.me/. Accessed 20 July 2018.

The Hunterian. 2018. *FAQ.* https://www.gla.ac.uk/hunterian/visit/frequentlyaskedquestions/. Accessed 20 July 2018.

The Mary Rose. 2018. *3D Artefacts.* https://maryrose.org/3d-artefacts/. Accessed 28 June 2018.

Thompson, T.J.U. 2001. Legal and Ethical Considerations of Forensic Anthropological Research. *Science and Justice* 41 (4): 261–270.

Thompson, T.J.U. 2003. The Quality and Appropriateness of Forensic Anthropological Education in the UK. *Public Archaeology* 3 (2): 88–94.

Tripadvisor. 2018. *Choeung Ek Genocidal Center.* https://www.tripadvisor.co.uk/Attraction_Review-g293940-d469300-Reviews-Choeung_Ek_Genocidal_Center-Phnom_Penh.html. Accessed 1 August 2018.

Trnio. 2018. *Trnio: Model Your World in True 3D Using Your Phone*. http://www.trnio.com/. Accessed 1 August 2018.

Walker, P.L. 2000. Bioarchaeological Ethics: A Historical Perspective on the Value of Human Remains. In *Biological Anthropology of the Human Skeleton*, ed. A. Katzenberg and S. Saunders, 3–40. Hoboken: Wiley.

Weber, G.W. 2014. Another Link Between Archaeology and Anthropology: Virtual Anthropology. *Digital Applications in Archaeology and Cultural Heritage* 1 (2): 3–11.

Williams, H., and A. Atkin. 2015. Virtually Dead: Digital Public Mortuary Archaeology. *Internet Archaeology* 40. https://doi.org/10.11141/ia.40.7.4.

World Archaeological Congress [WAC]. 1989. *The Vermillion Accord, Archaeological Ethics and the Treatment of the Dead: A Statement of Principles Agreed by Archaeologists and Indigenous Peoples at the World Archaeological Congress, Vermillion, USA*. http://worldarch.org/code-of-ethics/. Accessed 28 July 2018.

Zucker, E. 2013. *Forest of Struggle: Moralities of Remembrance in Upland Cambodia*. Honolulu: University of Hawai'i Press.

Chapter 14
3D Data in Human Remains Disciplines: The Ethical Challenges

Sian E. Smith and Cara S. Hirst

Abstract The rapid proliferation of 3D imaging in mainstream science is changing the quality and quantity of data that can be obtained. In the study of human remains, the structures and variations of the skeleton holds significant probative value in reconstructing the biological and physical history of that individual. As such, these new 3D tools are being successfully applied in the visualisation and assessment of human remains across forensic and archaeological contexts. However, while the practical applications are being discussed in the published literature, there has been little to no consideration of the more conceptual issues around the widespread use of these novel technologies in human remains disciplines. 3D imaging is producing increasingly accurate and realistic models that share many physical traits, and cultural and societal significances with the original skeletal remains. These are serious causes of concern for the ownership, sharing, and use of these resultant 3D digitisations, especially since there are already unique ethical challenges in the study and use of human remains. This chapter will discuss these issues within the context of a survey which revealed conflicting opinions between researchers and curators concerning the use, ownership, and ethics of 3D digital data of human remains.

14.1 Introduction

Technology is providing modern society with new and enhanced ways in which to view and interact with the real world. In recent years digital data has replaced physical artefacts in many aspects of modern life; digital albums have replaced

---

S. E. Smith (✉)
Centre for the Forensic Sciences, Department of Security and Crime Science, University College London, 35 Tavistock Square, London WC1H 9EZ, UK
e-mail: sian.smith.14@ucl.ac.uk

S. E. Smith · C. S. Hirst
Institute of Archaeology, University College London, Gordon Square, London WC1H 0PY, UK

K. Squires et al. (eds.), *Ethical Approaches to Human Remains*,
https://doi.org/10.1007/978-3-030-32926-6_14

printed photographs, MP3 files for CDs, and eBooks for printed books (Cheshire 2016). In the last decade, 3D technology has followed this similar pattern of integration. Democratisation of 3D imaging tools has allowed them to be widely and successfully implemented across mainstream science to improve critical services in society. These range from orthodontics (Jones and Rioux 1997), to large-scale building construction (Rodríguez-Martín et al. 2016), through to topographic mapping (Gonçalves and Henriques 2015) and virtual reality (Gibson and Howard 2000; Bruno et al. 2010). These tools are non-destructive, comparatively cost-effective, and often have a customisable resolution and scale, such as those utilising photography in 3D photogrammetry methods (Percoco et al. 2015); this makes them attractive for answering a range of scientific questions. For example, a study by Griffith and Thompson (2017) used laser scanning to quantify the taphonomic changes occurring on skeletal remains submerged in water, a largely unstudied phenomena. In another case, a team at the British Museum used CT scanning to access biological profile information from the skeleton of the mummified Gebelein Man remains. They confirmed the sex and age estimation of the individual as well as identifying a likely cause of death. A cut visible on the preserved soft tissue was initially thought to be a post-mortem change. However, the application of new 3D tools revealed a puncture wound from a sharp-object 1.5–2.0 cm wide that fractured the bone (Antoine and Ambers 2014).

Technological advancements in 3D imaging have had tremendous benefits to disciplines that entail the analysis of human remains, not only in respect of case-work analyses, but in facilitating empirical research that has validated and/or improved existing tools, and introduced novel ones to the disciplines (Kau et al. 2005; Remondino 2011; Franklin et al. 2016). Some of the pioneering applications of 3D digitisation in human remains research include: documenting crime scenes and archaeological sites (Fernández-Lozano et al. 2017; Soler et al. 2017), conducting virtual autopsies (Bolliger et al. 2008), and geometric morphometric analyses of evolutionary (Gómez-Robles et al. 2011) and adaptive (Nicholson and Harvati 2006) morphological changes and variations (Janin 2017). These digital tools are changing the scientific and cultural landscape, providing new methods to produce, visualise, store, and share data (Victoria and Albert Museum 2017). Beyond the visual enhancement that imaging tools provide, the most frequently stated benefits include: digitally reconstructing fragmentary human remains (Benazzi and Senck 2011; Mahfouz et al. 2017), the creation of interactive digital or 3D printed displays (Antoine and Ambers 2014; Krassenstein 2014), the global sharing of digital data sets (Russell 2012; Sulaiman et al. 2012), and, in cases of repatriation, the ability to retain digital or 3D printed copies for continued scientific analysis (Rowe et al. 2001; Mathys et al. 2013). It is these benefits that differentiate 3D digitisations from other forms of human remains data, and arguably demand a separate ethical and legal consideration. Currently, most of the research in this field has focused on exploring the significant analytical benefits brought by 3D imaging and printing. Concerns have been raised that the novelty of this technology means there is a dearth of work concerning the ethical, legal, and logistical implications (Margoni 2015; Dawson 2016; Márquez-Grant and Errickson 2017; Thompson 2017). This initial conversation has highlighted some of the major questions concerning 3D digitisations of human remains: who owns the 3D digitisations of human remains, what are the boundaries for the display of human remains, and should this data be shared, and to whom? Currently, there is little-to-no literature that has addressed these pressing concerns.

In an effort to fill this gap and develop the dialogue, two online surveys were designed to investigate the perspectives of practitioners and researchers in human remains disciplines on 3D imaging technology, and understand the implications on data collection, use, and ownership. It is important to note that this chapter does not aim to provide legal advice, or even an absolute standard at this stage, although it is strongly argued that formal protocols, and eventually a legal framework, are developed for the management of 3D digitised material of human remains. Preliminary survey data is presented in this chapter alongside a review of pertinent literature and case studies to illustrate the major issues and conflicts that currently exist in the application of 3D imaging tools in human remains research. The authors stem from forensic and archaeological backgrounds, respectively, therefore the work here explores these issues from the perspectives of both disciplines. While some variances inevitably stemmed from differences in objectives, many of the fundamental issues over ownership and sharing of the 3D data were mutual.

This chapter focuses on four frequently stated benefits of 3D digitisations in human remains research where potential ethical concerns have been identified: (1) the alteration of 3D digitisations, either for reconstructing damaged material or soft tissue, (2) the display and handling of digital and printed 3D printed human remains, (3) cases of digitising human remains prior to repatriation and reburial, and (4) the creation of global data sets allowing the sharing of data collected by different researchers. The surveys conducted by the authors supports theoretical arguments made in the recent literature, that the ethical issues regarding 3D digital data in human remains research generally stem from questions regarding the access, control, and use of information (Rickert 2015; Katz and Tokovinine 2017), all of which are strongly tied to the concept of ownership or authorship which has been demonstrated to be a highly complicated issue in 3D digitisation. This becomes more contentious when dealing with items in the public domain or items of unclear ownership such as human remains and cultural heritage objects, as these items are not definitively protected by copyright (Copyright, Designs and Patents Act 1988; Thompson 2017). Therefore, the first step in understanding ethical guidelines for 3D digitisations of human remains is to clarify the ownership, or authorship, of the data.

14.2 Survey Methodology[1]

Online surveys were created to gather and understand the current opinions and practices of researchers and practitioners working with human remains on 3D imaging tools. The targeted audiences were researchers working with human remains and/or 3D imaging projects, and individuals responsible for curating collections of human remains. Two surveys were created for these two contact groups so that specific data about demographics and skeletal collections could be collected, however the questions regarding opinions and practices around 3D data are the same. Contact details were sourced from online searches of institutions and research groups fitting these criteria. In total, 412 individuals were asked to participate in the survey. Additionally, participants were encouraged to pass on the survey to their colleagues. After nearly five months, 82 responses have been collected.

The first survey targeted collection managers of skeletal collections of UK and North America institutions, specifically individuals who manage research requests and data collection visits (n = 55). The second survey targeted researchers using digital imaging methods both within and outside human remains disciplines (n = 27).[2] The reason that both researchers and practitioners were consulted was to use their specific experiences to build a picture of the current perspectives around 3D data ownership, use, and sharing, and how these operate within human remains research. While the researchers did not all work within disciplines using human remains, as outlined in Fig. 14.1, they were all currently using 3D imaging methods to conduct research projects, and they provided an insight into the challenges faced by researchers in utilising this new technology. There are some issues that will likely be specific to human remains as there are unique ethical and legal challenges associated with this material, however there are some broader issues, like ownership of 3D data, that need to be addressed that are common to users of the technology.

The current perspectives on the use of 3D imaging tools in human remains research, gathered from the surveys conducted, will be used throughout this chapter to detail current perspectives of 3D digitisations in relation to other data formats.[3] The questions asked specifically focused on investigating the perceived ethical issues associated with some of the frequently stated benefits of 3D digitisations. The questions asked for opinions and the individual's experiences with standard practice in relation to 3D imaging, as well as photographic and written descriptive/metric data. This provides important points of comparison and changes in attitudes between these types of data, as these are the traditional documentation formats

---

[1]Ethics approval was obtained from UCL, and full details of informed consent around the surveys can be found here: https://digitaldataucl.wordpress.com/about/informed-consent/.

[2]N.b. Participants had the option to skip questions and as such sample sizes varies between questions presented later.

[3]A full publication of the results is intended for the near future.

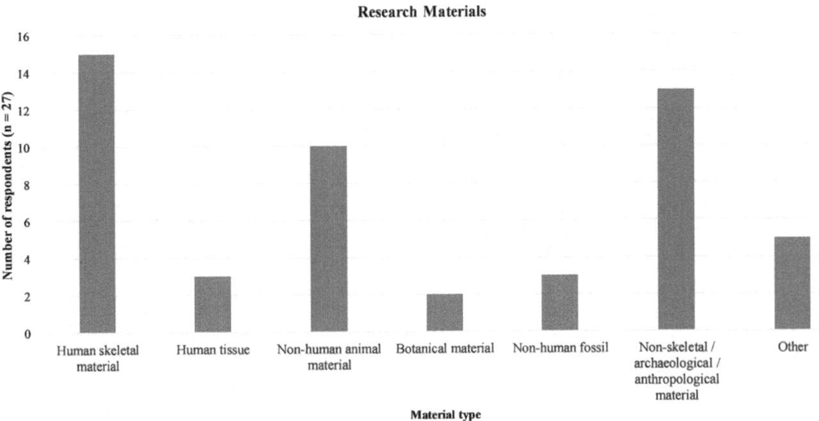

Fig. 14.1 Responses from researchers using 3D imaging methods, when asked what materials they worked with

(Buikstra and Ubelaker 1994). While the survey is still ongoing (Hirst et al. 2017) responses to date have already shown some interesting trends, and that data is presented here preliminarily.

14.3 Ownership of Data

Significant skill and effort is required for the creation of 3D digitisations. Therefore, it is not unreasonable to assume that the individual that produced the model is the owner. It is this level of skill and effort that is used in many instances to establish intellectual property (ILP) rights or copyright (Copyright, Designs and Patents Act 1988). The author must demonstrate that the creation of the digitisation involved "more than negligible labour, skill and effort", however, such terms are vague and it may be difficult to establish what is considered "more than negligible" (JISC 2014). The relative novelty of 3D technology means there is a lack of case studies in human remains disciplines regarding the ownership of 3D digitisations. However, concerns have been raised by a number of authors regarding the development of future issues, as the technological developments have outpaced legal changes (Margoni 2015; Dawson 2016; Thompson 2017). The lack of legal protection concerning the ownership of 3D digitisations was highlighted in a recent archaeological case involving Nefertiti's bust. This is one of Times Magazines 'Top 10 Plundered Artefacts', and is suggested to be one of the most frequently copied Ancient Egyptian specimens (Speed 2016). In 2015 two artists created a 3D digitisation of Nefertiti's bust while it was on display (1923-present) at the Neues Museum in Berlin. This digitisation was then released online under a Creative Commons licence in what the artists claim is an act of legal 'cultural repatriation'

(Voon 2016). Furthermore, a 3D print was displayed in Cairo (Egypt) in 2015 (Speed 2016). While the provenance of the digitisation is now called into question, this absence of legal repercussions in the case highlights some significant gaps in legal and ethical guidelines around 3D data. In terms of the existing Creative Commons licencing that protects artistic and digital media content (Creative Commons 2015), the artists can argue a legitimate claim. Therefore, this is not strictly a legal loophole, as opposed to a lack of contextual consideration in the existing law. The cultural sensitivity and value of the original material being 3D imaged is not accounted for, and consequently such items are left potentially unprotected. In the academic world this case is particularly important because it demonstrates that there is remarkably little legal regulation regarding the use and creation of 3D digitisations of archaeological material.

Furthermore, there is an additional layer of contextual consideration triggered by the unique challenges associated with the study, curation, and ownership of human remains; this also varies between countries and specific collections (Parker Pearson et al. 2011). Tensions exist between the need for extracting valuable knowledge to support scientific data acquisition, with the need to respect the rights of the descendant communities (Budowle et al. 2005; Wagner et al. 2011) and broader cultural communities. Moreover, the significant capacity of 3D imaging methods to capture realistic models means that digitisations are very similar to the original material, but are distinct from other data formats, like photography (Ebert et al. 2014; Urbanová et al. 2015). Consequently, these challenges mean that existing ethical and legal conceptualisations cannot be directly applied to determining the ownership status of 3D digitisations of human remains.

The current lack of ethical or legal guidelines regarding 3D digitisation in human remains research leaves four bodies of evidence to draw upon when attempting to decipher the challenges of this new data format: the study of physical human remains, 2D visual data of human remains, non-visual human remains data, and other disciplines utilising 3D digitisations, such as cultural heritage. There is some early research discussing the ethics and ownership of these different data forms (Márquez-Grant and Errickson 2017; Thompson 2017), the crux of the issue is in understanding where 3D digitisations of human remains lie in relation to these other formats. Currently, an overview of the literature reveals that the treatment of 3D digitisations is widely varied and adapted to suit the specific interests of those involved, on a case-by-case basis. For instance, there are incidents where 3D digitisations of cultural heritage items have been repatriated as a proxy for the original item, with the argument being that these two forms are all-but identical (Hess et al. 2009). Conversely, in other cases archaeological artefacts have been 3D imaged and/or printed prior to repatriation. The argument presented is that digitisations are dissimilar enough from the original remains, insofar as much of the cultural sensitivity is linked to those physical remains (Mendoza 2014).

Results from the surveys conducted by the authors, and presented here, supports the supposition that 3D digitisations are distinct enough from other forms of data to require separate considerations. However, this should not be interpreted as being the same as considering 3D digitisations to be distinctly different from original

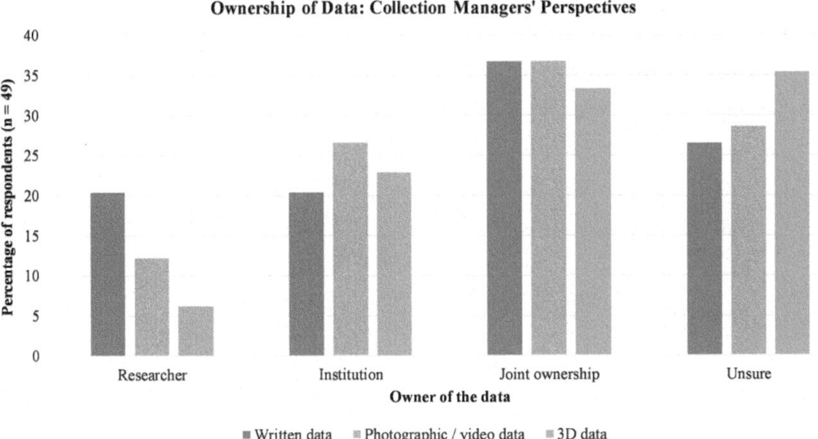

Fig. 14.2 How collection managers/curators responded when asked: "If a researcher is permitted to collect data from your collection, who is the owner of that data?"

physical remains. 56.36% of collection managers/curators (n = 55) and 62.96% of researchers (n = 27) stated that they considered 3D digitisations of human remains to require different ethical treatment and/or research agreements[4] to photographic and written data. These results support a strong requirement for the creation of specialised research or data collection agreements regarding 3D digitisations. Therefore, the next logical step is to establish formal protocols to define the boundaries of using this new data format, and avoid the contradictions seen in other cases. However, only 40% of collection managers/curators (n = 50) have a formal research agreement for 3D digital data, while 64.7% (n = 51) have formal agreements for photographic data. Given this unexpectedly low number, the next step was to understand how both stakeholders (i.e. the researcher and the curating institution) may act in the absence of such an agreement. The survey results highlighted a lack of compliance between researchers and curators on the 'ownership' of 3D digitisations of human remains. Both survey groups were asked who they considered to be the owner of three different forms of data, in the absence of a formal research agreement: (i) written data, (ii) photographic/video data, and (iii) 3D data.[5] These results, illustrated in Figs. 14.2 and 14.3, highlight a lack of agreement regarding who is considered the owner of data collected from skeletal collections. One of the most concerning results of these surveys was that between 26.53% and 35.42% of collection managers/curators (n = 49) were unsure of the

[4]A research agreement is considered as a formal agreement between the researcher(s) and the curating institution as to the agreed boundaries of data to be collected and how that data can be used and shared.

[5]Two institutions did not allow collection of 2D and photographic data, one institution did not allow 3D data collection.

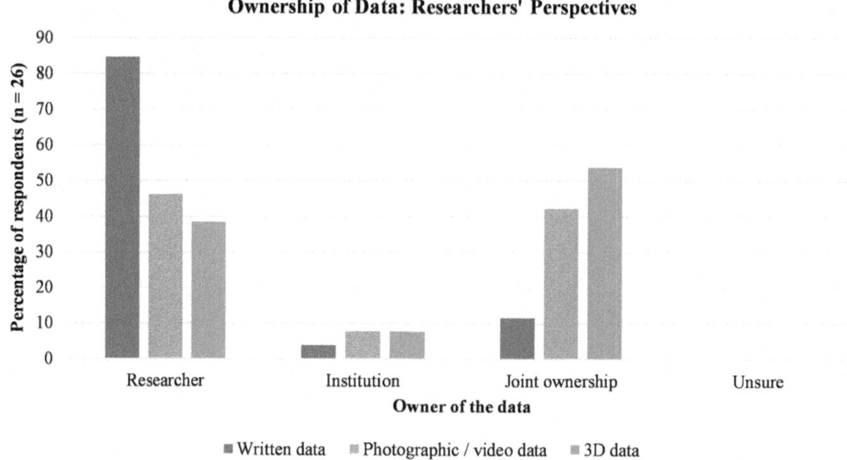

Fig. 14.3 How researchers responded when asked: "If a researcher is permitted to collect data from your collection, who is the owner of that data?"

ownership across these three different data formats. Conversely, no researcher stated that they were unsure of the ownership of such data, although they still disagreed on who that owner was (Fig. 14.3). Experience with the methods appears to have a relationship with the perspectives on ownership of the data. For example, of the total respondents (both researchers and curators) that stated they have "lots of experience" with photographic and 3D imaging methods (n = 30), only three stated that they were unsure of who would be the owner of these data. It is worth noting that this lack of understanding is coupled with a lack of published guidance that could offer assistance in cases of limited experience and may account for the overall inconsistencies in how data is perceived.

While the responses from both collection managers and researchers show that 3D data had the highest level of variation as to the perspectives on ownership, there was a lack of agreement across all three data formats (Table 14.1). The unexpected knock-on effect is that there is seemingly no common trend implemented across institutions for data collection in human remains research that can be transferred to 3D data. Interestingly, when aggregating the results of the two groups (n = 75), there were slight majorities that selected "joint ownership" of 3D data (40%) and photographic data (37.33%; compared to only 4% for written data). In lieu of any

Table 14.1 Aggregated responses of collection manager and researcher responses to the question: "If a researcher is permitted to collect data from your collection, who is the owner of that data?"

	Written data	Photographic/video data	3D data
The researcher	31 (41%)	17 (23%)	13 (17%)
The institution	10 (13%)	15 (20%)	13 (17%)
Joint ownership	20 (27%)	28 (37%)	30 (40%)
Unsure	13 (17%)	14 (19%)	18 (24%)

legal or formal guidelines this 'democratic' perspective would allow for a fairer process for researchers who are expending a lot of time and skill in processing 3D data, and for collection managers whose responsibility it is to protect the remains and ensure that they are treated with due respect.

Ownership, however, is a complicated concept, and what ownership entails is not always clear (Afrasiabi 1997). Results from the surveys mirrored this complexity. Responses suggested that defining the scope of ownership was unclear and inconsistent and did not necessarily relate to practical implications. Of the collection managers/curators who stated that the researcher owned the data considered some data usage to be either "probably" or "definitely not allowed". For instance, when asked if the researcher may give their data to an affiliated researcher 45% (n = 11) considered this to be either probably or definitely not allowed for written or photographic data, which increased to 57% (n = 7) for 3D data. Furthermore, researchers who believed that they were the owner of the data, were equally uncertain of publication rights with between 20% and 30% (25% for written data (n = 24), 30% for photographic data (n = 12), and 20% for 3D data (n = 5)) of researchers opting to consult the curator prior to publication. When asked about publishing data online or advertising data collections 8%–40% considered this to be "definitely not allowed". For written data, only 8% of curators considered the publishing of data to be either probably or definitely not allowed, while 17% disagreed with the advertisement of written data (n = 12). Levels of disagreement were found to vary between data formats, with 20% and 30% disagreeing with the publishing and advertising online data sets of photographic data (n = 12), and 40% disagreement for 3D data (n = 5). Therefore, without formalised research agreements to assign and define the scope of data ownership and use, individuals and institutions may be ineffective in their collection and management of 3D digital data. This then translates into ethical concerns due to the damage caused be repeated handling of archaeological material, specifically human remains (Caffell et al. 2001). Due to the confusion between ownership and practical data use, it is suggested that for research agreements and ethical guidelines to be of value they should break ownership into a series of separate claim-rights, detailed in practical data use statements, such as the intellectual property rights applied to academic research (Rai 1999).

14.4 Reconstruction

> 3D digitisation tools "quantify and reconstruct fragmentary human skeletal remains". (Mahfouz et al. 2017, 3)

Missing or fragmentary data is a critical problem in many biological fields, but is more pronounced in human remains research, for which available data is already limited by physical processes acting on the bone as a result of taphonomic processes

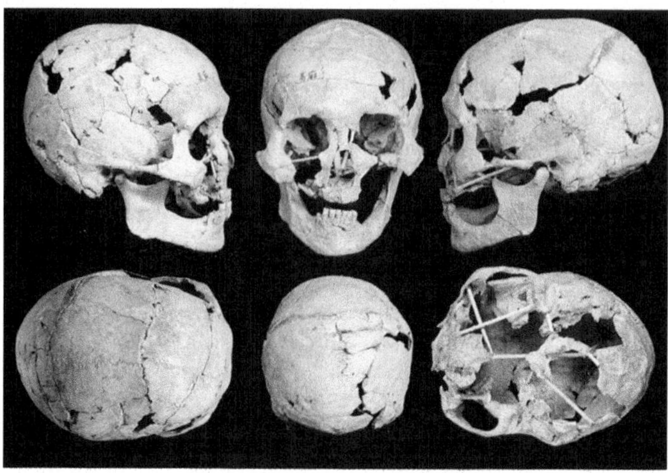

Fig. 14.4 Physical reconstruction of M-02 from Gaomiao illustrating the glue and wooden sticks used to reconstruct the cranial fragments (Matsumura et al. 2017)

following burial and during the excavation of remains (Walker et al. 1988; Froth and Rauhut 2013). Without complete skeletal remains, the information that can be extrapolated is restricted, for example geometric morphometric analysis requires the consistent placement of homologous landmarks across all skeletal remains (Arbour and Brown 2014). Such research is frequently constrained by poor preservation which limits sample sizes and research capabilities. Traditional methods for reconstructing skeletal elements include nails, resins, glue, cocktail sticks, and plasticine (Fig. 14.4) (Kalvin et al. 1995; Ward 2003; Wills et al. 2014). These reconstructions often result in considerable damage to the remains (Pickford 2002).

With the advent of 3D imaging technologies, it is now possible to virtually reconstruct human remains and prevent this damage. 3D digitisations of bone fragments can be digitally matched to reconstruct fragmentary or distorted skeletal elements (Dedouit et al. 2014). Additionally, holes or missing portions of the skeleton can be filled by interpolation (Guo et al. 1995), or reflecting across a plane of symmetry (Kuzminsky and Gardiner 2012). Not only does this process prevent damage to the skeletal material through contact, but this also allows for more accurate reconstructions and increased understanding of skeletal material. For instance, the National Museum of Denmark recently 3D printed the reconstructed skeletal remains of 'Gorm the Old', the first king of Denmark, using computed-tomography (CT) scans. These digital and 3D printed reconstructions revealed palaeopathological and morphological features that were not evident on the original remains, such as a pronounced external occipital protuberance (Medrano 2017). Furthermore, 3D reconstruction is valuable for much larger scales, such as forensic scenes or archaeological sites (Buck et al. 2013). For example, the Antikenmuseum in Basel (Switzerland) has a virtual and 3D printed reconstruction of the tomb of Pharaoh Seti I (Antikenmuseum Basel 2017). The process combined

3D scans of the original tomb walls and fragments on display at several museums across Europe (Baynes 2017). The ability to digitally consolidate separated elements into a full reconstruction is of particular value in archaeology, where there are many instances of sites and collections being divided up and separated between individuals, institutions, and countries.

As it has been claimed that some of the largest digital archaeology projects are almost exclusively based on digital reconstructions (Katz and Tokovinine 2017), the impact of large scale reconstructions on viewer perceptions needs to be better understood. In the case of human remains, museums strive to create displays which allow visitors to emotionally connect to people from past populations (Alberti et al. 2009). Therefore, ideally, reconstruction should not be displayed in isolation, and the original damaged specimens or photographs of the original specimen should accompany the reconstruction, or the reconstruction process should be displayed, such as with the display of the Neolithic skull from Jericho at the British Museum (Hirst 2017). The personification of human remains is useful in engaging public audiences to learn more from museum exhibitions. Furthermore, it has been argued that digital images, particularly those which are 'over-restored', can prevent a physical and emotional connection with the material for public audiences (Rountree et al. 2002; Smith 2010).

In forensic applications, there are similar concerns over the accuracy and interpretations of 3D digital reconstructions. It is clear that these digital reconstructions can be of significant analytical value in human remains research, as well as for creating strong public engagement (Metallo and Rossi 2011; Lautenschlager and Rücklin 2014). However, there is early research demonstrating a clear impact of 3D technologies on perception and decision making in different audiences. For instance, studies have shown that people are five times more likely to remember something they have seen rather than just heard, and twice as likely to be persuaded in an argument with visual aids (Ma et al. 2010). As such, 3D imaging and printing is being used in courtrooms in the UK and USA, but tentatively as the admissibility of this has been called into question (Schofield 2007; Garrie 2014). However, when using human remains as forensic evidence in the courtroom, the nature of this material can cause prejudice in the jury (Errickson et al. 2014). Therefore, the application of this 3D technology can tackle some existing ethical challenges as well.

Facial reconstruction is another common form of reconstruction in human remains research. Traditionally, this is achieved by applying tissue markers and modelling clay directly on to the skull to build up layers of soft tissue. While this can provide invaluable information in identifying an individual, and was often the only way to complete a physical reconstruction prior to advanced imaging technologies, this clay-based method can cause damage to the skull (Andersson and Valfridsson 2005). However, with recent technology, facial reconstruction can now be conducted digitally or on 3D printed skulls, preventing this damage and limiting ethical issues (Khatri et al. 2017). There have been a multitude of cases in the past five years where 3D printing technology has been successfully used in producing facial approximations (also known as facial reconstructions). For example, victims of the infamous Mount Vesuvius eruption (AD 79) (Mendoza 2017), Scottish King Robert the Bruce (1306–1329; Wilkinson et al. 2017), Ta Kush (a 2500-year-old mummified Egyptian female; Koslow 2016), and in the identification of eight unknown individuals that had died crossing the US-Mexico border (reported data since 2000; Holpuch 2018). These digital reconstructions, arguably prevent unethical modification of skeletal remains caused by direct physical reconstructions, such as the use of glue and tape, as discussed above. However, the application of these 3D imaging and printing technologies must, again, be implemented with discretion. Digital soft tissue reconstructions have frequently been criticised for causing false perception (Smith 2010) and overemphasised accuracy (Wilkinson 2005). This is argued to be particularly prevalent in bioarchaeology, because facial reconstruction cannot be either proved correct or incorrect (Stephan 2005).

As with archaeology, in forensic cases facial reconstruction is still a widely used method, despite the current issues with accuracy, as there have been a number of successful incidents of this contributing to police cases (Brooks 2012). From a purely utilitarian point of view, the benefits seem to outweigh any potential issues. If the facial reconstruction helps locate a missing person or solve a homicide case, it can be argued that the accuracy does not matter. However, in an archaeological case, the purpose of these reconstructions is quite different. It raises the question of whether it is ethically right to assign a potentially incorrect face to an individual's remains, that is then for public display. For instance, the virtual autopsy of Tutankhamun, conducted for documentaries by the BBC and Smithsonian Channels, portrayed the young Pharaoh with "club foot, a pronounced overbite and girlish hips" (Fig. 14.5) (Jones 2014; Lorenzi 2014; NBC 2014). This reconstruction has been intensely criticised as being "a morbid freak show that reduces the mystery of this once-forgotten pharaoh and his magnificent tomb to crass and vulgar infotainment" (Jones 2014). It has been argued that this reconstruction exaggerated or manufactured Tutankhamun's pathological conditions to allow for a

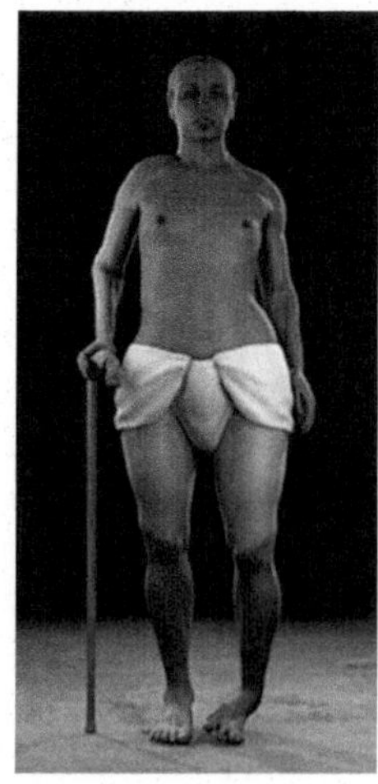

Fig. 14.5 Soft tissue reconstruction of Tutankhamun featuring "girlish hips…clubbed foot…and pronounced overbite", the reconstruction was created from CT scans (Lorenzi 2014)

more commercially entertaining reconstruction. Further research is therefore required in order to understand when reconstructions are ethically appropriate and to prevent misuse. The first step in this would be to consider the motivation of conducting and displaying reconstructions.

In addition to potential ethical concerns regarding the accuracy of reconstructions, another potential ethical and legal implication is related to intellectual property laws of 3D digitisations, and links back to the core issue of ownership. In accordance with current legal guidance, there is a suggestion that under the law in England and Wales the alteration of a 3D model through the "application of skill" affords that person ownership (DCMS 2005, 12). This has also been seen in other jurisdictions, for instance, in 2010, the Federal District Court of Missouri (USA) ruled that digital 3D models and prints could warrant copyright protection. In one case, a company called Osment Models took 3D digital models of railways and filling stations. By altering these models slightly through changing some of the colours or adding features, such as signage, it was determined by the court that these models met copyright requirements (Thompson 2017). However, due to a dearth of previous case studies it is unclear as to what is considered sufficient alteration to warrant changes in ownership. Does the modification of 2D photographs to form a 3D model justify the 3D model to have different ownership compared to the photographs physical object? What about in cases where 3D digitisations of fragmentary or distorted human crania are reconstructed by exploiting bilateral symmetry? This lack of clarity means that it is especially important for any work involving human remains to have a clear research agreement regarding cases of alteration/modification/reconstruction of digitisations. As such, collection managers/curators of human remains should be aware that unless explicitly stated, a researcher may have a compelling case to argue for having sole ownership of a reconstructed 3D model. As very few of the curators and collections managers of museums and archaeological collections were found to have previous experience with digital models, and as the legal precedence is uncertain it is unlikely that these sites are employing research agreements that sufficiently guard against this.

Additionally, while a number of institutions do have formal research agreements there are two clear concerns in the responses between the protocols for imaging methods. Firstly, the number of institutions with formal agreements for 3D data was lower than those with agreements for photographic data collection, with 38.5% prepared for 3D data (n = 52) and 72.3% for photographic data (n = 52)[6] (Fig. 14.6). Secondly, these formal research agreements are not being based consistently on established guidelines, such as those provided by the American Association of Physical Anthropologists (2003) or British Association of Biological

[6]The number of responses (n) has been included for each response rate as there is variation between the questions as some were not compulsory.

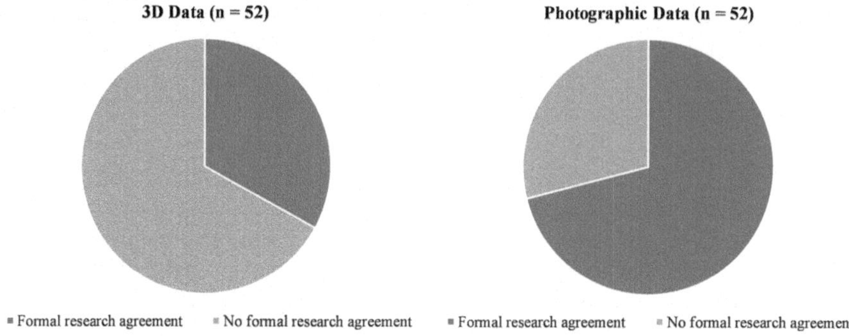

Fig. 14.6 The prevalence of institutions with formal research agreements for 3D data and photographic data

Anthropology and Osteoarchaeology (2018). The majority of institutions that stated they had research guidelines had instead created their own (70.6% for 3D data (n = 17) and 56.3% photographic data (n = 32)).

14.5 Digital Display and Handling

> Developments in technology have made possible a new type of virtual museum that actively supports the work of museums and enables the creation of immersive digital exhibits. (Cassidy et al. 2017, 170)

3D imaging and printing is becoming increasingly accessible and has become an integral part of outreach and teaching in many fields which involve human remains (Bimber et al. 2002; Walczak et al. 2006; Dimick 2015; Fasel et al. 2016). The display of human remains in museums is still an issue of contention in many countries (Alberti et al. 2009), but digital and 3D printed human remains are providing a new format in which they can be displayed and handled, with greater public interaction and understanding, and often bypass issues concerning the display of human remains. There are many benefits to the creation of digital and 3D printed human remains, and there has been considerable variation in how these resources are being utilised. This section will discuss the benefits and key ethical issues associated with the display and handling of human remains.

There has been an increase in museums digitising their collections to support creative exhibitions and learning spaces, as well as preserving the materials for display and scholarly work (Younan and Treadaway 2015; Kwan and Kwan 2017). For instance, the British Museum CT scanned the mummified remains of the 'Gebelein Man', revealing previously inaccessible information about the skeletal and soft tissues (Antoine and Ambers 2014). This project was then integrated into the visitor experience as an interactive exploration of a 3D visualisation of human remains (Ynnerman et al. 2016). It has been suggested that these digital displays provide a cheaper, more respectful, and sustainable approach to displaying human remains in museums (Csordas 2000; Alberti et al. 2009). Additionally, many institutions can only have small fractions of their physical collections on display. The Victoria and Albert Museum displayed only 24.4% of its collections in March 2015 (Victoria and Albert Museum 2016), the Smithsonian Institution state that less than 2% of its collection is on display at any given time (Smithsonian 2016a), and the British Museum have as little as 0.5% of their collections for public viewing (Gardner 2007). As such the creation of digital displays may allow for greater access to museums collections, allowing visitors to explore collections they might otherwise not have access to. In addition to digital 3D displays, 3D prints of human remains are being incorporated in museum displays (Allard et al. 2005; Appleby et al. 2014; Medrano 2017). These are particularly valuable in cases where it is not possible to view the original human remains, either because they have been damaged, or they may be obscured due to mortuary practices, such as the Jericho skull (Hirst 2017). Additionally, when the physical human remains have been reburied, 3D prints have allowed museums to still display a physical copy of these remains. For example, the remains of Richard III were reinterred in Leicester Cathedral in 2015, but 3D prints of the bones are still on display at the King Richard III visitor centre in Leicester (UK) (Krassenstein 2014). There is, however, a concern that the expansion of digital displays will replace physical displays in museums (Jones 2009; Khan 2012). While replicas and reconstructions have been displayed for as long as museums have existed, the ability to quickly and cheaply 3D print objects has the potential to drastically increase the proportion of replicas on display in museums and academia (McMenamin et al. 2014; Neumüller et al. 2014). Further research is needed in order to understand how this may influence the visitor experience, specifically with regards to human remains. However, when museums incorporate 3D digitisations or prints into displays with the original these can enhance visitor experience. For instance, the virtual autopsy table created as part of the ‘Gebelein Man’ exhibit in the British Museum, was found to increase visitor time in the gallery by 40% and increased the average number of stops that visitors took in the gallery (Fig. 14.7) (Ynnerman et al. 2016). There were some concerns that the virtual display would reduce time spent viewing the physical material, however the opposite was found. After the virtual autopsy table was installed, viewing of the physical display of the Gebelein Man remains increased from 59% to 83%, as the virtual exploration table was drawing visitor’s attention to the exhibition area (Ynnerman et al. 2016).

Additionally, 3D prints of human remains are increasingly being used in outreach events and university teaching. For example, in 2017 Liverpool John Moores University (UK) announced the development of their new teaching tool Skeleton2go (Irish et al. 2017). This project aims to provide students with a box of

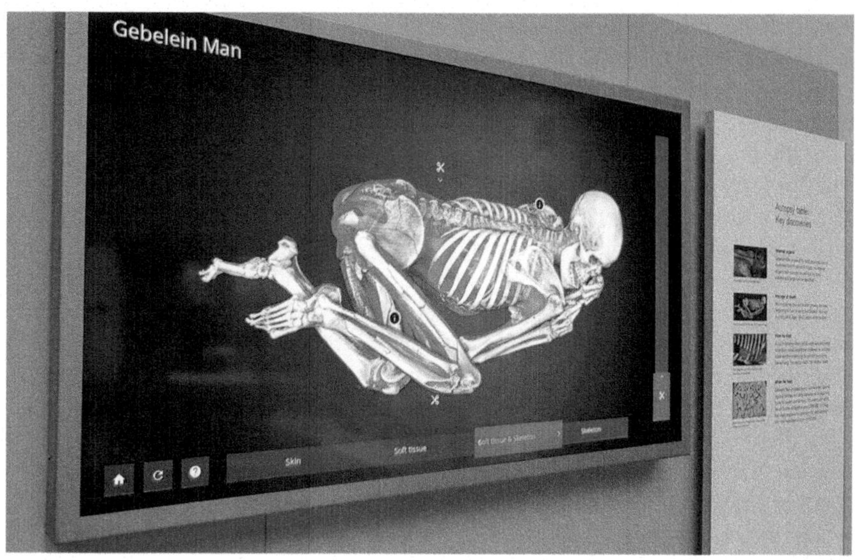

Fig. 14.7 Photograph illustrating the Inside Explorer Table allowing visitors to conduct a virtual autopsy of the Gebelein Man who was buried around 3500 BC in Upper Egypt. Photograph by Sian Smith (2018)

3D printed human remains which they can take home for self-study, with the plan to expand this to other universities. The haptic perception created by access to a physical object makes it easier for the human brain to process visual information (Kappers 2011). Studying the morphology of bone, either as natural variation or changes due to external forces, is one of the primary sources of information for bioarchaeologists and forensic anthropologists. As such, the physicality of a 3D print is of particular value in these disciplines. Of the universities surveyed, 24.5% used 3D prints or digitisations in their teaching and 22.5% in outreach events (n = 49). While there are clear benefits to the display and handling of digital and printed human remains to both museum visitors and students/researchers there has been once again little or no consideration as to the ethical considerations of these materials. 3D printed replicas of human remains are typically used for purposes and in environments where physical human remains would not be considered ethical, however, what exactly separates the real from the replica in the case of human remains? If it is not considered appropriate for children to handle physical human remains, then researchers need to consider how 3D prints and digitisation differ from the original that make this acceptable. Is it simply that there is no risk of damaging a finite resource? Once again, this issue boils down to the distinction between real physical human remains and digital or printed copies. Research is needed to understand variating opinions towards human remains in different media, in order to develop ethical guidelines and protocols.

In addition to protecting the rights of individuals whose remains may be digitised and printed for display and handling, there are concerns that blur the distinction between real and replica which may posse other ethical concerns. One particularly controversial argument for the display of digital data or 3D printed replicas, is that: "[n]ations rich in archaeological artifacts—typically developing nations, or economically weak countries like Italy and Greece—could capitalize on their archaeological resources by selling original artifacts, while still possessing indistinguishable copies that contain most of the value of the originals" (Cronin 2015, 4).

This statement is reminiscent of how archaeological collections were acquired in the past, which typically involved the theft, exploitation, or colonisation of other nations (Simpson 1996; Abungu 2004). It is important to avoid the mistakes of the past, in the advent of these new 3D technologies. Furthermore, if it can be argued that digital copies and prints are 'indistinguishable' then why not pay these 'developing nations, or economically weak countries' to have researchers digitise their artefacts for the benefit of both parties? This statement further demonstrates the necessity to understand the relationship between real and replica without bias. The digitisation of human remains for the purposes of display and handling also act to create large digital datasets that can be adopted for research purposes, creating large samples that are not restricted by geography, funding, or access requirements. The global benefits of having these large, shareable data sets will be discussed in the penultimate section of this chapter.

14.6 Reburial and Repatriation

> Digital data may be used for research after material is repatriated or reburied. (Rowe et al. 2001; Schurmans et al. 2002; Mathys et al. 2013)

Museums and archaeological institutions have been repatriating human remains since the 1980's (Simpson 1996), and have expressed concerns regarding the loss of these data for future research. Over time there has been an increasing pressure placed on museum and archaeological collections to remove human remains from display and repatriate them back to their countries of origin or descendant community (Holm 2011). This has been referred to as "a global movement away from liberal scientific access to human remains" (Afrasiabi 1997, 821). In addition, after revelations that the Liverpool's Alder Hey Hospital retained tissue samples after the burial of deceased individuals (Swain 2002), the Human Tissue Acts (2004, 2006) were created; these tightly regulate institutions which hold and display human remains under 100 years old in the UK. These Acts also require the reburial of archaeological material after two years of scientific analysis. Archaeological human remains held in a wide variety of institutions in the UK have arisen from a variety of sources, including private collections, and as such typically lack sufficient documentation concerning the provenance of human remains. Therefore, these collections are problematic as it may not be possible to prove the human remains are over 100 years old (Redfern and Clegg 2017). Similar increases in the occurrence of repatriation and reburial have are reported in other countries (Morell 1995). In Australia remains from Lake Mungo, dated to around 35,000 years have been recently returned for reburial after a decade's long dispute (Pickrell 2017). Similar reburial or repatriation of human remains in Israel and China have been argued to limit scientific analysis of human remains (Afrasiabi 1997). One of the criticisms levied against repatriation and reburial is that no one should possess the right to exclude others access to the remains. It has been frequently stated that 3D digitisation of human remains is particularly valuable as they provide a solution to this problem. 3D digitisations are argued to be a resource that can be used for future morphological-based research in cases where the physical remains can no longer be examined, such as in cases of repatriation and reburial (Villa et al. 2013).

Consequently, a common argument for scanning human remains is that repatriation requests can be honoured, while still keeping a digital copy of this data to be utilised for further research (Rowe et al. 2001; Schurmans et al. 2002; Mathys et al. 2013). Moreover, it has been suggested that virtual reality and 3D technology may be valuable in cases of repatriating cultural objects, as it provides new discourses in archaeological interpretation with the communities requesting repatriation (Dawson et al. 2011). In 2012 several Tlingit clan leaders of the Pacific North West Coast of North America requested their crest objects to digitally scanned for archival purposes, and during the 2017 ‘Sharing our knowledge’ conference more clan objects were voluntarily 3D scanned in order to digitally preserve the object for the future (Solly 2017). However, some members of the Tlingit community have raised concerns that 3D digitisations threatened their tradition, and they have argued against their clan crest being manufactured by a machine, with technology replacing human carvers, and raised concerned about public mass reproduction of the cultural heritage items (Isaac 2015; Solly 2017). Furthermore, in cases where cultural objects were scanned and/or printed without consultation with a representative from a community requesting repatriation has resulted in intense criticism. For instance, when artist Oliver Laric 3D scanned and printed seven columns from the Old Summer Palace in Beijing, whose repatriation had already been agreed, it was claimed that the production of these 3D prints was an attempt to steal cultural heritage material (Mendoza 2014).

Repatriation therefore is a complex issue involving a range of emotional, ethical, legal, and political factors (Museums Association 2006). Furthermore, in cases of the repatriation of cultural items, digital scans have been used instead of the original item (Resta et al. 2002; Hess et al. 2009; Ewing 2011), which acts to further blur the ascribed value of digital models compared to the original physical remains. As such the ethics of 3D scanning and printing needs to be considered on a case by case basis with open discussion with those requesting repatriation. Whether 3D digitisation hold the same scribed value as the original item seems to vary with the motivation of those concerned. The value of the 'original' is not consistent across cultures, in China temples are frequently restored and replaced arguably because there is less value placed on the original object (Speed 2016).

It is clear from these examples that an open discourse between museums/ researchers and communities requesting repatriation is necessary for the ethical preservation of 3D models of repatriated material. As part of the survey of museum curator and collection managers, participants were asked questions relating to their repatriation policy and previous experience with repatriation requests. Results from this survey revealed that of the curators and collection managers who had received repatriation requests (n = 28), 85.7% had not received any repatriation requests for which 3D scans were included in the repatriation request. Only 14.3% of participants had received requests which specifically mentioned 3D digital data, of these 66% requested a copy of the 3D scan, and 33% requested the scans to be destroyed (n = 4). When asked if the participants would consider 3D scanning human remains prior to returning remains for repatriation, 77% of participants said that they would 3D scan human remains prior to returning the remains, although only 6% of participants (n = 52) stated that they would scan them without asking for permission from the organisation requesting repatriation. Unfortunately, the sample sizes for these questions were very low, and considerable more data is required in order to make any meaningful inferences.

Unfortunately, previous case studies have focused on cultural objects where there may be a drive among many communities who are requesting repatriation to make traditional knowledge more accessible especially with younger generations, such as with the Tlingit where 3D prints of cultural artefacts were requested to share among descendant communities for educational purposes. As such these communities may share a common incentive with museums and archaeological researchers who strive to make archaeological knowledge more accessible to the general public (Dawson et al. 2011). Human remains, however, are far removed from other culturally sensitive artefacts. It is therefore uncertain if communities, when requesting repatriation, will be comfortable with the skeletal remains of their ancestors being 3D scanned and printed for future research. While there have been previous instances where Native American communities worked in collaboration with archaeologists where archaeologists were allowed to analyse the human remains for a period of time prior to reburial (Riding 1992), no discussion could be found regarding whether individuals considered 3D digitisations of human remains to have the same ascribed cultural sensitivity as physical remains. In order to maintain relationships between archaeologists and communities requesting repatriation further research is necessary to determine the ethical responsibility when storing or collecting digital copies of human remains or other culturally sensitive items. This is a discussion that needs to happen between archaeological institutes and the communities and organisations who are requesting the repatriation of human remains.

14.7 Global Data Sharing and Access

> [D]igitalization.... has opened a new way for data sharing via desktop-based or internet, thus giving access to all researcher around the world to conduct their research. (Sulaiman et al. 2012, 1)

Digital data allows researchers to collaborate on large projects around the world. They can communicate data more efficiently, reconstruct material and excavation sites, and encourage diversity of opinions (Russell 2012). In cases where researchers that have openly published digital data, others have been able to conduct further analyses, as well as validate the findings of the original project (Owen 2002; Pearce et al. 2010). One notable area where this collaborative and cumulative digital data sharing has been invaluable is the development of new databases to account for modern human skeletal morphological variations. In the analysis of human remains, datasets of known morphological measurements and characteristics are used to conduct biological profiling of unknown remains, for example using the William M Bass Donated Skeletal Collection at the University of Tennessee (University of Tennessee n.d.). However, inter-population variation and developmental changes have called the reliability of these systems into question. Particularly for the identification of very recent human remains in forensic cases, as many of the reference populations used are archaeological or historical and not representative of modern variations (Savall et al. 2016). However, recently there have been several projects collecting and sharing 3D and 2D digital data of contemporary skeletal remains to create more robust datasets for biological profiling (Verhoff et al. 2008; Algee-Hewitt 2016; Mallett and Evison 2017).

As a form of data, it is increasingly agreed that 3D digital data is providing educational and analytical opportunities, allowing people to have access to cheaply made replicas all over the world (Carone 2013). Moreover, the value of this 3D digital data has led to calls for institutions to 3D scan their collections, and to make this data available to everyone, or for researchers to share data or publish online databases (Kansa et al. 2007; Koller et al. 2009). Museums have begun digitising their collections, with the number of online stores of 3D digitisation of human remains increasing exponentially (Kuzminsky and Gardiner 2012). For instance, the Smithsonian Institution has started a project to digitise the human remains collections, and make these scans available online (Smithsonian 2016b). Similarly, 3D photogrammetry models of ten human skulls from the Mary Rose shipwreck have been released open source online for public and research purposes (Fletcher n.d.). Other organisations have also created digital collections, such as Digitised Diseases, a UK project which has digitised over 1600 palaeopathological specimens from archaeological collections in the UK (Digitised Diseases n.d.). Additionally, there are a number of online digital data stores, where individuals may publish their 3D scans for others to download, such as Morphosource (n.d.) and Sketchfab (2018). By advertising the availability of digital collections, researchers can apply to use this in their studies bolstering their sample sizes and the variety of data.

Furthermore, the sharing of 3D digital data may act to preserve human skeletal collections, both by providing a digital 'back-up' but also by reducing handling of fragile human remains which results in an accumulation of damage (Bowron 2001, 2003; Caffell et al. 2001; Palmer 2015).

It is clear that this new technology is the advent of increased global and rapid sharing of human remains collections online. While there are clear benefits to sharing digital data, there are several ethical concerns that need to be addressed. When considering the ethical sharing of human remains data, it is first necessary to establish who has permission to share these data, how these data should be shared, who may access these data sets, and once these data are shared, how may these data be utilised by other researchers? As demonstrated with the other issues dealt with in this chapter, these questions still stem from the unclarified ownership issue. The majority of the online stores for digital data require confirmation that the curator/ collection manager has approved the publication of any scans from their collection. However, legally there is uncertain precedence regarding the sharing of 3D scans of archaeological material, as demonstrated with the case of Nefertiti's bust (Speed 2016). Additionally, researchers may create their own digital data stores and share data collected from external collections informally among colleagues and students, potentially without legal repercussions.

In the case of human remains, particular care needs to be taken with regards to the digitisation and publication of 3D digital data on open access sites. For instance, the Hopi Cultural Preservation Office (Arizona, USA) wrote appeals to museums in the 1990's requesting that access to field notes, photographs, and excavated material be restricted due to perceived cultural sensitivity (Isaac 2015). The unique nature of human remains material is being considered by some museums when digitising their collections. For instance, the Senior 3D Program Officer, from the Smithsonian Digitization Program, notes that while 3D scans of repatriated Native American objects are held by the Smithsonian, the objects have huge religious significance and, as such, care has to be taken with these datasets to control the access and editing rights (Carone 2013). However, as discussed previously, if the external researchers are collecting this data and no formal guidelines exist, then data sets of culturally sensitive material may still be published. Furthermore, our understanding of a specimen or collection can change over time, what was once considered 'safe' to publish digital data on, may not remain so five or ten years in the future. Therefore, digital copies have the potential of disrupting the sense of trust between researchers and source communities due the potential of unauthorised distribution on the Internet (Dawson 2016).

As with cultural heritage sites and objects, human remains also present similar "territorial sovereignty and nationalism concerns", and arguments may be made against the sharing of digital human remains resources (Afrasiabi 1997, 834). It has been suggested that once this digital data is available in the online world, people are going to be less concerned with the provenance and legitimacy of items (Stromberg 2013). While this was stated as a benefit of public access archives of 3D digital data, there are potential economic concerns that may be associated with this. For instance, nations or institutions may reap financial benefit from their archaeological collections, either through charging bench fees, selling replicas, museums ticket sales, or through tourism revenue (Afrasiabi 1997). While in many instances this is simply to offset the costs associated with the time and space these researchers use, there are some institutions which heavily rely on this funding (Hublin 2013); therefore, the digital replication of these collections could also be detrimental to these institutions. Furthermore, at present the majority of principal researchers collecting digital scans are located in Western Europe and North America, and concerns regarding the potential of 'digital colonialism' has been raised (Thompson 2017). As such researchers and institutions need to be careful that sharing digital data neither exploits other nations and cultures, nor does it have financial repercussions to the nations or institutions that curate the physical remains.

In addition to researchers sharing data that they have collected from external institutions or museums and archaeological collections creating online data stores of their archives, results from the surveys determined that 95.9% of collection managers/curators would request a copy of 3D digitisations collected by external researchers (n = 49). As demonstrated in this study, research agreements are infrequently available regarding 3D data, this leaves the researcher unprotected in cases where a copy of the data is held by the institution. When asked how institutions may use these copies of the data collected by external researchers, responses varied considerably (Fig. 14.8). Most notably, 27.66% (n = 47) of curators stated that they would give 3D data to another external researcher; of these only 36.17% would contact the original researcher if using the copy of 3D data for anything other than storage and curation purposes. This demonstrates that it is not just in the

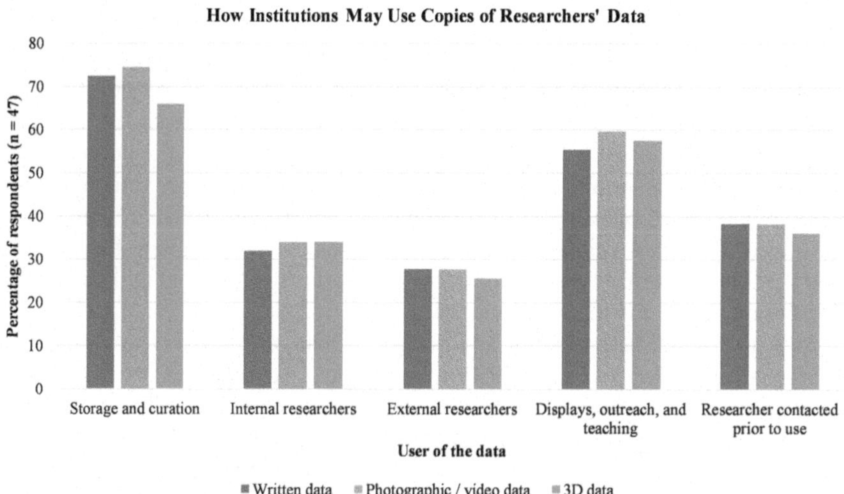

Fig. 14.8 How collection managers/curators who request copies of data collected by researchers would use these data

interests of the curating institution to develop clear and formal research agreements, and that these agreements need to consider sharing of data on both sides.

As with other forms of data collection, the materials and methods employed in creating a digitisation has an influence on the final 3D model, and subsequently any data extrapolated from these (Younan and Treadaway 2015). Therefore, there are concerns that sharing digital data, or the creation of large data sets from different researchers may introduce observer error, hindering any subsequent analyses from these data. To date, there is only one study that has tested the potential for inter- or intra-observer errors of different individuals creating 3D models from the same raw data (Errickson et al. 2014). The subjectivity of digitisation means that there is a risk of the resultant model being unconsciously modified by interpretation. The choices of different 'editors' have the potential to change the final manifestation of the model (Younan and Treadaway 2015). For example, in Meshlab (Visual Computing Lab CNR-ISTI 2017), a commonly used free 3D modelling software, there are at least three different tools for reconstructing the surface morphology all with multiple manual variable controls. This allows for flexibility in modelling to suit the unique features of each case, but also presents some uncertainty in the absence of standardised accuracy testing. Further research is needed to understand the potential error introduced by different digitisation methods and materials as well as inter-observer error.

The final concern regards the potential over-reliance on digital collections. With tighter budgetary controls in the forensic, archaeological, and academic fields, digital collections may offer a more viable alternative to gain access to large collections of human remains for research and reference. Museums are also facing similar budget cuts that restrict their physical storage facilities (Niven et al. 2009). However, while there are numerous benefits to digital data of human remains, an over reliance on digital may lead to reburial and loss of human remains, preventing future analysis. While 3D digitisations allow for a wide range of analyses, and greater public engagement, there are still many areas of research where analysis of the physical remains are required (Hamilton and Sayle 2017; Weyrich, Duchene and Cooper 2017). Furthermore, imaging methods vary considerably in accuracy and information provided (Wilson et al. 2017; Viner 2018). It is therefore important that the benefits of 3D digital data do not lead to an abandonment of physical human remains, both in curation, display, and research.

14.8 Conclusion

As addressed in this chapter, it is clear that, at the time of writing, digitising and printing of human remains appears to be largely unprotected by the law, due in part to the complicated nature of ownership. The lack of legal protection places the onus on those involved with the care and/or research of human remains to create clear ethical guidelines. Based on a review of the current ethical concerns, and the benefits of these technologies in human remains research it is argued that until more comprehensive legal and ethical guidelines are developed a joint ownership approach is recommended. Joint ownership of 3D digital data would acknowledge both the skill and effort contributed by the researcher during the digitisation process, as well as the role of the curating institution as custodians of the human remains, ensuring that the deceased individual and digitisations are treated with due respect. Joint ownership is further argued for because it places the responsibility of creating a research agreement on both parties. Currently it is generally assumed that research agreements are instigated by the curating institutions, without establishing a formal research agreement prior to data collection the legal ownership of the digitisations would be held by the individual in possession of these data. However, it was determined that very few of the collections managers surveyed were aware of, or had a formal data agreement regarding 3D digital data. Furthermore, when asked about their experience with 3D data, 53% (n = 49) indicated that they had no practical use of 3D methods, either with "no experience" or "limited experience" of 3D imaging. Given that 3D imaging technologies have undergone rapid integration into common practice over a relatively short period of time the lack of experience with 3D data is not unexpected but may limit the detail as well as the practical value of these research agreements.[7] However, the results from this survey revealed that curators/collection managers infrequently utilise these guidelines. Therefore, it is necessary to investigate why these guidelines are not being employed and develop a new system in order for archaeological collections to develop robust research agreements.

Additionally, this chapter has also illustrated that there is a lack of agreement between researchers and collection managers regarding the value of 3D digitisations in relation to physical human remains and other forms of data. Currently the ascribed value of 3D digitisations or prints is fluid and dependant on the motivations of those involved. It cannot be argued that it is both acceptable to repatriate a digital copy of cultural items in place of the physical objects, because these data forms are similar enough, and also argue that digital copies of an item may be kept after repatriation because they are copies removed from the ascribed cultural and spiritual value of the original. As such it is necessary to determine the relationship between 3D digital data compared to physical remains and other data forms without bias…or at least with minimal bias. The results from these surveys indicate that researchers and collection managers/curators generally consider 3D digital data to lie somewhere between physical human remains and other data forms, including 2D visual data. However, both groups surveyed are stakeholders in the display, research, and curation of human remains. Therefore, the authors argue that future research should consider the options of the general public to determine the treatment of 3D digitisation of human remains and the relationship between digitisations and physical human remains or other data forms.

[7]The authors acknowledge that these are moderately sized samples, however there is a broad spectrum of demographics (in terms of occupation, location, and background) that gives a wide collection of perspectives. Furthermore, in terms of the size of the disciplines and nature of the study, this is a reasonable sample size to expect.

Acknowledgements The authors would like to thank the collection managers and researchers who have kindly taken the time to complete the questionnaires. We also want to acknowledge the vision of the editors in creating this volume as a valuable step towards establishing formalised and considered practice in the use of new 3D technologies in human remains research.

References

Abungu, G. 2004. The Declaration of Contested Issue. *ICOM News* 57 (1): 5.

Afrasiabi, P. 1997. Property Rights in Ancient Human Skeletal Remains. *Southern California Law Review* 70: 805–839.

Alberti, S., P. Bienkowski, M. Chapman, et al. 2009. Should We Display the Dead? *Museum and Society* 7: 133–149.

Algee-Hewitt, B.F.B. 2016. Population Inference from Contemporary American Craniometrics. *The American Journal of Physical Anthropology* 160 (4): 604–624.

Allard, T.T., M.L. Sitchon, R. Sawatzky, et al. 2005. Use of Hand-Held Laser Scanning and 3D Printing for Creation of a Museum Exhibit. In *Proceedings of the 6th International Symposium on Virtual Reality, Archaeology and Cultural Heritage: Short and Project Papers*, ed. M. Mudge, N. Ryan, and R. Scopigno, 97–101. Geneva: Eurographics Association.

American Association of Physical Anthropologists [AAPA]. 2003. *Code of Ethics of the American Association of Physical Anthropologists*. http://physanth.org/about/committees/ethics/aapa-code-ethics-and-other-ethics-resources/. Accessed 29 May 2018.

Andersson, B., and M. Valfridsson. 2005. *Digital 3D Facial Reconstruction Based on Computed Tomography*. Norrköping: Linköpings Universitet.

Antikenmuseum Basel. 2017. *Special Exhibition: Scanning Seti. The Regeneration of a Pharaonic Tomb*. http://www.antikenmuseumbasel.ch/en/ausstellungen.html. Accessed 29 May 2018.

Antoine, D., and J. Ambers. 2014. The Scientific Analysis of Human Remains from the British Museum Collection: Research Potential and Examples from the Nile Valley. In *Regarding the Dead: Human Remains in the British Museum*, ed. A. Fletcher, D. Antoine, and J.D. Hill, 20–30. London: The British Museum Press.

Appleby, J., Mitchell, P., Robinson, C., et al. 2014. The Scoliosis of Richard III, Last Plantagenet King of England: Diagnosis and Clinical Significance. *Lancet* 383 (9932): 1944.

Arbour, J., and C. Brown. 2014. Incomplete Specimens in Geometric Morphometric Analyses. *Methods in Ecology and Evolution* 5: 16–26.

Baynes, C. 2017. Ancient Egyptian Tomb Resurrected Using 3D Printer 2,000 Miles Away in Switzerland. *The Independent*. 13 November.

Benazzi, S., and S. Senck. 2011. Comparing 3-Dimensional Virtual Methods for Reconstruction in Craniomaxillofacial Surgery. *Journal of Oral and Maxillofacial Surgery* 69 (4): 1184–1194.

Bimber, O., S.M. Gatesy, L.M. Witmer, et al. 2002. Merging Fossil Specimens with Computer-Generated Information. *Computer* 35 (9): 25–30.

Bolliger, S.A., M.J. Thali, S. Ross, et al. 2008. Virtual Autopsy Using Imaging: Bridging Radiologic and Forensic Sciences. A Review of the Virtopsy and Similar Projects. *European Radiology* 18 (2): 273–282.

Bowron, E. 2001. *Handling and Packaging of Human Skeletal Remains: Principles and Practice*. Dissertation, Durham University.

Bowron, E. 2003. A New Approach to the Storage of Human Skeletal Remains. *The Conservator* 27: 95–106.

British Association of Biological Anthropology and Archaeology [BABAO]. 2018. *Ethics and Standards*. http://www.babao.org.uk/publications/ethics-and-standards/. Accessed 30 May 2018.

Brooks, J. 2012. Beneath the Canvas: A Conversation with Forensic Artist Stephen Mancusi. *Forensic Examiner* 22 (1): 50–55.

Bruno, F., S. Bruno, G. De Sensi, et al. 2010. From 3D Reconstruction to Virtual Reality: A Complete Methodology for Digital Archaeological Exhibition. *Journal of Cultural Heritage* 11 (1): 42–49.

Buck, U., S. Naether, B. Räss, et al. 2013. Accident or Homicide—Virtual Crime Scene Reconstruction Using 3D Methods. *Forensic Science International* 225 (1): 75–84.

Budowle, B., F.R. Bieber, and A.J. Eisenberg. 2005. Forensic Aspects of Mass Disasters: Strategic Considerations for DNA-Based Human Identification. *Legal Medicine* 7 (4): 230–243.

Buikstra, J., and D. Ubelaker (eds.). 1994. *Standards for Data Collection from Human Skeletal Remains*. Fayetteville: Arkansas Archaeological Survey.

Caffell, A.C., C.A., Roberts, R.C. Janaway, et al. 2001. Pressures on Osteological Collections: The Importance of Damage Limitation. In *Human Remains Conservation, Retrieval and Analysis: Proceedings of a Conference Held in Williamsburg, VA, Nov 7–11th 1999*, 187–197. Oxford: Archaeopress.

Carone, A. 2013. Printing at Home with A 3D Printer. *KPBS News*. 9 July. https://www.kpbs.org/news/2013/jul/09/printing-art-home-3d-printer/. Accessed 11 November 2019.

Cassidy, C., A. Fabola, A. Miller, et al. 2017. A Digital Museum Infrastructure for Preserving Community Collections from Climate Change. In *Workshop, Long and Short Paper, and Poster Proceedings from the Third Immersive Learning Research Network Conference, Coimbra, Portugal, 26–29 June*, ed. D. Beck, C. Allison, J. Pirker, et al., 170–177. Cham: Springer.

Cheshire, T. 2016. Archaeology's Future Lies in 3D Scanning the Past. *Wired*. 8 January. http://www.wired.co.uk/article/isis-nefertiti-archaeology-3d-scanning. Accessed 30 May 2018.

Copyright, Designs and Patents Act. 1988. The Stationery Office, London.

Creative Commons. 2015. *About the Licenses*. https://creativecommons.org/licenses/. Accessed 30 May 2018.

Cronin, C. 2015. 3D Printing: Cultural Property as Intellectual Property. *Columbia Journal of Law and The Arts* 39: 1–31.

Csordas, T.J. 2000. Computerised Cadavers: Shades of Being and Representation in Virtual Reality. In *Biotechnology and Culture: Bodies, Anxieties, Ethics*, ed. P.E. Brodwin, 173–192. Bloomington: Indiana University Press.

Dawson, P. 2016. *The Design and Development of Digital Return Platforms for Northern Indigenous Heritage*. Calgary: University of Calgary.

Dawson, P., R. Levy, and N. Lyons. 2011. Breaking the Fourth Wall': 3D Virtual Worlds as Tools for Knowledge Repatriation in Archaeology. *Journal of Social Archaeology* 11: 387–402.

Dedouit, F., F. Savall, F.Z. Mokrane, et al. 2014. Virtual Anthropology and Forensic Identification Using Multidetector CT. *British Institute of Radiology* 87 (1036): 20130468.

Department for Culture, Media and Sport [DCMS]. 2005. *Guidance for the Care of Human Remains in Museums*. London: Department for Culture, Media and Sport.

Digitised Diseases. n.d. *Digitised Diseases*. http://www.digitiseddiseases.org/alpha/. Accessed 30 May 2018.

Dimick, P. 2015. How 3D Printing Facilitates Interactive Learning. *3DPrint.com*, 26 December. https://3dprint.com/112623/3dp-in-interactive-learning/. Accessed 11 November 2019.

Ebert, L.C., T.T. Nguyen, R. Breitbeck, et al. 2014. The Forensic Holodeck: An Immersive Display for Forensic Crime Scene Reconstructions. *Forensic Science, Medicine and Pathology* 10 (4): 623–626.

Errickson, D., T.J.U. Thompson, and B.W.J. Rankin. 2014. The Application of 3D Visualization of Osteological Trauma for the Courtroom: A Critical Review. *Journal of Forensic Radiology and Imaging* 2 (3): 132–137.

Ewing, R.G. 2011. *Finding Middle Ground: Case Studies in Negotiated Repatriation*. Dissertation, Simon Fraser University.

Fasel, J.H., D. Aguiar, D. Kiss-Bodolay, et al. 2016. Adapting Anatomy Teaching to Surgical Trends: A Combination of Classical Dissection, Medical Imaging, and 3D-Printing Technologies. *Surgical and Radiologic Anatomy* 38 (3): 361–367.

Fernández-Lozano, J., G. Gutiérrez-Alonso, M.Á. Ruiz-Tejada, et al. 2017. 3D Digital Documentation and Image Enhancement Integration into Schematic Rock Art Analysis and Preservation: The Castrocontrigo Neolithic Rock Art (NW Spain). *Journal of Cultural Heritage* 26: 160–166.

Fletcher, C. n.d. *Men of the Mary Rose: 3D.* http://www.virtualtudors.org/. Accessed 30 May 2018.

Franklin, D., L. Swift, and A. Flavel. 2016. "Virtual Anthropology" and Radiographic Imaging in the Forensic Medical Sciences. *Egyptian Journal of Forensic Sciences* 6 (2): 31–43.

Froth, C., and O.W. Rauhut. 2013. The Good, the Bad, and the Ugly: The Influence of Skull Reconstructions and Intraspecific Variability in Studies of Cranial Morphometrics in Theropods and Basal Saurischians. *PLoS One* 8 (8): e72007.

Gardner, L. 2007. The Uses of Stored Collections in Some London Museums. *Papers from the Institute of Archaeology* 18 (S1): 36–78.

Garrie, D.B. 2014. Digital Forensic Evidence in the Courtroom: Understanding Content and Quality Digital Forensic Evidence in the Courtroom: Understanding Content and Quality. *Northwestern Journal of Technology* 12 (2): 122–128.

Gibson, S., and T. Howard. 2000 Interactive Reconstruction of Virtual Environments from Photographs, with Application to Scene-of-Crime Analysis. In *Proceedings of the ACM Symposium on Virtual Reality Software and Technology, Seoul, Korea, 22–25 October*, 41–48. New York: ACM.

Gómez-Robles, A., M. Martinón-Torres, J.M.B. De Castro et al. 2011. A Geometric Morphometric Analysis of Hominin Upper Premolars. Shape Variation and Morphological Integration. *Journal of Human Evolution* 61 (6): 688–702.

Gonçalves, J.A., and R. Henriques. 2015. UAV Photogrammetry for Topographic Monitoring of Coastal Areas. *The ISPRS Journal of Photogrammetry and Remote Sensing* 104: 101–111.

Griffith, S.J., and C.E.L. Thompson. 2017. The Use of Laser Scanning for Visualization and Quantification of Abrasion on Water-Submerged Bone. In *Human Remains: Another Dimension. The Application of Imaging to the Study of Human Remains*, ed. D. Errickson and T. Thompson, 103–122. London: Academic Press.

Guo, J.-F., Y.-L. Cai, and Y.P. Wang. 1995. Morphology-Based Interpolation for 3D Medical Image Reconstruction. *Computerized Medical Imaging and Graphics* 19 (3): 267–279.

Hamilton, D., and K. Sayle. 2017. Stable Isotopes, Chronology, and Bayesian Models for the Viking Archaeology of North-East Iceland. *Journal of Island and Coastal Archaeology*. https://doi.org/10.1080/15564894.2017.1363097.

Hess, M., S. Robson, F. Millar, et al. 2009. Niabara—The Western Solomon Islands War Canoe at the British Museum—3D Documentation, Virtual Reconstruction and Digital Repatriation. In *Proceedings of the 15th International Conference on Virtual Systems and Multimedia, Vienna, Austria, 9–12 September*, ed. R. Sablatnig, M. Kampel, and M. Lettner, 41–46. Los Alamitos: IEEE Computing Society.

Hirst, C. 2017. British Museum Exhibition Review: The Jericho Skull, Creating an Ancestor. *Papers from the Institute of Archaeology* 27 (1): 1–4.

Hirst, C., Smith, S.E., A. Lockey. 2017. *Perspectives on 3D Data: Ownership, Sharing, and Use.* https://digitaldataucl.wordpress.com/. Accessed 15 June 2018.

Holm, S. 2011. Removing Bodies from Display is Nonsense. *New Scientist* 2803. 9 March. https://www.newscientist.com/article/mg20928030-100-removing-bodies-from-display-is-nonsense/. Accessed 30 May 2018.

Holpuch, A. 2018. *Artists' Impressions: Sculptors Help to Identify Victims Found on US-Mexico Border The Guardian*. 15 January. https://www.theguardian.com/us-news/2018/jan/15/new-york-sculptors-border-deaths. Accessed 30 May 2018.

Hublin, J.-J. 2013. Palaeontology: Free Digital Scans of Human Fossils. *Nature* 497 (7448): 183.

Human Tissue Act. 2004. The Stationery Office, London.

Human Tissue (Scotland) Act. 2006. The Scottish Parliament, Edinburgh.

Irish, J., A. Brough, I. De Groote, et al. 2017. *Skeleton2Go: A New Tool for Learning Human Skeletal Anatomy*. Paper presented at the 19th Annual Conference of the British Association for

Biological Anthropology and Osteoarchaeology, Liverpool John Moores University, Liverpool, 8–10 May 2017.

Isaac, G. 2015. Preclusive Alliances: Digital 3-D, Museums, and The Reconciling of Culturally Diverse Knowledges. *Current Anthropology* 56: S286–S296.

Janin, G.K. 2017. *Sex Estimation of Non-Adults: Can It Be Done? A Geometric Morphometric Approach*. Paper presented at MORPH17: A Conference on the Applications of Morphometrics, Aarhus University, Denmark, 4–5 May 2017.

JISC: Joint Information Systems Committee. 2014. *3D Digitisation and Intellectual Property Rights*. https://www.jisc.ac.uk/guides/3d-digitisation-and-intellectual-property-rights. Accessed 30 May 2018.

Jones, J. 2009. Museums on the Internet? Get Real. *The Guardian*. 9 July. https://www.theguardian.com/artanddesign/jonathanjonesblog/2009/jul/09/museums-internet-future. Accessed 25 June 2018.

Jones, J. 2014. Tutankhamun Does Not Deserve this 21st-Century Desecration. *The Guardian*. 21 October. https://www.theguardian.com/commentisfree/2014/oct/21/tutankhamun-desecration-computer-scan-images-pharoah-archaeological. Accessed 30 May 2018.

Jones, P.R., and M. Rioux. 1997. Three-Dimensional Surface Anthropometry: Applications to the Human Body. *Optics and Lasers in Engineering* 28 (2): 89–117.

Kalvin, A.D., D. Dean, and J.J. Hublin. 1995. Reconstruction of Human Fossils. *IEEE Computer Graphics Applications* 15: 12–15.

Kansa, S.W., E.C. Kansa, and J.M. Schultz. 2007. Open Context, Data Sharing and Archaeology. *Near Eastern Archaeology* 70 (4): 187–193.

Kappers, A.M.L. 2011. Human Perception of Shape from Touch. *Philosophical Transactions of the Royal Society B: Biological Sciences* 366 (1581): 3106–3114.

Katz, J., and A. Tokovinine. 2017. The Past, Now Showing in 3D: An Introduction. *Digital Applications in Archaeology and Cultural Heritage* 6: 1–3.

Kau, C.H., S. Richmond, A.I. Zhurov, et al. 2005. Reliability of Measuring Facial Morphology with a 3-Dimensional Laser Scanning System. *American Journal of Orthodontics and Dentofacial Orthopedics* 128 (4): 424–430.

Khan, Y. 2012. Museums in the Information Age: Survival of the Most Digital? *The Guardian*. 5 December. https://www.theguardian.com/culture-professionals-network/culture-professionals-blog/2012/dec/05/museums-adapting-digital-age. Accessed 25 June 2018.

Khatri, M., D. Misra, and S. Rai. 2017. Unfolding the Mysterious Path of Forensic Facial Reconstruction: Review of Different Imaging Modalities. *MAMC Journal of Medical Science* 3 (3): 120–127.

Koller, D., Frischer, B., and G. Humphreys. 2009. Research Challenges for Digital Archives of 3D Cultural Heritage Models. *Journal on Computing and Cultural Heritage* 2 (3): 7:1–7:17.

Koslow, T. 2016. Maidstone Museum to Use 3D Printing to Help Reconstruct 2,500-Year-Old Mummy. *3DPrint.com*. 18 August. https://3dprint.com/146324/maidstone-museum-mummy/. Accessed 30 May 2018.

Krassenstein, B. 2014. King Richard III's Entire 3D Printed Skeleton Unveiled for Museum Opening. *3DPrint.com*. 25 July. https://3dprint.com/10295/king-richard-iii-3d-bones/. Accessed 30 May 2018.

Kuzminsky, S., and M. Gardiner. 2012. Three-Dimensional Laser Scanning: Potential Uses for Museum Conservation and Scientific Research. *Journal of Archaeological Science* 39: 2744–2751.

Kwan, D., and J. Kwan. 2017. Empowering Cultural Preservation in China Through Participatory Digitization. *Journal of Archaeological Science: Reports* 12: 161–164.

Lautenschlager, S., and M. Rücklin. 2014. Beyond the Print—Virtual Paleontology in Science Publishing, Outreach, and Education. *Journal of Paleontology* 88 (4): 727–734.

Lorenzi, R. 2014. King Tut Re-Creation Presents a Shocking Image. *Seeker*. 20 October. https://www.seeker.com/king-tut-re-creation-presents-a-shocking-image-1769204424.html. Accessed 30 May 2018.

Ma, M., H. Zheng, and H. Lallie. 2010. Virtual Reality and 3D Animation in Forensic Visualization. *Journal of Forensic Sciences* 55 (5): 1227–1231.

Mahfouz, M., A. Mustafa, A. Fatah, et al. 2017. Computerized Reconstruction of Fragmentary Skeletal Remains. *Forensic Science International* 275: 212–223.

Mallett, X., and M.P. Evison. 2017. Critical Issues in the Historical and Contemporary Development of Forensic Anthropology in Australia: An International Comparison. *Forensic Science International* 275: 314.e1–314.e8.

Margoni, T. 2015. *The Digitisation of Cultural Heritage Originality, Derivative Works and (Non) Original Photographs*. Amsterdam: University of Amsterdam.

Márquez-Grant, N., and D. Errickson. 2017. Ethical Considerations: An Added Dimension. In *Human Remains: Another Dimension. The Application of Imaging to the Study of Human Remains*, ed. D. Errickson and T. Thompson, 123–134. London: Academic Press.

Mathys, A., S. Lemaitre, J. Brecko, et al. 2013. Agora 3D: Evaluating 3D Imaging Technology for the Research, Conservation and Display of Museum Collections. *Antiquity* 87 (336): 1–3.

Matsumura, H., H. Hung, N. Cuong, et al. 2017. Mid-Holocene Hunter-Gatherers 'Gaomiao' in Hunan, China: The First of the Two-Layer Model in the Population History of East/Southeast Asia. In *New Perspectives in Southeast Asian and Pacific Prehistory*, ed. P.J. Piper, H. Matsumura and D. Bulbeck, 61–78. Acton: Australian National Press.

McMenamin, P., M. Quayle, C. McHenry, et al. 2014. The Production of Anatomical Teaching Resources Using Three-Dimensional (3D) Printing Technology. *Anatomical Science Education* 7 (6): 479–486.

Medrano, K. 2017. Ancient Skull of Viking Kind Gorm the Old Reconstructed with 3-D Printing. *Newsweek*. 21 November. http://www.newsweek.com/viking-gorm-old-skull-skeleton-3d-printing-archaeology-718156. Accessed 30 May 2018.

Mendoza, H. 2014. 3D Printing of Chinese Cultural Artifacts Causes Controversy. *3DPrint.com*. 14 June. https://3dprint.com/6048/3d-printing-chinese-artifacts/. Accessed 30 May 2018.

Mendoza, H. 2017. Using 3D Technology to Recreate the Lost Faces of Herculaneum. *3DPrint.com*. 23 June. https://www.3dprint.com/178803/3d-recreate-faces-herculaneum/. Accessed 30 May 2018.

Metallo, A., and V. Rossi. 2011. The Future of Three-Dimensional Imaging and Museum Applications. *Curator* 54 (1): 63–69.

Morell, V. 1995. Who Owns the Past? *Science* 268 (5216): 1424–1426.

Morphosource. n.d. *Morphosource*. https://www.morphosource.org/. Accessed 30 May 2018.

Museums Association. 2006. *Policy Statement on Repatriation of Cultural Property*. http://www.museumsassociation.org/policy/01092006-policy-statement-on-repatriation-of-cultural-property. Accessed 30 May 2018.

NBC News. 2014. Tut, Tut: New View of King Tutankhamun Sparks Debate. *NBC News*. 2 November. https://www.nbcnews.com/science/science-news/tut-tut-new-view-king-tutankhamun-sparks-debate-n239166. Accessed 30 May 2018.

Neumüller, M., A. Reichinger, F. Rist, et al. 2014. 3D Printing for Cultural Heritage: Preservation, Accessibility, Research and Education. In *3D research Challenges in Cultural Heritage: A Roadmap in Digital Heritage*. Lecture Notes in Computer Science, vol 8355, ed. M. Ioannides and E. Quak. Springer, Berlin, 119–134.

Nicholson, E., and K. Harvati. 2006. Quantitative Analysis of Human Mandibular Shape Using Three-Dimensional Geometric Morphometrics. *American Journal of Physical Anthropology* 131 (3): 368–383.

Niven, L., T. Stelle, H. Finke, et al. 2009. Virtual Skeletons: Using a Structured Light Scanner to Create a 3D Faunal Comparative Collection. *Journal of Archaeological Science* 36 (9): 2018–2023.

Owen, J. 2002. The New Dissemination of Knowledge: Digital Libraries and Institutional Roles in Scholarly Publishing. *Journal Economic Methodology* 9: 275–288.

Palmer, A. 2015. Untouchable: Creating Desire and Knowledge in Museum Costume and Textile Exhibitions. *Fashion Theory* 12: 31–63.

Parker Pearson, M., T. Schadla-Hall, and G. Moshenska. 2011. Resolving the Human Remains Crisis in British Archaeology. *Papers from the Institute of Archaeology* 21: 5–9.

Pearce, N., M. Weller, E. Scalon, et al. 2010. Digital Scholarship Considered: How New Technologies Could Transform Academic Work. *Education* 16: 33–44.

Percoco, G., F. Lavecchia, and A.J.S. Salmerón. 2015. Preliminary Study on the 3D Digitization of Millimeter Scale Products by Means of Photogrammetry. *Procedia CIRP* 33: 257–262.

Pickford, M. 2002. New Reconstruction of the Moroto Hominoid Snout and a Reassessment of Its Affinities to Afropithecus Turkanensis. *Journal of Human Evolution* 17: 1–19.

Pickrell, J. 2017. Ancient Australian Goes Home. *Science* 358 (6365): 853.

Rai, A.K. 1999. Regulating Scientific Research: Intellectual Property Rights and the Norms of Science. *Northwestern University Law Review* 94: 77–152.

Redfern, R., and M. Clegg. 2017. Archaeologically Derived Human Remains in England: Legacy and Future. *World Archaeology* 49 (5): 574–587.

Remondino, F. 2011. Heritage Recording and 3D Modeling with Photogrammetry and 3D Scanning. *Remote Sensing* 3 (6): 1104–1138.

Resta, P., L. Roy, M.K. De Montano et al. 2002. Digital Repatriation: Virtual Museum Partnership with Indigenous Peoples. In *Proceedings of the International Conference on Computers in Education, Auckland, New Zealand, 3–6 December*, 1482–1483. Los Alamitos: IEEE Computer Society.

Rickert, J. 2015. *Printing the Past: 3D Imaging Technologies and Archaeology*. Dissertation, University of Waterloo.

Riding, J. 1992. Without Ethics and Morality: A Historical Overview of Imperial Archaeology and American Indians. *Arizona State Law Journal* 24 (1): 11–34.

Rodríguez-Martín, M., P. Rodríguez-Gonzálvez, S. Lagüela, et al. 2016. Macro-Photogrammetry as a Tool for the Accurate Measurement of Three-Dimensional Misalignment in Welding. *Automation Construction* 71: 189–197.

Rountree, J., W. Wong, and H. Robert. 2002. Learning to Look: Real and Virtual Artifacts. *Educational Technology and Society* 5: 129–134.

Rowe, J., A. Razdan, D. Collins, et al. 2001. A 3D Digital Library System: Capture, Analysis, Query, and Display. In *Abstracts of the Proceedings of the 4th International Conference of Asian Digital Libraries (ICADL), Bangalore, India, 10–12 December 2001*.

Russell, A.-W. 2012. *Designing the Digital Archaeological Record: Collecting, Preserving, and Sharing Archaeological Information*. Dissertation, Northern Arizona University.

Savall, F., C. Rérolle, F. Hérin, et al. 2016. Reliability of the Suchey-Brooks Method for a French Contemporary Population. *Forensic Science International* 266: 586.e1–586.e5.

Schofield, D. 2007. Animating and Interacting with Graphical Evidence: Bringing Courtrooms to Life with Virtual Reconstructions. In *Computer Graphics. Imaging and Visualisation: New Advances, CGIV 2007, Bangkok, Thailand, 14–17 August 2007*.

Schurmans, U., Razdan, A., Simon, A. et al. 2002. Advances in Geometric Modelling and Feature Extraction on Pots, Rocks and Bones for Representation and Query Via the Internet. In *Archaeological informatics: Pushing the Envelope. Computer Applications and Quantitative Methods in Archaeology. Proceedings of the 29th Conference of Computer Applications in Archaeology, Gotland, Sweden, April 2001*, 191–204, ed. G. Burenhult and J. Arvidsson. Oxford: Archaeopress.

Simpson, M. 1996. *Making Representations: Museums in the Post-Colonial Era*. Oxon: Routledge.

Sketchfab. 2018. *Sketchfab*. https://sketchfab.com/. Accessed 1 June 2018.

Smith, M. 2010. *A Necessary Duty, a Hideous Fault: Digital Technology and the Ethics of Archaeological Conservation*. Dissertation, Texas A&M University.

Soler, F., F.J. Melero, and M. Luzón. 2017. A Complete 3D Information System for Cultural Heritage Documentation. *Journal of Cultural Heritage* 23: 49–57.

Solly, M. 2017. This Replica of a Tlingit Killer Whale Hat Is Spurring Dialogue About Digitization. *Smithsonian Magazine*. 11 September. https://www.smithsonianmag.com/

smithsonian-institution/replica-tlingit-killer-whale-hat-spurring-dialogue-about-digitization-180964483/. Accessed 30 May 2018.

Speed, B. 2016. Nefertiti for Everyone: Returning Egypt's Cultural History with the Help of a 3D Printer. *New Statesman*. 2 March. https://www.newstatesman.com/culture/art-design/2016/03/nefertiti-everyone-returning-egypt-s-cultural-history-help-3d-printer. Accessed 30 May 2018.

Stephan, C.N. 2005. Facial Approximation: A Review of the Current State of Play for Archaeologists. *International Journal Osteoarchaeology* 15: 298–302.

Stromberg, J. 2013. What Digitisation Will Do for the Future of Museums. *Smithsonian Magazine*. 29 August. https://www.smithsonianmag.com/smithsonian-institution/what-digitization-will-do-for-the-future-of-museums-2454655/. Accessed 30 May 2018.

Sulaiman, N., E. Bachad, A. Ching, et al. 2012. *Close-Range 3D Laser Scanning for Archaeological Artefact Documentation*. Paper Presented at the 5th International Remote Sensing and GIS Workshop Series on Demography, Land Use—Land Cover and Disaster, Badung, Indonesia, 29–30 November 2012.

Swain, H. 2002. The Ethics of Displaying Human Remains from British Archaeological Sites. *Public Archaeology* 2: 95–100.

Smithsonian. 2016a. *Smithsonian Collections*. https://newsdesk.si.edu/factsheets/fact-sheet-smithsonian-collections. Accessed 30 May 2018.

Smithsonian. 2016b. *3D Collection*. http://humanorigins.si.edu/evidence/3d-collection. Accessed 30 May 2018.

Thompson, E.L. 2017. Legal and Ethical Considerations for Digital Recreations of Cultural Heritage. *Chapman Law Review* 20 (1): 153–176.

University of Tennessee. n.d. *WM Bass Donated Skeletal Collection*. https://fac.utk.edu/wm-bass-donated-skeletal-collection/. Accessed 30 May 2018.

Urbanová, P., P. Hejna, and M. Jurda. 2015. Testing Photogrammetry-Based Techniques for Three-Dimensional Surface Documentation in Forensic Pathology. *Forensic Science International* 250: 77–86.

Verhoff, M.A., F. Ramsthaler, J. Krähahn, et al. 2008. Digital Forensic Osteology—Possibilities in Cooperation with the Virtopsy Project. *Forensic Science International* 174 (2–3): 152–156.

Victoria and Albert Museum. 2016. *Size of the V and A Collections*. http://www.vam.ac.uk/content/articles/s/size-of-the-v-and-a-collections/. Accessed 30 May 2018.

Victoria and Albert Museum. 2017. *ReACH: Towards a New Convention on Digital Reproductions*. [Video] Available at: https://www.youtube.com/watch?v=6Lwpjst6C5E. Accessed 30 May 2018.

Villa, C., J. Buckberry, C. Cattaneo, et al. 2013. Technical Note: Reliability of Suchey-Brooks and Buckberry-Chamberlain Methods on 3D Visualizations from CT and Laser Scans. *American Journal of Physical Anthropology* 151: 158–163.

Viner, M. 2018. Overview of Advances in Forensic Radiological Methods of Human Identification. In *New Perspectives in Forensic Human Skeletal Identification*, ed. K.E. Latham, E.J. Bartelink, and M. Finnegan, 217–226. London: Academic Press.

Visual Computing Lab CNR-ISTI. 2017. *MeshLab*. http://meshlab.sourceforge.net/. Accessed 30 May 2018.

Voon, C. 2016. Artists Covertly Scan Bust of Nefertiti and Release the Data for Free Online. *Hyperallergic*. 19 February. https://hyperallergic.com/274635/artists-covertly-scan-bust-of-nefertiti-and-release-the-data-for-free-online/. Accessed 30 May 2018.

Wagner, B., V. Boucsein, and A. Maercker. 2011. The Impact of Forensic Investigations Following Assisted Suicide on Posttraumatic Stress Disorder. *Swiss Medical Weekly* 141: w13284.

Walczak, K., W. Cellary, and M. White. 2006. Virtual Museum Exhibitions. *Computer* 39 (3): 93–95.

Walker, P.L., J.R. Johnson, and P.M. Lambert. 1988. Age and Sex Biases in the Preservation of Human Skeletal Remains. *American Journal of Physical Anthropology* 76: 183–188.

Ward, C. 2003. *Conservation Survey of the Human Skeletal Material in the Wendorf Collection*. London: Department of Ancient Egypt and Sudan, British Museum.

Weyrich, L., S. Duchene, S., and A. Cooper. 2017. Neanderthal Behaviour, Diet, and Disease Inferred from Ancient DNA in Dental Calculus. *Nature* 544 (7650): 257–361.

Wilkinson, C. 2005. Computerized Forensic Facial Reconstruction: A Review of Current Systems. *Forensic Science, Medicine and Pathology* 1 (3): 173–177.

Wilkinson, C., M. Roughley, and Macgregor, M. 2017. *The Face of Robert the Bruce*. Paper Presented at the 19th Annual Conference of the British Association for Biological Anthropology and Osteoarchaeology, Liverpool John Moores University, Liverpool, 8–10 May 2017.

Wills, B., C. Ward, and V.S. Gómez. 2014. Conservation of Human Remains from Archaeological Contexts. In *Regarding the Dead: Human Remains in the British Museum*, ed. A. Fletcher, D. Antoine, and J.D. Hill, 49–73. London: The British Museum Press.

Wilson, A.S., Holland, A.D., and Sparrow, T. (eds). 2017. Laser Scanning of Skeletal Pathological Conditions. In *Human Remains: Another Dimension. The Application of Imaging to the Study of Human Remains*, ed. D. Errickson, and T. Thompson, 123–134. London: Academic Press.

Ynnerman, A., T. Rydell, D. Antoine, et al. 2016. Interactive Visualization of 3D Scanned Mummies at Public Venues. *Communications of the ACM* 59 (12): 72–81.

Younan, S., and C. Treadaway. 2015. Digital 3D Models of Heritage Artefacts: Towards a Digital Dream Space. *Digital Applications in Archaeology and Cultural Heritage* 2 (4): 240–247.

Chapter 15
Ethical Concerns in Forensic Anthropology

Nicholas Márquez-Grant, Nicholas V. Passalacqua, Marin A. Pilloud, Nicola Lester, Summer Decker and Jonathan Ford

Abstract The nature of forensic anthropology presents a number of ethical challenges to its practitioners. Some of these issues are similar to those encountered in bioarchaeology or biological anthropology, but a number of dilemmas are unique to the discipline. These ethical challenges are continually growing and becoming more significant as forensic anthropologists practice in a number of different casework scenarios, both domestically and internationally. These include cases ranging from law enforcement or coroner investigations dealing with one individual to mass fatalities. Moreover, forensic anthropologists may be involved in cases requiring the analysis of living individuals, which brings its own unique ethical issues. As technology develops, and the contributions that forensic anthropology makes to various forensic investigations increases worldwide, the need to confront the multitude of ethical issues as well as ensuring forensic anthropologists are qualified and competent, rises exponentially. This chapter highlights a number of areas, including: codes of ethics, field and laboratory analysis, age estimation in the living, education and teaching, research, and dealing with families within a forensic anthropological context. It is hoped that these topics will increase awareness of the need for ethical practice in forensic anthropology and some of the many professional challenges forensic anthropologists routinely face.

N. Márquez-Grant (✉)
Cranfield Forensic Institute, Cranfield University, Defence Academy of the United Kingdom, Shrivenham SN6 8LA, UK
e-mail: n.marquezgrant@cranfield.ac.uk

N. V. Passalacqua
Anthropology and Sociology Department, Western Carolina University, Cullowhee, NC 28723, USA

M. A. Pilloud
Department of Anthropology, University of Nevada, Reno, NV 89557, USA

N. Lester
School of Law and Politics, Cardiff University, Cardiff CF10 3AX, Wales, UK

S. Decker · J. Ford
Department of Radiology, Morsani College of Medicine, University of South Florida, Tampa, FL 33612, USA

K. Squires et al. (eds.), *Ethical Approaches to Human Remains*,
https://doi.org/10.1007/978-3-030-32926-6_15

15.1 Introduction

Forensic anthropology (e.g. see Klepinger 2006; Komar and Buikstra 2008; Tersigni-Tarrant and Langley 2017; Christensen et al. 2019) is a discipline that shares many ethical issues with bioarchaeology or with the study of human remains recovered from archaeological contexts, a topic covered in other chapters in this volume. It also has its own particular ethical challenges and dilemmas, some of which have been covered more recently in the literature (Thompson 2001; Walsh-Haney and Lieberman 2005; Webb 2006; France 2012; Blau 2016a, 2016b; Passalacqua and Pilloud 2018). As Passalacqua and Pilloud (2018) propose, ethics in forensic anthropology should cover a number of aspects which include: treating remains and colleagues with respect; adhering to one's area of expertise or remit; doing no harm; maintaining scientific integrity, transparency, and confidentiality; avoiding conflicts of interest; obtaining appropriate training and qualifications; and conducting research in an ethical manner. There are also technical issues to consider, which would include the appropriateness of the methods used, content in reports, and providing information as an expert witness (Passalacqua and Pilloud 2018, in press; Passalacqua et al. 2019).

Forensic anthropologists are increasingly being faced with a number of ethical dilemmas that range from scene attendance to analysis in the laboratory, research, publication, and dealing with families. Some key ethical questions forensic anthropologists may ask themselves include:

- Am I applying the appropriate methods?
- Should I be using invasive autopsy or should I assess CT images first?
- Should I macerate the remains or only some of them?
- In a commingled context, how confident am I that specific bones belong to a particular individual?
- Do I have the appropriate training?
- How should I present my findings to a research audience?
- Should I be showing images of the deceased?
- How should I speak to families regarding the state of the remains?
- How do I manage family expectations around DNA sampling and identification?
- What legal rights to the dead have?
- Have I exhausted all reasonable efforts in searching for the remains of a missing person?
- How shall I deal with estimating ancestry?
- Is my age assessment on a living individual fair and objective?
- What religious or cultural aspects should I take into consideration during my analysis?
- Do the analytical methods or technologies that I am using have any specific ethical considerations?
- Am I following all relevant guidelines and/or standards?

Forensic anthropologists are involved in the search, recovery, and analysis of human remains from a number of scenarios, ranging from individual homicide cases to mass disasters, human rights cases, and victims of past conflicts (the forensic timeframe will differ according to country and context; see Márquez-Grant and Fibiger 2011). Moreover, forensic anthropologists do not exclusively deal with the deceased. Analysis of the remains of individuals may impact or use records of living individuals and, in some cases, anthropologists may also examine living subjects to determine if someone is an adult or not (Black et al. 2010). This chapter will provide a number of considerations in these areas based on personal casework experience as practitioners and drawing from the literature, and is applicable to both practitioners and academics. It begins with a review of the codes of ethics within forensic anthropology, and then explores ethical issues concerning the recovery and analysis of human remains as well as those surrounding research, publication, and teaching. Finally, there is a discussion about the role the forensic anthropologist may play in discussions with next-of-kin.

15.2 Codes of Ethics

As Blau (2016a) indicates, most professional forensic anthropologists will agree to what may be called a 'code of conduct' or a 'code of ethics', which serves as guidance for best practice within the discipline and defines repercussions for unethical behaviour. These codes of ethics set some guiding principles that can be used by the professional when confronted with a situation that requires an action to be taken (Turner et al. 2018). Such codes are typically associated with professional organisations and must be agreed to as a requirement for membership. For example, in the United Kingdom, the code of practice for forensic anthropology (RAI 2018) outlines the duties and responsibilities, professional competency, documentation, and obligations to the court. Forensic anthropologists should adhere to the most appropriate code of conduct for the region in which they practice. For instance, the code of ethics of the Australian and New Zealand Forensic Science Society (2014) can serve in related disciplines including forensic anthropology. However, as Passalacqua and Pilloud (2018) point out, many of these codes may be lacking in their guidance and enforcement. Therefore, where there are no country specific codes of ethics, or those codes are otherwise lacking, international guidance may also be followed. For example, that of the International Committee of the Red Cross (Tidball-Binz 2007) relating to the obligation for the protection of human remains, the rights of the families, the respect for the dead, and the duties in assisting with identification.

Linked to these codes of conduct may be issues surrounding qualifications (Blau and Ubelaker 2016). Qualifications vary depending on the country, as will law enforcement and the judicial system. In some countries, the forensic anthropologist may be required to have a degree in medicine, whilst in others they may not. In order to enable the courts, police forces, and other organisations to recognise who may be qualified to perform forensic anthropological work, a system of certification has been implemented in some countries (e.g. see Blau 2016a, 2016b; Passalacqua and Pilloud 2018). In the USA, there is a certification process through the American Board of Forensic Anthropology (ABFA); in the UK the certification is carried out under the auspices of the Royal Anthropological Institute (RAI), in Europe, certification can be undertaken through the Forensic Anthropology Society of Europe (FASE), and in Latin America it is through the Latin American Association for Forensic Anthropology (ALAF, in its Spanish acronym). Although these certification processes have been the focus of debate and controversy in some countries, the implementation of these certifications is essential for setting standards for who is, and who is not, qualified to practice forensic anthropology.

15.3 Scene Assistance

The forensic anthropologist, when called to assist at a scene, will not only obtain information about the case, but will also ensure the request is within their competency or whether additional assistance is required (RAI 2018). It is also important to manage professional expectations in the types of analysis the forensic anthropologist can carry out within the context of a particular case, highlighting the limitations of the information that can be obtained based on the available evidence and contextual information. Similarly, in a humanitarian case where families and organisations are seeking anthropologists to recover and identify the missing, the limitations both with the methods currently available and on other factors, such as the state of decomposition of the bodies, may also need to be transmitted to families at the very start of the investigation in order to manage their expectations (e.g. see Aronson 2016).

After assessing the scene and, as the recovery progresses, forensic anthropologists may be asked to provide a preliminary assessment of the minimum number of individuals, biological profile (e.g. age-at-death and sex), possible chronology (e.g. ancient, historical, or recent remains) or the post-mortem interval, or an inventory of the remains that are present. However, such assessments should be avoided if possible as laboratory analyses often refine such estimates and may invalidate preliminary findings made while in the field.

Depending on the nature and size of the recovery, there may be a large team present of which the forensic anthropologist is only one participant. Discussions held by the team may address time constraints, resources, logistics, the nature of the incident, and aspects relating to health and safety. A search and recovery strategy will have to be implemented and designed by those working at the scene. The anthropologist must ensure that they provide assistance to maximise the recovery of evidence while working within whatever restraints are determined by the lead investigating organisation.

When working in the field, the forensic anthropologist may be interviewed by the media but the content of what can be said must first be discussed with the senior investigating officer. Appropriate clothing is necessary (e.g. plain clothes vs caricature on a T-shirt), and appropriate behaviour and conversations must be respectful and professional as these recoveries are performed in front of the press and other members of the community.

In some humanitarian contexts, the families and the community may want to view the exhumation process; although their presence must not jeopardise the investigation and the evidence. It is also worth considering what Djurić (2016) highlighted with regards to who is excavating the grave or undertaking the anthropological analysis, as there may be a particular ethnic group or a political party involved. Therefore, international teams are often called in to avoid conflicts between family members and local or national scientists (Albarella 2009; Congram 2016).

15.4 Age Estimation in the Living

Age estimates for living individuals occur in cases where the age of an individual is in question. For example, cases regarding human trafficking, underage marriage, and even age assessments in sports have required these types of analysis when individuals may be presented as minors or adults, but there is a reason to question the validity of their age regardless (Dvorak et al. 2007; Beh and Payne-James 2010; Wittschieber et al. 2014, Schmidt et al. 2015). Thus, a brief note on age estimation in the living (Cattaneo 2007; Schmeling et al. 2008; Black et al. 2010) is worth including here as it is of relevance to forensic anthropology, bearing in mind that requests to estimate age in living individuals are increasing. In Europe for example, the arrival of undocumented immigrants, those with false documentation, or those lying about their age, has required age assessments to be undertaken in both civil and criminal proceedings (Introna and Campobasso 2006; Defensor del Pueblo 2009; Black et al. 2010; Brownlees and Smith 2011; Roscam Abbing 2011; Schmeling et al. 2011).

Generally, an age estimation of a living individual requires a physical assessment by a medical doctor or forensic physician, a dental assessment by a forensic odontologist, and a skeletal assessment by a forensic anthropologist or other professional via radiology (Black et al. 2010; Schmeling et al. 2011). The forensic anthropologist would typically estimate age using the left hand and wrist; if these are skeletally mature, the clavicles (Kreitner et al. 1998; Schultz et al. 2008) and/or dentition can be assessed. Standards (Schmeling et al. 2008) and proficiency testing (Deutsche Gesellschaft für Rechtsmedizin n.d.) have been developed to ensure quality control, that the appropriate methods are used, and that the reporting is appropriate. Consent and the rights of the child are of the upmost importance (Office of the United Nations High Commissioner for Refugees 1997; Defensor del Pueblo 2009). The individual has to provide consent and, prior to the imaging, an understanding of the process and nature of the examination(s), the potential outcomes, and the radiation exposure need to be discussed. In addition, if the individual is thought to be a minor, the question relies on who (which adult) is able to provide consent (see Lal et al. 2007). The Office of the United Nations High

Commissioner for Refugees in Geneva set up Guidelines on Policies and Procedures in Dealing with Unaccompanied Children Seeking Asylum (Office of the United Nations High Commissioner for Refugees 1997) regarding the care and protection of children, in particular those separated from both parents with no other adult to care for them.

One recent US editorial by a forensic anthropologist highlighted the problems of an overreliance on methods in estimating age of the living that have not been validated (DiGangi 2018). Age estimation of the living is problematic because these methods are based on populations usually very different from those populations or individuals being assessed. The diet, medical background, and socio-economic status of each individual should all be taken into account (Schmeling et al. 2011). While these same considerations should be given to all methods employed by forensic anthropologists, there is an additional burden in many of these cases to consider the implications of the result. There are often punitive policies in place that the living individual could suffer based on the estimation of age provided by the practitioner.

15.5 Anthropological Analysis of the Dead

In the laboratory (or mortuary), there are a number of tasks that the forensic anthropologist may undertake, the type and number of which will vary depending on the case. These tasks may include establishing if bones are human, calculating the minimum number of individuals, constructing a biological profile to assist in the identification of the deceased, reconstructing fragmented skeletal remains, bone association from commingled remains, trauma assessment, facial approximation, and destructive sampling of bone for molecular or microscopic analyses (e.g. histology or isotope analysis) (Komar and Buisktra 2008; Roberts and Márquez-Grant 2012; Márquez-Grant 2015). If the forensic anthropologist was involved in the recovery of human remains or otherwise has additional information about the case, it is important to note the potential negative effects of cognitive bias, especially regarding the construction of a biological profile and trauma analysis. Such biases are decreased when a blind analysis of the remains is carried out (Nakhaeizadeh et al. 2014; Passalacqua and Pilloud 2018).

When dealing with deceased individuals, the dignity of the dead and their families should be of utmost importance. In this regard, there may be issues relating to invasive autopsy, soft tissue processing (i.e. maceration), the possibility of family viewing the remains, and any religious sensitivities. The medicolegal authority (e.g. coroner and medical examiner) is typically the one who determines whether or not a full autopsy or other destructive or invasive methods are required to resolve the case. For example, in a mass fatality with a presumed cause of death, an autopsy may not be necessary (Ranson 2016). In addition, the unauthorised removal of hands for fingerprinting or the extraction of mandibles for odontology, which has been done in the past, has been deemed unethical and should be avoided at all costs (Clarke 2001; Interpol 2014).

The forensic anthropologist is often, and more increasingly (Rainwater et al. 2012), assessing the biological profile of fleshed or well-preserved bodies of unidentified individuals. In order to facilitate such analyses, skeletal elements may be removed from the body. For example, to estimate age at death, forensic anthropologists may remove the medial end of the clavicle, the sternal end of the fourth rib, and the pubic symphyses (e.g. Rainwater et al. 2012). For stature estimation, removal or dissection to extract a long bone may be necessary to measure its length. Trauma analysis is also aided through the removal of soft tissue and if the trauma is isolated to a few bones, it is common for a forensic anthropologist to resect only those bones involved for further analysis. The level of processing and dissection should be carefully weighed against possible wishes of the next-of-kin, for example if relatives want to view the body for cultural and religious reasons (Berkovitz et al. 2013; Kahana 2014; Al-Waheeb et al. 2015; Franklin et al. 2015) or have objections to any manipulation or destruction of the remains. There may also be legal considerations in terms of the right to sepulcher for the decedent's family members (Passalacqua and Pilloud 2018).

When only a small number of bone fragments are recovered from a forensic case, the human vs non-human question is of utmost importance. Consequently, resolving this question may require destructive analysis of much of the sample. In such cases one needs to prioritise destructive sampling in terms of DNA, histology, XRD, or any other analysis while considering what other data (morphoscopic or metric) can be collected prior to destructive sampling. Thus, each fragment should be recorded prior to sampling, and any destructive analysis on the same bone or bone fragment assessed carefully, if the fragments are the only available potential evidence to identify an individual. A sampling strategy should be implemented at the very beginning of a case in discussion with other scientists, police, medicolegal authorities, potentially family members, and other relevant stakeholders.

Byrd and Adams (2016) have highlighted a number of sensitive issues that require careful consideration when dealing with fragmentary remains from commingled contexts, such as mass disasters. These issues are: whether every fragment of bone or tissue should be analysed and submitted for DNA analysis, how unidentifiable bones will be treated, and whether the goal is merely to identify the individuals present or to re-associate every single fragment possible to an individual. In fact, Sledzik and Mundorff (2016) indicate that these questions should be addressed prior to the tasks of victim identification. Another ethical issue surrounding commingled and fragmentary remains is the segregation of remains into individuals from the commingled assemblage (e.g. perpetrator vs victim), and every effort must be made to attribute as many bones or bone fragments as possible to an individual (which may have been identified only by a tooth or a bone fragment submitted for DNA analysis). These questions have of course implications that will influence the scientific strategy but also regarding the expectations and wishes of the relatives of the deceased (Wagner 2014).

With regard to the analytical methods employed (see Sect. 15.4 for age estimation in the living), Blau (2009) points out that there is an ethical responsibility to understand the reliability of the techniques, whether or not they are the most appropriate, and to consider methodological limitations. As İşcan and Steyn (2013) indicate, the methods employed should derive from an adequate sample size with an even age distribution, have data separated according to sex, a detailed description of the reference population regarding health, socio-economic status, and geographic origin, amongst other factors. Not only do the methods employed matter, but so does one's own professional competence. In circumstances where a case is beyond the expertise of the practitioner, they must refer that case to another competent individual. In a similar vein, it is the responsibility of the forensic anthropologist to receive continuing education, read the relevant scientific literature to stay abreast of new developments in the discipline, and adopt new methods as they are introduced and/or validated.

Whenever skeletal remains are retained, this must be formalised, and the proper authority consulted. In England, Wales, and Northern Ireland, for example, the Human Tissue Act (2004) will apply. In particular for research purposes, this must be strictly regulated. If remains are unidentified, a number of ethical questions and discussions arise (see, for example, Aronson 2016 in the case of 9/11). In some jurisdictions, the skeletal remains of those unidentified may be curated for extended periods of time within forensic anthropology laboratories, in case future identification is possible. However, unidentified cases should never be used for training as this may result in damage, further contamination or loss of evidence, as well as an unnecessarily complicated chain of custody. The final disposition of unidentified remains is decided by the medicolegal authority. In the UK, this is typically decided by the coroner; some will be buried in unknown single or communal graves or some will be kept in mortuaries.[1]

15.5.1 Special Considerations for the Use of Imaging

It is worth considering imaging techniques as they are increasingly being used by forensic anthropologists. Forensic imaging encompasses a diverse range of digital technologies from medical imaging such as radiographs, post-mortem computed tomography (PMCT), and post-mortem magnetic resonance imaging (PMRI) to photogrammetry, laser scanning, and photography. The use of these technologies has revolutionised forensic investigations with their ability to capture data as it is at a crime scene or as a body which is presented to the medical examiner. While these methods can serve as robust analytical tools for forensic experts, their use in forensic anthropology is subject to their own ethical considerations (Márquez-Grant and Errickson 2017).

There are many benefits to practitioners for using imaging including the documentation and long-term preservation of evidence (Decker et al. 2009), but especially the non-destructive manner in which these methods capture digital data.

[1]See, for example, Cawley (2016) for the UK, and Hernández (2017) regarding Mexico.

A body can be scanned using medical imaging and photogrammetry to capture fine details, such as fractures or other trauma as well as any discoloration from taphonomic changes to the bone. Another benefit to digital imaging is the derivatives from the data, such as 3D reconstructions, animations of trauma, identifying morphological features, and even 3D printing for use as illustrations in court (e.g. Baier et al. 2018). These methods allow forensic evidence to be preserved long term and can easily be shared between experts. One concern about these large datasets would be the proper storage of any files. Digital evidence would follow current legal requirements for physical evidence storage, which means that medical examiners or law enforcement would be responsible for safely securing these files with adequate support from informational technologists (IT) at their agency or institution.

The major ethical concern with the use of medical imaging in forensic science, in terms of both ante-mortem and post-mortem data, is patient/deceased privacy. Autopsy laws vary by country and in some countries they vary by region, so the inclusion of medical images might make them part of the public record if utilised as part of the investigation. Ante-mortem imaging for age estimation in the living and for post-mortem comparisons will require patient or next of kin consent. Care must be taken to protect these images from improper use or dissemination as there could be negative ramifications for the patient or family if certain data were made public. Many religious groups, such as Muslims and Jewish populations, are more in favour of virtual investigations due to the non-invasive nature of these methods and the speed in which a case can be processed (Berkovitz et al. 2013; Mohammed and Kharoshah 2014). However, the resulting images also carry religious concerns for use and display that should be addressed by the forensic team with sensitivity.

If digital images are to be used for forensic anthropological analyses in a virtual setting, the same guidelines and ethical considerations employed with the physical remains should be translated to the virtual data. This would start by ensuring that appropriate scanning modalities and settings are selected. For example, when using medical imaging, CT scanning would be more ideal for bone reconstruction, while MRI would be more beneficial for soft tissue visualisation. Additionally, with photography, laser scanning, or photogrammetry (Errickson and Thompson 2017), care must be taken to reduce artefacts during capture that could obscure critical findings. Reduction in these potential errors comes from ensuring that the practitioner capturing the data has the appropriate training and experience in these technologies. For example, using a certified radiographer for capturing medical image scans is particularly important when scanning living individuals, as the radiation dosage that the patient is exposed to is required to be monitored by the technologist to ensure safe levels are administered. An expert in imaging will also know the correct scanning protocols for post-mortem imaging, thus resulting in higher quality data to be analysed (Ford and Decker 2016). Additionally, adequate training is critical for the viewing, interpretation, and analysis of imaging results. Likewise, a sound anatomical and osteological background is essential for anyone utilising virtual anthropological methods. Segmentation of virtual remains with soft tissue requires more radiological expertise to ensure they are accurately capturing the anatomical structures. Untrained individuals can accidently bias data by incorrectly capturing, modelling, or animating evidence. As with all scientific methods, every effort should be taken to eliminate one's bias at all stages of analysis by only examining what has been accurately captured. Reconstructions must be based on the evidence provided and not influenced by opinion.

Due to the nature of digital image data, ease of transmission provides ample opportunities for collaborative sharing of resources for investigative and research purposes. However, this sharing of information must prevent the individuals' private information from being inadvertently exposed. For information being used in a forensic setting, data transfers between agencies must be secure and comply with all federal privacy standards. For research, metadata included in medical images and some photogrammetry must be stripped to ensure that records are protected and anonymised before being transferred. While basic demographic information is often necessary to conduct anthropological research, institutional review boards or ethics committees should be responsible for approving and overseeing any usage of this data beyond its original intent. Only the minimum demographic information needed to conduct the study should be retained. All practitioners and researchers (including research assistants or anyone who has access to image data) should require that their appropriate agency/institutional have ethics training and certifications to access personal information. The ethical use and display of image data and its derivatives for courtroom, research, and education are discussed in greater detail later in this chapter.

15.6 Research and Publication

Much of the research in forensic anthropology is based on experimental studies or research collections. Some research has also been undertaken on data, such as that obtained using CT on living individuals (Decker et al. 2011). The creation of research collections should be justified (DeWitte 2015). Whenever possible, research collections must obtain consent from the donors themselves or their next of kin. According to Young (2016), a number of skeletal collections are the result of physically removing the remains of the deceased from where they were laid to rest, where they died, or which were subsequently disturbed by natural factors or faunal or human intervention. A number of collections have been created from unclaimed bodies that were to be redeposited in ossuaries in a number of countries (Eliopoulos et al. 2007; Rissech and Steadman 2011). In such cases, the use of these remains for research should be acceptable if their descendants and/or the local community is in support of the project. Of particular significance is research on human remains from Indigenous groups as this could be problematic in some countries, Australia being one of them (Donlon 2016). The creation of decomposition facilities have their own ethical considerations as well (Black 2017; Williams, Cassella and Pringle, this volume).

Destructive analysis should answer specific research questions that balance the destruction of human remains with the value of the scientific work. France (2012) asks if it is ethical to remove sections of human remains for research and whether the research is justified for a common good. Some guidelines have appeared in bioarchaeology (APABE 2013) but may also be relevant in forensic anthropology; yet, the coroner or other medicolegal authority will have the final decision if samples are removed from forensic cases for research. Still, the question is whether the next-of-kin should have ownership or even prevent research (France 2012). In some countries, there is legislation regarding the destructive sampling of human remains, discarding soft tissue, and retention of human body parts which should be considered during skeletal analyses (Márquez-Grant and Fibiger 2011). As Passalacqua and Pilloud (2018) rightly point out, ethical discussions should arise when physical samples of bones are removed from a body for research but there is no intention or consideration with regard to re-associating the sample back to the individual. Concerns in the United Kingdom, such as the retention of human remains at Alder Hey Hospital, led to the creation of the Human Tissue Act (2004).

Ideally, research ethics committees at universities and other institutions will assess the ethics of proposed research projects that will involve the analysis of human remains. However, in a number of states in the USA, deceased individuals are not typically included in ethical research practices and such projects will often be considered exempt and will receive little ethical oversight; thus, necessitating the forensic anthropologist to be well versed in ethical issues.

As a final point, ethical considerations should filter into the presentation of results. Publishing research or case studies should obtain prior permission from the relevant authorities and families where applicable. The case studies should be anonymised (with regard to the identity of the deceased) and with dignified and respectful images. Publications of human rights' case studies where the deceased may not necessarily be anonymised, or where photos may lead to recognition, should require permission from relatives. In a volume edited by Blau and Ubelaker (2016), the editors include a note on the use of images of human remains in their publication (Blau and Ubekaler 2016, xxi):

> In keeping with our ethical responsibility of working with human remains we emphasize that access to and use of images of deceased individuals is an important part of the professional forensic anthropologist's casework and/or research. As part of the forensic anthropologist's professional ethical code of practice, when one depicts aspects of a case, the deceased individual must be de-identified (that is, nothing can identify the person). Consequently, in all cases in this edition where human remains (…) are depicted to illustrate a point there are no identifying features on the image. All research based on deceased individuals (whether identified or not), including the use of images, has ethical approval.

In the same edited volume, Black (2016) includes a note on the images used in her publication and is clear regarding the permission, anonymity, and cultural sensitivities of these images. Restrictions on images of the remains of casualties from World War I, World War II, and other conflicts are also to be taken into account (Elders 2006; Brown 2016). As Cox et al. (2016) note, the World War I (primarily Australian) casualties buried at Fromelles (northern France) were treated the same as those who die in warfare today, and no images were shown to the general public through media coverage. However, it was agreed that images of the remains of the deceased could be shown with prior approval for scientific reports and publications. In fact, some images were still blurred and others shown with dignity and respect in recent published volumes on the site (Cox and Jones 2014; Loe et al. 2014). To summarise, Passalacqua and Pilloud (2018) find that forensic anthropologists using images of human remains must be aware of any disrespect towards the deceased as well as their next of kin, that no photos should be inflammatory, that the images should not interfere with the investigation, and that all the permissions are in place. The title of the research paper should also show respect for the decedent(s) and their next of kin (Passalacqua et al. 2014).

15.7 Education and Training

Education and training in forensic anthropology, whether to undergraduate students, graduate students, or short courses for the law enforcement, general public, or other professionals requires responsibility and consideration of a series of ethical dilemmas (Passalacqua and Pilloud, in press). It is important for the forensic anthropologist to outline a set of rules prior to handling human remains in the classroom, and also to include a lecture at the beginning of the course on ethics, which also provides an awareness of the sensitivities surrounding the excavation, analysis, retention, and display of human remains. Likewise, it is important to set guidelines regarding photography, and it should be clear that no images be posted online or on social media.

Education and training in forensic anthropology involves theoretical (lectures and seminars) and practical sessions, analysis of real human skeletal remains (archaeological, anatomical, and forensic cases), handling of casts or 3D prints of actual cases, and often some form of scholarly research (typically a master's thesis, and/or doctoral thesis), which may require experimentation or other methods (interviews and/or analysis of images of living subjects).

It is also important to highlight appropriate behaviour in the academic setting, which may be accomplished by including a statement in the course syllabus, requiring personal conduct contracts, or displaying signs about ethics, respect, and dignity. Instructions should be given on handling human remains (e.g. handling skulls with both hands, always holding remains over a table, and careful with the use of pens and metal instruments). Instruction should also be provided on appropriate behaviour around human remains; for example, it is not appropriate to make jokes about the remains, give them names, pose for pictures with remains, or treat them in any sort of degrading manner.

Of course, images of deceased individuals, even in teaching, should be there to make a point, and their educational benefit must out-weigh their entertainment or shock value. It is often appropriate to give a notice about showing remains or potentially disturbing content before class. Obviously, it is necessary to anonymise human remains, for example, by only showing one part of the body, blurring or hiding facial features, as well as any possible identifying features, such as tattoos or birthmarks.

15.8 Dealing with the Relatives of the Missing and Deceased

Forensic anthropologists may encounter bereaved families for a myriad of reasons and at various stages in their work. Human loss is unique and each family makes sense of loss differently. As such, it is difficult to establish a set of standards that are all encompassing and recognise both the individuality of the circumstances of each loss and of the family's need to grieve. The level of information and detail families demand will be different; they will have different priorities and require different questions to be answered. It is impossible to provide a single set of standards to guide the forensic anthropologist in their engagement with families.

Although anthropologists may not wish to meet the next of kin, from personal experience of the lead author, such encounters are sometimes unavoidable. Interactions may relate to the families visiting the scene to find out where their loved ones were found, or relatives visiting to thank the scientists for the work they have undertaken in finding the missing. There may be instances where communication with family members is direct, as in a conversation or when presenting results to the public, or communication may be through a third party such as the police, a family liaison officer, a forensic pathologist, a coroner, or a psychologist. Although the anthropologist will be objective, unbiased, and impartial, in some contexts it is important to understand family sensitivities or understand family expectations, where the latter is particularly relevant to a human rights′ context. It may be that anthropologists are interviewing relatives to obtain ante-mortem data; however, this is complex and should be undertaken by practitioners that can address psychosocial aspects (Mladina 2016). In humanitarian cases, relatives of the deceased may directly contact forensic anthropologists or other investigators asking for their help in searching for their loved ones.

Of course, it is not always known how (in)appropriate it is for forensic anthropologists to familiarise themselves with the families (Blau 2016a). Whatever the work process, whether recovery at the scene, anthropological analysis in the laboratory (e.g. how invasive one needs to be), writing of the report, research and publication of a case study, or presenting evidence in court, one must consider to some extent the next-of-kin of the deceased. Through personal experience of the first author, families have asked if the remains were complete, and if any particular bones missing.

As Sledzik and Mundorff (2016) indicate, family members often have questions about the search, recovery, and identification of the remains. Sometimes anthropologists have to answer those questions and lead family meetings. They may also be the best suited in explaining and answering questions about the condition of the remains, as in the case of 9/11 (Sledzik and Mundorff 2016). Lunn (2017) indicates that sometimes there are common requests from family members to see and touch the deceased before they leave the scene, and argues that such wishes are to be honoured whenever practically possible. Relatives may see how the remains and personal effects of their loved ones are handled, and it is important to be aware of the cultural background of the relatives (Lunn 2017). When working with commingled remains and mass fatality incidents where fragmentation is high, the process of identification should be explained to relatives. Relatives may opt for not wanting to be notified about any further DNA tests or remains found at later dates after their loved one has already been identified, and this is a question that should be asked at the beginning of the investigation (Wagner 2014). It is equally important to recognise that a family's decision to refuse information may change over time, a continual process of checking with the family about these decisions is recommended. Likewise, if access to specific information is constrained by time and opportunity (for example viewing the body or the remains), the team, including forensic anthropologists, can be creative in how choices are provided, such as taking a photograph for the family to view so they can consider their need to physically see the remains.

Blau (2016b) asks that the political context and any social repercussions be considered, especially when dealing with incidental findings. For example, when the father is found not to be the biological father of a child (see Parker et al. 2013; Passalacqua and Pilloud 2018, for further discussion). In addition, it may be asked whether the local community will be involved in the recovery work, whether the political situation will influence the collection of ante-mortem data, and how will this influence the identification process (Passalacqua and Pilloud 2018).

There is certain tension that exists between providing families with accurate information and protecting them from details that could exacerbate their distress. However, it is important for families to be given a choice about the level of information that they require; after all it is this information that will assist them in making sense of their loss. In fact, understanding what the family needs, without compromising the scientist's objectivity, may be left to the forensic anthropologist, especially in mass fatality incidents and human rights cases where there is no police, coroner officer, or psychologist liaising with them. As professionals, it is critical to communicate with the family so that the information they require is understood. This management of family expectations cannot be emphasised enough. In our personal experience of human rights cases or where groups of families are searching for the disappeared; these are not receiving enough or the right information. There may be too many expectations regarding DNA analysis depending on the state of the remains. In a recent congress organised by the Latin American Association for Forensic Anthropology in Mexico in 2016, the conference organisers included discussion panels with the relatives of the missing. The work by the Mexican team, for example, is exemplary in that it helps relatives of the missing understand the process of search, recovery, and identification (EMAF 2013; Wade 2016). Likewise, in Spain, information is provided to relatives of those executed during the Spanish Civil War (1936–1939) when exhumations take place. These details are passed on to relatives at the end of the working day to outline their daily progress and achievements on site, and, on occasion, talks are also delivered to the community at the end of the investigation process (Etxeberria Gabilondo 2007, 2012).

Planning coping mechanisms with families is beyond our remit, but it is worth understanding the role of the extended family and the wider community in facilitating coping, also because enforced disappearances are traumatic for the family and community (Pinzón González 2016). As professionals, our relationships with families are relatively brief and transitory, and it is our responsibility to consider the time beyond our involvement and to ensure that families have access to sustainable and long-term support. Closure, memorialisation (Aronson 2016), and remembrance are important, as well as ensuring that the remains returned are from that particular person.

15.9 Conclusion

There are a myriad of ethical concerns when working with human skeletal remains. Many of these are outlined throughout this volume, particularly in relation to bioarchaeological research. In terms of forensic anthropology, ethical concerns extend into the medicolegal realm, which requires an understanding of local regulations and appropriate training in order to achieve the requisite qualifications to perform forensic anthropological work. Moreover, the nature of forensic anthropological work is sensitive due to the relative contemporaneity and context of the remains. Therefore, forensic anthropologists must consider the next-of-kin and any other political sensitivities regarding the work they are conducting, particularly in cases of mass disasters and abuse of human rights. These sensitivities should extend to the manner in which research is conducted and results are presented. As new technologies emerge and provide greater insight into forensic evidence, practitioners will be faced with addressing the ethical concerns that will inevitably arise from their novel applications. Finally, serious consideration needs to be taken regarding the ethics of working with the living, for example in providing age estimation and its associated consequences, particularly the protection of children, consent, and that subjects understand what the analysis involves.

Forensic anthropology is a growing discipline of inquiry that is just beginning to professionalise its practice through the use of certifications, standards, and accreditations; all of which are critical for the accurate and ethical practice of forensic anthropology as well as the legitimisation of the discipline.

References

Advisory Panel on Archaeology of Burials in England [APABE]. 2013. *Science and the Dead: A Guideline for the Destructive Sampling of Archaeological Remains for Scientific Analysis.* Swindon: English Heritage and The Advisory Panel on Archaeology of Burials in England.

Albarella, U. 2009. Archaeologists in Conflict? Empathizing with Which Victims? *Heritage Management* 2 (1): 105–114.

Al-Waheeb, S., N. Al-Kandary, and K. Aljerian. 2015. Forensic Autopsy Practice in the Middle East: Comparisons with the West. *Journal of Forensic and Legal Medicine* 32: 4–9.

Aronson, J.D. 2016. *Who Owns the Dead? The Science and Politics of Death at Ground Zero.* Cambridge: Harvard University Press.

Australian and New Zealand Forensic Science Society. 2014. *Code of Professional Practice for Members of the ANZFSS.* http://anzfss.org/wp-content/uploads/2012/05/ANZFSS-Code-of-Professional-Practice-Final.pdf. Accessed 29 July 2018.

Baier, W., J.M. Warnett, M. Payne, et al. 2018. Introducing 3D Printed Models as Demonstrative Evidence at Criminal Trials. *Journal of Forensic Sciences* 63 (4): 1298–1302.

Beh, P., and J. Payne-James. 2010. Clinical and Legal Requirements for Age Determination in the Living. In *Age Estimation in the Living: The Practitioner's Guide*, ed. S.M. Black, A. Aggrawal, and J. Payne-James, 30–42. Chichester: Wiley-Blackwell.

Berkovitz, N., S. Tal, P. Gottlieb, et al. 2013. Introducing Virtopsy into a Country Religiously Opposed to Autopsy. *Journal of Forensic Radiology and Imaging* 1 (2): 80.

Black, S. 2016. Disaster Anthropology: The 2004 Asian Tsunami. In *Handbook of Forensic Archaeology and Anthropology*, 2nd ed, ed. S. Blau and D.H. Ubelaker, 397–406. Abingdon: Routledge.

Black, S. 2017. Body Farms. *Forensic Science, Medicine and Pathology* 13: 475–476.

Black, S.M., A. Aggrawal, and J. Payne-James (eds.). 2010. *Age Estimation in the Living: The Practitioner's Guide*. Chichester: Wiley-Blackwell.

Blau, S. 2009. More than Just Bare Bones: Ethical Considerations for Forensic Anthropologists. In *Handbook of Forensic Archaeology and Anthropology*, ed. S. Blau and D.H. Ubelaker, 457–467. Abingdon: Routledge.

Blau, S. 2016a. More than Just Bare Bones: Ethical Considerations for Forensic Anthropologists. In *Handbook of Forensic Archaeology and Anthropology*, 2nd ed, ed. S. Blau and D.H. Ubelaker, 593–606. Abingdon: Routledge.

Blau, S. 2016b. La ética y el antropólogo forense: una variedad de consideraciones. In *Patología y Antropología Forense de la Muerte: La Investigación científico-judicial de la muerte y la tortura, desde las fossa clandestinas, hasta la audiencia pública*, ed. C. Sanabria-Medina, 25–36. Bogotá: Forensic Publisher.

Blau, S., and D.H. Ubelaker. 2016. Conclusion: International Perspectives on Issues in Forensic Anthropology. In *Handbook of Forensic Archaeology and Anthropology*, 2nd ed, ed. S. Blau, and D.H. Ubelaker, 509–513. Abingdon: Routledge.

Brown, M. 2016. Habeas Corpus: Contested Ownership of Casualties of the Great War. In *Archaeologists and the Dead: Mortuary Archaeology in Contemporary Society*, ed. H. Williams and M. Giles, 113–138. Oxford: Oxford University Press.

Brownlees, L., and T. Smith. 2011. *Lives in the Balance: The Quality of Immigration Legal Advice Given to Separated Children Seeking Asylum*. London: Refugee Council.

Byrd, J., and B.J. Adams. 2016. Analysis of Commingled Human Remains. In *Handbook of Forensic Archaeology and Anthropology*, 2nd ed, ed. S Blau and D.H. Ubelaker (eds), 238–239. Abingdon: Routledge.

Cattaneo, C. 2007. Forensic Anthropology: Developments of a Classical Discipline in the New Millennium. *Forensic Science International* 165: 185–193.

Cawley, L. 2016. England's Unclaimed Dead and the People Trying to Give Them a Name. *BBC News*. 25 January. https://www.bbc.co.uk/news/uk-england-34737343. Accessed 29 July 2018.

Christensen, A., N. Passalacqua, and E. Bartelink. 2019. *Forensic Anthropology: Current Methods and Practice*, 2nd ed. London: Academic Press.

Clarke, C. 2001. *Public Enquiry into the Identifications of the Victims Following Major Transport Accidents*. London: The Stationery Office.

Congram, D. (ed.). 2016. *Missing Persons: Multidisciplinary Perspectives on the Disappeared*. Toronto: Canadian Scholars' Press Inc.

Cox, M., and P. Jones. 2014. Ethical Considerations in the Use of DNA as a Contribution Toward the Determination of Identification in Historic Cases: Considerations from the Western Front. *New Genetics and Society* 33: 295–312.

Cox, M., Loe, L., and Jones, P. 2016. Fromelles: Forensic Archaeology and Anthropology in Identification. In *Handbook of Forensic Archaeology and Anthropology*, 2nd ed, ed. S Blau and D.H. Ubelaker, 575–606. Abingdon: Routledge.

Decker, S.J., S.L. Davy-Jow, J.M. Ford, et al. 2011. Virtual Determination of Sex: Metric and Nonmetric Traits of the Adult Pelvis from 3D Computed Tomography Models. *Journal of Forensic Sciences* 56 (5): 1107–1114.

Decker, S.J., J.M. Ford, and D.R. Hilbelink. 2009. Maintaining Custody: A Virtual Method of Creating Accurate Reproductions of Skeletal Remains for Facial Approximation. In *Abstracts of the Proceedings of the American Academy of Forensic Sciences 61st Annual Meeting, Denver, Colorado, USA, 26–21 February 2009*.

Defensor del Pueblo. 2009. *¿Menores O Adultos? Procedimientos para la Determinación de la Edad*. Madrid: Defensor del Pueblo.

Deutsche Gesellschaft für Rechtsmedizin. n.d. *Forensische Altersdiagnostik*. https://www.dgrm.de/arbeitsgemeinschaften/forensische-altersdiagnostik/. Accessed 29 July 2018.

DeWitte, S.N. 2015. Bioarchaeology and Ethics of Research Using Human Skeletal Remains. *History Compass* 13: 10–19.

DiGangi, E.A. 2018. Immigration Agents X-Raying Migrants to Determine Age Isn't Just Illegal, It's a Misuse of Science. *The Conversation*. 31 May. https://theconversation.com/immigration-agents-x-raying-migrants-to-determine-age-isnt-just-illegal-its-a-misuse-of-science-96771. Accessed 29 July 2018.

Djurić, M. 2016. Dealing with Human Remains from Recent Conflict: Mass Grave Excavation and Human Identification in a Sensitive Political Context. In *Handbook of Forensic Archaeology and Anthropology*, 2nd ed, ed. S. Blau and D.H. Ubelaker, 532–544. Abingdon: Routledge.

Donlon, D. 2016. The Development and Current State of Forensic Anthropology: An Australian Perspective. In *Handbook of Forensic Archaeology and Anthropology*, 2nd edn, ed. S. Blau and D.H. Ubelaker, 126–139. Abingdon: Routledge.

Dvorak, J., J. George, A. Junge, et al. 2007. Application of MRI of the Wrist for Age Determination in International U-17 Soccer Competitions. *British Journal of Sports Medicine* 41: 497–500.

Elders, J. 2006. Finding Common Ground: The English Heritage/Church of England Guidelines on the Treatment of Christian Human Remains Excavated in England. In *Human Remains and Museum Practice*, ed. J. Lohman and K.J. Goodnow, 86–90. Paris/London: UNESCO and the Museum of London.

Eliopoulos, C., A. Lagia, and S. Manolis. 2007. A Modern, Documented Human Skeletal Collection from Greece. *Homo* 58: 221–228.

Equipo Mexicano de Antropología [EMAF]. 2013. *Workshops*. http://emaf.org.mx/talleres/. Accessed 29 July 2018.

Errickson, D., and T. Thompson (eds.). 2017. *Human Remains—Another Dimensions: The Application of 3D Imaging to the Study of Human Remains*. London: Academic Press.

Etxeberria Gabilondo, F. 2007. Las exhumations de la Guerra Civil Española desde una perspectiva antropológica y paleopatológica. In *Enfermedad, Muerte y Cultura en las Sociedades del Pasado Volumen II*, ed. J. Barca Durán and J. Jiménez Ávila, 538–551. Cáceres: Fundación Academia Europea de Yuste.

Etxeberria Gabilondo, F. (ed). 2012. Antropología forense de la Guerra Civil Española. *Boletín Galego de Medicina Legal e Forense* 18. Santiago de Compostela: Asociación Galega de Médicos Forenses.

Ford, J.M., and S.J. Decker. 2016. Computed Tomography Slice Thickness and Its Effects on Three-Dimensional Reconstruction of Anatomical Structures. *Journal of Forensic Radiology and Imaging* 4: 43–46.

France, D. 2012. Ethics in Forensic Anthropology. In *A Companion to Forensic Anthropology*, ed. D. Dirkmaat, 666–682. Chichester: Wiley-Blackwell.

Franklin, D., A. Flavel, J. Noble, et al. 2015. Forensic Age Estimation in Living Individuals: Methodological Considerations in the Context of Medico-Legal Practice. *Research and Reports in Forensic Medical Science* 5: 53–66.

Hernández, P.S. 2017. Los Muertos de nadie; de la morgue a la fosa común. *El Sol de México*. 31 October. https://www.elsoldemexico.com.mx/metropoli/los-muertos-de-nadie-de-la-morgue-a-la-fosa-comun-306176.html. Accessed 29 July 2018.

Human Tissue Act. 2004. The Stationery Office, London.

Interpol. 2014. *DVI Guide*. https://www.interpol.int/Media/Files/INTERPOL-Expertise/DVI/DVI-Guide-new-version-2013. Accessed 29 July 2018.

Introna, F., and C.P. Campobasso. 2006. Biological vs Legal Age of Living Individuals. In *Forensic Anthropology and Medicine: Complimentary Sciences from Recovery to Cause of Death*, ed. A. Schmitt, 57–82. Totowa: Humana Press.

İşcan, M.Y., and M. Steyn. 2013. *The Human Skeleton in Forensic Medicine*, 3rd ed. Springfield: Charles C Thomas.

Kahana, T. 2014. Forensic Investigation of Suicidal Bombings in Israel: Balancing Religious Considerations with Medicolegal Responsibilities. In *Commingled Human Remains: Methods in Recovery, Analysis, and Identification*, ed. B.J. Adams and J. Byrd, 351–363. San Diego: Academic Press.

Klepinger, L. 2006. *Fundamentals of Forensic Anthropology*. Hoboken: Wiley.

Komar, D.A., and J.E. Buikstra. 2008. *Forensic Anthropology: Contemporary Theory and Practice*. New York: Oxford University Press.

Kreitner, K.-F., F.J. Schweden, T. Riepert, et al. 1998. Bone Age Determination Based on the Study of the Medial Extremity of the Clavicle. *European Radiology* 8: 1116–1122.

Lal, S.M.L., S. Parekh, C. Mason, et al. 2007. The Accompanying Adult: The Authority to Give Consent in the UK. *International Journal of Paediatric Dentistry* 17: 200–204.

Loe, L., C. Barker, K. Brady, et al. 2014. *Remember Me To all: The Archaeological Recovery and Identification of Soldiers Who Fought and Died in the Battle of Fromelles 1916*. Oxford: Oxford Archaeology.

Lunn, M.M. 2017. *Essentials of Medicolegal Death Investigation*. London: Academic Press.

Márquez-Grant, N. 2015. Age Estimation in Forensic Anthropology: Perspectives and Practical Considerations. *Annals of Human Biology* 42: 306–320.

Márquez-Grant, N., and D. Errickson. 2017. Ethical Considerations: An Added Dimension Book Chapter. In *Human Remains: Another Dimension. The Application of 3D Imaging in the Funerary Context*, 193–201, ed. D. Errickson and T. Thompson. London: Academic Press.

Márquez-Grant, N., and L. Fibiger (eds.). 2011. *The Routledge Handbook of Archaeological Human Remains and Legislation: An International Guide to Laws and Practice in the Excavation and Treatment of Archaeological Human Remains*. Abingdon: Routledge.

Mladina, V. 2016. Psychosocial Aspects of Interviewing and Self-Care for Practitioners. In *Missing Persons: Multidisciplinary Perspectives on the Disappeared*, ed. D. Congram, 171–183. Toronto: Canadian Scholars' Press Inc.

Mohammed, M., and M.A. Kharoshah. 2014. Autopsy in Islam and Current Practices in Arab Muslim Countries. *Journal of Forensic and Legal Medicine* 23: 80–83.

Nakhaeizadeh, S., I.E. Dror, and R.M. Morgan. 2014. Cognitive Bias in Forensic Anthropology: Visual Assessment of Skeletal Remains Is Susceptible to Confirmation Bias. *Science and Justice* 54: 208–214.

Office of the United Nations High Commissioner for Refugees. 1997. *Guidelines on Policies and Procedures in Dealing with Unaccompanied Children Seeking Asylum*. http://www.unhcr.org/uk/publications/legal/3d4f91cf4/guidelines-policies-procedures-dealing-unaccompanied-children-seeking-asylum.html. Accessed 29 July 2018.

Parker, L.S., A.J. London, and J.D. Aronson. 2013. Incidental Findings in the Use of DNA to Identify Human Remains: An Ethical Assessment. *Forensic Science International: Genetetics* 7: 221–229.

Passalacqua, N.V., M.A. Pilloud, and G.A. Gruters. 2014. Letter to the Editor—Professionalism: Ethics and Scholarship in Forensic Science. *Journal of Forensic Sciences* 59: 573–575.

Passalacqua, N.V., and M.A. Pilloud. 2018. *Ethics and Professionalism in Forensic Anthropology*. London: Academic Press.

Passalacqua, N.V., and M.A. Pilloud. In press. Education and Training in Forensic Anthropology. *Forensic Anthropology*.

Passalacqua, N.V., M.A. Pilloud, and W. Belcher. 2019. Scientific Integrity in the Forensic Sciences: Consumerism, Conflicts of Interest, and Transparency. *Science and Justice* 59 (5): 573–579.

Pinzón González, M.E. 2016. Psychosocial Perspectives on the Enforced Disappearance of Indigenous People in Guatemala. In *Missing Persons: Multidisciplinary Perspectives on the Disappeared*, ed. D. Congram, 102–118. Toronto: Canadian Scholars' Press Inc.

Rainwater, C.W., C. Crowder, K.M. Hartnett, et al. 2012. Forensic Anthropology at the New York City Office of Chief Medical Examiner. In *A Companion to Forensic Anthropology*, ed. D. Dirkmaat, 549–566. Chichester: Wiley-Blackwell.

Ranson, D. 2016. Legal Aspects of Identification. In *Handbook of Forensic Archaeology and Anthropology*, 2nd ed, ed. S. Blau and D.H. Ubelaker, 642–659. Abingdon: Routledge.

Rissech, C., and D. Steadman. 2011. The Demographic, Socio-Economic and Temporal Contextualization of the Universitat Autònoma de Barcelona Collection of Identified Human Skeletons (UAB Collection). *International Journal of Osteoarchaeology* 21: 313–322.

Roberts, J., and N. Márquez-Grant. 2012. Forensic Anthropology. In *Forensic Ecology Handbook: From Crime Scene to Court*, ed. N. Márquez-Grant and J. Roberts, 49–67. Chichester: Wiley-Blackwell.

Roscam Abbing H.D.C. 2011. Age Determination of Unaccompanied Asylum Seeker Minors in the European Union: A Health Law Perspective. *European Journal of Health Law* 18: 11–25.

Royal Anthropological Institute [RAI]. 2018. *Forensic Anthropology: Code of Practice*. London: Royal Anthropological Institute.

Schemling, A., C. Grundmann, A. Fuhrmann, et al. 2008. Criteria for Age Estimation in Living Individuals. *International Journal of Legal Medicine* 122 (6): 457–460.

Schmeling, A., P.M. Garamendi, J.L. Prieto, et al. 2011. Forensic Age Estimation in Unaccompanied Minors and Young Living Adults. In *Forensic Medicine—From Old Problems to New Challenges*, ed. D.N. Vieira, 77–120. Rijeka: IntTech.

Schmidt, S., V. Vieth, M. Timme, et al. 2015. Examination of Ossification of the Distal Radial Epiphysis Using Magnetic Resonance Imaging. New Insights for Age Estimation in Young Footballers in FIFA Tournaments. *Science and Justice* 55: 139–144.

Schultz, R., M. Mühler, W. Reisinger, et al. 2008. Radiographic Staging of Ossification of the Medial Clavicular Epiphysis. *International Journal of Legal Medicine* 22: 55–58.

Sledzik, P., and A.Z. Mundorff. 2016. Forensic Anthropology in Disaster Response. In *Handbook of Forensic Archaeology and Anthropology*, 2nd ed, ed. S. Blau and D.H. Ubelaker, 477–495. Abingdon: Routledge.

Tersigni-Tarrant, M.T.A., and N.R. Langley. 2017. Forensic Anthropology in the United States: Past and Present. In *Forensic Anthropology: A Comprehensive Introduction*, ed. N.R. Langley and M.T.A. Tersigni-Tarrant, 3–22. Boca Raton: CRC Press.

Thompson, T. 2001. Legal and Ethical Considerations of Forensic Anthropological Research. *Science and Justice* 41 (4): 261–270.

Tidball-Binz, M. 2007. Managing the Dead in Catastrophes: Guiding Principles and Practical Recommendations for First Responders. *International Review of the Red Cross* 89: 421–442.

Turner, T.R., J.K. Wagner, and G.C. Cabana. 2018. Ethics in Biological Anthropology. *American Journal of Physical Anthropology* 165: 939–951.

Wade, L. 2016. How Forensic Anthropologists are Helping the Families of Mexico's Disappeared Seek Justice. *Science*. 14 December. https://www.sciencemag.org/news/2016/12/how-forensic-anthropologists-are-helping-families-mexicos-disappeared-seek-justice. Accessed 29 July 2018.

Wagner, S. 2014. The Social Complexities of Human Remains. In *Commingled Human Remains: Methods in Recovery, Analysis, and Identification*, ed. B.J. Adams and J. Byrd, 491–506. San Diego: Academic Press.

Walsh-Hanney, H., and L.S. Lieberman. 2005. Ethical Concerns in Forensic Anthropology. In *Biological Repatriation and Ethics: From Repatriation to Genetic Identity*, ed. T.R. Turner, 121–132. New York: State University of New York Press.

Webb, J. 2006. *Professional Ethics: Forensic Anthropology and Human Rights Work.* Dissertation, Syracuse University.

Wittschieber, D., R. Schulz, V. Vieth, et al. 2014. The Value of Sub-Stages and Thin Slices for the Assessment of the Medial Clavicular Epiphysis: A Prospective Multi-Center CT Study. *Forensic Science, Medicine and Pathology* 10: 163–169.

Young, J. 2016. Collection, Curation, Repatriation: Exploring the Concept of Museum Skeletal Populations as Missing Persons. In *Missing Persons: Multidisciplinary Perspectives on the Disappeared*, ed. D. Congram, 119–134. Toronto: Canadian Scholars' Press Inc.

Chapter 16
The Ethical Considerations for Creating a Human Taphonomy Facility in the United Kingdom

Anna Williams, John P. Cassella and Jamie K. Pringle

Abstract Human Taphonomy Facilities are outdoor laboratories where forensic scientists investigate and monitor the decomposition of donated human cadavers in a variety of conditions. The use of human cadavers for this purpose is potentially controversial, as opinions differ about the value of the research conducted at such facilities and the extent to which the dignity of the deceased is preserved. As a result of the use of human cadavers for forensic research, there are ethical issues to consider if contemplating the creation of such a facility. Currently, there is no such facility in the UK, and the legal and ethical landscape in the UK regarding the use of human tissue is unique. Therefore, this chapter outlines the ethical considerations surrounding the creation of a Human Taphonomy Facility (HTF) in the United Kingdom. It starts with an overview of why controlled experiments are necessary for forensic investigations, and their potential importance for search and dating discovered remains. The chapter then acknowledges and discusses the usefulness of animal proxies for this research, with benefits of replicants, known age/diet, and availability. The rest of the paper then defines a HTF, explaining the need for controlled research and the importance of using human remains for controlled experiments. Finally, a discussion on why donation of human organs is routine and whole cadavers is not, the potential ethical considerations for body donation, the mechanics of how to run a HTF, and ultimately the considerations of public opinion.

A. Williams (✉)
School of Applied Sciences, University of Huddersfield, Queensgate, Huddersfield HD1 3DH, UK
e-mail: A.Williams@hud.ac.uk

J. P. Cassella
Department of Criminal Justice and Forensics, School of Law, Policing and Forensics, Science Centre, Staffordshire University, Leek Road, Stoke on Trent ST4 2DF, UK

J. K. Pringle
School of Geography, Geology and Environment, Keele University, Keele, Staffordshire ST5 5BG, UK

K. Squires et al. (eds.), *Ethical Approaches to Human Remains*,
https://doi.org/10.1007/978-3-030-32926-6_16

16.1 Introduction

All scientific research using human beings should be subject to ethical review, to ensure that the participants, whether alive or dead, are treated with dignity and respect and are not harmed or coerced in any way. In the UK, there are strict ethical guidelines, provided by the Human Tissue Authority, that govern research, education, and display of human tissues, and enshrine the concept of 'informed consent' in the protocols for such activities (Human Tissue Act 2004).

To assist in civil and criminal investigations, forensic researchers have reviewed multiple past cases, for example, to look at optimal search strategies, determine likely cause of death, and to assist determining post-mortem interval (Larson et al. 2011; Pringle et al. 2012a; Ruffell et al. 2017). Recent examples include decade reviews of suicidal hanging cases (Dean et al. 2012), homicide victims interred in concrete over an 18 year period in Los Angeles (California, USA) (Toms et al. 2008), and drowned victims in Glasgow (Scotland) to estimate submersion interval (Heaton et al. 2010). However, in all cases, depositional environments and variables cannot usually be accounted for, so controlled experiments can therefore help to assist to quantify the major variables.

Since the 1970s, research into human decomposition and the interaction of human cadavers with their environment has thus become increasingly important to forensic science and has led to the establishment of Human Taphonomy Facilities (HTFs) in the USA (Killgrove 2017), Australia (Forbes 2017), and more recently, mainland Europe (Enserink 2017). However, this area of research using human participants (donors) has not been as tightly regulated as other, longer-established, disciplines. In recent years, the possibility of the first HTF being built in the UK has been raised, thus creating a flurry of media attention and questions about how it would be organised and run, not only in terms of legalities, logistics, and finances, but also from an ethical standpoint.

Human Taphonomy Facilities are, by their nature, controversial, therefore, it is very important to allay fears and concerns held by the public, potential donors, or potential users of such facilities that the ethical issues have been considered. This chapter aims to address some of the ethical challenges and considerations that may arise if a Human Taphonomy Facility is created in the UK.

16.2 What is a Human Taphonomy Facility?

Human Taphonomy Facilities can be defined as outdoor laboratories where forensic scientists investigate and monitor the decomposition of donated human cadavers in a variety of conditions. The overall aim of the research conducted at such a facility is to advance our understanding of the processes of human decomposition and degradation of associated evidence in a natural environment. Decomposition is inherently impacted by the surrounding environment, particularly by environmental conditions such as temperature, rainfall, humidity, air current, and solar radiation (Haglund and Sorg 1997; Carter et al. 2007). Factors specific to the geological formation (such as soil texture, pH, moisture content, and electrical conductivity) as well as the ecological community (such as vertebrate and invertebrate scavengers and microorganisms) also play a major role in decomposition processes (Haglund and Sorg 1997; Dent et al. 2004; Carter et al. 2008).

At present, facilities that conduct human decomposition research are based in the USA, Australia, and most recently in The Netherlands, and are primarily focused on forensic anthropology. There have been a number of cemetery studies in the past (Fiedler et al. 2012; Hansen et al. 2014) that explore the impact of multiple human burials on the soil, water table, and ecology, but these are limited to their application for forensic science as Dick et al. (2017) detail, namely different depositional style, deeper burial depths, and length of burial. These HTFs can provide valuable data regarding the rate of decomposition in their specific ecological environments. However, data produced by the research at HTFs cannot be easily extrapolated to distinctly different environments of other countries or, indeed, within one country, due to the geographical variation in climate, geology, and ecology, and the inherent impact of these factors on the process of decomposition (Forbes 2017).

There are currently seven operational Human Taphonomy Facilities in the USA, one in Australia, and one in continental Europe (Enserink 2017). Human Taphonomy Facilities allow multi-disciplinary research to improve our understanding of the interactions between human cadavers, their local environment, and ecosystem. The research undertaken at the existing HTFs is designed to focus on three main areas of forensic investigation: search and location of missing individuals or clandestine depositions (whether victims of crime or disaster), identification of deceased individuals, and accurate estimation of the post-mortem interval. Research conducted at the existing HTFs, and in particular at the oldest one, based at the University of Tennessee (Knoxville, USA), which opened in 1981 (Vass et al. 1992, 2004, 2008), has influenced our knowledge about decomposition.

16.3 Do We Need a Human Taphonomy Facility in the UK?

World events in recent years have highlighted the need for research to improve our methodologies for searching, locating, recovering, and identifying victims of natural disasters (e.g. the Victoria bushfires (Australia), the Queensland floods (Australia), the Christchurch earthquake (New Zealand), and the earthquake and tsunami in Japan), transportation accidents (e.g. Marchioness Disaster in the UK), or terrorist incidents (e.g. 9/11 US terrorist attacks and the Bali bombings). On a smaller scale, but equally as important, these methodologies are also employed by police services to locate and identify missing persons and victims of homicide (Thornton 2017). Such methodologies include geophysical methods, aerial and thermal imaging, scent detection by specially trained ‘human remains detection’ dogs, and soil chemistry methods, all of which can be improved through research at a HTF. The capability to conduct this type of research and improve search and recovery methods is currently fragmentary and lacking on a global scale. Yet the ethical use of human cadavers to conduct scientific studies is vital for the ongoing success of investigations and when providing emergency response to countries impacted by disaster (Forbes 2017).

The alternative to a Human Taphonomy Facility is the use of animal models as analogues for human bodies. In the UK, several universities have animal-based taphonomy facilities, where scientifically rigorous experiments are carried out on freshly slaughtered pigs, rabbits, deer, or fallen domestic stock. It is clear from the numerous scientific research articles that the primary porcine model has been of great scientific value in bettering our understanding of the nature of forensic science in all its facets (Schultz et al. 2006; Schultz 2008; Bachmann and Simmons 2010; Pringle et al. 2012b, 2016; Lynch-Aird et al. 2015). Other animal models have been used but are less popular, for example, rabbits (Simmons et al. 2010; Troutman et al. 2014), wild deer (Young et al. 2014), and even red foxes (Young et al. 2015). The major advantages of using animal proxies are commonality and replicates. Indeed, some researchers believe that using animal analogues is preferable to using humans (Matuszewski et al. 2019). Animal cadavers can be routinely and relatively cheaply acquired for multiple replicate studies (Troutman et al. 2014; Matuszewski et al. 2019) to ensure results are statistically valid. The acquired animal cadavers also have typically common origin, diets, exercise, weights, ages, and manner of death. This therefore makes it easier, when, for example, looking at decomposition rates, that these listed variables can largely be factored out, whereas a HTF will be dependent on donor human cadavers, who will be of variable origin, differential weight and levels of fitness at the time of death (e.g. diet and exercise are key considerations), and manner of death will vary among donors. Therefore, comparing the results between donated human remains in large-scale studies is more difficult than when comparing results using animal proxies. In future, it may be possible to address this problem by coordinating efforts at many different body donation programs and amassing enough similar human cadavers at one time to do large-scale studies. HTFs, such as ARISTA in Amsterdam, suggest that amassing large numbers of individuals with similar characteristics or demographics is not necessary, but that databases of results from individuals buried separately can be interrogated for patterns based on certain characteristics. They also view their initial experiments with donors as pilot tests, which can provide fundamental locale-specific information on which to build (Oostra 2018, pers. comm.)[1]. Table 16.1 summarises the advantages and disadvantages of using porcine and human remains in taphonomy experiments, based on a similar table in Matuszewski et al. (2019).

However, there is a growing realisation that human remains need to be used in controlled experiments for certain aspects of taphonomy, such as specific conditions (e.g. diabetes, smoking, and drug overdoses), to establish how this may change the

[1]Oostra, R.J. (2018) Interview with Anna Williams (ARISTA, Amsterdam)

Table 16.1 Advantages and disadvantages of porcine and human remains in taphonomy research (after Matuszewski et al 2019)

	Use of porcine remains	Use of human remains
Advantages	1. Similar to human cadavers in: (i) Body mass range (ii) Skin coverage with hair (iii) Gross processes of decay 2. Easy to replicate: (i) Cheap and available in large numbers (i) Time and cause of death controllable (i) Possible to work with unfrozen cadavers 3. Straightforward ethical considerations	1. No species-relatcd differences 2. Opportunity to study effect of human conditions on decomposition rate 3. Opportunity to compare animal and human decomposition 4. Full medical details and history of cadavers usually available 5. Use of consenting humans 6. Greater applicability and reliability of results in court
Disadvantages	1. Dissimilar to human cadavers in: (i) Body proportions (ii) Gastro-intestinal anatomy (iii) Diet (iv) Overall anatomy (v) Ante-mortem pharmaceutical use 2. More uniform than humans 3. Potential for ground to be saturated with cadavers 4. Results not as applicable or reliable in court 5. Use of non-consenting animals 6. Unacceptable in some cultures 7. Potential tor objections from public	1. Difficult to replicate: (i) Available in low numbers (ii) Time and cause of death not controllable (iii) Dissimilar subjects (iv) Ante-mortem pharmaceutical use (v) May have to store cadavers for some time until replicates available 2. Limitations of HTFs: (i) Location-specific conditions (ii) Potential for ground to be saturated with cadavers 3. Complex ethical considerations 4. Unacceptable in some cultures 5. Potential for objections from public

estimations of post-mortem interval (Alapo 2016; Augenstein 2016; Hrala 2016). For many years, forensic experts have been studying animal cadavers to try and understand how human bodies decompose in different environmental and climatic conditions, and to better understand how long a person has been deceased. But current research (Rippley et al. 2012; Alapo 2016; Connor et al. 2017; Knobel et al. 2018) suggests that these animal proxies are not accurate enough when it comes to understanding the time of death for a human being.

A study, conducted at the University of Tennessee's Forensic Anthropology Centre in the USA, examined how pigs, rabbits, and humans decomposed in the same environment (Alapo 2016). They found that all of the test subjects decomposed at different rates, with pig cadavers decomposing faster than humans on average; the human body varied more wildly from body to body compared to rabbits or pigs. In 2012, a study in Texas (USA) also found differences in scavenging between animal and donated human cadavers (Rippley et al. 2012; Knobel et al. 2018). In addition, there are many human conditions or lifestyle choices that could potentially have an effect on decomposition rate that is simply not possible to determine using animal models. This is arguably the most important aspect of a Human Taphonomy Facility—the opportunity to study the effect of these conditions on decomposition in a variety of contexts. For example, cancer, diabetes, or other conditions such as autism may alter gut bacterial populations, and therefore may help or hinder decomposition (Buffington et al. 2016); smoking or drug or medicine use or abuse may also have an effect on gut bacterial populations, which influence decomposition rate. There has not been any animal proxy published research on this issue to-date. This variation may mean that the post-mortem interval estimation is over or under-estimated, severely compromising the criminal investigation. It is therefore challenging to undertake scientifically sound, rigorous empirical studies on the effect of these human conditions on the rate of decomposition using animal analogues.

16.4 Ethics of Research Using Animal Carcasses

The use of animals in scientific research is fraught with ethical problems; however, most of these are related to animal welfare and conditions during life. Taphonomy research in the UK has always been conducted on deceased animal carcasses, so can be exempt from issues of welfare and vivisection, but the purposes of sacrificing animals can be scrutinised (see Cross et al. 2010).

At the majority of animal taphonomy facilities in the UK, fallen domestic stock is used for research. These animals are dead but have not been killed for the purposes of research and, as such, this practice is generally deemed as ethically acceptable by most researchers. Some facilities choose stock that are being sent to the abattoir, effectively removing them from the food industry just before slaughter (Cross et al. 2010). It could be argued that human donors are preferable to animal donors from an ethical standpoint, as the human donors are actively volunteering their bodies for research, rather than having no choice in the matter, as in the case of animals. For the human donors, this is a desire expressed before their death, in the presence of witnesses. There is also growing support for reducing and replacing the use of animals (alive or dead) in medical and related research, and to increase the use of 'human-relevant' models (Animal Free Research UK 2018). A HTF would allow forensic research to be carried out on the best 'human-relevant' model of all, donated human cadavers.

16.5 The Ethics of Research Using Donated Human Cadavers

Clearly the experiences of the existing Human Taphonomy Facilities in the USA and Australia offer valuable information, not just about the ethics and morality of the use of human material, but how these principles have been put into operation in the acquisition of donated materials. Despite the first facility in Tennessee having opened in 1981 (Vidoli et al. 2017), it was not until 2015 that a paper on the ethics and best practices was authored by leaders of four of these institutions (Bytheway et al. 2015). These authors found a lack of standards and best practices to guide them in the ethical treatment of human remains as this research was not covered by Institutional Review Boards, where the federal guidelines specifically include "live human subjects". Neither were the human dead covered in any guidelines issued by the Department of Agriculture (USA) for animal research. Most universities in the USA have no guidelines for research using the recently dead, therefore they employ those proposed by medical research and those of the Belmont Report (National Commission for the Protection of Human Subjects of Biomedical and Behavioral Research 1978). However, the Belmont Report was designed for living patients with the principles to conduct research requiring careful consideration of (1) informed consent, (2) risks benefit assessment, and (3) selection of subjects of research.

There are three fundamental ethical principles for using any human subjects for research as set out by the Belmont Report (National Commission for the Protection of Human Subjects of Biomedical and Behavioral Research 1978):

1. Respect for persons: protecting the autonomy of all people and treating them with courtesy and respect and allowing for informed consent. Researchers must be truthful and conduct no deception;
2. Beneficence: the philosophy of "Do no harm" while maximising benefits for the research project and minimising risks to the research subjects;
3. Justice: ensuring reasonable, non-exploitative, and well-considered procedures are administered fairly—the fair distribution of costs and benefits to *potential* research participants—and equally.

There are seven fundamental elements that must be fulfilled to ensure the rights of any participant are met.

1. Ensure the study is approved by an Institutional Review Board (RDB) or Independent Ethics Committee;
2. obtain informed consent from the patient;
3. ensure that the patient understands the full extent of the experiment, and if not, will contact the study coordinator;
4. ensure the patient was not coerced into doing the experiment by means of threatening or bullying;

5. be careful of other effects of the clinical trial that were not mentioned, and report it to the proper study coordinator;
6. support the privacy of the patient's identity, their motivation to join or refuse the experiment; and
7. ensure that all patients receive the minimal care required.

It took until 2005 before a multidisciplinary expert 'Consensus Panel on Research with the Recently Dead' (CPRD) created ethical guidelines for dealing with the recently dead in the USA (Pentz et al. 2005).

The objective of the multidisciplinary expert CPRD was to craft ethics guidelines and recommended that research with the recently dead: (1) receive scientific and ethical review and oversight, (2) involve the community of potential research subjects, (3) be coordinated with organ procurement organisations, (4) not conflict with any organ donation or required autopsy (as required by certain countries), (5) use procedures respectful of the dead, (6) be restricted to one procedure per day, (7) preferably be authorised by first-person consent, though both general advance research directives and surrogate consent are acceptable, (8) protect confidentiality, (9) not impose costs on subjects' estates or next of kin and not involve payment, and (10) clearly explain ultimate disposition of the body.

Clearly the wishes of the living as to how their mortal remains are to be treated and used in a religious, social, and medical framework are paramount; Wicclair (2002) gives reasons for facilitating advance decision-making in relation to any form of post-mortem research. One reason Wicclair (2002) provides for why one should have control over our bodies is that one has a special relationship with it; events and actions that affect 'my' body also in some sense affect 'me'. The point made is that while we cease to be a person when we die, our body continues to exist on after our death and because we can anticipate how our body should be treated after our death, we have a distinctive and enduring relationship with it. This may provide a sufficient reason to extend a right to control what happens to one's body in advance of death. Wicclair (2002) provides additional reasons to facilitate advance decision making in anticipating the use of bodies for post-mortem research. Firstly, it provides individuals with the opportunity to act altruistically. Secondly, advance decision-making frees-up family members at a time when they are grieving the loss of a loved one. For Wicclair (2002), advance decision-making does not preclude the need to seek consent from family members when they have not made a pre-mortem decision. There are two important respects in which family members can consent, which can serve to protect the dead. First, consent can be used to protect the deceased's body from being used for research that is incompatible with the person's pre-mortem preferences and values. Secondly, consent can be used to protect the deceased's body from being subject to disrespectful treatment (Tomasini 2008).

16.6 The Ethics of Blood and Organ Donation

In considering the ethics and morality of the use of donated human cadavers in a forensic taphonomy context we should look to the experiences of other models, such as the medical model of body donation for medical dissection and learning, and also the model of human donation of human organs for transplantation. The use of blood for donation has been widely accepted as an almost obligatory gesture for over a century with the first recorded successful donation in 1818.

It is the recommendation of the World Health Organisation, endorsed by all member states, that all blood donations should be voluntary and non compensated, ethically coherent, and realisable in practice (World Blood Organisation 2012). Farrugia et al. (2010) have argued for a plurality of both compensated and non-compensated systems, claiming that, from both an ethical and practical perspective, the classical concept of the 'the gift relationship', advocated over 40 years ago by Titmuss (1970), is unnecessary and inadequate. However, this is where the dichotomy begins. If there is a need for the large volumes of blood worldwide there is an argument for payment for blood donation, therefore should this not equally apply to the donation of human cadavers? A reasoned argument against this is that blood and its products can be given without the death of the donor; the donation of a body cannot, and thus body donation should be set aside from other forms of Titmussian-driven donations in which the donor may remain living, and this should be separated from the considerations of forensic taphonomy donation. However, in recent years, there has also been the suggestion of a 'halfway-house' measure, where human tissue from surgical procedures such as appendectomies, biopsies, and amputations could be used for decomposition research and the training of human remains detection dogs (Evans 2016). This would mean that living people could donate to forensic decomposition research, and potentially see the effects of the results, within their lifetime.

Much has been reported on the ethics associated with the donation of organs by living donors (Troug 2005). Three categories of donation by living persons can be distinguished: 'directed donation' to a loved one or friend, 'non-directed donation', in which the donor gives an organ to the general pool to be transplanted into the recipient at the top of the waiting list, and 'directed donation to a stranger', whereby donors choose to give to a specific person with whom they have no prior emotional connection. Each type of donation prompts distinct ethical concerns, but whilst there is still debate about these issues, the worldwide use of donated organs has saved many lives, with the 'Global Observatory on Donation and Transplantation' showing over 120,000 transplants annually (Global Observatory on Donation and Transplantation 2018).

Although donor organ transplantation is now routine, but was once hotly debated (Joralemon 2001), the discussion surrounding options such as: 'mandated choice' (individuals would have to indicate their wishes regarding organ transplantation, perhaps on income tax forms or driver's licenses), 'presumed consent' (citizens' organs are taken after they die, unless a person specifically requests to not donate while still living), incentives (paid funeral costs for example), or indeed the use of prisoners, still continues.

16.7 Ethics of Donation to a Human Taphonomy Facility

There is currently precedent for the use of donated human cadavers in a forensic taphonomy environment. This in itself is not a moral directive or imperative to argue for the creation of a framework in the UK, but clearly these existing frameworks in the USA, Australia, and Europe suggest that our social, moral, and ethical concerns may be addressed by such precedents. As previously mentioned, it would appear to be extremely valuable to have a UK-based HTF, due to our unique island climate, depositional environments, soil and bedrock types, insects, and scavengers, which make it difficult to compare results with data from HTFs in other countries. Even the HTF in The Netherlands, close to the UK geographically, has different soil, climatic, and ecological conditions to the UK. For example, ARISTA is placed in very sandy soil with shell inclusions, is four metres below sea level, and is subject to different scavengers (Oostra 2018, pers. comm.; see footnote 1).

Let us consider the aspect of informed consent as it is used in research currently, and how it is used in the living donation of bodies for existing taphonomy facilities. Research has almost universally been treated with suspicion and even hostility by the vast majority of all those concerned with the ethics and regulation of research (Harris 2005). The so-called "precautionary approach" sums up this attitude, requiring dangers to be considered more likely and more serious than benefits, and assuming that no sane person would or should participate in research unless they had a pressing personal reason for so doing, or unless they were motivated by a totally impersonal altruism. International agreements and protocols, such as the Declaration of Helsinki (World Medical Association 2013) and the Council for International Organisations of Medical Sciences (2016) Guidelines have been directed principally at protecting individuals from the dangers of participation in research and ensuring that, where they participate, their full informed consent is assured. The overwhelming presumption has been and remains that participation in research is a supererogatory, and probably a reckless act, not an obligation.

Each Human Taphonomy Facility in the USA, Australia, and Europe has clear guidelines for the living before the donation of their body. As Harris (2005, 246) has observed, a new principle of research ethics suggests itself as an appropriate addition to the Declaration of Helsinki: "Biomedical research involving human subjects cannot legitimately be neglected, and is therefore both permissible and mandatory, where the importance of the objective is great and the possibility of exploitation of fully informed and consenting subjects is small".

Whilst Harris did not write this with taphonomy explicitly in mind, the sentiment fits perfectly. The exploitation of fully informed consenting subjects indicates that their use in taphonomy facility is "permissible". It is this recognition by Harris (2005) of the obligation to show equal concern and respect for all persons, which is the defining characteristic of justice. The recognition that the obligation to do justice applies not only to research subjects but also to those who will benefit from the research must constitute an advance in thinking about international standards of research ethics. The use of human material for such forensic research actually facilitates the development and the improvement in the ethical framework for working with the deceased.

When opening the Australian Facility for Taphonomic Experimental Research (AFTER) in 2016, Shari Forbes stated that the ethical use of donated human cadavers for scientific studies was vital for the success of human death investigations here and overseas, including neighbouring countries where Australia sent emergency response teams in times of disaster. She stated that: "The scientists and police involved in this research are confronted by death on a regular basis and understand the moral and ethical significance of working with human cadavers, just like doctors and medical students" (Crofts 2016).

Let us consider the family of the donor after death. Thompson (2006) is defensive of the idea that "the wishes of the deceased" are less deserving of respect than the wishes of surviving relatives and thus may be discarded. It is, however, confusing to speak of the wishes of the dead or deceased (or, alternatively, of the right of the "living dead") and to use this claim as the starting point to morally weigh the significance of such wishes. The dead have no wishes to be disrespected. Rather, what is at stake is the right of the living to decide in advance how they should be treated when dead, and the question of whether that prior decision should be respected after the person has died.

Thompson (2006) argues that the default position, that testamentary wishes should be respected to a certain degree, is limited only in those cases in which honouring these prior wishes would disrupt other values or judicial requirements without any counterbalance. An example given is a desire to display one's decomposing cadaver in a public area as an artistic statement, which would disrupt the tradition-bound value of properly putting a body to rest, and is not counterbalanced by the satisfaction that would result from such exposure. This does not mean, however, that there are no circumstances under which one's cadaver can be publicly exposed. The contrary is an example that there can be very good reasons for doing so. In a taphonomy facility, a body may lay in the open as a source of information for the science of decomposition. The results of which may permit a more accurate understanding of the process of decomposition and thus a more precise determination of the time of death; such an outcome necessary to the development of the science and crucial to crime solving counterbalances the issues of tradition bound values.

All UK medical schools welcome the offer of a body donation. However, certain medical conditions may lead to the offer being declined. Medical schools do offer information about which conditions and any other reasons why a body donation may be declined. A HTF would be able to accept donations from donors with amputations, tumors, and other conditions that would usually exclude them from being accepted for body donations programmes in medical schools. The authors have been approached by many members of the public hoping to donate their bodies to a HTF as a result of this rejection from medical schools. The potential to donate to a Human Taphonomy Facility may mean that those wishing to bequeath their bodies to science may be able to have their wishes granted after all.

There is a cogent argument to be raised against the forensic science community —if the public are not comfortable with a surgeon who has only completed their surgical training on models and porcine cadavers, why then would the public or the Criminal Justice System have trust and confidence in forensic scientists giving evidence in human case trials where they had only ever researched on animal (porcine) cadavers?

The HTF must live up to the Daubert Standard to be scientifically sound (Daubert v. Merrell Dow Pharmaceuticals Inc. 1993). This standard was used by a trial judge to make a preliminary assessment of whether an expert's scientific testimony was based on reasoning or methodology that was scientifically valid and could be properly applied to the facts at issue. Under this standard, the factors that may be considered in determining whether the methodology is valid are: (1) whether the theory or technique in question can be and has been tested, (2) whether it has been subjected to peer review and publication, (3) its known or potential error rate, (4) the existence and maintenance of standards controlling its operation, and (5) whether it has attracted widespread acceptance within a relevant scientific community. Therefore, without rigorous research being conducted and subsequently published in scientific peer-reviewed journals, the data for many aspects of forensic specialisms associated with human taphonomy risk being unheard, disregarded or challenged, and found wanting within a courtroom where they may have been able to make a valuable contribution.

16.8 Day to Day Running of a Human Taphonomy Facility

The funding of a HTF is another area for ethical consideration. Previous attempts to establish a HTF in the UK using private funding failed, due, in part, to reservations (on behalf of universities, other users, and investors) about the potential profit-making potential of such a facility. Of course, such a facility would have to be self-sufficient, but it is ethically dubious to be seen to be making profit from research based on donated human cadavers. Indeed, if potential donors thought that their bequests might be directly or indirectly used to make profit, it would undoubtedly put them off. Instead, it needs to be made emphatically clear that a HTF in the UK, if it was established, would not be a profit-making organisation, but operate more like a charity. Any profits made from conferences, training courses, or similar would be used for research purposes, to propel the societal benefits of the research.

The day to day running of a facility in the United Kingdom has yet to be fully identified, yet it is clear, as with other controversial institutions (e.g. the nuclear power industry), that allowing the public access to its transparent working and its value and safety will allow its raison d'être and its outcomes to be fully understood and appreciated. Whilst undoubtedly difficult, sensitive engagement with the public would be necessary to ensure that the purposes and research carried out at the HTF are accepted and understood, and that donations are sustained through careful reporting of research outcomes. It is likely that body donations would not happen directly at the site of a Human Taphonomy Facility, but instead at an affiliated Medical School which has an existing body donation programme. As is the practice in medical schools, it is expected that there would be an annual memorial service for the families of donors.

The management of the press and publicity of the site would need to be managed carefully by the organisers of any HTF in the UK. The vast majority of media attention focused on existing HTFs in other countries has been positive (Power 2015; Oriti 2017). The HTF in Amsterdam has received no negative publicity at all (Oostra 2018, pers. comm.; see footnote 1). There may be a tendency for the press to sensationalise and influence the public's perception of the research carried out at a HTF, so it is important that the societal benefits of such research are emphasised, so that the public is presented with a sensitive account that does not spark controversy or offence. The precious gift given by the donors should also be recognised, lauded, and celebrated.tag

16.9 Public Opinion

Research conducted by some of the authors has investigated public opinion into Human Taphonomy Facilities in general (Witt and Cassella 2015), and one in the UK in particular (Blamire and Williams 2017) has found overwhelming public support for the concept of HTFs. Blamire and Williams (2017) conducted an online survey open to anyone, advertised using social media, and gained over 500 responses. Initial results show that 76.6% of respondents replied 'strongly agree' to the question 'Do you support the development of a HTF in the UK?'. Issues that might potentially be expected to be problematic from an ethical stand point did not seem to cause concern to the respondents. In response to the statement 'A HTF would be disrespectful to the deceased', only 1.8% of respondents strongly agreed, 6.8% were neutral, and 73.4% strongly disagreed. Of course, these results may be skewed as respondents were self-selected as people interested in the subject, and the online questionnaire did not necessarily capture the views of the general public. However, as these are the only attempts to garner public opinion on this subject to date, they represent the best insight available into the public perception of HTFs.

Some academics in the discipline have expressed concern about how HTFs have been portrayed in the media, conscious of the tendency towards sensationalism that often accompanies journalism in popular media outlets, and wary of how this may influence public opinion. For example, Black (2017, 475) states that "…the first interaction that the public may have with this important research topic is wrapped in a frisson of sensationalism that will inevitably color that first impression. There is no doubt that decomposing rabbits and pigs are much less emotive than decomposing humans, and perhaps by permitting perpetuation of the rhetoric and exposure, we have secured a spectacular own goal". It is true that certain media publications have sullied the recognition of the potential benefits of a HTF through their sensationalist reporting (Slater 2017; Tingle 2017), but, on the flip side, it is clear that these media features have raised awareness of the existence and purpose of HTFs, encouraged debate and engagement in the possible research, stimulated a flurry of promises of bequests, and helped to lift the taboo that exists in the UK about discussion of after-death options. In light of the research carried out regarding public opinion, it could even be argued that the media coverage surrounding HTFs in the UK and abroad has encouraged support from the majority of respondents (Wordsworth 2016; Oriti 2017).

16.10 Conclusion

The bioethical considerations discussed here demonstrate the complexity of the situation of using human cadaveric material in such a forensic context. The disparity in the concerns expressed by some stakeholders between the accepted use of cadavers for medical training, human transplantation, automobile accident reconstructions, and general scientific endeavour seem at odds with the discouraging noises made about a Human Taphonomy Facility. The individual choice of a donor to donate their body after death for such forensic research, in the light of the existing uses in other areas of medically-based research, clearly suggests that there should not be any ethical barriers to the use of donated human cadavers for forensic research in the United Kingdom. There are no legislations preventing such donations, and no laws would be broken by the use of such donated material, especially if their use and treatment can be clearly regulated, monitored, and audited within the current legislation of the Human Tissue Act (2004).

The facility that could be created in the United Kingdom could provide an opportunity to engage researchers and law enforcement at both a national and international level. If managed correctly, by taking care to emphasise the scientific and societal benefits to the public, and maintaining open and transparent dialogue with the public about the fate of bequests, it is our opinion that a HTF in the UK would boost forensic science, and make significant contributions to other related disciplines. Moreover, we believe it would bring forensic science research in the UK fully up-to-date with countries that already have HTFs, and would allow direct comparisons between specimens in different climatic conditions and depositional environments. Finally, it would demonstrate the UK's commitment to improving forensic identification methods, and obtaining justice for victims of crime in the UK and abroad.

References

Alapo, L. 2016. Humans-Pigs-Rabbits Decomposition Study to Impact Court Cases Worldwide. *Tennessee Today*. 27 April. https://news.utk.edu/2016/04/27/humanspigsrabbits-decomposition-study-impact-court-cases-worldwide/. Accessed 10 May 2018.

Animal Free Research UK. 2018. *Mission, Vision, Values*. https://www.animalfreeresearchuk.org/mission-vision-values/. Accessed 11 May 2018.

Augenstein, S. 2016. Decomposition Rates Between Humans, Pigs May Vary Wildly. *Forensic Magazine*. 5 March. https://www.forensicmag.com/article/2016/05/decomposition-rates-between-humans-pigs-may-vary-wildly. Accessed 10 May 2018.

Bachmann, J., and T. Simmons. 2010. The Influence of Preburial Insect Access on the Decomposition Rate. *Journal of Forensic Sciences* 55: 893–900.

Black, S. 2017. Body Farms. *Forensic Science, Medicine and Pathology* 13 (4): 475–476.

Blamire, J., and A. Williams. 2017. *What Does the Public Think About the Development of an HTF in the UK?* Presented at "Does the UK need a 'Body Farm'?" Public Seminar, UCL, 13 June 2017.

Buffington, S., G. Di Prisco, T. Auchtung, et al. 2016. Microbial Reconstitution Reverses Maternal Diet-Induced Social and Synaptic Deficits in Offspring. *Cell* 165 (7): 1762–1775.

Bytheway, J.A., M. Connor, G.R. Dabbs, et al. 2015. The Ethics and Best Practices of Human Decomposition Facilities in the United States. *Forensic Science Policy and Management: An International Journal* 6 (3–4): 59–64.

Carter, D.O., D. Yellowlees, and M. Tibbett. 2007. Cadaver Decomposition in Terrestrial Ecosystems. *Naturwissenschaften* 94: 12–24.

Carter, D.O., D. Yellowlees, and M. Tibbett. 2008. Cadaver Decomposition and Soil Processes. In *Soil Analysis in Forensic Taphonomy: Chemical and Biological Effects of Buried Human Remains*, ed. M. Tibbett and M.O. Carter, 29–52. Boca Raton: CRC Press.

Connor, M., C. Baigent, and E.S. Hansen. 2017. Testing the Use of Pigs as Human Proxies in Decomposition Studies. *Journal of Forensic Science* 62 (5). https://doi.org/10.1111/1556-4029.13727.

Council for International Organizations of Medical Sciences. 2016. *International Ethical Guidelines for Health-related Research Involving Humans*. Geneva: Council for International Organizations of Medical Sciences.

Crofts, C. 2016. Australia's First Body Farm Flooded with Donations. *National Geographic*. 15 April. http://www.nationalgeographic.com.au/science/australias-first-body-farm-flooded-with-donations.aspx. Accessed 11 February 2018.

Cross, P., T. Simmons, R. Cunliffe, et al. 2010. Establishing a Taphonomic Research Facility in the United Kingdom. *Forensic Science Police and Management* 1: 187–191.

Daubert v. Merrell Dow Pharmaceuticals Inc. 509 U.S. 579. 1993.

Dean, D.E., L.J. Kohler, G.C. Sterbenz, et al. 2012. Observed Characteristics of Suicidal Hanging: An 11-Year Retrospective Review. *Journal of Forensic Sciences* 57: 1226–1230.

Dent, B.B., S.L. Forbes, and B.H. Stuart. 2004. Review of Human Decomposition Processes in Soil. *Environmental Geology* 45: 576–585.

Dick, H.C., J.K. Pringle, K.D. Wisniewski, et al. 2017. Determining Geophysical Responses from Burials in Graveyards and Cemeteries. *Geophysics* 82: B245–B255.

Enserink, M. 2017. Amsterdam to Host Europe's First 'Forensic Cemetery'. *Science*. 23 January. http://www.sciencemag.org/news/2017/01/amsterdam-host-europes-first-forensic-cemetery. Accessed 12 July 2017.

Evans, M. 2016. Body Parts Left Over from Operations Should be Used to Help Train Police Dogs. *The Telegraph*. 3 February.

Farrugia, A., J. Penrod, and J.M. Bult. 2010. Payment, Compensation and Replacement—The Ethics and Motivation of Blood and Plasma Donation. *Vox Sanguinis* 99: 202–211.

Fiedler, S., J. Breuer, C.M. Pusch, et al. 2012. Graveyards: Special Landfills. *Science of the Total Environment* 419: 90–97.

Forbes, S. 2017. Body Farms. *Forensic Science, Medicine and Pathology* 13 (4): 477–479.

Global Observatory on Donation and Transplantation. 2018. *WHO-ONT*. http://www.transplant-observatory.org/. Accessed 10 May 2018.

Haglund, M.H., and W.D. Sorg. 1997. *Forensic Taphonomy: The Postmortem Fate of Human Remains*. Boca Raton: CRC Press.

Hansen, J.D., J.K. Pringle, and J. Goodwin. 2014. GPR and Bulk Ground Resistivity Surveys in Graveyards: Locating Unmarked Burials in Contrasting Soil Types. *Forensic Science International* 237: e14–e29.

Harris, J. 2005. Scientific Research is a Moral Duty. *Journal of Medical Ethics* 31: 242–247.

Heaton, V., A. Lagden, C. Moffatt, et al. 2010. Predicting the Post-Mortem Submersion Interval for Human Remains Recovered from UK Waterways. *Journal of Forensic Sciences* 55: 302–307.

Hrala, J. 2016. Human 'Body Farm' Reveals We Need to Stop Using Pigs to Establish Time of Death. *Science Alert*. 17 June. https://www.sciencealert.com/pigs-may-not-be-the-most-amazing-forensic-tool-after-all-finds-body-farm-researchers. Accessed 2 July 2018.

Human Tissue Act. 2004. The Stationery Office, London.

Joralemon, D. 2001. *Shifting Ethics: Debating the Incentive Question in Organ Transplantation.* 27 (1): 30–35.

Killgrove, K. 2017. Forensic 'Body Farm' Opens in Florida—Becomes Seventh in US. *Forbes*. 28 February. https://www.forbes.com/sites/kristinakillgrove/2017/02/28/new-body-farm-opens-in-florida-becomes-7th-in-u-s/#ed4d84828645. Accessed 12 July 2017.

Knobel, Z., M. Ueland, K.D. Nizio, et al. 2018. A Comparison of Human and Pig Decomposition Rates and Odour Profiles in an Australian Environment. *Australian Journal of Forensic Sciences* 16 (1): 1–16.

Larson, D.O., A.A. Vass, and M. Wise. 2011. Advanced Scientific Methods and Procedures in the Forensic Investigation of Clandestine Graves. *Journal of Contemporary Criminal Justice* 27: 149–182.

Lynch-Aird, J., C. Moffatt, and T. Simmons. 2015. Decomposition Rate and Pattern in Hanging Pigs. *Journal of Forensic Sciences* 60: 1155–1163.

Matuszewski, S., M.J.R. Hall, G. Moreau, et al. 2019. Pigs Versus People: The Use of Pigs as Analogues for Humans in Forensic Entomology and Taphonomy Research. *International Journal of Legal Medicine*, 1–18. https://doi.org/10.1007/s00414-019-02074-5.

National Commission for the Protection of Human Subjects of Biomedical and Behavioral Research. 1978. *The Belmont Report: Ethical Principles and Guidelines for the Protection of Human Subjects of Research*. DHEW Publication No. (OS) 78-0014. Washington, D.C.: U.S. Department of Health, Education, and Welfare.

Oriti, T. 2017. Forensic Scientists Overwhelmed by Number of Donors to NSW Body Farm. *ABC News*. 12 May. http://www.abc.net.au/news/2017-05-12/forensic-scientists-at-body-farm-overwhelmed-by-number-of-donors/8520058. Accessed 1 February 2018.

Pentz, R.D., C.B. Choen, M. Wicclair, et al. 2005. Ethics Guidelines for Research with the Recently Dead. *Nature Medicine* 11: 1145–1149.

Power, J. 2015. Australia's First Body Farm: More Than 30 People Offer to Donate Their Corpses. *The Sydney Morning Herald*. 12 April. https://www.smh.com.au/national/australias-first-body-farm-more-than-30-people-offer-to-donate-their-corpses-20150408-1mgod0.html. Accessed 10 May 2018.

Pringle, J.K., J.R. Jervis, D. Roberts, et al. 2016. Geophysical Monitoring of Simulated Clandestine Graves Using Electrical and Ground Penetrating Radar Methods: 4–6 Years. *Journal of Forensic Sciences* 61: 309–321.

Pringle, J.K., A. Ruffell, J.R. Jervis, et al. 2012a. The Use of Geoscience Methods for Terrestrial Forensic Searches. *Earth-Science Reviews* 114: 108–123.

Pringle, J.K., J.R. Jervis, J.D. Hansen, et al. 2012b. Geophysical Monitoring of Simulated Clandestine Graves Using Electrical and Ground Penetrating Radar Methods: 0–3 Years. *Journal of Forensic Sciences* 57: 1467–1486.

Rippley, A., N.C. Larison, K.E. Moss, et al. 2012. Scavenging Behavior of Lynx Rufus on Human Remains During the Winter Months of Southeast Texas. *Journal of Forensic Sciences* 57: 699–705.

Ruffell, A., J.K. Pringle, J.P. Cassella, et al. 2017. The Use of Geoscience Methods for Aquatic Forensic Searches. *Earth-Science Reviews* 171: 323–337.

Schultz, J.J. 2008. Sequential Monitoring of Burials Containing Small Pig Cadavers Using Ground-Penetrating Radar. *Journal of Forensic Sciences* 53: 279–287.

Schultz, J.J., M.E. Collins, and A.B. Falsetti. 2006. Sequential Monitoring of Burials Containing Large Pig Cadavers Using Ground-Penetrating Radar. *Journal of Forensic Sciences* 51: 607–616.

Simmons, T., P. Cross, R. Cunliffe, et al. 2010. The Influence of Insects on Decomposition Rate in Buried and Surface Remains. *Journal of Forensic Sciences* 55: 889–892.

Slater, A. 2017. Inside Australia's First Body Farm Where Rotting Corpses and the Thick, Pungent Smell of Death Fills the Air. *Mirror*. 25 June. https://www.mirror.co.uk/news/uk-news/inside-australias-first-body-farm-10684440. Accessed 10 May 2018.

Thompson, J. 2006. Relatives of the Living Dead. *Journal of Medical Ethics* 32: 607–608.

Thornton, L. 2017. Operation Ben Needham Turned to Texas Body Farm for Help with Clues Found on Kos. *The Mirror*. 23 July. http://www.mirror.co.uk/news/uk-news/operation-ben-needham-turned-texas-10858732. Accessed 25 July 2017.

Tingle, R. 2017. Inside the Body Farm: Gruesome Images Show Texas Institute Where Corpses are Left to Rot in Cages as Part of Scientific Research to Help Solve Crimes. *Daily Mail Online*. 15 December. http://www.dailymail.co.uk/news/article-5183149/Gruesome-images-inside-Texas-body-farm.html. Accessed 10 May 2018.

Titmuss, R.M. 1970. *The Gift Relationship: From Human Blood to Social Policy*. New York: The New Press.

Tomasini, F. 2008. Research on the Recently Dead: An Historical and Ethical Examination. *British Medical Bulletin* 85: 7–16.

Toms, C., C.B. Rogers, and L. Sathyavagiswaran. 2008. Investigation of Homicides Interred in Concrete—The Los Angeles Experience. *Journal of Forensic Sciences* 53: 203–207.

Troutman, L., C. Moffat, and T. Simmons. 2014. A Preliminary Examination of Differential Decomposition Patterns in Mass Graves. *Journal of Forensic Sciences* 59: 621–626.

Truog, R.D. 2005. The Ethics of Organ Donation by Living Donors. *New England Journal of Medicine* 353: 444–446.

Vass, A.A., W.M. Bass, J.D. Wolt, et al. 1992. Time Since Death Determinations of Human Cadavers Using Soil Solution. *Journal of Forensic Sciences* 37: 1236–1253.

Vass, A.A., R.R. Smith, C.V. Thompson, et al. 2004. Decompositional Odor Analysis Database. *Journal of Forensic Sciences* 49: 760–769.

Vass, A.A., R.R. Smith, C.V. Thompson, et al. 2008. Odor Analysis of Decomposing Human Remains. *Journal of Forensic Sciences* 53: 384–391.

Vidoli, G.M., D.W. Steadman, J.B. Devlin, et al. 2017. History and Development of the First Anthropology Research Facility, Knoxville, Tennessee. In *Taphonomy of Human Remains: Forensic Analysis of the Dead and the Depositional Environments*, ed. M.J. Schotsmans, N. Márquez-Grant, and S.K. Forbes, 463–475. Chichester: Wiley.

Wicclair, M. 2002. Informed Consent and Research Involving the Newly Dead. *Kennedy Institute of Ethics Journal* 12: 351–362.

Witt, I., and J.P. Cassella. 2015. *The Feasibility of a United Kingdom Human Taphonomic Research Centre (UKHTRC)*. http://www.blurb.co.uk/b/6632826-the-feasibility-of-a-united-kingdom-human-taphonom. Accessed 10 May 2018.

Wordsworth, M. 2016. Inside the Secret Australian Body Farm Helping Real-Life CSIs. *ABC News*. 18 October. http://www.abc.net.au/news/2016-10-18/australias-only-body-farm-helping-crime-scene-investigators/7939664. Accessed 1 February 2018.

World Blood Organisation. 2012. *Blood Donor Selection: Guidelines on Assessing Donor Suitability for Blood Donation*. http://www.who.int/bloodsafety/publications/bts_guideline_donor_suitability/en/. Accessed 11 February 2018.

World Medical Association. 2013. *Declaration of Helsinki: Ethical Principles for Medical Research Involving Human Subjects*. https://www.wma.net/policies-post/wma-declaration-of-helsinki-ethical-principles-for-medical-research-involving-human-subjects/. Accessed 10 May 2018.

Young, A., N. Márquez-Grant, R.A. Stillman, et al. 2014. An Investigation of Red Fox (Vulpes Vulpes) and Eurasian Badger (Meles Meles) Scavenging, Scattering, and Removal of Deer Remains: Forensic Implications and Applications. *Journal of Forensic Sciences* 60: S39–S55.

Young, A., R. Stillman, M.J. Smith, et al. 2015. Applying Knowledge of Species-Typical Scavenging Behavior to the Search and Recovery of Mammalian Remains. *Journal of Forensic Sciences* 61: 458–466.

Part III
Global Perspectives and Case Studies

Chapter 17
Ethical Perspectives in Forensic Anthropology and Museum Curation in the United States of America

Douglas H. Ubelaker and Haley Khosrowshahi

Abstract This chapter explores the concept of repatriation as related to forensic anthropology and museum studies. Forensic anthropology is the study of human remains in a legal and medical setting. While repatriation, the return of human remains, associated artefacts, and sacred objects to a native group is discussed globally, this chapter mainly focuses on the issues within the United States. In the United States, a rich history of repatriation has formed and continues to develop. For example, within the late twentieth century, new laws and protocols affecting museums and their collections have been enacted. The repatriation process emphasises education and communication of the various groups involved.

17.1 Introduction

Ethical issues are common to both forensic anthropology and museum curation of human remains. These issues involve public attitudes toward the dead, community definitions of proper respect, and the appropriate final disposition of human remains. While forensic anthropology and museum curation represent distinct areas of anthropological activity, they share the need for proper treatment of human remains and both work within legal and procedural frameworks. Webster's New World Dictionary of the American Language (Anonymous 1957, 499) defines ethics as "the study of standards of conduct and moral judgment…the system or code of morals of a particular …profession….". In casework and museum curation activities, forensic anthropologists continuously deal with ethical issues. Individual judgments dictate conduct and practices that collectively define professional ethics.

The work of forensic anthropologists concentrates on human remains that are usually skeletonised. Increasingly however, forensic anthropologists are also called

D. H. Ubelaker (✉) · H. Khosrowshahi
Smithsonian Institution, Washington, D.C., USA
e-mail: ubelaked@si.edu

H. Khosrowshahi
The George Washington University, Washington, D.C., USA

K. Squires et al. (eds.), *Ethical Approaches to Human Remains*,
https://doi.org/10.1007/978-3-030-32926-6_17

upon to address issues of fleshed remains and even the living. As noted by Blau (2009), the subject matter focus of forensic anthropologists is loaded with emotion and diverse points of view. This practice calls for conduct that is both reasonable and appropriate in each context. The recovery and identification process can have strong effects on survivors, especially families of the deceased (Williams and Crews 2003). Forensic anthropologists who work in museums or similar institutions face special ethical challenges relating to the collections in their care. This chapter explores aspects of the ethical challenges facing forensic anthropologists in both casework and museum curation.

17.2 Practices in Forensic Anthropology

Casework in forensic anthropology involves the analysis of human remains. Usually, these remains have been reduced to skeletons but occasionally fleshed remains are examined as well. The process begins with a briefing by authorities, search, and recovery. Search teams that pursue the location of human remains should include forensic anthropologists but usually involve other specialists as well. If remains are below the surface, excavation should feature the leadership of a forensic archaeologist. If remains are recovered, analysis can involve determining if human remains are present, assessment of age-at-death, sex, ancestry, living stature, time since death, taphonomic history, features useful for identification, and evidence of trauma. The analysis involves thorough documentation, security of all evidence, report writing and, if necessary, legal testimony (Ubelaker 1978; Pickering and Bachman 2009; Dirkmaat 2012; Tersigni-Tarrant and Shirley 2013).

Each step of this process requires ethical considerations (Webb 2006; Cassman et al. 2007; Kumar-Yadav 2017). In the search process, the anthropologist must ensure that appropriate professional roles are defined and all those involved adhere to them. Proper decisions are needed regarding permissions and the procedures and equipment utilised. Recovery is usually a destructive process requiring critical decisions on methods employed and the extent of documentation. As the process moves forward toward analysis, evidence must be protected with a documented chain of custody. In the laboratory, safeguards must be in place to maintain the integrity of the evidence and limit the possibility of error, loss, or contamination. Analysis techniques should be selected that address the problems presented and the nature of the evidence. Reports should accurately and clearly communicate the analysis results, summarise the bench notes, and fairly present the probabilities involved. Legal testimony must be truthful and accurately convey the results of the analysis.

Clearly, throughout the entire process from recovery to testimony, ethical decisions must be made to drive conduct in an appropriate manner. Each step frequently requires thoughtful, ethical judgment (Congram and Sterenberg 2009; Flavel and Barker 2009; Sterenberg 2009). While organisations and investigative units provide some guidelines, every forensic anthropologist must determine their personal moral conduct, even when it may conflict with procedures of the unit or organisation (Webb 2006). Examples of the need for personal ethical judgment include individual roles in larger organisations, cultural influences, problems of communication due to language differences, the proper role (extent of involvement and communication) of family members related to an investigation, recognising the limits of personal expertise, and the use of images and case-related information in public presentations. While some general ethical guidelines certainly can be defined, usually these contexts are highly variable and idiosyncratic, calling for case-by-case judgment.

The American Board of Forensic Anthropology (2017) and the Scientific Working Group in Forensic Anthropology (SWGANTH 2010) have issued a "Code of Ethics and Conduct". These documents include the following as ethical guidelines for forensic anthropologists:

- Education, training, experience, and area of expertise must be accurately conveyed;
- Refrain from misrepresentation of data, primarily related to report writing and testimony;
- Ensure that statements and conclusions are factually correct with a solid scientific foundation;
- Ensure impartiality with clear reporting of results;
- Refrain from using a contingency fee system;
- Ensure the appropriate information is kept confidential;
- Refrain from plagiarism and improper citation of the work of others;
- Avoid conflicts of interest that influence the quality and integrity of the work provided;
- Ensure that human remains are treated with respect and dignity;
- Attempt to maintain the integrity of all evidence;
- Ensure that data collection is appropriate and authorised;
- Avoid speculation and giving opinions outside of expertise;
- Ensure that individuals under supervision are appropriately trained.

17.3 Museum Curation

The practice of forensic anthropology and museum curation share many ethical issues regarding human remains. Primary shared concerns are the need to maintain appropriate confidentiality and to treat human remains with respect and dignity. However, the museum curation of human remains involves additional ethical issues. The display of human remains usually calls for careful consideration of context and message. Most members of the public are fascinated with the human skeleton and the information that can be derived from its scientific examination. Nearly everyone can relate to the topics of dental development, growth and maturation, age changes, disease affects, and health issues. Equally fascinating is how analysis of the skeleton can reveal secrets of the deep past and help solve modern forensic mysteries. However, other individuals may react negatively to the display of human remains for religious, cultural, psychological, or other reasons. Those involved in museum exhibition planning need to be sensitive to these public reactions. If human remains are included in museum displays, presentations should be tasteful, educational, and respectful, and not reveal any individual identities without proper permissions. This issue is especially important in displaying remains representing particular native groups. Vaswani (2003) provides an important perspective on these issues building on guidelines and public opinion polls conducted in the UK.

Museum curation of human remains also involves the assessment of proper storage conditions, research access, controls of specimen data and images, and conservation. Curation seeks to provide long-term care and preservation of human remains within museum custody. However, approved researchers must be provided access to these collections and given the opportunity to handle, examine, measure, and otherwise collect the necessary scientific data. The need to provide access and the use of collections must be appropriately balanced against the need for long-term preservation.

In recent years there has been a surge of research interest in destructive sampling of human remains (APABE 2013). New research techniques can involve analysis of elemental isotopes, DNA, dental calculus, bone histological structure, palaeopathological lesions, and other skeletal components that require destructive sampling. Some analytical equipment may not be available near the collection areas, calling for transport of fragile specimens. Such requests for destructive sampling present unique ethical challenges. The Department of Anthropology of the Smithsonian Institution's National Museum of Natural History maintains a destructive sampling committee to evaluate such requests. Researchers must submit a detailed proposal outlining the specific samples targeted, the rationale for the research, and the specific techniques to be employed. Requests are evaluated by the collection manager, as well as those curators with knowledge of the subject matter. The consensus opinion is then forwarded to the researcher making the request. Concerns usually centre on the need to sample the particular specimens requested, the nature of the technical analysis, the qualifications of the researcher, the research design, and the extent of sample destruction involved in the study. The Office of Repatriation carefully reviews any request that relates to remains associated with a particular native group. Although the Office of Repatriation is unique to the Smithsonian, other museums in the USA have similar processes for review and decision-making.

Repatriation represents another major ethical issue relating to museum curation (Jones and Harris 1998). Standard museum practice is to ensure that collections in curation have proper permissions and documentation. Such information may be questionable in some cases, especially with those collections that were acquired many years ago (Fletcher et al. 2014). When questions emerge, the usual process of evaluation involves careful assessment of the accession history and all relevant documents and communications. When the associated documentation does not produce clarity, oral history, and legal opinions may be incorporated as well. In recent years, particularly in the United States, museum custody of human remains has been challenged by Native American groups who argue that they have an ancestral relationship with individuals in some museum collections. Because of the ancestral connection, they believe they have the right to determine the proper custody and ultimate location of those remains. These concerns have led to specific policies and laws that are referred to as "repatriation" (Buikstra 2006a, 2006b). These developments are explored further in the remainder of this chapter.

17.4 History of Repatriation Issues in the United States of America

In the United States, the roots of the repatriation movement extend back to the 1970s in the Plains area of the country (Anderson 1982). In 1971, an archeological excavation in Iowa recovered the human remains of 27 individuals (Anderson 1982). Of these, the analysis revealed that 26 represented historic European pioneers and one represented a Native American. Local Native Americans protested when they learned of plans that called for the burial of the Europeans but the museum curation of the Native American. Eventually the remains of the Native American were buried.

Shortly after the aforementioned incident, remains of Native Americans were discovered, also in Iowa, during a commercial sand and gravel operation in 1972 (Anderson 1982). Media coverage and confrontation was stated to have resulted in violence with subsequent reburial of the remains on Rosebud Reservation in South Dakota. Although preliminary plans had included study of the remains followed by local burial, representatives of the American Indian Movement (AIM) intervened and took the remains to South Dakota (Anderson 1982). Continued commercial quarry activity resulted in the loss of information about the archeological site that had originally contained the remains (Anderson et al. 1978; Anderson 1982). The early confrontations in Iowa led to dialogue and a new state law was passed in May 1976. The resulting new law reduced confrontation and promoted cooperative projects (Anderson et al. 1983; Anderson 1985).

Subsequent years marked similar developments in other states with associated strong rhetoric. In July 1985, two individuals approached the Smithsonian Institution relaying concerns about Smithsonian collections of human remains of Native American origin. The visit led to Smithsonian officials opening a dialogue with Native American tribes and their representatives (Ubelaker and Grant 1989). Smithsonian Institution policy at that time included discussion and dialogue with all concerned parties (Ubelaker and Grant 1989). Deaccession and transfer were considered appropriate if remains could be individually identified or records indicated whether they were acquired illegally or unethically. Following this policy, in 1984, crania of identified individuals of the Modoc Tribe were transferred to their known descendants. Additionally, remains of individuals of the Blackfeet Tribe were transferred to tribal representatives after questions emerged regarding the validity of the title, meaning that it is not clear if the Smithsonian had legal ownership of this 1982 acquisition. In 1989, the Smithsonian Institution policy was expanded to allow deaccession and transfer to American tribes if the tribal origin of remains could be determined (Ubelaker and Grant 1989).

The 1970s and 1980s represent decades of difficult and, at times, tense exchanges among individuals and interest groups on the general repatriation issue. Too much has been written to summarise adequately here, but more details are available in the references provided throughout this chapter. However, in general, many in the Native American community expressed strong sentiment toward human remains, even relatively ancient ones and resented that these were held in museum collections (Bray and Killion 1994; Bray 2001). Many archeologists, physical anthropologists, and museum curators naturally felt that museum collections, even those of human remains, should be preserved for their scientific value and their potential to yield unique information about the individuals and populations they represent. However, these positions were not universally polar. Of course, the Native American community is diverse with ranging opinions on not only human remains but also the value of local history. Many anthropologists and museum administrators are sensitive to Native American concerns revealing differing views on the value of museum retention of collections or repatriation. At that time, the legal issues were complex and did not offer a clear path to decision-making in most cases. Complexities of the legal issues included the doctrine of standing to assert a claim (including tribal and representational standing) and claims of religious freedom. Discussions led to considerable federal and national policy statements, including those from the Department of the Interior, the National Park Service, the United States Forest Service, and the Advisory Council on Historic Preservation. Additionally, individual States passed burial legislation similar to that of Iowa, as discussed earlier. Details on individual state legislation are available in Ubelaker and Grant (1989, 275). Apart from the formal documents and laws generated, individual institution administrators have also made decisions regarding collections of human remains following discussions with concerned parties (Ubelaker and Grant 1989).

17.5 The Native American Graves Protection and Repatriation Act

In November 1990, the Native American Graves Protection and Repatriation Act (NAGPRA 1990) was passed by the United States Congress and became law with the signature of President George H. W. Bush. This new law resulted from extended discussion and debate regarding the many issues of concern. The book "The Future of the Past" (Bray 2001) and, in particular, the chapter "The Native American Graves Protection and Repatriation Act: Background and Legislative History" by Trope and Echo-Hawk (2001), as well as the book by McKeown (2012), provided detailed accounts of events leading up to this landmark legislation. Appendix two of the Bray (2001) volume presents the entire legislation language. Key terms such as "cultural affiliation," "Indian tribe," "associated funerary object," "sacred objects," "cultural patrimony," "right of possession," as well as "tribal land" are defined and then utilised in the legislation. The language of this legislation is too complex to be presented here. However, the document establishes ground-rules regarding the discovery and recovery of Native American remains and objects, inventory of these materials in museums and Federal agencies, communication of inventory results with relevant groups, and repatriation. The legislation also established a review committee and a grant mechanism to assist the process. Authorisation is provided for grants to be awarded to both Indian Tribes and museums.

The new law provided a solid framework to address the complex issues related to museum collections and repatriation. It also ushered in a new era of communication between museum personnel and the Native American community. As noted by Haas (2001), difficulties arise when the language of the law is applied to actual situations and objects. These complications are focused on the varied interpretations of what is "needed" regarding sacred objects, who represents a "traditional religious leader", and how far back into the past "cultural affiliation" can extend. While these are considered on a case-by-case basis, basically, tribes have to make the argument that objects present special qualities and are needed to revitalise important ceremonies (Haas 2001).

17.6 The National Museum of the American Indian Act

In 1989, the United States Congress passed the National Museum of the American Indian Act (NMAI 1989). This legislation initiated the new National Museum of the American Indian as part of the Smithsonian Institution in Washington D.C. It also required that the Smithsonian conduct an inventory of human remains and associated funerary objects in their collections, determine the cultural affiliation of these materials, and then transfer those collections to affiliated groups if requested to do so. The edited volume by Bray (2001) presents the language of this Act in full in Appendix 1. Akin to the NAGPRA legislation that followed a year later, the NMAI Act (1989) established a review committee and authorised funding to support the process.

Killion (2001) provides a thoughtful review of the impact of the Smithsonian legislation, at least by that date. He notes the considerable conflicts that resulted from varied interpretation of the language and the paucity of funding to address all of the issues. However, he also indicates how the Smithsonian Institution legislation and NAGPRA have changed the nature of institutional interaction with native peoples of the United States, which ushered in a new era of communication and, in many instances, collaboration. The new legislation established a process for communication and an opportunity for those concerned to work through differences and find reasonable solutions. As noted by Killion (2001), as a result of the legislation, anthropologists must carefully consider the historical record resulting in museum collections. Although Smithsonian communication with native groups on these issues and transfer of human remains preceded the legislation, both were greatly augmented. Due to the magnitude of the collections involved and the work required in the inventory and communication process, a Repatriation Office was established and staffed in 1991. Initially, this effort was administered by the Office of the Director of the National Museum of Natural History but subsequently, it was transferred to the Department of Anthropology. While the other anthropology staff regularly interact with the issues involved, the Repatriation Office personnel are dedicated solely to this purpose. Over the two decades since its inception, the work of this office and its staff has been remarkable. Detailed inventories and scholarly reports have been generated for each case. Communication with the American Indian tribal community has been continuous and timely. As noted by Killion (2001), in 1997 more than 60 tribal representatives travelled to the National Museum of Natural History in Washington D.C. to discuss various repatriation-related topics. The review committee has met regularly (twice each year) to discuss difficult issues and evaluate the process. The anthropology curatorial and collection management staff review reports and interact as needed on specific issues. While some repatriation issues have been contentious (Bray and Killion 1994) the process has gradually advanced. When the legislation was passed in 1991, approximately 18,400 sets of human remains thought to represent Native Americans were curated at the National Museum of Natural History. These remains constituted about half of the total collections of human remains in the museum (Bray and Killion 1994). In 2001, Killion noted that by that time, the Repatriation Office had received 80 requests from native groups with 53 repatriations completed involving the transfer of many sets of human remains and associated artefacts. A later report indicates that by 31 October 2014, an estimated 6007 individuals and many more artefacts had been made available for repatriation (Smithsonian Institution 2014). Arrangements for repatriation to native groups had been completed for the remains of 4323 individuals. By 2016, the National Museum of Natural History reported that 6148 individuals reflecting 5569 catalogue numbers had been deemed available for repatriation. The National Museum of the American Indian reported that by 2016, over 500 individuals representing over 200 catalogue numbers were also available for repatriation (Table 17.1).

17.7 Repatriation Impact

As noted above, repatriation legislation has resulted in the significant transfer of human remains of Native American origin from museum repositories to American Indian communities. While this represents a loss of potential scientific information, especially to future biological anthropologists, many positive impacts have been recorded as well. The repatriation era has ushered in enhanced communication and the positive sharing of perspectives (Swidler et al. 1997; Gulliford 2000; Mihesuah

Table 17.1 This table represents the human remains that were available for repatriation within the National Museum of Natural History (NMNH) and the National Museum of the American Indian (NMAI) during each of the specified calendar years and over the study period

	NMNH		NMAI	
	2011			
	2011	Overall	2011	Overall
Number of individuals	187	5743	49	418
Catalogue numbers	184	5117	22	248
	2012			
	2012	Overall	2012	Overall
Number of individuals	88	5828	6	463
Catalogue numbers	78	5292	3	262
	2013			
	2013	Overall	2013	Overall
Number of individuals	19	5847	46	547
Catalogue numbers	18	5307	14	256
	2014			
	2014	Overall	2014	Overall
Number of individuals	160	6007	2	594
Catalogue numbers	140	5447	1	259
	2015			
	2015	Overall	2015	Overall
Number of individuals	116	6123	0	549
Catalogue numbers	97	5554	0	257
	2016			
	2016	Overall	2016	Overall
Number of individuals	25	6148	26	528
Catalogue numbers	5	5569	23	242

The term human remains, in this case, refers to the remains of a person who is of Native American ancestry. This information was collected from the annual reports submitted to Congress by the Smithsonian Institution starting in 2011 (Samper 2011; Johnson 2012; Smithsonian Institution 2013, 2014, 2015, 2016a)

2000; Turner 2005; Watkins 2006; Turnbull and Pickering 2010; Colwell 2017). The bioarcheologist Larsen (2015) notes the loss of future data. However, he articulates three important principles "(1) the scientific community respect the perspectives and desires of living descendants, (2) descendants have the authority to control the remains of deceased relatives, and (3) when possible, human remains may be preserved for continued study and increased understanding of the shared human past" (Larsen 2015, 429).

The repatriation laws have required detailed inventory and data collection. In some cases, this has forced scientific attention toward collections that have been minimally analysed in the past. The scholarly repatriation reports that must be generated to evaluate possible cultural affiliation with existing groups result from careful research of archeological, historical, biological, and other records. These reports themselves represent very positive scholarly products that illuminate many aspects of both the collections and the history of the groups involved. The data generated from these inventories, skeletal analysis, and related research will be available for generations of future scholars. The entire effort brings renewed attention to these collections.

17.8 Standards

During the formative years of the repatriation movement in the United States, biological anthropologists noted many analyses and inventories of human skeletal remains were being conducted in museums and other repositories (Buiskstra and Ubelaker 1994). However, they also noted that formats for data collection varied enormously, with the result that many of the data collected were not directly comparable (Buikstra and Ubelaker 1994). This situation reflected long-term historical developments. In the early history of physical anthropology, scholars such as Johann Friedrich Blumenbach (1752–1840), Rudolf Martin (1864–1925), Aleš Hrdlička (1869–1943), and Earnest Albert Hooton (1887–1954) had developed and promoted standard approaches to data collection. While these standard protocols were religiously followed by these individuals and their students, gradually physical anthropology shifted data collection methodology towards more specific, problem-oriented approaches. Following this trend, those tasked with taking skeletal inventories in the late 1980s and early 1990s following repatriation pressures, utilised highly variable approaches. Jonathan Haas, of the Field Museum of Natural History in Chicago, addressed this issue by receiving a grant to convene a workshop in Chicago to determine what standard observations and measurements should be recorded from human remains during repatriation-related inventory (Buiskstra and Ubelaker 1994). The goal was to agree upon the most important standard procedures. The project leaders hoped that most colleagues would utilise them and the resulting data would be comparable. Colleagues were brought together in the workshop who not only represented experienced professionals, but who also had been trained in different academic universities and traditions. The resulting volume "Standards for Data Collection from Human Skeletal Remains" was published in 1994 (Buikstra and Ubelaker 1994). "Standards" had the ethical impact of reducing variation in the data recording process and providing a central source of measurements and observations that were deemed important. The volume is a direct, early product of the repatriation movement. On 12th October 2017, Google Scholar recorded 4440 scientific citations, suggesting that many scholars have found it useful for data collection in a standard format. The success and widespread use of the Standards volume (Buiskstra and Ubelaker 1994) stimulated a digital version called “Osteoware.” This software system, developed by scientists at the Smithsonian Institution’s National Museum of Natural History, is a programme to aid in the information recording related to remains being considered for possible repatriation (Smithsonian Institution 2016b).

17.9 Conclusion

Forensic anthropologists, especially those working internationally, and museum curators face a complex cultural landscape in defining guidelines for conduct. At the baseline, anthropologists must be truthful, give proper credit to others and be sensitive to diverse perspectives with regards to the treatment of human remains. In the museum context, there are now laws in the United States that dictate the process. However, this process is clouded by nuance in the wording and diverse interpretation regarding applications.

The field of forensic anthropology and museum curation have much to teach each other in respect to proper treatment of human remains. The practice of forensic anthropology seeks truth and justice, but also a sense of closure and respect for the impacted families of the deceased. In fact, much of the international work of forensic anthropologists is stimulated by a familial search for closure and information about their loved ones. While this need-to-know is focused on the immediate families of the missing person/deceased individual, it also extends to the relevant general community and/or region. The situation calls for excellent science, but also communication and education of the affected public.

Human remains curated in museums are subject to many of the same sentiments expressed in forensic practice. If remains in museums relate to identified individuals, the families and direct descendants of those individuals are likely to have strong feelings about them and should offer views on their ultimate disposition. With the repatriation movement, we have learned that such sentiment can be extended beyond immediate families to culturally affiliated Native American tribes. Concerns have been expressed from the general American Indian community regarding ancient remains. The problem here is that, because of their antiquity, the remains cannot be linked to a particular existing tribe. Of course, all human remains offer unique scientific information, but this value to science must be considered in the context of community sentiment.

Forensic anthropologists acknowledge the value of retaining human remains following analysis. Issues may arise calling for additional testing beyond what was originally conducted. Long-term retention not only enables such possible issues to be addressed, but recognises the dynamic and evolving nature of forensic science. New methodology, stimulated by emerging technology, may enable future analysis that is not currently possible. However, in the legal arena, decisions regarding retention are not made by the forensic anthropologists, but rather by the investigative authorities and/or legal system. The forensic anthropologist has the ethical obligation to inform truthfully those involved about the merits of retention, but others make the informed decision.

A similar process takes place in the museum context. The biological anthropologist museum curator has the ethical obligation to inform those concerned regarding the scientific value of curation and the merit of long-term retention. However, similarly to the forensic context, decisions regarding retentions are made by others. Such decisions are generated through a process of dialogue among concerned individuals, as outlined by law and driven by modern museum practice.

References

Advisory Panel on Archaeology of Burials in England [APABE]. 2013. *Science and the Dead: A Guideline for the Destructive Sampling of Archaeological Remains for Scientific Analysis*. Swindon: English Heritage and the Advisory Panel on Archaeology of Burials in England.

American Board of Forensic Anthropology. 2017. *Policies and Procedures Manual*. http://theabfa.org/wp-content/uploads/2017/06/ABFA-Policies-and-Procedures.pdf. Accessed 4 October 2017.

Anderson, D. 1982. *Indians and Anthropologists: The Development of Cooperative Programs in Iowa*. Paper Presented at the Eighty-First Annual Meeting of the American Anthropological Association, District of Colombia, Washington, D.C., USA, 7 December 1982.

Anderson, D. 1985. Reburial: Is It Reasonable. *Archaeology* 38: 48–51.

Anderson, D., M. Finnegan, J. Hotopp, et al. 1978. The Lewis Central School Site (13PW5): A Resolution of Ideological Conflicts at an Archaic Ossuary in Western Iowa. *Plains Anthropologist* 23: 183–219.

Anderson, D., D. Zieglowsky, and S. Schermer. 1983. *The Study of Ancient Human Skeletal Remains in Iowa: A Symposium*. Iowa City: Office of the State Archaeologist of Iowa.

Anonymous. 1957. *Webster's New World Dictionary of the American Language*. Cleveland: The World Publishing Company.

Blau, S. 2009. More Than Just Bare Bones: Ethical Considerations for Forensic Anthropologists. In *Handbook of Forensic Anthropology and Archaeology*, ed. S. Blau and D.H. Ubelaker, 457–467. Walnut Creek: Left Coast Press.

Bray, T. (ed.). 2001. *The Future of the Past—Archaeologists, Native Americans, and Repatriation*. London: Garland Publishing.

Bray, T., and T. Killion (eds.). 1994. *Reckoning with the Dead*. District of Columbia: Smithsonian Institution Press.

Buikstra, J. 2006a. History of Research in Skeletal Biology. In *Handbook of North American Indians. Vol. 3: Environment, Origins, and Population*, ed. D. Ubelaker, 504–523. District of Columbia: Smithsonian Institution.

Buikstra, J. 2006b. Repatriation and Bioarchaeology: Challenges and Opportunities. In *Bioarchaeology: The Contextual Analysis of Human Remains*, ed. J. Buikstra and L. Beck, 389–415. London: Elsevier.

Buiskstra, J., and D. Ubelaker (eds.). 1994. *Standards for Data Collection from Human Skeletal Remains*. Fayetteville: Arkansas Archaeological Survey.

Cassman, V., N. Odegaard, and J. Powell (eds.). 2007. *Human Remains: Guide for Museums and Academic Institutions*. Lanham: Altamira Press.

Colwell, C. 2017. *Plundered Skulls and Stolen Spirits*. London: The University of Chicago Press.

Congram, D., and J. Sterenberg. 2009. Grave Challenges in Iraq. In *Handbook of Forensic Anthropology and Archaeology*, ed. S. Blau, and D.H. Ubelaker, 441–453. Walnut Creek: Left Coast Press.

Dirkmaat, D.C. (ed.). 2012. *A Companion to Forensic Anthropology*. Oxford: Blackwell Publishing.
Flavel, A., and C. Barker. 2009. Forensic Anthropology and Archaeology in Guatemala. In *Handbook of Forensic Anthropology and Archaeology*, ed. S. Blau and D.H. Ubelaker, 427–440. Walnut Creek: Left Coast Press.
Fletcher, A., D. Antoine, and J.D. Hill (eds.). 2014. *Regarding the Dead: Human Remains in the British Museum*. London: The British Museum Press.
Gulliford, A. 2000. *Sacred Objects and Sacred Places—Preserving Tribal Traditions*. Boulder: University Press of Colorado.
Haas, J. 2001. Sacred Under the Law—Repatriation and Religion Under the Native American Graves Protection and Repatriation Act (NAGPRA). In *The Future of the Past—Archaeologist, Native Americans, and Repatriation*, ed. T. Bray, 117–126. London: Garland Publishing.
Johnson, K., and K. Gover. 2012. *Annual Report of the Repatriation Activities of the Smithsonian Institution 2012*. http://anthropology.si.edu/repatriation/pdf/Annual%20Report%20of%20the%20Repatriation%20Activities%20of%20the%20Smithsonian%20Institution%202012.pdf. Accessed 28 September 2017.
Jones, D., and R. Harris. 1998. Archaeological Human Remains—Scientific, Cultural, and Ethical Considerations. *Current Anthropology* 39 (2): 253–264.
Killion, T. 2001. On the Course of Repatriation—Process, Practice, and Progress at the National Museum of Natural History. In *The Future of the Past—Archaeologists, Native Americans, and Repatriation*, ed. T. Bray, 149–168. London: Garland Publishing.
Kumar-Yadav, P. 2017. Ethical Issues Across Different Fields of Forensic Science. *Egyptian Journal of Forensic Sciences* 7: 10.
Larsen, C. 2015. *Bioarchaeology: Interpreting Behavior from the Human Skeleton*. Cambridge: Cambridge University Press.
McKeown, C. 2012. *In the Smaller Scope of Conscience—The Struggle for National Repatriation Legislation, 1986–1990*. Tucson: The University of Arizona Press.
Mihesuah, D. (ed.). 2000. *Repatriation Reader—Who Owns American Indian Remains?* Lincoln: University of Nebraska Press.
National Museum of the American Indian Act (NMAI). 1989. Public Law 101-185, 20 United States Code 80q, 103 Stat. 1336, November 28, 1989. 101st United States Congress, Washington D.C.
Native American Graves Protection and Repatriation Act (NAGPRA). 1990. Public Law 101-601, 25 United States Code 3001 et seq., 104 Stat. 3048, November 16, 1990. 101st United States Congress, Washington, D.C.
Pickering, R., and D. Bachman. 2009. *The Use of Forensic Anthropology*, 2nd ed. Boca Raton: CRC Press.
Samper, C., and K. Gover. 2011. *Annual Report of the Repatriation Activities of the Smithsonian Institution 2011*. Washington, D.C.: Smithsonian Institution.
Scientific Working Group for Forensic Anthropology (SWGANTH). 2010. *Code of Ethics and Conduct*. https://www.cmu.edu/chrs/conferences/eppi/docs/Code%20of%20Ethics%20and%20Conduct.pdf. Accessed 4 October 2017.
Smithsonian Institution. 2013. *Annual Report of the Repatriation Activities of the Smithsonian Institution 2013*. http://anthropology.si.edu/repatriation/pdf/Annual%20Report%20of%20the%20Repatriation%20Activities%20of%20the%20Smithsonian%20Institution%202013.pdf. Accessed 28 September 2017.
Smithsonian Institution. 2014. *Annual Report of the Repatriation Activities of the Smithsonian Institution 2014*. http://anthropology.si.edu/repatriation/pdf/Annual%20Report%20of%20the%20Repatriation%20Activities%20of%20the%20Smithsonian%20Institution%202014.pdf. Accessed 28 September 2017.
Smithsonian Institution. 2015. *Annual Report of the Repatriation Activities of the Smithsonian Institution 2015*. http://anthropology.si.edu/repatriation/pdf/Annual%20Report%20of%20the%20Repatriation%20Activities%20of%20the%20Smithsonian%20Institution%202015.pdf. Accessed 28 September 2017.

Smithsonian Institution. 2016a. *Annual Report of the Repatriation Activities of the Smithsonian Institution 2016.* https://anthropology.si.edu/repatriation/pdf/Annual%20Report%20of%20the%20Repatriation%20Activities%20of%20the%20Smithsonian%20Institution%202016.pdf. Accessed 16 October 2017.

Smithsonian Institution. 2016b. *Osteoware—Standardized Skeletal Documentation Software.* https://osteoware.si.edu/. Accessed 31 October 2017.

Sterenberg, J. 2009. Dealing with the Remains of Conflict: An International Response to Crimes Against Humanity, Forensic Recovery, Identification, and Repatriation in the Former Yugoslavia. In *Handbook of Forensic Anthropology and Archaeology*, ed. S. Blau and D.H. Ubelaker, 417–425. Walnut Creek: Left Coast Press.

Swidler, N., K. Dongoske, R. Anyon, et al. (eds.). 1997. *Native Americans and Archaeologists—Stepping Stones to Common Ground.* Walnut Creek: AtlaMira Press.

Tersigni-Tarrant, M.A., and N.R. Shirley (eds.). 2013. *Forensic Anthropology: An Introduction.* Boca Raton: CRC Press.

Trope, J.F., and W.R. Echo-Hawk. 2001. The Native American Graves Protection and Repatriation Act: Background and Legislative History. In *The Future of the Past—Archaeologists, Native Americans, and Repatriation*, ed. T. Bray, 9–36. London: Garland Publishing.

Turnbull, P., and M. Pickering (eds.). 2010. *The Long Way Home—The Meaning and Values of Repatriation.* New York: Berghahn Books.

Turner, T. (ed.). 2005. *Biological Anthropology and Ethics—From Repatriation to Genetic Identity.* Albany: State University of New York Press.

Ubelaker, D.H. 1978. *Human Skeletal Remains: Excavation, Analysis, Interpretation.* Chicago: Aldine Publishing Company.

Ubelaker, D.H., and L. Grant. 1989. Human Skeletal Remains: Preservation or Reburial? *American Journal of Physical Anthropology* 32: 249–287.

Vaswani, R. 2003. *Attitudes Towards the Treatment and Return of Human Remains: A British Perspective.* Paper Presented at the International Congress of Anthropology Conference, Athens, Greece, 21–22 November 2003.

Watkins, J. 2006. *Contemporary Native American Issues: Sacred Sites and Repatriation.* Langhorne: Chelsea House Publishers.

Webb, J. 2006. Professional Ethics: Forensic Anthropology and Human Rights Work. Dissertation, Syracuse University.

Williams, E., and J. Crews. 2003. From Dust to Dust—Ethical and Practical Issues Involved in the Location, Exhumation, and Identification of Bodies from Mass Graves. *Croatian Medical Journal* 44 (3): 251–258.

Chapter 18
Culturally Sensitive and Scientifically Sound: Ethical Challenges of Human Osteology in Contemporary Archaeology in the United States of America

Rebekah Loveless and Brandon Linton

Abstract Native American remains found within the context of archaeology are a point of extreme controversy and have a mixed past. Many scientists view archaeological human remains as bodies of evidence containing exclusive information in which they are entitled to. Yet Native Americans believe their ancestral remains should be treated with dignity and desire the right to decide how these remains are treated. Cultural Resource Management (CRM) is a form of archaeology that primarily works as a mitigation measure for development projects. Human osteologists or bioarchaeologists working within CRM face a multitude of difficulties including the lack of standardised guidelines on how to identify and record Native American remains, legal obligations, and political influence. It is important for osteologists to understand the unique cultural and political climates in which they work, and not to exceed their personal and professional abilities. Consequences experienced by Native Americans when underqualified personnel conduct osteological analyses on ancestral human remains are all too common and can be detrimental to the repatriation process, as the identification of bone is what gives Native Americans the right to reclaim their ancestors. This chapter will therefore highlight the importance of adopting a holistic approach to ethical practice and conduct when working with human remains in CRM in the United States of America.

The original version of this chapter was revised: Citations have been corrected. The correction to this chapter is available at https://doi.org/10.1007/978-3-030-32926-6_31

R. Loveless · B. Linton (✉)
Loveless Linton, Inc., 1421 West Lewis St., San Diego, CA 92103, USA
e-mail: brandon@loveless-linton.com

K. Squires et al. (eds.), *Ethical Approaches to Human Remains*,
https://doi.org/10.1007/978-3-030-32926-6_18

18.1 Introduction

As anthropologists, we are responsible for the acquisition and dissemination of anthropological information whilst simultaneously following the principle of "Do No Harm" to both the living and deceased (AAA 2012). Anthropology often walks a fine line of being factually (scientifically) accurate and culturally sensitive. Doing what is humane and right by people or a culture is the ethical responsibility of any scientist that works within a living population. Working with ancestral remains of a living population takes an elevated degree of empathy and ethical conduct. In the state of California, where we work, and all over the Americas for that matter, there are very few situations where the excavation of human remains is little more than a scientific process and it is rarely a culturally conscious practice. For example, in 1997 Daphne Percy described the discovery of five Native American skeletons in Hamilton County, Ohio, and the difficulties faced by scientists in maintaining access to those human remains in light of the Native American Graves and Repatriation Act (NAGPRA), which was enacted in 1990. The aim of all scientific investigations that involve human remains is to obtain the maximum amount of information. However, these studies rarely consider the effects felt by living populations and the spiritual violations that result from Western studies; these are not seen as ethical and humane considerations, but rather an obstacle in their quest for knowledge. Historically, the majority of archaeological excavations in the Americas have focused on Indigenous populations and were typically performed by Western institutions without any regard for living populations who were (and still are) connected to the human remains. To this day, archaeological field schools offer programmes that focus on the excavation and/or study of Native American material cultural and human remains, for example, at Pinson Mounds State Archaeological Park in Tennessee (Colorado State University 2018) and Kampsville in Illinois (Arizona State University 2018). On a similar line, institutions and affiliated laboratories continue to use Native American remains as teaching specimens, but the status of consultation and efforts of repatriation are unknown to the authors. In section 18.6 of this chapter we discuss the variation of Native American cultural practices and how there is no one solution that is culturally appropriate for every Native American peoples; therefore the recommendations and requests for repatriation vary within and between states and cultural regions. Regardless, human remains that are recovered from these sites were once living individuals, connected to other beings by way of spirituality, land, or kinship. This relationship permeates through death and through time, and is what makes the relationships between ancestral remains and living populations of Native Americans so relevant. To discount this human connection in favour of scientific research is inhumane and, at the very least, an unethical practice within anthropology and Cultural Resource Management (CRM).

In the United States of America, the excavation of Native American remains generally occurs in the wake of development. Cultural Resource Management is the discipline of archaeology within a development setting and is the focus of the ethical discussion in this chapter. Academic archaeological projects are held to a standard that concentrates on the preservation and extraction of information and are performed at a pace that allows careful design and excavation of a site. Conversely, CRM is a fast-paced regulatory solution to the irreversible impact of development on archaeological remains. Regulatory laws, such as the California Environmental Quality Act (1970), and the Association of Environmental Professionals (2018) provide guidelines and check lists for initial evaluations to determine if archaeological material (or resources) will be, or has the potential to be, negatively impacted by any works that may take place (Remy 1999; Association of Environmental Professionals 2018). Consequently, mitigation requirements will be implemented and, ideally, archaeological and Native American monitors will be on-site during construction to identify any buried resources if they are unearthed. Historically and contemporaneously, the development of a site is permitted and implemented regardless of the presence of human remains. Many assume that there are laws that would prohibit the excavation of burials, when in practice there is little that can be done to protect Native American burials. Understanding the political and cultural climate of a project allows one to have a better understanding of the potential consequences that the identification of bone may have on a living population and is one of the most significant elements of practicing osteologists or bioarchaeologists in an archaeological context (see section 18.6 for further details).

In the field of CRM cultural competency is not something that is taught, or even addressed. Methodologies and guidelines that address how osteologists should identify Native American fragmented and cremated human remains in the field do not exist. Many of the texts that discuss the excavation and identification process of human remains are scholarly and provide reference material from controlled excavations and with the aid of laboratory tools (Brothwell 1981; Barker 1993; Bass 2005). Identifications that are conducted under CRM circumstances are affected by time constraints and are culturally sensitive. Once identified as human, there is significant variation in terms of the regulatory obligations and traditional cultural practices. Public agencies differ in their regulations, which consequently dictate how the remains are legally handled. Cultural traditions are more complex, with variables that differ by region, kin group, and the relationship between ancient remains and living populations; the latter of which recommend appropriate treatment of the remains according to their spirituality and traditions. Each project requires a unique recovery plan, and should follow standard practices that assure the ethical treatment of ancestral remains and the living population who are connected to them. Unfortunately, standard practices and professional qualifications have not been developed in CRM. It is up to the individual tasked with the identification of bone to develop their own ethical standards and not to compromise the integrity of the remains. It is imperative that osteologists, bioarcheologists, and any other individual that takes on this responsibility are aware and conscious of the history and the political climate in the locale in which they are working. They must also acknowledge their own professional limits (i.e. if they are qualified to undertake a specific task, such as the identification of human remains), understand the appropriate laws, and appreciate that there are living populations who are affected by each and every exhumation and identification.

Within California alone, there are numerous operating CRM companies, all with different ways of approaching and evaluating a site. However, this becomes extremely problematic when human remains are found. Although there are laws in California that address the identification of human remains (Health and Safety Code 1939; Public Resources Code 1939; California Environmental Quality Act 1970), they are vague and do not offer guidelines for how identifications should be made, nor do they have requirements for professional qualifications for individuals making the initial identification. Legislation and municipal codes are primarily concerned with the lawful identification of remains within a forensic context and are limited in addressing archaeological and Native American ancestral remains. Since the CRM industry is predominately privatised, each company uses a wide variety of exhumation methods as well as different criteria for determining whether bone is human or non-human. Furthermore, there is no standardised definition of what constitutes a qualified osteologist within the CRM industry. This consequently leads to a multitude of challenges, such as underqualified people making identifications, which can compromise the ability for Native peoples to reclaim their ancestors. In this chapter, we will discuss the impact that osteological analysis has on Native American communities, ethical challenges faced by osteologists or bioarchaeologists in the USA, and how the identification of human remains is much more than what is learned in the laboratory. This chapter will also emphasise the importance of the identification process as it ultimately determines the level of legal protection that ancestral remains will receive.

18.2 History and Context

Unlike traditional clinical forensic cases, Native American archaeological cases are heavily encumbered by socio-political challenges and the historical narrative of the relationship between Native American people and western culture. The relationship between science and Native American Nations has been one of distrust and deceit. Native American communities have been subjected to scientific and social scrutiny in inhumane ways and treated as sub-par human beings. Very few in the American archaeological community recognise that living Native American populations are connected to the sites and/or human remains they are excavating. As such, Native communities have been treated as outsiders with a distant and separate relationship, and are only allowed to participate in archaeological activities as interested third parties. This can be seen by the lack of Native American authorship or input in archaeological records and documents. Furthermore, archaeological excavations and the analysis of cultural material and human remains reopen painful wounds of generational trauma, displacement, genocide, ethnic cleansing, and loss (Tinker 1993; Smith 2015; Madley 2016). The consequences of colonisation have a ripple effect through generations. Colonisation stripped people of their culture and traditional knowledge, it forced the relocation of many people, and it reconfigured the cultural landscape of the Native American people (Duran and Duran 1995; Madley

2016). The cultural trauma is very relevant today and can be seen in the constant fight that Indigenous people have to endure to preserve what little material culture is left, and to regain control over their ancestral remains.

Consultation is a relatively new method of communicating with Native Americans that, in theory, recognise Native peoples as cultural groups that have patrimonial connections to the people and the land pre-colonisation. Prior to development, consultation is carried out between agencies, developers, archaeologists, human osteologists, bioarchaeologists, and Native peoples in an effort to exchange information regarding the development process and Native American concerns. However, the process of notification and method of exchanging information is innately flawed, and does not facilitate an opportunity for fair and meaningful conversations. For example, it does not obligate the developers or agencies to comply with any of the requests from the Native communities, nor give directive on what constitutes a consultation. In 1979, the Archaeological Resources Protection Act was the first federal law to mandate the consultation of affected Native Americans. Until then, Native Americans were primarily a subject of study and romanticised literature. As a result, Native Americans have been, and often continue to be, viewed as relics and extinct people who are treated as scientific specimens (Austin 1924; Percy 1997; Owsley and Jantz 2001).

Archaeology, by its very nature, is a field with a scientific agenda and is, essentially, a destructive process. Cultural Resource Management employs expedited archaeological methodologies that are focused on the salvage of archaeological remains and is structured to work within the fast-paced world of development. Pressure to speed up development and reduce the costs of a project is a constant burden felt by CRM companies. As one may expect, proper archaeological investigations are meticulous, time consuming, and are seldomly welcomed on any construction site. A common approach to a site with suspected buried archaeological remains is to monitor the site and to observe all earth moving activities for archaeological material. Upon discovery of any archaeological material or any archaeological features, the project is stopped until the discovery can be evaluated. Osteologists are generally only called to a site when bone is discovered during this process, and are responsible for identifying whether or not the remains are human and/or need to go through the legal identification process. The discovery of bone on a construction site can cause the project to slow down or be shut down for an undetermined amount of time. It is important to understand the consequences of CRM osteology, because the pressure to make a rapid identification can lead to unethical behavior, such as underqualified people conducting osteological analyses, quick and careless evaluations, the incomplete documentation of a site, and a number of other actions that not only discredit the profession as a whole, but do not offer the respect that ancestral human remains deserve (for examples, see section 18.6 of this chapter).

Historically, archaeological resources were not protected and developers did not consider the destruction of archaeological sites or the damage and/or displacement of any human remains from a site during their work. Federal and state laws, such as the National Historic Preservation Act (1966), California Environmental Quality Act (1970), National Environmental Policy Act (1970), and Archaeological Resources Protection Act (1979) now offer archaeological sites some level of protection (Neumann et al. 2010). Under legislative protection, archaeological sites undergo an evaluation process, which assesses the archaeological material and/or site against an established set of criteria. This subsequently determines its level of significance and whether they qualify for protection, mitigation, or no further action; for example, a site that is deemed to be "significant" will require protection or further study, and an "insignificant" site will not require any further study and may not qualify for any further protection (Association of Environmental Professionals 2018). This is a long and complicated process and is comprised of several evaluation stages, each of which assesses the individual characteristics of a site. These range from the aesthetics and surrounding environment of a site to the archaeology, and everything in between, as a means of establishing the potential impacts of a project on archaeological resources (Association of Environmental Professionals 2018). California is a pioneer in environmental protection. It has enacted formal legislation, such as the California Environmental Quality Act (1970), which places greater restrictions on projects that could potentially impact the environment or any environmental resource such as archaeological sites, biological habitats, and palaeontological fossils. The Act requires more stringent impact studies for many environmental resources, and demands more sustainable and preventative mitigation measures. Under the California Environmental Quality Act (1970), archaeological materials (including human remains) are classified as cultural resources and are included in the list of resources that must be evaluated for the level of impact caused by development.

The development of legal protection of Native American ancestral remains and homelands has been a painfully long and drawn out process, yet it continues to evolve. The implementation of NAGPRA (1990) gave Native Americans the legal right to claim the remains of their ancestors and funerary objects that were held within federally funded institutions, and to request their return to their culturally affiliated tribes. Despite its implementation almost three decades ago, NAGPRA (1990) continues to be resisted by many large institutions that want to maintain possession of ancestral remains in the name of science. Section 18.6 of this chapter will address this issue further, with discussions of infamous cases such as Kennewick Man, various examples from California (e.g. the dispute that involved the La Jolla Culture), and contemporary cases that continue to demonstrate the struggle between science and culture.

18.3 Know Your Limits and Legal Obligations

Professional qualifications (in human osteology or physical/forensic anthropology) and the experience and abilities of an osteologist are essential if human remains are to be identified with confidence. To date, there are no national guidelines regarding the qualifications or experience needed to conduct osteological analysis of archaeological human remains in the USA. This leaves the field open for errors, such as the misidentification of human remains. Most CRM companies do not have qualified osteologists as part of their core team, rather they have a staff member that is classed as the "most qualified" person to examine skeletal remains within the organisation. This individual may be highly qualified with the technical skills required to identify bone or it may be someone who took a human anatomy class in college, or anything in between. CRM companies are free to take advantage of the lack of standards and qualifications and can arbitrarily deem any member of their team as the "authority" on human remains. Only when bone is suspected to be human will an expert or the coroner be called out to make a legal identification. This unregulated environment, coupled with the fact that CRM companies are private and for profit, can result in the employment of underqualified individuals, and the consequent gross negligence of human remains and associated cultural material. Thus, the absence of an official framework of standards and qualifications means it is the responsibility of the individual making the initial identification to act with the highest level of integrity and ethics. Those working with human remains must acknowledge their own professional limits, understand the laws which they are working under, and possess the highest level of personal ethical standards when working in CRM. Nevertheless, the implementation of "required qualifications" for those tasked with analysing human remains would create a more ethical and proficient identification practice. In addition, it would improve the quality of professionals making the identification, improve the reputation of "osteologists" in the field by limiting the title to those who demonstrate proficient training and experience, and help Native American communities gain access to their ancestral remains. This would also help CRM companies and agencies because they would have standards to lean on and include in project requirements. Furthermore, the employment of qualified, ethical osteologists would greatly lessen the frustration experienced by Native American people when confronted with the impossible task of making alterations to their cultural practices when faced with the repatriation of human remains or cultural material.

When bone or teeth are found on archaeological sites, an initial identification is made in the field to determine if the remains are human, and whether further evaluation is needed. Establishing whether skeletal remains are human or non-human is important as it determines whether the bone and associated cultural material have the protection of the law or not, and also whether Native Americans have the right to claim an interest in the treatment of the remains (National Historic Preservation Act 1966; California Environmental Quality Act 1970; Association of Environmental Professionals 2018). The identification of human remains leads to a chain reaction of events that has legal implications and can greatly affect Native American groups by violation of cultural norms, spirituality, and denying descendants the right to lawfully and respectfully reclaim ancestral remains. If deemed necessary, a subsequent legal identification will then be carried out, at which point the Coroner's Office or Medical Examiner's Office is contacted. The identification of human remains by a coroner or medical examiner is required by law and ultimately determines whether an individual has Native American ancestry (Health and Safety Code 1939; California Environmental Quality Act 1970). However, many coroners and medical examiners do not regularly identify human remains if they are recovered from archaeological contexts, and are often unaware of the legal obligations required to perform this type of formal identification. In San Diego (California), we are fortunate enough to have an anthropologist with an American Board of Forensic Anthropology certification, but not all jurisdictions are as fortunate, and identifications are performed on a "case by case" basis. The following case study demonstrates the level of inconsistency in policy and practice pertaining to CRM osteology.

18.3.1 Operation Standardisation

In 2017, the authors performed an informal survey to establish the industry standard for identification protocols of osteological material in the states of California, New Mexico, Arizona, Colorado, and Washington (Loveless and Linton 2018). In this study, three CRM firms were chosen at random from each state. Law enforcement agencies from these states were also contacted. When contacting CRM firms, we requested to speak with a principal investigator or a member of staff who was able to discuss the process that was implemented when bone was discovered on development sites. Two questions were asked in a conversational format:

1. When you come across bone that is not obviously faunal, what is your company's procedure?
2. What, if any, laws are you following when implementing the above procedure?

Law enforcement agencies were asked similar questions:

1. When archaeologists find bone, what identification procedures are followed?
2. What laws are you following and/or enforcing regarding the identification process, notification of the related affiliated Native American groups, and repatriation of bone?

The results of the survey indicated that all initial discoveries were handled on a "case by case" basis. It was found that no interviewed subject, from a CRM company or law enforcement agency, had a written or common procedure for identifying human remains in a development setting. All subjects were aware of legal obligations, such as the California Environmental Quality Act (1970) and Native American Graves Protection and Repatriation Act (1990) but were unaware of what they were or how to systematically implement appropriate procedures when human remains were found. Legal representatives from law enforcement agencies always assumed that the CRM company hired a forensic anthropologist or someone with similar credentials to identify human skeletal remains. This assumption is also made by project developers, law enforcement, and environmental professionals. Forensic anthropologists go through an arduous process to certify as American Board of Forensic Anthropology (ABFA) qualified. They must demonstrate their qualifications as an individual who has the education, training, and hands-on experience to confidently perform the identification of human remains, death analysis, and testify in court as an expert witness, amongst other duties. With a legal obligation to the courts and ethical obligations to the dead and the public, forensic anthropologists are trusted to be ethical and accurate. While this is not an error proof system, it ensures that the person conducting identifications is qualified.

These conversations also revealed that each company has their own standards and qualification requirements that must be met by employees in order to carry out an initial osteological assessment of human remains. In some jurisdictions, the CRM companies had company specific qualifications set in house, but these were not part of their written policies that could be shared with the public. There were also inconsistent levels of understanding in terms of the legal responsibilities of the law enforcement agencies in all states contacted. Without a thorough understanding of legal responsibilities to archaeological Native American remains and the procedural training to respond to a discovery, coroners/medical examiner's and archaeologists are not able to efficiently and legally identify the remains. This highlights another common challenge faced in CRM; understanding legal obligations. This requires osteologists, or any person conducting an initial identification of human remains, to be proactive and to learn about the legal structure in which they work as this will facilitate the process of legal identification. There are laws that address identification and/or treatment of archaeological or historical human remains at all government levels: federal (National Historic Preservation Act 1966; National Environmental Policy Act 1970; NAGPRA 1990), state (Health and Safety Code 1939; Public Resources Code 1939; California Environmental Quality Act 1970), and local jurisdictions, such as the City of San Diego Historical Resources Guidelines (Office of the City Clerk, City of San Diego 2014). Depending on the agency, location, and funding, one or more laws may apply to a single project. At a minimum, all states and local jurisdictions are held accountable to federal legislation, such as the National Historic Preservation Act (1966), National Environmental Policy Act (1970), and NAGPRA (1990). Without getting into the depths of statutes and policies, being familiar with the project documents and mitigation measures ensures that the identification of human remains is performed within regulations and is legally defensible. Not only will this knowledge aid in the legality of the identification, but it also adds a layer of objectivity. Osteologists are not only held to a project's standards, but because they are handling human remains which have legal implications, they are obliged to understand and work within the law.

18.4 Identification

Any form of osteological analysis, in the context of archaeological remains, requires one foot in the scientific world and one foot in the socio-cultural world. Population variation not only applies to the morphological expressions exhibited on skeletal remains, but also to the cultural beliefs, expectations, and interactions between Native American populations and science. Although scientists working with and within cultural constructs are proficient and ethical, one must be aware of the active cultural relationship between living populations and skeletal remains, as no one solution can be shared across the hundreds of Native American communities. Native American tribes, bands, and kin groups have unique traditional cultures and do not share a congruent view on life and death. What is culturally appropriate for one group of Native peoples may be inappropriate burial practices or a violation of religion for another (Heizer and Elsasser 1980; Deloria 2003).

A common ethnicity does not equate to a common culture. There are many small cultural groups within large ethnic populations. As of October 2016, 109 federally recognised Native American tribes were recorded in California (National Conference of State Legislatures 2018), and many more non-federally recognised tribes, all of which are still eligible for consideration as a Most Likely Descendant (MLD). Thus, there are potentially over 109 different definitions of how to treat human remains in a respectful manner in California alone. Furthermore, there is an additional layer of familial and religious traditions within each tribe that may require the specific treatment of bone for repatriation in accordance with local traditions (Kroeber 1976; Bray 2001; Deloria 2003). This will be discussed further in section 18.6 of this chapter.

The first step in the identification process is to establish whether the remains are human or faunal. In most cases, the answer is not as simple as one would think. In the context of CRM, material has either been previously disturbed and fragmented by development or is being impacted by a new development. In addition to disturbance by previously unregulated excavations and desecration by development and farming, there is a long history of looting for university, museum, and private collections, as exhibited by the extravagant assemblages housed by museums across the United States and globally (Smithsonian National Museum of Natural History n. d.; Rogers 1963; Clewlow et al. 1971; Ferguson 1996; Jones and Harris 1998; Thomas 2000; Trope and Echo-Hawk 2001; National Park Service 2018). Unfortunately, Native American artefacts and skeletal remains were, and continue to be, prized by collectors and institutions alike. It is expected that many of the grave sites in North America have been disturbed, thus minimising the likelihood of finding complete skeletons.

It is also worth mentioning that funerary rites themselves can also lead to incomplete burials. Many Native American cultures practice cremation whereby material objects, animals, and other non-human elements are placed on the funerary pyre alongside the deceased (Kroeber 1976; Heizer and Elsasser 1980). The dearth of complete skeletons from burial contexts (either inhumed or cremated) and the variations in burial practices among Native American Nations requires osteologists to consider the condition and location of bone, and associated material, such as tools, shells, and faunal bone, when identifying fragments of bone. Identifying remains in a context of disturbance and fragmentation requires flexibility, confidence, and a transparent procedural system of identification. Fragmented remains are just as significant as an entire skeleton. The presence of human remains on a site is the trigger for a change in how the site is treated, no matter how small the fragment may be. Simply acknowledging the presence of bone is the first step. This may seem obvious, but when working on an active construction site that has been previously disturbed and littered with debris, it can be very difficult to identify small pieces of unburned or cremated archaeological bone.

Cultural factors are subsequently used as second-tier indicators as a means of establishing whether the remains may be human or not. Additional information, such as the form and aesthetics of the vessel used to hold the cremated remains, the cultural material placed with the cremation vessel, and location relative to habitation or village sites are examples of contributing factors in the identification process. Third-tier indicators are used when attempting to identify bone that does not have any clear morphological traits. Some key indicators include: areas of soil with a high density of utilitarian artefacts, dense midden soils, previously discovered human bone, and, in some cases, evidence of burned material. In San Diego, separate burial plots or cemeteries were not employed in traditional burial practices (Kroeber 1976; Heizer and Elsasser 1980). Burials form a key component of archaeological sites and blend into the cultural landscape. Traditional burials are typically found within general living areas, therefore, in addition to traditional knowledge, habitation evidence, such as the presence of midden soils, lithic material, and the proximity to water and food sources, needs to be considered (Rogers 1929; Heizer and Elsasser 1980; Cuero and Shipek 1991). These broad indicators are not only employed to assess the overall condition of a site but can be used in conjunction with other tiers of identification to substantiate a human identification or to establish whether the remains are more likely to be faunal.

In San Diego, multiple lines of evidence are used against standardised definitions and practices to establish whether fragmented remains are human or faunal. Through years of case work, Loveless Linton, Inc. (2012) have devised standard definitions to aid in the identification of human bone. These definitions are as follows:

- Possible human: The morphology and observed characteristics of the bone(s) fall within the general variation of human bone and therefore cannot be ruled out as human.
- Likely human: The morphology and observed characteristics suggest human and fall within the general variation of human bone, but due to the lack of defining morphological markers that are unique to humans the bone(s) are categorised as likely.
- Human: Morphology unique to humans was observed.

Each one of these definitions is applied with prudence and the understanding that it is impossible to deliver an absolute identification without irrefutable evidence. A more detailed and standardised process of identification is desperately needed in the CRM and osteology communities. Standardisation is an approach employed to improve the quality of products, performance, and results in a variety of fields, such as product development, healthcare, military practices, education, and in anthropology (Darling-Hammond and Wise 1985; Buikstra and Ubelaker 1994; Ulmer et al. 2009). In field archaeology, standardised definitions and identification processes that are supported by the scientific and forensic communities would improve the legitimacy of identifications and implement a level of confidence that can be applied across regions and disciplines. This would improve the accuracy of the identification of archaeological inhumed and cremated remains in research and CRM contexts.

When making a preliminary identification in the field, specialists must not forget that there are cultural norms that should be respected during the entire process. For example, some Native American groups object to the photography of human bone, including any bone that has yet to be identified. The exponential use of mobile (cell) phones means it is now possible to take a photograph of archaeological remains and share it instantaneously with colleagues, with the aim of ascertaining a rapid identification, without thinking that a spiritual norm is being violated. This common mistake often jeopardises the relationship between the archaeological and native communities. To avoid misunderstandings, cultural violations and conduct defensible identifications, ethical practices are encouraged through fluid cultural consciousness and the application of an objective analysis.

18.5 Identified as Human, Now What?

The requirement to analyse human remains is dependent on the objective of a project. The primary aim of a university or controlled excavation is the acquisition of biological information through various types of analyses. In CRM, the primary aim is to establish whether bone is human or non-human, and analysis is typically an afterthought. However, as scientists we want to ask the who, what, why, when, where, and how questions. An inquisitive personality is what drives us to be osteologists, archaeologists, and anthropologists. It is easy to assume that everyone wants the basic scientific questions answered. But we must ask: why else would someone be interested? Again, it is imperative that we stand back, remove the scientific lens, and implement scientific practices through a cultural lens, giving cultural norms and requests precedence over scientific knowledge. General cultural and historical contextual information alone is insufficient when addressing the analysis of human remains. Difficulties that result from the misappropriation of cultural knowledge from one group or band to another continue to arise as one moves from project to project, as cultural norms and expectations vary by region, population, and family. The goal is to reunite ancestral remains with their descendants in a respectful manner; to successfully accomplish this task, cultural expectations must be discussed during the initial identification process and subsequent analysis. It is thus crucial that those working with human remains have intimate knowledge of the people they are working with, and the legal and political circumstances they are working within.

The ethical analysis of human remains requires cultural input from appropriate Native American people. Historical events and the establishment of the reservation system can make identifying affiliated Native American bands and/or Most Likely Descendants (MLD) a difficult task to accomplish. At the time of writing this chapter (2018), there are currently 567 federally recognised tribes in the United States of America (Bureau of Indian Affairs 2018). Recognition is nothing more than a government status applied by the United States Government and carries some stigma as to the legitimacy of non-recognised tribes and bands. Non-federally recognised tribes do not have access to the same federal programmes or consultation rights (Bureau of Indian Affairs 2018). However, both federally recognised and non-federally recognised tribes are treated as equal under California law. Reservation policies divided and reassembled those belonging to tribes and bands by moving them around based on regional occupation at the time of establishment. Before the establishment of reservations, California Native Americans endured three separate occupational periods: the Spanish occupation (1769–1821), Mexican occupation (1821–1864), and, currently, that of the United States of America (1864–present), with California becoming the thirty-first state in the Union in 1850 (Starr 2007). During these periods, economic and religious priorities, among others, influenced the movement of Native people in California. Each period will be briefly explored to add some historical context to the discussion.

During the Spanish (Mission) period, the goal of the Catholic church was indoctrination by force. Native peoples were driven from their homes and forced to relocate or be enslaved in the Mission system (Miskwish 2007). The Mexican period saw the establishment of Ranchos and many Native Americans in California found work and subsequently relocated to the Ranchos (Gates 1967; Starr 2007). The American period witnessed further development of lands and removed Native Americans from lands that were desired by American farmers, ranchers, and homesteaders (Kroeber 1976). By the time reservations were legally established, Native American peoples had already been dispersed across the country as they sought refuge from colonisation and Western expansion. This forced individuals and groups to leave their traditional homelands and kin groups to survive. Relocation and the introduction of reservations created a new cultural dynamic with a variety of Native American practices and beliefs integrated into one space. In some cases, individual beliefs were passed down through familial lines, sometimes they were combined with other belief systems, and on occasion people adopted alternative belief systems. One example of this concerns the Iipay and Tipai of San Diego County. Historical maps illustrate the pre-contact Aboriginal territory of these two groups, but historically they were grouped together under the Mission San Diego as Diegueno Indians (Heizer 1978; Connolly 2005). Today they are united in solidarity under the single term of Kumeyaay, yet they maintain their

Aboriginal identities and cultural practices. However, a traditional ceremony for repatriation or reburial did not exist. Before modern development, population expansion, and the massive urbanisation we see today, there was never a need to unearth and reinter a person and, therefore, there was no concept of repatriation. However, in the twenty-first century, there is a constant obligation to honour and rebury ancestral remains. Without tradition guiding the practice, it is the onus of contemporary populations to create new ceremonies and guidelines on how remains should be treated. This creates confusion on how to approach and handle human remains.

Under current environmental and graves protection laws in the United States (California Environmental Quality Act 1970; National Environmental Policy Act 1970; NAGPRA 1990), all human remains and associated material culture are required to be repatriated to an affiliated tribe and/or the most likely descendant(s). The historic turmoil of relocation and cultural genocide can make it difficult to determine the proper Native American group to contact upon the discovery and identification of human remains. While it is not the responsibility of the osteologist or archaeologist to determine who has the legal right to claim the remains, it is important to understand that there may be multiple claims and more than one group or person affiliated with the remains.

In 1978, California established a government appointed commission, the Native American Heritage Commission (NAHC), as a way of simplifying the process of establishing who had a claim to Native American ancestral remains. The commission is comprised of 10 California Native members, all of whom are appointed by the Governor of California (Native American Heritage Commission 2018). Among many other responsibilities, the NAHC designates the Most Likely Descendent (MLD) when human remains are identified. The MLD then acts as the designated person or group of people who advise the archaeologists on how they want the ancestral remains to be treated. The limits of analysis will also be determined by the MLD. It is important to fully understand what the MLD wants from the analysis and which analyses are permitted. Basic, non-destructive analysis to establish a biological profile (e.g. age estimation, sex, and stature) is often a violation of spiritual norms. Destructive analysis, such as DNA or isotope analysis, is generally a forbidden practice but depending on the circumstances, analysis may be requested or required (Cui et al. 2013; Doughton 2015). A number of questions must be addressed prior to the excavation, analysis, and dissemination of information relating to an archaeological discovery at any site. These questions are as follows:

1. Who are the interested Native American parties?
    a. Identify the person or persons that should be communicated with.
2. Are the remains going to be taken off the site and if so, where will they be taken to?
3. What is the requested level of security at the site?
4. What information do the different parties hope to get from the analysis?

   a. Human or non-human
   b. Ancestry
   c. Full inventory
   d. Biological profile
   e. Pathological conditions

5. What, if any, limits do Native Americans put on the analysis of human remains?
6. What type of documentation is permitted and/or requested?

   a. Photographs
   b. Descriptive report
   c. Basic skeletal inventory

7. Is destructive analysis requested?

   a. If so, which elements should samples be taken from?

8. Is the associated soil to be kept with the remains?
9. How are the remains to be re-packed once analysis is complete?
10. Once analysis is complete, who is responsible for taking possession of the remains (i.e. from the Coroner's/Medical Examiner's Office or the archaeological site) and transporting them for repatriation?
11. What is the timeline?

This simple line of questioning allows for clear communication between the osteologist and project personnel, which includes, but is not limited to, archaeologists, lead agencies, private owners, Native American communities, and MLD's. It is also designed to limit the liability of the osteologist, restrict the analysis to the requested limits, and be culturally respectful. It is easy to get caught up in osteological analyses and the information that can be gleaned from skeletal remains, but it is important to remember that these remains belonged to individuals and any analysis will have an impact on living populations.

18.6 Real World Consequences

When discussing the consequences of bone identification experienced by contemporary Native American people, it is important to examine the cause and effect relationship between the identification process and the ability Native Americans have to influence the treatment of ancestral remains. Traditional reburial practices of repatriated remains are non-existent within traditional culture, so in itself, the process of repatriation is traumatic. Native American peoples are faced with the repercussions of colonialism and continue to fight for access to their traditional properties and ancestral remains. There are a few simple universal requests. First and foremost, all Native American nations wish to be acknowledged as an existing population that have occupied traditional territories throughout time. Secondly, skeletal remains, regardless of condition, should be treated as human and not scientific vessels of knowledge. These seem like simple universal human rights that should be granted to all without question (United Nations General Assembly 1948), but the request to be acknowledged as human is continuously challenged. Both historically and contemporaneously, political resources and academic status have been used to gain exclusive access to skeletal collections or influence decisions that have consequently violated the requests of descendants or culturally affiliated groups (Larson 2008; White v. University of California 2014; Killgrove 2016; Zimmer 2016).

Historically, particularly in the nineteenth century, anthropologists used morphometrics to categorise individuals (or groups of individuals) as physically, intellectually, and culturally superior or inferior, competent or incompetent, or more human or less human, which has consequently tarnished the integrity of the discipline. In 1995, Richard Jantz, an American Anthropologist closely affiliated with the University of Tennessee (Knoxville, Tennessee), praised Franz Boas for gathering the morphometric data of 15,000 Native American people and believed this feat was an achievement that greatly benefitted physical anthropology (Jantz 2003). However, the morphometric information collected by Boas, his contemporaries, and successive anthropologists resulted in the creation of a standardised methodology that could be used to categorise humans. Unfortunately, this method was inappropriately applied to Native American skeletal remains to validate political beliefs and academic driven claims to avoid repatriation in favour of study (Birkby 1966; Owsley and Jantz 2001; Dalton 2008; Larson 2008; Killgrove 2016). The use of morphometrics in this manner is outdated, unethical, and maleficent. This is not to say that morphometrics is not a useful tool. When applied to a population with an appropriate comparative dataset, the number of accurate identifications can be greatly increased (Spradley et al. 2008; Spradley 2014). Identifying an ancestral relationship between skeletal remains and living populations has its place in forensic anthropology where it yields a positive outcome for the skeletal remains, living kin groups, and science. A good example of this, is the work being carried out on human remains recovered at the US/Mexico border region (Birkby 1966; Spradley et al. 2008; Spradley 2014). With the support of metric and non-metric methods, the skeletal remains of missing migrants are being identified and repatriated to families (Birkby et al. 2008; Spradley et al. 2008). Scientific data, such as dental morphology and morphometrics, and other forms of evidence, such as historical documentation, ethnographic documentation, and traditional cultural knowledge, are used to establish cultural or ancestral relationships between ancient remains and modern-day Native Americans. This is a more inclusive way of establishing affiliations between the living and their ancestral remains. It is important to understand that all identifications have an impact on living populations and disagreements between all parties involved throughout the process is unavoidable, regardless of the situation. Osteologists, archaeologists, anthropologists, and any other persons involved in the identification process has an obligation to both the living and the deceased; these specialists are responsible for providing a scientifically sound identification and should not, under any circumstances, have an ulterior motive.

Repatriation is expected to resolve the negative impacts felt by Native American communities as a result of disinterred remains and decimated cultural sites by returning the material culture and human remains to the living people who are culturally affiliated and/or have familial ties (NAGPRA 1990; Ellis 2000). While this seems to be a standard "good deed", and the essence of the process may be one of genuine intent to do right where so much wrong has preceded, it is much more complicated and does not offer a conclusion to the process. Rather, repatriation is a new cultural hurdle faced by all Native peoples in the Americas. The wounds of colonisation, the disarticulation of culture, and endured trauma is not healed once the material and/or ancestral remains have been returned. The repatriation process can be broken down into two parts. Firstly, the ancestral remains and/or funerary items must be returned. Secondly, once given back, the recipients are then left with the task of reinterring the remains with no support from the people or projects that exhumed them in the first place. Descendants must do their best to re-establish spiritual continuity and inter the remains in a dignified burial. As this is a new challenge and traditional guidance does not exist, the recipients must do their best to collaborate and devise best management practices to do right by their ancestors that have been disturbed as a result of archaeological works. This is a heavy burden to bear for Nations that are steeped in traditional practices, and it further promotes forced assimilation by colonialism.

18.6.1 Kumeyaay People

The Kumeyaay people, who inhabit southern California, have burial practices that deal with death very directly, with the primary intention of disconnecting any association the deceased may have with this world. The process of burial is deeply personal and rooted in tradition and spirituality. The Kumeyaay practice can be looked at from a broad perspective, focusing on general cultural practices, to very narrow perspectives, focusing on familial rites. Although these burial practices have an overall uniformity, there can be a wide range of variations depending on clans and familial lines. At every level, there are similarities and differences in the funerary rites practiced within and between kin groups. Burials follow a long line of traditional practices, whereby each person involved has specific roles and responsibilities, and may prohibit the family of the deceased to participate in certain activities. However, the process of repatriation and reinterring remains does not allow traditional religious practices to be followed. Repatriation, more specifically "reburial", is a practice that has never been a part of the Kumeyaay culture. Essentially, the exhumation of our ancestors has forced a change in our religious practices. We are forced to create new ceremonies that are not based in any sort of traditional spiritual practice and we are always in danger of violating our own beliefs.

The process of identification is intimately tied to repatriation. Repatriation only becomes an option once bone is identified to be human. In cases of incomplete and/or disturbed burials, the identification of one bone fragment is just as important as the identification of a complete skeleton. The majority of remains that have been identified in Kumeyaay Territory are fragmented and carry little to no identifying features. However, ancestral remains are equally significant and sacred regardless of their condition. As such, all remains deserve to be treated with utmost respect and dignity. As mentioned in section 18.3 of this chapter, there is currently no regulatory process regarding the minimum qualifications required to conduct an identification. This means that underqualified archaeologists are making decisions on whether bone is worthy of a legal identification or not. From a Native American perspective, this is extremely disrespectful and does not treat our ancestors with the dignity they deserve. Thus, the identification process should only be conducted by highly skilled, qualified osteologists.

Those working in science are responsible for deciding who are the eligible recipients of ancestral remains. The burden of proof lies on the Native American claimants to prove that they meet the requirements for "cultural affiliation" under NAGPRA (1990, Sect. 2). Yet given the manner of exhumation and the long history of rapid expulsion from our homes, we rarely know the direct family line of ancestral remains. This is an enduring process that often creates much controversy, and the simple act of returning the excavated material comes nowhere near healing or repairing the damage that it has caused. Disturbance of a burial is an abuse of human rights, and a violation of the religious rights and spirituality of Native American people. Rectifying a spiritual connection for the human remains through repatriation is not an accomplishable goal. As previously mentioned, we do not have any kind of "reburial ceremony", nor do we have cultural guidelines to help us re-establish passing practices (rites that help the deceased pass over into the next life), bring closure to the family, or know who should participate in the burial. Not only has our spiritual practice been destroyed, but the physical remains returned are rarely complete, which forces the reburial of partial remains. There are also times when repatriations are completed before the entirety of the known remains are returned, causing a single ancestor to be buried in more than one location. This is extremely disheartening. Obligations of repatriation do not address the completeness of human remains or the efforts one is required to make to recover all remains or material culture from a human burial. It simply addresses the types of funerary material that may be recovered, though this is limited and does not address the eligible remains in a holistic, comprehensive manner that would embrace cultural practices and treat human remains as those of once living beings (NAGPRA 1990). As a consequence, contextual information and items viewed through a Western lens as "non-burial related items", such as faunal bone or tools that may be out of context, are rarely shared as part of the repatriation process. This creates further discontinuity between the past and present. For cultures that heavily rely on oral tradition for knowledge and moral consciousness, the consequence of colonisation, Western expansion, and cultural genocide has severely damaged the traditional thread of communication that would reveal the direct relationship between ancestral remains and living populations. However fragmented, knowledge does persist, and working with archaeologists to determine the traditional significance of all items recovered would lead to a more complete picture for the archaeological record, and give Native Americans the opportunity to recover and repatriate a more complete burial with more appropriate cultural customs.

To amplify the struggle, there is little to no support given to the Native recipients of human remains or material culture by the repatriating party. The funerary costs of an unexpected death in the family can be a huge financial burden. The same principal applies to repatriation, but monetary funding to cover these costs is not provided by a person or company who disturbed the remains. There are no insurance policies or any kind of pecuniary reimbursements that could help with the expenditure required for reburial. Each project is budgeted for the possibility of digging up human remains and for their subsequent analysis. However, that budget stops once the remains and/or material are returned to the appropriate Nation. The burden of cost then lies with the designated recipient. This is a task humbly taken on by Native American communities, because there is no other choice. In most of the cases experienced by the Kumeyaay people, repatriation will cost thousands of dollars and several days of volunteer time to complete; all to deal with a problem that was not ours in the first place. Each repatriation brings its own set of circumstances and is a process of constant modification and adjustment that raise a multitude of cultural and logistical issues. However, this is the best option available to us at present. At the very least, this process gives us access to ancestral remains that would otherwise be held in an institution, laboratory, or other facility and treated as a specimen rather than a human being. After all, these individuals are part of a living population and are intimately cared for by their families and communities; the living descendants therefore deserve dignity and closure, the same as all human beings. The following case studies demonstrate to the reader the historical and on-going challenges faced by Native American Nations in their struggle to claim ancestral remains.

18.6.2 The Work of Malcolm Rogers

Malcolm Rogers was a geologist turned archaeologist in San Diego during the first half of the twentieth century (Ezell 1961). His most noted contribution to San Diego archaeology was the detailed documentation and interpretation of Native American archaeological sites along the coast and, subsequently, inland (Rogers 1929, 1945; Ezell 1961; Warren 1967). He created a sequence of cultural periods that were delineated by material evidence, such as tools, dietary evidence, and technology, into two distinct and separate cultural affiliations: the San Dieguito Complex and the La Jolla Complex (Rogers 1929, 1945; Warren 1967). Theoretically, culture could be measured chronologically through the evidence of objects recovered from archaeological sites. Rogers (1929, 1945) suggested that the San Dieguito Complex and La Jolla Complex cultural periods were mutually exclusive and not associated with the ancestral populations of the contemporary Kumeyaay. The problem with Rogers' hypothesis is that it did not account for cultural evolution; the premise that culture changes through socially transmitted beliefs, technology, and language were not factored into his work (Carter 1996; Mesoudi 2011). The only constant in life is change, and culture is not an exception. The descendants and culturally affiliated nation of the Kumeyaay have had to fight academia and the scientific community for recognition, familial rights, and access to their ancestral remains, the latter of which have been located within assemblages of material culture that Rogers (1929, 1945) classified as a cultural complex that pre-dated, and were not related to, the contemporary Indigenous Kumeyaay. This is simply not the case as the Kumeyaay have inhabited San Diego since time immemorial (Miskwish 2007). Rogers' theories were, and continue to be, a popular paradigm, which have given credence to the claims made by scientists and anthropologists that the Kumeyaay and the ancient remains of San Diego County are not culturally affiliated, and therefore the Kumeyaay do not have any legal or patrimonial claims to human remains or any archaeological material.

At the end of his career, Rogers re-evaluated his original conclusions regarding the cultural groups he had established based on material evidence (e.g. shells and beads) and tool technology typologies (Warren 1967). In 2012, David Hanna Jr., wrote that Rogers was admittingly wrong in assigning short term unique cultures to the material that he observed. The evidence he had studied actually supported a continuous long-term occupation. While this is part of the evolutionary process of science and scholarly investigations, the original labels applied to the material culture have transcended through archaeological paradigms; denying contemporary Native American people the recognition of cultural affiliation and the right to claim their ancestors. Currently, the Museum of Man in San Diego, where Malcolm Rogers and many of his subordinates worked, is proactively decolonising the museum and repatriating their entire collection (Mandel 2018).

18.6.3 Chancellor House, La Jolla, California

In 1976, excavations at Chancellor House located at the University of California, San Diego (UCSD), resulted in the excavation of two inhumation burials (Larson 2008). Prior to the work that was carried out in 1976, there had been several excavations that yielded human remains. According to development documentation, a total of 29 skeletons had been removed from the property over a period of approximately 80 years (Larson 2008). At that time, there were no laws that gave Native Americans any access to the burials and repatriation was not part of the process. Documentation was either poor or has since been lost; this has hampered efforts to locate the human remains from these burials and, as a result, only two individuals have been returned to the Kumeyaay people through the court system under NAGPRA (1990). Repatriation is not innately public knowledge and the skeletal remains from Chancellor House have been moved between institutions over a period of nearly 100 years, thus it is not possible to establish how many of the remaining 29 skeletons have been returned over the years. It is believed that universities and museums across the United States have, or at one time, had possession of these ancestral remains, but it is difficult to determine the exact numbers of remains and institutions involved (Larson 2008).

The remains that were discovered in 1976 were immediately claimed by UCSD but were not indefinitely curated at this institution. In 2008, John Larson found documentation stating that the Museum of Man in San Diego agreed to store the skeletal remains. At an unknown point in time, they were loaned to the Smithsonian in Washington D.C. and subsequently returned to San Diego in 2007 (Larson 2008). In the case of these two individuals, who have been radiocarbon dated to approximately 8977 to 9603 years old, scientists brought a lawsuit against the university that owned the remains to keep them from being repatriated (White v. University of California 2014). In 2006, the Kumeyaay Cultural Repatriation Committee (KCRC), which is a committee that represents all 12 Kumeyaay bands, claimed the remains of these two individuals under NAGPRA (1990). In 2008, UCSD responded to the claim, denying cultural affiliation and KCRC's claim to the remains (Killgrove 2016; Zimmer 2016). In 2011, UCSD decided to repatriate the remains to KCRC, but "Shoeninger, Bettinger, and White sued UCSD to prevent this, citing UC's 2008 report with inconclusive cultural affiliation and pointing out that the NAGPRA law was not being properly followed" (Killgrove 2016). These academics claimed not to be against repatriation but insisted that further analyses were needed before the La Jolla skeletons were returned to the Kumeyaay. In 2017, the Supreme Court ruled that the ancestral remains should be returned to the Kumeyaay, with the opinion that the remains are culturally affiliated and protected, thus NAGPRA (1990) does apply in this instance (Killgrove 2016). In a response to the ruling, Shoeninger, Bettinger, and White's lawyer stated that the verdict and dismissal of their case by the Supreme Court was "a tragedy and a disgrace—a tragedy for science" (Zimmer 2016). Consequently, universities and curatorial museums are seen by Native Nations as adversaries of the Native American people. Historically, they use all available resources to deny Native people their repatriation rights. Repatriation is not simply the legal right of Native American people to obtain possession of their ancestral remains once western scientists have finished extracting the desired information from their bodies. It is a chance for Native American people to restore continuity and offer their ancestors, as close as they can, a respectful burial and to be treated as dignified human beings. As seen in this case, attitudes of scientific superiority perpetuate the reputation of all institutions and universities as selfish, untrustworthy establishments that treat human remains as subjects rather than humans and have no respect for the descendants.

Museums and universities cannot improve their relationships with Native peoples until they move towards decolonisation and begin to communicate transparently with Native peoples. Universities and museums project a positive and enriching experience for the public. However, it is a shame that what they represent is not always how they perform in practice. In this case, California is attempting to force universities to comply with NAGPRA (1990) by returning all ancestral remains through recently approved legislation (Assembly Bill No. 2836 2018). This would require universities to create repatriation committees and involve the Native American Heritage Commission in any actions it may take. Whilst this is a step in the right direction, it is unfortunate that it takes the implementation of legislation to ensure that museums and universities treat human remains in an ethical manner with consideration for their living kin.

18.6.4 Assembly Bill No. 2836

In 2018, Assembly Bill 2836 (chapter 823) was approved and passed by the Governor of California. The Bill was designed to further hold universities accountable, by law, for the repatriation of Native American remains. While the Bill cites all universities within the University of California system, it specifically targets UC Berkeley, with the aim of ensuring that the institution makes a greater effort to culturally affiliate the human remains currently housed at the institution with living descendants and to comply with legislation, such as NAGPRA (1990). UC Berkeley is the target of this legislation as they curate a large collection of Native American human remains and associated funerary artefacts. This institution houses human remains that have been classified as "culturally unaffiliated". Culturally unaffiliated is a term used to denote that human remains cannot be affiliated with modern Native Americans. This can be due to the lack of provenance or the lack of effort to establish affiliation. NAGPRA (1990) does not stipulate the level of investigation that should be carried out to ascertain the affiliation between human remains, material culture, and Native groups; if an association does not already exist with the assemblage, additional effort is not mandated. In our experience, it is an unspoken expectation that institutions who hold human remains try to establish affiliations and/or start a dialogue with tribes to determine the best course of action with the aim of repatriating the remains; but since it is not legally required, this is rarely done. Reasons for the lack of effort can range from a lack of funds and staff to the more common presumption that universities and museums do not want to relinquish possession of these remains. Academic and scientific communities that avoid repatriation claims by maintaining possession of "culturally unaffiliated" remains ultimately contribute to the disassociation between ancestral remains and their descendants, and the fragmentation of cultures. It is thus imperative that all osteologists, archaeologists, and anthropologists create a proactive dialogue with Native American communities as opposed to waiting for discoveries or legal obligations to force a conversation with relevant Native American tribes. While examples are scarce, it is possible for agencies and institutions to initiate positive and active relationships with Native American Nations (Brugge and Missaghian 2006).

18.6.5 Kennewick Man

In 1996, the skeletal remains of an adult male were discovered on the banks of the Columbia River in Kennewick (Washington State). The Army Corp of Engineers were the lead agency and were in control of the site as the discovery was on their land. Requests for repatriation under NAGPRA (1990) were received by the Army Corps from the Confederated Bands of the Umatilla Indian Reservation who claimed cultural affiliation (Owsley and Jantz 2001). Scientists felt that repatriation would be a devastating loss of information as they believed the remains could be used to improve the public's understanding of human migration and settlement in North America (Owsley and Jantz 2001). To prevent the loss of information through repatriation, a law suit was filed challenging the interpretation of NAGPRA (1990) and the reburial of the skeletal remains was halted (Bonnichsen v. United States 2002). The goal of the law suit was to gain access to the skeletal remains and conduct scientific analyses. Scientists' argued that the tribes involved were unable to prove cultural affiliation to the remains, therefore the remains should belong to the public and scientific community (Owsley and Jantz 2001; Zimmerman 2005). After years of court battles, in 2005, the scientific community won the rights to Kennewick Man. This group proceeded to conduct destructive and non-destructive analyses and published several papers based on their conclusions (Chatters 2000; McManamon 2004; Owsley and Jantz 2014; Rasmussen et al. 2015; Zimmer 2015).

Kennewick Man was evaluated using standard skeletal evaluation methodologies, such as cranial measurements and an assessment of skeletal morphology. However, standard metric and non-metric methods of analysis are not scientifically conclusive, rather, they are employed to evaluate biological associations based on the statistical relationships produced through skeletal measurements. These measurements and formulae can then be utilised to estimate stature and ancestry (Boas 1961; Buikstra and Ubelaker 1994). Anthropologists and contributing scientists who analysed Kennewick Man identified that cranial morphology was a valuable method when determining ancestry (Owsley and Jantz 2014). Following the publication of these results (Owsley and Jantz 2014), DNA analysis was performed on the skeletal remains. This analysis provided conclusive, scientific evidence that Kennewick Man's closest living relatives are the Colville people of Washington State (Rasmussen et al. 2015). It was also found that Kennewick Man is also genetically related to the tribes that initiated the claim of cultural affiliation under NAGPRA (1990; Rasmussen et al. 2015). Academics used science as a weapon of objectivity by withholding the remains for the scientific community and refusing to consider the Native American cultural claims. This is one of many stories that demonstrates the unnecessary damage and harm scientific agendas can have on Native American peoples.

18.6.6 Faunal or Human: Which Comes First?

In 2017, a large renewable energy project was established in the back country of San Diego where known archaeological sites exist. Local Kumeyaay bands participated in the legal process and consultation, identifying previously occupied and sensitive sites. However, the project design changed, and the area of impact increased, which consequently triggered additional archaeological evaluation. The location was previously acknowledged by tribal elders as culturally sensitive as it was likely to contain human remains. During construction, a zooarchaeologist, who was not familiar with human remains, cremated (human or animal) remains, or cultural constructs, was asked to make initial observations of bone. If, and when, possible human remains were discovered, a human osteologist was then called to the site. In this case, the human osteologist successfully identified "possible human" bone. However, the faunal expert was allowed to revisit the bone identified as "human" and consequently questioned the conclusions drawn by the human osteologist. This jeopardised the identification, protection, and recognition of human remains.

While the faunal expert did not intend to jeopardise the identification process, they cost any additional human remains that may have been present onsite the protection of NAGPRA (1990) as the project was allowed to proceed without further analysis or consequence until the remains were reconfirmed as human. This occurred because they did not understand their cultural context, they were unable to identify human bone, and they did not acknowledge their professional limits. This consequently resulted in a volatile relationship between project personnel and the Native American community. The identification of human remains was questioned and, at the time, bone was determined to be "questionably human", therefore NAGPRA (1990) did not apply and the project was permitted to continue. By the time the identification was corrected, and the remains were determined to be "human", the site in which the bone was excavated from had been destroyed. Even though the identification was rectified, the negligence of the faunal expert had dire consequences for the Native American community as they had to fight for the re-examination of the remains, which took time, effort, and exposed everyone to unnecessary trauma. It also resulted in the unwarranted destruction of the site and all the contents that remained in its soils. This case highlights that hiring underqualified and inexperienced personnel in the identification process downgrades the significance of human remains and denies Native American peoples the right to protect and rebury their ancestors in a dignified and respectful manner.

18.7 Conclusion and Recommendations

The aim of this chapter was to raise awareness of the current status of bone identification and the lack of standardised protocol in the field of Cultural Resource Management in the United States, and its implications on Native American peoples. While our work is based in California, the issues raised throughout this chapter resonates across state borders. Identification of human remains is a crucial component of any project, yet it lacks any standardised procedural protocol. Legal authorities and archaeologists alike have minimal guidelines to follow. The academic, professional, and legal authorities have yet to come together in a collaborative effort to close the gaps in communication and protocol. It is the opinion of the authors that this huge oversight is largely due to the fact that professionals who work outside of archaeology are generally unaware of the complete absence of standardised protocols or minimum qualifications required for osteologists to work in archaeology and identify bone. Indeed, there are some legal guidelines that address the need for a legal identification by the coroner or medical examiner, but these laws do not require these agencies to employ a qualified individual to make the required identifications of human skeletal remains within an archaeological context. The United States Secretary of the Interior has standard qualifications that must be met by individuals who perform identification, evaluation, registration, and treatment activities regarding archaeological and historical resources (Code of Federal Regulations 1999). However, human bone and teeth identification is not currently included in these guidelines and there are no Secretary of the Interior standards for education or experience for osteologists or bioarchaeologists.

To improve the identification process, the authors would like to ask the forensic science community in the USA to create a set of standards that outlines the minimum qualifications, based on education and professional and local experience, that is required for an individual to carry out an ethical and accurate identification in an archaeological context. This would also require adequate education in laws pertaining to the identification process and cultural competency that would allow the osteologist to be a better ambassador to Native American populations who are impacted by the identification of ancestral remains. Until standards and minimum qualifications are implemented in legislation, it is the responsibility of the individual who practices osteological identification to understand their obligation to both science and humanity. It is important that they acknowledge the project design and agenda, particularly deadlines and budgets, and are acutely aware of the lack of guidelines directing them in the identification process. The British Association for Biological Anthropology and Osteoarchaeology (BABAO 2017) recently adopted qualification standards for osteologists that may serve as a useful template for creating a USA set of requirements that would address the technical qualifications as well as the Native American cultural component. Above all, we hope that every person who attempts to make an identification of human remains understands that, regardless of the size, condition or antiquity, all human bone, or potentially human bone, must be treated as such and respected accordingly. Skeletal remains, and the person they belonged to, was, and remains, intimately connected to a living cultural body, and the communities of that culture are impacted with every disinterment of their ancestors. We do not expect those involved in the exhumation and identification process to learn the intimate details of that culture; however, we do expect them to treat human remains with the dignity and respect that all humans deserve.

References

American Anthropological Association [AAA]. 2012. *AAA Ethics Blog*. http://ethics.americananthro.org/ethics-statement-1-do-no-harm/. Accessed 17 September 2018.

Archaeological Resources Protection Act (ARPA). 1979. Public Law 96-95, 16 United States Code, 470aa-mm, 93 Stat. 721, October 31, 1979. 96th United States Congress, Washington D.C.

Arizona State University. 2018. *Kampsville: Archaeology Field and Laboratory Programs*. https://shesc.asu.edu/field-schools/kampsville. Accessed 4 November 2018.

Assembly Bill No. 2836. 2018. Native Americans: Repatriation, Chapter 823.

Association of Environmental Professionals. 2018. *California Environmental Quality Act (CEQA) Statute and Guidelines*. Palm Desert: Association of Environmental Professionals.

Austin, F.B. 1924. The Noble Savage. *The Bookman* 66 (396): 317–318.

Barker, P. 1993. *Techniques of Archaeological Excavation*, 3rd ed. London: Routledge.

Bass, W.M. 2005. *Human Osteology: A Laboratory and Field Manual*, 5th ed. Springfield: Missouri Archaeological Society.

Birkby, W.H. 1966. An Evaluation of Race and Sex Identification from Cranial Measurements. *American Journal of Physical Anthropology* 24: 21–27.

Birkby, W.H., T.W. Fenton, and B.E. Anderson. 2008. Identifying Southwest Hispanics Using Nonmetric Traits and the Cultural Profile. *Journal of Forensic Sciences* 53 (1): 29–33.

Boas, F. 1961. *Race, Language and Culture*. New York: Macmillan.

Bonnichsen v. United States. 2002. 217 F. Supp. 2d 1116.

Bray, T.L. 2001. American Archaeologists and Native Americans: A Relationship Under Construction. In *The Future of the Past: Archaeologists, Native Americans, and Repatriation*, ed. R.L. Bray, 1–8. New York: Routledge.

British Association for Biological Anthropology and Osteoarchaeology [BABAO]. 2017. *Specialist Competence Matrix—To Support Applicants Who Work in Osteology*. https://www.archaeologists.net/sites/default/files/Osteology%20specialist%20competence%20matrix_final.pdf. Accessed 6 November 2018.

Brothwell, D.R. 1981. *Digging Up Bones: The Excavation, Treatment and Study of Human Skeletal Remains*, 3rd ed. Ithaca: Cornell University Press.

Brugge, D., and M. Missaghian. 2006. Protecting the Navajo People Through Tribal Regulation of Research. *Science and Engineering Ethics* 12 (3): 491–507.

Buikstra, J.E., and D.H. Ubelaker (eds.). 1994. *Standards for Data Collection from Human Skeletal Remains*. Fayetteville: Arkansas Archaeological Survey.

Bureau of Indian Affairs. 2018. Indian Entities Recognized and Eligible to Receive Services from the United States Bureau of Indian Affairs. *Federal Register* 83 (20): 4235–4241.

California Environmental Quality Act [CEQA]. 1970. Public Resources Code Sections 21000-21178.

Carter, G.F. 1996. Early Man at San Diego: A Geomorphic-Archaeological View. In *Proceedings of the Society for California Archaeology* 9: 104–112.

Chatters, J.C. 2000. The Recovery and First Analysis of an Early Holocene Human Skeleton from Kennewick, Washington. *American Antiquity* 65 (2): 291–316.

Clewlow, C.W., P.S. Hallinan, and R.D. Ambro. 1971. A Crisis in Archaeology. *American Antiquity* 36 (4): 472–473.

Code of Federal Regulations. 1999. 36 Code of Federal Regulations Part 61, 16 United States Code 430 et seq., 64 FR 11742, March 9, 1999. National Parks Service, Washington, D.C.

Colorado State University. 2018. *Archaeology Field School. 2019 Field School Session: May 20–July 12*. https://anthropology.colostate.edu/field-schools/archaeology-field-school/. Accessed 26 October 2018.

Connolly, M. 2005. *Kumeyaay Maps Detail Tribal History*. http://www.kumeyaay.info/kumeyaay_maps/. Accessed 26 October 2018.

Cuero, D., and F.C. Shipek. 1991. *Delfina Cuero: Her Autobiography, an Account of Her Last Years, and Her Ethnobotanic Contributions*. Menlo Park: Ballena Press.

Cui, Y., J. Lindo, C.E. Hughes, et al. 2013. Ancient DNA Analysis of Mid-Holocene Individuals from the Northwest Coast of North America Reveals Different Evolutionary Paths for Mitogenomes. *PLoS One* 8 (7): e66948. https://doi.org/10.1371/journal.pone.0066948.

Dalton, R. 2008. No Burial for 10,000-Year-Old Bones. *Nature* 445: 1156–1157.

Darling-Hammond, L., and A.E. Wise. 1985. Beyond Standardization: State Standards and School Improvement. *The Elementary School Journal* 85 (3): 315–336.

Deloria, V.J. 2003. *God Is Red: A Native View of Religion*, 3rd ed. Colorado: Fulcrum Publishing.

Doughton, S. 2015. What's Next for Kennewick Man, Now that DNA Says He's Native American? *The Seattle Times*, 18 June.

Duran, E., and B. Duran. 1995. *Native American Postcolonial Psychology*. New York: State University of New York Press.

Ellis, L. 2000. *Archaeological Method and Theory: An Encyclopedia*. New York: Garland.

Ezell, P.H. 1961. Malcolm Jennings Rogers, 1890–1960. *American Antiquity* 26 (4): 532–534.

Ferguson, T.J. 1996. Native Americans and the Practice of Archaeology. *Annual Review of Anthropology* 25 (1): 63–79.

Gates, P.W. (ed.). 1967. *California Ranchos and Farms, 1846–1862*. Madison: State Historical Society of Wisconsin.

Hanna Jr., D.C. 2012. Malcom J. Rogers' Career and Context. *Pacific Coast Archaeological Society Quarterly* 48 (3–4): 7–12.

Health and Safety Code [HSC]. 1939. Division 7. Dead Bodies [7000-8030], Ch. 60.

Heizer, R.F. 1978. *Handbook of North American Indians Vol. 8: California*. Washington, D.C.: Smithsonian Institution.

Heizer, R.F., and A.B. Elsasser. 1980. *The Natural World of the California Indians*. Berkeley: University of California Press.

Jantz, R.L. 2003. The Anthropometric Legacy of Franz Boas. *Economics and Human Biology* 1 (2): 277–284.

Jones, D.G., and R.J. Harris. 1998. Archeological Human Remains: Scientific, Cultural, and Ethical Considerations. *Current Anthropology* 39 (2): 253–264.

Killgrove, K. 2016. Two 9,500-Year-Old Skeletons Found at UC San Diego President's House Will Return to Tribes. *Forbes*, 30 January. https://www.forbes.com/sites/kristinakillgrove/2016/01/30/two-9500-year-old-skeletons-found-at-uc-san-diego-presidents-house-will-return-to-tribes/#376d0d51e371. Accessed 17 October 2018.

Kroeber, A.L. 1976. *Handbook of the Indians of California*. New York: Dover.

Larson, T. 2008. How UCSD Spent Over $500,000 on a Home Remodel That Never Happened: The House of the Land of the Dead. *San Diego Reader*, 30 April. https://www.sandiegoreader.com/news/2008/apr/30/cover/#. Accessed 17 October 2018.

Loveless Linton, Inc. 2012. *Company Guidelines. Inventory and Identification of Bone* (Unpublished Document).

Loveless, R., and B. Linton. 2018. *Broken Link*. Paper Presented at the 70th Annual Meeting of the American Academy of Forensic Science, Seattle, Washington, 19–24 February 2018.

Madley, B. 2016. *An American Genocide: The United States and the California Indian Catastrophe, 1846–1873*. New Haven: Yale University Press.

Mandel, J. 2018. Museums in Balboa Park Attempt to “Decolonize”: The Museum of Man and San Diego History Center Retool Their Messaging and Collections. *San Diego City Beat*, 1 August. http://sdcitybeat.com/culture/features/museums-in-balboa-park-attempt-to-%E2%80%9Cdecolonize%E2%80%9D/. Accessed 17 October 2018.

McManamon, F.P. 2004. *Kennewick Man*. https://www.nps.gov/archeology/kennewick/Index.htm#potential. Accessed 20 October 2018.

Mesoudi, A. 2011. *Cultural Evolution: How Darwinian Theory Can Explain Human Culture and Synthesize the Social Sciences*. Chicago: University of Chicago Press.

Miskwish, M.C. 2007. *Kumeyaay: A History Book*. El Cajon: Sycuan Press.

National Conference of State Legislator. 2018. *Federal and State Recognized Tribes*. http://www.ncsl.org/research/state-tribal-institute/list-of-federal-and-state-recognized-tribes.aspx#ca. Accessed 14 October 2018.

National Environmental Policy Act [NEPA]. 1970. Public Law 91-190, 42 United States Code 4321 et seq., 83 Stat. 852 – January 1, 1970. 91st United States Congress, Washington, D.C.

National Historic Preservation Act [NHPA]. 1966. Public Law 89-665, 16 United States Code 470 et seq., 470 et seq., October 15, 1966. 89th United States Congress, Washington, D.C.

National Park Service. 2018. *National NAGPRA Online Databases: Notices of Intent to Repatriate Database*. https://www.nps.gov/nagpra/FED_NOTICES/NAGPRADIR/index2.htm. Accessed 26 October 2018.

Native American Graves Protection and Repatriation Act [NAGPRA]. 1990. Public Law 101-601, 25 United States Code 3001 et seq., 104 Stat. 3048 – November 16, 1990. 101st United States Congress, Washington D.C.

Native American Heritage Commission. 2018. *Native American Heritage Commission*. http://nahc.ca.gov/. Accessed 17 October 2018.

Neumann, T.W., R.M. Sanford, and K.G. Harry. 2010. *Cultural Resources Archaeology: An Introduction*, 2nd ed. Lanham: Alta Mira Press.

Office of the City Clerk, City of San Diego. 2014. *San Diego's Municipal Code, Chapter 11: Land Development Procedures*. San Diego: Office of the City Clerk.

Owsley, D.W., and R.L. Jantz. 2001. Archaeological Politics and Public Interest in Paleoamerican Studies: Lessons from Gordon Creek Woman and Kennewick Man. *American Antiquity* 66 (4): 565–575.

Owsley, D.W., and R.L. Jantz (eds.). 2014. *Kennewick Man: The Scientific Investigation of an Ancient American Skeleton*. College Station: Texas A&M University Consortium Press.

Percy, D.H. 1997. Osteological Analysis of Five Individuals of Native American Descent: Determination of Sex, Age at Death, and Evident Pathologies. *Bios* 68: 36–45.

Public Resources Code [PRC]. 1939. Division 5. Parks and Monuments [5001-5873], Ch. 94, Section 5097.98.

Rasmussen, M., M. Sikora, A. Albrechtsen, et al. 2015. The Ancestry and Affiliations of Kennewick Man. *Nature* 523: 455–458.

Remy, M.H. 1999. *Guide to the California Environmental Quality Act (CEQA)*. Point Arena: Solano Press Books.

Rogers, M.J. 1929. The Stone Art of the San Dieguito Plateau. *American Anthropologist* 31: 454–467.

Rogers, M.J. 1945. An Outline of Yuman Prehistory. *Southwestern Journal of Anthropology* 1 (2): 167–198.

Rogers, S.L. 1963. *The Physical Characteristics of the Aboriginal La Jollan Population of Southern California*. San Diego: Museum of Man.

Smith, A. 2015. *Conquest: Sexual Violence and American Indian Genocide*. Durham: Duke University Press.

Smithsonian National Museum of Natural History. n.d. *Anthropology Collections*. https://anthropology.si.edu/cm/#about. Accessed 26 October 2018.

Spradley, M.K. 2014. Toward Estimating Geographic Origin of Migrant Remains Along the United States-Mexico Border. *Annals of Anthropological Practice* 38: 101–110.

Spradley, M.K., R.L. Jantz, A. Robinson, et al. 2008. Demographic Change and Forensic Identification: Problems in Metric Identification of Hispanic Skeletons. *Journal of Forensic Sciences* 53 (1): 21–28.

Starr, K. 2007. *California: A History*. New York: Modern Library.

Thomas, D.H. 2000. *Skull Wars: Kennewick Man, Archaeology, and the Battle for Native American Identity*. New York: Basic Books.

Tinker, G.E. 1993. *Missionary Conquest: The Gospel and Native American Cultural Genocide*. Minneapolis: Fortress Press.

Trope, J.F., and W.R. Echo-Hawk. 2001. The Native American Graves Protection and Repatriation Act: Background and Legislative History. In *The Future of the Past: Archaeologists, Native Americans, and Repatriation*, ed. R.L. Bray, 9–36. New York: Routledge.

Ulmer, C., B. McFadden, and D.R. Nerenz (eds.). 2009. *Race, Ethnicity, and Language Data: Standardization for Health Care Quality Improvement*. Washington, D.C.: National Academies Press.

United Nations General Assembly. 1948. *Universal Declaration of Human Rights*. New York: United Nations.

Warren, C.N. 1967. The San Dieguito Complex: A Review and Hypothesis. *American Antiquity* 32 (2): 168–185.

White v. University of California. 2014. United States Court of Appeals for the Ninth Circuit, No. 12–17489.

Zimmer, C. 2015. New DNA Results Show Kennewick Man Was Native American. *The New York Times*, 18 June. https://www.nytimes.com/2015/06/19/science/new-dna-results-show-kennewick-man-was-native-american.html. Accessed 17 October 2018.

Zimmer, C. 2016. Tribes' Win in Fight for La Jolla Bones Clouds Hopes for DNA Studies. *The New York Times*, 29 January. https://www.nytimes.com/2016/02/02/science/tribes-win-in-fight-for-la-jolla-bones-clouds-hopes-for-dna-studies.html. Accessed 17 October 2018.

Zimmerman, L.J. 2005. Public Heritage, a Desire for a "White" History for America, and Some Impacts of the Kennewick Man/Ancient One Decision. *International Journal of Cultural Property* 12 (2): 265–274.

Chapter 19
Ethical Issues of Bioarchaeology in New Zealand-Aotearoa: Relationships, Research, and Repatriation

Helen Gilmore, Amber Aranui and Siân E. Halcrow

Abstract New Zealand has a high profile internationally for the repatriation of human skeletal remains, with repatriation starting in the 1970s, and international and national repatriations continuing to the present day. The ethical issues surrounding the use of Māori human skeletal remains (kōiwi tangata Māori) for research are significant as kōiwi tangata are considered tūpuna (ancestors). Kōiwi tangata Māori embody central elements of Māori identity including genealogy and wellbeing, thus the study of their remains is abhorrent for many Māori. This chapter provides a review from both a Māori and bioarchaeological perspective on repatriation issues of kōiwi tangata Māori. We present a discussion of the Māori worldview and their relationship with the dead, interactions and relationships between Māori and bioarchaeologists during the stages of the repatriation process, and the attitudes of repatriation by bioarchaeologists working in New Zealand. Ethnographic work is presented on the attitudes of bioarchaeologists and archaeologists in New Zealand and these are contrasted to the situation in England of working with local human skeletal remains. Internationally, New Zealand is unique, where bioarchaeology and archaeological practice is very much intertwined with Māori cultural and spiritual values, making the relationships between iwi (a Māori

---

Helen Gilmore and Amber Aranui: Shared first authorship.

The original version of the chapter was revised: Citations have been corrected. The correction to this chapter is available at https://doi.org/10.1007/978-3-030-32926-6_31

H. Gilmore · S. E. Halcrow (✉)
Department of Anatomy, University of Otago, Dunedin, New Zealand
e-mail: sian.halcrow@otago.ac.nz

H. Gilmore
Department of Archaeology and Anthropology, University of Otago, Dunedin, New Zealand

A. Aranui
Karanga Aotearoa Repatriation Programme, Museum of New Zealand Te Papa Tongarewa, Wellington, New Zealand

A. Aranui
Te Kawa a Māui, School of Māori Studies, University of Victoria, Wellington, New Zealand

K. Squires et al. (eds.), *Ethical Approaches to Human Remains*,
https://doi.org/10.1007/978-3-030-32926-6_19

tribe or group of people descended from a common ancestor and associated with a distinct territory) and bioarchaeologists generally positive.

19.1 Introduction: Interactions and Relationships in New Zealand/Aotearoa

Repatriation is an important ethical issue for both descendent communities and bioarchaeological research. The issue of repatriation and/or reburial of archaeological human remains is one that increasingly impacts on archaeological and bioarchaeological practices. Controversies can arise from differing ethical values and cultural attitudes regarding archaeological approaches to dealing with the dead in both the archaeological context and the repatriation of human remains from museum collections. The ethics surrounding the methods and ideologies by which many human skeletal remains were originally obtained for research or display in New Zealand are now questioned or outright condemned by the bioarchaeological community (Cooper 2011).

In this chapter we consider the relationships and interactions that connect and involve bioarchaeologists and descendant communities, how repatriations of kōiwi tangata Māori from both international and national museums are managed in the New Zealand context, and compare this with bioarchaeological attitudes and practices in England. In doing so, we are illustrating the need for respectful dialogue by presenting perspectives of New Zealand bioarchaeologists (Helen Gilmore and Siân Halcrow) and a Māori repatriation researcher (Amber Aranui). It is hoped that this approach will demonstrate the positive outcomes and opportunities to be gained by forming partnerships and actively engaging in negotiations between the two groups. Ethical practice for bioarchaeology and archaeology in New Zealand is very much intertwined with Māori cultural and spiritual values, making the formation of relationships with iwi and museum personnel essential. Bioarchaeological ethics require that collection, curation, and skeletal analyses of kōiwi tangata Māori are dependent on iwi consent and the agreement that the tūpuna (ancestors) are returned and reburied (Heritage New Zealand Pouhere Taonga 2010), all of which are accepted and often actively facilitated by New Zealand bioarchaeologists. Research conducted in 2013 and 2014 of bioarchaeological practices and attitudes to human remains, gathered through interviews and observations in New Zealand and England by Helen Gilmore (unpublished data), revealed that the repatriation issue was viewed differently in England in many respects, and some of the participants' comments and general observations are included here. During this research, Gilmore interviewed a total of 35 archaeologists, bioarchaeologists, museum curators, and death studies academics, including one Māori archaeologist, two Māori curators, and one Māori iwi monitor (an iwi representative tasked with monitoring archaeological sites). This chapter seeks to highlight the differences in cultural understandings of bioarchaeological ethics between New Zealand and England, and illustrate the importance of the relationships negotiated between iwi and bioarchaeologists in New Zealand.

19.2 Science Versus Culture: Issues of Repatriation in Bioarchaeology

Bioarchaeologists' relationship with human remains from the past is one of mediation between the archaeological dead and the living of the present, producing information from the expert examination of human skeletal remains from past populations and interpreting their stories. This is a relationship requiring a balance between the research imperative of bioarchaeology, which requires scientifically suitable curation space and access to the remains, and the obligation to respect the dead and the cultural claims and values of their descendants.

The remains of dead human beings command emotional and generally respectful responses far beyond those accorded to other life forms (Peers 2004). Those who handle and interact with the dead do so for diverse practical, educational, or spiritual/religious purposes, and this is not an area of comfort for everyone. Bioarchaeology as a profession has a certain relationship with the dead, not universally shared with others, many of whom will regard death and the dead in a variety of different ways (Walter 1991; Willmott 2000). This means that the relationships formed between bioarchaeology and Indigenous groups are sometimes fragile. As Bulmer (1993, 54) comments "the attitude that Indigenous bones are primarily of scientific importance is still widespread in universities and museums" despite the intentions of the 1989 Vermillion Accord that relationships of mutual respect should be encouraged between archaeological science and Indigenous communities (WAC 1989). Often the resistance to repatriate skeletal collections that some bioarchaeologists (e.g. Meighan 1992; MacKie 2003; Weiss 2008) have expressed is based on the assumption that Indigenous demands for return and reburial destroys access to data to which they believe science has an undisputed right (Klesert and Powell 1993).

Of course, human remains can be very important for research as they are the only direct evidence for insights into past diets, population health, migration patterns, and genetic affinities (Larsen 2015). Modern bioarchaeologists have a responsibility to conduct work of a high professional and ethical standard, and be clear about what they are doing and why. The argument from a scientific perspective is that, as new research and analytical techniques are constantly developing, retention of collections is necessary to allow for further information to potentially be discovered (BABAO 2010). However, the remains are also important to their descendant communities who wish to have them returned for reburial with the appropriate cultural rituals as described below in the following section. The counter argument from Indigenous groups is that the remains were generally obtained without consent in the first place and that science has had more than enough time (sometimes more than a century) to conduct research, and it is time for their ancestors to return home. This dichotomy between ethics in scientific research and in respect for Indigenous concerns is one that bioarchaeology increasingly needs to confront and resolve, particularly in connection with the return of Indigenous remains acquired in the nineteenth and twentieth centuries (Hole 2007).

There is growing acceptance among museums, as well as the bioarchaeological and archaeological communities in New Zealand, that repatriation is expected and considered normal practice. This highlights the increased understanding of the importance of repatriation for Māori amongst the scientific, museological, and academic spheres. In this changed sociocultural environment of acceptance of the Māori worldview, the nature of bioarchaeological culture and practice is also changing. There is an increasing awareness of Māori values and perspectives regarding kōiwi tangata, and an understanding that the profession has no "automatic right" to non-consensual "ownership" and intrusive examination (Tayles and Halcrow 2011; Ruckstuhl et al. 2015; Aranui 2018; Buckley and Petchey 2018). This is articulated by a participant in Gilmore's research:

> I think the difference [between kōiwi tangata Māori and European skeletal samples] is that there are people that are spiritually connected with them, and would like them back, and feel strongly about their human remains and their ancestors. (Deborah, New Zealand bioarchaeologist 2014)

The return of deceased loved ones to their home has always been part of Māori society, and repatriation is essentially an extension of long held practice, which still continues today, outside of the museum and university context (Aranui 2018). The connection between Māori and their dead must be understood and acknowledged within the scientific community and in New Zealand, for example, repatriation of kōiwi tangata Māori is seen as the norm and is to be expected. There is a growing number of iwi who are including the repatriation of their ancestral remains in Treaty claims, and New Zealand museums are becoming more proactive in returning Māori and Moriori (Indigenous people from the Chatham Islands, situated east of the New Zealand archipelago) human remains back to descendant communities (Armstrong 2010; Office of Treaty Settlements 2015).

19.3 Human Remains as Tūpuna – A Māori Worldview

Great respect and honour are given to tūpuna in Māori society. These values, as well as the beliefs and cultural practices surrounding wāhi tapu (sacred places, such as burial places) are significant in understanding why Māori are so active in the repatriation of their ancestral remains. Māori cultural concepts such as tapu, mana, wairua, and whakapapa are essential elements of the Māori world relating to the connection, relationship, and care given to the dead (Aranui 2018). In Māori society, the dead are forever in a state of tapu, which can be understood to mean they are in a state of restriction, sacredness, and prohibition (Shirres 1982). This state exists as a result of an individual's transformation from the physical world to the spiritual world, and therefore tapu signifies the "interception between the human and the divine" (Benton, Frame and Meredith 2013, 404). Burial places are also in a state of tapu, and are therefore under restriction and prohibition, making the desecration (excavation and disturbance) of burials a breach of the tapu placed upon them. Mana, which can be defined as “prestige”, “authority”, and “power” (Williams 2006, 172), is closely aligned with tapu, and relates to a person’s place within a social group, as well as a person’s connection to a place (Mead 2003, 29). To remove ancestral remains from their resting place and subsequent retention in museums and university collections is seen, from a Māori perspective, as diminishing the mana of the person. Repatriation is a way of restoring the mana of the person, by returning them to their descendants (Aranui 2018). Wairua, in the Māori world, relates to the spiritual aspect of the person (and in fact all living things), and is sometimes defined as the “spirit” or “soul”. The concept of wairua in relation to Māori ancestral remains, like mana, connects people, place, and the land. When remains are removed, the wairua of the individual is disturbed and become restless. It is believed that the spirit of the ancestor is unable to rest until the remains are returned (Aranui 2018). Whakapapa is understood as genealogy, not just to people but to all living things (Barlow 1991), which creates interlinking connections through time and is an essential part of Māori identity. Māori involved in the repatriation process often refer to Māori human remains as “tūpuna” or “ancestors”. This connection is made through whakapapa links and a Māori cultural identity. These concepts, which when understood separately as well as through their interconnection, enable the reader to gain some understanding of why Māori may still be, at times, sceptical or apprehensive of scientific research.

19.4 Ethical Debates and Issues in New Zealand

The unauthorised and unethical removal of Māori skeletal remains from their place of burial in the past by collectors and archaeologists is now freely acknowledged (Jones and Harris 1998; Tayles and Halcrow 2011). However, over the past 30 or so years, New Zealand bioarchaeology, together with New Zealand museum culture, has undergone processes of ‘domestic decolonisation’ (McCarthy 2013, 72), reinforced by the Historic Places Act (1993), succeeded by the Heritage New Zealand Pouhere Taonga Act (2014), and, overall, by the principles of the Treaty of Waitangi (Te Tiriti o Waitangi) Act (1975). The Treaty of Waitangi (1840) is an agreement that was signed by representatives of the British Crown and Māori in 1840. The purpose of the Treaty was to enable the British settlers and Māori to live together in New Zealand under a common set of laws or agreements. As Pākehā (New Zealanders of European descent) society has acculturated to biculturalism, ethical views have shifted and formulated a more contemporary and culturally informed set of bioarchaeological ethics of practice. New Zealand bioarchaeologists accept and, in general, agree that iwi should have the ultimate authority over kōiwi tangata, that skeletal analysis or extended curation for no apparent purpose are off the table, and that ultimately reburial of kōiwi tangata or placement in a dedicated wahi tapu (a designated space or place for tapu objects) is inevitable (Heritage New Zealand Pouhere Taonga 2010). A participant in Gilmore’s study commented on this subject of negotiation and iwi control in research and reburial of kōiwi tangata:

> Oh that's just accepted and expected that they will be reburied. If the iwi want a certain level of information we will provide that and then – that's it. It's not up for negotiation, really. And I'm quite happy with that too. (William, New Zealand archaeologist, 2014)

One of the most important protocols for the bioarchaeologist, therefore, is the requirement to consult with the appropriate Māori community in the first instance when kōiwi tangata are involved (Allen and Phillips 2010; Heritage New Zealand Pouhere Taonga 2010) and endeavour to form partnerships based on mutual respect. In order for bioarchaeology to continue in New Zealand, it is essential that the profession fosters good working relationships with Māori communities and is proactive in building relationships of trust and goodwill as a base for bridging the gap between scientific and cultural values and ethics. It is also important to ensure that there is a benefit for iwi. The formal Ngāi Tahu Policy on Human Remains (Gillies and O'Regan 1994, 31) has offered such a bridge by stating that: "…the tribe [i.e. Ngāi Tahu] will make kōiwi tangata available for research when a good case can be presented, but not merely for the sake of it". As noted above, bioarchaeologists may offer various analyses of skeletal remains, which range from establishing basic skeletal indicators such as age and sex, to more in-depth analyses to form a picture of the individual's diet, disease experience, and lifestyle, and reveal the impact of environmental and cultural changes on health, development, and mortality rates. When it is deemed acceptable by descendent communities, bioarchaeology can offer a unique and direct perspective into the lives of their ancestors, which may benefit the community in terms of a better understanding of their own social history and contemporary experiences (Ruckstuhl et al. 2015; Clark et al. 2017).

New Zealand archaeologists and bioarchaeologists admitted that this can also mean that scientific information may sometimes be unobtainable when a community prefers immediate reburial with no unnecessary extra moving or handling of the remains.

> I don't like the idea that scientific information is being lost, but it's a balance. I think we got a pretty good balance with Wairau Bar. I don't really like the idea of any data that can be of value in understanding the past being just, you know, buried. (Frank, New Zealand archaeologist, 2014)

Although bioarchaeologists can see the value of osteological analyses over repatriation without analyses, there is a general consensus that work needs to be done collaboratively and the wishes of iwi are paramount. As one participant explained, the bioarchaeologists can only make their case and outline what science can offer, and the choice of conducting research remains up to iwi.

> …but there's no argument that should rule over the rights of iwi, or hapu or whanau to decide what they want done. We can't counter them…. (Rose, New Zealand bioarchaeologist, 2014)

From a bioarchaeological perspective, these protocols impact on the types of research that can be performed on excavated or previously collected kōiwi tangata. There is limited public outreach or education through the display of, or commentary, on archaeological skeletal material, and access to collections of kōiwi tangata for research purposes is limited to cases where iwi such as Ngāi Tahu agree that "scholarly investigation of kōiwi tangata can further an understanding of the lives of our tūpuna" and that "appropriate research in this area [is] a legitimate scientific interest" (Ngāi Tahu whānui, cited by Gillies and O'Regan 1994, 31–32).

From the 1940s through to the 1960s Roger Duff, the then Director of Canterbury Museum (Christchurch, New Zealand) and others excavated the famous Wairau Bar site in Marlborough in the north of the South Island. The kōiwi from the site were removed to the museum and, despite opposition from iwi (Rangitāne o Wairau) (Armstrong 2010), were displayed with their grave goods as illustrations of the burial culture of their society. The return of these ancestral remains to Wairau Bar in 2009 was the result of decades of opposition and discussions between Rangitāne o Wairau and Canterbury Museum. This repatriation came following the decision by the Waitangi Tribunal (a permanent commission of inquiry established under the Treaty of Waitangi Act (1975) that the tūpuna should be returned (Armstrong 2010). Conditions for the return were set by the museum however, with the insistence that scientific research must be carried out by biological anthropologists before burial (Aranui 2018). Although the research was carried out in partnership with Rangitāne, some members of Rangitāne were initially "suspicious" and "sceptical" about the kind of research that would be carried out (Mutch 2013, 6). Others, however, saw this as an opportunity to mend the broken relationships, which were a result of the removal of their ancestors from Wairau Bar (Mutch 2013).

The 'Science versus Culture' arguments about repatriation are more nuanced and less straightforward than they may seem at first sight because they rest on specific contexts and relationships. Although some in the profession can be narrowly focused on the scientific opportunities that may be lost, bioarchaeologists are increasingly working with Indigenous communities to resolve these issues, particularly in New Zealand since the 2000s. As Sayer (2010) has argued, there are contexts in which repatriation is not incompatible with research objectives as evidenced by the rewarding partnership that has developed between Rangitāne iwi and University of Otago researchers in 2009, which facilitated the re-excavation of the Wairau Bar site and analysis of its human remains (then stored at the Canterbury Museum) prior to their repatriation and reburial (Mutch 2013; Clark et al. 2017; Buckley and Petchey 2018). The goodwill of Indigenous communities engendered by bioarchaeologists endorsing and facilitating repatriation and reburial requests can be seen as a benefit, which far outweighs the sometimes narrow interests of science, and lays the foundation for future collaborative research efforts.

> [Bioarchaeology] is not simply a subject that exists for its own right – its own good. It's part of a broader environment. And I think that to some extent repatriation to Indigenous communities is something that can help to re-empower them politically. (Paul, English archaeologist, 2013)

As with most debates concerning opposing belief systems there is always bound to be disagreement and opposition among the protagonists in repatriation claims and debates, depending on their own perspective. Therefore, from a bioarchaeological viewpoint, it is essential to have ongoing open consultation and negotiation, and the establishing of working partnerships in order to achieve an acceptably balanced outcome in each situation.

19.5 Museums, Collection, Display, and Repatriation

The issue of repatriation of archaeological human remains housed in museum collections inevitably requires careful negotiation and the forming of constructive relationships and interactions among a variety of interest groups and stakeholders to achieve an outcome acceptable to all parties in the process. Generally speaking, the process of repatriation is carried out between the groups who are requesting the repatriation or reburial of their ancestors and the museum personnel and/or bioarchaeologists who field the requests. It may also involve interactions with legislative bodies, such as Heritage New Zealand and public opinion (e.g. Mills and Tranter 2010). Positions taken within these discussions are determined by the values, cultural perspectives and relationships each interested party has with the remains. A good example of different approaches to repatriation issues is demonstrated in New Zealand and English examples of this process.

The collection and display of skeletal and other human body parts has had a long tradition in Western European culture, either as an essential element of religious and/or funerary ritual or scientific exposition, as well as public entertainment, such as the eighteenth century public anatomical dissections of executed criminals in England (Chaplin 2012; Corradini and Bukowski 2012), and the practice of including human remains in museum displays has, after over two centuries, become well entrenched in English culture and expectation (Mills and Tranter 2010). The nineteenth century was characterised by the growth of human skeletal remains collections from burial sites of Indigenous peoples from around the world for scientific, medical, and ethnological research (Gilmore et al. 2013) and their display (often viewed as curiosities) in European museums was also an integral part of the colonial museum culture in New Zealand. Until recent decades, New Zealand museums followed the British model of museum display (McCarthy 2014). This was intended to provide the basis for scientific research as well as venues for public education, and were an important link with bioarchaeological research and practice. In the first half of the twentieth century, New Zealand museum archaeologists, with little or no consultation with iwi, continued to amass skeletal collections for research, and connect with the public through educational displays illustrated with human remains where relevant.

However, during the 1970s and 1980s, at the request of Māori and through the development of a national cultural shift, kōiwi tangata Māori and toi moko (preserved tattooed Māori heads) were gradually withdrawn from museum displays in which they had been standard educational exhibits (McCarthy 2014). These changes in museum practice took place against a background of broader social and cultural changes, including the emergence of a strong movement of Māori activism, which included land claims, redress of Treaty breaches (through the Treaty of Waitangi Amendment Act 1985), demands for cultural respect, and for control over their own cultural and natural heritage. A growing awareness of the need for a more bicultural arrangement of public and social policy and legislation developed (King 2003).

The reburial of ancestral remains excavated from archaeological contexts, at the request of iwi, has been recorded as taking place since the 1970s (Aranui 2018) and continues to the present day (Buckley et al. 2010, Campbell and Hudson 2011). Repatriation as an issue took on a public profile in New Zealand in the 1980s, with the first international repatriation of one individual in 1985, taken from Vienna back to Waikato (O'Hara 2011). Subsequently, repatriations significantly increased in frequency at an international level, which in turn led to an increase in domestic repatriations (Aranui 2018). Today the involvement of museums in the repatriation of Indigenous ancestral remains is a steadily growing process. Many museums have, and are, actively engaging with Māori, Moriori, as well as other Indigenous peoples from Rapa Nui in Chile, Niue in the Pacific Islands, North America, and Japan (Aranui 2018).

The development of international repatriation to New Zealand began at the National Museum (predecessor to the National Museum of New Zealand Te Papa Tongarewa). Maui Pomare, then the chair of the National Museum Council, had become aware of the absence of precedence with regard to the return of cultural material, including ancestral remains, throughout Europe and North America, and felt strongly that ancestral remains should no longer be categorised as artefacts but, "treated in a special sensitive manner appropriate for human remains" (Pomare 1993, 1). The National Museum began to repatriate Toi moko from international institutions from 1989.

By the early 2000s, as a result of Pomare's early work, consultation and a number of wānanga (meetings, discussions) between iwi representatives, government agencies, and museums, a fully funded repatriation programme was established at the National Museum of New Zealand Te Papa Tongarewa (Te Papa) through a government mandate (Karanga Aotearoa Repatriation Programme 2005). The creation of the Karanga Aotearoa Repatriation Programme, with support by both iwi and the Government, became the Crown Agent to undertake repatriations from international institutions and return ancestral remains to their descendant communities. Since its inception in 2003, the programme has successfully returned over 500 ancestral remains from almost 100 overseas institutions in 17 countries (Aranui 2018), and over 100 ancestors to their descendant communities, with the number steadily growing every year (Aranui 2018).

Te Papa is not the only New Zealand museum that is proactively returning ancestral remains. The Auckland War Memorial Museum, the Tairāwhiti Museum in Gisborne, and the Whanganui Regional Museum have all had an active role in the return of ancestral remains to iwi. What is interesting about all four of the museums discussed here is that the development of their policies (Canterbury Museum 1998; Whanganui Regional Museum 2006; Auckland War Memorial Museum 2008; Museum of New Zealand Te Papa Tongarewa 2010) around human remains and repatriation were heavily influenced by Māori and their cultural beliefs and practices concerning the dead. The Māori worldview has also had an impact on both the Otago and Canterbury Museums in New Zealand's South Island. The policies relating to human remains for both museums are guided by the Ngāi Tahu Policy on Kōiwi Tangata, which was developed by the South Island iwi (Gillies and O'Regan 1994).

19.6 English Museums and Repatriation

The Guidance for the Care of Human Remains in Museums (DCMS 2005) and the Human Tissue Acts (2004, 2006) have provided the framework for British museums to remove human remains from their collections. These guidelines were the result of a report from a working group set up in 2001 by the Minister of Arts and Cultural Property, the purpose of which was to examine the possibility of deaccession and legislation changes around human remains and associated objects (Palmer 2003). The report recognised that for many Indigenous communities the issue of consent in the collection of human remains "is not simply an academic issue…the removal of human remains without consent was a moral wrong that demands correction" (Palmer 2003, 146). Prior to these changes in legislation, museums, such as the British Museum and the Natural History Museum in London, were bound by the British Museum Act (1963), which did not allow them to deaccession any object from their collections, including human remains (Harris 2015). The new Human Tissue Acts (2004, 2006) granted both museums the power to deaccession human remains from their collections. Museums in England and the wider United Kingdom began to be more open to repatriation claims from Indigenous groups from around the world and have increasingly engaged with Indigenous peoples regarding the return of ancestral remains.

19.7 English Bioarchaeological Attitudes to Repatriation

In Gilmore's research, English bioarchaeologists expressed mixed reactions to the question of repatriation and reburial of human remains. Although bioarchaeological views do not necessarily reflect the museums' opinions, many of the English bioarchaeologists who were interviewed had current or past links to museums in their work, and had been responsible for curating collections or arranging and coordinating displays. According to English participants, allowing everyone the opportunity to "connect" with the past and understand what the lives of their ancestors were like was considered an important aspect of their practice. Surveys of British visitors to museums have indicated that most support the practice of displaying human remains, and expect to see skeletons when visiting museums (Mills and Tranter 2010). However, the fact that English museums frequently conduct such surveys (e.g. Mills and Tranter 2010; Jenkins 2011; Giesen 2013) does indicate that there is some anxiety in the present climate of ethical and repatriation debates.

The value to science and the potential for benefits in future research is a view that is also strongly upheld as a reason for retaining collections in England. "Human remains in the collection help advance important research fields such as archaeology, human biology, the history of disease, palaeoepidemiology, bioarchaeology, physical anthropology, forensics, and genetics" (British Museum 2013, 3). Although all the English bioarchaeologists interviewed were of the opinion that the unethically or illegally retained Indigenous individuals should be returned, there appeared to be regret that collections would be depleted and potential research and educational opportunities lost. This is echoed in the response of one interviewee:

> There are some collections that are very interesting, and important, and probably will *continue* to be interesting and important in the future, because you never know with scientific methods developing all the time, you never know what's going to be developed, and the… you know, you can always revisit collections and learn more from those collections. (Kate, English bioarchaeologist, 2013)

However, although English bioarchaeologists supported the return of Indigenous remains from museum collections to their descendant communities, there are continuing debates over the retention of some of their own country's archaeological and anatomical human remains. Requests for the return and reburial of prehistoric "Pagan" remains in England have generated much controversy (Jenkins 2011, 81–84). English bioarchaeologists see many opportunities afforded by skeletal human remains from prehistoric Britain to employ their particular skills in order to learn about many aspects of human life in the distant past—diet, health, migrations and interactions, conflicts, and social organisation. There is concern that this knowledge would be lost if the Pagan community were to appropriate and bury material that is considered a valuable resource for investigating the human past (Parker Pearson et al. 2011; Pitts 2011). British Pagan groups, particularly Honour the Ancient Dead, on the other hand, see this approach as disrespectful to the remains of their 'ancestors' as, from their perspective, the ancestral dead are still an integral part of the community, and to whose remains they have a responsibility. "It makes no difference how long ago someone died. We are their living relatives" (Restall Orr 2006, 4).

This issue has many of the hallmarks of the wider Indigenous repatriation debates. The Pagan debate, however, seems to contain important differences from the issue that confront Indigenous groups when addressing repatriation. The procedures for repatriation outlined by the Department for Culture, Media and Sport (DCMS 2005) allow for Indigenous rather than philosophical claims in a situation "where all parties hold some (genetic, cultural) relationship to the human remains at issue" (Wallis and Blain 2011, 35). English bioarchaeologists have made a number of objections to such cases being treated in the same ways as Indigenous repatriations (Mays and Smith 2009; Bienkowski 2014). They cite the lack of proven cultural, religious, or biological continuity with the specific groups making these requests. As our participants frequently pointed out, anyone in Europe could be biologically descended from these individuals, and the majority of these descendants are perfectly content to have their 'ancestors' on display or retained for research.

> They can't obviously demonstrate a continuity of religious beliefs. They can't … they've tried to a continuity in genetic terms, which is probably true to some extent, but to no greater extent than it is … that we all have some genetic connection…. (Eric, English skeletal biologist, 2013)

The differing views of New Zealand and English bioarchaeology on who has the right to claim cultural descent and make decisions about the future of archaeological remains highlights the diversity of beliefs and values concerning the treatment of the remains of the dead. This raises the question of whether the ethical rationale for repatriation can be considered a universal standard, or if it demonstrates that there is no 'one-size-fits-all' solution to these issues.

19.8 Conclusion

Repatriation is part of the wider debate on ethical treatment of human remains. It is therefore a dialogue, which not only includes the perspectives of bioarchaeological research and practice but also forms part of debates on the significance of cultural heritage and ancestors, both in New Zealand and the United Kingdom. Clearly, these are viewed differently in two widely different sociocultural settings, and indicate that the ethical elements to consider in the retention or repatriation of human remains are predicated on cultural understanding and context. In New Zealand, active involvement of Māori in discussions with bioarchaeologists and museums, and Government-sponsorship of an international repatriation programme, underpinned by a commitment to honouring Treaty principles have helped to resolve many of these issues "to a greater degree than elsewhere" (McCarthy 2013, 72).

Unlike many of their predecessors, bioarchaeologists today are taught to understand that "the study of human remains is a privilege and not a right" (Roberts 2009, 37), and must be conducted with respect and preserving the dignity of the remains. While the scientific value of archaeological remains is undoubted, it is important to understand that the cultural and spiritual value for their descendants has as greater claim. If living descendants, direct or indirect, claim the right to care for them and request their return or re-interment, it seems appropriate and ethical that bioarchaeologists should respect this and facilitate rather than hinder the process. Respectful dialogue and the formation of relationships, therefore, should lie at the ethical centre of the repatriation of human remains debates.

> There is obviously a synchronicity between archaeology and cultural values, but they're like two parallel paths that sit beside each other. So they're not the same thing but they each complement each other, and they can each inform each other. (Jenny, New Zealand archaeologist, 2014)

Acknowledgements Helen Gilmore's research was funded by a University of Otago Ph.D. scholarship and ethical approval was gained from the University of Otago Human Ethics Committee (13/190). All participant names have been changed for anonymity.

References

Allen, H., and C. Phillips. 2010. Maintaining the Dialogue: Archaeology, Cultural Heritage and Indigenous Communities. In *Bridging the Divide: Indigenous Communities and Archaeology into the 21st Century*, ed. C. Phillips and H. Allen, 17–48. Oakland: Left Coast Press.

Aranui, A.K. 2018. *Te Hokinga Mai O Ngā Tūpuna: Māori Perspectives of Repatriation and the Scientific Research of Ancestral Remains*. Dissertation, Victoria University of Wellington.

Armstrong, D. 2010. *Wairau Bar Kōiwi Tīpuna and Taonga. Te Rangitāne o Wairau*, Unpublished Report.

Auckland War Memorial Museum. 2008. *Governance Policy: Human Remains*. Auckland: Auckland War Memorial Museum.

Barlow, C. 1991. *Tikanga Whakaaro: Key Concepts in Māori Culture*. Auckland: Oxford University Press.

Benton, R., A. Frame, and P. Meredith. 2013. *Te Mātāpunenga: A Compendium of References to the Concepts and Institutions of Māori Customary Law*. Wellington: Victoria University Press.

Bienkowski, P. 2014. Authority and the Power of Place: Exploring the Legitimacy of Authorized and Alternate Voices in the Restitution Discourse. In *Museums and Restitution: New Practices, New Approaches*, ed. L. Tythacott and K. Arvanitis, 31–52. Aldershot: Ashgate.

British Association for Biological Anthropology and Osteoarchaeology [BABAO]. 2010. *Reburial and Repatriation*. http://www.babao.org.uk/publications/reburial-and-repatriation Accessed 5 August 2018.

British Museum. 2013. *British Museum Policy: Human Remains in the Collection*. London: The British Museum.

British Museum Act. 1963. The Stationery Office, London.

Buckley, H.R., and P. Petchey. 2018. Human Skeletal Remains and Bioarchaeology in New Zealand. In *Archaeological Human Remains: Legacies of Imperialism, Communism and Colonialism*, ed. B. O'Donnabhin and M.C. Lozada, 93–110. Cham: Springer.

Buckley, H.R., N. Tayles, S.E. Halcrow, et al. 2010. The People of Wairau Bar: A Re-examination. *Journal of Pacific Archaeology* 1 (1): 1–20.

Bulmer, S. 1993. Archaeology and Indigenous Rights: The World Archaeological Congress' Code of Ethics from an Archaeologist's Point of View. *Archaeology in New Zealand* 34: 54–58.

Campbell, M., and B. Hudson. 2011. *The NRD Site Community Report*. Auckland: CFG Heritage Ltd.

Canterbury Museum. 1998. *Kōiwi Tangata/Human Remains Policy*. Pouhere Taonga: Heritage New Zealand.

Chaplin, S. 2012. Dissection and Display in Eighteenth-Century London. In *Anatomical Dissection in Enlightenment England and Beyond. Autopsy Pathology and Display*, ed. P. Mitchell, 95–114. Farnham: Ashgate.

Clark, A.L., C.L. King, H.R. Buckley, et al. 2017. Biological Anthropology in the Indo-Pacific Region: New Approaches to Age-Old Questions. *Journal of Indo-Pacific Archaeology* 41: 78–94.

Cooper, E.M. 2011. *Julius Haast, the Canterbury Museum and Māori*. Dissertation, Massey University.

Corradini, E., and M. Bukowski. 2012. *Proposed European Anatomical Collections Network*. http://edoc.hu-berlin.de/umacj/2012/corradini-119/XML/CorradiniBukowski_xdiml.xml Accessed 12 December 2014.

Department for Culture, Media and Sport [DCMS]. 2005. *Guidance for the Care of Human Remains in Museums*. London: Department for Culture, Media and Sport.

Giesen, M. (ed.). 2013. *Curating Human Remains: Caring for the Dead in the United Kingdom*. Woodbridge: Boydell Press.

Gillies, K., and G. O'Regan. 1994. Murihiku Resolution of Kōiwi Tangata Management. *New Zealand Museums Journal* 24: 30–31.

Gilmore, H., C. Schafer, and S. Halcrow. 2013. Tapu and the Invention of the "Death Taboo": An Analysis of the Transformation of a Polynesian Cultural Concept. *Journal of Social Archaeology* 13: 331–349.

Harris, F. 2015. Understanding Human Remains Repatriation: Practice Procedures at the British Museum and the Natural History Museum. *Museum Management and Curatorship* 30: 138–153.

Heritage New Zealand Pouhere Taonga (Formerly New Zealand Historic Places Trust Pouhere Taonga). 2010. *Kōiwi Tangata/Human Remains*. Archaeological Guidelines Series 8. Pouhere Taonga: Heritage New Zealand.

Heritage New Zealand Pouhere Taonga Act. 2014. New Zealand Government, Wellington.

Historic Places Act. 1993. New Zealand Government, Wellington.

Hole, B. 2007. Playthings for the Foe: The Repatriation of Human Remains in New Zealand. *Public Archaeology* 6(1):5–27.

Human Tissue Act. 2004. The Stationery Office, London.

Human Tissue (Scotland) Act. 2006. The Scottish Parliament, Edinburgh.

Jenkins, T. 2011. *Contesting Human Remains in Museum Collections: The Crisis of Cultural Authority*. London: Routledge.

Jones, D.G., and R.J. Harris. 1998. Archeological Human Remains. *Current Anthropology* 39: 253–264.

Karanga Aotearoa Repatriation Programme. 2005. *Background to the Karanga Aotearoa Repatriation Programme*. Wellington: Museum of New Zealand Te Papa Tongarewa.

King, M. 2003. *The Penguin History of New Zealand*. Auckland: Penguin Books.

Klesert, A., and S. Powell. 1993. A Perspective on Ethics and the Reburial Controversy. *American Antiquity* 58: 348–354.

Larsen, C.S. 2015. *Bioarchaeology: Interpreting Behavior from the Human Skeleton*, 2nd ed. Cambridge: Cambridge University Press.

MacKie, R. 2003. Scientists Fight to Save Ancestral Bone Bank: Aborigines Demand Return of Skeletal Remains. The Observer. 28 September. https://www.theguardian.com/uk/2003/sep/28/australia.highereducation. Accessed 20 June 2018.

Mays, S., and M. Smith. 2009. Ethical Dimensions of Reburial, Retention and Repatriation of Archaeological Human Remains: A British Perspective. In *Proceedings of the Ninth Annual Conference of the British Association for Biological Anthropology and Osteoarchaeology*, ed. Lewis, M.E., and M. Clegg, 107–117. Oxford: Archaeopress.

McCarthy, C. 2013. The Practice of Repatriation: A Case Study from New Zealand. In *Museums and Restitution: New Practices, New Approaches*, ed. L. Tythacott and K. Arvanitis, 71–84. Aldershot: Ashgate.

McCarthy, C. 2014. *Museums—Museums Expand and Diversify, 1945 to 1990*. http://www.TeAra.govt.nz/en/museums/page-4. Accessed 20 June 2018.

Mead, S.M. 2003. *Tikanga Māori: Living by Māori Values*. Wellington: Huia.

Meighan, C. 1992. Some Scholars' Views on Reburial. *American Antiquity* 57: 704–710.

Mills, S., and V. Tranter. 2010. *Research into Issues Surrounding Human Bones in Museums*. London: Business Development Research Consultants.

Museum of New Zealand Te Papa Tongarewa. 2010. *Kōiwi Tangata Policy*. Wellington: Museum of New Zealand Te Papa Tongarewa.

Mutch, N. 2013. Voyage of Rediscovery. *University of Otago Magazine* 34: 6–9.

O'Hara, C. 2011. *Andreas Reischek Collection of Kōiwi Tangata in Vienna. Karanga Aotearoa Repatriation Programme*, Unpublished Research Report.

Office of Treaty Settlements. 2015. *Deed of Settlement of Historic Claims: Ngatikahu Ki Whangaroa and Ngatikahu Trust and the Crown*, Unpublished Document.

Palmer, N. 2003. *Report of the Working Group on Human Remains*, Unpublished Report.

Parker Pearson, M., T. Schadla-Hall, and G. Moshenska. 2011. Resolving the Human Remains Crisis in British Archaeology. *Papers from the Institute of Archaeology* 21: 5–9.

Peers, L. 2004. Repatriation: A Gain for Science? *Anthropology Today* 20: 3–4.

Pitts, M. 2011. Digging Deeper: Comment on Resolving the Human Remains Crisis in British Archaeology. *Papers from the Institute of Archaeology* 21: 20–22.

Pomare, M. 1993. *Memorandum: Tattooed Heads*. Wellington: Karanga Aotearoa Repatriation Programme.

Restall Orr, E. 2006. *Human Remains: The Acknowledgment of Sanctity*. Paper Presented at the Respect for Ancient British Human Remains: Philosophy and Practice Conference, Manchester Museum, Manchester, UK, 17 November 2006.

Roberts, C.A. 2009. *Human Remains in Archaeology: A Handbook*. York: Council for British Archaeology.

Ruckstuhl, K., N. Tayles, H.R. Buckley, et al. 2015. The Ancestors Speak: Kōiwi Tangata, Mātauranga Māori and the Development of Biological Anthropology in New Zealand. In *The Routledge Handbook of Bioarchaeology in Southeast Asia and the Pacific Islands*, ed. M. Oxenham and H.R. Buckley, 637–655. Abingdon: Routledge.

Sayer, D. 2010. *Ethics and Burial Archaeology*. London: Duckworth.

Shirres, M.P. 1982. Tapu. *The Journal of the Polynesian Society* 91: 29–52.

Tayles, N. 2009. Repatriation—A View from the Receiving End: New Zealand. In *The Proceedings of the Ninth Annual Conference of the British Association for Biological Anthropology and Osteoarchaeology*, ed. M. Lewis and M. Clegg, 131–135. Oxford: Archaeopress.

Tayles, N., and S. Halcrow. 2011. New Zealand/Aotearoa. In *The Routledge Handbook of Archaeological Human Remains and Legislation*, ed. N. Márquez-Grant and L. Fibiger, 647–648. London: Routledge.

Treaty of Waitangi. 1840. https://nzhistory.govt.nz/politics/treaty/read-the-treaty/maori-text. Accessed 9 September 2018.

Treaty of Waitangi Act. 1975. New Zealand Government, Wellington.

Treaty of Waitangi Amendment Act. 1985. New Zealand Government, Wellington.

Wallis, R.J., and J. Blain. 2011. From Respect to Reburial: Negotiating Pagan Interest in Prehistoric Human Remains in Britain, Through the Avebury Consultation. *Public Archaeology* 10: 23–45.

Walter, T. 1991. Modern Death: Taboo or Not Taboo? *Sociology* 25: 293–310.

Weiss, E. 2008. *Reburying the Past: The Effects of Repatriation and Reburial on Scientific Inquiry*. New York: Nova Science Publishers.

Whanganui Regional Museum. 2006. *Whanganui Regional Museum Policy: Human Remains/Kōiwi Tangata*. Whanganui: Whanganui Regional Museum.

Williams, H.W. 2006. *A Dictionary of the Māori Language*. Wellington: Legislation Direct.

Willmott, H. 2000. Death. So What? Sociology, Sequestration and Emancipation. *The Sociological Review* 48: 649–665.

World Archaeological Congress [WAC]. 1989. *The Vermillion Accord, Archaeological Ethics and the Treatment of the Dead: A Statement of Principles Agreed by Archaeologists and Indigenous Peoples at the World Archaeological Congress, Vermillion, USA*. http://worldarch.org/code-of-ethics/. Accessed 5 August 2018.

Chapter 20
Ethical Considerations in Human Remains Based Research in Argentina

Rocío García-Mancuso, Marcos Plischuk, Bárbara Desántolo, Gonzalo Garizoain and Marina Laura Sardi

Abstract In this chapter we aim to analyse the ethical issues associated with working with human remains, and how this has affected the different areas of professional advancement in Argentinian physical anthropology. Firstly, we explore the ethical concerns related to research involving human remains of Indigenous populations. Secondly, we comment on the development of forensic anthropology in Argentina. The analysis of skeletal remains for legal and humanitarian purposes is developed within the legal system, and usually in relation to educational and research institutions. Ethical issues arise in its contribution to the administration of justice. Finally, the legal framework concerned with, and the ethical issues derived from, working with contemporary collections of identified skeletons are analysed. In this context, institutions that have temporary or permanent custody of human remains must ensure the protection of the identity and physical integrity of the remains, and the personal or historical records associated with them. Human remains are a matter of dispute, as they are simultaneously the ancestors and heritage of Indigenous communities, objects under state rule, and material of research interest for scientists. Due to the significance that human remains have to the understanding of the history of our species, it is important to analyse the ethical issues emerging from their study, conservation, and management.

R. García-Mancuso (✉) · M. Plischuk · G. Garizoain · M. L. Sardi
Consejo Nacional Científico y Tecnológico (CONICET), Buenos Aires, Argentina
e-mail: rgarciamancuso@gmail.com

R. García-Mancuso · M. Plischuk · B. Desántolo · G. Garizoain
Cátedra de Citología, Histología y Embriología "A", Facultad de Ciencias Médicas, Universidad Nacional de La Plata, La Plata, Argentina

M. L. Sardi
División Antropología. Museo de La Plata, Facultad de Ciencias Naturales y Museo, Universidad Nacional de La Plata, La Plata, Argentina

K. Squires et al. (eds.), *Ethical Approaches to Human Remains*,
https://doi.org/10.1007/978-3-030-32926-6_20

20.1 Introduction

The study of human remains is an integral element of anthropology and is of great importance to society in general. Its relevance lies in its potential for contributing to the history of humankind, regardless of nationality, creed, ancestry, or religious beliefs (AABA 2007). Human remains are imbued with symbolism, cultural, and political significance, and they exhibit spiritual and religious meaning for individuals as well as entire communities (DCMS 2005; Alfonso and Powell 2007; Martin et al. 2013). It is in this context where bioethics incorporates a deep and holistic reflection on knowledge construction, based on a multidisciplinary and intercommunicated approach, promoting a critical consideration of the consequences of scientific investigations to society (González Broquen 2014).

The dilemma of reducing humans to a mere (study) object in scientific investigations raises a series of ethical and socio-political questions regarding the established relationship between subject and object (González Broquen 2014). An example of this is evidenced in the language itself, where concepts such as 'specimen', 'object', or 'corpse' reflect an imposed distance between the researcher and the deceased, which results in impartiality and objectivity. This is in stark contrast to terms like 'individual', 'person', or 'human remains', which mark a connection between the scientist with the object of study (Cassman et al. 2007).

Professional ethics encompass the personal and corporate standards of behaviour expected by professionals, and are produced in an environment where each discipline develops its own language, conceptual tools, and technical procedures. One of the most transcendent purposes of a professional organisation is to establish a set of normative principles. Although ethical principles apply to any professional activity, it is worth mentioning that, in working with human remains, due to their social transcendence and their ties with contemporary descendants or close relatives, the application of ethical principles demands a greater responsibility and a stricter enforcement of their fulfilment (Mancuso 1995; CONICET 2006). Collecting and studying human remains is a politically and socially complex activity, thus our professional practice must be revised and revisited continuously. In Argentina, the study, conservation, and management of human skeletal remains is regulated by the Code of Ethics devised by the Argentine Biological Anthropology Association (Asociación de Antropología Biológica Argentina, AABA) (AABA 2007; Aranda et al. 2014), which includes normative aspects of professional behaviour.

The aim of this chapter is to analyse the ethical issues derived from working with human remains, and how this has affected different areas of Argentinian anthropology. Firstly, we will address the ethical concerns faced by researchers that work with human remains of Indigenous populations. The importance of obtaining consent from the community to which the remains belong, and of giving descendants the authority to control the disposition of their relatives' remains is highlighted.

Secondly, we comment on the development of forensic anthropology, and certain ethical issues relating to its contribution to the administration of justice. In this respect, the researcher must be aware of the implications of their report, which may affect the resolution of a case and, as is often the case in forensics, the conclusions drawn in the report must be defendable in court. The Argentine legal system, the different kind of cases in which anthropologists are summoned, and formal education in forensic anthropology are also explored in this chapter.

Finally, the legal framework and ethical issues concerned with working with contemporary collections of identified skeletons will be analysed, considering that human remains must be treated with respect and dignity during their study and conservation. In this context, institutions that have temporary or permanent custody of human remains must warrant the protection of the deceased's identity, and the physical integrity of the remains, as well as any personal or historical documentation associated with them.

20.2 Ethical Concerns Relating to Indigenous Human Remains

Argentina has a long tradition of anthropological research following the creation of osteological collections during the last two decades of the nineteenth century. In recent years, the excavation and treatment of Indigenous remains in scientific contexts have been contested by local communities, whose claims are influenced by two conflicting laws (Sardi 2011).

The National Act 25517 (2001), which has been in force since 2001, deals with the restitution of human remains. In Article 1 of this Act, it establishes that "the human remains of Indigenous people that are held in museums and in public and private collections should be made available for reclamation by the communities to which they belong". Article 3 states that "all scientific research that involves Aborigine communities and their heritage should have the express consent of such communities". The National Institute of Indigenous Affairs (in Spanish, Instituto Nacional de Asuntos Indígenas, INAI) is the national agency in charge of the enforcement of this Act, and where, depending on the administration, different number of officials, professionals, lawyers, and Aborigines work. INAI was founded in 1985 following the enactment sanction of National Act 23302 (1985), which develops and coordinates public policies to guarantee Indigenous rights (see below; National Act 24430 1994).

The law finds its support, firstly, in the International Labour Organization Convention about Indigenous and Tribal Peoples No. 169 (International Labour Organization 1989), which acknowledges the aspirations of these peoples to exercise control over their own institutions, ways of life, and economic development, and to maintain and develop their identities, languages, and religions, within the framework of the Nations in which they live. Secondly, since the 1994 amendment to the Constitution of the Argentine Nation (National Act 24430 1994), the State acknowledges Indigenous rights. Section 75 (17) states that the Congress is empowered "To recognise the ethnic and cultural pre-existence of Indigenous peoples of Argentina. To guarantee respect for the identity and the right to bilingual and intercultural education; to recognise the legal capacity of their communities, and the community possession and ownership of the lands they traditionally occupy; and to regulate the granting of other lands adequate and sufficient for human development; none of them shall be sold, transmitted or subject to liens or attachments. To guarantee their participation in issues related to their natural resources and in other interests affecting them. [...]". This Article represents a significant change, because for most of the twentieth century, the State had developed policies that solely represented a homogeneous white sector of the population through the promotion of European immigration as a means of populating large "empty" areas of land (whilst simultaneously disregarding the presence of Indigenous families), the establishment of a mandatory public education system in Spanish, the compulsory enlistment of males to the newly centralised army, and the imposition of national symbols (e.g. a national anthem, flag, and war heroes) (Geler and Rodríguez 2016). As a result, there was a widely accepted social misconception that Indigenous people were extinct, and that most Argentinians have European origins, an assumption that still prevails.

The National Act 25517 (2001) was the result of a sustained campaign led by Indigenous people as a way of gaining public visibility and the right to participate in cases where their territories, and their material and spiritual life were affected (Lazzari 2007; Rodríguez in press). Several of their claims were directed against physical, political, and epistemic violence that neglected Indigenous existence and identities, but also against anthropologists, museums, and other scientific institutions that used their bodies and material culture for exhibitions and research.

Claims about the restitution (i.e. repatriation) of human remains are based on an ontological difference. Whilst some archaeologists and biological anthropologists view human remains as objects to study (e.g. DNA, morphology, pathologies, nutrition, and funerary rituals), or as "archives" of past lives that are susceptible to observation, analysis, and interpretation through scientific procedures, several Indigenous communities consider the dead to be linked with them by territory or genealogy; they are their ancestors, dead persons in a different spiritual condition or, at least, the material evidence of robbery, colonialism, and genocide (Rodríguez 2013; in press; Sardi 2016; Sardi and Ballestero 2017).

The Museum of La Plata (Museo de La Plata), in the city of La Plata, is one of the institutions that has changed the most in Latin America regarding claims over Indigenous human remains. In the 1980s, when the last dictatorship ended, repatriation requests started, and different social sectors gained visibility. The first demands for restitution were those regarding the remains of Inacayal and Panguitruz Gner. Inacayal had been imprisoned with his family just after the war against the Indigenous people of Pampa and Patagonia ended in 1884. In 1886 these people were taken to the Museo de La Plata, where Inacayal died. His body was dissected, and his skeleton, brain, and scalp became part of anthropological collections. Panguitruz Gner was an important chief of the Ranquel people who died in 1877. Soldiers exhumed his body and took his skull, which was then donated to the

Museum of La Plata. After several demands and following the compulsory restitution of these two important Indian chiefs, Inacayal and Panguitruz Gner, in 1994 and 2001, respectively (Sardi 2011; Ametrano 2015), the Museum of La Plata developed a policy in 2006 regarding the non-exhibition of Indigenous remains, their adequate conservation, their restitution to ancestral territories or communities, and the request of informed consent of the communities claiming sovereignty over Indigenous remains (Ametrano 2015; Del Papa and Pucciarelli 2015; Sardi et al. 2015; Sardi and Ballestero 2017). The request of informed consent before studying the remains was granted in some cases and denied in others.

Akin to other countries (e.g. USA), repatriation processes in Argentina have provoked much discussion among archaeologists and bioanthropologists. On the one hand, they want to preserve human remains for research, under the assumption that bones, as well as material culture, contain information about human history and evolution, and are irreplaceable material evidence. Yet, on the other hand, Indigenous rights must be respected. As a result, the AABA recently outlined a deontological ethical code (Aranda et al. 2014), which falls in line with other archaeological organisations that have issued similar statements (Gómez Otero 2012).

The enforcement of the National Act 25517 (2001) has also led to the organisation of six workshops, entitled "Discussion on Restitution of Human Remains of Archaeological and Bioanthropological Interest" (in Spanish, Taller de Discusión sobre Restitución de Restos Humanos de Interés Arqueológico y Bioantropológico, TaDiRH), held from 2011 to 2017. Apart from debates about restitution, another important topic discussed in these workshops is the excavation of Indigenous tombs and cemeteries, which is a common practice amongst some archaeologists and anthropologists in Argentina. It is worth noting that some researchers recognise the importance of the restitution of Indigenous remains that are part of historical collections, but do not question the assumptions and validity of those scientific practices (i.e. excavation without informed consent and possession of remains in scientific institutions) that are contested in National Act 25517 (2001).

The excavation, exhumation, and transportation of human remains to research institutions are supported by the National Act 25743 (2003) which regulates the registration, permission, and control of Argentinian archaeological and palaeontological heritage. This Act does not explicitly mention human remains, but they are implicitly covered in Article 2, which states "The archaeological heritage is defined as movable and immovable property or remains regardless of its nature found on the surface, underground or within territorial waters that can provide information about the socio-cultural groups that have inhabited the country from pre-Colombian times to recent historical periods". The protection of the archaeological heritage is the responsibility of the State of each province (the main territorial divisions of Argentina), which issues permits for the excavation and registration of sites, and the resultant collections (for further details, see Sardi 2011).

This law openly contradicts Indigenous rights, which are recognised in the National Act 25517 (Rodríguez 2013). Scientific practices that involve exhumation and analysis of human remains, both in the laboratory and the field, are sometimes strongly contested by Indigenous communities that inhabit within or close to the territory where such burials or cemeteries are located. On such occasions, informed consent of these communities is completely disregarded (Gómez Otero 2012). According to National Act 25743 (2003), part of the "movable and immovable property or remains" is ruled by the State. Human remains are not persons, ancestors, or the corporeality of spirits with some kind of agency over living people; instead, they are objects (Rodríguez 2013, in press).

Indigenous claims, however, have led some biological anthropologists and archaeologists to think about Indigenous rights over the remains of their ancestors, and have begun to work together with local communities that inhabit areas close to where human remains have been found (Endere and Curtoni 2006; Gómez Otero 2012; Guichón et al. 2015; Salceda et al. 2015; Fabra and Zabala 2018). The institution with the greatest experience of this type of collaborative work is the National Patagonian Center (Centro Nacional Patagónico, CENPAT), on the northeast coast of Chubut province, in Patagonia (Gómez Otero 2012, 2016). In this region, several exhumations have taken place, many of which were due to accidental discovery. Consequently, these triggered Indigenous demands to stop what they considered the desecration of burials. Consequently, anthropologists demanded action to protect these burials. As a result, communities identified as the Mapuche, Tehuelche, and Mapuche-Tehuelche communities began to interact with researchers and with State authorities in order to be informed, to provide consent, and to intervene in decisions about Indigenous burials (Gómez Otero 2012, 2016).

In Santa Cruz province (Patagonia), the Mapuche-Tehuelche community, Lof Fem Mapu, has been working together with researchers since 2004, when there was a claim over human remains displayed in the local "Carlos Borgialli" museum in the city of Puerto Santa Cruz (Guichón et al. 2015). As a result of this collaborative venture, a new Local Act (Local Act 169/09 2009) was enacted with the aim of generating a Co-managed Transitory Repository for human remains (Nahuelquir et al. 2015). The word "repository" refers to a site of respect, where human bodies are protected temporarily until the authorities of the Indigenous community decide their definitive disposition. The repository is "co-managed" by anthropologists, municipal employees, and the authorities of the Lof Fem Mapu Community, resulting in an intercultural management place which recognises the significance attributed to skeletal remains by the Indigenous community (Nahuelquir et al. 2015).

These new experiences, but with their particularities, also occurred in Tierra del Fuego province (Patagonia), between 2006 and 2014 during exhumations in the cemetery of the Salesian Mission in Rio Grande city. Members of the Salessian community, Maria Auxiliadora's nuns, ancient settlers, and members of the Selk'nam-Haush Indigenous community were buried in this cemetery (Guichón et al. 2015). In addition to the permits granted by the local authorities and the Mission's authorities, conversations between anthropologists and members of the Selk'nam community also took place. Here, authorities of the Selk'nam community were informed and visited the area that was to be excavated, and during the fieldwork, meetings were held, and progress was reported. However, there are still tensions between the anthropologists and community, particularly over complex issues. One part of the Indigenous group granted their informed consent to study the human remains, while the other part does not. The restitution of remains, along with individual documentation and information obtained during the research project, has been agreed for the near future.

Collaborative research has also taken place in the Gran Chaco region, particularly in Formosa province, in the northeast region of Argentina (Salceda et al. 2015). The first project began in 2008 when the Wichi community "Pajarito" (Afwenchelhos) made a request to forensic anthropologists at the Museum of La Plata. The request involved the exhumation of several burials as a means of proving ancestor-descendant relationship and, also, to obtain legal support over land property. An interdisciplinary team, consisting of archaeologists, ethnographers, bioanthropologists, geneticists, lawyers, and film-makers reached an agreement with the local community in order to locate and excavate a burial site in Paraje Esteros (Formosa province). As a result, the complete skeleton of an individual was exhumed, which showed genetic affinities with extant members of the community. This finding evidenced that ancestors had inhabited the same territory and thus enabled the Pajarito community to gain rights over the land (Desántolo et al. 2013).

A further collaborative project took place in Formosa province in 2011 when human remains were recovered in the Wichi community of El Quebracho during the construction of a school (Lamenza et al. 2016). Members of the community kept the remains for safekeeping and demanded (to governmental authorities) that archaeological research was conducted on them. Previous meetings were held between Indigenous people, teachers, construction workers, and researchers in order to establish research guidelines. The exhumed individuals were analysed in situ and, following exhumation, the human remains were handed over to the local community, which comprised of integrated members of the Indigenous community and local citizens, most of them teachers of the school, with the expectation that a local museum might be created (Salceda et al. 2015).

From these experiences, we can see that Indigenous people do not deny scientific research; moreover, sometimes they request the collaboration of anthropologists in order to gain other rights, such as the property of their land, or to find out about the life of local inhabitants from ancient times, and to ascertain their ties with the spiritual life of their ancestors. When Indigenous groups submit a claim for repatriation of human remains, informed consent, and when they participate in scientific projects, they are contesting epistemic supremacy of scientific narratives (Rodríguez 2013, in press; Sardi and Ballestero 2017); they ask for the right to be recognised as Indigenous people, to participate in public debates in a respectful and egalitarian way, and to put into practice Indigenous narratives over the past, over their territory, and over their ancestors.

Bodies of the dead are charged with enormous emotional significance and memories, some of which entail traumatic pasts. In our opinion, the greatest ethical challenge for researchers is, firstly, to respect the wishes of Indigenous people and, secondly, to develop an open and equalitarian dialogue, not only with Indigenous people, but also with different social actors that maintain some kind of relationship with a given territory and with burials located there.

20.3 Ethical Issues Associated with the Contribution of Forensic Anthropology to the Administration of Justice

Forensic anthropology is the application of knowledge and methodology of physical anthropology to medicolegal issues (Ubelaker 2018). It shares its ethical concerns with the others branches of biological anthropology, but the discipline also needs to formulate its own set of principles, as the identity of the deceased may be known, they may have surviving kin, and any information obtained from the remains affects relatives, and analyses must be conducted in accordance with legal regulations (Galloway et al. 1990; Cesani et al. 2014; Turner et al. 2018). Forensic anthropologists analyse skeletal remains for legal and humanitarian purposes and, therefore, their activity is developed within the legal system. In Argentina, this system is divided in two: a national system that deals with federal cases across the entire national territory, and a provincial system that functions through judicial bodies created and organised by each province, which is responsible for hearing local cases (Fondebrider and Bosio 2015).

Participation in federal cases related to the exhumation and identification of disappeared people in Argentina has been the priority of the Argentine Forensic Anthropology Team (Equipo Argentino de Antropología Forense, EAAF). The EAAF was established in 1984, and is a private, scientific, and non-profit organisation that applies forensic sciences to the investigation of human rights violations in Argentina and worldwide (Fondebrider 2012; see also Silika and Squires, this volume, for details of the EAAF's work in Zimbabwe). Individuals that disappeared during Argentina's civic-military dictatorship, calling itself the National Reorganisation Process (1976–1983), were victims of the crime of enforced disappearance. Argentine state terrorism exercised a systematised sequence that consisted in kidnapping-torturing-assassinating; the remains of "disappeared" persons were then buried in clandestine graves or they were buried in unnamed graves in public cemeteries throughout the country (Cohen Salama 1992). With the return to democracy in Argentina, after the general election of 1983, forensic anthropology became of great social importance (Levin 2015).

The EAAF is also involved in the search and identification of children born in captivity in clandestine detention centres (1975–1984) (Ferrante 2011), and has recently contributed to the Humanitarian Project Plan, organised by the International Committee of the Red Cross, which entailed the identification of bodies of fallen Argentine soldiers from the Malvinas War (2nd April 1982 to 14th June 1982), who were buried in individual, unnamed graves. The EAAF's guiding ethical principle is to work closely with victims' relatives throughout the investigation and to maintain the utmost respect for their wishes, during the exhumation and identification process, given that they are in distress over the "disappearance" of a loved one (EAAF 2018).

In Argentina, biological anthropologists that are called as expert witnesses in cases involving human remains do not belong to the judicial system or to the security forces, but to educational and research public institutions. For this reason, the request of anthropologists is usually made to the Deans of faculties that offer a degree in anthropology and from there, the requisition is delegated to the professional that the institution considers most suitable for the task. These professionals are summoned by judges, but they are rarely completely dedicated to contributing in forensic investigations, as they are not employees of the law enforcement agencies. In any case, the study, conservation, and management of human skeletal remains from past populations is regulated by the AABA Code of Ethics (AABA 2007; Aranda et al. 2014) and the same should be applied to human remains from forensic cases.

Forensic anthropologists are required to answer a series of predetermined questions about human remains, such as age at death, sex, ancestry, cause and manner of death, and an estimation of time since death. The latter is always difficult to answer due to the large number of factors that need to be considered, and that the early post-mortem changes (e.g. hours or days) show less variation, while skeletonised bodies associated with longer post mortem intervals (weeks, months, and years) result in a decrease in the accuracy of time since death estimates (Christensen et al. 2014; Mariani et al. 2017). Also, the remains usually arrive at the laboratory with very little contextual information due to the absence of professional archaeologists during surface collection and/or excavation. Despite this, the location where the remains were found, the number of skeletal elements, and some other bone features (e.g. artificial cranial deformation, non-metric traits, and bone weathering) allow anthropologists to establish whether the remains are forensically significant, or if they derive from an archaeological unmarked burial (Walsh-Haney and Lieberman 2005). If it is determined that the remains are archaeological, the anthropologist must inform the appropriate authorities about the risk of alteration or destruction of archaeological sites that contain human remains as established by the professional code of ethics (Aranda et al. 2014).

Many Argentinian anthropologists are trained in the analysis of skeletal remains from archaeological contexts or contemporary collections. Despite not having formal education in forensic anthropology, the professionals involved in forensic cases where human remains are present will have a degree in anthropology, and usually a Ph.D. They are frequently called upon by law enforcement agencies through their academic institutions and are usually renowned for their research, despite being rarely certified. Due to the absence of a national board that regulates the profession, the only formal training and accreditation for forensic anthropologists in Latin America is given by the Latin American Forensic Anthropology Association (in Spanish, Asociación Latinoamericana de Antropología Forense, ALAF) during annual conferences hosted in different countries each year. Given that, in Argentina, biological anthropologists conduct work in forensic cases, their practice falls under the scope of the Deontological Code. This states that "a lack of ethics to undertake any aspect of professional practice that involves the treatment of human remains without being adequately trained from the theoretical and technical point of view in relation to the problem addressed in each case" is considered unethical behaviour (Aranda et al. 2014, 112), meaning that biological anthropologists that are not trained to work with human remains should not work with them.

Under an unwritten rule of ethical commitment between the academics and judicial agencies, scientists have responded to the requirements of the general community, offering their expert knowledge in litigation situations of land seizure, or in the face of criminal complaints (Salceda et al. 2010). Particularly, at the National University of La Plata (Universidad Nacional de La Plata), forensic anthropological requests were historically sent to the Anthropology Division of the Museum La Plata, Faculty of Natural Sciences and Museum, National University of La Plata (Facultad de Ciencias Naturales y Museo, Universidad Nacional de La Plata) where Professor Maria Esther 'Lilia' Cháves de Azcona and Dr. Susana Salceda (after Chaves de Azcona's retirement in the mid-1980s), responded to the demands made from security and justice institutions, which led to the creation of a Forensic Anthropology Laboratory.

The relationship between scientific and judicial systems has been strengthened in recent years by the signing of several cooperation agreements between different justice departments and national university research laboratories, to collaborate in the recovery and examination of human remains when they are found, with the aim of solving cases in civil and criminal jurisdictions, e.g. Córdoba, San Juan, Mendoza, Puerto Madryn, and La Plata cities (Fabra and Ginarte 2009; FCM 2012; CENPAT 2014; FFyL 2018). Also, in 2016 the National Council for Scientific and Technical Research (Consejo Nacional de Investigaciones Científicas y Técnicas, CONICET) created the National Science and Justice Programme, with the aim of not only strengthening ties between the scientific community and the judiciary, the Public Ministry of Defence, and public prosecutors throughout the country, but also of highlighting the importance of applied sciences and their contribution to the administration of justice (CONICET 2015).

20.4 Legal Framework and Ethical Issues About Contemporary Collections of Identified Skeletons

Important progress in the field of bioanthropology over the past 150 years has been the result of research carried out on skeletal collections housed in institutional repositories, such as the Museum of La Plata in La Plata City, and the Ethnographic Museum Juan B. Ambrosetti in Buenos Aires (Argentina), School of Medicine in Coimbra (Portugal; see Cardoso, this volume, for further discussion around the collections in Portugal), the National Museum of Natural History in Paris (France), and the Natural History Museum in London (UK) among others. These collections were traditionally created with human skeletal remains obtained from archaeological excavations. Nevertheless, the need for skeletons with associated information, which would allow researchers to develop estimation methods for age, sex, or stature (among other characteristics), has led to the creation of skeletal collections composed of bones from hospitals or cemeteries where such information is available (Salceda et al. 2012; Henderson and Alves Cardoso 2018).

Taking into consideration population heterogeneity and the global consensus that local standards should be used to generate the biological profile of unidentified human remains, several identified skeletal collections have been created in South America over the last 20 years, for example Santiago's Subactual Collection, University of Chile (n = 1282) (Colección Subactual de Santiago, Universidad de Chile) (Lemp Urzúa et al. 2008), Chacarita Collection, University of Buenos Aires (n = 146) (Colección Chacarita, Universidad de Buenos Aires) (Bosio et al. 2012), and the Contemporary Colombian Skeletal Reference Collection, National Institute of Legal Medicine and Forensic Sciences (n = 600) (Colección Instituto Nacional de Medicina Legal y Ciencias Forenses (Sanabria-Medina et al. 2016). In Argentina, the largest skeletal collection is the Lambre collection (n = 445), created in 2005 and hosted in the Faculty of Medical Sciences of the National University of La Plata (Facultad de Ciencias Médicas, Universidad Nacional de La Plata) (Salceda et al. 2009, 2012). Work that has been carried out on this collection has allowed scientists to validate and propose new methods in forensic anthropology (García-Mancuso 2014; García-Mancuso and Salceda 2014; Plischuk et al. 2014; García-Mancuso et al. 2015; Plischuk and Inda 2015; Salceda et al. 2015; Desántolo and Beral 2016; Desántolo and Inda 2016; Garizoain et al. 2016, 2017; García Mancuso et al. 2018; Plischuk et al. 2018a, 2018b).

The Lambre Collection is regulated by Local Acts 7638/90 (1990) and 9741/02 (2002). Local Act 7638/90 (1990) establishes that, unless close relatives decide upon a prior exhumation, individuals that have been buried for at least six years can be exhumed *ex officio* by cemetery employees. Later, relatives have a period of time to claim the remains and decide their subsequent destination. After the allotted time expires, cemetery administration has the authority to decide the final destination of the remains, which is usually the cemetery ossuary. Like other contemporary collections, the Lambre Collection has been amassed from a municipal cemetery with the permission of the local City Hall (Campanacho and Cardoso 2018).

Local Act 9471/02 (2002) establishes that the administration of the Cemetery of La Plata is authorised to hand over those duly identified unclaimed remains to the Faculty of Medical Sciences at the National University of La Plata. Article 2 states, "The remains referred to in Article 1 [intended for common ossuary] will be destined to the Faculty of Medical Science (Morphological Science Department) for the creation of an osteological collection, and to the Faculty of Odontology, the osseous elements relevant to the speciality for the creation of a skull collection to be used by students for their training and for scientific research". In 2005, an agreement was signed between the Faculty of Medical Sciences and the Faculty of

Natural Sciences and associated museum (at the National University of La Plata) to create an osteological reference collection for research and teaching purposes. Studies that involve handling human skeletal remains from the collection must follow the guidelines outlined by the Argentine Biological Anthropological Association (Asociación de Antropología Biológica Argentina) (Aranda et al. 2014) stressing the dignified and respectful treatment of the remains in order to guarantee their correct management and preservation. Likewise, all studies performed using the Lambre Collection have been approved by the Bioethics Committee of the Faculty of Medical Sciences (Comité de Bioética y Ética de la Investigación 2012).

The anthropological analysis of human remains for research purposes is characterised by non-invasive techniques, for example measurements and imaging. These data are useful in that the information can assist in the production of biological profiles of past populations and the identification of victims. Also, imaging, such as photographs, radiographs, and 3D scans, are also useful tools in the identification process and allows the anthropologist to reach relevant conclusions (Márquez-Grant and Errickson 2017). This type of information should be treated in a respectful manner, since it is a type of record that once belonged to living people (France 2012).

20.5 Conclusion

In Argentina, most regulations related to the management and study of human bone have been devised in response to issues associated with the human remains of Indigenous people (AABA 2007; AAPRA 2009; Aranda et al. 2014). Ethical concerns derived from working with, and handling, contemporary human remains from osteological collections and forensic cases have not been profoundly discussed in the published literature. In this sense, a debate about the meanings and sensitivities that arise at the individual and community level is necessary. The lack of discussion should be reversed through the promotion of debate in congresses, workshops, and other academic and non-academic spaces in order to consider a revision of the legislation and introduce the wishes of Indigenous communities in the debate.

With regards to forensic anthropology, the country's recent history and circumstances have led to significant developments in this discipline and to the creation of a team of professionals at the service of the families of the victims' (of state terrorism) and to seek justice in cases of human rights violations. It is necessary to expand on the positive contribution forensic anthropology can provide to the administration of justice in current cases and to the police. To this end, establishing formal education in forensic anthropology and encouraging the training and continuing professional development of anthropologists working in forensic cases are essential requirements. It is also necessary to develop the biological anthropology deontological normative code and to promote new topics concerning the management of forensic evidence as it is crucial to the judicial process.

Every institution that houses human remains from contemporary cemeteries and archaeological contexts for research and/or teaching purposes must ensure that remains are managed, stored, handled, and recorded in accordance with the existing legislation, namely, National Act 25517 (2001) and National Act 25743 (2003) and their respective provincial and local acts. Human remains are a matter of dispute, since they are subject to various, and at times, conflicting, interests and laws: they are the ancestors and heritage of Indigenous communities, objects under State rule, and scientific information related to past populations. Due to the importance that human remains have to the understanding of the history of our species, their preservation for scientific research has become an ethical principle.

References

Alfonso, M., and J. Powell. 2007. Ethics of Flesh and Bone, or Ethics in the Practice of Paleopathology, Osteology, and Bioarchaeology. In *Human Remains: Guide for Museums and Academic Institutions*, ed. V. Cassman, N. Odegaard, and J. Powell, 5–11. Lanham: AltaMira Press.

Ametrano, S.J. 2015. Los procesos de restitución en el Museo de La Plata. *Revista Argentina de Antropología Biológica* 17 (2): 1–13.

Asociación de Antropología Biológica Argentina [AABA]. 2007. *Declaración de la Asociación de Antropología Biológica Argentina. Ética del estudio de restos humanos.* http://www.fcnym.unlp.edu.ar/aabra/Declaraci%F3n%20AABA%20Restos%20Humanos.pdf. Accessed 30 May 2018.

Asociación de Arqueólogos Profesionales de la República Argentina [AAPRA]. 2009. *Código de Ética Profesional.* http://www.aapra.org.ar/wp-content/uploads/2017/09/AAPRA-C%C3%B3digo-de-%C3%89tica-Profesional.pdf. Accessed 30 May 2018.

Aranda, C., G. Barrientos, and M. Del Papa. 2014. Código Deontológico para el Estudio, Conservación y Gestión de Restos Humanos de Poblaciones del Pasado. *Revista Argentina de Antropología Biológica* 16 (2): 111–113.

Bosio, L., S. García Guraieb, L.H. Luna, et al. 2012. Chacarita Project: Conformation and Analysis of a Modern and Documented Human Osteological Collection from Buenos Aires City—Theoretical, Methodological and Ethical Aspects. *Homo* 63: 481–492.

Campanacho, V., and H. Cardoso. 2018. The Significance of Identified Human Skeletal Collections to Further Our Understanding of the Skeletal Ageing Process in Adults. In *Identified Skeletal Collections: The Testing Ground of Anthropology?* ed. C.Y. Henderson and F.A. Alves Cardoso, 115–131. Oxford: Archaeopress.

Cassman, V., N. Odegaard, and J. Powell. 2007. Introduction: Dealing with the Dead. In *Human Remains: Guide for Museums and Academic Institutions*, ed. V. Cassman, N. Odegaard, and J. Powell, 1–4. Lanham: AltaMira Press.

Centro Científico Tecnológico Patagónico (CENPAT). 2014. *Ciencia Forense: Una Contribución Interdisciplinar a la Justicia. Comunicación CONICET, CENPAT 23/10/2014.* http://www.conicet.gov.ar/ciencia-forense-una-contribucion-interdisciplinar-a-la-justicia. Accessed 20 May 2018.

Cesani, M.F., M. Sardi, D. Colantonio, et al. 2014. Líneas de Investigación Actuales de la Antropología Biológica Argentina. *Revista Argentina de Antropología Biológica* 16 (1–2): 31–38.

Christensen, A.M., N.V. Passalacqua, and E.J. Bartelink. 2014. Forensic Taphonomy. In *Forensic Anthropology*, ed. A.M. Christensen, N.V. Passalacqua, and E.J. Bartelink, 119–147. San Diego: Academic Press.

Cohen Salama, M. 1992. *Tumbas Anónimas: Informe sobre la Identificación de Restos de Victimas de la Represión Illegal*. Buenos Aires: Catálogos Editora.

Comité de Bioética y Ética de la Investigación. 2012. Aprobación del Protocolo Integración y Análisis de la Colección Osteológica Prof. Dr. Rómulo Lambre. Acta N.°17. Exp.: N° 0800-013812/12-000. Facultad de Ciencias Médicas, Universidad Nacional de La Plata, La Plata.

Consejo Nacional de Investigaciones Científicas y Tecnológicas [CONICET]. 2006. *Comité de Ética. Lineamientos para el Comportamiento Ético en las Ciencias Sociales y Humanidades. Res. 2857*. http://www.conicet.gov.ar/wp-content/uploads/RD-20061211-2857.pdf. Accessed 30 May 2018.

Consejo Nacional de Investigaciones Científicas y Tecnológicas [CONICET]. 2015. *Programa Nacional de Ciencia y Justicia*. http://www.conicet.gov.ar/programas/ciencia-y-justicia. Accessed 30 May 2018.

Del Papa, M.C., and H.M. Pucciarelli. 2015. Administración de las Colecciones de Antropología Biológica del Museo de La Plata. *Revista Argentina de Antropología Biológica* 17 (2): 1–5.

Department for Culture, Media and Sport [DCMS]. 2005. *Guidance for the Care of Human Remains in Museums*. London: Department for Culture, Media and Sport.

Desántolo, B., G. Lamenza, G. Balbarrey, et al. 2013. Territorialidad y Laudo Forense. El Caso "Misión Esteros" (Formosa, Argentina). *Folia Histórica del Nordeste* 21: 155–167.

Desántolo, B., and V. Beral. 2016. Los Estudios de Histología Ósea en Antropología Biológica. *Revista Argentina de Antropología Biológica* 18 (2): 1–3.

Desántolo, B., and A.M. Inda. 2016. Estimación Microscópica de Edad a Partir de la Zona Cortical del Fémur en Individuos Adultos: Revisión Metodológica. *Revista Argentina de Antropología Biológica* 18 (2): 1–12.

Endere, M.L., and R.P. Curtoni. 2006. Entre Lonkos y "Ólogos". La Participación de la Comunidad Indígena Rankülche de Argentina en la Investigación Arqueológica. *Arqueología Suramericana* 2 (1): 72–92.

Equipo Argentino de Antropología Forense [EEAF]. 2018. *History of EAAF*. http://eaaf.typepad.com/founding_of_eaaf. Accessed 30 May 2018.

Fabra, M., and A. Ginarte. 2009. *Protocolo de Hallazgo, Recuperación y Análisis de Restos Óseos. Poder Judicial, Gobierno de la Provincia de Córdoba*, Unpublished manuscript. Córdoba: Universidad Nacional de Córdoba.

Fabra, M., and M.E. Zabala. 2018. *Historias Escritas en los Huesos: Los Poblados de la Costa Sur de Laguna Mar Chiquita*. Córdoba: Universidad Nacional de Córdoba.

Facultad de Ciencias Médicas [FCM]. 2012. Resolución sobre la creación del Centro de Investigaciones en Ciencias Forenses. Res. N°487, Expte. N°800-14486/12. 4 December, 2012. Facultad de Ciencias Médicas, Universidad Nacional de La Plata, La Plata.

Facultad de Filosofía y Letras [FFyL]. 2018. *Acuerdo entre la Facultad de Filosofía y Letras de la Universidad Nacional de Cuyo y el Ministerio Público Fiscal de la Provincia de Mendoza. 17 April 2018*. Mendoza: Universidad Nacional de Cuyo y el Ministerio Público Fiscal de la Provincia de Mendoza.

Ferrante, M. 2011. La Prueba de la Identidad en la Persecución Penal por Apropiación de Niños y Sustitución de su Identidad. In *Hacer Justicia. Nuevos Debates sobre el Juzgamiento de Crímenes de Lesa Humanidad en Argentina*, ed. J. Taiana, 227–258. Buenos Aires: Siglo Ventiuno.

Fondebrider, L. 2012. The Application of Forensic Anthropology to the Investigation of Cases of Political Violence. In *A Companion to Forensic Anthropology*, ed. D.C. Dirkmaat, 639–648. London: Wiley-Blackwell.

Fondebrider, L., and L. Bosio. 2015. The Practice of Forensic Sciences in Argentina. In *The Global Practice of Forensic Science*, ed. D. Ubelaker, 5–11. London p: Wiley-Blackwell.

France, D.L. 2012. Ethics in Forensic Anthropology. In *A Companion to Forensic Anthropology*, ed. D.C. Dirkmaat, 666–682. London: Wiley-Blackwell.

Galloway, A., W.H. Birkby, T. Kahana, et al. 1990. Physical Anthropology and the Law: Legal Responsibilities of Forensic Anthropologists. *American Journal of Physical Anthropology* 33: 39–57.

García-Mancuso, R. 2014. Congruencia entre Edad Esquelética y Desarrollo Dentario en una Muestra Osteológica con Edad Cronológica Documentada. *Revista Argentina de Antropología Biológica* 16 (2): 103–109.

García-Mancuso, R., and S. Salceda. 2014. Evaluación de Diferentes Métodos de Estimación de Edad por Desarrollo de la Dentición en Restos Humanos Esqueletizados de Entre y 6 Meses. *Revista Española de Medicina Legal* 40 (4): 133–138.

García-Mancuso, R., A.M. Inda, and S. Salceda. 2015. Age Estimation by Tympanic Bone Development in Foetal and Infant Skeletons. *International Journal of Osteoarchaeology* 26: 544–548.

García Mancuso, R., S. Petrone, S.A. Salceda, et al. 2018. Revisión Crítica de la Utilización del Ilion para el Diagnóstico de Sexo en Restos Esqueléticos de Individuos Subadultos Mediante Técnicas Morfométricas. *Anales de Antropología* 52 (2): 7–22.

Garizoain, G., S. Petrone, R. García Mancuso, et al. 2016. Análisis de Preservación Ósea y Dentaria en Dos Grupos Etarios: Su Importancia en el Estudio de Conjuntos Esqueléticos. *InterSecciones en Antropología* 17: 353–362.

Garizoain, G., M. Plischuk, S. Petrone, et al. 2017. Asociación entre Enfermedad Periodontal y Periostitis. Análisis Esquelético en una Población Contemporánea (La Plata, Argentina). *Revista Española de Antropología Física* 38: 1–8.

Geler, L., and M. Rodríguez. 2016. Argentina. In *The Wiley Blackwell Encyclopedia of Race, Ethnicity, and Nationalism*, ed. J. Stone, R.M. Dennis, P.S. Rizova, et al., 1–4. London: Wiley.

Gómez Otero, J. 2012. La Importancia de Rescatar los Eterratorios Humanos en Riesgo: Experiencias en el Nordeste de la Provincia de Chubut. *Cazadore Recolectores del Cono Sur* 6: 15–33.

Gómez Otero, J. 2016. *Informe Técnico sobre el Rescate del Enterratorio del Loteo Don Emilio (Ruta 25, Trelew)*. Instituto de Diversidad y Evolución Austral (IDEAUS), ed. 1–13. Godoy Cruz: Centro Nacional Patagónico (CENPAT).

González Broquen, X. 2014. Ciencia, Bioética y Política: La Bioética como Camino para la Trasformación de la Praxis Científica. *Acta Bioethica* 20 (2): 271–277.

Guichón, R., P. García Laborde, and J. Motti, et al. 2015. Experiencias de Trabajo Conjunto entre Investigadores y Pueblos Originarios. El Caso de Patagonia Austral. *Revista Argentina de Antropología Biológica* 17 (2): 1–8.

Henderson, C., and F. Alves Cardoso (eds.). 2018. *Identified Skeletal Collections: The Testing Ground of Anthropology*? Oxford: Archaeopress.

International Labour Organization [ILO]. 1989. C169—Convention about Indigenous and Tribal Peoples Convention, 1989 (No. 169). http://www.ilo.org/dyn/normlex/en/f?p=NORMLEXPUB:12100:0::NO::P12100_ILO_CODE:C169. Accessed 29 May 2018.

Lamenza, G., S. Salceda, and H. Calandra. 2016. Nuevos Aportes a la Arqueología de Formosa (Argentina): Cronología del Sitio Arqueológico "El Quebracho". *Arqueología* 22 (2): 399–408.

Lazzari, A. 2007. Historias y Reemergencias de los Pueblos Indígenas. In *Explora. Las Ciencias en el Mundo Contemporáneo*, ed. P. Funes and A. Lazzari, 1–16. Buenos Aires: Ministerio de Educación, Ciencia y Tecnología de la Nación.

Lemp Urzúa, C., M. Rodríguez Balboa, R. Retamal Yermani, et al. 2008. Arqueología del Depósito: Manejo Integral de las Colecciones Bioantropológicas en el Departamento de Antropología de la Universidad de Chile. *Revista Conserva* 12: 69–96.

Levin, L.G. 2015. Cuando la Periferia se Vuelve Centro. La Antropología Forense en la Argentina: un Caso de Producción de Conocimiento Científico Socialmente Relevante. *Cuadernos de Antropología Social* 42: 35–54.

Local Act 169/09. 2009. Puerto Santa Cruz, Argentina. http://www.hcdptosantacruz.gov.ar//hcdpsc_ordenanzas_2009-169htm. Accessed 16 July 2018.

Local Act 7638/90. 1990. Enacted on December 27, 1990. La Plata, Argentina. http://www.concejodeliberante.laplata.gov.ar/digesto/or8000/or7638.asp?ver=1&resol=1360x768. Accessed 22 May 2018.

Local Act 9471/02. 2002. Enacted on October 9, 2002. La Plata, Argentina. http://www.concejodeliberante.laplata.gov.ar/digesto/or9500/or9471.asp?ver=&resol. Accessed 22 May 2018.

Mancuso, F. 1995. *Ética de la Abogacía y Potestad Disciplinaria*. La Plata: Editorial Universitaria de La Plata.

Mariani, R., R. García-Mancuso, G.L. Varela, et al. 2017. New Records of Forensic Entomofauna in Legally Buried and Exhumed Human Infants Remains in Buenos Aires, Argentina. *Journal of Forensic and Legal Medicine* 52: 215–220.

Márquez-Grant, N., and D. Errickson. 2017. Ethical Considerations: an Added Dimension. In *Human Remains: Another Dimension. The Application of Imaging to the Study of Human Remains*, ed. D. Errickson and T. Thompson, 193–204. London: Academic Press.

Martin, D.L., R.P. Harrod, and V.R. Ventura. 2013. An Ethos for Bioarchaeologists. In *Bioarchaeology: An Integrated Approach to Working with Human Remains*, ed. D.L. Martin, R.P. Harrod, and V.R. Ventura, 23–55. New York: Springer.

National Act 23302 Aboriginal Communities. Enacted on November 8, 1985. Buenos Aires, Argentina (1985) http://servicios.infoleg.gob.ar/infolegInternet/anexos/20000-24999/23790/texact.htm. Accessed 16 July 2018.

National Act 24430. 1994. Argentine National Constitution (Enacted in 1853, with modification in 1860, 1866, 1898, 1957 and 1994) Buenos Aires, Argentina. http://servicios.infoleg.gob.ar/infolegInternet/anexos/0-4999/804/norma.htm. Accessed 16 July 2018.

National Act 25517. 2001. Indigenous Communities. Enacted the 14 of December of 2001, with Additions of the Regulatory Decree 701/2010. Buenos Aires, Argentina. http://servicios.infoleg.gob.ar/infolegInternet/anexos/70000-74999/70944/norma.htm. Accessed May 22 2018.

National Act 25743. 2003. Paleontological and Archaeological Patrimony Protection. Enacted the 25 of June of 2003, with Additions of the Regulatory Decree 1022/2004. Buenos Aires, Argentina. http://servicios.infoleg.gob.ar/infolegInternet/anexos/85000-89999/86356/norma.htm. Accessed 22 May 2018.

Nahuelquir, S., C. Huiliano, F. Huillino, et al. 2015. Trabajamos Juntos. Antes y Después de la Ordenanza Municipal de Puerto Santa Cruz 169/09. In *La Arqueología Pública en Argentina: Historias, Tendencias y Desafíos en la Construcción de un Campo Disciplinar*, ed. M. Fabra, M. Montenegro, and M.E. Zabala, 77–92. San Salvador de Jujuy: Editorial de la Universidad Nacional de Jujuy.

Plischuk, M., and A. Inda. 2015. Hiperostosis Esquelética Difusa Idiopática en una Colección Osteológica Contemporánea (La Plata, Buenos Aires, Argentina). *Revista del Museo de Antropología* 8 (1): 147–156.

Plischuk, M., A.M. Inda, and A.L. Errecalde. 2014 Modificaciones de la Estructura Ósea del Fémur Proximal. Análisis de una Muestra Esqueletal. *Revista Argentina de Radiología* 78 (1):42–48.

Plischuk, M., M.E. De Feo, and B. Desántolo. 2018a. Developmental Dysplasia of the Hip in Female Adult Individual: Site Tres Cruces I, Salta, Argentina (Superior Formative Period, 400–1000 CE). *International Journal of Paleopathology* 20: 108–113.

Plischuk, M., R. García Mancuso, and B. Desántolo. 2018b. Nódulos de Schmörl en una Serie esqueletal contemporánea de La Plata, Argentina. *Revista Argentina de Antropología Biológica* 20 (1): 1–9.

Rodríguez, M. 2013. Cuando los muertos se vuelven objetos y las memorias bienes intangibles: Tensiones entre Leyes Patrimoniales y Derechos de los Pueblos Indígenas. In *Tramas de la Diversidad. Patrimonio y Pueblos Originarios*, ed. C. Crespo, 67–100. Buenos Aires: Editorial Antropofagia.

Rodríguez, M. in press. Los Enterratorios Indígenas como Campo de Disputa. Reflexiones desde la Ontología Política Etnográfica. *Revista do Centro em Rede de Investigação em Antropologia. Dossier Heterogeneidad Ontológica y Ontologías en Conflicto en América Latina.*

Salceda, S., B. Desántolo, R. García Mancuso, et al. 2009. Integración y Conservación de la Colección Osteológica "Profesor Doctor Rómulo Lambre": Avances y Problemáticas. *Revista Argentina de Antropología Biológica* 11 (1): 133–141.

Salceda, S., H. Calandra, and G. Villanueva. 2010. Las Paradojas de lo Legal: Aportes de la Antropología. *Intercambios* 11: 1–4.

Salceda, S., B. Desántolo, R. García Mancuso, et al. 2012. The 'Prof. Dr. Rómulo Lambre' Collection: An Argentinian Sample of Modern Skeletons. *Homo* 63: 275–281.

Salceda, S., B. Desántolo, and M. Plischuk. 2015. Espacio de Reflexión: El por qué y para Quién de la Investigación Bioantropológica. *Revista Argentina de Antropología Biológica* 17 (2): 1–6.

Sanabria-Medina, C., G. González-Colmenares, H. Osorio Restrepo, et al. 2016. A Contemporary Colombian Skeletal Reference Collection: A Resource for the Development of Population Specific Standards. *Forensic Science International* 266: 577.e1–577.e4.

Sardi, M.L. 2011. Argentina. In *The Routledge Handbook of Archaeological Human Remains and Legislation: An International Guide to Laws and Practice in the Excavation, Study and Treatment of Archaeological Human Remains*, ed. N. Márquez-Grant and L. Fibiger, 579–583. London: Routledge.

Sardi, M.L. 2016. Los Museos Antropológicos y la Mirada de un Cacique Actual. *Ciencia Hoy* 26: 32–35.

Sardi, M.L., and D. Ballestero. 2017. Cuerpos y Biografías. El Pueblo Aché en el Discurso y la Práctica de la Antropología. *Suplemento Antropológico de la Universidad Católica de Paraguay* 52 (2): 7–116.

Sardi, M.L., M.M. Reca, and H.M. Pucciarelli. 2015. Debates y Decisiones Políticas en Torno de la Exhibición de Restos Humanos en el Museo de La Plata. *Revista Argentina de Antropología Biológica* 17 (2): 1–8.

Turner, T., J. Wagner, and G. Cabana. 2018. Ethics in Biological Anthropology. *American Journal of Physical Anthropology* 165: 939–951.

Ubelaker, D. 2018. A History of Forensic Anthropology. *American Journal of Physical Anthropology* 165: 15–23.

Walsh-Haney, H., and L.S. Lieberman. 2005. Ethical Concerns in Forensic Anthropology. In *Biological Anthropology and Ethics: From Repatriation to Genetic Identity*, ed. T. Turner, 121–131. Albany: New York Press.

Chapter 21
Ethical Issues of Bioarchaeology in Southeast Asia

Siân E. Halcrow, Rebecca Crozier, Kate M. Domett, Thanik Lertcharnrit, Jennifer S. Newton, Louise G. Shewan and Stacey M. Ward

Abstract Since the 1990s there has been an increase in bioarchaeological research in many parts of Southeast Asia by both locals and non-locals. Southeast Asian countries are characterised by varied social, cultural, and political histories, but there are also some broad similarities in terms of poor economic development that limits much local research, and strong nationalism and rigid bureaucratic procedures for research. All have implications for non-local and local bioarchaeological research. Despite the growth in bioarchaeological research, the ethics of the practice of bioarchaeology in this region remain relatively underexplored. This chapter presents some of the main ethical issues of research with human remains in the region focusing on the countries of Thailand, Myanmar, Cambodia, and the Philippines, from a non-local and local researcher viewpoint. We review a range of ethical issues, including the varied way different cultures respond to bioarchaeological work, local-non-local partnership in research, community archaeology, bioarchaeological methods including post-excavation management, and looting of archaeological sites. With the recent development of local expertise in bioarchaeology in the region, the repatriation of skeletal samples to Thailand, the increase in

S. E. Halcrow (✉) · S. M. Ward
Department of Anatomy, University of Otago, Dunedin, New Zealand
e-mail: sian.halcrow@otago.ac.nz

R. Crozier
Department of Archaeology, University of Aberdeen, Aberdeen, UK

K. M. Domett
College of Medicine and Dentistry, James Cook University, Townsville, Australia

T. Lertcharnrit
Department of Archaeology, Silpakorn University, Bangkok, Thailand

J. S. Newton
Department of Anthropology, Trent University, Peterborough, Canada

L. G. Shewan
School of Earth Sciences, University of Melbourne, Parkville, Australia

K. Squires et al. (eds.), *Ethical Approaches to Human Remains*,
https://doi.org/10.1007/978-3-030-32926-6_21

local training, and partnerships between local and non-local bioarchaeologists, there is much promise for the further development of local research in the field.

21.1 Introduction

Bioarchaeological research has occurred relatively late in Southeast Asia compared with other parts of the world (Halcrow et al. 2011; Tayles et al. 2012; Clark et al. 2017). However, since the 1990s, there has been an increase in the work that has been done in this region, with large multidisciplinary projects largely focused on Thailand, and a recent proliferation of projects in Cambodia, Myanmar, and Viet Nam, though there is still relatively limited work in Laos and much of Island Southeast Asia (Pietrusewsky and Douglas 2002; Higham and Thosarat 2004; Oxenham and Tayles 2006; Higham 2007; Domett and O'Reilly 2009; Higham and Kijngam 2009, 2011, 2012a, 2012b; Higham et al. 2014; Galipaud et al. 2016; Oxenham and Buckley 2016; Clark et al. 2017). Southeast Asia is a diverse area prehistorically, historically, geographically, as well as culturally, and can be defined by varied boundaries (Miksic and Goh 2017). For the purposes of this chapter we define Mainland Southeast Asia to include Myanmar, Thailand, Laos, Viet Nam, Cambodia, Peninsular Malaysia, and Singapore. Island Southeast Asia includes Taiwan, Malaysian Borneo, Philippines, Timor Leste, and Indonesia as far east as Sulawesi/Celebes (Tayles et al. 2012). In this chapter we exclude a discussion of palaeoanthropological research, which is relatively rare, but has a long history in this region (Durband 2009; Demeter et al. 2015; Clark et al. 2017).

The region's varied social, cultural, and political history means that the bioarchaeological practices and ethical issues are diverse. However, the modern states of Southeast Asia are affected by prehistoric and historic voluntary and forced migration, and mixing with fluid boundaries only defined in the post-colonial era. There are also similarities in terms of strong nationalism, an increase in bureaucratic procedures around cultural heritage management, and relatively poor economic development, which has implications for the methods, practicalities, and ethics of bioarchaeological research in the area. Because we are dealing with countries with different histories and approaches to archaeology, it is not possible to carry out a comprehensive survey of the ethics of bioarchaeological research from all countries (see Tayles et al. 2012 for a review of the history of palaeopathological research in the region as a whole). However, given that most of the bioarchaeological research has been carried out in mainland Southeast Asia, this chapter discusses the main ethical issues in this region by presenting case studies from research conducted in Thailand, Cambodia, and Myanmar, and some research from the Philippines in Island Southeast Asia. This chapter reviews bioarchaeology largely from the non-local (non-Southeast Asian) perspective, although we also present examples of research conducted using community-based archaeological approaches, including collaborations with ethnic minority groups within Southeast Asia. To understand the ethical issues of bioarchaeological practice in Southeast Asia, background on the social, economic, and political history of the region, and cultural beliefs in relation to the dead is vital. We present a brief history of the practice of bioarchaeology in Southeast Asia and the varied cultural contexts in which these studies have been undertaken. Case studies from several Southeast Asian countries are presented that discuss the ethical issues on local-non-local partnership in research, community archaeology, bioarchaeological methods including post-excavation management, and looting of archaeological sites. The recent increase in the development of local expertise in the region in bioarchaeology through training is reviewed, and repatriations of skeletal samples are discussed.

21.2 The Ethical and Historical Context: A Need for Cultural Relativism in Bioarchaeology Practice in Southeast Asia

Ethics are the moral principles of an individual and/or group that guide them in their perception as to what is right and wrong within particular contexts (Blackburn 2001). What is considered ethical is therefore largely dependent on the social and cultural context, but no ethical guidelines exist for dealing specifically with human remains in Southeast Asia (Halcrow et al. 2011). Considering ethics are particularly important when dealing with human remains as people in different cultures and social contexts relate to the dead in different ways (Parker Pearson 1999; Turner 2005; Tarlow 2006). Philosophical and biomedical discussions on the ethics of dealing with human remains often revolve around ideals of dignity and consent (Salmon 1997). To understand the varied responses of working with human remains from archaeological sites it is vital to understand the social, political, and economic history of the region. Historically, the Southeast Asia region is one of fluid political control, with kingdoms and principalities with expansionist objectives and no clear boundaries, although some are approximate to modern country borders (Gunn 2011). From the 1500s onwards, Portuguese, Spanish, English, and French missionaries and traders increasingly became a presence in the region. Many of these travellers produced ethnographic and archaeological studies to satisfy the need for the 'exotic' in Europe, resulting in biased Western descriptions of Southeast Asian history and culture, including mortuary practices (e.g. McCarthy 1994; De Carné 1995; Harmand 1997; De Marini 1998; Pallegoix 2000). Following French colonisation of parts of the region including Viet Nam, Cambodia, and Laos in the late 1800s, several French archaeological expeditions carried out biological anthropology (mainly palaeoanthropology) research with the objective of tracing human evolution in the region (Tayles 2012). However, in the absence of full translation and acknowledgement in texts, it is difficult to ascertain local contribution to these early archaeological expeditions (e.g. Verneau 1909; Mansuy 1924; Mansuy and Colani 1925; Colani 1927, 1935; Fromaget 1940). After World War II, Southeast Asia experienced increased political instability and associated economic development problems. During this time, there was also an increase in nationalism and use of political propaganda. This resulted in a shift from western to local interpretations of the past, adding a well needed perspective. However, as with all archaeological research from any tradition, the local archaeological research and its interpretation was sometimes coloured by modern local political agendas (Tayles 2012).

As noted, the majority of bioarchaeological research in the Southeast Asian region is undertaken by non-locals, although there has been an increase in local development and capacity-building of expertise in this field, undertaken in large part by local academics devoted to the development of research in their countries (e.g. Decolonizing Southeast Asia's Past Conference in 2018). Non-local researchers may be faced with difficulties in gaining access to bioarchaeological samples for research. Such issues often arise from complexities associated with obtaining research permits including different requirements for non-local and local researchers, largely attributed to the strong nationalism within Southeast Asian countries (Halcrow et al. 2011). The policies and management of cultural heritage in most countries can hinder bioarchaeological research to some extent, even for local researchers. The local policies regarding excavation and access to collections also means that researchers are often restricted to working in one country, in part as it is easiest to navigate the bureaucratic and legislative procedures in one context and it takes time to build relationships with local researchers (Tayles 2012). Cooperative archaeological projects among countries initiated by locals are rare, which can inhibit the development of a regional comparative assessment of pre-history to span different modern political borders (Tayles 2012). However, more recently, non-local bioarchaeologists and doctoral students are undertaking projects across different countries in the region (e.g. Halcrow et al. 2013).

The increase in non-local-led bioarchaeological research of large cemetery sites from different regions in Mainland Southeast Asia provides an opportunity to undertake comparative research to answer regional questions of migration, demography, and changes in health (Domett 2001; Oxenham et al. 2006; Halcrow et al. 2016; Corny et al. 2017). For example, with the increase in large cemetery samples excavated in mainland Southeast Asia, Halcrow et al. (2016) undertook a comparative synthesis of infant and child health as a sensitive proxy for population health in relation to the intensification of agriculture using seven different cemetery samples.

There are further ethical considerations in the context of changing technologies in bioarchaeological research. With the successful extraction of aDNA from human remains from tropical contexts, there is a current 'race' for the procurement of samples from well-funded international institutions with several recent published articles in Southeast Asia (Lipson et al. 2018; Matsumura et al. 2018; McColl et al. 2018). As with all aDNA meta-analyses and human genomic approaches, this research has the opportunity to address important questions regarding the origins and migration of people and the emergence of ancient disease. Similarly, isotope work and radiocarbon dating from bone, which is usually destructive, has become standard in bioarchaeology in the region (e.g. Krigbaum 2003; Beavan et al. 2012; King et al. 2013). It is important with destructive work that the relevant authorities and/or communities are consulted and engaged with before samples are acquired, and that with research agreements and grant applications there is consideration and provision for training for local universities or research groups, as well as retention of sufficient sample material for reproducibility and accessibility (Makarewicz et al. 2017). There are, however, problems with development of local expertise in these methods without major research infrastructure development. There are also instances of multiple sampling by different research groups, which severely works against the general principle of preservation ethics (Walker 2008; Redfern and Clegg 2017). As with all aDNA analyses, although consent is given for specific projects, these permissions are actually blanket permissions because of the way the genomic data are deposited and published (Redfern and Clegg 2017).

21.3 Ethical Considerations in Southeast Asia

In this section we review the main ethical considerations of bioarchaeological practice in Southeast Asia, including the relationship between non-local researchers and local researchers, the development of local expertise in bioarchaeology, and the varied cultural beliefs of locals towards the dead, including ethnic minority groups. We present case studies on local-non-local partnership in archaeological research and community archaeology, and post excavation management, including storage, repatriation, site museums, and looting, focusing on the countries of Thailand, Myanmar, Cambodia, and the Philippines.

There is limited local expertise in bioarchaeology, at least partly due to limited resources and training. In developing countries, financial investment is more frequently focused in primary sectors, such as agricultural development, business, and health care (The World Bank 2017), with limited funds available for heritage research and management. Any ensuing ethical complexities of dealing with human skeletal remains are further compounded considering that it is mostly non-local researchers working in Southeast Asia. This is especially pertinent given the colonial history of the field of archaeology and the colonial history in most Southeast Asian countries. Many researchers working in the region are now dedicated to building local expertise through research and training (see Sect. 21.5). However, there is still a power differential that exists in terms of who generally holds the funding for excavation and specialty research facilities. Over the past few decades, internationally, there has been a movement for local management of projects and genuine collaboration between local and international researchers that can result in the increase in local expertise. Related to this, there has been the repatriation of human remains from international museums back to local communities in Southeast Asia.

The potential for power dynamics and differential resources that often exist between non-local researchers and locals should be kept in mind throughout the bioarchaeological research process. In archaeological and bioarchaeological research there are many ethical considerations that we could reflect on including: the agendas for the different parties (locals and non-local workers); who is driving the research agenda; who is writing the papers and how will publication work; how does this fit into the political landscape of the country you are working in; how will this further develop archaeological research in the country or countries of excavation, including education (including outreach) and cultural resource management; and how will this affect the locals that you are working with directly at the site?

The belief systems of non-local bioarchaeologists and local Southeast Asian archaeologists can be fundamentally different. Research with human skeletal remains from archaeological sites in mainland Southeast Asia is generally accepted culturally, largely due to the Buddhist belief system, the main religion in the region. In Buddhist belief, the body is not seen as integral to the person's spirit itself (as discussed in the context of bioarchaeological practice in Thailand in the next section). In the international bioarchaeological community, there is an acknowledgement that we need to work in a professional and ethical manner with human remains, and there are generic codes of ethics from professional bodies (WAC 1989, 2005; AAPA 2003; BABAO 2010; CAPA 2015), but there is little written specifically on the ethics of bioarchaeology in this region (Halcrow et al. 2011). Although bioarchaeological research is generally accepted within Southeast Asia, some ethnic minority groups (as discussed later) relate to human remains in different ways. Furthermore, the very people that are excavated from many of the late prehistoric contexts have been suggested to be Animists, a belief system in which there is a clear relationship between human remains and ancestors, where the practice of exhumation of the dead would have been abhorrent (Årnhem and Sprenger 2016).

There is an untapped opportunity for the study of bioarchaeology to be more than just the scientific analyses of finds. There is a dearth of literature on the social relationships among local and non-local bioarchaeologists and with the dead in Southeast Asia, or anywhere in the world (Zimmerman et al. 2003). This, in fact, represents a largely untapped opportunity to look at cross-cultural understandings of relationships between the living and the dead and therefore the inner workings of our societies. Social anthropological research into the relationships of local and non-local bioarchaeologists and the dead is limited. However, this may reveal important cultural values of people today, just as death rituals in archaeology can tell us a lot about social factors of past societies (Sayer 2010).

We now present some short examples of bioarchaeological research from different countries of Southeast Asia that touch on the pertinent ethical issues in the context of their historic, cultural, and political circumstances.

21.4 Case Studies of Country-Specific Ethical Considerations and Outcomes

21.4.1 Thailand

Most contemporary bioarchaeological research in Southeast Asia has been undertaken in the Kingdom of Thailand, with much of the work centered on assessing the effects that the intensification of agriculture had on human wellbeing (Domett 2001; Tayles et al. 2007; Halcrow et al. 2016). This is in large part due to the long history of collaboration between the Thai government Fine Arts Department and the University of Otago in New Zealand, following earlier work mostly by Thai-US teams (Gorman 1970; White 1982; Higham and Bannanurag 1990; Higham and Thosarat 1998, 2004; Pietrusewsky and Douglas 2002; Higham 2007; Higham and Kijngam 2009; Bayard and Solheim 2010; Higham et al. 2014). In Thailand, as is the case in all Southeast Asian archaeological excavations that involve non-locals, research needs to be undertaken in collaboration with local archaeologists. However, there has generally been little local bioarchaeological research, largely as a result of lack of funding into the area (Halcrow et al. 2011). Fortunately, there are now some newer projects where Thai bioarchaeologists are taking the lead, mostly in Thai-run archaeological projects (e.g. Shoocondej et al. 2003; Pureepatpong 2006; Shoocondej 2006; Lertcharnrit et al. 2013). All archaeological work is set up in full consultation with the local villagers, local administration offices (e.g. sub-district administration organisation, Police stations, district offices, and Buddhist temples), the Thai Fine Arts Department, the National Research Council of Thailand, and private landowners who are paid for the use of their land for excavation.

Prior to excavations, Buddhist ceremonies are held that make merit to the ancestors (*sen wai phi*–make merit to the spirits, or *sen wai ban pa bu rute*–make merit to the ancestors) (Sparkes 2007). As with other Buddhist societies, the Thai people view their bodies as a 'vessel' for the spirit with death being seen as the passage to the next life. Their bones are not considered sacred, nor are the prehistoric remains from archaeological sites (Halcrow et al. 2011, 627). During excavations, local and non-local researchers frequently deliver talks to local schools and visitors. There have been several archaeological projects with a bioarchaeological element in Southeast Asia that include a significant research component of community archaeology, where the practice and outputs have been undertaken for the education and economic benefit of the community, including teaching school children about the prehistory of the region, as well as training guides within the community to help boost local tourism work, e.g. Mae Hong Son in Northern Thailand (Shoocongdej 2017), the Ban Pong Manao community in Lopburi Province in Central Thailand (Thanik Lertcharnrit, pers. comm.), and the Ban Non Wat community in Nakhon Ratchasima Province in Northeast Thailand.

Ethical issues also affect the post-excavation phases of archaeological projects, including preservation issues with skeletons left in situ for periods of time, and looting. Thailand, as well as other Southeast Asian countries, has developed an interest in open-air museums, where human skeletons, or sometimes replicas of bones, that have previously been left in situ are on display to the public. These are popular with locals and tourists, and often useful for public education and for revenue gain from museum visitors. However, these museums can have detrimental effects on the preservation of bone tissue, which limits future research. In addition, because the soil pedestals for the excavated burials have been left in situ, there is only partial excavation of sites and therefore a loss of information. There is also a move for the development of local museums at archaeological sites. For example, museums and learning centres have been developed at the large prehistoric site of Ban Non Wat in Northeast Thailand, and Promtin Tai in Lopburi (Central Thailand) (Fig. 21.1). Such museums help provide employment opportunities for locals, many of whom have been central contributors in the excavation and post-excavation phases of the archaeological research.

In the tropical environment of Thailand, excavation of sites often needs to be carried out in the dry, 'cool' season, which often means that excavations need to be carried out over several years, especially when non-locals are constrained to visiting for a period of a couple of months. This, however, can lead to problems with looting if there are no contingencies put in place for site protection. An unfortunate case was at the archaeological site from Tam An Mah in Luang Prabang Province

Fig. 21.1 Students visiting the site museum at Promtin Tai (Thailand). Photograph by Thanik Lertcharnrit

(Laos) excavated as part of the Middle Mekong Archaeological Project (Lewis et al. 2015). After the partial excavation of a prehistoric occupation and burial site over one season, subsequent looting prior to the planned second season resulted in the destruction of the entire cave site (Lewis et al. 2015).

21.4.2 Myanmar

Political instability over recent decades has limited access to Myanmar for bioarchaeological research, which has only been possible since the early 2000s. One of the first studies was carried out at the invitation by the Ministry of Culture of Myanmar (now known as the Ministry of Religious Affairs and Culture (Myanmar) or MMRAC). Tayles et al. (2001) undertook a study of the human remains left in situ at a site museum of the first excavated Bronze Age (3500–2500 BP) site in Myanmar, Nyaung'gan near Mandalay. Unfortunately, this study had many limitations, including not being able to lift the burials which therefore meant it was not possible to undertake full data collection. Burials were left in situ to respect the wishes of the MMRAC who wished to promote Myanmar's heritage with the erection of an open-air museum (Fig. 21.2). However, it was possible to gain some insights into the health of this past population (Tayles et al. 2001). The construction of site museums has continued in Myanmar including at the World Heritage site of Halin in the Sagaing

Fig. 21.2 The 'open-air' site museum, Nyaung'gan, near Mandalay (Myanmar). Photograph by Kate Domett

Division (Moore 2003). Halin is an impressive site that includes the famous Pyu monuments (brick Buddhist temples) as well as a collection of preserved excavations including human remains left in situ and frequently superimposed. Halin is a popular tourist site and does much to promote the heritage of Myanmar, and although this type of open-air museum is supported by the community, we have concerns regarding the longevity of the exposed human remains. Recently, through collaboration of one of the primary international research groups, the Mission Archéologique Française au Myanmar of the Centre National de la Recherche Scientifique in France with the MMRAC, it has been possible to remove some human skeletal remains to complete post-excavation analyses on the recent research in Halin. This type of collaborative approach has led to the improved preservation of the human remains (Pautreau 2007; Coupey 2008, 2013; Pautreau et al. 2010; Pryce et al. 2013, 2018), which bodes well for future bioarchaeological work in Myanmar.

21.4.3 Cambodia

Bioarchaeological research in Cambodia also only commenced quite recently since the political situation settled in the 1990s. One major focus has been on understanding the people of the prehistoric period leading into protohistoric times and the influence of the development of the Angkorian state on human wellbeing (Chhem et al. 2004; Domett and O'Reilly 2009; Domett et al. 2011; Domett and Buckley 2012; Domett et al. 2013; Newton et al. 2013). Excavation and survey in Cambodia requires the permission from the Ministry of Culture and Fine Arts (MoCFA) or the body for the Protection and Management of Angkor and the Region of Siem Reap (APSARA) depending upon jurisdiction and consultation with provincial leaders and local communities.

Unfortunately, many scientific excavations have been rescue excavations after widespread looting of archaeological sites has occurred in a response by locals to difficult economic circumstances. Valuable artefacts such as semi-precious stones, glass beads, and bronze jewellery found as grave goods are sold on the international antiquities market (O'Reilly and Shewan 2016). Skeletal remains associated with these artefacts are cast aside, though many have now been transferred to keeping places in local temples or *wats* (Fig. 21.3). Through consultation with the village Abbott and elders, it has been possible to study these ossuaries despite the loss of context alongside scientifically excavated remains in the same area. For example, at the village of Phum Snay in Banteay Meanchey Province, specialists from Australian and New Zealand universities collaborated with the Royal University of Fine Arts (Phnom Penh) and the MoCFA to excavate a few of the remaining unlooted areas. By combining the 21 excavated skeletons with the ossuary (a collection of stratigraphically unprovenanced human remains recovered from looters pits comprising a minimum number of individuals of 134) it was possible to mitigate, to some extent, the loss of this information from looting (Domett and O'Reilly 2009; Domett et al. 2013; Newton et al. 2013). As is the case in other

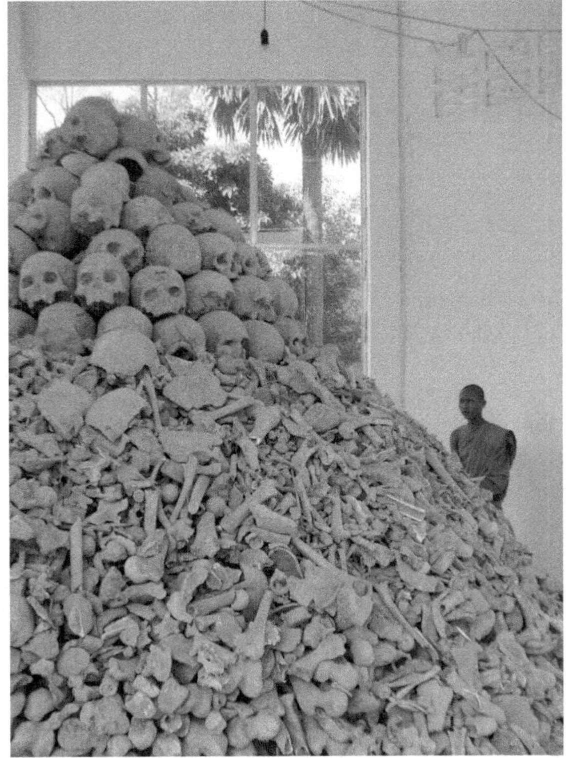

Fig. 21.3 The human remains that were placed in the stupa after extensive looting at the archaeological site of Phum Sophy (Cambodia) in 2007. Photograph by Kate Domett

countries in Southeast Asia during excavations, non-local researchers have worked closely with authorities at the local and national level and have recruited local archaeology students for assistance with excavation and analysis. Site talks are frequently provided for local schools and visitors. Education has proven to be the key in preserving the heritage of Cambodia. HeritageWatch (2017) was established as a nationwide education campaign aimed at highlighting the value of Cambodia's heritage. It was founded by archaeologist Dr. Dougald O'Reilly in response to the large-scale looting that occurred in the country in the early 2000s, and it continues to promote awareness of Cambodia's past and discourages destruction of its heritage.

Bioarchaeological research conducted by Australian, New Zealand, and Khmer researchers at the historic-era sites of Phnom Pel and Phnom Khnang Peung in the remote Cardamom Mountain range of southwest Cambodia required particular ethical consideration and treatment. This region is occupied by ethnic hill tribes who adhere to an Animist belief system, different from the Buddhist belief system where the physical remains in burials are not considered 'taboo'. Following permission granted by the MoCFA, provincial and local authorities, and prior to the study of the human skeletal remains deposited within the ceramic jars and intact wooden coffins perched on natural rock ledges, spiritual ceremonies were conducted and offerings made to the Neak ta forest spirits. A condition of the analysis required that all skeletal material was examined and sampled within the field and covered and protected at night. Following the completion of the analysis and sampling, bones were redeposited to their respective vessels and returned to their original rock ledge position after which a final ceremony was performed (Beavan et al. 2011).

21.4.4 Philippines

Bioarchaeology is still in its early stages in the Philippines. However, as resources and local expertise are developing, more and more research is being conducted (Lewis et al. 2008; Garong 2013; Go et al. 2017; Vlok et al. 2017), and an inspection of the National Museum research papers reveals a high number of human remains that have been excavated over the years.

Within the Philippines, all archaeological excavation and survey requires a permit issued by the National Museum. Further permission and consultation must also be sought from all local stakeholders of the area in question: Mayor, Barangay (village or district) Captain, and the landowners (at a minimum). This level of interaction invariably means direct consultation with the local community, a particularly important and often rewarding endeavour. This exercise provides an opportunity to understand not only what excavations may reveal, but also how human remains are viewed, allowing concerns about the practice of bioarchaeology to be addressed. The Philippines is characterised by predominantly Christian denominations in the areas of Luzon and Visayas. However, there is a strong awareness of much older belief systems and cosmologies, including forms of Animism and Shamanism that the archaeologists must acknowledge. There is much respect for ancestors, and in some regions this is still maintained via impressive oral traditions. For example, before archaeologists could enter a rockshelter (for the purpose of a preliminary survey of the site) known to contain mummified human remains in Luzon, the local guide performed a series of prayers to acknowledge and respect the ancestors. It should be noted that in this case, the specific identities of the individuals within the rockshelter are unknown. Once this was complete, the community was happy to allow access to the remains for inspection and analysis. Indeed, the archaeologists were there at the request of the community. Similarly, when human remains, encountered by locals during construction work in the Visayan Islands, are brought from where they were stored by the local community to the museum for analysis, it is requested that a local priest bless the remains.

Looting is a major issue due to the potential association of collectible ceramics and gold from dental work and death masks. Reporting of looting activities by the communities affected is frequently how sites are discovered. For this reason, openness, communication, and inclusion of communities during and after excavation is important in order to distinguish archaeological practice from looting. Many of these principles and methods are cemented in the Katipunan Arkeologist ng Pilipinas (KAPI 1994) code of ethics. This code outlines eight key principles, which includes stewardship, accountability, public education, reporting, and publication, with specific references for the archaeologist to treat all archaeological remains with respect. Stewardship is based around long-term conservation and protection of the archaeological record. The accountability clause is largely based around working legally, ethically, with consent, and being culturally respectful. The code details are blanket for archaeological remains, without specific reference to human remains. Furthermore, all archaeological remains are protected by law in the National Cultural Heritage Act (2009).

21.5 Development of Southeast Asian Expertise

21.5.1 Bioarchaeology Workshops and Conferences for Training of Locals

There is a current push to develop local bioarchaeological expertise through training and conferences on archaeology and bioarchaeology (e.g. the locally arranged biennial Southeast Asian Ministers of Education Organization, and the Southeast Asian Regional Centre for Archaeology and Fine Arts International Conference on Southeast Asian Archaeology), the increase of locally led archaeological projects, the increase in locally led bioarchaeological programmes (Shoocondej et al. 2003; Pureepatpong 2006; Shoocondej 2006; Highland Archaeology Project 2017), and the development of bioarchaeology centres (e.g. the bioarchaeology laboratory at the Princess Maha Chakri Sirindhorn Anthropology Centre (SAC) in Bangkok). In addition to these efforts, bioarchaeological workshops have been run throughout the region over the past 15 years. Non-local bioarchaeologists frequently visit universities (e.g. the Department of Archaeology at Silpakorn University in Bangkok) to carry out short training programmes in bioarchaeology for both student archaeologists and professionals who wish to upskill. These workshops are aimed at offering basic bioarchaeological training and provide an understanding of the scientific value of human remains, and aspects of curation and analyses, as well as opportunities for local networking and collaboration. Although often initiated by non-local researchers, these workshops are conducted in close collaboration with local organisers and translators. For example, New Zealand, Australian, and Thai researchers collaborated to provide a workshop at Silpakorn University in Bangkok (Thailand) in 2016. Non-local researchers and local archaeological consultants have also worked together to provide on-site training in a range of archaeological sub-disciplines at Ban Non Wat. This training was accompanied by a one-day conference where all talks were presented in, or translated into, Thai. This native language conference provides a departure from traditionally English-speaking conferences and allows the inclusion of locals in archaeological discourse. Other examples of significant workshops include the First and Second Southeast Asian Bioarchaeology Conferences held in Siem Reap (Cambodia) in 2004 and Khon Kaen (Thailand) in 2012. A third bioarchaeological workshop was held at the National University of Laos in

Vientiane in January 2014. Although these workshops are received with enthusiasm, difficulties in obtaining funding and long distance communication and organisation can hinder their provision. The expectations are that they will give participants expertise in skeletal analysis but it is difficult to communicate the next step, which is to develop research questions and design appropriate research projects.

As noted, there has been a close collaboration of research between non-local and Southeast Asian bioarchaeologists and/or archaeologists. The continuation of these types of close-knit workshops will be particularly useful to strengthen collaborations and lead to new research collaborations, which will result in further developments of local archaeological research. Some of the leading local archaeologists and bioarchaeologists in Thailand are trained in the USA, UK, and New Zealand.

21.5.2 Repatriation

Following the international trend for the repatriation of skeletal material back to their country of origin (Scarre 2009), there has been the recent repatriation of significant Southeast Asian bioarchaeological collections back to the region. For example, the skeletal collection from the site of Khok Phanom Di from Southeast Thailand was returned to Thailand in 2003 after being housed in the University of Otago's Department of Anatomy in New Zealand, and the skeletons from the UNESCO World Heritage site of Ban Chiang, curated at the Department of Anthropology at the University of Hawai'i-Manoa, were returned to Thailand in 2017. In the case of Thailand, this is largely driven by nationalism, rather than any strong spiritual or cultural feelings about the remains themselves, apart from some ethnic groups. It is now accepted by locals and non-local researchers that skeletal remains excavated from Southeast Asian sites remain curated in the countries of origin. Because there was a general scarcity of early bioarchaeological studies in the twentieth century in Southeast Asia, and the current push to repatriate and retain archaeological human skeletal remains in their country of origin, it is very uncommon for Southeast Asian archaeological skeletal remains to be held in overseas countries. With the repatriation of these human remains and the increasing number of archaeological sites excavated in Thailand, a purpose-built facility for curating Thai human remains was constructed at the Fine Arts Department in Phimai (Northeast Thailand) in 2010. The location of the building is situated in the region where most of the Thai bioarchaeological samples have been excavated from and this division of the Fine Arts Department possesses local control of these samples. Although we feel that there are definite advantages for local development of bioarchaeological research with the centralised housing of these remains, there are several ethical considerations related to the management of human skeletal remains that are not under the control of specific investigators or biological anthropologists directly. These include issues of access to collections for further research and curation management, especially in light of destructive sampling, which has become routine in bioarchaeological analyses.

21.6 Conclusion

There has been a recent surge in bioarchaeological research in Mainland and Island Southeast Asia by both local and non-local researchers. Despite this growth in research, the ethics of the bioarchaeological practice in this region remains relatively underexplored. This chapter has touched upon some of the main ethical issues of bioarchaeological practice within the sociocultural and historical political contexts of different Southeast Asian countries. These issues include local-non-local relationships, collection management, looting, and increasing the development of local expertise and management of bioarchaeology, including repatriation of significant skeletal collections. It is essential to try to facilitate development in local expertise and research programmes in bioarchaeology. Non-local and local collaboration, including co-mentorship of local students, is one important way of initiating this.

Acknowledgements We would like to thank the many locals who have given their time and expertise in some way to making possible the bioarchaeological research in Southeast Asia. Thank you to the countries of Southeast Asia that allow this work to be undertaken and our various funding sources, including the NZ Marsden Fund and the Australian Research Council. We also thank Associate Professor Nancy Tayles for stimulating many of the ideas contained in this paper based on her keynote "Bioarcheology in Mainland Southeast Asia" given at the Society for American Archaeology Meeting in Memphis, Tennessee, in 2012.

References

American Association of Physical Anthropologists [AAPA]. 2003. *Code of Ethics of the American Association of Physical Anthropologists*. www.physanth.org/documents/3/ethics.pdf. Accessed 5 August 2018.

Årnhem, K., and G. Sprenger (eds.). 2016. *Animism in Southeast Asia*. Abingdon: Routledge.

Bayard, D.T., and W.G. Solheim II (eds.). 2010. *Archaeological Excavations at Non Nok Tha, Northeastern Thailand 1965–1968*. Mangilao: University of Guam, Micronesian Area Research Center.

Beavan, N., S. Halcrow, B. McFadgen, et al. 2012. Radiocarbon Dates from Jar and Coffin Burials of the Cardamom Mountains Reveal a Unique Mortuary Ritual in Cambodia's Late-to Post-Angkor Period (15th–17th Centuries AD). *Radiocarbon* 54 (1): 1–22.

Beavan, N., T. Sokha, and O. Sokha, et al. 2011. "To Discover and Preserve": The First Recording, Analysis and Site Conservation of the 15th to 17th Century Jar and Coffin Burials in the Cardamom Mountains, Kingdom of Cambodia. In *The Royal Academy of Cambodia and the Ministry of Culture and Fine Arts Conference on Conservation and Development of Khmer Culture "Cultural Heritage"*, 126–141. Phnom Penh: The Royal Academy of Cambodia and The Ministry of Culture and Fine Arts.

Blackburn, S. 2001. *Ethics: A Very Short Introduction*. Oxford: Oxford University Press.

British Association for Biological Anthropology and Osteoarchaeology [BABAO]. 2010. *Code of Ethics*. http://www.babao.org.uk/assets/Uploads/code-of-ethics.pdf. Accessed 29 November 2017.

Chhem, R.K., S.K. Venkatesh, W. Shih-Chang, et al. 2004. Multislice Computed Tomography of Two 2000-Year-Old Skeletons in a Soil Matrix from Angkor, Cambodia. *Canadian Association of Radiologists Journal* 55 (4): 235–241.

Clark, A.L., C.L. King, H.R. Buckley, et al. 2017. Biological Anthropology in the Indo-Pacific Region: New Approaches to Age-Old Questions. *Journal of Indo-Pacific Archaeology* 41: 78–94.

Colani, M. 1927. La Grotte Sepulchrale de Lang Gao. *L'Anthropologie* 37: 227–229.

Colani, M. 1935. *Megaliths du Haut–Laos (Hua Pan, Tran Ninh).* Paris: De L'Ecole Francaise D'Extreme-Orient.

Corny, J., M. Galland, M. Arzarello, et al. 2017. Dental Phenotypic Shape Variation Supports a Multiple Dispersal Model for Anatomically Modern Humans in Southeast Asia. *Journal of Human Evolution* 112: 41–56.

Coupey, A.-S. 2008. Infant and Child Burials in the Samon Valley, Myanmar. In *Archaeology in Southeast Asia, from Homo Erectus to the Living Traditions: Choice of Papers from the 11th International Conference of the European Association of Southeast Asian Archaeologists, Bougon, France, Sept 25–29, 2006*, ed. Patreau, J.-P., A.-S., Coupey, and Zeitoun, V., et al., 119–125. Chiang Mai: Siam Ratana.

Coupey, A.-S .2013. Infant Jar Burials in Upper Burma. In *Unearthing Southeast Asia: Selected Papers from the 12th International Conference of the European Association of Southeast Asian Archaeologists*, ed Klokke, M.J., and V. Degroot, 84–90. Singapore: NUS Press.

De Carné, L. 1995. *Travels on the Mekong: Cambodia, Laos and Yunnan—The Political and Trade Report of the Mekong Exploration Commission (June 1866–1868).* Bangkok: White Lotus Press.

De Marini, G.F. 1998. *A New and Interesting Description of the Lao Kingdom (1642–1648).* Bangkok: White Lotus Press.

Decolonising Southeast Asia's Past: Archaeology, History of Art and National Boundaries Conference (2018) Faculty of Arts, Thammasat University, Tha Prachan Campus, Bangkok. 13th–14th September 2018.

Demeter, F., L. Shackelford, K. Westaway, et al. 2015. Early Modern Humans and Morphological Variation in Southeast Asia: Fossil Evidence from Tam Pa Ling, Laos. *PLoS One* 10 (4): e0121193. https://doi.org/10.1371/journal.pone.0121193.

Domett, K.M. 2001. *Health in Late Prehistoric Thailand.* Oxford: Archaeopress.

Domett, K.M., and H.R. Buckley. 2012. Large Lytic Cranial Lesions: A Differential Diagnosis from Pre-Angkorian Cambodia. *International Journal of Osteoarchaeology* 22 (6): 731–739.

Domett, K.M., J. Newton, D.J.W. O'Reilly, et al. 2013. Cultural Modification of the Dentition in Prehistoric Cambodia. *International Journal of Osteoarchaeo*logy 23 (3): 274–286.

Domett, K., and D.J.W. O'Reilly. 2009. Health in Pre-Angkorian Cambodia: A Bioarchaeological Analysis of the Skeletal Remains from Phum Snay. *Asian Perspectives* 48 (1): 56–78.

Domett, K.M., D.J.W. O'Reilly, and H.R. Buckley. 2011. Bioarchaeological Evidence for Conflict in Iron Age North-West Cambodia. *Antiquity* 85 (328): 441–458.

Durband, A.C. 2009. Southeast Asian and Australian Paleoanthropology: A Review of the Last Century. *Journal of Anthropological Science* 87: 7–31.

Fromaget J (1940) Les récentes découvertes anthropologiques dans les formations préhistoriques de la chaîne annamitique. In *Proceedings of the Third Far Eastern Prehistory Congress*, 51–59. Singapore: Government Off Print.

Galipaud, J.-C., R. Kinaston, S. Halcrow, et al. 2016. The Pain Haka Burial Ground on Flores: Indonesian Evidence for a Shared Neolithic Belief System in Southeast Asia. *Antiquity* 90 (354): 1505–1521.

Garong, A.P. 2013. *Ancient Filipino Diet: Reconstructing Diet from Human Remains Excavated in the Philippines*. Cebu: University of San Carlos Press.

Go, M.C., A.B. Lee, J.A.D. Santos, et al. 2017. A Newly Assembled Human Skeletal Reference Collection of Modern and Identified Filipinos. *Forensic Science International* 271: 128.e121–128.e125.

Gorman, C. 1970. Excavations at Spirit Cave, North Thailand: Some Interim Interpretations. *Asian Perspectives* 13: 79–108.

Gunn, G.C. 2011. *History Without Borders: The Making of an Asian World Region, 1000-1800*. Hong Kong: Hong Kong University Press.

Halcrow, S.E., N.J. Harris, N. Tayles, et al. 2013. From the Mouths of Babes: Dental Caries in Infants and Children and the Intensification of Agriculture in Mainland Southeast Asia. *American Journal of Physical Anthropology* 150 (3): 409–420.

Halcrow, S.E., N. Tayles, and C.L. King. 2016. Infant and Child Health and Disease with Agricultural Intensification in Mainland Southeast Asia. In *The Routledge Handbook of Bioarchaeology in Southeast Asia and the Pacific Islands*, ed. M. Oxenham and H.R. Buckley, 158–186. Abingdon: Routledge.

Halcrow, S.E., N. Tayles, N. Pureepatpong, et al. 2011. Thailand/ประเทศไทย. In *The Routledge Handbook of Archaeological Human Remains and Legislation: An International Guide to Laws and Practice in the Excavation, Study and Treatment of Archaeological Human Remains*, ed. N. Márquez-Grant and L. Fibiger, 623–632. Abingdon: Routledge.

Harmand, F. 1997. *Laos and Hilltribes of Indochina—Journeys to the Bolven Plateau, from Bassac to Hue Through Laos, and to the Origins of the Thai*. Bangkok: White Lotus Press.

HeritageWatch. 2017. *HeritageWatch International*. www.heritagewatchinternational.org. Accessed 5 August 2018.

Higham. C. (ed.). 2007. *The Origins of the Civilization of Angkor Volume II: The Excavation of Noen U-Loke*. Bangkok: The Fine Arts Department of Thailand.

Higham, C., and R. Bannanurag, (eds.). 1990. *The Excavation of Khok Phanom Di: A Prehistoric Site in Central Thailand. Volume I: The Excavation, Chronology and Human Burials*. London: The Society of Antiquaries.

Higham, C., and A. Kijngam, (eds.). 2009. *The Origins of the Civilization of Angkor Volume III: The Excavation of Ban Non Wat. Part One: An Introduction*. Bangkok: The Fine Arts Department of Thailand.

Higham, C., and A. Kijngam, (eds.). 2011. *The Origins of the Civilization of Angkor Volume IV: The Excavation of Ban Non Wat. Part Two: The Neolithic Occupation*. Bangkok: The Fine Arts Department of Thailand.

Higham, C., and A. Kijngam, (eds.). 2012a. *The Origins of the Civilization of Angkor Volume V: The Excavation of Ban Non Wat. Part Three: The Bronze Age*. Bangkok: The Fine Arts Department of Thailand.

Higham, C., and A. Kijngam, (eds.). 2012b. *The Origins of the Civilization of Angkor Volume VI: The Excavations of Ban Non Wat. Part Four: The Iron Age, Summary and Conclusions*. Bangkok: The Fine Arts Department of Thailand.

Higham, C., and R. Thosarat, (eds.). 1998. *The Excavation of Nong Nor: A Prehistoric Site in Central Thailand*. Dunedin: University of Otago.

Higham, C., and R., Thosarat, (eds.). 2004. *The Origins of the Civilization of Angkor Volume I: The Excavation of Ban Lum Khao*. Bangkok: The Fine Arts Department of Thailand.

Higham, C.F.W., J. Cameron, N. Chang, et al. 2014. The Excavation of Non Ban Jak, Northeast Thailand – A Report on the First Three Seasons. *Journal of Indo-Pacific Archaeology* 34: 1–41.

Highland Archaeology Project. 2017. *Highland Archaeology Project in Pang Mapha District, Mae Hong Son Province Phase 2*. http://highland.trf.or.th/Mainpage2-English.htm. Accessed 29 November 2017.

Katipunan Archeologist ng Pilipinas [KAPI]. 1994. *Kapi Code of Ethics*. https://static1.squarespace.com/static/574f993f356fb0dff99d7619/t/580dd3a5e4fcb5fdf2791fe7/1477301455875/KAPI+Code+of+Ethics.pdf. Accessed 12 March 2018.

King, C.L., R.A. Bentley, N. Tayles, et al. 2013. Moving Peoples, Changing Diets: Isotopic Differences Highlight Migration and Subsistence Changes in the Upper Mun River Valley, Thailand. *Journal of Archaeological Science* 40: 1681–1688.

Krigbaum, J. 2003. Neolithic Subsistence Patterns in Northern Borneo Reconstructed with Stable Carbon Isotopes of Enamel. *Journal of Anthropological Archaeology* 22: 292–304.

Lewis, H., V. Paz, M. Lara, et al. 2008. Terminal Pleistocene to Mid-Holocene Occupation and an Early Cremation Burial at Ille Cave, Palawan, Philippines. *Antiquity* 82 (316): 318–335.

Lewis, H., J., White, and B. Bouasisengpaseuth. 2015. A Buried Jar Site and Its Destruction: Tham An Mah Cave, Luang Prabang Province, Lao PDR. In *Advancing Southeast Asian Archaeology 2013: Selected Papers from the First SEAMEO SPAFA International Conference on Southeast Asian Archaeology, Chonburi, Thailand 2013*, ed. N.H. Tan, 72–82. Bangkok: SEAMEO SPAFA Regional Centre for Archaeology and Fine Arts.

Lertcharnrit, T., S. Kirkland, and S.E. Burnett. 2013. Dental Palaeopathology: Preliminary Results of Iron Age Human Teeth from Central Thailand. *Art and Culture Magazine* 34 (6): 28–33.

Lipson, M., O. Cheronet, S. Mallick, et al. 2018. Ancient Genomes Document Multiple Waves of Migration in Southeast Asian Prehistory. *Science* 361 (6397): 92–95.

Makarewicz, C., N. Marom, and G. Bar-Oz. 2017. Ensure Equal Access to Ancient DNA. *Nature* 548: 158.

Mansuy, H. 1924. Contribution à l'étude de la préhistoire de l'Indochine IV: Stations préhistoriques dans les cavernes du massif calcaire de Bac-son (Tonkin). *Mémoires du Service Géologique de l'Indochine* 11: 15–20.

Mansuy, H., and M. Colani. 1925. Contribution à l'étude de la pré histoire de l'Indochine VII: néolithique inférieur (Bac-Sonien) et néolithique supérieur dans le haut-Tonkin (dernières recherches), avec la description des crânes du gisement de Lang-Cuom. *Mémoires du Service Géologique de l'Indochine* 12: 1–45.

Matsumura, H., K.-I. Shinoda, T. Shimanjuntak, et al. 2018. Cranio-morphometric and aDNA Corroboration of the Austronesian Dispersal Model in Ancient Island Southeast Asia: Support from Gua Harimau, Indonesia. *PLoS One* 13 (6): e0198689.

McCarthy, J. 1994. *Surveying and Exploring in Siam with Descriptions of Lao Dependencies and of Battles Against the Chinese Haw*. Bangkok: White Lotus Press.

McColl, H., F. Racimo, L. Vinner, et al. 2018. The Prehistoric Peopling of Southeast Asia. *Science* 361: 88–92.

Miksic, J.N., and G.Y. Goh. 2017. *Ancient Southeast Asia*. London: Routledge.

Moore, E. 2003. Bronze and Iron Age Sites in Upper Myanmar: Chindwin, Samon and Pyu. *SOAS Bulletin of Burma Research* 1 (1): 24–39.

National Cultural Heritage Act. 2009. House of Representatives of the Philippines, Quezon City.

Newton, J.S., K.M. Domett, D.J.W. O'Reilly, et al. 2013. Dental Health in Iron Age Cambodia: Temporal Variations with Rice Agriculture. *International Journal of Paleopathology* 3 (1): 1–10.

O'Reilly, D.J.W., and L. Shewan. 2016. Prehistoric Mortuary Tradition in Cambodia. In *The Routledge Handbook of Bioarchaeology in Southeast Asia and the Pacific*, ed. M. Oxenham and H.R. Buckley, 45–67. Abingdon: Routledge.

Oxenham, M., and H.R. Buckley (eds.). 2016. *The Routledge Handbook of Bioarchaeology in Southeast Asia and the Pacific Islands*. Abingdon: Routledge.

Oxenham, M., L. Nguyen, and K. Nguyen. 2006. The Oral Health Consequences of the Adoption and Intensification of Agriculture in Southeast Asia. In *Bioarchaeology of Southeast Asia*, ed. M. Oxenham and N. Tayles, 263–289. Cambridge: Cambridge University Press.

Oxenham, M., and N. Tayles (eds.). 2006. *Bioarchaeology of Southeast Asia*. Cambridge: Cambridge University Press.

Pallegoix, J.B. 2000. *Description of Thai Kingdoms or Siam, Thailand Under King Mongkut*. Bangkok: White Lotus Press.

Parker Pearson, M. 1999. *The Archaeology of Death and Burial*. Stroud: Sutton.

Pautreau, J.-P. 2007. *Ywa Htin, Iron Age Burials in the Samon Valley, Upper Burma*. Chiang Mai: Mission Archéologique Française au Myanmar.

Pautreau, J.-P., C. Maitay, and A.A. Kyaw. 2010. Level of Neolithic Occupation and 14C Dating at Ywa Gon Gyi, Samon Valley (Myanmar). *Aseanie* 25: 1–22.

Pietrusewsky, M., and M.T. Douglas. 2002. *Ban Chiang, a Prehistoric Village Site in Northeast Thailand I: The Human Skeletal Remains*. Philadelphia: The University of Pennsylvania.

Pryce, T.O., A.-S., Coupey, and A.A. Kyaw, et al. 2013. The Mission Archéologique Française au Myanmar: Past, Present and Future. *Antiquity* 87 (338).

Pryce, T.O., A.A. Kyaw, M.M. Kyaw, et al. 2018. A First Absolute Chronology for Late Neolithic to Early Bronze Age Myanmar: New AMS 14C Dates from Nyaung'gan and Oakaie. *Antiquity* 93 (363): 690–708.

Pureepatpong, N. 2006. Recent Investigation of Early People (Late Pleistocene to Early Holocene) from Ban Rai and Tham Lod Rock Shelter Sites, Pang Mapha District, Mae Hong Son Province, Northwestern Thailand. In *Uncovering Southeast Asia's past: Selected papers from the 10th International Conference of the European Association of Southeast Asian Archaeologists*, ed. Bacus, E.A., I., Glover, and V.C. Pigott, 38–45. Singapore: National University of Singapore.

Redfern, R., and M. Clegg. 2017. Archaeologically Derived Human Remains in England: Legacy and Future. *World Archaeology* 49 (5): 574–587.

Salmon, M.H. 1997. Ethical Considerations in Anthropology and Archaeology, or Relativism and Justice for All. *Journal of Anthropological Research* 53 (1): 47–63.

Sayer, D. 2010. Who's Afraid of the Dead? Archaeology, Modernity and the Death Taboo. *World Archaeology* 42 (3): 481–491.

Scarre, G. 2009. The Repatriation of Human Remains. In *The Ethics of Cultural Appropriation*, Young, J.O., and C.G. Brunk, 72–92. Chichester: Wiley-Blackwell.

Shoocondej, R. 2006. Late Pleistocene Activities at the Tham Lod Rockshelter in Highland Pang Mapha, Mae Hong Son Province, Northwestern Thailand. In *Uncovering Southeast Asia's past: Selected Papers from the 10th International Conference of the European Asscoiation of Southeast Asian Archaeologists*, ed. E.A. Bacus, I. Glover, and V.C. Pigott, 22–37. Singapore: National University of Singapore.

Shoocondej, R., S., Nakbunlung, and N. Pumjamnong, 2003. *The Highland Archaeological Project in Pang Ma Pha District, Mae Hong Son Province. Final Research Report Presented to the Thailand Research Fund*, Unpublished Report.

Shoocongdej, R. 2017. The History and Practice of Archaeology in Thailand. In *Handbook of East and Southeast Asian Archaeology*, ed. J. Habu, P.V. Lape, and J.W. Olsen, 97–109. New York: Springer.

Sparkes, S. 2007. Rice for the Ancestors: Food Offerings, Kinship and Merit Among the Isan of Northeast Thailand. In *Kinship and Food in South East Asia*, ed. M. Janowski and F. Kerlogue, 223–241. Copenhagen: NIAS Press.

Tarlow, S. 2006. Archaeological Ethics and the People of the Past. In *The Ethics of Archaeology: Philosophical Perspectives on Archaeological Practice*, ed. C. Scarre and G. Scarre, 199–216. Cambridge: Cambridge University Press.

Tayles, N., K. Domett, and U.P. Pauk. 2001. Bronze Age Myanmar (Burma): A Report on the People from the Cemetery of Nyaunggan, Upper Myanmar. *Antiquity* 75 (288): 273–278.

Tayles, N., Halcrow, S., and Domett, K. 2007. The People of Noen U-Loke. In *The Origins of the Civilization of Angkor (Vol. II): The Excavation of Noen U-Loke and Non Muang Kao*, ed. Higham, C.F.W., A., Kijngam, and S. Talbot, 244–304. Bangkok: The Thai Fine Arts Department.

Tayles, N. 2012. *Bioarchaeology in Mainland Southeast Asia*. Paper Presented at the 77th Annual Meeting of the Society for American Archaeology, Memphis, Tennessee, USA, April 18–22, 2012.

Tayles, N., S.E. Halcrow, and N. Pureepatpong. 2012. Regional Developments: Southeast Asia. In *History of Palaeopathology Pioneers*, ed. J.E. Buikstra and C. Roberts, 1360–1396. Oxford: Oxford University Press.

The Canadian Association for Physical Anthropology [CAPA]. 2015. *Code of Ethics*. http://www.capa-acap.net/sites/default/files/basic-page/capa_code_of_ethics_-_oct_2015.pdf. Accessed 5 August 2018.

The World Bank. 2017. *World Development Indicators | DataBank*. http://databank.worldbank.org/data/reports.aspx?source=2&Topic=11. Accessed 29 November 2017.

Turner, T.R. (ed.). 2005. *Biological Anthropology and Ethics: From Repatriation to Genetic Identity*. Albany: State University of New York.

Verneau, R. 1909. Les crânes humains du gisement préhistorique de Pho-Binh-Gia (Tonkin). *L'Anthropologie* 20: 545–559.

Vlok, M., V. Paz, R. Crozier, et al. 2017. A New Application of the Bioarchaeology of Care Approach: A Case Study from the Metal Period, the Philippines. *International Journal of Osteoarchaeology* 27 (4): 662–671.

Walker, P.L. 2008. Bioarchaeological Ethics: A Historical Perspective on the Value of Human Remains. In *Biological Anthropology of the Human Skeleton*, ed. M. Katzenberg, A. Saunders, and R. Shelley, 3–39. Hoboken: Wiley.

White, J.C. 1982. *Discovery of a Lost Bronze Age: Ban Chiang*. An Exhibition Organised by The University Museum, University of Pennsylvania, the Smithsonian Institution Traveling Exhibition Service and The National Museums Division, Department of Fine Arts, Thailand. Philadelphia: The University Museum, University of Pennsylvania and the Smithsonian Institution Traveling Exhibition Service.

World Archaeological Congress [WAC]. 1989. *The Vermillion Accord, Archaeological Ethics and the Treatment of the Dead: A Statement of Principles Agreed by Archaeologists and Indigenous Peoples at the World Archaeological Congress, Vermillion, USA*. http://worldarch.org/code-of-ethics/. Accessed 5 August 2018.

World Archaeological Congress [WAC]. 2005. *Code of Ethics: The Tamaki Makau-rau Accord on the Display of Human Remains and Sacred Objects*. http://worldarch.org/code-of-ethics/. Accessed 5 August 2018.

Zimmerman, L.J., K.D. Vitelli, and J. Hollowell-Zimmer (eds.). 2003. *Ethical Issues in Archaeology*. Walnut Creek: AltaMira Press.

Chapter 22
Ethical Considerations of the Management of the Dead in the Middle East

Sakher AlQahtani and Joe Adserias-Garriga

Abstract Ethical considerations pertaining to the management of the dead in the Middle East are embodied by a number of misconceptions. Dealing with the dead is influenced and affected by either religion or culture. However, all ethical considerations, particularly in Islam, are built upon the principle that "the dignity of the dead is the same as for the living". Managing human remains in a forensic science context is no exception. It is important for forensic scientists working in these countries to understand existing cultural practices. This requires an acknowledgement of the origin and evolution of contemporary beliefs. Therefore, this chapter discusses these ethical considerations and how working with the dead is influenced by religion and culture. The following research demonstrates that it is of paramount importance to understand the different religious beliefs, their accompanied funerary customs, and burial rites, specifically, when managing both the dead and the living. This chapter, in particular, focuses on Islamic funerary practices. Relevant to the latter is the ethical and legislative obligation regarding autopsy. Finally, the process of identification through the means of DNA and fingerprints is addressed, highlighting a need for further involvement of other practitioners, such as forensic anthropologists and forensic odontologists, in a number of scenarios.

22.1 Introduction

In AD 610, an Arab merchant named Muhammad, in what is now Makkah (Saudi Arabia), started preaching a new religion based on Abrahamic teachings. At the time, the Indigenous people of the Arabian Peninsula were either nomadic or sedentary. Nomadic groups constantly travelled seeking water and pasture for their flocks and also depended on raiding caravans or oases; nomads did not view this as

S. AlQahtani (✉)
College of Dentistry, King Saud University, Riyadh 11545, Saudi Arabia
e-mail: drsakher@gmail.com

J. Adserias-Garriga
Department of Applied Forensic Science, Mercyhurst University, Erie, PA 16546, USA

K. Squires et al. (eds.), *Ethical Approaches to Human Remains*,
https://doi.org/10.1007/978-3-030-32926-6_22

a crime. In fact, mutilation of the dead was common practice following these raids to send a message of power (Al-Shaybani and Al-Kabir 1997).

When Muhammad established Islam, and became revered by his followers as a prophet, many Arabs rejected the Islamic concepts, namely Monotheism and equal rights, and raged war against the newly established cult. During the early battles, Muhammad already set certain rules in regard to the management of the dead. This was a revolution in the Arab psyche at that time (Al-Lalakaa 1027). The first rule was prohibiting body mutilation; any crime committed against a dead body was punishable in the same way as it was when the person was alive (Al-Dawoody 2017). Many of his followers objected to this rule as they wanted to ascertain authority and show power as it was the custom, but Muhammad refused. He also asked, as the second rule, for the dead soldiers to be identified, which was done by visual means using marks or scars, tattoos, and personal belongings. At the time there was a special unit of women who identified the dead and nursed the injured; thus the first recorded disaster victim identification (DVI) unit in history was established (AlBukhari 847; Abi Shaybah 850 ; Ibn Hanbal 850; Muslim 855; Al-Zuhayli 2010).

The third rule was that every soldier was to be buried, as soon as possible, in individual graves rather than mass graves, which were prohibited except in extreme situations (Ibn Hanbal 850; Al-Mawardi 1038). Even enemies received the same funerary treatment. On one occasion, Muhammad's enemies requested the body of a prominent leader, killed during battle, and offered a handsome price for the body. However, Muhammad refused the money but did return the body. This led to the creation of a fourth rule, that: dead bodies are not for sale and the family has the right to have the body of their loved one, even during war and even if they were the enemy ('Abd Al-Malik and Ibn Isḥāq 1955). The consequences of not burying the deceased enemies would result in bodies decomposing or eaten by scavengers, which would have been tantamount to mutilation, prohibited under Islamic law (Al-Mawardi 1038). This particular rule is not only consistent with International Humanitarian Law, the law that regulates the conduct of war, but it goes even further in protecting the dignity of the dead and respecting the needs of their loved ones. International Humanitarian Law allows for burial of the deceased without repatriation provided they are "honourably interred" (Henckaerts and Doswald-Beck 2005).

These new concepts when dealing with the dead were not only a stark contrast to the traditional way of thinking, but Muhammad cemented them in Islam by setting a new principle that the 'dignity of the dead is as the dignity of the living', which is still something believed by contemporary Muslims (Andrabi 2018). Consistent with these Islamic rules, International Humanitarian Law stipulates that parties involved in conflict shall take all possible measures to search for the dead in Non-International Armed Conflicts (NIACs) (International Committee of the Red Cross 1949a; 1949b; Henckaerts and Doswald-Beck 2005).

Although many of his teachings were revolutionary with regards to human rights, they did not last long after his death, simply because they were ahead of their times. Therefore, soon after his death, his followers reverted back to their Arab way of thinking, abandoning the democratic voting system for their leaders, oppressing women, and reviving body mutilation of their deceased enemies (Al-Shawkāni 1973, 1984).

In AD 910, during the golden age of science in the Middle East, books on the ethics in the medical field were published as well as new regulations on licensing physicians. Two prominent scholars are to be recognised here: Rahawi and Al-Rāzī. The book titled 'Ethics of the Physician' (Adabul Tabib), by Ishaq bin Ali Al Rahawi (AD 854–931) who lived in Northern Syria, describes the process of licensing physicians, keeping patient records, and their use in education, quality control, and litigations. Here, it states "It has been said of them in regard to trustworthiness that the physician did not practice medicine until he passed an examination and had experience. When the ancient medical man was given accreditation, then there was a chair for him called the chair of wisdom for it possessed the value and beauty of form. Only an authorized physician passed by the medical practitioners was allowed to sit on that chair. When one sat on it, then the sick people knew that he was a trustworthy physician" (Levey 1967, 87).

Abū Bakr Muhammad Ibn Zakariyyā Al-Rāzī, also known by his Latinised name Rhazes or Rasis (AD 854–925), was an important figure in the history of medicine. On a professional level, Razi introduced many practical, progressive, medical, and psychological ideas. He attacked charlatans and fake doctors who roamed the cities and countryside selling their nostrums and "cures". He also wrote the following on medical ethics: "The doctor's aim is to do well, even to our enemies, so much more to our friends, and my profession forbids us to do harm to our kindred, as it is instituted for the benefit and welfare of the human race, and God imposed on physicians the oath not to compose mortiferous remedies" (Zarrintan et al. 2018, 1453).

From the nineth century AD, all medical ethics' regulations focused on the living and rarely mention the dead. All contemporary ethical issues in regard to the management of the dead in the Middle East are derived from religion or traditions, but all are based on the principle that "the dignity of the dead is the same as for the living". In Middle Eastern cultures, enormous respect should be shown following death. Management of the dead should preferably be performed by people from the same religion and sex (Rutty 2010). In general, the management of the dead can be subdivided into several categories: biological profile (namely, age-at-death), care of the deceased, religion, autopsy, human identification, evidence of torture and human rights violation, and burial. The remainder of this chapter will address each of these topics in turn.

22.2 Age-at-Death

Age-at-death estimation in Islamic countries is a very significant practice due to the number of unregistered births (United Nations Children's Fund 2013). In Islamic culture, abortion of a foetus that is less than 16 weeks gestation does not require naming or proper burial. In cases where the deceased is a neonate, which is legally defined as an individual when aged 16 weeks gestation or more, a still born at full term pregnancy, or death after live birth, the neonate has to be given a name and dealt with as an adult thereafter (Zarabozo 2009).

22.3 Care of the Deceased

In all Middle Eastern cultures, management of the dead is extremely similar regardless of religion as Non-Muslim minorities in Muslim societies usually have similar conservative social norms, except for minor differences (mainly in Orthodox Christians in Lebanon) (Al-Dawoody 2017). In general, the care of the deceased should be undertaken by relatives from the same sex, or close relatives from the opposite sex. If this is not feasible then it should be carried out by undertakers from the same sex and religion, with the exception being when no one fits the primary criteria (Resolution 85/12/d8, 1994; Al-Dawoody 2017).

In Islam, the eyes of the dead should be closed (in Judaism, this must be performed by a child, a relative, or a close friend—in that order of preference). The mandible should be bandaged to the head so that the mouth does not gape, the body should be extended at the elbows, shoulders, knees, and hips; thus, enabling washing and enshrouding of the body later. In Islam, the head is turned to the right shoulder (so the body can be buried with the face towards Makkah) (Rutty 2010). No hair or nails can be cut and the whole of the body should be covered with a white sheet at all times (Sarhill et al. 2003; Green and Green 2006). If an autopsy is required, only necessary parts of the body can be exposed for the duration needed and covered immediately when complete. The ceremonial preparations in caring for the body will begin right after the autopsy (Al-Waheeb et al. 2015; Al-Saif et al. 2016).

22.4 Religion

Below is a summary of the main religions in the Middle East with information on the management of the deceased or funerary/burial rites.

22.4.1 Islam

Normally, the body is ceremonially washed at least three times with soap and is subsequently wrapped with three pieces of white cotton cloth (*Kafan*). Scent or perfume is also applied to the body. The person managing the deceased should always wear disposable gloves. This practice derives from religious beliefs and the importance placed on hygiene. In this instance, gloves are employed to avoid contamination of the body after it has been washed.

22.4.2 Christianity

Arab Christians include many sects, the majority of which live in Syria, followed by Iraq, Lebanon, Egypt, Jordan, Israel, Palestine, Morocco, and then Turkey. They all share the same traditions as Muslims in regard to the management of the deceased except for the dress code, as the deceased are dressed in their best outfits, though this is not the case in Jordan, where the funerary rites are similar to Muslims. The Greek Orthodox in Lebanon, however, have a European cultural influence in their funerary practices (Rutty 2010).

22.4.3 Judaism

In Judaism, the body should never be left unattended from the time of death to burial of the body, as it is believed to be vulnerable and unable to watch over itself during this period (Rutty 2010). The body must be handled as little as possible, as considerable importance is attached to the ritual cleansing and clothing of the body by Jews. These funerary rites should be carried out by a qualified person who is the same sex as the deceased. If relatives wish to view the body, mortuary staff should ensure that the room is free from Christian iconography (e.g. a crucifix), however candles are permitted (Nazarko 2006).

22.4.4 Bahá'í

Those practicing the Bahá'í faith, from Iran and some other countries within the Middle East, are required to observe certain procedures. This includes the body being washed carefully by the family, being wrapped in a shroud of white silk or cotton, and a Bahá'í burial ring (carrying a specific prayer) being placed on the finger. An important rule is not to move the body from where death happened; the maximum distance a body can travel is a one-hour journey. This rule also applies to all remains donated to medical science. Only in extreme circumstances should that rule be broken (Smith 2008; Rutty 2010), for example, if burial cannot be guaranteed within the stipulated time frame.

22.4.5 Druze

The Druze faith is one of the major religious groups in the Levant, with between 800,000 and a million followers. Druze are found primarily in Syria, Lebanon (where the Druze are considered part of its Muslim population), and Israel, with a small community in Jordan. The oldest and most densely populated Druze communities exist in Mount Lebanon and in the south of Syria around Jabal Al-Druze (literally the "Mountain of the Druzes"). The Druze's social customs differ markedly from those of Muslims and Christians. However, they share the same traditions as the Muslims with regards to the management of the deceased (including the dressing), although they believe in reincarnation (Rutty 2010).

When working in a Middle Eastern context it is very important to understand these religious beliefs, their funerary customs, and burial rites, especially when managing both the dead and the living in a mass disaster situation where international teams may be deployed.

22.4.6 Autopsy

Forensic science involves the investigation of the identity of the deceased and the cause and manner of death, as well as the identification of foul play where relevant. This investigation relies primarily on forensic pathology where post-mortem external and internal examinations are required.

In the Middle East, all religions share the belief that it is a religious requirement to bury the body immediately after death as this is believed to comfort the deceased (Charlton 1994); therefore, delays cause anguish to families. The idea of dissecting a body (invasive autopsy) is prohibited across the Middle East regardless of religious beliefs; this notion aims to preserve the dignity of the dead. In the last century, with the advancement of medical knowledge as well as developments in the law, the practice of autopsy has become a legal necessity in cases of accidental, suicide, homicide, and undetermined deaths. This has caused resistance by religious authorities, although body dissection was started among well-known Muslim physicians, such as Al-Razi (Rhazes) and Ibn Sina (Avicenna) more than one thousand years ago (Cosman and Jones 2008).

In Islam, the Holy Qur'an and the Hadith do not directly address the issue of autopsy (McHaffie et al. 2001). Therefore, a *fatwa* was sought for assistance on the matter. The latter is a ruling on a point of Islamic law given by a recognised authority (Thali et al. 2003), issued by the Islamic Committee, regarding the request of performing hospital or medicolegal autopsy. The *fatwa* decreed that autopsies are allowed if the following conditions are met:

- When it is requested by a judge during criminal proceedings to determine the cause of death of a deceased when the latter is deemed ambiguous or unclear;

- To confirm the presence of infectious diseases that, if confirmed, may require preventative or containment measures to avoid public health concerns;
- For teaching purposes in certified institutions such as universities and medical schools.

The other clauses of the *fatwa* narrate the ethical and moral values of Islam, which are mandatory while dealing with deceased humans. Nonetheless, this *fatwa* clarifies the Islamic perspective of post-mortem examination and recommends such an examination where needed. Currently, all religions in the Middle East no longer contest autopsy under these conditions, but cultural traditions hold greater meaning to the public than religious facts; thus, autopsy is not favoured by the population (Thali et al. 2003; Mohammed and Kharoshah 2014).

In Judaism, Jewish law (Halacha) requires that after someone has died, the body is buried in its entirety. Judaism believes that humans were created in God's image and the body belongs to God (Dorff 2005). Therefore, any mutilation of the body is strongly opposed. Therefore, autopsy examinations are not permitted in Jewish law unless required by civil law, in instances when three doctors cannot establish the cause of death, when three doctors agree that an autopsy could save the lives of other individuals with the same illness, and in cases that may safeguard relatives from hereditary diseases (Dorff 2005; Green and Green 2006).

Virtual autopsy (VA), which involves post-mortem examination using multi-slice computed tomography (MSCT) and magnetic resonance imaging (MRI) (Shastry et al. 2012), could be an innovative technique in forensic medicine that may resolve the issues with cultural norms. It is used as either part of the post-mortem examination (Loughrey et al. 2000) or as an alternative tool to the classic forensic autopsy. However, its use as an alternative to traditional post-mortem examinations is still in its early phase (Harcke et al. 2007). Several institutions across the world are implementing VA in their medicolegal workflow (Khunti 2000) and it is expected to not only increase the rate of post-mortem examination, but also to serve an effective alternative to the classic autopsy on populations that are against conventional post-mortems, such as the Middle East (Aljerian et al. 2015; see also Squires, Booth and Roberts, this volume).

22.5 Identification

There is scarcity of standardised protocols in regard to the management of the dead and human identification in the Middle East (UNAMI/OHCHR 2018) and, in certain cases, the scientific accepted procedures are not followed (AlQahtani et al. 2017). The forensic service in the Middle East varies from country to country. In some countries, this service falls under the Ministry of Justice (e.g. Egypt), some under the Ministry of Health (e.g. Saudi Arabia), while others sit under the Ministry of Interior Affairs (e.g. United Arab Emirates), or stand within independent institutions (e.g. in Turkey). This difference in legislative framework reflects on modalities used in regard to post-mortem examination protocols, reporting, human identification, and Disaster Victim Identification (DVI) operations.

Prophet Muhammad established a law principle concerning the use of evidence when delivering a verdict more than 1400 years ago. He stated that one should only apply penalties in cases beyond reasonable doubt (Bamousa et al. 2016). However, human identification modalities in the Middle East, with few exceptions, are mainly based on non-scientific methods like visual recognition, circumstantial evidence, or testimony. When scientific methods are used, the techniques employed are typically fingerprint and DNA analyses.

Fingerprints databases are widely used for human identification in the Middle East. Most countries require all individuals over the age of 16 years old to obtain an identification card; these cards display a person's fingerprints. In the Gulf countries, including Saudi Arabia, all 10 fingers are scanned. Although the idea of having a database for the population is utopic, the reality is that all countries in the Middle East have high numbers of illegal immigrants because of the political struggles in the region.

The most widely used human identifier in the Middle East, however, is DNA. Many Muslim countries felt the need to have religious regulations to use this form of evidence (as it conflicts with paternity disputes). Therefore, in 2002, the International Islamic Fiqh (Jurisprudence) Academy (Al Natsha-Jordan 2001) approved several clauses regarding the use of DNA evidence:

1. According to Islamic law, there is no objection to relying on genetic profiling in verifying or investigating crimes;
2. The usage of genetic profiling in paternity disputes should be handled with much care and confidentiality. In this regard, Islamic law shall have priority over genetic profiling;
3. It is not permissible to rely on genetic profiling in denying paternity, and it shall not have priority over the oath of condemnation;
4. Genetic profiling should not be used to verify pedigrees that are already verified according to Islamic law because Islam encourages respect for all women—it is demeaning to any mother's dignity to even question the paternity of a certain child. The concerned authorities should bar the use of genetic profiling in that matter; authorities are encouraged to propose sanctions on any father who may ask for genetic profiling without a valid reason and who fails to respect his wife's dignity the way he should;
5. It is permissible to use genetic profiling to verify paternity in only the following three cases: in cases of dispute over a person of unknown parentage, in cases of suspicion of a mix-up of infants in a hospital or social welfare centre, or in cases of in vitro fertilisation;
6. In addition, genetic profiling may be used for identification purposes in accidents, mass disasters, or wars, as well as for use in identifying prisoners of war or missing persons;
7. It is not permissible to sell a human genome whatever the reason. It is also not permissible to donate a human genome to anybody.

Of course, as with all DVI protocols, forensic odontology has an important role in human identification. Forensic odontology, if applied, is often performed by forensic personnel with little or no training in forensic odontology. Conducting dental age estimation and human identification by dental means and bite mark analysis, all require special training and experience. The lack of properly trained forensic odontologists currently in the Middle East is a concern that should be addressed. There is indeed a handful of specialised forensic odontologists in the Middle East, yet the demand for these specialists is very high because of the high number of unregistered births, mass fatalities due to political struggles and terrorism, and more profoundly the immigration crisis that puts dental age estimation, in particular, to be of the utmost importance. Undertaking dental age estimation by non-trained personnel or by a general dentist, is in violation of human rights as it may have long term consequences on the individual whose age is in dispute and therefore significantly affects the individual's life (AlQahtani et al. 2017).

Forensic anthropology is seldom applied in the Middle East. Consequently, there are very few forensic anthropologists in the region, and these have often received little specialist training. Therefore, in most cases forensic pathologists carry out the skeletal analysis.

Countries that follow Sharia Law can introduce forensic science evidence, specifically as expert witnesses, into their legal system. The Egyptian government took the more drastic approach and banned Sharia courts, implementing a law system very akin to Common Law in Europe (Shaham 2010). Other countries, such as Iraq and Qatar (current events not withstanding), have also managed to integrate forensic science into their legal system, albeit in a less extreme form than the Egyptians (Ali 1980; Bhootra 2006).

The forensic community in the Middle East should begin the arduous process of proving their validity as both scientists and experts in any field, forensic or otherwise. This will require a large overhaul of their teaching system and standardisation of assessment so any one individual can be judged fairly on his or her competence and expertise. If this requirement is present in Common Law, it will be twice as important in Sharia Law, where even legal defence is afforded on sufferance (Alkantani et al. 2015). This is of particular relevance in the case of certain deaths that hold forensic and judicial significance. These occur in the Middle East as a result of religious and/or political beliefs and/or cultural traditions. The following examples highlight a number of areas where specialist forensic teams need to be trained in DVI in the Middle East and exemplifies the religious, political, and cultural nuances that DVI teams must be aware of during their work.

22.5.1 Hajj

As the world's largest gathering, approximately four million pilgrims from more than 50 countries around the world travel to the holy city of Makkah to complete the Hajj rituals (i.e. Islamic Pilgrimage to Makkah). In these overcrowded conditions, human stampedes, terrorist attacks, or accidental disasters occur. Over the years, stampedes and terrorist attacks have occurred on both a small- and large-scale during Hajj (Manoochehry and Rasouli 2017). Identifying the injured, dead, or missing people in a crowd disaster is an elusive, complex, and time-consuming task (Alsalamah et al. 2018).

A number of incidents have occurred in recent years. In June 1990, 1426 pilgrims died in a stampede inside a pedestrian tunnel heading out from Makkah towards Mina (Staff and Agencies 2006). In February 2004, 251 pilgrims were trampled to death during the stoning ritual (Staff and Agencies 2006). Two years later, 345 pilgrims died in a stampede at the entrance of the bridge leading to the stoning site in Mina (Oliver 2006). On 24 September 2015, at least 1630 pilgrims were reported dead in a mass stampede in Makkah (Associated Press 2015; BBC 2015). In July 2019, 717 pilgrims were killed in a stampede in Mina (Freeman and Akkoc 2015). Stampedes and crushes, due to the failure of crowd control, are the most common disaster scenario, but also fires, plane crashes, and construction failures have taken place during the Hajj Pilgrimage representing a high number of fatal victims, which requires the disaster management by the authorities. Management of the dead during Hajj comes with its own challenges. Although the deceased will be followers of Islam, they are guaranteed to be international with different cultural customs and attitudes towards the treatment of the dead. Some may perceive those that die whilst on Hajj to be martyrs and thus request special management of the dead.

22.5.2 The Arab Spring and Rise of the Islamic State of Iraq and Al-Sham (ISIS)

In late 2010, peaceful popular protests calling for secular political changes started in Tunisia and soon spread to the Arab world calling for freedom and better quality of life. Many of these dictatorial and corrupt regimes that were losing their legitimacy, used the excuse of defending society from jihadi terrorism to hold their power. These peaceful protests soon changed into violent revolutions. In Libya, and later in Syria, the old regimes would not surrender to popular pressure, and were ready to use limitless violence. The backbone of Arab nations—security services and the army—was thrown into the struggle, gambling with the fate of the state itself. In fact, the entire regional political system that had emerged after the departure of British and French colonialism was falling apart. Individual nation-states were failing, without a ready replacement (Cheterian 2015).

When the old regimes unleashed tribal war in Libya, and confessional war in Syria, the nature of the revolt changed, from secularism to jihad by armed militias based in local village or neighbourhood networks, all professing the same ideology, yet competing with each other over the same political geography and to attract foreign support, which fueled radicalism (Cheterian 2015). This violence led to the worst human crisis in recorded history. Millions of people have died or were forced to leave their countries.

The aforementioned events came to a head in March 2013, when Islamist battalions overran Raqqa (Syria). This city was the first provincial capital they took control of in the Syrian war. This city acted as a safe haven for fighters from which they could regroup, attract Syrian and foreign fighters, and a base from which they could turn their attention to Iraq, attacking several towns in Anbar province in January 2014 and overrunning Mosul and Tikrit in June 2014. Militia who were fighting ISIS were, by and large, disorganised. This in part led to the military success of the jihadists in Iraq and Syria as they were better equipped and able to survive the 'state of nature' in which they found themselves (Cheterian 2015).

These jihadists claimed the title of the Islamic State of Iraq and Al-Sham (ISIS). However, the group could not be further from Islam. The sheer brutality—decapitating prisoners and burning them alive, crucifying, and exhibiting its victims on social media—lead to it being labeled 'enemy number one of Islam' by the Grand Mufti of Saudi Arabia and even Al-Qaeda, an international terrorist group in the name of Islam, condemned ISIS violence (Al-Quds Al-Arabi 2014; Mufti 2014; Cheterian 2015).

When ISIS forces advanced in Iraq in May 2014, they carried out ethnic cleansing of the Mosul, pushing the remainder of what were once some 30,000 Christians in Iraq's second city towards Kurdish controlled Erbil. In August 2014 they killed countless Yazidis—an ancient religious group inhabiting Northern Iraq and other areas in the Middle East and Caucasus (Cheterian 2015). On this occasion, imprisoned Yazidi men and kidnapped women and girls were forced to convert to Islam. The process was filmed and uploaded on YouTube for others to view (Cheterian 2015). This further highlights the tactics used by ISIS to share propaganda in the twenty-first century.

This violence caused by ISIS between June 2014 and December 2017 may amount to war crimes, crimes against humanity, and possibly genocide under international criminal law. Up to date, it has been estimated that 202 mass graves have been left behind by ISIS in areas that they formerly controlled (UNAMI/OHCHR 2018). The UNAMI/OHCHR (2018) project report that there are more than 12,000 victims in Iraq alone, the majority of whom may never be identified. At present, only 28 mass graves have been excavated with the remains of 1258 bodies exhumed by the Mass Graves Directorate (UNAMI/OHCHR 2018).

These atrocities, namely of mass murder, come with challenges that the Iraqi authorities face in conducting exhumations, investigations, and identifying human remains, as well as the difficulties faced by relatives seeking to obtain information on the fate and whereabouts of their missing family members and, if dead, their mortal remains (UNAMI/OHCHR 2018). The UNAMI/OHCHR (2018, 1) report "highlights international law and standards relating to Iraq's obligations to investigate and prosecute the mass killings that occurred in the context of this conflict and best practices relating to the protection and examination of mass grave sites, including forensic investigation of mass graves in support of criminal processes". Furthermore, UNAMI/OHCHR (2018, 16) state that:

> "Mass grave sites could potentially contain critical forensic material that may not only assist in the identification of victims' remains, but also build an understanding around the scale of abuses and violations that occurred and support the process of determining whether the acts that led to these mass graves/burials amount to war crimes, crimes against humanity or genocide. Exhumations not in line with international standards and best practice could lead to the destruction or loss of critical evidence and complicate the identification of bodies, thereby extending the grief of affected families and undermining their right to truth, justice and reparations".

The fact that there are very few forensic personnel in the Middle East, especially within the fields of anthropology and odontology, means the challenge of excavations, exhumations, and identifications of the deceased is profound. It is clear that capacity building is required within the region to tackle this problem.

22.5.3 Honour Killings

It is estimated that over 5000 women and girls are killed each year worldwide in the name of honour by members of their own family (United Nations Population Fund 2000). However, this figure is clearly underestimated since these murders used to be disguised as suicides or accidents, and were underreported. Victims are often buried in unmarked graves, and the records of their existence may be eradicated. Even though honour killings have historically occurred in many patriarchal cultures (Gilmore 1987), nowadays they mainly occur in the Middle East, North Africa, and certain parts of South Asia and Europe. Honour killings are perpetrated as a result of premarital sex, marital infidelity, initiating separation or divorce, contacting persons of different faiths, being victim of rape, or flirting (Kulczycki and Windle 2011).

22.5.4 Reporting on Torture and Evidence of Human Rights Violations

Torture occurs when a person intentionally inflicts severe pain or suffering on to another human being for purposes such as obtaining information or confession, punishment, intimidation, or coercion. The perpetrator has to be an official or should at least have some degree of official approval of the act (United Nations Human Rights 1987; Amnesty International 2014).

Even though authorities in Middle East countries have, in some cases, taken certain positive steps in strengthening the legal prohibition of torture, this has not been translated into practice. Reports on torture in Syria, Iraq, Bahrain, Kuwait, Qatar, United Arab Emirates, and Saudi Arabia (Amnesty International 2014; Human Rights Watch 2018; BBC 2019) have been issued by national and international Human Rights entities.

22.6 Burial

Embalming is prohibited in all Middle Eastern countries, though a small number of Christian sects that inhabit the region do practice this rite. Although this prohibition is culturally based with no religious basis, it is only accepted by court order or for repatriation where a body is transferred from country to country for burial. Cremation is also prohibited by all religions in the Middle East as historically it is frowned upon as an unnatural means of treating the human body, but non-Orthodox Jews allow cremation (Cytron 1993). On 14 May 2015, the Grand Mufti of Egypt, Dr Shawki Allam, issued Fatwa 3246 permitting the cremation of the bodies of Ebola victims as it was considered the best method of body disposal to stop the spread of the disease (Al-Dawoody 2017).

As mentioned in Sect. 22.4 of this chapter, burial is the preferred method of body disposal, regardless of religion. It is widely believed that it is a humiliation to the dead to leave them unburied. Therefore, arrangements to bury the deceased, ideally within 24 hours, are of upmost importance. There is, however, no religious basis for this belief and it can be deferred if needed. Nevertheless, it is important for forensic scientists to be aware of this in order to minimise any anguish to relatives.

Burial at sea is not acceptable in Middle Eastern cultures, especially in Islam, except in very narrow and specific situations. One of the highest profile cases of sea burial was that of Osama bin Laden by the USA forces. Although it was claimed that the ritual of washing, shrouding, and funeral prayer were performed, there is no justification for burying his body at sea in light of Islamic law (Black and Whitaker 2011). The US administration took the decision to bury bin Laden in a secret place at sea because if he were buried in an actual grave in the ground, it would become a shrine for some extremists (Amidon Lusted 2012).

22.7 Conclusions

Many aspects of the management of the dead in the Middle East are heavily influenced by religion and culture; at the same time, some ethical considerations around the dead and its management are surrounded by misconceptions.

In the Middle East, all religions share the belief that the body must be buried immediately after death to comfort the deceased, which means that delays cause anguish to families. The idea of dissecting a body is prohibited across the Middle East regardless of religious beliefs, based on preserving the dignity of the dead. However, in recent years, with the advancement of medical knowledge and law, the practice of autopsy became a legal necessity. Thus, *fatwas* have been issued to address such a conflict. The *fatwa* allows the post-mortem examination, when it is requested by a Judge, to investigate infectious disease or for teaching purposes.

Human identification methods in the Middle East, with few exceptions, are mainly based on non-scientific methods such as visual recognition, circumstantial evidence, or testimony; when scientific methods are used, fingerprint and DNA analyses are typically employed. Forensic anthropology and odontology are seldom applied, even though there is demand for these specialisms. There is a lack of properly trained forensic odontologists and anthropologists in the Middle East, which is a considerable concern that should be addressed in the future, especially in view of some of the tragedies that have taken place in the region in recent years. This is particularly pertinent in light of the immigration crisis and the sheer amount of mass graves, coupled with the high number of unregistered births. It should be taken into account that improper practices in age estimation may lead to incorrect results, which can significantly affect the individual's life.

Finally, a cultural shift and attitudes towards the body can prohibit professionals when attempting to establish the cause and manner of death. Where autopsies are prohibited due to religious views the process, which is deemed to be one of the keystones of medical education and forensic science, is invalidated. In some instances, it may be necessary for ideological beliefs to be set aside to allow for proper conclusions to be reached, particularly where new technologies, such as virtual autopsy, are unavailable. It is extremely difficult to stand witness for any case where even the time of death cannot be established because Saudi Arabian culture draws a distinction between death of self and death of soul. Muslims believe that the individual dies when Allah holds his/her soul. Accordingly, death is defined as the complete separation of the spirit from the body. The death of soul is the significant one in legal cases (Alzeer et al. 1998). It is, of course, of utmost importance for forensic scientists, including forensic anthropologists, to be aware of these sensitivities when working with human remains in these countries and without compromising the scientific work, try to address some of these issues, especially around managing the dead, their burial customs, and family expectations.

References

Abd al-Malik ibn Hishām, Muḥammad ibn Isḥāq. 1955. *The Life of Muhammad: A Translation of Isḥāq's Sīr at Rasūl Allāh*. Trans. Alfred Guillaume, 450–460. Oxford: Oxford University Press.

AbiShaybah, A. 850. Al-Kitab al-Muṣannaf fi al-Aḥadith wa al-Āthār (Hadith 33650). In ed. Al-Hut, K. (1988) *Maktabah al-Rushd, Riyadh* 6: 537.

Al Natsha-Jordan, A.J. 2001. *Recent Medical Issues in View of Islamic Law*. Dissertation, Om Durman University.

Ali, W. 1980. The Establishment and Practice of Forensic Medicine in Iraq. *American Journal of Forensic Medicine and Pathology* 1 (1): 81–84.

Al-Dawoody, A. 2017. Management of the Dead from the Islamic Law and International Humanitarian Law Perspectives: Considerations for Humanitarian Forensics. *International Review of the Red Cross* 99 (2): 759–784.

Al-Lalakaa. 1027. Sharḥ Usul I'tiqad Ahl al-Sunnah wa al-Jama'ah, ed. AlGhamdi, A (2003) *Dar AlTiba'ah, Riyadh* 3: 423.

Al-Mawardi, A. 1038. Al Ahkam Al lsultaaniyh, in ed. Al-Bghddy, A. (1985) *Above Note 6. Dar Al-Kotob Al-Ilmiyah, Beirut* 7: 445.

Al-Quds al-Arabi. 2014. *Abu Qatada Yuhajim 'Daesh' bi'unf wayasfha bimunh'arif.* http://www.alquds.co.uk/?p=138083. Accessed 15 July 2019.

Al-Saif, D.M., M.A. Al-Faraidy, M.S. Madadin, et al. 2016. The Attitude of People with an Arabic Islamic Cultural Background Toward Medico-Legal Autopsy. *Australian Journal of Forensic Sciences* 48 (5): 557–563.

Al-Shawkāni, M. 1973. *Nayl Al-Awttar Min Ahadith Sayyid Al-Akhyar, Sharh Muntaqa Al-Akhbar. vol. 8, 4*. Beirut: Dār al-Jīl.

Al-Shawkānı M. 1984 Al-Sayl al-Jarrār al-Mutadaffiq 'alāaḤadā'iq al-Azhār, in ed. Zāyid, M.I. *Dār al-Kutub al-'Ilmiyyah, Beirut* 4: 568.

Al-Shaybani, M.H, and S.K.S Al-Kabir (eds.). 1997. *AbiAbdullah Muḥammad Ḥassan Muḥammad Hassan Ismā'il al-Shafi'ī, commentary by Muḥammad ibn Aḥmad al-Sarakhsi. vol. 1, 79*. Beirut: Dar al-Kutub al-'Ilmiyyah.

Al-Waheeb, S., N. Al-Kandary, and K. Aljerian. 2015. Forensic Autopsy Practice in the Middle East: Comparisons with the West. *Journal of Forensic and Legal Medicine* 32: 4–9.

Al-Zuḥayli, W. 2010. *Mawsū'ah al-Fiqh al-Islāmī wa al-Qaḍāyā al-Mu'āṣirah. vol. 7, 437*. Damascus: Dār al-Fikr.

AlBukhari, M. 847. Ṣaḥīḥ al-Bukhārī (Hadith 2727), in Al-Bagha, M. (ed.) (1987) 3rd ed. *Dār ibn Kathır, Damascus and Beirut* 3: 1056.

Aljerian, K., A. Alhawas, S. Alqahtani, et al. 2015. First Virtual Autopsy in Saudi Arabia: A Case Report with Literature Review. *Journal of Forensic Radiology and Imaging* 3 (1): 76–79.

Alkantani, T., K. Aljerian, B. Golding, et al. 2015. Forensic Science in the Context of Islamic Law: A Review. *Journal of Forensic and Legal Medicine* 34: 179–181.

AlQahtani, S., Y. AlShahrani, and A. AlQahtani. 2017. Reality of Forensic Odontology in Saudi Arabia. *Revista Brasileria de Odontologia* 4 (2): 12–21.

Alsalamah, S., H. Alsalamah., J. Radianti et al. 2018. Information Requirements for Disaster Victim Identification and Emergency Medical Services: Hajj Crowd Disaster Case Study. In *Proceedings of the 15th International Conference on Information Systems for Crisis Response Management Conference—Rochester, NY, USA May 2018*, eds. Boersma, K. and Tomaszewski, B, 861–873. New York: International Conference on Information Systems for Crisis Response Management Conference.

Alzeer, A., A. Mashlah, N. Fakim, et al. 1998. Tuberculosis is the Commonest Cause of Pneumonia Requiring Hospitalization During Hajj (Pilgrimage to Makkah). *Journal of Infection* 36 (3): 303–306.

Amidon Lusted, M. 2012. *The Capture and Killing of Osama Bin Laden*. Edina: ABDO Publishing.

Amnesty International. 2014. *Torture in 2014: 30 Years of Broken Promises*. https://www.amnestyusa.org/files/act400042014en.pd. Accessed 15 July 2019.

Andrabi, A.A. 2018. Medical Ethics Within the Islamic Tradition and the Specific Issues in the Modern Scientific Era. *International Journal of Multidisciplinary Research and Development* 5 (2): 110–117.

Associated Press. 2015. Iran Holds Funeral for Diplomat Killed in Saudi Hajj Crush. *AP News*. 27 November. https://web.archive.org/web/20151208212802/bigstory.ap.org/article/a7713a35e7314dd7824326f3ee5638f1/iran-holds-funeral-diplomat-killed-saudi-hajj-crush. Accessed 11 July 2019.

Bamousa, M.S., S. Al-Fehaid, O. Al-Madani, et al. 2016. The Islamic Approach to Modern Forensic and Legal Medicine Issues. *American Journal of Forensic Medicine and Pathology* 37 (2): 127–133.

BBC. 2015. Hajj Stampede: Saudi Officials Clarify Toll After Questions. *BBC News*. 29 September. https://www.bbc.com/news/world-middle-east-34391055. Accessed 10 July 2019.

BBC. 2019. Jamal Khashoggi: All You Need to Know About Saudi Journalist's Death. *BBC News*. 19 June. https://www.bbc.com/news/amp/world-europe-45812399. Accessed 18 July 2019.

Bhootra, B.L. 2006. Forensic Pathology Services and Autopsy Law of Qatar. *Journal of Clinical Forensic Medicine* 13 (1): 15–20.

Black, I., B. Whitaker. 2011. Sea Burial of Osama Bin Laden Breaks Sharia Law, Say Muslim Scholars. *The Guardian.* 2 May. https://www.theguardian.com/world/2011/may/02/sea-burial-osama-bin-laden. Accessed 15 July 2019.

Charlton, R. 1994. Autopsy and Medical Education: A Review. *Journal of the Royal Society of Medicine* 87 (4): 232–236.

Cheterian, V. 2015. ISIS and the Killing Fields of the Middle East. *Survival* 57 (2): 105–118.

Cosman, M.P., and L.G. Jones. 2008. *Handbook to Life in the Medieval World.* New York: Infobase Publishing.

Cytron, B.D. 1993. To Honour the Death and Comfort the Mourners: Traditions in Judaism. In *Ethnic Variations in Dying, Death and Grief: Diversity in Universality*, ed. D.P. Irish, K.F. Lundquist, and V.J. Nelson, 113–124. London: Taylor and Francis.

Dorff, E.N. 2005. End-of-Life: Jewish Perspectives. *Lancet* 366: 862–865.

Freeman, C., Akkoc, R. 2015. Mecca Stampede: At Least 717 Killed and Hundreds Injured in Crush During Hajj. *The Telegraph.* 25 September. https://www.telegraph.co.uk/news/worldnews/middleeast/saudiarabia/11887302/Eid-al-Adha-At-least-100-killed-and-hundreds-injured-in-crush-during-hajj-outside-Mecca.html. Accessed 10 July 2019.

Gilmore, D.D. 1987. *Honor and Shame and the Unity of the Mediterranean.* Washington, D.C. American Anthropological Association.

Green, J., and M. Green. 2006. *Dealing with Death: Practices and Procedures*, 2nd ed. London: Jessica Kingsley Publishers.

Harcke, H.Y., A.D. Levy, R.M. Abbott, et al. 2007. Autopsy Radiography: Digital Radiographs (DR) vs Multidetector Computer Tomography (MDCT) in High-Velocity Gunshot-Wound Victims. *American Journal of Forensic Medicine and Pathology* 28 (1): 13–19.

Henackaerts, J.M., and L. Doswald-Beck (eds). 2005. *Customary International Humanitarian Law, Volume 1: Rules.* Cambridge: Cambridge University Press.

Human Rights Watch. 2018. *Iraq: Chilling Accounts of Torture, Deaths. Investigative Abuse During Interrogations in Mosul.* https://www.hrw.org/news/2018/08/19/iraq-chilling-accounts-torture-deaths. Accessed 15 July 2019.

Ibn Ḥanbal, A. 850. Musnad Ahmad ibn Hanbal (Hadith 1065). *Dar AlHadith, Cairo* 5: 84.

International Committee of the Red Cross. 1949a. *Geneva Convention Relative to the Protection of Civilian Persons in Time of War (Fourth Geneva Convention), 12 August.* Geneva: International Committee of the Red Cross.

International Committee of the Red Cross. 1949b. *Geneva Convention Relative to the Treatment of Prisoners of War (Third Geneva Convention), 12 August.* Geneva: International Committee of the Red Cross.

Khunti, K. 2000. Referral for Autopsies: Analysis of 651 Consecutive Deaths in One General Practice. *Postgraduate Medical Journal* 76 (897): 415–416.

Kulczycki, A., and S. Windle. 2011. Honor Killings in the Middle East and North Africa: A Systematic Review of the Literature. *Violence Against Women* 17 (11): 1442–1464.

Levey, M. 1967. Medical Ethics of Medieval Islam with Special Reference to Al-Ruhāwī's "Practical Ethics of the Physician". *Transactions of the American Philosophical Society* 57 (3): 1–100.

Loughrey, M.B., W.G. McCluggage, and P.G. Toner. 2000. The Declining Autopsy Rate and Clinicians' Attitudes. *Ulster Medical Journal* 69 (2): 83–89.

Manoochehry, S., and H.R. Rasouli. 2017. Recurrent Human Tragedy During Hajj. *International Journal of Travel Medicine and Global Health* 5 (1): 36–37.

McHaffie, H.E., P.W. Fowlie, R. Hume, et al. 2001. Consent to Autopsy for Neonates. *Archives of Disease in Childhood Fetal and Neonatal Edition* 85 (1): F4–F7.

Mohammed, M., and M.A. Kharoshah. 2014. Autopsy in Islam and Current Practice in Arab Muslim Countries. *Journal of Forensic and Legal Medicine* 23: 80–83.

Mufti. 2014. Grand Mufti: Terrorism Has No Place in Islam. *Arab News.* 21 August. http://www.arabnews.com/news/featured/618351. Accessed 15 July 2019.

Muslim, I. 855 Ṣaḥiḥ Muslim (Hadith 1812), ed. Fu'ad 'Abd al-Baqi, M. *Dar Iḥya' al-Turath al-'Arabi. Beirut* 3: 1447.

Nazarko, L. 2006. As Death Approaches: Cultural Issues. *Nursing and Residential Care* 8: 441–444.

Oliver, M. 2006. Hundreds Killed in Hajj Stampede. *The Guardian*. 12 January. https://www.theguardian.com/world/2006/jan/12/saudiarabia.religion Accessed 10 July 2019.

Resolution 85/12/d8. 1994. Majallat majma' al-Fiqh al-Islami. Majma' al-Fiqhi al-Islami (Muslim World League). *Jeddah* 8 (3): 412.

Rutty, J.E. 2010. Religious Attitudes to Death and Post-Mortem Examinations. In *The Hospital Autopsy: A Manual of Fundamental Autopsy Practice*, 3rd ed, ed. J. Burton and G. Rutty, 39–58. London: Arnold.

Sarhill, N., F. Mahmoud, and D. Walsh. 2003. Muslim Beliefs Regarding Death, Dying and Bereavement. *European Journal of Palliative Care* 10: 34–37.

Shaham, R. 2010. *The Expert Witness in Islamic Courts: Medicine and Crafts in the Service of the Law*. Chicago: University of Chicago Press.

Shastry, S.M., S.S. Kolte, and P.R. Sanagapati. 2012. Potter's Sequence. *Journal of Clinical Neonatology* 1 (3): 157–159.

Smith, P. 2008. *An Introduction to the Bahá'í Faith*. Cambridge: Cambridge University Press.

Staff and Agencies. 2006. A History of Hajj Tragedies. *The Guardian*. 13 January. https://www.theguardian.com/world/2006/jan/13/saudiarabia Accessed 10 July 2019.

Thali, M.J., W. Schweitzer, K. Yen, et al. 2003. New Horizons in Forensic Radiology: The 60-Second Digital Autopsy-Full Body Examination of a Gunshot Victim by Multislice Computed Tomography. *American Journal of Forensic Medicine and Pathology* 24: 22–27.

United Nations Assistance Mission for Iraq and Office of the High Commission for Human Rights [UNAMI/OHCHR]. 2018. *Unearthing Atrocities: Mass Graves in Territory Formerly Controlled by ISIL*. https://ohchr.org/Documents/Countries/IQ/UNAMI_Report_on_Mass_Graves4Nov2018_EN.pdf. Accessed 10 July 2019.

United Nations Children's Fund. 2013. *Country Office Annual Report Summary 2012*, Unpublished Document.

United Nations Human Rights. 1987. *Convention Against Torture and Other Cruel, Inhuman, or Degrading Treatment of Punishment*. https://www.ohchr.org/EN/ProfessionalInterest/Pages/CAT.aspx. Accessed 14 July 2019.

United Nations Population Fund. 2000. *The State of the World's Population 2000. Lives Together, Worlds Apart: Men and Women in a Time of Change*. http://www.unfpa.org/swp/2000/english. Accessed 11 July 2019.

Zarabozo, J.D.M. 2009. *Commentary on the Forty Hadith of Al-Nawawi*. Nicosia: Al Basheer Company.

Zarrintan, S., A. Shahnaee, and S. Aslanabadi. 2018. Rhazes (AD 865–925) and His Early Contributions to the Field of Pediatrics. *Childs Nervous System* 34: 1435–1438.

Chapter 23
"Not of One's Body": The Creation of Identified Skeletal Collections with Portuguese Human Remains

Francisca Alves-Cardoso

Abstract This chapter will explore how identified skeletal collections are built using unclaimed human remains from modern cemeteries in Portugal. The custom of collecting unclaimed human remains is an old practice in Portugal, dating back to the late nineteenth century. Several institutions in Portugal currently house five identified collections, which contain complete skeletons. These are housed at the Universities of Coimbra, Porto, and Évora, and the Museum of Natural History of Lisbon. The Coimbra and Lisbon collections have become synonymous with scientific excellence in research worldwide. However, the scientific acknowledgment of the importance of these collections contrasts with the almost absent discussion on the ethical and legal issues associated with the collections, and the use of unclaimed human remains from modern cemeteries in science. Therefore, this chapter hopes to highlight the need for conversation on the topic, which is a pressing necessity since this practice, i.e. the collection of unclaimed remains from modern cemeteries, is not limited to Portugal and identified collections worldwide are a valuable resource amongst the scientific community.

23.1 Introduction

Portugal has proven to be generous to those that study human remains. Presently the country possesses a significant number of skeletal human remains collections recovered from archaeological excavation, as well as assemblages from modern

The original version of the chapter was revised: Citations have been corrected. The correction to this chapter is available at https://doi.org/10.1007/978-3-030-32926-6_31

F. Alves-Cardoso (✉)
Laboratório de Antropologia Biológica e Osteologia Humana (LABOH), Centro em Rede de Investigação em Antropologia (CRIA), Faculdade de Ciências Sociais e Humanas (FCSH), Universidade NOVA de Lisboa, FCSH-Nova, Edifício ID, Av. Berna, 26, Sala 3.09, 1069-061 Lisbon, Portugal
e-mail: francicard@fcsh.unl.pt

K. Squires et al. (eds.), *Ethical Approaches to Human Remains*,
https://doi.org/10.1007/978-3-030-32926-6_23

cemeteries (for details see Rocha 1995; Umbelino and Santos 2011; Alves-Cardoso and Cunha 2018). Those teaching and learning about biological, physical, and forensic anthropology and bioarchaeology have had the privilege to handle real and complete skeletal remains in classrooms, rather than casts. This osteological material derives from various chronological periods, stages of bone tissue development, and human/population variability. These human remains are accessed for the use of teaching, learning, and research, which typically takes place at universities, research centres, museums, and laboratories throughout the country. In contrast, other countries have long engaged in the discussion on the care and ethics of dealing with human remains, specifically regarding issues related to the repatriation and curation of Indigenous skeletons (APABE 2005; DCMS 2005; Walker 2008; Giesen 2013; Fletcher et al. 2014; Mugabowagahunde 2016, to cite but a few authors that have addressed this topic). Portugal has remained unusually quiet on this topic. However, news brought to the public in 2016 (discussed further below) may prove to be the perfect setting to explore issues related to the access and curation of human remains in Portugal, its ethical settings, alongside the discussion of body donation to science.

On the 9th September 2016, a Portuguese newspaper article (Francisco 2016) highlighted the fact that Lisbon City Council (Câmara Municipal de Lisboa, Portugal) had approved the donation (Boletim Municipal 2016) of unclaimed human remains from the Lisbon cemeteries, dated between the end of the nineteenth century and first decade of the twenty-first century, to a Canadian University in order to develop a new skeletal reference collection, for the purpose of research and teaching. The request was put forward by a Portuguese academic, Hugo Cardoso, working at a Canadian university (Cardoso 2016). In sum, and as described by the project outline, the Portuguese human remains would be curated at Simon Fraser University (Canada) on a long-term, but temporary basis (Cardoso 2016). This project was explained as akin to other projects in Portugal, i.e. in which modern human skeletal remains from cemeteries have been amassed to develop skeletal reference collections in Lisbon, Coimbra, Porto, and Évora (Cardoso 2016). The Portuguese National Ethics Council for the Life Sciences (Concelho Nacional de Ética para as Ciências Vivas—CNECV) and the Portuguese National Institute of Legal Medicine were consulted with both providing reports that were interpreted as positive. Therefore, the Lisbon City Council deliberated that "…the abandoned bones may be transferred definitively (donated) to the Simon Fraser University, Canada, provided that the constraints set forth in the Law-Decree No 274/99 are observed".[1] The law decree mentioned (LDn274/99) regulates the dissection of cadavers and extraction of body parts, tissues, or organs from cadavers for purposes of teaching and scientific research.

[1]The original text states: "O pedido formulado foi objeto de pareceres, do Instituto de Medicina Legal e Ciências Forenses, I. P., e do Conselho Nacional de Ética para as Ciências da Vida, os quais perfilham o entendimento, de que as ossadas abandonadas podem ser cedidas a título definitivo (doadas) à Universidade Simon Fraser, no Canadá, desde que observados os condicionalismos previstos no Decreto-Lei n.º 274/99, de 22 de julho;" (Boletim Municipal 2016, 208–209).

Following this press story, on the 18th October 2016, several Portuguese academics manifested their concerns to a number of Portuguese Ministries as well as Lisbon City Council. The concerns mostly addressed the topic of "exportation" and definite donation of the human remains to Canada; the legal void on this specific matter; and associated ethical issues, remembering that these remains were not of archaeological nature, but belonged to identifiable individuals (for details of media coverage on this matter see Dias 2016; Firmino 2016). As a consequence of the concerns expressed by the Portuguese academics, the request, which was originally approved as a donation by the City Council, presently awaits to be voted on as a loan,[2] shifting the emphasis from a definite donation to a long-term loan. However, and after consulting the Lisbon City Council Boletim Municipal from October 2016 until January 2018 (Boletim Municipal nº 1246, Suplemento Nº 1), no mention was found addressing the donation or loan of the remains. Therefore, one is left wondering if this is still an ongoing request waiting for final approval, or if the request fell through. Note that the description of the above events is but a mere summary.

Apart from media coverage, at the time, a public debate titled 'Restless Dead Bodies: The Ethics of Circulation of Human Remains', was promoted during the EASA Medical Anthropology Network 2017 Biennial Conference Network Meeting—'Bodies in Transition: Power, Knowledge, and Medical Anthropology' (APA 2017). The debate took place in Lisbon, Portugal, on the 6th July 2017. This debate, organised by Francesca De Luca and Ricardo Moreira from the University of Lisbon Social Science Institute, intended to be a discussion among biological anthropologists, currently engaged in a dialogue around the ethics and politics of circulation of human remains from osteological collections. The departure point of the debate was, as stated by one of the organisers "…the recent polemic that ensued in the press after the Lisbon municipality accepted a proposal for the transportation of human remains of Portuguese origin to a university in Canada, in order to compose a new reference collection for research in forensic and biological anthropology".[3] The expectation of this final point was to further engage the academic community and public in a discussion of these events.

Participants at the debate included Hugo Cardoso (via Skype), from Simon Fraser University, and the proponent of the donation/loan request to Lisbon City Council, Susana Garcia from the University of Lisbon—Instituto Superior de Ciências Sociais e Políticas (ISCSP_ULisboa) and curator of the Luis Lopes Identified Skeletal Collection of the Portuguese Museum of Natural History, Francisca Alves-Cardoso from the Centro de Rede de Investigação em Antropology

---

[2]Comment provided by Hugo Cardoso on the 16th July 2017 on—*Review of Public Debate "Restless Dead Bodies: The Ethics of Circulation of Human Remains"*. EASA Medical Anthropology Network Conference, Lisbon, Portugal, 6th July 2017. https://bodiesandacademia.wordpress.com/2017/07/15/review-of-public-debate-restless-dead-bodies-the-ethics-of-circulation-of-human-remains-easa-medical-anthropology-network-conferencelisbon-2017/.

[3]Details of the public debate may be found at the EASA Medical Anthropology Network | 2017 Biennial Conference Network Meeting's site: http://medanthlisbon2017.apantropologia.org/public-debate/.

(CRIA, FCSH, Universidade NOVA de Lisboa), a biological anthropologist whose focus of research has been the Portuguese Human Identified Collections, Cristiana Bastos (ICS-ULisboa), chair of the debate, and whose work recently addressed Portuguese colonialism through its health institutions, and Vítor Oliveira Jorge, from Instituto de História Contemporânea (IHC, FCSH-NOVA), who is an archaeologist and heritage specialist and was the convenor of the debate.

Truth be said, and although the debate was publicised as a "public debate" on social media and other advertising platforms, with the exception of a small number of Portuguese and international academics attending the EASA meeting, only a handful of Portuguese academics that work with human remains, and volunteers of the conference were present. The general public, by large, were absent. Hence, the aim of it becoming a "public debate" fell short on expectations. A video of the debate has been posted by the Associação Portuguesa de Antropologia (APA), but six months after the event, it only had 90 views (APA 2017). Consequently, the public and academic impact of this news, i.e. the transportation of human remains of Portuguese origin, and exhumed from Portuguese cemeteries, to a university in Canada to develop an identified skeletal collection for research and teaching, is still to be evaluated, and due to the sensibility of the issue people may choose to reserve from comments and/or actions. A review of the public debate has been available on the Bodies and Academia blog since 15th July 2017 (Ion 2017).

The aforementioned mise-en-scène is the perfect setting to discuss issues related to the creation of human identified collections, with specific reference to Portuguese human remains, either in Portugal or other countries. It further allows us to explore how a legal void on this specific matter, the legislation related to organ donation, and the use of cadavers and sampling of tissues from cadavers for purposes of research and teaching, have permitted the possibility of identified human remains from Portuguese modern cemeteries to be relocated to Canada so that a new reference collection could be built. Note that the same circumstances have also facilitated the establishment of identified skeletal collections, which also contain human remains from modern cemeteries in Portugal (Rocha 1995; Cardoso 2006; Cunha and Wasterlain 2007; Ferreira et al. 2014). This convergence of events, and particular circumstances, offer a new challenge to those inclined to think about ethical issues associated with the recovery, curation, and assembly of collections of human remains in traditional and virtual environments.

The following sections contextualise the importance of skeletal collections, specifically those composed of identified human skeletonised remains in Portugal, hence justifying their development and use in the production of scientific knowledge. Secondly, this chapter will briefly introduce the Portuguese identified collections, as opposed to archaeological collections, exploring how these become a reality, and the mechanism that has allowed their creation. Thirdly, the legal framework will be introduced, including the Portuguese organ donation law, which has also been used as an argument for building collections of human remains. Finally, some concluding remarks and ethical considerations will be drawn.

23.2 Contextualising the Importance of Human Identified Skeletal Collections

Anthropological knowledge based on the study of human skeletal remains has grown considerably in the last decade. Much of this growth has been promoted by forensic sciences and the study of human skeletonised remains. The glorification of forensic science via social media and television series, such as Bones, have certainly left its mark on the subject (IMDb 2005). Prior to that, the work of Kathy Reichs, an American crime writer/forensic anthropologist/academic popularised the subject. In recent years, a significant number of students have attended courses in anthropology, with an emphasis on forensic anthropology and/or archaeological sciences hoping to become (not considering gender) "Bones", i.e. Dr Temperance "Bones" Brennan, the main character of the aforementioned television show. The realisation of these students' expectations is the result of many informal conversations with undergraduate and master students in Portugal, when asked—"Why do you want to study Forensic Anthropology?". Therefore, the influence of popular culture should be considered with caution. Nevertheless, what is called "The CSI effect" has deserved academic attention, and one cannot ignore the impact of the media in forensic sciences and associated contexts (Shelton et al. 2006; Dauria and Quintyn 2007; Weaver et al. 2012).

Alongside this flourishing interest in forensic sciences and the study of human skeletonised remains, many universities worldwide have invested and promoted undergraduate and postgraduate courses on the study of bones, either stressing bioarchaeology or forensic anthropology. As a consequence of the ever-growing interest in these disciplines, there has been an equivalent worldwide interest in the development, construction, and curation of human identified osteological collections (Eliopoulos et al. 2007; Alemán et al. 2012; Ferreira et al. 2014; Belcastro et al. 2017, to name but a few). The human skeletal remains used to build these collections are primarily recovered from archaeological excavations, but there are a growing number of collections—referred to as Identified Skeletal Collections or Reference Collections—whose remains were exhumed from cemeteries that are still in use (for examples see Rocha 1995; Cardoso 2006; Eliopoulos et al. 2007; Alemán et al. 2012; Ferreira et al. 2014; Belcastro et al. 2017). Other remains appertained to autopsied bodies and/or donated bodies and anatomical (medical) collections (Knoeff and Zwijnenberg 2015).

Of these assemblages, the Identified Skeletal Collections deserve further consideration since they are composed not only of the human remains themselves, but also their associated biographical data (L'Abbé et al. 2005; Cardoso 2006; Eliopoulos et al. 2007; Rissech and Steadman 2011; Alemán et al. 2012; Bosio et al. 2012; Ferreira et al. 2014; Sanabria-Medina et al. 2016; Belcastro et al. 2017; Go et al. 2017). The association of personal data with skeletonised remains in some archaeological collections has also been possible due to information presented on coffin plates and tombstones, but in much smaller numbers, such as the cases of the Spitalfields and St. Brides archaeological collections in the United Kingdom (Molleson and Cox 1993; Scheuer and Black 1995; Scheuer and Bowman 1995; Cox 1996). The publications on these collections introduce the demographic and socio-economic profiles of these populations, emphasising their relevance to science (see the following for examples: Cardoso 2006; Eliopoulos et al. 2007; Bosio et al. 2012; Ferreira et al. 2014; Belcastro et al. 2017). The provenance of the remains from the identified collections is no more than a note on the manuscripts, with reference to the need of vacating temporary graves (those that contained the remains of unclaimed humans) in accordance with the legislation of these cemeteries. Hence, the largest part of the worldwide Identified Skeletal Collections have been amassed from unclaimed human remains in modern cemeteries. Anonymity of these individuals is, to a certain extent, preserved. However, much is known about the deceased as biographical data includes the name of the individual, his/her sex and age-at-death, place and year of birth, parents' names, place and location of death, occupation at death, cause of death, address at time of death, among other information that was listed at time of death (this is the case of the Portuguese collections).

These collections, particularly the Portuguese assemblages, are amongst the most widely used in international research on anthropological methods and/or population related studies on the biological profiling of sex and age-at-death, behaviour patterns and/or activity related bone changes, disease diagnosis and/or pathological related bone changes, human and population variability, and evolutionary anthropology, as well as comparative anatomy. All these themes have been explored, revised, and criticised, further contributing significantly to the body of knowledge of physical, biological, and forensic anthropology. For example, research on activity related-osseous changes, such as entheseal changes, have produced conflicting results on the correlation of entheseal changes and activity. These results have highlighted the need for caution when reconstructing activity based on osseous changes, with a consequent revision of the methodological approach to entheseal changes to infer past activity patterns (Milella et al. 2012; Alves-Cardoso and Henderson 2013; Henderson et al. 2013; Perréard Lopreno et al. 2013; Cardoso et al. 2015). Therefore, the contribution of these collections to the advancement of scientific knowledge has been paramount. Hence, these collections of human remains are the equivalent of *excellence* in research and have formed the basis of many scholarly works worldwide. But, it is also necessary to remember that these collections (and associated research) are permeable to bias and therefore their *excellence* may be questioned (for details see Henderson and Alves-Cardoso 2018).

23.3 The Portuguese Human Skeletal Collection—The Identified Collections

As stated in the introduction of this chapter, Portugal possesses a large number of collections that are comprised of human remains. These collections vary extensively in number of individuals, their sex, age, and morphology. It would be fair to say that, presently, it is impossible to know how many skeletal human remains have been excavated and subsequently curated in various institutions across Portugal.

In Portugal, collections composed of human remains recovered from archaeological contexts fall within the legislation that governs archaeological findings. A specific reference to human remains is present in the legislation that regulates archaeological works (Decreto Lei nº 270/99 1999) stating that the excavation of necropolises, where anthropological material (i.e. human skeletonised remains) may be found, will only be authorised if the collaboration of specialists in physical anthropology is assured during the excavation process (for an overview of the history associated with the excavation and recovering of human remains in Portugal see Umbelino and Santos 2011). In this sense, human remains recovered from archaeological contexts are considered archaeological material, and are regulated as such, as are other materials, such as ceramics, glass, and stones. As "cultural assets" they fall within the legislation that addresses the cultural patrimony (Lei nº107/2001 2001). Due to the absence of specific legislation that addresses issues associated with human remains recovered from various contexts in Portuguese territory, a Working Group of Biological Anthropology and Human Remains, endorsed by the Directorate-General for Cultural Heritage (DGPC), Portuguese Secretarial State of Culture (Portugal), was created in 2014. This group aimed to facilitate the discussion around the methodological and excavation procedures of human remains, their storage, curation, and accessibility for research. Despite this positive action, there is still much to do.

The identified human osteology collections housed in universities and museums in Portugal are not considered archaeological collections, due to their chronological age and associated biographical data. As a result, these individuals are granted a particular status. For example, the 21st Century Identified Skeletal Collection (CEI/XXI) associated with Coimbra University possesses individuals that died in 2008 (Ferreira et al. 2014). For this reason, identified collections can be used to explore how science and society engage in the present day, and they also open the door to discuss the role of Human Identified Skeletal Collections as a testing ground for anthropology (Henderson and Alves-Cardoso 2018) whilst exploring the fine line of equilibrium between scientific knowledge production and caring for the dead.

In Portugal, there are currently five Human Identified Skeletal Collections that comprise complete human skeletons. Other collections exist, though these only contain partial skeletons or individual skeletal elements, such as skulls (for a full overview of the collections see Alves-Cardoso and Cunha 2018, and authors therein). Some of the best-known assemblages include the Coimbra Identified Collection, housed at Coimbra University (Rocha 1995) and the Luis Lopes

Skeletal Collection, curated at the Museum of Natural History in Lisbon (Cardoso 2006). Others include the Évora University Collection, the BoneMedLeg Research Project Collection (henceforward Porto collection), and the 21st Century Identified Skeletal Collection (CEI/XXI) associated with Coimbra University (Ferreira et al. 2014). Additionally, and associated with the CEI/XXI collection, the first collection of laboratorial burned human skeletons is also under development (Gonçalves 2012). All the aforementioned collections have been collected from modern cemeteries from the late nineteenth century to the present day, and are composed of more than 2500 individuals: a figure which continues to grow. Some of the individuals whose remains are stored in these collections died in the late 1800s whilst others passed away in 2008, some of which were exhumed as recent as 2013 in the case of the CEI/XXI collection (Ferreira et al. 2014).

The Portuguese identified collections are widely used by the scientific community, specifically the Lisbon and Coimbra Identified Skeletal Collections. Since 2006, which coincided with the brief communication published in the American Journal of Physical Anthropology (Cardoso 2006), access requested to the Lisbon collection has been significant. Between 2008 and 2014, 79 international researchers have studied the Lisbon collection. The majority were associated with institutions in Portugal (26), Spain (17), and the USA (16). Others were from various European countries, Canada, South America, and Japan (Maria Judite Alves 2014, pers. comm.). Further quantitative data on research outputs based on the Coimbra documented collections are also known from an earlier date. Between 1898 and 1995, around 106 scholarly works that cited the Coimbra assemblage were produced (Rocha 1995, 21–33). To this number, in 2007, Cunha and Wasterlain (2007, 30–31) added a list of 21 doctoral thesis, and the same number of master's dissertations. Not only is this number significant, but the wide range of international institutions, and associated scholars and students that have based their research on the collection, is also noteworthy. Apart from Portugal, other European countries, including Spain, France, Italy, Switzerland, and England, are mentioned by Cunha and Wasterlain (2007). Additionally, scholars working in other countries, such as Brazil, USA, New Zealand, and Canada, are also referenced (Cunha and Wasterlain 2007). Since 2007, more scholars have had the privilege to access these collections, as well as the newly formed 21st Century Identified Skeletal Collection. At present, researchers from Brazil, Croatia, France, Spain, USA, Germany, Mexico, Sri Lanka, Saudi Arabia, and Colombia have accessed the new collection (Alves-Cardoso and Cunha 2018). This reinforces the need for ethical and legal considerations associated with the acquisition, and the use of the skeletonised human remains that compose these collections. Science, and the development of science, should not be the sole and ultimate justification to acquire and utilise human osteological remains without careful consideration (Martin et al. 2013, and authors therein). Larsen and Walker (2015, 114) have identified that, when working with human remains, three points must be considered at all times, these include: "… (1) human remains should be treated with dignity and respect, (2) descendants should have the authority to control the disposition of their relatives' remains, and (3) because of the importance of human remains for the understanding of our common past, human remains need to be preserved when possible so that they are available for scientific research." Adding to this, and in accordance with Sørmoen (2012), to balance the integrity of the dead and the desire for knowledge is, in my opinion, one of the major challenges facing those associated with the human identified collections.

23.4 How Did the Collections Come to Be?

The remains from these collections belong to individuals that were classified as being abandoned and/or unclaimed by their relatives according to cemetery regulations. Cemetery regulations have changed over time, but they all refer back to the Decreto Lei n° 411/98 (Decreto Lei 1998). An account of "how" human remains may be incorporated into identified collections has been described by Hugo Cardoso for the Luis Lopes collection (Cardoso 2006, 45–46):

> The skeletons in this collection originate from modern cemetery sources and correspond to the remains that, by virtue of being abandoned or neglected by relatives, were destined for communal graves in the local cemeteries in Lisbon. […] The practice at these cemeteries is to exhume individuals from temporary graves after the legally stipulated period of five years and if complete skeletonisation has occurred so that the grave can be reused. The bones are then deposited in the communal grave or, for an annual fee paid by relatives or legal representatives; they are placed in small urns that are kept in individual block compartments or niches (ossários). […] In the case of temporary graves, if the family or legal representatives do not claim the remains shortly after exhumation or do not pay a periodic fee for the ossários, the cemeteries issue an order of removal. Because failure to pay for the periodic fee can occur anytime from one year to several decades after exhumation, a substantial lapse of time can pass between the secondary interment in the ossários and the order of removal. Individual remains in irregular situations (due to abandonment or failure to pay the periodic fee) are deposited in a storage room until a relative or other rightful person shows up to claim them. After waiting for a relatively long period of time (usually a few years) the cemetery authorities deposit them in the communal grave or, more recently, destroy them in the cemetery incinerator if present. Just before the remains are destroyed or reburied, the museum steps in and collects the skeletal material.

The same procedure was also mentioned, although more succinctly, for the Coimbra collections (Cunha and Wasterlain 2007) and the CEI/XXI collection (Ferreira et al. 2014). The Porto and Évora collections follow the same practice, as are/will be the circumstances, which may allow the remains of the Lisbon cemeteries to be loaned to a Canadian university. The transition of human remains from the cemeteries to secondary housing/curating facilities is based on collaborative agreements and/or permissions granted by the City Councils (Câmaras Municipais) responsible for the cemeteries management, and the proponents of the action, whether they are Portuguese universities or scholars associated with foreign institutions, as the case discussed.

In a practical sense the legitimacy of the procedure is not questioned, it follows the legislation of cemetery management (Law Decree n° 411/98, Decreto Lei 1998). This decree has allowed for exhumations to be performed without participations of judicial authorities, simplifying exhumations, and the administration of cemeteries by local authorities. Furthermore, with this legislative framing, exhumed and unclaimed skeletonised human remains fall under cemetery jurisdiction and responsibility. The law decree (Law Decree n° 411/98, Decreto Lei 1998) aimed to converge several laws on cemetery construction, management, and regulatory procedures of dealing with human remains, as well as providing a revision and updating of the terminologies in use. The reuse of graves is not a novelty in Portugal, or in other European countries such as the UK, Spain, Greece, Italy, and others, as it provides a response to serious problems originated by the saturation of cemetery space. The reduction of the inhumation period from five to three years is an example of that preoccupation, as well as the simplification of the exhumation procedure excluding the need of other authoritative figures than those associated with the cemetery.

According to cemetery legislations[4] the reference to the abandonment of human remains appears in association with exhumations, as well as in the description of abandonment of crypts and graves. The former is related to the legal period in which an individual may remain buried in a temporary grave; the latter relates to perpetual graves. The process in which a person may find their remains declared "abandoned" may happen three years after burial, if inhumed in temporary graves, or after ten years if inhumed in perpetual graves or crypts. However, each cemetery will deal with space management according to their needs. Consequently, temporary graves may hold human remains for much longer than three years. Information or notification to the interested parties on the ongoing process of vacating an inhumation site is announced via newspapers, a letter, a notice in appropriate locations, or even on social media, such as Facebook. There is the possibility of the remains, classified as abandoned, to be reburied, cremated, or placed into secondary resting places. However, all the latter options may include a fee payment, or it will be a mere administrative procedure of disposing of the remains.

The need to vacate the space in which a person was originally buried is the key point used in the classification of abandonment, i.e. remains being classified as "abandoned". Descriptions found in the published literature on the identified collection also refer to the process of abandonment as an act practiced by ones' relatives. The expression 'abandoned by'/'neglected by'/'unclaimed by' relatives is a banner used in association with the creation of these identified skeletal collections. However, in practice, and to date, no diligences have been undertaken to ascertain if the remains have any living relatives, and if they do, why the remains were "abandoned". Somehow, it is tacitly accepted that the efforts to advertise in newspapers, and notifications posted in designated locations or social media are enough. Furthermore, informally, it is accepted that "people know" that after a stipulated period of burial, if payment is discontinued or if the deceased was buried

[4]For details consult the cemetery regulations of the cities of Lisbon, Coimbra, Évora, and Santarém: these are the City Councils which have granted access to unclaimed human remains to be incorporated into identified collections over the years, and to my knowledge, to the present day. All regulation and legislation may be found online, as well as in association with each City Council webpage.

in a temporary grave, the remains may be exhumed. However, this may be a simplification of reality. The concept of a perpetual grave is understood as "forever" for the majority of the Portuguese population, with no need of constant surveillance. To assess if "people" actually know that graves are temporary, and what may happen to human remains after they are declared abandoned, a pilot study was developed within a larger theoretical framework as the one being discussed (Alves-Cardoso 2014). The study was conducted via a mailing list at the Faculty for Social Sciences and Humanities of the Universidade NOVA de Lisboa and a total of 356 individuals participated. The age range varied from 18 to 65 years old. This study is still under development, but the first results are contradictory to the notion that "people know". The majority of the participants of the survey (88%) were unaware that human remains from the identified collections were collected from modern cemeteries, and that they were individuals classified as "abandoned" (54%). With this in mind, it becomes clear that there is the need to understand how much people actually know about the subject, and the implication this may have from both a practical and an ethical viewpoint.

Let us now raise the issue of "consent" to access these remains incorporated into the collections. Ideally, issues related to the search for consent of individuals or living relatives, or the impossibility of such practice, should also be explored by the collections curators and/or those directly involved in the creation of identified collections. In the case of Portugal, it may be argued that 'consent' is not needed since according to Portuguese law (Lei nº 12/93 1993) all citizens (Portuguese, stateless people, and foreigners living in Portugal) are potential organ donors unless they have expressed their will not to be so, i.e. if one does not wish to become a donor, one needs to register as such. In Portugal, a person is not a potential donor until after they register on the *Registo Nacional de Não Dadores* (RENNDA: National Registra of Non Donors, Decreto Lei nº 244/94 1994). Additionally, the legislation on the use of soft tissues of cadaveric human remains for research and teaching (Decreto Lei nº 274/99 1999) can be used as a counter argument for the need to explore consent. It was this law decree that was used as a basis for the argument provided by the Conselho Nacional de Ética para as Ciências de Vida (CNECV 2015) on the issue related to the donation of human remains to Canada, and in the absence of a registration on the RENNDA (by those whose remains appertained[5]). The CNECV concluded that there were no legal impediments to the assignment of the remains in question for scientific research purposes. Most importantly, and although the position of the CNECV was described as a favorable one, it has in actual fact highlighted a series of considerations that need careful thinking. For example, it was noted that Portugal lacks a national legislation on the regulation of the donation of human remains, i.e. bones and skeletons. The law that was used as a basis of the report (Decreto Lei nº 274/99 1999b), which regulates the dissection of cadavers and the extraction of parts, tissues, or organs for teaching and scientific research purposes, is in need of extensive interpretation, and only in its

[5]As interpreted by the author.

limits can it be applied to the request. The Lisbon Municipal Cemeteries Regulation (Call Notice no. 60/84[6]) does not contemplate the loan of bones for scientific research, although there is the possibility of the remains been given a more adequate destiny (as opposed to cremation and/or reburial), though this decision rests on those responsible for the cemeteries management. If the decision is favorable to the loaning of the remains, ethical issues associated with scientific research on human remains must be upheld, namely the rigorous anonymisation of those whose cadaveric remains are to be studied. These were some of the major conclusions drawn from the CNECV report (CNECV 2015). These concluding remarks deserve further development by those that share mutual interest in the access of identified human remains to build collections for the purposes of research and teaching, by those engaged in the development of regulations that permit the access to the remains and, finally, the population at large.

Also, and from a social and cultural perspective, it would be worth exploring the context in which human remains are not claimed. Are there no living relatives? Alternatively, do they not care nor wish to 'attend' to the remains of their family members? In 1995, Augusta Rocha expressed similar questions in relation to the Coimbra human identified collection, stating that the lack of claimed human remains may be associated with other factors than mere economics, such as changes in attitudes towards death or religious behaviours (Rocha 1995).

The cemetery legislation and the procedures in which unclaimed remains are dealt with, alongside the legislation on the dissection of corpses for teaching and scientific research, and the "presumed consent" law on organ donation in Portugal have all supported the creation of identified collections. The argument in favor of the creation of the collections has always been that all legal requirements are met, and that these collections have a significant scientific value. So, we need to find a way to balance the rights of the dead, with the rights and expectations of the living.

23.5 Conclusion

There are many relevant questions for those that study human remains, either from modern cemeteries or archaeological contexts. The focus of the current chapter was the collectives of human remains from modern cemeteries that are used to create identified collections. Although the focus has been Portugal, the procedure of building identified collections is a common practice worldwide: unclaimed human remains are being used to build human identified collections for both research and teaching, mostly in association with forensic sciences. They all comply to existing legislation, and are therefore perceived as being excused of discussion.

[6]The full document can be found on the Lisbon City Council webpage: http://www.cm-lisboa.pt/regulamentos?tx_damfrontend_pi1[pointer]=2.

The cemetery legislation simplifies, to an extreme, the classification of unclaimed remains as "abandoned", which ultimately legitimises their incorporation into collections. The fact is that there are many reasons why human remains may be abandoned in cemeteries for example, financial difficulties may have prevented surviving kin to rebury a loved one or relatives may have moved away and did not update their address so were not informed that the remains were to be exhumed. Of course, remains may also be abandoned because people do not care anymore. Fundamental authority is conferred to the cemetery administrative entities as to how unclaimed human remains are to be disposed of, but it would be desirable that whichever decision was taken considered the overall social, cultural, and economic context which may indicate why human remains are abandoned since it may have future impact on the politics and practices of cemetery management. Taking a step back and reflecting on the reasons why the remains are being abandoned will certainly contribute to a more realistic understanding of societal changes, and how to address and adjust the handling of unclaimed remains with continued dignity. Have you never stopped at what looks like an abandoned grave, in a cemetery, and wondered why are there no visible signs of remembering? I have on a number of occasions. A reflection on all of the above, especially on the disposal of unclaimed remains, leads us to a point already highlighted by Larsen and Walker (2015, 114) when addressing remains from archaeological contexts:

> Ethical dilemmas do arise, however, when we consider who has or is given authority to determine disposition when the remains in questions are those of individuals distantly related to the living people who claim them. How should this authority be determined when there is a distance of hundreds, thousands, or even millions of years between the living and the dead?

The author offers no solution. Rather, they introduce another issue, that of the concept of ownership by entity or entities, and control and disposal of the remains. The fact is, human behaviour is complex, there are economic and social issues to consider, as well as emotional. The decision to access human remains from cemetery grounds for research and teaching should not be, in the author's opinion, a unilateral decision. All those involved in the process should be consulted in the sense that many families will be called to address the issue of their beloved ones/relatives remains: these include local authorities, those that provide burial services, researchers accessing the remains, and communities at large from various religious and other belief groups. There is a need for designing a new approach to burial grounds and the disposal of unclaimed remains, and how these are ultimately treated by the living.

Acknowledgements Francisca Alves-Cardoso's research is funded by the Fundação para a Ciência e Tecnologia (FCT) Investigator Program also supported by the European Commission ESF and POPH [FCT Investigador IF/00127/2014 and FCT Investigador Exploratory Project IF/00127/2014/CP1233/CT0003].

References

Advisory Panel on Archaeology of Burials in England [APABE]. 2005. *Guidelines for Best Practice for the Treatment of Human Remains Excavated from Christian Burial Grounds in England*. Swindon: Advisory Panel on Archaeology of Burials in England.

Alemán, I., J. Irurita, A.R. Valencia, et al. 2012. Brief Communication: The Granada Osteological Collection of Identified Infants and Young Children. *American Journal of Physical Anthropology* 149 (4): 606–610.

Alves-Cardoso, F. 2014. *With Who's Permission? Using Human Skeletal Tissue to Build Identified Skeletal Collections*. Paper Presented at ASA14: Anthropology and Enlightenment, University of Edinburgh, Edinburgh, UK, 19–22 June 2014.

Alves-Cardoso, F., and E. Cunha 2018. L'expérience de la Constitution des Collections Documentées au Portugal. In: *Les Ensembles Anthropologiques et Paléobiologiques: Entre Législation, Intérêt Scientifique et Enjeu Éthique*, ed. Y. Ardagna and A. Chaillou. Paris: Collection Documents d'Archéologie Française. Ministère de la Culture et de la Communication Direction Générale des Patrimoines – sous-direction de l'Archéologie.

Alves-Cardoso, F., and C. Henderson. 2013. The Categorisation of Occupation in Identified Skeletal Collections: A Source of Bias? *International Journal of Osteoarchaeology* 23 (2): 186–196.

Associação Portuguesa de Antropologia [APA]. 2017. *Public Debate: Restless Dead Bodies: The Ethics of Circulation of Human Remains*. https://www.youtube.com/watch?v=L0QEOCAHB6A. Accessed 19 September 2017.

Belcastro, M.G., B. Bonfiglioli, M.E. Pedrosi, et al. 2017. The History and Composition of the Identified Human Skeletal Collection of the Certosa Cemetery (Bologna, Italy, 19th–20th Century). *International Journal of Osteoarchaeology* 27: 912–925.

Boletim Municipal. 2016. 2.° *Suplemento ao Boletim Municipal*, N.° 1166, 208–209. http://bm-pesquisa.cm-lisboa.pt/pls/OKUL/app_bm.download_my_file?p_file=2417#search=. Accessed 19 September 2017.

Bosio, L.A., S. García Guraieb, L.H. Luna, et al. 2012. Chacarita Project: Conformation and Analysis of a Modern and Documented Human Osteological Collection From Buenos Aires City—Theoretical, Methodological and Ethical Aspects. *HOMO* 63 (6): 481–492.

Cardoso, F.A., S. Assis, and C. Henderson. 2015. Exploring Poverty: Skeletal Biology and Documentary Evidence in 19(th)–20(th) Century Portugal. *Annals of Human Biology* 43 (2): 102–106.

Cardoso, H. 2016. Brief Communication: Development of a New Skeletal Reference Collection in Canada and Science Outreach Projects in Portugal. *Canadian Association for Physical Anthropology* 2016 (2): 7–9.

Cardoso, H.F.V. 2006. Brief Communication: The Collection of Identified Human Skeletons Housed at the Bocage Museum (National Museum of Natural History), Lisbon. Portugal. *American Journal of Physics and Anthropology* 129 (2): 173–176.

Conselho Nacional de Ética para as Ciências de Vida [CNECV]. 2015. 85/CNECV/2015, *Pedido de Doação de Ossadas e Trasladação destas para o Canadá*. http://www.cnecv.pt/admin/files/data/docs/1446826133_Parecer%2085CNECV2015.pdf. Accessed 19 September 2017.

Cox, M. 1996. *Life and Death in Spitalfields 1700 to 1850*. York: Council for British Archaeology.

Cunha, E., and S. Wasterlain. 2007. The Coimbra Identified Skeletal Collections. In *Skeletal Series and Their Socioeconomic Context*, ed. G. Grupe and J. Peters, 23–33. Munchen: Verlag.

Dauria, S., and C.B. Quintyn. 2007. Anthropologists Confront the CSI Effect. *Anthropology News* 48 (8): 21.

Decreto Lei n° 244/94. 1994. Diário da República n.° 223/1994, Série I-A de 1994-09-26. https://dre.pt/web/guest/pesquisa/-/search/606526/details/normal?q=Registo+Nacional+de+n%C3%A3o+Dadores±. Accessed 19 September 2017.

Decreto Lei nº 411/98. 1998. Diário da República n.º 300/1998, Série I-A de 1998-12-30. https://dre.pt/pesquisa-avancada/-/asearch/286106/details/normal?perPage=25&types=SERIEI&numero=411%2F98&tipo=%22Decreto-Lei%22/en. Accessed 19 September 2017.

Decreto Lei nº 270/99. 1999. Diário da República n.º 163/1999, Série I-A de 1999-07-15. https://dre.pt/web/guest/pesquisa/-/search/358173/details/maximized. Accessed 19 September 2017.

Decreto Lei nº 274/99. 1999b. Diário da República n.º 169/1999, Série I-A de 1999-07-22. https://dre.pt/web/guest/pesquisa/-/search/354704/details/normal?q=n.%C2%BA%20274%2F99. Accessed 19 September 2017.

Department for Culture, Media and Sport [DCMS]. 2005. *Guidance for the Care of Human Remains in Museums*. London: Department for Culture, Media and Sport.

Dias, J.Á. 2016. *Cientistas Portugueses Denunciam Exportação de Esqueletos para o Canadá. Observador*. 6 December. http://observador.pt/2016/12/06/cientistas-portugueses-denunciam-exportacao-de-esqueletos-para-o-canada/. Accessed 19 September 2017.

Eliopoulos, C., A. Lagia, and S. Manolis. 2007. A Modern, Documented Human Skeletal Collection from Greece. *Homo* 58 (3): 221–228.

Ferreira, M.T., R. Vicente, D. Navega, et al. 2014. A New Forensic Collection Housed at the University of Coimbra, Portugal: The 21st Century Identified Skeletal Collection. *Forensic Science International* 245: 202.e1–202.e5.

Firmino, T. 2016. Cientistas Portugueses unem-se contra Exportação de Esqueletos Humanos. *Público*. 6 December. https://www.publico.pt/2016/12/06/ciencia/noticia/cientistas-portugueses-juntamse-contra-exportacao-de-esqueletos-humanos-1753755. Accessed 19 September 2017.

Fletcher, A., D. Antoine, and J.D. Hill (eds.). 2014. *Regarding the Dead: Human Remains in the British Museum*. London: The British Museum.

Francisco, S. 2016. Lisboa vai doar Ossadas Abandonadas ao Canadá. Diário De Notícias. 9 September. https://www.dn.pt/sociedade/interior/lisboa-vai-doar-ossadas-abandonadas-ao-canada-5379568.html. Accessed 9 September 2017.

Giesen, M. 2013. *Curating Human Remains: Caring for the Dead in the United Kingdom*. Woodbridge: Boydell Press.

Go, M.C., A.B. Lee, J.A.D. Santos, et al. 2017. A Newly Assembled Human Skeletal Reference Collection of Modern and Identified Filipinos. *Forensic Science International* 271: 128.el–128.e5.

Gonçalves, D. 2012. *Assemblage of the First Collection of Laboratorially Burned Human Skeletons for Bioanthropological Research*. http://hotresearch.wixsite.com/main/projects. Accessed 19 September 2017.

Henderson, C.Y., and F. Alves-Cardoso (eds.). 2018. *Identified Skeletal Collections: The Testing Ground of Anthropology?* Oxford: Archaeopress.

Henderson, C.Y., D.D. Craps, A.C. Caffell, et al. 2013. Occupational Mobility in 19th Century Rural England: The Interpretation of Entheseal Changes. *International Journal of Osteoarchaeology* 23 (2): 197–210.

Internet Movie Database [IMDb]. 2005. *Bones*. https://www.imdb.com/title/tt0460627/. Accessed 19 September 2017.

Ion, A. 2017. Review of Public Debate "*Restless Dead Bodies: The Ethics of Circulation of Human Remains*". In EASA Medical Anthropology Network Conference, Lisbon 2017. Bodies in Academica. https://bodiesandacademia.wordpress.com/2017/07/15/review-of-public-debate-restless-dead-bodies-the-ethics-of-circulation-of-human-remains-easa-medical-anthropology-network-conferencelisbon-2017/. Accessed 19 September 2017.

Knoeff, R., and R. Zwijnenberg (eds.). 2015. *The History of Medicine in Context: The Fate of Anatomical Collections*. Farnham: Ashgate.

L'Abbé, E.N., M. Loots, and J.H. Meiring. 2005. The Pretoria Bone Collection: A Modern South African Skeletal Sample. *Homo* 56: 197–205.

Larsen, C.S., and P.L. Walker. 2015. The Ethics of Bioarchaeology. In *The Ethics of Bioarchaeology*, ed. T. Turner, 111–119. Albany: State University of New York Press.

Lei nº 12/93. 1993. Diário da República n.º 94/1993, Série I-A de 1993-04-22. https://dre.pt/web/guest/pesquisa/-/search/692651/details/maximized. Accessed 19 September 2017.

Lei nº 107/2001. 2001. Diário da República n.º 209/2001, Série I-A de 2001-09-08. https://dre.pt/pesquisa/-/search/629790/details/maximized. Accessed 19 September 2017.

Martin, D.L., R. Harrod, and V. Pérez. 2013. Bioarchaeology: An Integrated Approach to Working with Human Remains. In *Manuals in Archaeological Method, Theory and Technique*, ed. D.L. Martin, R. Harrod, and V. Pérez, 151–172. New York: Springer Science and Business Media.

Milella, M., M.G. Belcastro, C.P.E. Zollikofer, et al. 2012. The Effect of Age, Sex, and Physical Activity on Entheseal Morphology in a Contemporary Italian Skeletal Collection. *American Journal of Physics Anthropology* 148 (3): 379–388.

Molleson, T., and M. Cox. 1993. *The Spitalfields Project, Volume II—The Middling Sort*. York: Council for British Archaeology.

Mugabowagahunde, M. 2016. African Indigenous Heritage in Colonial and Postcolonial Museums: The Case of the Batwa of Africa's Great Lakes Region. In *A Companion to Heritage Studies*, ed. L. William, M.N. Craith, and U. Kockel, 146–159. Oxford: Wiley Blackwell.

Perréard Lopreno, G., F. Alves Cardoso, S. Assis, et al. 2013. Categorization of Occupation in Documented Skeletal Collections: Its Relevance for the Interpretation of Activity-Related Osseous Changes. *International Journal of Osteoarchaeology* 23 (2): 175–185.

Rissech, C., and D.W. Steadman. 2011. The Demographic, Socio-Economic and Temporal Contextualisation of the Universitat Autònoma de Barcelona Collection of Identified Human Skeletons (UAB Collection). *International Journal of Osteoarchaeology* 21 (3): 313–322.

Rocha, M.A. 1995. Les Collections Ostéologiques Humaines Identifiées du Musée Anthropologique de l' Université de Coimbra. *Antropologia Portuguesa* 13: 7–38.

Sanabria-Medina, C., G. González-Colmenares, H.O. Restrepo, et al. 2016. A Contemporary Colombian Skeletal Reference Collection: A Resource for the Development of Population Specific Standards. *Forensic Science International* 266: 577.e1–577.e4.

Scheuer, J.L., and S.M. Black. 1995. *The St. Bride's Documented Skeletal Collection*. Unpublished Archive Held at the Biological Anthropology Research Centre, Department of Archaeological Sciences, University of Bradford.

Scheuer, J.L., and J.E. Bowman. 1995. Correlation of Documentary and Skeletal Evidence in the St. Bride's Crypt Population. In *Grave Reflections: Portraying the Past Through Cemetery Studies*, ed. S.R. Saunders and A. Herring, 49–70. Toronto: Canadian Scholars Press.

Shelton, D.E., Y.S. Kim, and G. Barak. 2006. A Study of Juror Expectations and Demands Concerning Scientific Evidence: Does the 'CSI Effect' Exist? *Vanderbilt Journal of Entertainment and Technology Law* 9 (2): 331–368.

Sørmoen, O. 2012. 'To Balance the Rights of the Living and the Dead': Reflections on Issues Raised in the Norwegian National Committee for Evaluation of Research on Human Remains. In: *Reflections on Issues Raised in the Norwegian National Committee for Evaluation of Research on Human Remains*, ed. H. Fossheim, 11–20. Oslo: Norwegian National Research Ethics Committee.

Umbelino, C., and A.L. Santos. 2011. Portugal. In *The Routledge Handbook of Archaeological Human Remains and Legislation: An International Guide to Laws and Practice in the excavation and Treatment of Archaeological Human Remains*, ed. N. Márquez Grant and L. Fibiger, 341–352. London: Routledge.

Walker, P. 2008. Bioarchaeological Ethics: A Historical Perspective on the Value of Human Remains. In *Biological Anthropology of the Human Skeleton*, ed. M.A. Katzenberg and S.R. Saunders, 3–40. Hoboken: Wiley.

Weaver, R., Y. Salamonson, J. Koch, et al. 2012. The CSI Effect at University: Forensic Science Students' Television Viewing and Perceptions of Ethical Issues. *Australian Journal of Forensic Sciences* 44 (4): 381–391.

Chapter 24
Ethical Considerations in the Investigation and Commemoration of Mass Graves from the Spanish Civil War

Layla Renshaw

Abstract The Spanish Civil War (1936–1939) was marked by a high number of non-combatant deaths, with recent studies suggesting over 175,000 dead. Under the Franco dictatorship, the mourning of Republican losses was strongly prohibited and there was a total breakdown in the transmission of memory in many families and communities. Since the year 2000, there has been a radical rupture in Spain's prevailing memory politics with the founding of the Republican memory campaign, led by the Association for the Recovery of Historical Memory, known by its Spanish acronym ARMH, that has tirelessly organised the exhumation of thousands of victims from mass graves across Spain. This chapter will critically assess the ethical challenges posed by the contemporary exhumations in Spain, particularly their character as a predominantly grassroots movement. The primary ethical questions considered here are the absence of a judicial framework and the barriers to future prosecutions, the emotional distress and social disruption threatened by the resurfacing of long-buried trauma, and the levels of public and volunteer involvement, as a perceived threat to the integrity and objectivity of investigations. The intensive production and circulation of images of the dead, the accompanying aestheticisation of the graves, and the challenge of arriving at consensus on the religious and political iconography used in the ceremonies and monuments that accompany reburial are also discussed. Despite these complex challenges, the remarkable logistical and technical achievements accomplished in Spain, the transformative impact of these investigations on Spanish collective memory, and the strengths conferred by a grassroots memory campaign are recognised.

L. Renshaw (✉)
Department of Applied and Human Sciences, Kingston University,
Penrhyn Road, Kingston upon Thames KT1 2EE, UK
e-mail: l.renshaw@kingston.ac.uk

K. Squires et al. (eds.), *Ethical Approaches to Human Remains*,
https://doi.org/10.1007/978-3-030-32926-6_24

24.1 Introduction

The Civil War that engulfed Spain between 1936 and 1939 was a catastrophic conflict with a far-reaching and enduring impact and legacy. It was triggered by a military coup headed by General Francisco Franco against a democratically elected leftist government known as The Popular Front (e.g. Graham 2005; Preston 2012). In broad terms, Franco's supporters adhered to a far-right fascist or falangist ideology, aligned with a highly traditional vision of Spanish society, shaped by the Catholic Church and conservative social and economic relations. By contrast, the Republican side, defending the elected government of the time, incorporated a broad spectrum of left-wing politics, including those with communist, anarchist, and socialist sympathies, with strong connections to the Trade Union movement, and aspiring to challenge Spain's entrenched power relations through progressive social change, secularism, and economic redistribution (Graham 2005). The conflict ended with victory for Franco's forces and the initiation of his regime as dictator, which endured until 1975. The period was marked by a high number of non-combatant deaths, comprised of both civilians and prisoners of war (Juliá 1999). It has been estimated that over 175,000 people were killed away from the battlefields during the Spanish Civil War in the first brutal decade of Franco's dictatorship, with 127,000 victims of Francoist violence and 49,000 victims of Republican violence (Preston 2012; Ríos et al. 2014a). The post-war years were a punitive period characterised by the mass imprisonment of defeated combatants in repressive camps, forced labour, summary justice, and localised retributive violence (Preston 2012).

The experience of violence, as victim, perpetrator, or witness, was disseminated widely through the population, leaving lasting traces of collective trauma. Despite the well-known international dimensions to the war, many episodes of violence were highly localised and intimate, deeply dividing small communities and even families. The majority of those killed in the intense political repression of civilians, which is the main focus of this chapter, were males, between late adolescence and late middle-age. However, female civilians were also frequently targeted for execution, due to their political activities and ideology, as well as being subjected to horrific instances of gendered and sexual violence. In some communities, wider kinship networks, such as brothers, fathers, sons, or spouses of the primary target were also killed, as part of a tactic of terror (Juliá 1999; Rodrigo 2008; Ryan 2009; Renshaw 2011; Preston 2012).

This chapter will identify some of the key features of the deaths and burials of the Spanish Civil War (1936–1939), and the years that followed under Franco's dictatorship, that have made the subsequent recovery and commemoration of these bodies so complex. It will describe the founding and functioning of the contemporary Republican memory movement to identify some of the ethical challenges inherent in this type of organic, grassroots campaign. Given the contrasting treatment accorded to the dead of the winning and losing sides in this war, which will be elaborated upon further in this chapter, the recent scientific investigations of mass graves since the year 2000 are almost wholly concentrated on the Republican victims, so these graves will form the primary focus of this discussion. A number of key ethical problems encountered in the recovery, identification, and reburial of the dead will be examined in more detail, leading to an assessment of the impact and legacy of this work. Examples enumerated here of the ethical challenges encountered in Spain's recent exhumations draw on my own experiences of field work between 2003 and 2008, assisting on mass grave excavations as an archaeologist in Castile and Leon, Asturias, and Extremadura. I also conducted participant-observation ethnographies amongst a number of teams of archaeologists and forensic specialists, and in parallel, an extensive series of ethnographic interviews including life history and family history narratives amongst survivors, witnesses, and relatives of the dead in those communities under investigation (Renshaw 2010, 2011). Additionally, more recent examples of Spanish exhumations are drawn from other ethnographies, case studies, and published forensic reports in this rapidly growing field of scholarship (Ríos et al. 2010, 2012, 2014a, 2014b; Ferrándiz 2013; Bevernage and Colaert 2014; Etxeberria et al. 2015, 2016; Núñez et al. 2015; Ceasar 2016; Ríos and Etxeberria 2016).

24.2 The History and Politics of Spain's Civil War Mass Graves

Due to its scale and complexity, the investigation, memory, and commemoration of this conflict has engendered a particular set of logistical and ethical challenges, particularly in relation to the treatment of human remains. It is useful to identify these characteristic features of the deaths and burials that occurred in Spain, and the legacy of these deaths in the present, in order to understand the demands of working in the Spanish context. The mass graves in Spain are the product of multiple forms and phases of violence. Some perpetrated by the military, by quasi-official militias, or in more clandestine acts by falangist death squads. This was a complex picture, shifting with the course of the war, as the two sides gained ascendancy in different regions at different times. In broad terms, the first year of the war resulted in a particularly high number of civilian deaths, as Francoist forces used 'shock and awe' tactics to embed the coup, rooting out possible resistance, and instilling fear (Fernández de Mata 2004; Rodrigo 2008; Preston 2012). Mirroring this, a higher number of violent acts were conducted in Republican-held territory in the early part of the war, in a phase of so-called 'revolutionary' violence. As troops mobilised into more conventional battle lines, the casualties shifted toward military deaths. The mass incarceration of Republican supporters, during and after the war, also confuses this picture as some were officially condemned, executed, and buried in group graves associated with prisons, whilst thousands more disappeared after detention, often taken out of prisons by local death squads, with the connivance of officials, in a process known as '*sacas de presos*' (Rodrigo 2008; Preston 2012). This means there is a highly variable and often highly confused trail of archival evidence and witness testimony to follow when determining when, where, and how individual victims were killed and buried (Renshaw 2011).

One of the defining features of the Spanish Civil War is the extremely brutal and sustained repression that continued for decades after the formal end of hostilities. The civilian death toll remained high in the postwar period during an intense phase of political repression designed to permanently root out ideological resistance to the dictatorship, reverse all and any of the progressive social and economic change witnessed in the pre-war period, and dismantle any basis within civil society for a future resurgence in leftist ideas (Fernández de Mata 2004; Rodrigo 2008). These repressive measures include mass incarceration of political prisoners (Rodrigo 2012), forced labor, sexual violence against women (Preston 2012), the institutionalisation of children from Republican families (Ryan 2009), large-scale exile abroad, and internal displacement. For close to 40 years there was no functioning democracy, with cultural and press censorship enforced, and curbs on civil society. Much of this repression directly targeted the collective identity of the defeated, their community and familial bonds, and concertedly suppressed the memory and commemoration of the dead (Renshaw 2011). It was politically dangerous to mourn or even acknowledge the dead in public, and any attempt to locate or recover Republican bodies could provoke punishments and reprisals (Graham 2004). These repressive strategies were highly effective in inculcating a deep fear and anxiety about disturbing the dead amongst large sections of Spanish society.

Another characteristic feature of Spain's mass graves is the dramatically different treatment of the war dead from the winning and losing sides of the conflict. In the aftermath of Franco's victory, a highly elaborate programme of monument-building and commemorative activity was initiated by the regime, to celebrate both their military dead and their civilian supporters murdered by Republicans during the war. This commemorative project found its most dramatic expression at the Valley of the Fallen, a vast monumental complex that dominates the landscape outside Madrid and now houses Franco's own mausoleum, and has been the subject of sustained debate and controversy (Casanova 2007; Ferrándiz 2011; Stockey 2013). The most recent and dramatic twist in this narrative being the 2018 announcement by Spanish Prime Minister, Pedro Sánchez, that the body of Francisco Franco will be removed from its mausoleum (Jones 2018). Consequently, his body was relocated to a municipal cemetery on 24th October 2019. Along with monument building, Franco orchestrated a massive post-war exhumation programme to relocate the bodies of thousands of his supporters to the Valley of the Fallen, centralised war cemeteries, or local churchyards.

On a more local level, every small community in Spain contains its own plaque with a list of names of those 'Fallen for God and Spain', as the casualties on Franco's side are described. These are often situated in a dominant spot or symbolically significant place such as the village church. Statues and street names dedicated to Franco's military and ideological leadership dominated public spaces (Ferrándiz 2006; Ledesma and Rodrigo 2006). This means that for decades, recognition and mourning, particularly public mourning, was only afforded to one side of the war, compounding the Republican experience of loss. A further recent example of this perceived inequality was the state-funded recovery and repatriation of the 'Blue

Division', a unit of Spanish volunteers who went to fight with the German SS on the Eastern Front during World War II. At the time of this repatriation project, no comparable state intervention or responsibility had been exhibited towards the tens of thousands of Republican civilian bodies lying in mass graves throughout Spain, fueling the perception of an unequal treatment of the dead, and foregrounding the official neglect of the Republican victims (Silva and Macías 2003; Renshaw 2011).

24.3 Recent and Contemporary Mass Grave Exhumations in Spain

For the reasons outlined above, in many families and communities throughout Spain, there has been a near-total breakdown in the normal mechanisms by which a memory of the Republican dead could be transmitted between generations (Cenarro 2002). The transition to democracy that occurred following the death of Franco in 1975 resulted in many significant and rapid changes in Spanish society, but did very little to challenge the prevailing memory politics and dominant narratives on the Civil War. This was described variously as the 'pact of amnesia' or the 'pact of silence', and was felt by some as the necessary price for a largely peaceful transition to democracy (Desfor Edles 1998; Aguilar 2002).

Recent scholarship has given more attention to the brief window of mass grave exhumations that followed immediately after Franco's death. For example, Ríos et al. (2014a, 622) identify a period between 1975 and 1982 when "hundreds of exhumations were carried out to recover the victims of Francoist violence by the families themselves, without any state support […] These exhumations declined after the attempted coup of 23 February 1981". In a very useful analysis, Aguilar and Ferrándiz (2016, 2) summarise the differences between the investigations during the transition to democracy and the contemporary memory movement:

> Indeed, after Franco's death, despite the overall indifference of the State and the most relevant political parties (including the heirs of the war losers), a substantial number of exhumations of Republican mass graves took place across the country. This first wave of exhumations (leaving aside those conducted by the victors in the war's aftermath) had a number of features, which differentiated it from the better known exhumations that have taken place in the twenty-first century: (a) they were basically promoted by relatives and their impact was mostly local; (b) they were carried out without any kind of technical (e.g. forensic, anthropological), judicial or economic support; (c) they took place in the absence of any official memory policies; (d) they had very limited (and often no) media exposure; and (e) they did not give rise to broader debates regarding Spain's tortuous relationship with its traumatic past.

This is a useful corrective to the widely-held perception that there was no groundswell of desire to recover the bodies prior to the current exhumation campaign; it also points to media coverage as a pivotal difference between these two phases of exhumation, a key ethical dimension that will be returned to in more detail.

However, despite decades of the pact of silence dominating public discourse on the war, and keeping the subject of Spain's mass grave as a topic of denial and taboo, the exhumation of mass graves eventually engendered a radical shift in Spain's memory politics, 25 years after Franco's death. In 2000, a journalist called Emilio Silva travelled back to his ancestral village of Priaranza del Bierzo to research the history of his grandfather, Emilio Silva Faba, a Republican who had been killed by Francoists in the Civil War and buried in a clandestine grave (Silva and Macías 2003). After preliminary investigations with a local historian and his own elderly relatives, he published an article in a regional paper entitled 'My Grandfather was also a *Desaparecido*', a title which explicitly referenced the disappeared of Latin America, and the subsequent forensic investigations and transitional justice processes witnessed in countries such as Argentina (Silva 2000). The publication of this article drew the attention of archaeologists and anthropologists who volunteered to help, and was the first investigation to use a scientific (archaeological and anthropological) methodology. This initial article ultimately created an interdisciplinary network, which supported Silva in the location, recovery, and identification of his grandfather, along with twelve other victims located in the same mass grave (Tremlett 2006).

This founding act has had an explosive impact on Spain's relationship with its Civil War mass graves and the memory of its Republican dead. Silva and his supporters formed the Association for the Recovery of Historical Memory (La Asociación para la Recuperación de la Memoria Histórica or ARMH). In 2001, the ARMH excavated a second mass grave and also launched their internet presence that would prove pivotal in raising awareness and support among a wider public, creating an incipient community amongst the descendants of murdered Republicans. Since the inception of ARMH, thousands of graves across Spain have been opened, ranging in size from single burials to vast sites containing the victims of massacres, and systematic executions at camps and prisons (see González-Ruibal 2012; Ríos et al. 2012, 2014a, 2014b; Núñez et al. 2015 for detailed reports on the broad spectrum of Civil War sites under investigation). The increase in exhumation has been exponential, with Congram and Steadman (2008, 162) stating that more than 3000 victims had been exhumed by 2007, and Ríos et al. (2014a, 622) noting that 6174 individuals had been recovered by 2014. This number draws on the centralised database of exhumations coordinated by the Aranzadi Science Society (see Etxeberria 2016), which currently documents the recovery of over 8000 victims.

The ARMH also made rapid progress in formalising the status of their movement. They collaborated with both the United Nations and Amnesty International to gain recognition for Spain's disappeared.[1] In November 2002, the Spanish parliament passed an unprecedented motion to condemn Franco's military uprising (Ferrándiz 2006). A cross-governmental commission was established to hear testimonies from a range of groups and experts associated with the Republican

[1]"Conclusiones y Recomendaciones de Amnistía Internacional al Gobierno Español para que haga justicia a las víctimas de la guerra civil y del Franquismo", http://www.es.amnesty.org/.

memory campaign (Espinosa Maestre 2006). The sustained pressure from the campaign to provide some legal framework within which to operate eventually produced the so-called 'Law of Historical Memory' (Ley de la Memoria Histórica 2007).[2] This is a complex piece of legislation which has provoked a divided response across Spain's political spectrum (Moreno 2006). Some criticism has proved prescient as both the implementation and influence of this law has waxed and waned, following shifts in Spain's ruling political party and economic fortunes.

Aside from its formal status, the work of the ARMH has been powered by the committed involvement of the families of the dead, and has also triggered a wider popular engagement with the question of the war dead (Fernández de Mata 2004; González-Ruibal 2007). Levels of popular interest can be detected in the volume of news media coverage (Renshaw 2007) and online activity (Ferrándiz 2006). This seismic rupture in Spain's wider memory politics originated in the central act of exhuming and reburying the Civil War dead, and Fernández de Mata (2004) has characterised it as "the mass grave phenomena". In the story of its founding, are contained many of the strengths of the Spanish memory movement, but also a number of its inherent limitations and tensions, which contribute to the ethical challenges associated with the current investigations into Spain's mass graves. These strengths include its grassroots, citizen-led, character, which constitutes a genuinely popular social movement. However, there are no formal mechanisms to ensure the centralisation or standardisation of these investigations. Similarly, there are few formal judicial or governmental processes routinely applied in these cases, and those processes which are applied vary significantly across Spain's regions. There is no central source of funding or technical support for exhumations (Ferrándiz 2006; Ríos et al. 2014a). The ethical challenges of this unique context will be evaluated in greater detail in the following section.

24.4 The Ethical Challenges of Working Outside a Legal Process and Without State Resources

Underpinning many of the ethical challenges of the Spanish context is the fact that, despite the passing of the 'Law of Historical Memory' or *Ley de la Memoria Histórica* (2007) there is no legal endpoint in terms of the collation and presentation of evidence to a Truth Commission, or the pursuit of prosecutions for the perpetrators. In an excellent comparative analysis of the Spanish exhumations, in the context of other transitional justice movements, Rubin (2014, 107) explores the paradoxical situation that many investigations gather evidence to a legally

[2]The official title of this legislation is "Ley 52/2007, de 26 de diciembre, por la que se reconocen y amplían derechos y se establecen medidas en favor de quienes padecieron persecución o violencia durante la guerra civil y la dictadura." The full text of this legislation is reproduced in the Official State Bulletin number 310 (BOE no. 310, 27 December 2007), http://noticias.juridicas.com/base_datos/Admin/l52-2007.html.

admissible standard, following international protocols, yet with no legal outcome in prospect within Spain:

> …this new wave of exhumations was led by forensic doctors and archaeologists, using protocols explicitly developed for post-conflict transitional processes around the world. And yet, unlike forensic interventions conducted by their peers in the immediate aftermath of civil wars and dictatorships, these exhumations were not carried out to support a truth commission, war crimes tribunal or any other juridical process. Rather, they were implemented entirely by civil society organisations, with hardly any support from government. Although the legal categories and practices associated with transitional justice had come to Spain, they did so without the force of law, the backing of the state or the support of international bodies.

The tortuous reversals in status experienced by transitional justice figurehead, Judge Baltasar Garzón, underscore how fraught an issue this continues to be in Spain (Rubin 2014). Garzón's attempt to address Civil War atrocities within the framework of Spain's current judicial system provoked a significant backlash from those who feared that this moved the contemporary mass grave exhumations out of the realm of the symbolic, affective, and historical, and into the realm of legal culpability.

With no legal hearings or prosecutions in sight, the continued work in Spain raises a number of troubling questions. The first is whether conducting this work under the current status quo is contributing to a culture of impunity in which the individuals, organisations, and structures that perpetrated or acquiesced in crimes on a massive scale, will never be named in any public forum, or subjected to any kind of judicial or historical judgment. Following this logic, the contemporary memory movement is an edited or self-censored version of a true transition, echoing the 'pact of amnesia' that surrounded the transition to democracy in the 1970s (Desfor Edles 1998; Aguilar 2002). A further question is how future-proof the work is, and if, in the future, a judicial or quasi-judicial process began, could it draw upon the vast body of investigative work already carried out, or would those cases end up excluded? A more urgent question concerns the sustainability and legacy of the investigative work conducted since 2000. There is no officially-sanctioned central body or structure to receive all the information and evidence collected, to collate it, report it, and curate it for the future, which would be comparable in function to a Truth Commission.

Many organisations, such as the ARMH and Sociedad de Ciencias Aranzadi in the Basque region, have an excellent track record of collating data, disseminating information to communities, and making it available online (Etxeberria 2016). Yet, the speed and scale of the recent exhumations mean it is a mammoth task to analyse and extrapolate meaningful patterns on the nature and distribution of violence (Ríos and Etxeberria 2016). There is also a constant tension between the need to reflect upon, and intellectually process, the picture emerging across Spain, and the more immediate demands of families and communities who wish to initiate the next mass grave investigation. The result is still a highly fragmentary, often regionally-based, picture of the discoveries from mass graves (for a moving and impressive example of what can be achieved on a regional level, see Todos los Nombres 2018).

However, these criticisms of Spain's memory movement are based on a very dogmatic view of what transitional justice should look like, and do not accurately reflect the profound and transformative impact of exhumations on individuals, families, and communities throughout Spain, as experienced by all those participating in these investigations on the frontline.

In the absence of a judicial or quasi-judicial process, the main rationale for these exhumations, and the primary ethical framework in which the work is undertaken, is enabling the families to recover the remains of their relatives, to conduct funeral rites, and fill in the missing details of the events surrounding these deaths (Tuller 2015). These processes are intended to fill gaps in family history and facilitate mourning and emotional closure. However, a central problem with this underlying rationale for exhumation is that, in common with many investigations into historic war graves, not every deceased individual in a grave will have a traceable living relative to act as a point of contact, or for consultation and consent (Steele 2008; Renshaw 2011, 2013). Consequently, the opening of the grave will unavoidably generate an inequality of outcomes for the dead in the grave, as some will be reclaimed and mourned by blood relatives, whilst others will not (Scully and Woodward 2012). As there is no clear central authority for conducting the exhumations and no overarching legal aims, the basis for exhumation rests strongly on the consent and approval of relatives, which is readily forthcoming in the great majority of cases. However, if different groups of relatives associated with the same mass grave disagree about the best course of action, it is very hard to resolve this ethically, and to the satisfaction of all stakeholders (Renshaw 2011, 2013).

These tensions were very vividly demonstrated on the first day of exhumation of a mass grave of 46 individuals in a village in Burgos Province (Renshaw 2011). A small group of relatives of those presumed to be in the grave came to stage a protest and temporary occupation of the gravesite, to stop the work commencing. Their main spokesperson was a very articulate and passionate woman, a health-professional who went on to demonstrate a high level of scientific understanding of the exhumation and, particularly, the identification processes. She raised a number of salient, and as it transpired, prescient points about the nature of exhuming and identifying 46 bodies: Why did those relatives who wanted the grave opened have the right to overrule those who wished it to remain undisturbed? Had other ways to remember and honour the dead been explored first? Who had given permission concerning those victims who had no living relatives? What would happen to the large proportion of bodies that might never be confidently identified? If the grave was broken up and the identified remains returned to families, who would take the financial and moral responsibility for the reburial of the unidentified remains? How could the scientific team ensure that no mistakes would be made, and no bodies returned to the wrong families? (Renshaw 2011).

This impasse was defused through negotiation. Those opposed to the exhumation were reassured by the expertise and experience of the technical team, by commitments to keep channels of communication and decision-making open to all stakeholders, and by an emotional appeal to consider the feelings of those relatives of the dead who ardently wish for the exhumation to proceed as they had already waited so long for this to take place. In this case, the promise of collective decision-making was scrupulously followed, in keeping with many of the investigations I observed, which were often exemplary cases of community-level democracy in action (Renshaw 2011). A comparable drama has played out over a more prolonged time-frame and on a more public stage concerning the search for the remains of famous Spanish poet and dramatist Federico Garcia Lorca, believed to be buried in a shared grave with others killed in the same violent episode (Kolbert 2003). The closest relatives of Lorca have raised sustained objections to the proposed exhumations over a number of years and for a number of reasons, citing their distaste for sensationalist media coverage and the desire to let Lorca's literary legacy stand as his monument (Delgado 2015). The seemingly intractable national debate around Lorca's grave, which is still ongoing, has highlighted the complexity of resolving the competing moral claims of descendants, when multiple bodies share the same resting place.

24.5 The Risks of Emotional Distress and Social Disruption

Given the intimate, localised nature of violence between neighbours and the subsequent decades of political repression, which have allowed no release mechanism for past antipathies, a mass grave investigation in a small community can be potentially destabilising, as it revives memories of violence and betrayal between those living in close proximity. It is inherently part of the investigative process to challenge and, at least temporarily, disrupt the status quo, but there are important ethical questions surrounding how to manage this process to minimise the risk of lasting harm to the functioning of these communities, particularly after exhumations finish and the external team of investigators, campaigners, and experts inevitably withdraw (Steele 2008; Renshaw 2011). A large proportion of these investigations utilise interviewers with expertise in psychology or therapy, or experienced social anthropologists and oral historians, to minimise these risks (Cenarro 2002; Fernández de Mata 2010; Ríos and Etxeberria 2016). Yet, due to the grassroots, volunteer-led nature of these investigations and the vast number of traumatised individuals, it is not possible that everyone involved in gathering evidence can possess the ideal expertise or training. In the investigations I observed, the community of volunteers that mobilised around the project is, in itself, a source of support to informants, valuing, and validating their testimony. However, this is by no means a perfect solution to the depth and extent of collective trauma that persists in these communities.

A complicating factor is the extreme age and corresponding physical frailty of many of the key informants and stakeholders. The revisiting of very old and deeply buried childhood traumas can have emotionally devastating consequences. I have undertaken recordings of testimony or life histories with elderly informants who have entered so deeply into their memories that they make childlike cries of anguish for their long-dead parents (Renshaw 2011). Fernández de Mata (2010) very movingly describes a comparable interview with an elderly informant in which their speech breaks down entirely and they seem to enter a childlike state. In these particular cases, it is hard to draw on the usual redemptive narratives that surround transitional justice, of healing, and closure (Bevernage and Colaert 2014), as some of my oldest informants asserted that these investigations have come 'too late' to compensate them for the years of repression (Renshaw 2011). Others maintained a more positive perspective that they were satisfied to witness the exhumations before they themselves died, and that their involvement was primarily a service to the next generation.

There are also logistical and evidential challenges linked to the use of childhood memories (see the mass grave at Valdedios, Asturias, as reported by Ferrándiz (2010), and in detail by Rubia Barbón and Rubia Huete (2006), for a case study concerning children's memory and long-delayed testimony). Some measures to ameliorate the ethical challenges of working with the very old or frail are to ensure genuinely informed consent before engagement, where participants understand the scope and topics that will be brought up by the investigative process. It is ethically important to find forms of explanation, particularly of scientific techniques, bureaucratic processes, and likely outcomes that are relatable and meaningful (see Stover and Peress 1998; Wagner 2008; Renshaw 2010, 2011, for examples of this). It is also important to maintain channels of communication and modes of organisation that are accessible to all, and not dependent on technology that could be exclusionary to the old. A further step is trying to ensure that those elderly informants who choose to engage with the investigation have the immediate support of trusted family and community members.

However, the ideal of elderly informants supported by their adult children is by no means straightforward in the Spanish context. There are strong prohibitions against transmitting civil war experiences to one's children, partly because all communication was inherently dangerous under Franco, and partly for fear of perpetuating cycles of enmity (Cenarro 2002; Renshaw 2011). Yet these silences have, in themselves, created barriers between generations that are extremely painful for both the young and old (Cenarro 2002; Fernández de Mata 2010; Ceasar 2016). A large proportion of the testimony elicited during the mass grave investigations, often in the immediate environs of the mass grave, will have never been shared before, even amongst close relatives (Renshaw 2011). This can be a revelatory, but extremely painful process for the descendants, hearing of traumas for the first time. Some investigative teams, such as the Aranzadi Science Society team, adopt the protocol of producing a recorded DVD of testimony from elderly informants, which can then be viewed later by their descendants, often in the company of their elderly relative. By watching a pre-recorded testimony together, some of the emotional force is mediated and ingrained self-censorship can be overcome (see Ferrándiz and Baer 2008 for more detail on how recordings of both exhumation and testimony inform the memory process in Spain).

A central part of mitigating the risk of emotional distress amongst the relatives and communities of the dead is clear expectation-management and a realistic, even conservative, approach to the likely outcome of exhumation. This is particularly salient in the Spanish case. The decades long wait naturally fuels expectation and a negative outcome can be experienced as a crushing disappointment, or even a second bereavement. After overcoming the seemingly insurmountable political and social barriers to exhumation, it is important to communicate that very real logistical and technical barriers remain. The events surrounding these deaths and burials create serious obstacles, both to the location and recovery of bodies, and also to their confident identification. A proportion of the dead will have no traceable living descendant, or the descendant will not choose to engage with the process, or they may not be a suitable donor of a DNA reference sample for matching (Wagner 2008; Scully and Woodward 2012; Núñez et al. 2015). The same constraints broadly apply to the gathering of all other ante-mortem data such as family documents, letters, portrait photographs, biographical information, and physical descriptions. The timeframe since their family member passed away and the breakdown in family memory can impair the collection of all these sources (Renshaw 2010). Some investigative teams have made it their practice to work with trained psychologists or counsellors either present at the grave side or supporting the collection of testimony, but this resource is not accessible to all.

Whilst generally good, the conditions of bodies in some graves will contain remains with degraded DNA, and therefore require specialist capabilities to achieve a result. Even when preservation is good, larger mass graves require the large-scale collection of reference DNA samples and family tracing that is resource-intensive and beyond the limited funding of many exhumations. The more successful examples of genetic identification often involve small graves or a ‘closed group’, meaning a limited number of potential identities and good supporting ante-mortem evidence for the presumptive identities of those in the grave (Ríos et al. 2010, 2012; Núñez et al. 2015). However, there is an inherent tension in the Spanish memory campaign, which can act against the kind of realistic expectation management, which is an ethical necessity. Since the primary rationale and moral authority for opening up the graves rests with the relatives of the dead, there is an impetus to recruit relatives to these projects by sharing ‘good news stories’ from other successful mass grave investigations. While this does not entail a distortion, it does entail selective representation, as there is no guarantee that previous successes can be replicated in another investigation. A more subtle point is that the Republican memory campaign broadly seeks to enthuse and engage communities with this lost element in their collective past, and in transmitting this passion, they risk downplaying the logistical challenges of recovering and identifying the dead, potentially creating false hope (Renshaw 2010, 2011, 2013). Comparable ethical challenges of managing familial expectations, the emotional demands placed on relatives by long investigative processes, and the potential for relatives and communities to turn against the investigative process have been discussed in more detail from contexts such as Kurdish Iraq, Bosnia, and Argentina (see Steele 2008; Wagner 2008; Rosenblatt 2015, respectively).

24.6 Forensic Archaeology as Public Archaeology

Aside from the primary rationale of serving the relatives of the dead, another key concept, cited frequently by those engaged in Spain's memory campaign, is the public education value of exhumation, citing its power to raise public awareness of these events, contributing to collective memory, creating a forum for both testimony and discussion of the past, and ultimately, reversing the pact of silence (González-Ruibal 2007; Ferrándiz 2013; González-Ruibal et al. 2015). This is the central idea that forensic investigations are a kind of 'public truth', particularly those investigations that challenge previously held 'truths', or widespread denials, which is a concept explored by Weizman (2014). Weizman's (2014) tracing of the etymology of the word 'forensic', to the type of public discourse and representations that occurred in the ancient Roman forum, has a very strong resonance with the dynamic public spaces created around Spain's contemporary mass grave investigations.

Because there is no court or tribunal in which the discoveries of the graves will be presented, the gravesite itself becomes the primary forum and medium for the enacting of public truth. The Spanish mass grave exhumations exist at the interface between community archaeology and forensic archaeology, and at many sites, investigators adopt a practice that is a uniquely integrated, hybrid form of community forensics. The practicalities of this can make a contemporary Spanish mass grave exhumation appear very different from the stereotypical images of forensic work promoted in the media, with highly-controlled physical spaces, the use of screens, tents, and crime scene tape to limit access and visibility. By contrast, many of the projects I participated in, or observed, utilised community campaigners, and even relatives of the dead, in a broad range of non-specialist tasks, such as clearing topsoil, sourcing and moving equipment, sieving bulk samples of soil, and even the superficial cleaning of bones (Renshaw 2011). This was particularly true in the early years of contemporary exhumations, from around 2000 to 2005. Some projects attracted an almost constant stream of visitors to check on progress, leave flowers, sing or pray, or to make an oral recording of their testimony or family history. Some locals regularly brought food and drink for the exhumation team. A combination of relatives, survivors, witnesses, and curious visitors would chat informally about the evidence as it emerged. At some moments, a visitor would become overwhelmed by what they saw, or the memories it triggered, and become intensely emotional. The technical aspects of the work would ebb and flow with these interruptions, but generally practitioners incorporated them very naturally into the exhumation process, with investigators taking time for reflection alone, or offering each other mutual support by explicitly acknowledging the emotional dimension of their work (Renshaw 2011, 2013).

This environment does not conform to the textbook operation of a mass grave investigation, and there are a number of ethical risks associated with maintaining a gravesite that is in such open exchange with the surrounding community. There are potential risks such as contamination of genetic samples if a relative of the dead is moving soil or cleaning bones, and later gives a DNA sample with the hope of identifying one of the dead. There are, theoretically, risks to evidence recovery from inexperienced volunteers, trophy-hunters, and distractions to the excavating team. Aside from the material evidence, other forms of transfer are also taking place, as the constant sharing of testimony, memory, and anecdotes may influence the interpretation of physical evidence as it emerges. However, the reality from every project I observed, and multiple case reports and ethnographies produced more recently, is that these risks are small and strongly outweighed by the palpable benefits of maintaining an open connection to the community and the relatives of the dead (Renshaw 2011). Multiple commentators have highlighted openness and accessibility as touchstones of work that will have a profound and lasting social impact (Congram 2015; González-Ruibal et al. 2015; Moshenska 2015). I would also contend that transparency between the investigation and the local community is one of the best strategies to pre-empt the risks of emotional distress and social disruption; as previously discussed, engendering a climate of openness, participation, and debate.

The technical quality of the work is routinely excellent (Ríos et al. 2010; Etxeberria et al. 2015; Núñez et al. 2015), and many commentators have noted the early adoption of agreed protocols (Etxeberria et al. 2016), mirroring international standards of forensic investigation (Skinner et al. 2003), and the remarkable consistency with which these are followed throughout Spain, despite the fact that there is no central investigative authority to impose them. Rubin (2014) notes that even in the most impassioned critiques of the exhumations, the quality of the evidence is seldom doubted. Even on sites that appear very fluid, experienced investigators have subtle ways to manage the space, and carve out designated places for testimony, finds processing, private discussion of the project, and have informal strategies to manage visitor numbers and experience (Renshaw 2011). At its best, this is comparable to the kind of emotionally-engaged, locally-attuned, community forensics conducted by forensic scientists working with the Indigenous communities of Guatemala, described by Sanford (2000).

A further form of public engagement, that has reached a much wider audience and arguably had a much more profound impact on Spanish memory politics, is the intensive image production that characterises these investigations, including film and photography of the dead, their possessions, the relatives at the grave side, and the investigators at work. This particular feature of the Spanish exhumations has been noted by Renshaw (2007), Ferrándiz and Baer (2008), Ferrán (2013), and Rubin (2014). Specific visual tropes around clandestine death and disappearance have emerged from cases around the world, particularly Latin America, and we readily decode these pictures of bereaved parents, widows, and portrait photos of the dead, as a shorthand for suffering and loss (Dorfman 2006; Renshaw 2011). However, the Spanish image production has a particularly strong focus on the opening of the mass graves and the contents of these graves. Some of these images are immensely powerful (see Torres 2008 for examples, and Ferrán 2013 for an analysis of this work). This power is pivotal in engaging the empathy, intellectual curiosity, and historical awareness, of the wider Spanish public who, due to decades of political repression, were either unaware of their existence, or wary of learning more.

From an ethical perspective, this is one of the most potentially problematic aspects of the current exhumations. The Spanish memory campaign has repeatedly faced the charge of politicising the dead, or harnessing the emotive and visual power of the dead to gain symbolic capital in contemporary political debates. There is a porous line between images that are produced to record the physical evidence, to capture it, or explain it to others, and images that become aestheticised to convey a certain emotional or political message about the dead (Renshaw 2007, 2011). This does not mean that visual images of the dead are ever distorted or manipulated, only that certain powerful symbolic or affective associations are brought to the fore, particularly through the selection and assemblage of images.

Despite carrying an aesthetic or emotional charge, the images produced at the graves carry the authority and apparent objectivity of scientific evidence, making it very hard to spot the aesthetic storytelling, and critically engage with, or challenge it (Renshaw 2007, 2011). The use of these images as symbols or icons involves co-opting the dead into an overarching narrative about the past rather than focusing on the physical evidence of their bodies to tell their own particular story or restore their own identities. However, the images generated at these exhumations immediately become a public resource, particularly in the digital age, rapidly moving beyond the control of archaeologists and forensic scientists (Renshaw 2007). Furthermore, the wealth of imagery produced by news media reports, visual artists, and filmmakers indicate a healthy civil society engaging with the graves, and are arguably just another investigative process, comparable to exhumation. The production, circulation, and consumption of images of the dead is not merely a by-product of exhumation in Spain, it is inseparable from, and indispensable to, the development of the contemporary memory movement. Individual images may be vulnerable to misinterpretation, and may be aestheticised or de-contextualised, but in the absence of any formal Truth Commission, the mass-consumption of such a large volume of mass grave images can be understood as a diffuse, citizen-led way of publicly airing and judging the events of the past.

24.7 Achieving Consensus on Collective Reburials

A third rationale for the current exhumations, which are amorphous but frequently-referenced concepts, are the human rights and dignity of the dead themselves, and the impetus to restore the rights taken from them, including their rights to democratic expression, their right to life, and their right to a dignified burial. The notion of the dead as bearers of rights is complex and subject to academic debate (see Verdery 1999; Moon 2013, 2014; Rosenblatt 2015) but is a widely-accepted rationale for exhumation, particularly in a society like Spain, which places strong cultural significance on the dignity of burial, the location of one's ancestors in the cemetery, and burials as a focus of kinship and legitimacy. Given the many obstacles to confident identification, it is common for the bodies recovered from mass graves in the current investigations to be reinterred in some kind of collective burial, or to have a shared monument. Even for those with confirmed identities, a shared ceremony is common (Renshaw 2011). The necessity for a collective reburial can produce discord amongst relatives of the dead. For some families, a major objective of the exhumation is to rebury the dead alongside other deceased relatives, particularly the mothers, spouses, or children of the murdered Republicans, but limits to the certainty of identification make this goal difficult to achieve and can be a crushing disappointment for some. By contrast, I also encountered a frequently-expressed sentiment that the dead had a bond or camaraderie formed by a shared history of death and burial and, therefore should not be separated. Similar to the protests at the graveside described above, the only ethical way through this impasse, with all relatives having equal moral rights, is through true democratic debate, mutual respect, and compromise.

The form of memorialisation and monument selected is highly significant because it is a public statement about the dead, shaping the legacy of these exhumations, and their impact on future generations. A major issue of contention when multiple families come together to plan a collective reburial is the religious and ideological content of the ceremony, and the wording or imagery of the monument (Renshaw 2011). Key questions that are often asked include: should a ceremony be conducted in the church? Should a priest officiate (or even be present at all)? Should hymns and prayers be offered? Should Republican or leftist songs, poems, flags, or slogans be incorporated into the ceremony, or on the monument? How does the monument accurately make reference to the events surrounding these deaths without being considered a provocative or inflammatory gesture in communities that are still divided? Descendants may find it harder to compromise over the expression of religion and political ideology in the reburial ceremony because it feels like a betrayal of the dead to depart from their values. However, it is very hard for the living to assert with confidence exactly what values or ideology the dead possessed. Terms like Republican and Nationalist are inevitably a simplification of the intersecting ideological, cultural, and regional divisions that Spain was riven by. Francoist rhetoric further confused the memory of Republican politics, its goals and ideals, instead presenting it as criminal and degenerate (Cenarro 2002). These tensions can cause the consensus over collective reburial to break down. As one informant succinctly stated at a public meeting in Burgos province: “I’ll bury his body in my garden rather than take him to the church!” (Renshaw 2011, 211).

24.8 Conclusion: The Enduring Legacy of Spain’s Civil War Exhumations

Congram (2015) asserts that forensic archaeologists and anthropologists do bear a responsibility to assess the ethical value and impact of the investigations they are called to work on, and make an active choice on whether to participate. The first of the ethical criteria he proposes is how ‘democratic’ a project is in terms of grassroots engagement and ownership of the work. As demonstrated in this chapter, the current exhumations in Spain are the model of a public, community-led investigation into the collective past, as opposed to a top-down or centrally imposed process. The second criterion is how partisan is the work, and does it endeavor to treat all victim groups equally? The current memory campaign in Spain is, de facto, a Republican memory campaign, and so at first sight, appears to fail this test. However, the current investigations are an intervention into a highly unequal situation that has persisted for many decades. The commemoration of Francoist victims was highly orchestrated during the dictatorship, whilst the neglect of the Republican dead was total. It is true that many of those working on the memory campaign, including scientists, archaeologists, and historians, are strongly motivated by the multiple injustices experienced by the murdered Republicans and their descendants. But these sympathies find parallels in many other human rights or civil society movements around the world (see Saunders 2002, on working in Guatemala and the former-Yugoslavia), and do not equate to partisan sentiments about the dead, or a denial of the suffering of both sides. Motivations to uncover the truth are also very far removed from seeking to influence or distort the evidence in any way.

In assessing the impact and legacy of Spain's Civil War exhumations, it is important to restate the profound transformation in the social and political status quo that was achieved by opening these graves. It is arguable that if the families and communities of murdered Republicans had waited for a formal state response in terms of a Truth Commission or a centralised investigative agency (and full economic support), then they might still be waiting. In the meantime, thousands of Spanish citizens have learnt more about their family and community history, have faced deeply-held past traumas with the help of a wide network of supporters, and have recovered the remains of loved ones for reburial. The grassroots, underfunded, regionally dispersed nature of these investigations clearly brings its own ethical tensions. Uppermost is probably the degree to which the findings from hundreds of ad hoc, independent investigations can be successfully recorded for posterity and enter the historical record. At the other end of the judicial spectrum, multiple authors have produced critical assessments of highly centralised and systematised transitional justice processes from around the world, such as Wilson's (2001) excellent critique of South Africa's Truth and Reconciliation Commission, or Theidon's (2012) analysis of trauma discourse and the justice industry in Peru. These show that other ethical challenges come with increased intervention from the state, or from those Non-Governmental Organisations specialising in transitional justice. With testimony forced to conform to the legal protocols (Ross 2001), emotion and vernacular forms of memory are crowded out, and the victims and their families surrender control and ownership of the process. In light of these criticisms, it is arguable that the organic, citizen-led nature of Spain's memory movement could also be considered its greatest strength.

References

Aguilar, P. 2002. *Memory and Amnesia: The Role of the Spanish Civil War in the Transition to Democracy*. New York: Berghahn Books.

Aguilar, P., and F. Ferrándiz. 2016. Memory, Media and Spectacle: Interviú's Portrayal of Civil War Exhumations in the Early Years of Spanish Democracy. *Journal of Spanish Cultural Studies* 17 (1): 1–25.

Bevernage, B., and L. Colaert. 2014. History from the Grave? Politics of Time in Spanish Mass Graves Exhumations. *Memory Studies* 7 (4): 440–456.

Casanova, J. 2007. El Valle de Franco. *El País*. 20 November. https://elpais.com/diario/2007/11/20/opinion/1195513212_850215.html. Accessed 5 August 2018.

Ceasar, R. 2016. Kinship Across Conflict: Family Blood, Political Bones, and Exhumation in Contemporary Spain. *Social Dynamics* 42 (2): 352–369.

Cenarro, A. 2002. Memory Beyond the Public Sphere. *History and Memory* 14 (1–2): 165–188.

Congram, D. 2015. Cognitive Dissonance and the Military-Archaeology Complex. In *Ethics and the Archaeology of Violence*, ed. A. González-Ruibal and G. Moshenska, 199–213. London: Springer.

Congram, D., and D.W. Steadman. 2008. Distinguished Guests or Agents of Ingérence: Foreign Participation in Spanish Civil War Grave Excavations. *Complutum* 19 (2): 161–173.

de la Rubia Barbón, Á., and P. de la Rubia Huete. 2006. *La Fosa de Valdediós*. Gijon: Muséu del Pueblu d'Asturies.

Delgado, M. 2015. Memory, Silence, and Democracy in Spain: Federico García Lorca, the Spanish Civil War, and the Law of Historical Memory. *Theatre Journal* 67 (2): 177–196.

Desfor Edles, L. 1998. *Symbol and Ritual in the New Spain: The Transition to Democracy after Franco*. Cambridge: Cambridge University Press.

Dorfman, A. 2006. The Missing and Photography: The Uses and Misuses of Globalization. In *Spontaneous Shrines and the Public Memorialization of Death*, ed. J. Santino, 255–260. New York: Palgrave Macmillan.

Espinosa Maestre, F. 2006. La Memoria de la Represión y la Lucha por su Reconocimiento (En Torno a la Creación de la Comisión Interministerial). *Hispania Nova Revista de Historia Contemporánea* 6: 257–262.

Etxeberria, F. 2016. *Listado de Exhumaciones Llevadas a cabo en España desde el año 2000*. http://www.politicasdelamemoria.org/wp-content/uploads/2015/09/Exhumaciones-desde-el-a%C3%B1o-2000-CSIC.pdf. Accessed 30 January 2018.

Etxeberria, F., L. Herrasti, F. Serrulla, et al. 2015. Contemporary Exhumations in Spain: Recovering the Missing from the Spanish Civil War. In *Forensic Archaeology: A Global Perspective*, ed. W.J.M. Groen, N. Márquez Grant, and R. Janaway, 489–498. Oxford: Wiley-Blackwell.

Etxeberria, F., L. Herrasti, N. Márquez-Grant, et al. 2016. Mass Graves from the Spanish Civil War: Exhumations, Current Status and Protocols. *Archaeological Review from Cambridge* 31 (1): 489–497.

Fernández de Mata, I. 2004. The "Logics" of Violence and Franco's Mass Graves: An Ethnohistorical Approach. *International Journal of the Humanities* 2 (3): 2527–2535.

Fernández de Mata, F. 2010. The Rupture of the World and the Conflicts of Memory. In *Uneathing Franco's Legacy: Mass Graves and the Recovery of Historical Memory in Spain*, ed. C. Jerez-Farrán and S. Amago, 279–303. Notre Dame: University of Notre Dame Press.

Ferrán, O. 2013. Grievability and the Politics of Visibility: The Photography of Francesc Torres and the Mass Graves of the Spanish Civil War. In *Memory and Postwar Memorials: Confronting the Violence of the Past*, ed. M. Silberman and F. Florence Vatan, 117–136. New York: Palgrave.

Ferrándiz, F. 2006. The Return of Civil War Ghosts: The Ethnography of Exhumations in Contemporary Spain. *Anthropology Today* 22 (3): 7–12.

Ferrándiz, F. 2010. The Intimacy of Defeat: Exhumations in Contemporary Spain. In *Uneathing Franco's Legacy: Mass Graves and the Recovery of Historical Memory in Spain*, ed. C. Jerez-Farrán and S. Amago, 304–325. Notre Dame: University of Notre Dame Press.

Ferrándiz, F. 2011. Guerras sin Fin: Guía para Descifrar el Valle de los Caídos en la España Contemporánea. *Política y Sociedad* 48 (3): 481–500.

Ferrándiz, F. 2013. Exhuming the Defeated: Civil War Mass Graves in 21st Century Spain. *American Ethnologist* 40 (1): 38–54.

Ferrándiz, F., and A. Baer. 2008. Digital Memory: The Visual Recording of Mass Grave Exhumations in Contemporary Spain. *Forum Qualitative Social Research* 9 (3): 35.

González-Ruibal, A. 2007. Making Things Public: Archaeologies of the Spanish Civil War. *Public Archaeology* 6 (4): 203–226.

González-Ruibal, A. 2012. From the Battlefield to the Labour Camp: Archaeology of Civil War and Dictatorship in Spain. *Antiquity* 86: 456–473.

González-Ruibal, A., X. Ayan Vila, and R. Ceasar. 2015. Ethics, Archaeology, and Civil Conflict: The Case of Spain. In *Ethics and the Archaeology of Violence*, ed. A. González-Ruibal and G. Moshenska, 167–180. London: Springer.

Graham, H. 2004. The Spanish Civil War, 1936–2003: The Return of Republican Memory. *Science and Society* 68 (3): 313–328.

Graham, H. 2005. *The Spanish Civil War: A Very Short Introduction*. Oxford: Oxford University Press.

Jones, S. 2018. Franco's Family Fights PM Over Removal of Dictator's Remains. *The Guardian*, 20 July. https://www.theguardian.com/world/2018/jul/20/franco-family-refuses-facilitate-removal-dictator-spain. Accessed 5 August 2018.

Juliá, S. 1999. *Víctimas de la Guerra Civil*. Madrid: Temas de Hoy.

Kolbert, E. 2003. Looking for Lorca. *The New Yorker*, 22 December.

Ledesma, J.L., and J. Rodrigo. 2006. Caídos por España, Mártires de la Libertad. Víctimas y Conmemoración de la Guerra Civil en la España Posbélica (1939–2006). *Ayer* 63: 233–255.

Ley de Memoria Histórica. BOE, no 310 27 December 2007. Cortes Generales, Madrid.

Moon, C. 2013. Interpreters of the Dead: Forensic Knowledge, Human Remains and the Politics of the Past. *Social and Legal Studies* 22 (2): 149–169.

Moon, C. 2014. Human Rights, Human Remains: Forensic Humanitarianism and the Human Rights of the Dead. *International Social Science Journal* 65 (215–216): 49–63.

Moreno, J.A. 2006. La Memoria Defraudada: Notas sobre el Denominado Proyecto Ley de Memoria. *Hispania Nova Electrónica Revista de Historia Contemporánea* 6: 711–722.

Moshenska, G. 2015. The Ethics of Public Engagement in the Archaeology of Modern Conflict. In *Ethics and the Archaeology of Violence*, ed. A. Gonzalez-Ruibal and G. Moshenska, 167–180. London: Springer.

Núñez, C., M. Baeta, L. Palencia-Madrid, et al. 2015. A Grave in My Garden: Genetic Identification of Spanish Civil War Victims Buried in Two Mass Graves in Espinosa de los Monteros (Burgos, Spain). *Forensic Science International: Genetics Supplement Series* 5: 335–337.

Preston, P. 2012. *The Spanish Holocaust: Inquisition and Extermination in Twentieth-Century Spain*. London: Harper Press.

Renshaw, L. 2007. The Iconography of Exhumation: Representations of Mass Graves from the Spanish Civil War. In *Archaeology and the Media*, ed. T. Clack and M. Brittain, 237–252. Walnut Creek: Left Coast Press.

Renshaw, L. 2010. Scientific and Affective Identification of Republican Civilian Victims from the Spanish Civil War. *Journal of Material Culture* 15 (4): 449–463.

Renshaw, L. 2011. *Exhuming Loss: Memory, Materiality and Mass Graves of the Spanish Civil War*. Walnut Creek: Left Coast Press.

Renshaw, L. 2013. The Exhumation of Civilian Victims of Conflict and Human Rights Abuses: Political, Ethical, and Theoretical Considerations. In *The Oxford Handbook of the Archaeology of Death and Burial*, ed. S. Tarlow and L. Nilsson Stutz, 781–800. Oxford: Oxford University Press.

Ríos, L., and F. Etxeberria. 2016. The Spanish Civil War Forensic Labyrinth. In *Legacies of Violence in Contemporary Spain: Exhuming the Past, Understanding the Present*, ed. O. Ferrán and L. Hilbink, 44–68. New York: Routledge.

Ríos, L., J. Casado Ovejero, and J. Puente Prieto. 2010. Identification Process in Mass Graves from the Spanish Civil War I. *Forensic Science International* 199: 27–36.

Ríos, L., A. García-Rubio, B. Martínez, et al. 2012. Identification Process in Mass Graves from the Spanish Civil War II. *Forensic Science International* 219: 4–9.

Ríos, L., A. García-Rubio, B. Martínez, et al. 2014a. Patterns of Perimortem Trauma in Skeletons Recovered from Mass Graves from the Spanish Civil War (1936–1939). In *The Routledge Handbook of the Bioarchaeology of Human Conflict*, ed. C. Knüsel and M.J. Smith, 621–640. London: Routledge.

Ríos, L., B. Martínez, A. García-Rubio, et al. 2014b. Marks of Autopsy and Identification of Victims of Human Rights Violations Exhumed from Cemeteries: The Case of the Spanish Civil War (1936–1939). *International Journal of Legal Medicine* 128 (5): 889–895.

Rodrigo, J. 2008. *Hasta la Raíz. Violencia durante la Guerra Civil y la Dictadura Franquista*. Madrid: Alianza.

Rodrigo, J. 2012. Exploitation, Fascist Violence and Social Cleansing: A Study of Franco's Concentration Camps from a Comparative Perspective. *European Review of History* 19 (4): 553–573.

Rosenblatt, A. 2015. *Digging for the Disappeared: Forensic Science after Atrocity*. Stanford: Stanford University Press.

Ross, F.C. 2001. Speech and Silence: Women's Testimony in the First Five Weeks of Public Hearings of the South African Truth and Reconciliation Commission. In *Remaking a World: Violence, Social Suffering and Recovery*, ed. V. Das, A. Kleinman, M. Lock, et al., 250–280. Berkeley: University of California Press.

Rubin, J. 2014. Transitional Justice against the State: Lessons from Spanish Society-Led Forensic Exhumations. *International Journal of Transitional Justice* 8: 99–120.

Ryan, L. 2009. The Sins of the Father: The Destruction of the Republican Family in Franco's Spain. *The History of the Family* 14: 245–252.

Sanford, V. 2000. *Buried Secrets: Truth and Human Rights in Guatemala*. New York: Palgrave.

Saunders, R. 2002. Tell the Truth: The Archaeology of Human Rights Abuses in Guatemala and the Former Yugoslavia. In *Matériel Culture: The Archaeology of Twentieth Century Conflict*, ed. J. Schofield, W.G. Johnson, and C.M. Beck, 103–114. London: Routledge.

Scully, J.L., and R. Woodward. 2012. Naming the Unknown of Fromelles: DNA Profiling, Ethics and the Identification of First World War Bodies. *Journal of War and Culture Studies* 5 (1): 59–72.

Silva, E. 2000. Mi Abuelo también fue un Desaparecido. *La Crónica de León*, 8 October.

Silva, E., and S. Macías. 2003. *Las Fosas de Franco: Los Republicanos que el Dictador Déjo en las Cunetas*. Madrid: Temas de Hoy.

Skinner, M., D. Alempijevic, and M. Djuric. 2003. Guidelines for International Forensic Bio-archaeology Monitors of Mass Grave Exhumations. *Forensic Science International* 134: 81–92.

Steele, C. 2008. Archaeology and the Forensic Investigation of Recent Mass Graves: Ethical Issues for a New Practice of Archaeology. *Archaeologies* 4 (3): 414–428.

Stockey, G. 2013. *Valley of the Fallen: The (N)ever Changing Face of General Franco's Monument*. Nottingham: CCCP.

Stover, E., and G. Peress. 1998. *The Graves: Forensic Efforts at Srebrenica and Vukovar*. New York: Scalo.

Theidon, K. 2012. *Intimate Enemies: Violence and Reconciliation in Peru*. Philadelphia: University of Pennsylvania Press.

Todos los Nombres. 2018. Bienvenidos a la web de Todos los Nombres. http://www.todoslosnombres.org/. Accessed 29 Aug 2018.

Torres, F. 2008. The Images of Memory: A Civil Narration of History. A Photo Essay. *Journal of Spanish Cultural Studies* 9 (2): 157–175.

Tremlett, G. 2006. *Ghosts of Spain: Travels Through a Country's Hidden Past*. London: Faber and Faber.
Tuller, H. 2015. Identification Versus Prosecution: Is It That Simple and Where Should the Archaeologist Stand? In *Disturbing Bodies: Perspectives on Forensic Anthropology*, ed. Z. Crossland and R. Joyce, 85–101. Santa Fe: SAR Press.
Verdery, K. 1999. *The Political Lives of Dead Bodies: Reburial and Postsocialist Change*. New York: Columbia University Press.
Wagner, S. 2008. *To Know Where He Lies: DNA Technology and the Search for Srebrenica's Missing*. Berkeley: University of California Press.
Weizman, E. 2014. Introduction: Forensis. In *Forensis: The Architecture of Public Truth*, ed. A. Franke and E. Weizman, 9–34. Berlin: Sternberg Press.
Wilson, R. 2001. *The Politics of Truth and Reconciliation in South Africa: Legitimizing the Post-Apartheid State*. Cambridge: Cambridge University Press.

Chapter 25
Killing Them Twice: Ethical Challenges in the Analysis of Human Remains from the Two World Wars

Andrew S. Robertshaw

Abstract The scale of casualties inflicted on the military forces of the combatant nations during the two World Wars, in 1914–1918 and 1939–1945, surpassed all previous conflicts. Identification, burial, and memorialsation was a challenge and a strain on resources, and to personnel involved in the process. These issues have also raised ethical, moral, and religious challenges, which nations have had to deal with, though these differ between jurisdictions, and these approaches are dependent on existing conventions, the scale of casualties, geography, and the status of the nation as 'victor' or 'vanquished'. Consequently, there is no accepted convention for the way in which military dead from the period before 1945 are recorded and memorialised. What is acceptable for one nation is not for another. Politics, religious views, the passage of time since the end of conflicts, and advances in science means that the accepted standards and conventions have also changed over time. The challenges created by the aftermath of two world conflicts continue to concern families, society, and political bodies, as further sets of human remains are recovered from former battlefields. There is no evidence that these issues, raised by the recovery, burial, and memorialisation of the war dead, will be resolved and the echoes of the World Wars will continue to resonate throughout the twenty-first century.

25.1 Introduction

In mid-January 1643, three months after the Battle of Edgehill (which took place on 23rd October 1642 and marked the first major action of the English Civil War), a series of pamphlets were published (Oldridge 2016). These described, in great detail, how the battle was being re-fought in the sky by 'ghosts' on an almost nightly basis. A delegation of 'gentlemen of credit' was sent by King Charles I, to investigate this claim (Young 1976). They reported not only seeing the battle

A. S. Robertshaw (✉)
Bay Leaf Cottage, 9 Ashford Road, Sheldwich, Faversham, Kent ME13 0DL, UK
e-mail: andy@andyrobertshaw.com

K. Squires et al. (eds.), *Ethical Approaches to Human Remains*,
https://doi.org/10.1007/978-3-030-32926-6_25

themselves, but recognising some of the 'slain', and even named Sir Edmund Verney who had died on the battlefield and whose body had not been identified. In the opinion of the King's officers, they felt the apparitions would only cease once the "carcases as yet unburied" were found (Anon 1643, 41). After a careful search of the battlefield, the remains of the missing soldiers were discovered and given a 'Christian burial'. At this point, the apparitions stopped and the battlefield was peaceful once more. The only part of Sir Edmund Verney recovered was his hand, which had been cut off by a sword blow in the battle and was found still gripping the King's Banner Royal. This was positively identified by his Royalist comrades by means of a ring bearing a miniature portrait of Charles I on one of his fingers. This severed hand was buried at the family church at Claydon (Buckinghamshire). Although the battle was fought 375 years ago, the story of the 'apparitions' and the importance of burial for the 'unknown', and even the fate of Sir Edmund's hand, serve to indicate that throughout history people have sought an appropriate burial for those who fall in battle, and are even prepared to extend this to individual body parts. This process mirrors ancient Greek burial practice and is a precursor of the Cenotaph, a memorial without a burial, that lies at the heart of the post Great War Armistice Day commemorations.

Most soldiers must at some point anticipate death on the battlefield and most come to terms with their potential fate, whether it be for themselves or their comrades. This chapter covers the two World Wars at the time when soldiers of all nations began to expect marked burials in appropriate military cemeteries. This period, however; also coincides with the rise of air power, which meant that civilians increasingly became the victims of war. For the purpose of this chapter, I will restrict my study to combatants. The ratio of civilian to military deaths has changed over time and civilian casualties and deaths greatly outnumber those of combatants in modern warfare (Epps 2013). Since the beginning of the twentieth century, it was expected that their death would result in an unidentified battlefield burial. It must be recognised that the anticipation of 'an honoured burial' as identified by the 'Imperial', later 'Commonwealth', War Graves Commission (CWGC) is a feature of the custom and practice of relatively modern conflict of most nations. Although the defeated Richard III was buried in a church in Leicester, following the battle of Bosworth in 1485, none of the 'rank and file' received anything more than internment in an unmarked pit on the battlefield. This approach was taken by most nations until the end of the nineteenth century, although provision made for the fallen of the American Civil War (1861–1865) can be regarded as exceptional. Central to the treatment of war dead adopted by each nation is the concept of ethics, legality, and morality, as it relates to the treatment of human remains. These concepts were to a greater or lesser extent influenced by the experience of previous conflicts. For France and Germany, this meant the Franco-Prussian War (1870–1871) and for the United States of America, The American Civil War (1861–1865). For Britain, the most recent military campaign was the Second Anglo-Boer War (1899–1902). During the Franco-Prussian conflict the two sides lost in excess of 180,000 war-dead (Wawro 2003). In the case of the United States of America, the conflict resulted in more than 624,511 military deaths

(Ohio State University n.d.). In contrast, the Boer War resulted in just over 20,721 deaths, most of which succumbed to disease (Geni 2018). In the aftermath of the Franco-Prussian war, the belligerents established military cemeteries, some of which were joint, and many memorials were constructed on the battlefields. Some bodies were returned to home cemeteries but the majority were buried close to where they fell. In the United States of America, many more families claimed the bodies of the fallen of the Civil War and, although battlefield cemeteries and monuments were common, many towns had their own war cemeteries. A unique feature of the union army was the decision to establish a military cemetery at Arlington (Virginia), the home of Confederate General Robert E. Lee. In 1862 a decision was taken by the US Congress to purchase land close to Washington for national military cemeteries. By 1864 these had reached capacity and the United States Quartermaster General conducted a study of suitable sites. The site at Arlington was selected for geographical and political reasons. Arlington lies on the outskirts of the Federal Capital, close to the main scene of combat on the eastern seaboard between the warring Unionists in the North and Confederates to the South and, critically it represented a revenge on General Lee for siding with the Confederacy having previously served in the Federal Army. This site subsequently became the new National Military Cemetery. The British dead of the Boer War were, for the first time, the responsibility of the Royal Engineers and they largely oversaw the construction of graves in over 350 cemeteries. As a result of the British victory, these cemeteries were established in territory that was part of the British Empire. Although the Royal Engineers moved on to other tasks, a voluntary organisation called ‘The Guild of Loyal Women’ took on the task of caring for the graves and memorials (Van Heyningen and Merrett 2003). This was formalised into the ‘South African Soldier’s Graves Association’ but it was chronically short of funds and the problems it faced were soon to be over shadowed by a much greater conflict, which began in the summer of 1914.

Although many believed that the ‘European War’ would be over by Christmas 1914, the scale, duration, and geographical scope of the conflict meant that the challenge of mass casualties resulting from industrial warfare would present belligerent nations with ethical, moral, and social problems, on an unprecedented scale. As a consequence, the outbreak of the Great War (1914–1918) can be seen as a clear transitional point in the way that the military dead were identified and buried. This can be linked to earlier attempts made by nations to ensure that identification was possible through the provision of identity tags for each soldier. The first systemic scheme of individual identification involved the Prussian Army, which issued metal identity tags to its soldiers in 1870 (Wawro 2003). It was an unfortunate coincidence that the contemporary system of registration for dogs in parts of Germany involved the issuing of *Hundemarken*, metal dog tags for animals. Hence the adoption of the term ‘Dog Tag’ by the German, and later by other, armies (Landser n.d.). By 1914, most armies had a system of identification in place, the most efficient of which were stamped metal discs. The Soviet Army continued to use paper identification in the Second World War and the British Army withdrew metal identification tags made of metal and replaced them with heat treated cardboard, 'vulcanised fibre' in 1915, on the basis of economy (Robertshaw and Kenyon 2008). As both paper and cardboard are easily destroyed by moisture, the result was many more 'missing' soldiers. The Great War resulted in the largest number of military casualties caused in any conflict up to that point in history. Even in the opening weeks of the campaign, deaths ran into tens of thousands per day. Although many felt that the war would be over after a few months, it soon became clear that this would not be the case and the war turned into a 'World' rather than 'European' conflict.

25.2 From Wars of Nations to World Wars

Estimates of the numbers of deaths in the conflicts of the first half of the twentieth century vary greatly. The number of both military and civilian lives lost in the Second World War (1939–1945) far surpass those of the First World War (1914–1918). Some estimates suggest that over 850,000 individuals lost their lives in World War II (National World War II Museum 2018). Military and civil authorities were confronted by deaths running into millions and they had to deal with these in a way that was 'appropriate' for the country at that time. Politics, religion, the number of casualties, geography, and public opinion, would all influence how bodies were treated and commemorated during and after the conflict. The nature of modern warfare meant that casualties may be unrecognisable, or unfound, having been burned, blown up, or buried by explosions. Others were simply lost in the depths of the ocean or the frozen heights of mountains due to crash sites into the sea or against mountains, respectively. No two nations had the same experience with the fate of their casualties. The result was that few nations had the same policy towards their war dead, but the approach taken in the Second World War would, in many ways, mirror that of the Great War. There were, however, great differences in attitudes towards burial and memorialisation, the identification of individuals, whether remains should be repatriated, or whether individual or mass graves were appropriate. The scale of casualties and religious beliefs will influence whether nations deem mass graves to be an appropriate means of burial. In both World Wars, some nations became combatants at a later stage than others. Consequently, the scale of the contribution of nations and the associated number of casualties varied considerably from country to country. Clearly it is easier for a combatant nation to deal with a small number of casualties in an area within its own national boundaries than with mass casualties overseas. Ethical parameters also change over time, for example what was regarded as 'appropriate' at one time may not be so at a later date. As we will see, national grief, defeat in war, and changing political opinion, can all influence how the process of remembrance and memorialising is approached. To examine this process, we must look at some examples of the way in which 'The Fallen' were treated and how ethical approaches developed.

25.3 Missing in Action

A key feature of both World Wars is the question of 'The Missing', often referred to as 'Missing in Action' (MIA). This is a term first used during the Vietnam War (1955–1975) and has greatly influenced the approach and attitudes towards the 'missing' of other historical conflicts. However, the concept of 'The Missing' and how they should be remembered or recovered has an earlier history. The identification of casualties is intimately linked to the means of doing so. As outlined in section 25.1 of this chapter, some combatant nations had the means to do so before 1914 via the use of identification tags. However, 'dog' or 'identification' tags proved to be an insufficient means of ensuring that every set of remains were identified. The conditions of warfare meant that some bodies were disarticulated and scattered across a large area, whilst others were buried in dugouts or trenches, and others were buried by comrades but their grave markers were destroyed or lost in subsequent fighting (Robertshaw and Kenyon 2008). For example, a large number of CWGC cemeteries contain head stones on which the words 'Known' or 'Believed to be buried in this cemetery' are inscribed. Even formal military burials were not exempt from the ravages of war. Overall, a significant minority of the 'Fallen' were 'missing in action'. Some combatant nations provided additional means of identification, for instance a second identification tag was added to the first by the British in 1916, and the two-piece bifurcated system was adopted by the Imperial German army in November 1916 (Robertshaw and Kenyon 2008). Despite this, many of the dead in both World Wars become officially missing. The cultural and ethical attitudes in the twentieth century demanded that their status be recognised. The memorials to the missing at Thiepval and at Vimy or at the Menin Gate in Ypres, together with memorial walls in Washington and elsewhere, are key points of focus for remembrance for those for whom there was no 'closure' provided by a burial at home or abroad. Given that the remains of the missing were overseas, nations accordingly sought their own 'Tomb of the Unknown Soldier', and many erected a cenotaph as a focus for national mourning. The key point about the 'Tomb of the Unknown Soldier' was that he had to be anonymous to ensure that this burial symbolised all the unknown. Theoretically it would be possible to obtain DNA from an unknown soldier and to potentially establish his identity. However, this has not happened so far, and such an attempt would undermine the whole concept of the 'unknown' soldier representation of the others of that nation. In the case of the British example, 'unknown' bodies were recovered from the main battlefields of the Western Front, and a single body selected in France before burial at Westminster Abbey (Watrin 1987). The use of techniques, such as DNA and isotope analysis, allow investigators to identify missing casualties and offer the prospect that even the 'unknown soldier' could be given a name.

Since many of these casualties of war had not been exhumed, there was the possibility of recovering and identifying their remains. It is rare that any project is based simply on 'prospecting for the dead' even if it is to bring 'closure' to relatives of the fallen. An exception is the exhumation and identification of the French author and poet Alain Fournier and many of his comrades (who died in 1914) in 1991 (Adam 2006). This type of archaeological project raises the expectation of relatives and may result in disappointment if nothing is found. It is for this reason that the British Ministry of Defence closely regulates aircraft crash sites and licences are only issued to specialist groups, frequently on the basis that human remains are not believed to be present. However, as Moshenska (2008) has explained, these sites are themselves subject of ethical and moral controversy. Although attempts were made in wartime to recover the remains of the crew, these projects were frequently hurried and cursory as units were under great time constraints, and enemy dead frequently received little attention from combatants. Consequently, human remains have been discovered on crash sites from which the remains of the crew had been removed by official teams from the nation in which the aircraft had come down, for example the Spitfire that crashed in the Cambridgeshire Fens. Although the partial remains of the pilot were recovered from the downed aircraft by a crew from the nearby RAF Wittering in 1940, the 2015 excavation revealed that this recovery, had been far from complete and personal artefacts and human remains were found on site (Great Fen 2018). All too often the reality of the 'burial' and the contents of the coffin are at odds with the archaeology. It is noteworthy that the dead on the terrestrial battlefields of the World Wars do not have the protection offered to those who died at sea. The treatment offered to those whose remains are contained in military and civil ships lost in action are designated as 'War Graves', which are protected by national law and recognised by international law (Protection of Military Remains Act 1986). One suggestion from Australia is the idea that farmers on the battlefields of the Great War should be subject to a non-tillage ruling to avoid disturbing the remains of the men buried there (unnamed Australian descendant of a deceased soldier who died in Fromelles 2010, pers. comm.). This proposal was largely aimed at 'Australian' casualties, also referred to as the 'Digger Dead' ('Diggers' was a nickname the Australians gave themselves). As such it does not take into account the remains of those of other nations. When conducting any form of excavation on a battlefield, there can be no certainty that human remains will be discovered, only a probability, and even where remains are found, they may be incomplete. Consequently, the Commonwealth War Graves Commission is increasingly under pressure to use modern techniques, such as DNA and isotope analysis, though the level to which these methods are employed is currently unknown. The project at Fromelles, which was based on the recovery of, largely, Australian dead, was the first time the CWGC allowed the use of these techniques in a systematic manner.

The Fromelles project, itself an Australian led initiative, helps to demonstrate that ethics are fluid and evolving. On 19th/20th July 1916, an Anglo-Australian attack was mounted close to the village of Fromelles, between Lens and Armentiers in Northern France. This was a disaster, and in the aftermath 1,650 soldiers were listed as missing. The Germans reportedly buried up to 450 of these in unmarked graves. By the beginning of the twenty-first Century Australian public opinion favoured the exhumation of the missing and funds were raised to do this. With the backing of the Australian Department of Defence, a project was funded to investigate the burial and recover and identify the remains found. This was carried out in 2009, and 250 sets of remains were found by a unit from Oxford Archaeology (Loe et al. 2014; see also Loe and Clough, this volume). The project was a departure from the previous practice of the British Ministry of Defence and CWGC in that bodies from a burial site were exhumed and DNA samples were taken from bones, teeth, hair, and soft tissues, and used to identify the majority of the casualties. This was standard practice until the 2009 Fromelles Project (Loe et al. 2014). An ethical problem that arose was that, although 250 sets of remains were recovered at Fromelles, many were not found. This meant that many families, especially in Australia, expressed disappointment that 'their' relative had not been discovered from the Fromelles site. In 2010, one unnamed Australian descendent contacted the author and suggested subsequent projects and also identified and explored potential sites for further work to be conducted in the area to find the remaining bodies. What the project does therefore is to indicate the potential ethical problems faced by those searching for the missing of any conflict. It is worth saying at this point that the centenary of the Great War has resulted in an upsurge in interest in the missing in general, and many individuals and groups are working to establish the identity of soldiers buried as 'unknown' in CWGC cemeteries. In at least one case, that of John Kipling, son of the poet Rudyard Kipling, there has been significant debate over the accurate identification of human remains found on the battlefield at Loos in Northern France (Holt and Holt 2007). This case could be resolved if the remains were exhumed and samples taken. However, this is against current CWGC policy that states that once buried a casualty will not be exhumed (Commonwealth War Graves Commission 2018). Thus, the question will remain, where is he? During the Fromelles project, it was decided that no photographs of the remains were to be released to the public, although the project report did contain some images of human remains, a number of which had been altered "in order to present potentially sensitive information in a respectful manner" (Loe et al. 2014, front plate; see also Loe and Clough, this volume). This was a new policy decision taken by the Oxford Archaeology project team for this specific project of exhumation and has not been followed in subsequent projects on the Western Front.

An alternative approach has been adopted by the United States of America in the case of the casualties lost in the attack on Pearl Harbour on the 7th December 1941. This makes a contrasting case study in the ethics of exhumation and identification. During the Great War, the families of US Service Men and Women killed in action were given the option of burial, 'where they lay' or repatriation to the USA for burial 'at home' or in Arlington National Cemetery. The consequence was that 30% of Great War casualties and 23% of those killed in the Second World War remained overseas based on their relative's decision (Harris 2017). However, public suspicion as to the fate of those declared to be a Prisoner of War (POW) or Missing in Action (MIA) during the Vietnam War (1955–1975) led to a public campaign to encourage the Department of Defense and Federal Government to return over 2500 individuals (dead or alive) that were classed as MIA to the USA (Franklin 1993). In most cases there was no evidence that these men were actually dead and a large group of relatives and supporters ascribed this to a cover up. As a consequence, the US military began a long term and costly process of systematically searching for the remains of those MIA since the beginning of the Second World War, as their mandate does not extend to previous conflicts (Franklin 1993). The Joint POW/MIA Accounting Command (JPAC) was responsible for this, though in 2015 the organisation was renamed as the Defense POW/MIA Accounting Agency (DPAA) (Cole 2015). Unlike other nations, these agencies have an active policy of staging missions to former battlefields to attempt to recover the remains of US servicemen. The rate of recovery is in the region of 200 per year. As there are approximately 28,000 US personnel still unaccounted for, this is a long-term commitment.

In 2015, it was announced by the agency that some of the crew of USS Oklahoma, one of the ships lost in the Pearl Harbour attack and buried in (sometimes intermingled) mass graves, would be disinterred and subjected to forensic analysis (Ruane 2016). As stated by Robert Work, the US Deputy Defense Secretary, the US government "remains committed to fulfilling its sacred obligation to achieve the fullest possible accounting for US personnel… Recent advances in forensic science and technology, as well as family member assistance in providing genealogical information, have now made it possible to make individual identifications for many service members, long buried in graves marked unknown" (Dodd 2015). However, he added that "not all families will receive an individual identification, we will strive to provide resolution to as many families as possible" (Dodd 2015).

The Netherlands adopted a similar proactive approach by establishing, in August 1945, The Royal Netherlands Army: Recovery and Identification Unit (RIU). This specialist unit was officially established in August 1945 under the Military Administration, but had been operational under the Dutch Free Forces of the Interior in the liberated southern part of the Netherlands since the aftermath of Operation Market-Garden (September–October 1944). On behalf of The Netherlands government, the unit continues to ratify the 1929 and 1949 Geneva Conventions for the Amelioration of the Condition of the Wounded and Sick in Armies in the Field, by taking care of the location, exhumation and identification of missing World War Two victims, both military and civilian, on Dutch territory regardless of their background or nationality. The main objective is to help next of kin achieve closure and ensure a re-interment in a marked grave, preferably in the presence of the soldier's loved ones. The Netherlands government still considers this to be a moral obligation, a duty of care, and a debt of honour. The work of the unit combines the fields of conflict archaeology, physical anthropology, and military history. In order to establish identification, the unit matches biological evidence to medical and historical profiles. As well as traditional identification techniques, such as the use of Second World War dental treatment cards and medical examination on enlistment forms; the unit nowadays also uses modern forensic techniques such as DNA analysis and isotope testing, in order to establish the geographical area of origin of the individual. It is striking that the RIU is pro-active rather than reactive and treats civilians and the military of nations equally. In Europe, at least, the unit has led the way in the use of forensic techniques in such contexts.

In a recent case, the unit were positive that they had identified a British infantryman, but so far had been unable to provide evidence beyond any reasonable doubt (Geert Jonker 2015, pers. comm.). The biological profile and the soldier's physical description were fully consistent, with only a 4 mm discrepancy in stature, and there was a match with certain artefacts found with the remains. The soldier was known to have been killed in the area where the remains were found (South Arnhem), hence the historical profile matched as well. Unfortunately, no dental treatment card for the individual had survived with MOD records. Extensive genealogical research showed that his father was unknown and that his mother's entire bloodline had died out. There was no one left to provide a DNA sample. The RIU decided that the only way in which to confirm the identity of this soldier was to use his mother, who had died in hospital in 1954, as a DNA donor. After obtaining licenses from the local city council, the Regional Health and Safety Department, the Diocese, and the Ministry of Justice (all with the invaluable help of the UK Embassy in The Hague), a RIU team travelled to the UK in order to exhume the remains of the serviceman's mother and collect DNA samples. Exactly 60 years after her own death, she had unknowingly identified her only son who is now buried at the CWGC cemetery at Oosterbeek near Arnhem

When contacting next of kin, as a means of collecting DNA samples, there should always be a presumption of identity. A researcher needs to appeal to the family's rationality and not raise their expectations. This 'Catch 22' situation can be seen as an ethical risk or an opportunity as the outcome of the research and scientific analysis, ultimately, could be negative. Some years before this case, at the 2005 'Finding the Fallen' conference held at the National Army Museum (London), the US forensic archaeologist, O'Connor and Scott (2005) stated that, finding a serviceman or woman from any conflict and then failing to do everything possible to identify them is like 'killing them twice'. It is the RIU's experience that, despite a negative outcome of a DNA test, the next of kin appreciate the effort and are utterly grateful that their missing loved ones have not been forgotten. In the words of Commanding Officer (RIU) Geert Jonker (2018, pers. comm.): "Moral obligations should never be time-limited. We owe it to the missing and to their families to go out and search for them. After all, now that we have all these wonderful modern day forensic techniques such as DNA-testing at our disposal, and with time ticking away, what is the excuse not to?".

British and American visitors to a Commonwealth War Graves Commission or United States Military Cemetery often state (to the author of this chapter) 'Isn't it well cared for', followed by the observation that even the unidentified casualties have, in most cases, their own headstone or memorial cross or marker. Most visitors are unaware of the funding from national governments that support the maintenance of these sites. When the same visitors make their way to a German Great War or Second World War cemetery they are often surprised to find multiple burials using one memorial cross or stone. The use of mass graves and the lower level of maintenance horrify some non-German visitors. Langemarck German cemetery has a mass grave containing just under 25,000 soldiers who are identified by name rank and date of death on bronze plaques. This kind of burial is sometime rationalised as expressing some form of German 'War Guilt', which in some ways it does. At the end of the Great War there were a large number of German war cemeteries on the

Western Front. Following defeat in 1918, some of these cemeteries were simply ploughed in or bulldozed and 13,000 individual graves were lost in Belgium alone (Great War n.d.).

Maintenance was hampered by the attitude taken by the nations in which the cemeteries lay, and access was difficult for the state maintained German War Graves teams. Following the end of the Second World War and the defeat of the Nazi cause, the new German government decided that in future the state would not be responsible for the maintenance of war graves (Lavalle 2014). This decision was purely political and not ethical and was a response to previous militarism in Germany. As a result, the Volksbund Deutsche Kriegsgräberfürsorge (VDK) was to receive no revenue from the state and would have to depend upon voluntary contribution of money and resources. The consequence of this pragmatic decision was to concentrate the burials from both World Wars into a much-reduced number of cemeteries. This process was carried out during the 1950s and 1960s. The result was the mass burials that are a feature of so many of the German cemeteries today. Another affect of the two World Wars was the decision taken by the VDK to concentrate their resources to the Second World War Eastern Front. With over a million missing and relatives young enough to be directly affected by the loss of family members, this pragmatism is logical, but driven by economics rather than ethics. However, a similar decision has been taken by the state funded US Defense POW/MIA Accounting Agency concerning war dead before 1918 on the basis that the passage of time means that few relatives have any knowledge of the family member.

25.4 Individual or Collective Memorial?

One aspect of the treatment of war dead (which is cultural rather than ethical) is the display of human remains on former battlefields. Sites such as the French memorial at Notre Dame de Lorette or Verdun include ossuaries containing the remains of thousands of French and, in some cases, German soldiers, which are often on public display. The ossuary at Douaumont contains over 13,000 French and German soldiers (Chemins de Mémoire 2018). This fact is clearly a shock to many and some visitors are known to rationalise the situation by suggesting “the French don’t care like *we* do” (Chemins de Mémoire 2018), forgetting the number of casualties and the limitations of identification. However, the use of ossuaries or even the display of human remains in crypts is familiar in parts of Europe sharing a common Catholic religious heritage. This meant that even families who had the remains of their relatives returned home, had them buried in what were mass graves linked to a community war memorial. Examples of these can be found in France, Belgium, and elsewhere. Although an anathema to Britons, in particular, they were a solution to a problem that had its roots in national culture and tradition rather than a simple post war expedient. Catholic burial practices are different from those practiced by Protestants, and less importance is placed on the body after the death and departure of the soul. Additionally, in contrast to Britain or the United States, graves in France are not granted in perpetuity and at the end of the 'lease' the human remains can be removed and the grave site reused (Kselman 1993).

Shortly after I was asked to write this chapter on the ethics of the recovery of human remains related to the First and Second World Wars, a British based militaria dealer sent me an electronic catalogue of his latest Second World War products. On the first page was a series of items entitled 'from a small collection of items recovered from the battlefields of southern Lithuania, now part of north-eastern Poland. This was where the SS Lettische was more or less wiped out by the Russians'. One was a cap badge described as a 'Rare Lithuanian version, one piece with fold over fastening claws, aluminum. Some corrosion holes and dirt'. Another was a complete identity tag carrying the details of a member of the Nazi SS. This two-part metal artefact was worn around the owners neck on a cord and the information stamped into it was in duplicate either side of a horizontal line of slots. The intention was that if the soldier was killed in action the lower half could be removed to confirm his identity while the top half would remain with the body to ensure future identification and appropriate burial. As the object was being offered for sale as a complete artefact it was either from someone who survived, or a casualty who had been dug up in the search for items to sell. As the sales details included information about 'corrosion, dirt, and holes' and even included a location from which this object was recovered, it was clear that the item and others had come from fairly recent battlefield scavenging. What made the item all the more powerful was that it had clearly been removed from a set of human remains. In so doing this, the no doubt illegal relic hunter, one of the so-called "black diggers", had taken away the last possibility for that fallen soldier's identification. With an estimated 26,000,000 dead on the Eastern Front there is plenty of 'loot' still available (Ash 2014). Arguments, expressed by visitors on a number of battlefield tours in 2016, such as "he was only a Nazi", "he wouldn't care", or even "I need the money" need to be set against the morality of taking away the one opportunity a fallen soldier has to be identified. Fortunately, although the level of this illegal and immoral activity has not decreased, an informal agreement has been reached with the national authorities and VDK so that the remains and a photograph of the soldiers identification tag can be handed over, while the original, worth a lot of money to the detectorists can be retained and sold' (Olga Ivashina 2017, pers. comm.). Such 'grave robbing' is not a unique feature of the Eastern Front (Ash 2014). It is conducted on many battlefields, sometimes quite openly, with the results offered to an eager client who either does not know or does not care about the results of 'Bone Bothering', as it is termed. On a visit to the area of the Halbe Pocket near Berlin, the site of potential mass graves dating from May 1945 and containing the remains of Nazi, Polish, and Russian troops together with civilians, I was advised by the authorities to have an armed guard as protection from illegal diggers and the Neo Nazis who see the area as 'sacred soil'. Sites on the Western Front are subject to disturbance on a virtually industrial scale, and legal archaeologists have to be aware that their arrival on site will almost inevitably attract the attention of metal detectorists who run the risk of arrest but are prepared to take the risks. There is a fine line between the legal and illegal 'excavation' of battlefields

As Moshenska (2008) has identified, it is only in the twenty-first century that real concern has been raised concerning the ethics of archaeological practice and the material remains of recent conflicts. In his article 'Ethics and Ethical Critique in the Archaeology of Modern Conflict', Moshenska (2008, 159) highlighted that "Little or no explicit effort has been made to examine the ethical challenges presented by archaeological interventions into the resonant remains of modern warfare". By contrast, as late as 1987, John Laffin could advise that the archaeologist's tools were "A conventional garden spade, a small trowel and a single-hand garden fork. The most useful tool is a probe; mine is a stair rod 30 inch long fitted with a wooden handle…every archaeologist needs a stout bag (an old army kit bag is ideal) for carrying his finds. Each find should be at once labelled with the position of the find, the date, tentative identification. I put each item in a separate bag together with a luggage label on which I put my notes" (Laffin 1987, 120).

In many ways this spirit was embodied by a group of amateur battlefield investigators who called themselves 'The Diggers'. This group was based in the area of Ypres and described themselves as "a team of enthusiasts digging for World War I relics. We often refer to ourselves as amateur-archaeologists, hoping that the 'real' professional archaeologists will not take offence at this, as our field is a lot more limited" (The Mauser Shooters Association 2001).

The group operated in the period from the late 1980s until the early 2000s when they were refused permission to continue with their relic hunting. Although the group were amateur and their methods crude they were sanctioned by the local authorities and were, at the time, the only people conducting exploration ahead of development work in the area. In the course of their work they exhumed over 100 sets of remains but the identification rate was terribly low because there was no methodology and they lacked knowledge and scientific support (The Mauser Shooters Association 2001). Fortunately for other victims of the war, a decision to build an extension of the A19 motorway from Ypres to the coast across the battlefield of the Ypres Salient led to the establishment, by the local government of West Flanders in 2003, of 'The Association for World War Archaeology' (AWA). The Diggers were refused permission to carry on and the investigation carried out by the AWA was able to convince the authorities that the construction of the motorway would destroy evidence of the war.

On the Eastern Front, despite the apparently bleak prospect, there exist a variety of officially sanctioned groups that search for the casualties of the 'Great Patriotic War'. Although under resourced and often without the services of specialists, they aim to identify casualties by nationality and possibly name. Unfortunately, Russian soldiers were only issued with military identification on pieces of paper carried in a tube worn round the neck, therefore the chance of a named burial is remote. In 2016, volunteers recovered remains of more than 20,000 soldiers in Russia (Olga Ivshina 2018, pers. comm.). However, only 1229 of them were identified, because most of the soldiers did not have identification tags (Olga Ivshina 2018, pers. comm.). This work is done almost entirely by volunteers. Challenges include lack of funding and lack of co-ordination among nearly 1000 digging teams, which work in 39 regions of Russia. However, activists manage to develop some technologies, such as metal detectors and simple gridded plotting squares, which help to make this process more organised and efficient (Olga Ivshina 2017, pers. comm.). The case of casualties from the Russo-Finnish Winter War 1939–1940 and the Continuation War 1941–1944 demonstrate that even in a hostile condition, casualties can be recovered and identified largely by volunteers. As recently as 2015, more than 250 Finnish casualties were repatriated following discovery on the battlefield of the Karelia Isthmus (YLE 2015).

A problem that continues to exist is when human remains are refused burial. One example is that of a Nazi officer killed by a resistance fighter during the Second World War. Before his death the killer confessed to the deed, in part to clear his conscience, and explained where the man was buried. The remains were exhumed and found to be a Latvian SS officer who had been returning from a night out in occupied Belgium. The remains were offered to the German War Graves (VDK) who refused burial on the basis that the man was not German. The remains were then offered to Latvia who responded that the man was indeed a national of that country, but a Nazi, so he would not be repatriated. When last heard of, the remains were in storage (Geert Jonker 2015, pers. comm.). An example of political sentiment being more important than moral considerations for a fellow national by a decision maker in the modern world.

During the Spanish Civil War (1936–1939) approximately 500,000 people died and many civilians were killed in summary executions. Many of the Republicans were buried in unmarked mass graves. In 2007, a Socialist government passed a law on "historical memory" (Ley de Memoria Histórica), which required the national government to facilitate and subsidise the identification of these victims. This decision was in line with the United Nations declaration of 'Forced Disappearances' of 1992 that Spain signed in 2007. Between 2007 and 2011, 25 million Euros were spent supporting this search for the missing. However, in 2011, the new government cut off funding (Laursen 2016). One aspect of this decision was the refusal of Priests to bury the remains of those who had been identified. This was on the basis that they were 'Communists' and therefore not Catholic, a view that still prevails in some sections of modern Spanish society.

As Doug Scott (2017, pers. comm.) has pointed out "There are those that argue that we should leave war dead where they lie". This is often based on the belief that they are safe where they are and with their comrades. As we have already seen, human remains on former battlefield face multiple threats. These range from looting and unsupervised development to bad practice, the constraints of budgets and even changes in government policy. However, it is clear that with the numbers of war dead that resulted from both World Wars (estimates for the Second World War alone indicate up to 85,000,000 casualties), it precludes recovery of only a fraction of the missing (National World War II Museum 2018). It is possible that if projects are mounted deliberately to 'find the fallen' or others are found in the course of agriculture or development, the process of recovery "Should be done to the highest professional archaeological and anthropological standards" (National World War II Museum 2018).

25.5 Conclusion

It is clear that ethical tension exists between the public, archaeologists, official bodies, and governments. These tensions are in part fuelled by opinion, culture, religion, lack of finance, and the limitations of current archaeological practice. Every nation has its own approach to this process, and political will, budget and experience means widely differing practice even within Europe. What was regarded as ethical in one culture is not so in another and what is regarded as acceptable practice today may not be so tomorrow. The boundaries are ever changing and there is no question that building development, farming practice, commercial exploitation, and archaeology will reveal yet more 'missing'. The discovery of these remains produces challenges in terms of identification and burial both moral and ethical for which there is no universal protocol or policy. Virtually every country has its own way of proceeding, some within a legal framework and others outside or on the edge of legality. Modern science has added a new dimension to this mix, and whereas it is now possible to use DNA and other techniques to identify the fallen, cost, policy, and expedience means that these methods may not be used at all. It is recognised that recovery of human remains from world conflicts without an attempt to identify these is the equivalent of 'killing them twice'. But this is what is happening and will continue to do so, sometimes because of greed and ignorance but in other circumstances because of policy and budgetary constraints.

As the centenary of the Great War has come(s) to a conclusion, there is no doubt that attention will turn to the eightieth anniversary of the outbreak of the Second World War in September 2019. Emphasis will turn to the worldwide battlefields of this conflict in a way not seen before. As the relatives of the fallen in this conflict are 20 years younger than those of the Great War and are more numerous, there is no question that this will result in pressures on governments to find and identify the 'MIA'. At present only one country, the USA, is systematically searching for their post First World War fallen in a well-funded and scientific manner. What the result will be for other countries, as the combination of expectation of identification of 'their' loved ones by relatives, the potential of new scientific techniques, and public pressure, remains to be seen. There can be no doubt that there will be many opportunities to employ existing techniques of search and identification and for the development of new methods. The moral and ethical issues that underlie these processes will, no doubt, change and be adapted as pressure groups, families, and government grapple with the implication of the mass casualties of two world wars. Talk of 'contested ground' and 'conflict archaeology' reveals the challenging nature of the discipline. As Moshenska (2008, 172) has identified, the ethical debate "will ensure that this powerful and dangerous discipline is ticking over, keeping archaeologists and heritage manager on their toes and firmly outside their comfort zones. For this is no place for comfort". In an ideal world there would be an international agreement as to how these issues should be addressed and a unified approach adopted by all governments and agencies. However, the reality is that budgetary constraints, politics, and public attitude will make this unlikely. It is also worth considering that a single approach could become a 'straight jacket' whereby local initiatives would be stifled by 'policy' and 'bureaucracy' and the number of groups able to conduct high quality and potentially innovative work restricted. In these circumstances an initiate, which would allow all those currently involved in the recovery of humans remains from the battlefields of the twentieth century to share experience, skills, and best practice would be a step towards developing a unified and ethical global approach.

Acknowledgements With grateful thanks to the following people who have given me advice or guidance in writing this chapter: Jean Loup Gassend (Forensic Pathology Resident, France), Doug Scott (Archaeologist, USA), Timothy Nosal (Chief of External Affairs, American Battle Monuments Commission, USA), Heather Harris (Deputy Director, Europe Mediterranean Region Defense POW/MIA Accounting Agency, USA), Olga Ivshina (BBC Russian Correspondent and a Volunteer Digger, UK and Russia), and finally Geert Jonker (Recovery and Identification Unit (RIU) of the Royal Netherlands Army).

References

Adam, F. 2006. *Alain-Fournier et ses Compagnons d'arme: Une Archéologie de la Grande Guerre*. Paris: Editions Serpenoise.

Anon. 1643. *E85 (41) The New Years Wonders, Thomason Tracts*. Thomason, London.

Ash, L. 2014. Digging for Their Lives: Russia's Volunteer Body Hunters. *BBC News*, 13 January. http://www.bbc.co.uk/news/magazine-25589709. Accessed 29 May 2018.

BBC. 2015. Spitfire Crash Pilot's Remains Laid to Rest. *BBC News*, 19 November. https://www.bbc.co.uk/news/uk-england-sussex-34866398. Accessed 12 June 2018.

Chemins de Mémoire. 2018. *National Necropolis and Ossuary*. http://cheminsdememoire.gouv.fr/en/douaumont-national-necropolis-and-ossuary. Accessed 19 July 2018.

Cole, W. 2015. Hawaii's JPAC Folds into Defense POW/MIA Accounting Agency. *Star Advertiser*, 30 January. http://www.staradvertiser.com/2015/01/30/breaking-news/hawaiis-jpac-folds-into-defense-powmia-accounting-agency/. Accessed 19 July 2018.

Commonwealth War Graves Commission. 2018. *Frequently Asked Questions About Our Documents*. https://www.cwgc.org/find/find-war-dead-and-cemeteries/documents-faqs. Accessed 27 June 2018.

Dodd, K. 2015. USS Oklahoma Disinterments Complete. *Defense POW/MIA Accounting Agency*. 9 November. http://www.dpaa.mil/News-Stories/Recent-News-Stories/Article/628567/uss-oklahoma-disinterments-complete/. Accessed 27 June 2018.

Epps, V. 2013. Civilian Casualties in Modern Warfare. *Georgia Journal of International and Comparative Law* 41: 307–355.

Franklin, B.H. 1993. *M.I.A or Mythmaking in America: How and Why Belief in Live POWS Has Possessed a Nation*. New Brunswick: Rutgers University Press.

Geni. 2018. *Anglo Boer War (1899–1902)—British Casualties*. https://www.geni.com/projects/Anglo-Boer-War-1899-1902-British-Casualties/23521. Accessed 12 June 2018.

Goellnitz, J. n.d. *Statistics on the Civil War and Medicine*. https://ehistory.osu.edu/exhibitions/cwsurgeon/cwsurgeon/statistics. Accessed 12 June 2018.

Great Fen. 2018. *Spitfire*. http://www.greatfen.org.uk/spitfire. Accessed 19 July 2018.

Great War. n.d. *Volksbund Deutsche Kriegsgräberfürsorge (VDK)*. http://www.greatwar.co.uk/organizations/volksbund-vdk.htm. Accessed 5 August 2018.

Harris, H. 2017. *Keeping the Nation's Promise: Case Studies in Recent Efforts to Locate Missing U.S. Service Members*. Paper Presented at the Finding the Fallen Conference, Working, UK, 15 July 2017.

Holt, T., and V. Holt. 2007. *My Boy Jack: The Search for Kipling's Only Son*. Barnsley: Pen and Sword.

Kselman, T.A. 1993. *Death and the Afterlife in Modern France*. Princeton: Princeton University Press.

Laffin, J. 1987. *Battlefield Archaeology*. London: Ian Allen.

Landser. n.d. *Identity Discs*. http://moebius.freehostia.com/dogtag.htm. Accessed 19 July 2018.

Laursen, L. 2016. Gathering the Genetic Testimony of Spain's Civil War Dead. *Sapiens*, 3 June. https://www.sapiens.org/archaeology/spanish-civil-war-forensics-memory/. Accessed 29 May 2018.

Lavalle, S.E. (2014). *Monumental Shifts in Memory: The Evolution of German War Memorials from the Great War to the End of the Cold War*. Dissertation, Wichita State University.

Loe, L., C. Barker, K. Brady, et al. 2014. *Remember Me to All: The Archaeological Recovery and Identification of Soldiers Who Fought and Died in the Battle of Fromelles 1916*. Oxford: Oxford Archaeology.

Moshenska, G. 2008. Ethics and Ethical Critique in the Archaeology of Modern Conflict. *Norwegian Archaeological Review* 41 (2): 159–175.

National World War II Museum. 2018. *Research Starters: Worldwide Deaths in World War II*. https://www.nationalww2museum.org/students-teachers/student-resources/research-starters/research-starters-worldwide-deaths-world-war. Accessed 11 July 2018.

O'Connor, M., and D.D. Scott. 2005. *They Died with Custer*. Paper Presented at Finding the Fallen Conference, National Army Museum, Chelsea, London, 9 July 2005.

Ohio State University. n.d. *Statistics on the Civil War and Medicine*. https://ehistory.osu.edu/exhibitions/cwsurgeon/cwsurgeon/statistics. Accessed 27 June 2018.

Oldridge, D. 2016. *The Supernatural in Tudor and Stuart England*. London: Routledge.

Protection of Military Remains Act. 1986. The Stationery Office, London.

Robertshaw, A., and D. Kenyon. 2008. *Digging the Trenches*. Barnsley: Pen and Sword.

Ruane, M.E. 2016. After 75 Years, Remains of 5 USS Oklahoma Sailors Are Identified. *Stars and Stripes*. 11 January. https://www.stripes.com/news/us/after-75-years-remains-of-5-uss-oklahoma-sailors-are-identified-1.388226. Accessed 27 June 2018.

Swift, E. 2003. *Where They Lay*. London: Bantam.

The Mauser Shooters Association. 2001. *What and Who Are the Diggers?* http://www.mausershooters.org/diggers/E/voorstelling/welkom.htm. Accessed 19 July 2018.

Van Heyningen, E., and P. Merrett. 2003. 'The Healing Touch': The Guild of Loyal Women of South Africa 1900–1912. *South African Historical Journal* 47: 24–50.

Watrin, J. 1987. *The British Military Cemeteries in the Region of Boulogne-sur-Mer*. Leicester: The Book Guild.

Wawro, G. 2003. *The Franco-Prussian War: The German Conquest of France in 1870–1871*. Cambridge: Cambridge University Press.

YLE. 2015. Remains of Finnish War Dead to Be Buried in Lappeenranta. *YLE*, 5 March. https://yle.fi/uutiset/osasto/news/remains_of_finnish_war_dead_to_be_buried_in_lappeenranta/7846268. Accessed 29 May 2018.

Young, P. 1976. *Edgehill 1642: The Campaign and the Battle*. Moreton-in-Marsh: The Roundwood Press.

Chapter 26
Between the Archaeological and the Criminal Cases: Human Remains and Ethical Issues in Russia

Tatiana Shvedchikova

Abstract Ethical issues in Russia have stemmed from a long tradition of research into historical and contemporary archaeological sites. However, these investigations vary depending on whether the archaeologist or anthropologist is dealing with human remains from archaeological contexts, the victims of the Second World War, or those from recent criminal cases. Furthermore, there are a number of cultural and political considerations that have since become entwined within ethical practice, such as the case of the Ukok Princess. This chapter argues that the attitudes regarding human remains started to change with the excavation of monasteries and convents, resulting in the identification of the deceased employing forensic anthropological methods. Likewise, Russia was involved in a number of conflicts throughout the twentieth century that included: The Revolution, two World Wars, and a Civil War. In recent years, the discovery of conflict casualties has led to an increase in the search and identification process by a number of scientists. Therefore, this chapter addresses the ethical challenges associated with searching, recovering, and identifying human remains, and how these change depending on their associated period. Also detailed is the treatment of the dead and any living relatives. In Russia, ethical issues pertaining to human remains will continue to develop, and its awareness will continue to increase throughout the professional community and reach out to the wider population.

26.1 Introduction

"Stop moaning!"—A colleague of mine told me this while we were searching for burial C13 amongst a mound of black plastic bags containing the human remains of Napoleonic soldiers, which dated back to the beginning of the nineteenth century. "They are not humans—this is anthropological material!" was the response of my

---

T. Shvedchikova (✉)
Institute of Archaeology, Russian Academy of Sciences, Dm. Ulyanova str., 19, Moscow, Russia
e-mail: tashved@gmail.com

K. Squires et al. (eds.), *Ethical Approaches to Human Remains*,
https://doi.org/10.1007/978-3-030-32926-6_26

colleague after I raised my concerns around the treatment of juvenile and young adult skeletons. In particular, my comments regarded the cruel destiny of the remains of these war casualties and the fact that this anthropological collection had already been relocated three times in one year. Following this difference in opinion, we did not speak to each other for several days. This incident took place in 2006, when appropriate archaeological guidance was applied to the excavations by the Institute of Archaeology, Russian Academy of Sciences, but the skeletons recovered were not classed as 'interesting' like older archaeological remains that date back several hundred, if not thousands of years old. Instead, they were labelled as 'unusually fresh' (a term used within the community to describe remains found within the past few hundred years, but are of no scientific interest). The chronological period between what is deemed to be "archaeological" and what is classed as "recent" (e.g. in a police or judicial case) did not interest many archaeologists, but the discovery of human remains from recent history in Russia was becoming common due to the increased number of rescue excavations uncovering the remains of Napoleonic soldiers (1812–1813). Interest in the early nineteenth century was enhanced further following several large rescue excavations which took place in Kaliningrad (former Koenisberg) between 2006 and 2007 (Kozlov et al. 2009) and the research excavation at the monastery of Trinity Lavra of St. Sergius in Sergiev Posad (Moscow region) from 2003 to the present day (Engovatova et al. 2016a, 2016b). The attitude of archaeologists regarding human remains started to change as a result of the increased number of excavations taking place in the early twenty-first century, particularly of monasteries and convents where the identity of the deceased could be determined. This was something that had not previously been encountered within traditional archaeology in Russia.

26.2 Archaeological Remains and the Absence of Any Ethical Considerations?

Traditional Russian archaeology focuses upon a whole host of periods up until the present day. However, the majority of specialists would rate the Palaeolithic, Mesolithic, Bronze Age, Early Iron Age, and the Early Medieval sites as the most interesting ones in comparison to those that are more recent. According to Federal Law, all artefacts and sites that are older than 100 years is the responsibility of the archaeologist. Likewise, cultural and historical objects, and how they are used, are regulated by Federal Laws No. 73-FZ (2002), No. 245-FZ (2013), and No. 315-FZ (2014). The rules and methodological approach of any archaeological investigation is controlled by the 'Regulations of carrying out the archaeological fieldwork and preparation of scientific reports' that were developed by the Institute of Archaeology of the Russian Academy of Sciences (Polozhenie 2018). This document is updated periodically and guides on the process of dealing with human remains. For example, point 4.33 stipulates that human remains should be sent to anthropologists, after which they can be sent for storage at specialised institutions or they can be reburied (Polozhenie 2018).

Written scientific reports that detail archaeological fieldwork must contain basic anthropological data, including biological information (e.g. estimated sex and age of the individuals), as well as information regarding the storage location of the human remains (Polozhenie 2018). According to each of the aforementioned regulations, human bones are considered and treated the same as animal bones and palaeobotanical samples, that is, they are an additional source of information that holds archaeological data. However, there are no specific rules for the storage of human remains in respect to whether they are held in scientific organisations or universities that do not hold a 'museum status' (Buzhilova 2011).

In fact, up until the 1980s, some individuals working in Russian physical anthropology would collect skulls or one side of the skeleton. However, with the emergence of the 'bioarchaeological approach' in classical anthropological publications, and the understanding of the wider context associated with skeletal anatomy (such as the cultural and biological environment), the attitude towards curating and storing skeletal remains started to improve.

The recovery and analysis of human remains that are older than 100 years old is relatively straightforward. However, the example of the 'Ukok Princess" highlights that this is not always the case. Excavated in 1993 on the plateau Ukok on the Russian border with Mongolia the burial of a young woman, dating to the 5th–3rd century BC, was discovered (Polosmak 2013; Doronin 2016). This individual 'belonged' to the Pazyryk archaeological culture and she became known as the famous 'Altai Princess' or 'Ukok Princess". The unique state of preservation within the burial complex enabled the study of the ancient Altai population and their material culture. In particular, the well-preserved embalmed body of the young female (estimated to be around 25 years at death) facilitated the study of her numerous tattoos (Polosmak 2013). The body was transported and curated at the Institute of Archaeology and Ethnology of the Siberian Branch of the Academy of Sciences in Novosibirsk. However, this act incurred unfavourable opinions from the local Altai population who believed that the female appeared to be that of a shaman. Therefore, the Altai wanted the mummy to be returned for reburial, and deemed the removal of the 'Altai Princess' to be the cause of several natural disasters (such as floods) that has since affected the area (The Siberian Times 2012).

In 2012, the mummy was moved to the new National Museum in Gorno-Altaysk and was stored in a specially made sarcophagus incorporating climate control. However, in 2014, the local Council of Elders, in conjunction with the local authorities (the Head of the Altai Republic) decided to rebury the princess. Meetings and debates, some of which even reached Gorno-Altay City Court, were undertaken by the Indigenous people who classed the Altai Princess as their ancestor (Doronin 2016). The reburial request was refused by the Ministry of Culture, and now the mummy is mainly kept in a closed sarcophagus and is only occasionally opened for the public.

The Altai Princess is a well-known case that is part of a more complex and contemporary issue surrounding the opinions and beliefs of historical and religious Indigenous groups. The case also triggered a 'cultural rebirth' of this local population, even though there are no genetic links to the contemporary population. However, the outcome of this case was regulated according to the Law (Federal Laws No.73-FZ 2002; No.245-FZ 2013; No. 315-FZ 2014).

26.3 Identification of Historical Skeletons: Who Are Your Ancestors?

Ethically, the improved treatment and attitude towards human remains progressed with the analysis of historical cemeteries and, in particular, the anthropological identification of known individuals. Still, these investigations were performed within the framework of traditional archaeological operational procedures, and this often faced the non-codified, law abiding religious regulations or a descendant's will. Yet, it has been proven that when a church works in close collaboration with the archaeologist, and the archaeologist can demonstrate the importance and quality of the work and the information gained, the withdrawal of some religious rules can occur. For example, in the longstanding excavations of the Moscow Ecclesiastic Academy Necropolis in Trinity Lavra of St. Sergius (Sergiev Posad, Moscow region), buried individuals were identified. This was achieved through the use of contemporary anthropological and forensic methods without any restrictions imposed by the priesthood (Engovatova et al. 2016a, 2016b).

The identification of the last archimandrites from the Solovetsky Monastery, recovered from the archipelago in the White Sea in 2013–2014, is a good example of the collaboration between archaeologists and anthropologists at the bequest of the Russian Orthodox Church (Khartanovich et al. 2014; Shvedchikova et al. 2017). Within the Trinity Church on the monastery's territory, was the discovery of four burial vaults thought to belong to the last archimandrites of the Solovetsky monastery: Ioannikyi, Porphyrius, Varlaam, and Theophan. The resulting anthropological investigation included craniological description, palaeopathological analysis, forensic facial reconstruction, and three-dimensional documentation (Khartanovich et al. 2014; Shvedchikova et al. 2017). Due to Christian beliefs (i.e. not to disturb the body) and the fact that individuals from vaults 1 and 2 were laid in anatomical position, two of the skeletons were analysed in situ with only the removal of the skulls and some long bones for metric and photographic documentation. Vaults 3 and 4 had signs of secondary disturbance from grave robbers, and besides the full study of the skeleton, anthropologists were asked to lay out the disarticulated and commingled skeletons in an anatomical position.

The skeleton within vault 3 was disturbed, and although largely disorganised, the upper part of the body had some anatomical order. Much of these alterations were the result of robbery. In 2014, the whole vault was investigated. The excavation showed that the cranium was absent, with only the mandible and several teeth present. The right femoral head showed evidence of post-mortem modification, which further led to the interpretation that vandalism had occurred once the bodies had skeletonised (Shvedchikova et al. 2017). Similarly, burial 4 was also disturbed. Nonetheless, pathological findings on this skeleton enabled identification of the deceased; his name being Archimandrite Porphyrius (Shvedchikova et al. 2017). It is now known that in the autumn of 1860 Archimandrite Porphyrius was affected by flu and had developed a rash across his body. In 1865 the illness had affected his organs and the resultant acute pains were unbearable (Shvedchikova et al. 2017). This was followed by severe damage to the liver and lungs. The bone lesions identified on the cranial and post-cranial skeleton included a number of diseases, including metastatic carcinoma or cryptococcosis. A detailed palaeopathological study was undertaken and differential diagnosis was considered. The results of the study indicated that these skeletal lesions were consistent with the illness that Archimandrites Porphyrius suffered. Alongside a consistent biological profile (e.g. age at death and sex), a presumptive identification was made (Shvedchickova et al. 2017). Since this assessment, the remains have been reburied with dignity and respect in a religious ceremony. Generally, it is not always possible to identify individuals, not only due to their antiquity or preservation but because of a lack of collaboration between the scientists and the Church. However, knowing that some cases can be identified, provides a more respectful consideration and alternative attitude to the excavation of human remains.

26.4 Human Remains from the Second World War

The chronological interval between what is deemed as archaeological (over 100 years old) and recent (within the past 30 years), includes World War I (1914–1918), the Russian Civil War (1917–1922), and the Second World War (1941–1945). It should be noted that human remains from World War I already fall under archaeological legislation and must be excavated according to scientific archaeological guidance (Institute of Archaeology, Russian Academy of Sciences 2018).

Within the Soviet Union, it is estimated that 26,000,000 people died in World War II. This number has been calculated by researchers from the joint commission of the Ministry of Defence, Federal Security Services, Federal Service of State Statistics, and the Federal Archival Agency. From this number, 20,000,000 of the deceased were men, 8.5 million of those were the result of direct military loss, and two million of these individuals were listed as missing people. It is these numbers that has caused significant disputes amongst historians.

From the beginning of the twentieth century, a chain of events took place in Russia. These included The Revolution (1917–1918), World War I (1914–1918), Civil War (1917–1922), and World War II (1941–1945). The precise loss is difficult to estimate, and in 2012 in Tomsk (Siberia), the first public enquiry named the

‘Immortal Regiment’ was held (Andreev 2013). Families with the portraits of their relatives who died and took part in World War II walked along the streets. In response to a local action which took place in Tyumen in 2007, this event takes place in every Russian city on an annual basis on the 9th May (‘Victory Day’). In 2019, almost 10 million people participated (Reevell 2019).

During the first few years after World War II, the search for victims was undertaken sporadically. The general public and those who restored the ruined country, found the remains, buried them, marked their tombs, and gave the information to the military enlistment centres. Enthusiasts, mainly former battle-fronted veterans, and those who were not indifferent to the destiny of the dead in battles undertook this task. In fact, school teachers also organised some of the very first teams involved in searching for those that were still missing.

In the 1950s and 1960s the ‘All Union’ campaign intended to visit the places of The Revolution, battlefields, and labour sites (Vsesoyuznyu pohod komsomoltsev i molodezhi po mestam revolyutsionnoi, boevoi i trudovoi slavy) started. Thousands of expeditions were organised and, as a result, it became a powerful trigger for orchestrating the search movement among young people. However, there was no legal basis for this and reburials were organised by the government and military services.

Likewise, the ‘All Union Leninist Young Communist League’ played a very important role in the search movement. In 1981 they organised a long-term mission called ‘The Chronicle of The Great Patriotic War’ (Letopis velikoi otechestvennoi voiny). The aim of this expedition was to collect documentary materials, memoirs of participants, to help veterans, and to create new museums. In 1988, the first congress that included all parties involved in the search process took place in Kaluga. This resulted in the creation of the ‘All Union Coordinating Center of the Search Detachments’ and on the forty-fifth anniversary of Victory Day, civilians were finally permitted to take part in search campaigns (Zhuravlev 2018). Additionally, a number of laws and legal regulations were issued by the Ministry of Defence and the Youth Communist League aimed at allowing such search organisations. For instance, ‘Memory Watches’ (Vakhty pamyati) were expeditions set up with the aim of searching and reburying soldiers. These missions started at the location of large battles, for example in the regions of Smolensk and Novgorod. Later, the All Union Book of Memory was created as a result of an initiative launched by the Ministry of Defence; the aim of which was to unite all available data about the war dead. In 1989, The Centre of Memory Perpetuation of the Fallen (Tsentr po uvekovechivaniju pamyati pavshih) was created. This organisation coordinated investigations between the USSR and foreign countries, and also took control of each discovery, listings of the missing, and improving the cemeteries of Soviet soldiers. In addition, a number of inter-governmental memorandums were created and included: Finland, Germany, Italy, Poland, Hungary, Czech Republic, Slovakia, Serbia, Romania, Latvia, Slovenia, Turkey, Mongolia, China, Vietnam, and Japan.

A number of statutes that were initiated in this period, and during the exploratory movement, concerning the memorialisation of the Soviet dead were registered legally within the Ministry of Justice. Unfortunately, following the collapse of the Soviet Union, this financial and political crisis influenced the development of the search movement, and parts of the detachments from the former Soviet Republics arranged their own associations. For example, Lithuania and Belorussia developed strong governmental support (Jankauskas 2015). Yet the local Russian search team continued to exist independently with its own group of volunteers. These developments led to an extremely important law being established in 1993. The law became the legal basis for undertaking the search, and determined both the financial and technical aid to support the organisation. Essentially, this was the beginning of a new era and with the creation of this judicial status, and new legislative regulation, more than individual 500 search teams united in the Union of search teams of Russia (Soyuz poiskovyh otryadov Rossii) (Khotina 2015).

Federal Law No. 8 FZ (1996), 'On Burial and Funeral Business', defined the terms for 'old war' and 'recently unknown burials'. This law was specific to the victims of war and their rightful burials, and in turn forbid any excavation of these individuals without official permissions. In 2006, the Presidential Decree No. 37 (2006) on the 'immortalisation of the memory of people killed during the homeland defence' was signed. This was placed within the Ministry of Defence, and had regulations to control the search for victims from World War II. Finally, in 2013, the different governmental organisations (search teams) were united under one umbrella in what is called the 'Exploratory Movement of Russia" (Poiskovoe dvizhenie Rossii) (Andreev 2013). From this, exhumation protocols and burial maps have been developed and are mandatory for all search teams. For example, in the Tatarstan region, search teams upload information (including documentation, photographs of burials, descriptions, and GPS markers) onto one database.

It is demonstrated that throughout the 'Exploratory Movement of Russia', and at the very beginning of its development, the search for World War II victims was performed by enthusiastic volunteers with no specialist education in archaeology, physical anthropology, or even history. Even though those involved possessed a respectful attitude to the deceased soldiers, they lacked the specialist understanding needed to handle human remains correctly during the excavation process and anthropological identification. Absence of stringent regulation in the excavation process from the controlling ministry, lack of specialists involved in the search process, and even the lack of interest from the professionals, has led to today's situation where all communities have to build a dialogue from the very beginning.

The new generation of anthropologists who take part in the search for World War II victims take part in educational seminars where correct methodological approaches to excavation is discussed, as well as the legislative rules pertaining to excavation, documentation, and analysis. Currently, this step-by-step change has allowed for better and more precise contemporary practice. The latter includes an ethical awareness on how to treat human remains. Furthermore, many soldiers are still listed as 'missing', and are believed to be buried in collective graves. The loss of life was undoubtedly huge. Millions of dead soldiers lay lost in the forests and in swamps where, from experience, bone preservation does not facilitate successful identification of the deceased. Soldiers could potentially be identified using personal belongings, but unfortunately the preservational state of these artefacts is poor.

26.5 Conclusion

To conclude, the memory of the deceased will always live on while their descendants are alive. In archaeological cases that have no strong connections to a contemporary population, those within a professional organisation have the ability to dictate the treatment of human remains with no strict rules or regulations to follow. Furthermore, there are no penalty systems in the cases of inappropriate treatment. There are exceptions, such as the Ukok Princess, that do occur, but these are largely connected to political views and the search for new identities. Currently, there are stricter rules in terms of dealing with human remains from criminal cases as opposed to those of an archaeological nature. However, there are exceptions. This is demonstrated in historical cases involving the Russian Royal Family's lineage, where anthropological analysis was undertaken as a criminal investigation akin to that of a forensic homicide incident (Abramov et al. 2015). Likewise, the identification of the Napoleonic war hero, General Ermolov was also undertaken within the framework of a criminal case, though the case was closed during the archaeological investigation (Shvedchikova 2018).

Finally, particular laws and regulations pertaining to different communities and countries are just some of the considerations that must be addressed when dealing with human remains. Yet, within the boundaries of these regulations, the most important part is the ethical responsibility within the professional community. This should always take into account the humanitarian principles and views of descendants and society as a whole. These considerations continue to develop, and ethical awareness is increasing amongst the archaeological community in Russia.

References

Abramov, A., Veselovskaya E., Dolgov, et al. 2015. Forensic Archaeology in the Russian Federation. In *Forensic Archaeology: A Global Perspective,* ed. W.J.M Groen, N. Márquez-Grant, and R.C. Janaway, 139–149. Chichester: Wiley Blackwell.

Andreev, Y. 2013. *Bessmertnyy polk: Aktsiya, pridumannaya v Tomske i pokorivshaya Rossiyu* [*The Immortal Regiment, Invented in Tomsk and Conquered Russia*]. *RIA News.* 9 May. https://ria.ru/20130509/499424020.html. Accessed 19 July 2019.

Buzhilova, A. 2011. Chapter 35. Russia. In *The Routledge Handbook of Archaeological Human Remains and Legislation. An International Guide to Laws and Practice in the Excavation and Treatment of Archaeological Human Remains,* ed. N. Márquez-Grant, and L. Fibiger. Abingdon: Routledge.

Doronin, D.Y. 2016. What Is Wrong Again with 'Altai Princess'? New Facts from Newslor's Biography of Ak Kadyn. *Siberian Historical Research* 1: 74–104.

Engovatova, A., M. Mednikova, E. Vasileva, et al. 2016a. *Arheologicheskye issledovaniya u Dukovskoi tserkvi Troitse-Sergievoi lavry v 2014 gody (k voprosu o vozmozhnostyah istoricheskih identifikatsyi)* [*Archaeological Investigations Near Dukhovskaya Church of The Holy Trinity St. Sergius Lavra in 2014 (To The Question of the Possibilities of Historical Identifications)*]. Arheologiya Podmoskovya: Materialy nauchnogo seminara. vol. 12. Moscow: Institute of Archaeology, Russian Academy of Sciences.

Engovatova, A., M. Mednikova, E. Vasileva, et al. 2016b. *Istoriya identifikatsii rektorov, prepodavatelei i studentov Moscowskoi duhovnoi akademii pri raskopkah akademicheskogo nekropolya* [*The History of the Identification the Rectors, Teachers and Students of Moscow Ecclesiastical Academy During the Excavations of Academical Cemetery*]. In *Russian Empire and Neighborhood: Materials of the Scientific Conference,* ed. L. Beliaev and N. Rogozhin, 234–240. Moscow: Institute of Archaeology Russian Academy of Sciences.

Federal Law 8-FZ. 1996. *On Funeral Business*. Enacted on January 12, 1996, With Modifications in 2008, 2009, 2011, 2012, 2014, 2015, 2016, 2018. Moscow, Russia http://www.consultant.ru/cons/cgi/online.cgi?req=doc&base=LAW&n=298701&fld=134&dst=100022,0&rnd=0.2521182748626438#04027269082330871. Accessed 19 July 2019.

Federal Law 73-FZ. 2002. *On Cultural Heritage Objects (Cultural and Historical Sites) of Peoples of Russian Federation and Independent Statures of Russian Federation*. Enacted on June 25, 2002. Modified in 2019. Moscow, Russia http://www.consultant.ru/cons/cgi/online.cgi?req=doc&ts=21157996440184033074740727728&cacheid=4F75F65932EB6201E5DF0E62A4A8A3F0&mode=splus&base=LAW&n=315360&rnd=0.2521182748626438#2ojb35izl28. Accessed 19 July 2019.

Federal Law 245-FZ. 2013. *On Modifications in the Independent Statures of Russian Federation in the Extinction of Illegal Activity in Archaeology*. Enacted on July 23, 2013. Modified in 2017. Moscow, Russia http://www.consultant.ru/cons/cgi/online.cgi?req=doc&ts=211579964401840 3307474072772&cacheid=3979AE4C3A9B3883FE6825A4E97CBA56&mode=splus&base=LAW&n=286537&rnd=0.2521182748626438#pjjl7guzlr. Accessed 19 July 2019.

Federal Law 315-FZ. 2014. *On Modifications in the Federal Law 'On Cultural Heritage Objects (Cultural and Historical Sites) of Peoples of Russian Federation and Independent Statures of Russian Federation*. Enacted on October 22, 2014. Modified in 2016. Moscow, Russia http://www.consultant.ru/cons/cgi/online.cgi?req=doc&ts=211579964401840330747407277 2&cacheid=8E37B64505406D00A68C66F0F3CC30E8&mode=splus&base=LAW&n=201551&rnd=0.2521182748626438#2h64oe3a3j6. Accessed 19 July 2019.

Institute of Archaeology, Russian Academy of Sciences. 2018. *Polozhenie o poryadke provedeniya arheologicheskih polevyh rabot I sostavleniya otchtnoi dokumentatsii* [*Regulations of Carrying Out the Archaeological Fieldwork and Preparation of Scientific Reports*]. Moscow: Institute of Archaeology, Russian Academy of Sciences.

Jankauskas, R. 2015. Forensic Archaeology in Lithuania. In *Forensic Archaeology: A Global Perspective*, ed. W.J.M. Groen, N. Márquez-Grant, and R.C. Janaway, 99–108. Chichester: Wiley Blackwell.

Khartanovich V, T. Shvedchikova, and R. Galeev. 2014. *Ob antropologicheskoi ekspertize kostnyh ostankov na territorii Solovetskogo monastyra* [*About the Anthropological Expertize of Human Remains from the Territory of Solovetsky Monastery*]. Nauchnye issledovaniya I muzeinye proekty MAE RAS in 2013, 36–48. Saint-Petersburg: Museum of Anthropology and Ethnology (Kunstkamera), Russian Academy of Sciences.

Khotina, Y. 2015. Deyatelnost poiskovyh otryadov organizatsyi Krasnodarskogo kraya v vossozdanii istoriko-kulturnogo naslediya perioda Velikoi Otechestvennoi voiny [The Activity of Search Organizations of the Krasnodar Region in the Reconstruction of Historical and Cultural Heritage of the Great Patriotic War]. *Nauchnyi zhurnal Kubanskogo Ggosudarstvennogo Aagrarnogo universitetaU* 109 (5): 1–15.

Kozlov, A., K. Skvortsov, A. Khohlov, et al. 2009. *Raboty Sambyiskoi ekspeditsii IA RAN v Kaliningrade [Investigations of Sambia Archaeological Expedition in Kaliningrad]*. Moskva: Arheologicheskie otkrytia.

Polosmak, N. 2013. Dvadtsat let spustya [Twenty Years After]. *Science First Hand* 3 (51): 6–23.

Presidential Decree No. 37. 2006. *Immortalization of the Memory of People Killed During the Homeland Defence*. Enacted on January 22, 2006. Moscow, Russia http://www.kremlin.ru/acts/bank/23367. Accessed 19 July 2019.

Reevell, P. 2019. *Russia's Victory Day Parade Allows Putin to Show Off Military Hardware, and a Softer Side*. ABC News. 9 May. https://abcnews.go.com/International/russia-celebrates-wwii-anniversary-annual-military-parade/story?id=62932755. Accessed 19 July 2019.

Shvedchikova, T. 2018. Forensic Archaeology in Russia: Past Developments and Future Approaches. In *Multidisciplinary Approaches to Forensic Archaeology*, ed. P.M. Barone and W.J.M. Groen, 181–187. Cham: Springer.

Shvedchikova, T., V.I. Khartanovich, and R.M. Galeev. 2017. Role of the Palaeopathological Evidences in the Identification of Historical Characters on the Example of Solovetsky Monastery. *Brief Communications of the Institute of Archaeology* 249: 240–250.

The Siberian Times. 2012. Siberian Princess Reveals her 2500 Year Old Tattoos. *The Siberian Times*. 14 August. https://siberiantimes.com/culture/others/features/siberian-princess-reveals-her-2500-year-old-tattoos/. Accessed 19 July 2019.

Zhuravlev, V.A. 2018. Razvitie poiskovogo dvizheniya v Rossii: normativno-pravovoi aspect [Development of Search Movement: Legal and Regulatory Aspect]. *Izvestiya Volgogradskogo gosudarstvennogo pedagogicheskogo universiteta GPU* 4 (126): 226–233.

Chapter 27
Human Remains from the Khmer Rouge Regime, Cambodia

Caroline Bennett

Abstract On the 17th April 1975, the Communist Party of Kampuchea, colloquially known as the Khmer Rouge, marched into Phnom Penh and took control of Cambodia. During their rule of three years, eight months, and twenty days, an estimated 1.7 million people died. Their remains were buried or abandoned across the country. Since the deposal of the regime in January 1979, the human remains of those who died have been central to memorialisation and political rendering of the Khmer Rouge regime. This chapter offers a case study of the treatment of these remains, outlining the Khmer social, political, and religious frameworks affecting their treatment. By doing so it offers a consideration of ethics and human rights related to the location, identification, and treatment of human remains from the Khmer Rouge regime in contemporary Cambodia.

27.1 Introduction

On the 17th April 1975, after years of conflict and guerilla fighting, the Communist Party of Kampuchea—colloquially known as the Khmer Rouge—took control of Cambodia, establishing Democratic Kampuchea (DK) in 1976. Their Maoist-rule, though short (three years, eight months, and twenty days) effected dramatic changes to Cambodia and its people. Aiming to create an agrarian based economy, independent of foreign influence, they forcibly evacuated the cities, moving people to rural workcamps across the country, and implemented policies aimed to disassemble old ways of life. To this end, they dismantled the formal institutions of the previous rule, including hospitals, schools, government, religion, and money, enforced social control over education, marriage, community, and work, and

C. Bennett (✉)
School of Social and Cultural Studies, Victoria University of Wellington, 9th Floor Murphy Building, Kelburn Parade, Wellington 6012, New Zealand
e-mail: caroline.bennett@vuw.ac.nz

K. Squires et al. (eds.), *Ethical Approaches to Human Remains*,
https://doi.org/10.1007/978-3-030-32926-6_27

effected a social system and prison network that controlled the population and imposed absolute rule.[1]

Although debates continue on the exact death toll (Kiernan 2003; Sharp 2008; Heuveline 2015), a genocide by attrition (Fein 1997, 10) paralleled mass execution and genocide by intent, and most scholars estimate that around 1.7 million people died during the regime, which totalled between one third and one quarter of the population of the time. Their deaths were caused by disease, starvation, exhaustion, and execution, and the bodies of those who died were buried or abandoned in mass graves across the country.

Since the deposal of the regime in January 1979, the human remains of those who died have been central to memorialisation and political rendering of the Khmer Rouge regime. This chapter offers a case study of the treatment of these remains, based on the author's ongoing research, outlining the Khmer social, political, and religious frameworks affecting their treatment. By doing so it offers a consideration of ethics and human rights related to the location, identification, and treatment of human remains from the Khmer Rouge regime in contemporary Cambodia.

27.2 The Dead

The Khmer Rouge regime is often presented as one of homogenous violence and destruction, and the deaths occurring within it as the result of direct violence. Certainly, there were brutal killings throughout the regime, and even before they came to power—throughout the 1970s the Khmer Rouge fought a campaign of resistance against the military rule of General Lon Nol, who led Cambodia following a coup that overthrew Prince Norodom Sihanouk, Cambodia's former King and Prime Minister, in 1970. During the resistance, the Khmer Rouge evacuated villages and constructed security centres in Central and Northern Cambodia, where people were imprisoned, tortured, and killed.[2]

Once the regime took power, those deemed a threat to the new order (for example monks, the intelligentsia, and soldiers of the previous regime) were eliminated, either by exile or execution; ethnic minorities such as the Cham and the Vietnamese were targeted; and a prison network was established across the country, where those arrested for alleged transgressions (for example disobeying orders, or committing 'moral offenses' such as having sex), or considered to have the potential to undermine the new regime, were imprisoned, often tortured, and then executed.[3]

---

[1]This summary owes much to the work of Kiernan (1996, 2004) and Becker (1998).

[2]The most notorious of these is M-13 in Kampong Speu province.

[3]In their mapping, DC-Cam has located 158 prisons, whilst historian Henri Locard suggested that in all likelihood, there was one per district, which would be 171 prisons in total (Locard and Moeng 1993).

No-one was exempt—for instance in attempts to crush suspected treachery, purges of Khmer Rouge cadre in all zones were conducted under the leadership of Ta Mok, particularly throughout 1977 and 1978 (Kiernan 2004; Hinton 2006).[4] The scale of killings escalated throughout the regime, with a final wave occurring in the latter part of 1978 and the early days of 1979, as cadre murdered prisoners still in captivity, before fleeing the rapidly advancing Vietnamese troops who had invaded in December 1978 to depose the regime.

While up to one third of those who died were executed, the majority of victims died from exhaustion, starvation, malnutrition, infections, and diseases. Moved from their homes to live in rural work-camps across the country, they suffered as a consequence of the wide scale dismemberment of the country and its logistical support (Chandler 2008). These deaths started immediately after the Khmer Rouge's accession to power and only increased throughout the regime. Sometimes a consequence of changes in policy (such as the reduction of rations to one cup of watery rice per day), disease and starvation, and the deaths they resulted in, were also used as mechanisms of social control alongside the security system of the regime (Locard 2004).

27.3 Disposal of Remains

Corpses were disposed of in varying ways. Once the Khmer Rouge came into power and began executing the populace, orchestrating mass reorganisation of the country, and dismantling the institutions of the previous rule (including Buddhism and its associated rituals), there was little opportunity for individual care for the dead. The abandonment of bodies was common; one person I interviewed commented that: "if anybody did anything wrong they just beat them to death, and so [dead bodies] were everywhere. If it was too appalling, they just put some dirt on them." The phrase "The Killing Fields", one now synonymous with mass violence across the globe, originated from journalist Dith Pran's description of his escape across Cambodia to Thailand as a refugee in 1979, when he stumbled across multiple rice fields covered with rotting corpses (Schanberg 1985).

Some bodies were buried (individually or communally), their graves usually being dug by other workers in the area (Yathay 1988), or sometimes by those who were next to be killed. Before Democratic Kampuchea, deaths were subject to a host of funeral rituals (see Davis 2009). However, the Khmer Rouge banned Buddhism and its associated practices, as well as attempting to break ties to the old ways of life, particularly bonds to kin and community, which were to be redirected to the party and its cause (Kiernan 1996). As a consequence, most dead were buried

[4]Ta Mok (nicknamed the butcher because of his reputation for brutality) was a leading Khmer Rouge commander, and according to Hinton (2006) one of the key architects of the Khmer Rouge genocide. In 1977 he became chief of the Khmer Rouge army and oversaw the internal purges of the regime.

without ceremony and with no particular attention; people told me the deceased were *kmoac ckae*—literally translated as dead dogs. The severity or kindliness of Khmer Rouge cadre, however, varied in different communes and in some families were able to bury their own dead: one of my informants told me he felt lucky to be able to bury his children who died when a mine exploded.[5] In other locations, people did this secretly at night, adapting Buddhist rituals to provide care for the dead, risking their own lives while doing so (LeVine 2010). As well as abandonment and burial pits, some corpses were thrown into existing features such as caves, rivers, or wells.[6] In most areas the graves were simply a means to dispose of the increasing numbers of dead, but according to some survivors, in some cases the dead were buried to fertilise rice fields or coconut groves, or, on rare occasions, sacrificed in offering to *Neak Ta* (guardian spirits) (Zucker 2013).

27.4 Uncovering the Dead

Following the deposal of the regime in 1979, a new government was put into place —the People's Republic of Kampuchea (PRK)—a group of Cambodian defectors backed by Saigon. They immediately exploited material evidence of Democratic Kampuchea to assert political legitimation for their rule, as a means to solidify their narrative as saviours of Cambodia; one that remains for the ruling party to date. Human remains were important for this, providing stark physical evidence of the atrocities of the 'Pol Pot-Ieng Sary clique'. Tuol Sleng prison in Phnom Penh was turned into a museum for foreign journalists and visiting dignitaries, and officials were brought to its killing site, Choeung Ek, several times a year (Chandler 1999). The government ordered the collection and preservation of human remains in other areas (Fawthrop and Jarvis 2004). These were housed in *ptĕəh kmoac* (literally "house of the dead/ghost house")—wooden structures built to house the skeletal remains. In some locations this involved excavating mass graves; in many it simply involved collecting the remains that lay across the land.

There was no systematic approach to excavation or collection of the remains beyond the directive to preserve evidence, which was open to interpretation at the local level. While local people in many areas looted some graves, and regional officials ordered the excavation of others, it was not exhaustive, and even today many graves remain unexcavated. The excavations that did occur were by people with no expertise in excavation or treatment of human remains. At Po Tonle, in Kandal province, the remains were piled on top of a communal hall that returning villagers slept in for months before they were moved. In another, a site I call "Koh

[5]Because he had buried them himself, he was one of the few able to locate loved ones' remains after the regime; in the 1980s he unearthed their remains and took them to a local pagoda.

[6]Sometimes these features were used as killing, as well as burial, sites. One example is Phnom Sampeau in Battambang province, where people were thrown from cliffs to their deaths on the cave floors below.

Sap", local villagers were paid to collect the remains. After sufficient were gathered from the surface to satisfy the official who had ordered their collection,[7] the others were left as they were, and it was left to people returning or moving to the area to clear the dead to make living space available. Some piled them under trees that housed *Neak Ta*, some burnt the remains and then threw them in the river, whilst one villager piled soil on top of them and built her house on top.

At the same time, people used the remains for many different purposes. Davis (2009) argues that Khmer show great ambivalence to the body, and this ambivalence is best illustrated in attitudes towards the dead, the corpses of which are contemporaneously meaningless and imbued with power, particularly straight after death. The treatment of the Khmer Rouge remains expresses this ambivalence. During the regime, the ubiquity of death and frequent exposure to corpses led to a certain imperviousness to them—an elderly man I interviewed told me that they often slept among dead bodies on their evacuation out of the city, as the elderly, sick, and infirm succumbed to death.

After the regime, the remains became material of both power and banality. People told me stories of using the bones to create medicine and tonics, taking skulls as protective amulets against malevolent spirits and intrusion, and children using them as toys. Some people were haunted, and allayed that haunting by giving offerings to the dead. Graves were looted, sometimes by local people, sometimes by teams who travelled the country and paid local workers to search for valuables amongst the remains (Bennett 2018). The corpses unearthed by this looting were often added to those collected under the government orders and added to the *ptĕəh kmoac*.

Throughout the 1980s, annual ceremonies remembering the violence of the regime and reinforcing its portrayal of one of genocide and destruction occurred at sites that had been witness to the violence of the regime—mass graves, detention centres, prisons, and killing fields (Hughes 2005). The *ptĕəh kmoac* were sometimes part of this: around 80 of these structures existed at the time (Guillou 2012b). They also offered locations for people to visit and make offerings to the dead during annual rituals of remembrance. Guillou (2012b) reports that after Vietnam withdrew from Cambodia in 1989, local people no longer saw these as requiring attention, and the memorials were neglected. Repeated floods damaged some of the memorials and their remains, and cows and other animals ate remains in others. National remembrance ceremonies have now been confined to certain central locations, in particular Choeung Ek Genocidal Centre, although other sites also hold remembrance ceremonies. The remains at most locations, however, are visited only during annual rituals, primarily the Chinese grave sweeping ceremony, *Cheng Meng*, the Khmer festival for the dead, *Pchum Benh,* and Khmer New Year (see Sect. 27.5 below).

In 2001, the Cambodian government issued a directive ordering the preservation of evidence of the 'genocidal Pol Pot regime,' as physical testimony of the crimes

[7]There were no specific guidelines or standards for this beyond the directive to preserve evidence.

committed against the innocent Cambodian people. The directive ordered the examination and restoration of existing memorials, and the investigation of other gravesites, so that "all such places may be transformed into memorials" (Royal Government of Cambodia 2001, 1).[8] At around this same time, skeletal remains started to move around the country from the rural *ptĕəh kmoac* to concrete stupa (*chetĕy*)—Buddhist structures built to house cremated remains of the dead, usually within particular pagoda sites. Many of the villagers I interviewed considered that this was done for their benefit—to make it easier for families to visit the dead. A local commune chief from Southern Cambodia informed me that remains were moved to these areas under government orders so that each provincial pagoda would have more remains. As well as being desirable for religious and political reasons, there were material benefits to these moves: having the dead, I was told, encouraged people to visit, and therefore give offerings of food and money to help maintain the pagoda and its monks, simultaneously therefore, providing spiritual care for the dead, and material care for the living.[9] These pagodas, often close to regional government offices, now also offer potential sites of political use. In 2013 protests run by the ruling party, the Cambodian People's Party, against the main opposition, the Cambodian National Rescue Party (now dissolved) occurred at some of these pagodas in front of the Khmer Rouge remains: the skeletal remains providing symbolic power to invocation of the violence and terror of the Khmer Rouge regime.

The majority of people I worked with did not search for the remains of their family and friends. There were three main reasons for this. Firstly, while the mass graves were never clandestine, much of the population had been so often moved during the regime that many people did not know where to look, or how to trace their relatives or the particular sites they were killed at. Secondly, the regime immediately after the Khmer Rouge, the PRK, still strictly controlled the Cambodian population; people had to get permission to move around the country, which may have dissuaded some. Finally, the Buddhist-animist cosmology of Cambodia creates a different relationship to death and the body than in Judeo-Christian or Islamic countries, allowing for reincarnation, funerary rituals without corporeal remains, and relationships with the dead through dreams and other social interactions (Davis 2015).

[8]This directive was primarily aimed at turning the former Khmer Rouge settlement of Anlong Veng into a "historical museum for national and international tourists" (Royal Government of Cambodia 2001, 1).

[9]The remains from Koh Sap were split between three local pagodas because of this—the one closest to the commune government office took the majority, but two smaller pagoda were able to claim some for themselves.

27.5 Physical Versus Spiritual Remains

A forensic approach to human remains emphasises the corporeal remains of the dead as central to care for the living and the dead. They are positioned as central to justice, and their materiality unparalleled by other forms of testimony (Renshaw 2011). Their exhumation and individual identification is also positioned as central to due care for surviving populations, and respectful treatment of the dead (Wagner 2008).

Attention to the memorial stupa across Cambodia could, from a superficial glance, indicate neglect of the dead and undue care and attention to the living. In many, the remains are piled high, and different individuals are commingled (Fig. 27.1). In some locations, the bones are encased in glass, and the humidity of Cambodia is leading to the growth of mould on the bones and their decomposition within the stupa. Some authors claim that the display of human remains is against Buddhist practice, offensive, and upsetting to Khmer people, and done only for state political aims, which undermine the needs of the population in general (e.g. Becker 2013). Hughes (2005) claimed that because violent deaths can result in malevolent spirits, sites such as Choeung Ek Genocidal Center, which display remains of the dead, are frightening to many Cambodians.

In Cambodia, the treatment of physical remains has some import, particularly in the initial days after death, however, care for the plethora of supernatural entities that share the earth with humans and animals is also, if not a greater, imperative. Care for the local guardian spirits, for example, was the first priority for many of my research participants when they returned to their homes after the regime,

Fig. 27.1 Human remains from the Khmer Rouge regime in Kandal province. Photograph by Caroline Bennett

before dealing with the dead from the mass-graves. My research suggests that for many people in Cambodia, care for the physical remains of those killed during the Khmer Rouge has been devolved to the Buddhist *sangha* and the state, while care for spirits of the dead has been subsumed into the annual ritual cycle, providing numerous opportunities for the living to send offerings to the dead to help them accumulate karma and thus be reborn (Guillou 2012a; Holt 2012). The stupa containing the remains of the dead, mostly housed nowadays within Buddhist pagodas, provide culturally appropriate modes of caring for the dead, at the same time as performing political functions: the two are not mutually exclusive for either the government or the general population.

The state religion of Cambodia is Theravada Buddhism, and Buddhism is central to much life in Cambodia, including how the Khmer Rouge period and its aftermath is understood. Buddhism is intertwined with the pre-existing Animist religion it layered over on its introduction in the thirteenth century, which attends to care for ancestors, guardian spirits, and other supernatural entities common across the country (Chouléan 1988; Kent 2003). Theravada Buddhism allows four types of corpse disposal—burial, cremation, abandonment in forests, and abandonment in water (Davis 2009). Cremation is the most common funerary practice in contemporary times, depending on class and ethnicity.

Following death, all bodies are displayed for a short time, and powerful individuals, such as revered monks, may be displayed indefinitely (Marston 2006). Following cremation, family members, particularly children, are encouraged to sift through the ashes to look for bone fragments and teeth, which may then be made into protective amulets to wear. Cremated remains, or portions of them—particularly pieces of bone or teeth—are commonly housed in *chetěy*: memorial stupa located in pagodas or, in some cases, in the homestead.[10] These stupa were a common site in one village I visited in Kandal province, even at the houses of people who had converted to Christianity.

Once dead, a person is reborn in one of the six realms of existence within Buddhist cosmology (Harris 2008). Funerary rites help ease this transition, however, in Theravada Buddhism, the corpse is not needed for these to occur. Once reborn, the spirit is no longer attached to the corpse, and many interviewees told me the skeleton thus becomes "like wood". This enables their transformation into symbolic artefacts, for both the lay population and the government. The state uses this in reinforcing particular narratives of the regime and its demise. For many lay people, the remains are symbolic of those they lost: sometimes individually, sometimes en masse. Etcheson (2005a) reports one memorial containing only long bones, because families of the missing were allowed to claim one skull each, symbolic representatives of their loved ones. One of my informants had taken a termite-mound from the last known location of her father for the same purpose. Although it did not contain any skeletal remains, the spirit of her father had told her

[10]Sometimes these relics are kept within wooden spirit houses at the front of the homestead rather than concrete stupa.

Fig. 27.2 A communal stupa containing human remains from the Khmer Rouge and urns of unknown dead and those whose family cannot afford individual stupa. Photograph by Caroline Bennett

in a dream that this was the place of his death, and so to my participant it provided a metaphysical connection to his remains.

The Buddhist pagoda is often viewed as the appropriate place for remains because monks are viewed as the ones who can control the dead (Chouléan 1988). Across Cambodia, therefore, most pagodas have numerous *chetěy* within their walls. In addition to those holding the remains of one individual, most pagoda also house at least one communal stupa, where urns containing cremated remains of those whose family members are unknown, or who are too poor to be able to afford individual *chetěy*, are housed. These communal stupa allow the dead to be given due care and attention, and provide a place for people to give offerings during annual ritual ceremonies that attend to the dead: the fifteen day *Pchum Benh* festival in September/October, Khmer New Year, and, for Chinese or Chinese-Khmer people, *Cheng-Meng*, the grave-sweeping ceremony usually held in April.[11]

In most of the locations I visited, the human remains from the Khmer Rouge were housed in such communal stupa, often alongside urns holding portions of remains or relics of the poor or unknown (Fig. 27.2). Their remains, therefore, rather than being neglected or displayed in culturally inappropriate ways, are, in fact, being cared for through their collation at these sites. A monk I interviewed

[11]Not all those who lost relatives visit pagoda with remains: some visit their closest pagoda and by giving offerings to the monks, provide offerings to the dead by simply stating their names.

likened it to caring for ones parents, commenting that "these bones are kept [...] because they do not have any relatives, so they put them all in one place so that other people who could not find their relatives will celebrate *baŋ-skoul* [ceremonies for the dead] and pass the merit to those dead people". Another interviewee told me that because they are not able to distinguish one set of remains from another, nor whose dead belongs to who, they could not cremate the remains, and it was better, therefore, to house and care for them together.

27.6 Political Attention to the Remains

While the housing of remains in a Buddhist pagoda provides appropriate care for those who died during the Khmer Rouge, this is not to say that there is no political motivation to the retention of human remains in Cambodia. While collecting them together provides a place for the dead, and for the living to visit and give offerings, they also allow locales to create political narratives of the Khmer Rouge regime. As Winter (2009) notes, memorials present nationally specific renderings of often-contested histories ("rehearsed memories" as she labels them), even when they simultaneously have useful commemorative functions for the general population. This is particularly the case when anonymous human remains are included. Displaying the remains as one mass allows a unified story to be presented, while obscuring the complex realities of the situation, including, in Cambodia, the deaths of the DK regime and the political circumstances surrounding their occurrence as well as their subsequent rendering in public history.[12]

In the 2000s there was some debate between the former King, Norodom Sihanouk, and the current Prime Minister, Hun Sen, about the preservation of remains. Sihanouk called for their cremation, while Hun Sen supported their preservation, claiming the need for material evidence of the horrors of the regime. To date, no official national cremation of remains has been conducted, and those exposed in the 1980s remain displayed across Cambodia. No further graves have been deliberately excavated, although occasionally remains are unearthed during road construction, or by farming.

Human remains are used to illustrate the violence of the regime. Even at national museum-memorials such as Tuol Sleng and Choeung Ek, the emphasis is on the atrocities of the Khmer Rouge, providing little or no information about the provenance of the remains, the geo-political and historical circumstances leading to the regime and its maintenance, and the reality of its violence, which was at the hands of hundreds of individuals not just the few "evil" perpetrators being tried by the contemporary courts.

---

[12]Guyer (2009) gives a good discussion of this in relation to the Rwandan genocide.

27.7 Mapping the Graves and Analysing Remains

A final consideration should be made to attempts to collate data on the mass graves and the human remains within them. Between 1995 and 2005, mass graves from the Khmer Rouge were mapped by the Documentation Center of Cambodia, supported by Yale University's Cambodian Genocide Project (DC-Cam 2005; Etcheson 2005b; Yale University 2018). The issues with the data from this project have been addressed in previous publications (Vickery 1984; Kiernan 2003; Tyner 2016). A brief summary suffices here to indicate that a consideration of ethics related to human remains includes data collection methods and the stories they can tell.

The mapping project considered only graves created by direct violence (Etcheson 2014, pers. comm.). It did not include graves close to hospitals, those created before or after the regime (1975–1979),[13] and 47 of the 171 districts of Cambodia were not investigated.[14] Whilst being researchers all trained for this project, those collecting data were not experts in archaeology or osteology, no test trenches were dug to confirm the presence of remains, and witness testimony, sometimes recorded decades after the events, was often the sole evidence.[15] They also assumed all bodies within the graves were executed, providing simple narratives of the violence of the regime. The mapping project thus reduces the violence of the regime to a specific timeframe in keeping with the political narrative of the Khmer Rouge, and by only considering graves containing victims of direct violence, the overall contextualisation of its brutality is diminished. The forensic value of these data is thus debatable, although this project does provide the only comprehensive record of the graves across Cambodia to date and is a useful starting point for further research (DC-Cam 2005).

While the location of the mass graves was subject to a country-wide survey, projects analysing the human remains have been sporadic and mostly small scale. In the 1980s, a group of Vietnamese scientists undertook basic analysis of the skulls at Choeung Ek, categorising them into the sex and age categories that ordered their display for many years (Fawthrop and Jarvis 2004). Several skulls from Tuol Sleng prison were also examined and were displayed as part of the museum's exhibition, as was a map of Cambodia made from human skulls (this was dismantled in 2002). In the 2000s, DC-Cam undertook surveying of different sites to assess their suitability for forensic investigation; only six of 53 investigated were assessed as

[13]The exception being M-13 in Kampong Speu, arguably because this could be directly linked to Duch, the first person to be tried in the Extraordinary Chambers in the Courts of Cambodia (ECCC).

[14]There are various reasons for this, including short time-frames for research trips, high levels of malaria in some areas, and, especially at the beginning of the project, the Khmer Rouge still functioning and being dangerous in some areas.

[15]The detailed records of this research are kept at the Documentation Center of Cambodia (DC-Cam). Shortened versions of records for each site can be accessed on the DC-Cam database, which also contains reports on the project (DC-Cam 2005). Etcheson (2005b), one of the founding researchers on the project, has also written extensively about the project (see also Klinkner 2008).

suitable (Klinkner 2008). In 2006, a report was released on trauma to 85 crania from Choeung Ek (Klinkner 2008). Between 2012 and 2015 Khmer osteologists re-examined remains at Choeung Ek as part of a project to analyse and preserve the remains and, at the same time, Julie Fleischmann, a forensic anthropologist from the USA, conducted skeletal analysis of over 500 skulls from the site as part of her Ph. D. research (Fleischman 2016). In 2016, Khmer osteologists assessed remains at Kraing Ta Chan in Takeo province (Fleischman 2016). Other small-scale projects are listed in Fleischmann's article. The aim of these investigations is to provide additional data on the violence conducted by the Khmer Rouge, and certainly they add to the body of knowledge about the regime. The lack of known, provable, provenance in many locations, however, means they are unlikely to be used in a criminal trial against the Khmer Rouge leaders, which rely, instead, on historical documentation and witness testimony. In addition, the concentration of analyses at the locales related to state memory narratives—Tuol Sleng, Choeung Ek, and Kraing Ta Chan—potentially adds a political dimension to these analyses, particularly given the current Prime Minister's use of the regime, its graves, and the remains, as central to his discourse of saving Cambodia from the regime.

Disputes over recent memorialisation efforts illustrate the complications of naming and recording. A new memorial at Tuol Sleng prison was the source of tension before its unveiling in 2015. Conceived by the Victims Support Section of the Extraordinary Chambers in the Courts of Cambodia (ECCC), and funded by German development agency Deutsche Gesellschaft für Internationale Zusammenarbeit (GIZ) GmbH, its design prompted much debate. The memorial lists the names of those processed at Tuol Sleng. Farino So, head of the Cham Oral History project, argued that naming the dead is a Western tradition, not in keeping with Khmer customs (McPherson 2014). In listing only those killed at Tuol Sleng, it renders invisible the many ethnic minorities and religious groups targeted by the regime in other locations. More salient, for many, is the fact that up to two-thirds of those processed at Tuol Sleng were Khmer Rouge cadre. Chum Mey, a survivor of the prison and president of the Victims of Democratic Kampuchea Association, was quoted as saying: "in no country in the world do they take the names of someone who kills and put it on a stupa" (McPherson 2014). When the memorial was finally unveiled, it reportedly did not even list all of those processed by Tuol Sleng, thus presenting an incomplete listing even in its final rendition. The inscription of names of the victims of Tuol Sleng, the only one in the country to name its victims, defines and confines who is publicly remembered and who is forgotten, obliterating others from historical record and, consequently, national (though not local and individual) memory.

27.8 Conclusion

A consideration of the ethics related to locating, excavating, and identifying human remains resulting from conflict and human rights abuses often rests on an assumption that there is a universal mode of dealing with these issues, where to unearth and individually identify the remains is 'for the greater good,' and a necessary part of justice, healing, and reconciliation. These concepts are conceived within an international justice system based on a Judeo-Christian ideology, where excavation of the dead, individual identification, and repatriation to nations and family are viewed as essential. As Booth (2001, 782) states: "not to bring the dead into the sanctuary of truth-memory-justice is to annihilate them a second time". Although international systems of justice and post-conflict management are increasing in influence and applicability (as can be seen in the transitional justice framework within which the ECCC sits), the provenance of these frameworks of justice, as well as archaeological and anthropological methods used to recover and identify human remains, arguably do not fit with the Buddhist cosmology that orders life and understanding in Cambodia.

Dealing with the dead is often essential for post-conflict management, particularly after genocide and human rights abuses. In Cambodia, a primarily Buddhist state, where the dead are socially salient beings who interject into the lives of the living and are the cause of much social action, care of the dead was an essential part of the re-establishment of security after the fall of the regime. This involved re-establishing reciprocal relations between the living and the dead, as well as dealing with the physical remains. The care of human remains has been devolved to the Buddhist sangha and the state, and their use in state-sponsored memorials is largely considered acceptable, at least by the many people I worked with across Cambodia.

Forensic/scientific attention to the remains has been sporadic, small-scale, and aimed towards specific ends. The lack of systematic analysis may indicate a lack of political will to identify the remains, however, that is a somewhat simplistic analysis. While it is arguably more useful for the remains to remain as a pile of anonymous dead (allowing their use in the manipulation of state narratives of the regime and its demise, by making them displays of large-scale horror and genocidal violence), Khmer cosmology does not attach utmost importance to skeletal remains, and the need to attach individual identification to remains is not consistent with Khmer tradition, where even individual *stupa* do not bear the name of the deceased. The mass display of de-personalised remains at once renders them open to political manipulation, and subject to state care: by collecting them together in communal pagodas, the dead without relatives and identity can be cared for, given offerings, and housed with others like them. The dead are remembered individually at annual rituals and in the home, not in state memorials. Memorials are almost always politically driven (see also Silika and Squires, this volume, for similar observations in Zimbabwe).

This chapter has discussed the treatment of remains from the Khmer Rouge regime, and the relevant socio-religious relationships to them, in order to consider human rights and ethics related to their location, investigation, identification, and preservation. The dead of the Khmer Rouge have always belonged to both the state and the people, and their remains have served different functions for both since the end of the regime. As the current ruling party, the Cambodian People's Party, continues to assert its dominance, often in relation to the Khmer Rouge regime, consideration of the human remains of the regime will no doubt remain complicated.

References

Becker, E. 1998. *When the War Was Over: Cambodia and the Khmer Rouge Revolution*. New York: Public Affairs.

Becker, E. 2013. *Overbooked: The Exploding Business of Travel and Tourism*. New York: Simon and Schuster.

Bennett, C. 2018. Living With the Dead in the Killing Fields of Cambodia. *Journal of Southeast Asian Studies* 49 (2): 184–203.

Booth, W.J. 2001. *Communities of Memory: On Witness, Identity, and Justice*. Ithaca: Cornell University Press.

Chandler, D. 1999. *Voices from S-21: Terror and History in Pol Pot's Secret Prison*. London: University of California Press Limited.

Chandler, D. 2008. Cambodia Deals With Its Past: Collective Memory, Demonisation and Induced Amnesia. *Totalitarian Movements and Political Religions* 9 (2–3): 355–369.

Chouléan, A. 1988. The Place of Animism with Popular Buddhism in Cambodia: The Example of the Monastery. *Asian Folklore Studies* 47 (1): 35–41.

Davis, E.W. 2009. *Treasures of the Buddha: Imagining Death and Life in Contemporary Cambodia*. Dissertation, University of Chicago.

Davis, E.W. 2015. *Deathpower: Buddhism's Ritual Imagination in Cambodia*. New York: Columbia University Press.

DC-Cam. 2005. *Mapping Project*. http://www.d.dccam.org/Projects/Maps/Mapping.htm. Accessed 25 May 2018.

Etcheson, C. 2005a. Khmer Rouge Prisons and Mass Graves. In *Encyclopedia of Genocide and Crimes Against Humanity, vol. 2*, ed. D.L. Shelton, 613–615. Detroit: Macmillan Reference USA.

Etcheson, C. 2005b. *After the Killing Fields: Lessons from the Cambodian Genocide*. Westport: Praeger.

Fawthrop, T., and H. Jarvis. 2004. *Getting Away with Genocide? Elusive Justice and the Khmer Rouge Tribunal*. London: Pluto Press.

Fein, H. 1997. Genocide by Attrition 1939–1993: The Warsaw Ghetto, Cambodia, and Sudan: Links Between Human Rights, Health, and Mass Death. *Health and Human Rights* 2 (2): 10–45.

Fleischman, J. 2016. Working with the Remains in Cambodia: Skeletal Analysis and Human Rights after Atrocity. *Genocide Studies and Prevention: An International Journal* 10 (2): 121–130.

Guillou, A.Y. 2012a. An Alternative Memory of the Khmer Rouge Genocide: The Dead of the Mass Graves and the Land Guardian Spirits (*neak ta*). *Journal of Southeast Asia Studies* 20 (2): 207–225.

Guillou, A.Y. 2012b. The Living Archaeology of a Painful Heritage: The First and Second Life of the Khmer Rouge Mass Graves. In *"Archaeologizing" Heritage? Transcultural Entanglements Between Local Social Practices and Global Virtual Realities?* ed. M. Falser and M. Juneja, 263–274. Heidelberg, New York: Springer.

Guyer, S. 2009. Rwanda's Bones. *Bound.* 236 (2): 155–175.

Harris, I. 2008. *Cambodian Buddhism: History and Practice*. Honolulu: University of Hawai'i Press.

Heuveline, P. 2015. The Boundaries of Genocide: Quantifying the Uncertainty of the Death Toll During the Pol Pot Regime in Cambodia (1975–1979). *Population Studies* 69 (2): 201–218.

Hinton, A.L. 2006. We Can't Let the Khmer Rouge Escape. *The Washington Post*, 8 April.

Holt, J.C. 2012. Caring for the Dead Ritually in Cambodia. *Southeast Asian Studies* 1 (1): 3–75.

Hughes, R. 2005. Memory and Sovereignty in Post-1979 Cambodia: Choeung Ek and Local Genocide Memorials. In *Genocide in Cambodia and Rwanda: New Perspectives*, ed. S. Cook, 269–292. Piscataway: Transaction Publishers.

Kent, A. 2003. Recovery of the Collective Spirit: The Role of the Revival of Buddhism in Cambodia. Working Paper, Series No. 8, Legacy of War and Violence. Goteborg: Socialantropologiska Institutionen, Goteborg University.

Kiernan, B. 1996. *The Pol Pot Regime: Race, Power, and Genocide in Cambodia Under the Khmer Rouge Regime 1975–1979*. New Haven: Yale University Press.

Kiernan, B. 2003. The Demography of Genocide in Southeast Asia: The Death Tolls in Cambodia, 1975–79, and East Timor, 1975–80. *Critical Asian Studies* 35 (4): 585–597.

Kiernan, B. 2004. *How Pol Pot Came to Power*. London: Yale University Press.

Klinkner, M. 2008. Forensic Science for Cambodian Justice. *International Journal of Transitional Justice* 2: 227–243.

LeVine, P. 2010. *Love and Dread in Cambodia: Weddings, Births and Ritual Harm Under the Khmer Rouge*. Singapore: National University of Singapore Press.

Locard, H. 2004. *Pol Pot's Little Red Book: The Sayings of Angkar*. Chiang Mai: Silkworm Books.

Locard, H., and S. Moeng. 1993. *Prisonnier de L'Angkar*. Paris: Fayard.

Marston, J. 2006. Death, Memory and Building: The Non-Cremation of a Cambodian Monk. *Journal of Southeast Asian Studies* 37 (3): 491–505.

McPherson, P. 2014. Memorial Plan Prompts Debate About Victims and Perpetrators of Genocide. *Phnom Penh Post*. 9 May. https://www.phnompenhpost.com/7days/memorial-plan-prompts-debate-about-victims-and-perpetrators-genocide. Accessed 25 May 2018.

Renshaw, L. 2011. *Exhuming Loss: Memory, Materiality and Mass Graves of the Spanish Civil War*. Walnut Creek: Left Coast Press Inc.

Royal Government of Cambodia. 2001. *Circular Concerning Preservation of Remains of the Victims of the Genocide Committed During the Regime of Democratic Kampuchea (1975–1978), and Preparation of Anlong Veng to Become a Region for Historical Tourism—Unofficial Translation*. Phnom Penh: ECCC.

Schanberg, S. 1985. *The Death and Life of Dith Pran*. London: Penguin.

Sharp, B. 2008. Counting Hell. *Mekong*. 9 January. http://www.mekong.net/cambodia/deaths.htm. Accessed 25 May 2018.

Tyner, J. 2016. *Landscape, Memory, and Post-Violence in Cambodia*. London: Rowman and Littlefield.

Vickery, M. 1984. *Cambodia 1975–1982*. Boston: South End Press.

Wagner, S. 2008. *To Know Where He Lies: DNA Technology and the Search for Srebrenica's Missing*. Berkeley: University of California Press.

Winter, C. 2009. Tourism, Social Memory and the Great War. *Annals of Tourism Research* 36 (4): 607–626.

Yale University. 2018. *Cambodian Genocide Program.* https://gsp.yale.edu/case-studies/cambodian-genocide-program. Accessed 25 May 2018.

Yathay, P. 1988. *Stay Alive, My Son.* New York: Touchstone Books.

Zucker, E. 2013. *Forest of Struggle: Moralities of Remembrance in Upland Cambodia*. Honolulu: University of Hawai'i Press.

Chapter 28
Ethical Issues of Working with Human Remains in Zimbabwe

Keith Silika and Kirsty Squires

Abstract Four key conflicts have taken place in Zimbabwe over the past 50 years. These events have resulted in the deaths of thousands of people and have consequently led to ongoing tensions between the state, victims, and community groups. Moreover, the situation is complicated further due to the politicisation of human remains, the time elapsed since the atrocities took place, and the interment of human remains from different conflicts in the same location. In the past, unorthodox means of recovering and analysing human remains (including the use of spirit mediums) to identify the dead have been widely employed in Zimbabwe. The lack of legislation and government involvement in these matters has led to unethical practices, which has, in turn, had a profound impact on local communities. However, it is hoped that the recent implementation of the National Peace and Reconciliation Act (2018) will not only lead to the formation of a commission with the aim of investigating these atrocities, but will also lead to the development of subsidiary legislation that will address the ethics of recovering and identifying victims of conflict. The following chapter will explore ethical issues of historical exhumations alongside recommendations for future best practice in Zimbabwe.

28.1 Introduction: A History of Violence in Zimbabwe

Zimbabwe is a former British colony located in Southern Africa that gained its independence in 1980. Robert Mugabe ruled Zimbabwe from the year of independence until his forced resignation by a coup in 2017. In the last 50 years the country has experienced various democides that have resulted in the death of over 50,000 people (Sachikonye 2011; Mukonori 2012). The conflicts during this period include: the Liberation War (1966–1979), the Matabeleland democides (1982–1987), political violence in every election cycle since 1980, and conflicts over blood diamonds (2006-present day).

K. Silika (✉) · K. Squires
Staffordshire University, Science Centre, Leek Road, Stoke-on-Trent ST4 2DF, UK
e-mail: keith.silika@research.staffs.ac.uk

K. Squires et al. (eds.), *Ethical Approaches to Human Remains*,
https://doi.org/10.1007/978-3-030-32926-6_28

The first conflict to take place was the Liberation War, which was fought by two-armed guerilla armies, namely the Zimbabwe African National Liberation Army (ZANLA) and the Zimbabwe Peoples Liberation Army (ZIPRA), against the Rhodesian Forces (RF) (Bhebe and Ranger 1995; Alexander et al. 2000). ZANLA was the military wing of the Zimbabwe African National Union—Patriotic Front (ZANU-PF) and ZIPRA was the armed wing for Zimbabwe African People's Union (ZAPU). This war resulted in over 25,000 people losing their lives, not only within Zimbabwe, but also in neighbouring countries such as Mozambique and Zambia. Human remains pertaining to the Liberation War were buried in mass graves in those countries as well as in Zimbabwe (Bhebe and Ranger 1995; Alexander et al. 2000).

The second conflict occurred after independence from 1982 to 1987. There was a period of internal strife in the Matabeleland provinces, which resulted in the deaths of over 20,000 individuals, mostly from the Matabeleland and Midland provinces (Catholic Commission for Justice and Peace in Zimbabwe (CCJP) 2007; Coltart 2016). This conflict was fueled by several factors, including the one-party state agenda favoured by Robert Mugabe at the time of independence in 1980, South African destabilisation processes, dissident activity, and poor army integration programme (CCJP 2007; Doran 2017). The main perpetrators of this democide were a Shona speaking North Korean trained army, answerable only to President Mugabe, called the Fifth Brigade. This period is also known by the lexicon *Gukurahundi*, a Shona word meaning the early rain that washes away the dry season chaff (Werbner 1991). There is still an ongoing debate to frame the killings in the Matabeleland provinces in the context of genocide, a term formulated by Lemkin (1944). In his famous and formational text, Lemkin (1944) derived the term from two words, genos (race/people) and cide (kill), and defined "genocide" as any deliberate act committed by a State or associated apparatus to destroy a national and ethnic group. The Second Article of the Convention on the Prevention and Punishment of Genocide (United Nations 1948) adds other acts to the definition of "genocide", such as causing serious bodily or mental harm, imposing measures to prevent births, and the transfer of children to another group. In Zimbabwean contexts, this is primarily concerned with the victims (mostly Ndebele speaking) and perpetrators, namely the Shona speaking Fifth Brigade (Hill 2011; Jones 2016). During these massacres, there was also a sustained campaign of rape of Ndebele speaking women, which was viewed as an attempt to *Shonalise* the Ndebele speaking people (Ndlovu-Gatsheni 2003). Previous longitudinal studies, which involved speaking to surviving victims, have revealed that the massacres are viewed within the context of genocide (Ndebele 2007; Vambe 2012). In addition, international criminal tribunals have progressively shifted from an objective approach when defining genocide to a subjective one (Verdirame 2000; Deng 2011). Human remains belonging to the *Gukurahundi* are buried mostly in the Matabeleland provinces and can be found at former detention centres (e.g. Bhalagwe), mineshafts (e.g. the Antelope Mine), caves (e.g. Matobo), and individual clandestine burials (e.g. in Ziga) (CCJP 2007; Eppel 2015; Manayiti 2016). The demography of those killed during this era is varied and includes adolescents, women, and sometimes children, however the majority are young men aged between 16 and 40 years old whom the Fifth Brigade accused to be dissidents.

Since 1980, every election cycle has been marred by political violence. The violent acts are principally directed at the opposition parties, particularly the Movement for Democratic Change (MDC). The party claims that over 2000 of its supporters have been killed since its formation in 1999 (Sachikonye 2011; Movement for Democratic Change 2017). The perpetrators of the aforementioned acts primarily belong to the ruling party, ZANU-PF youth's militia, former war veterans, Central Intelligence Organisation (CIO), and in some cases, the Police (Reeler 2009). Victims of such violence were shot, thrown in rivers, burnt in huts and, in some instances, were stabbed to death (Reeler 2009). People killed within each election cycle have been found dumped near detention centres, which were set up by the militia groups, and in mineshafts. Some of these victims have been located and reburied by relatives whilst others have still not been accounted for (Human Rights Watch 2011; Coltart 2016).

In 2006, alluvial diamonds were discovered in the Marange fields in eastern Zimbabwe. The Marange area was initially invaded by illegal mining syndicates, unemployed youths, corrupt politicians, and connected securiocrats. These groups were subsequently driven off by a state planned operation in 2008, using army police and the CIO under the operation codenamed *Hakudzokwi* (Human Rights Watch 2009; Global Witness 2017). This operation, which is still ongoing at the time of writing, has led to over 500 deaths. However, there is an enduring debate with regards to the exact number of people killed during this operation as the area is still under military control, and skirmishes between illegal panners and the police continue (Mashaya 2017). People killed in this conflict are buried in disused mine shafts, in the Marange mining fields, mass graves at nearby cemeteries, former detention centres (such as Bhalagwe), cattle dip tanks, burnt huts, abandoned commercial farms, and near, or in, schools and hospitals (Human Rights Watch 2009).

This chapter will provide an overview of the ethical challenges associated with historical exhumations of human remains in Zimbabwe, as well as casting an eye on future disinterments. The chapter will initially outline the various democides that have occurred in the country over the last 50 years. Subsequently, there will be a discussion around the typology of mass graves in Zimbabwe, cultural approaches to burial, followed by a discussion around the partisan nature of groups that exhume human remains, and surviving victim involvement. Next, forensic anthropological and archaeological approaches to exhumations, ethical challenges around legislation, culture, politicisation of human remains, and memorialisation will be addressed. These difficulties make a discussion on ethics and mass grave exhumation in Zimbabwe an engaging vantage point to learn and compare experiences within the context of this book. The conclusion will outline holistic approaches that could be used to overcome the ethical challenges discussed in this chapter.

28.2 The Exhumations

28.2.1 Exhumations by the Fallen Heroes Trust

The presence of mass graves throughout Zimbabwe has consequently led to sporadic exhumations, which have taken place since 1980 (Gumbo 1995; Kriger 1995). Exhumations of Liberation War mass burials are conducted mainly by the Fallen Heroes Trust (FHT), who occasionally consult the National Museum and Monuments of Zimbabwe (NMMZ). On the other hand, Gukurahundi remains have been excavated by the Amani Trust (AT), Argentine Forensic Anthropology Team (EAAF), and private family members (Eppel 2015; Manayiti 2016). The FHT are a group of ex-combatants from the Liberation War, mixed with spirit mediums (see Sect. 28.4 of this chapter for further details), who carry out exhumations of remains from this conflict (The Herald 2013). This is the result of promises they made to fellow guerillas during the war, that is, to afford them a respectable burial. This group has carried out exhumations both within Zimbabwe and neighbouring countries, such as Mozambique and Zambia (Nhambura 2013a; Mapepa 2015). The organisational structure and training of this group, with regards to mass graves and exhumations, is not known. The opposition, particularly the Movement of Democratic Change, believes the FHT to be aligned to the ruling ZANU-PF party (Amnesty International 2011; Mudzungairi 2011). Up to the present day, the FHT are believed to have exhumed over 6000 human remains, some of which have been returned to families whilst others have been reburied in provincial heroes acres around the country (Nhambura 2013b). The Government or the NMMZ are not always informed when these exhumations take place (Fontein 2014). This raises questions of legality, ethics, and responsible authority, which will be discussed later in this chapter. It is worth noting that no legal action has been taken against this group with regards to the exhumation and reburial of human remains.

The methodology employed in the identification of human remains by the FHT or relatives of deceased individuals often involves the use of ‘spirit mediums’. Here, spirit mediums attending the scene become possessed by the ‘spirit’ of the deceased person. This can range from a group of them being in a trance to one who is ‘senior’ uttering some words. The medium goes into a trance and provides a narrative of the circumstances of the individuals’ death and identity (Gumbo 1995; Nhambura 2013b). Often the medium shouts out the *nom de guerre* of a deceased Liberation War hero, and assigns a particular assemblage to that individual (Cox 2016). Liberation War fighters often took up a nom de guerre for security and motivational purposes (Pfukwa 2008). Spirit mediums have been used in Rhodesia and Zimbabwe since the first Shona and Ndebele uprisings (1894–1897) against colonial rule, and are generally believed to be able to foretell the truth, cast away spells, and heal the sick (Lan 1985; Fontein 2004). However, no secondary scientific aids are employed to ascertain the validity of the claims of spirit mediums when identifying human remains (Amnesty International 2011). Hence there has been a call by both local and international organisations for such methods to be examined closely (Benyera 2014). Whilst it is understood that their use is entrenched in Zimbabwean society, this method is ambiguous, as techniques grounded in the hard sciences are needed (Benyera 2014).

In 2011, the FHT exhumed 600 human remains at the William Mine. The preservational state of these remains varied significantly as some were still wet with flesh and bodily fluids whilst others were mummified (Smith 2011). Spirit mediums would call out the name of a deceased individual and the FHT would label the remains with that name without any other form of verification (Smith 2011). Moreover, spirit medium methods fail to meet the minimum standards in the identification of human remains outlined by the United Nations (2016). This further highlights the need for standardised scientific techniques in the recovery and identification process of human remains in Zimbabwe. Indeed, there are currently no official published or accessible archaeological or anthropological reports from work conducted in Zimbabwe by the FHT. It is of utmost importance that such investigations are transparent, and those involved are accountable for any conclusions drawn, as the resultant documents of the missing and presumed dead can be reconciled with biological evidence. This point will be revisited throughout this chapter.

28.2.2 Exhumations by the Argentine Forensic Anthropology Team and the Amani Trust

The Amani Trust is a non-governmental organisation based in Bulawayo and works with victims of the Matabeleland democides and other human rights abuses in Zimbabwe (Eppel and Raftopoulos 2010). In 1999, the organisation invited the Equipo Argentino de Antropología Forense (EAAF, the Argentine Forensic Anthropology Team) to investigate these atrocities, and to train local volunteers in archaeological and anthropological methodologies (EAAF 1999). The local volunteers consisted of church leaders, students, and individuals affiliated with human rights organisations. The Amani Trust requested assistance from the EAAF due to their experience in the exhumation of mass graves in South America, Africa, and Europe. The group comprised of both archaeologists and anthropologists. The EAAF conducted three visits in Zimbabwe in 1999, 2000, and 2001 (EAAF 1999, 2000, 2001). This group worked on 15 sites and exhumed around 20 human remains before the Amani Trust was banned and declared an illegal organisation by the government (EAAF 2001; Eppel and Raftopolus 2010). The exhumations were hampered by fear, politics, time, and legality. The exhumations followed international standards with regards to exhumation protocols, which involved an on-site assessment, systematic exhumation, and anthropological examination of human remains.

One of the key investigations conducted by the EAAF took place from July 1999 to August 1999. The EAAF was asked by the Amani Trust to investigate five sites in Matabeleland South where they suspected victims of the Gukurahundi were

Table 28.1 Exhumations by the Equipo Argentino de Antropología Forense (1999)

Site number	Location	Contents (based on witness testimony and EAAF 1999 report)	Findings
Site 1	Mapane Primary School	One individual	Disarticulated remains of one person found at depths of 95 cm and 115 cm
Site 2	Simbumbumbu	Two individuals	Authorisation of excavation was later declined
Site 3	North of Site 2	One individual	No human remains found
Site 4	Sitczi	Five or six individuals	Commingled remains of six people, which had also been burnt, were recovered
Site 5	Magumbo cattle dip tank	Two individuals	Remains of two people with handcuffs recovered

buried (Table 28.1). The information pertaining to these sites was collected from witness testimony gathered by the Amani Trust prior to the arrival of EAAF personnel. Before archaeological work commenced, the EAAF asked the local archbishop to perform religious rites on the locations at the request of the community (EAAF 1999). The second stage of this investigation involved geoprospection, photography, and sketching of each site. The next phase involved the exhumation of human remains, using the pedestal excavation method (Tuller and Durić 2005). The soil from all sites was sieved, and all human remains were labelled appropriately and stored for further anthropological examination. Finally, anthropological analysis was conducted using standardised methods as a means of estimating the minimum number of individuals from each site, and the construction of biological profiles of the deceased. DNA extraction was not performed due to the preservation of the remains, some of which had been burnt (EAAF 1999). The human remains from the sites investigated were later buried at different locations in mass funerals held by local communities.

28.2.3 Exhumations by Family Members

In addition to the exhumation of human remains carried out by the organisations mentioned in this chapter, some families conduct investigations and exhumations without external consultation for the purpose of closure. Some exhumations have been reported in the media whilst others have been carried out secretly. The media widely reported on the exhumation of Nehemiah Nkala's remains (Southern Eye 2014). Nkala was allegedly murdered by the Fifth Brigade and buried in a shallow grave near Filabusi. He was believed to be a dissident. His son applied to have the remains exhumed and reburied in Lupanda. The local chief initially refused the reburial, but this decision was later withdrawn (Southern Eye 2014). Another exhumation that was widely reported in the media relates to the reburial of Melusi Job Mlevu, who was the father of the former Minster of Higher Education, Professor Jonathan Moyo (Manayiti 2016). Mlevu was allegedly killed by the Fifth Brigade in Kapanyana in 1982 because he was a member of the ZAPU party. The family applied to exhume and rebury his remains in their village in 2016. The local district administrator granted permission. However, it is questionable how the administrator had authority to do so as this is not covered in legislation. Questions put before Professor Moyo to clarify the dates and time of his father's murder were not answered. At the time of writing, there was no available information regarding the forensic archaeological methods and identification processes involved in these exhumations. The primary aims of the exhumations were to identify the deceased, provide a dignified burial, and offer some closure for family members. However, each of these elements are subject to debate as discussed in the conclusion of this chapter.

28.2.4 *Exhumation and Reburial for Humanitarian Reasons*

Some exhumations have taken place for practical reasons and as a result of accidental discoveries, for example, instances whereby mass graves have collapsed in a children's playground (e.g. at St. Paul's Mission, Lupane), remains have washed up on river banks (e.g. Bhode River near Kezi) (Smith 2011; Tshuma 2017), or occasions where remains have been exposed due to soil erosion (Fontein 2014; Sithole 2014). This has recently led to one group, Ibhetshu Likazulu, exploring the possibility of touring sites in Matabeleland and recording these remains (Ndlovu 2017a). Many of the mass graves in Zimbabwe are known by local people. However, some communities do not want to exhume or handle remains due to fears of ancestral spirits and state reprisals (Eppel 2014).

28.2.5 *The William Mine Exhumation*

The most contentious exhumation took place in March 2011 at William Mine (Mount Darwin, Mashonaland Central province) and resulted in the recovery of over 600 human remains. The exact number of remains is unknown due to the methodology used during the exhumation and identification processes. Furthermore, some remains were not removed from the mineshafts. These remains were already known to exist by the local community as the mineshafts had been left open since production ceased. The same shafts had also been used to dump human remains from the Liberation War (1966–1979) (Fontein 2014). A miner who was looking for gold stumbled upon these remains in 2008 (Benyera 2014). This exhumation was conducted by the FHT without the authority of any other government agency. The human remains were contained in several disused mineshafts, which had been left open and were unsecure. The exhumation involved crudely removing remains from shafts, without forensic archaeological approaches, such as systematic excavation, labelling, photography, appropriate packaging, and scientific identification (Smith 2011; Fontein 2014). This haphazard approach resulted in one group, the ZIPRA Trust, applying to the courts to stop the exhumation (ZIPRA v. FHT Judgement 2011). This was a problematic case as different groups (i.e. the FHT, ZIPRA, and the MDC) claimed ownership of the remains solely based on their condition (e.g. the presence of bodily fluids/blood), location (e.g. open mine shafts), and the timeframes (1966–2011) they were assigned.

The FHT claimed that the remains related to the Liberation era, over 30 years previously, yet some anthropological features such as the presence of soft tissue on some of the bodies made this claim doubtful (Amnesty International 2011; Benyera 2014). It is likely that the human remains belonged to all groups since the mineshafts had been left open since the Liberation War. There is no official report on how these remains were recovered and identified, nor is there any indication whether any archaeologists and/or anthropologists were present during the exhumation process. The Minister of Empowerment at the time, Saviour Kasukuwere, stated that no forensic analysis was to be performed, but instead local burial religious rites were to be implemented (Benyera 2014). Despite the court order preventing further interference of this site, many of the recovered remains were (and still are, at the time of writing) displayed at the National Heroes Acre in Harare (Amnesty International 2011; Charamba 2015). With assistance from the government, other remains were buried near the site in August 2011 but there is currently no associated monument at this site (Machenyuka 2011).

28.3 Cultural Approaches to Burial

Before delving into the ethical challenges of handling human remains, it is imperative to give an overview of local funerary customs. Within Zimbabwean society, there are several cultural practices that must be adhered to following the death of an individual. According to local dominant Shona and Ndebele practices, when an adult passes away, the mourning period lasts for one to three days before the deceased is buried in a grave, which is normally six feet deep (Mwandayi 2011). The number of mourning days is dependent on the available funds needed to buy a casket, food for mourners, availability of relatives, or outstanding family cultural interests. The soul of the individual is deemed to continue into the afterlife as a spiritual entity (Muchemwa 2002). Following burial of the deceased, rituals such as purification, bringing back the spirit, inheritance, and appeasement may take place, though this is dependent on specific tribe or family traditions (Muchemwa 2002). Mourning is complete once a ceremony, called '*kurova guva*' (in Shona) or '*umbuyiso*' (in Ndebele), has taken place (Dengu-Zvogbo 1996). The timing of this ceremony varies. It may take a couple of weeks after the deceased has been buried or several years following the event. Deceased individuals are normally buried either at the family kraal or in a local cemetery. This is dictated by the wishes of the deceased or family practices. Failure to perform certain practices or rituals is believed to bring bad luck to the family in the form of failure in business, marriage, or child conception (Eppel and Raftopoulos 2010; Muchemwa 2010). This particular cultural practice has not been performed for individuals in some mass graves as the location of certain individuals is unknown or access to a site has been denied (e.g. at William Mine, Mount Darwin). Therefore, this is causing surviving victims to suffer from continuous loss, which is fuelling feelings of disenchantment, oppression, and neglect by the authorities.

28.4 Partisan Nature of Groups Exhuming Human Remains and Victim Participation

The partisan nature of the personnel involved in the exhumation of human remains, particularly the FHT, makes the process problematic in terms of objectivity and integrity, although their work has brought closure to some relatives and has facilitated the dignified reburial of exhumed remains. The conduct of personnel involved in processing and identifying human remains should not be above reproach; they should be trained, there should be no conflicts in interest in investigations, and their primary duty should be to the law (College of Policing 2017; Dutelle 2017). This is important as it will guarantee the integrity of the evidence and subsequent judicial processes (Klinkner 2008). The first Director of the Trust, George Rutanhire, who passed away in 2017, was a member of the ZANU-PF hierarchy and was afforded national hero status (Share 2017). The FHT only exhumed remains pertaining to the Liberation War, yet those remains are, in some instances, in the same location or in close proximity to other mass burials (Fontein 2014; Chipangura 2015). In essence, the FHT lack political autonomy in mass grave investigation espoused by Rosenblatt (2015). In the William Mine exhumation investigation in March 2011, certain health and safety protocols were not followed, that is, participants did not wear adequate personal protective equipment. It is known that sulphuric acid was poured on some of the human remains shortly after victims were killed as a means of accelerating decomposition and covering up atrocities from the Liberation War (Bird 2014; Cilliers 2015). This consequently puts the health of individuals exhuming the remains at risk. Despite the court order requesting a halt to proceedings, some human remains were exhumed and buried in a nearby mass grave, while others are exhibited at the National Heroes Acre (Charamba 2015).

Victim participation and cooperation surrounding human remains recovery and reburial is, as previously mentioned, heavily partisan. Zimbabwe has over 10 victim association groups from various atrocities but they are never consulted on exhumations. These groups include: Ibhetshu Likazulu, Gukurahundi Genocide Survivors for Justice, Zimbabwe Victims of Organized Violence Trust, Post-Independence Survivors' Trust, and Chiadzwa Community Development Trust. Others are housed within respective political parties. During investigations by the EAAF from July 1999 to August 1999, there was some victim participation in the exhumation exercise, yet this was not seen in the William Mine case. This is not only a violation of the rights of the living but also of the deceased (Smolensky 2009; Rosenblatt 2015). Recently, victims of violence and relatives of the missing/deceased were not consulted when the government announced that they would be issuing 'death certificates' to victims of Gukurahundi (Nkala 2017). For several reasons, various victim groups roundly condemned this. Firstly, the government had refused to release the enquiry into the Matabeleland massacres, 30 years after concluding their investigation (CCJP 2007). Furthermore, there had been no additional enquiries into the matter, including compensation or prosecution. Instead, Robert Mugabe issued a blanket amnesty on all individuals involved in the massacres (CCJP 2007) and issued amnesties after every cycle of political violence (Magaisa 2016). In essence, the commission of the offences by the government, the issuing of amnesty to perpetrators, suppression of commemorations, and issuing of death certificates, is tantamount to covering up the massacres. It is therefore unethical for such processes to take place without full investigation using appropriate anthropological and archaeological methods.

28.5 Forensic Anthropological and Archaeological Approaches

One of the most palpable ethical challenges in Zimbabwe is the deficiency of forensic archaeological and anthropological methods used in the detection, recovery, and identification of human remains. From the information available, exhumations conducted by the FHT at William Mine (Mount Darwin), Gutu, and Butchers Site did not implement suitable archaeological and anthropological methods in their work (Fontein 2014; Chipangura 2015; Eppel 2015). A primary issue encountered is the presence of human remains from different democides that have been deposited in the same location (Fontein 2014). This is particularly true for remains from the Mount Darwin mineshafts (see Sect. 28.2.5 for further details). This therefore calls for a multi-disciplinary forensic archaeological approach to exhumation. The lack of awareness around the ethical handling of human remains, from initial discovery through to analysis, is alarming given the number of human remains encountered as a result of the diverse conflicts that have taken place. In terms of exhumation, the approaches should follow archaeological standards, in terms of both non-invasive and invasive techniques, depending on the context (Hunter et al. 2013). The collection of witness accounts, archival searches, cartographic research, and photography would ideally form the basis of non-invasive investigation within such contexts (Hunter and Cox 2005). The adoption of more technical forms of non-invasive technology may also be used to detect clandestine burials, such as LiDAR (Ruffell et al. 2014) and geophysical survey (Pringle et al. 2012). Depending on the context, standard pedestal or stratigraphic excavation of sites should be carried out during the invasive phase of investigation (Tuller and Durić 2005). Exhumation of remains should be conducted by experienced personnel, as each site should be treated as a crime scene (Rosenblatt 2015). The approaches used by the EAAF were valid in forensic contexts, though there is no legislation that covers the authorisation to exhume human remains, and other groups that have requested to conduct exhumations have been denied by the authorities (Church and Civil Society Forum 2012; Katongomara 2017).[1] Additionally, the involvement of surviving victims is paramount to any forensic archaeological work as it validates these exercises and increases transparency (EAAF 1999; Blau and Ubelaker 2016). However, this was not the case at William Mine.

Once human remains are found, an archaeological approach to recovery should be adopted. Archaeothanatology (or Field Anthropology) involves detailed recording and analysis of human remains in-situ following a number of methods (e.g. Duday 2009). The application of archaeothanatology would be particularly useful in future investigations in Zimbabwe, especially sites that are multi-phased, as detailed recording using rectified photography, 3D documentation, illustration, and interpretation of evidence in-situ would facilitate more accurate phasing. This in turn, will lead to a more thorough recovery process and a greater chance of accurately identifying the dead. Given that human remains from the contexts under discussion date to the last few decades, remains are often found with surviving soft tissue and associated personal effects, such as clothing. In the first instance, investigators should be implementing basic, on site identification, through the use of Interpol's Disaster Victim Identification (DVI) forms (Interpol 2013). These forms would allow investigators to record the appearance of the body, unique identifying markers (such as scars), and clothing, which could be relayed back to the family and could aid in the identification process. Where remains are skeletonised, this poses a greater challenge to investigators. Here, the anthropologist should use appropriate, detailed skeletal recording forms. Standard osteological methods would be needed to estimate the minimum number of individuals and facilitate the construction of a biological profile (that is, the deceased's age-at-death, sex, stature, ancestry, and any unique identifying features such as pathological conditions or ante-mortem trauma) (Buikstra and Ubelaker 1994; Dirkmaat 2015). The application of standard anthropological methods and the use of osteological methods that have been developed in neighbouring countries to estimate stature and ancestry of deceased

[1]From information provided by the anonymous reviewer, it is understood that authorisation of exhumations conducted by the EAAF was granted by the Minister of Home Affairs, the Police Commissioner of Matabeleland South, the Provincial Medical Director, and the Gwanda Registrar General Office.

Fig. 28.1 The Fallen Heroes Trust believed the area of black humus depicted in this image represented burials at the Butchers Site in Rusape. Photograph courtesy of Njabulo Chipangura

individuals would ensure that issues relating to skeletal analysis would be eliminated. There are considerable issues with the work carried out by the FHT as they frequently misidentify and overestimate the number of human remains from exhumations, which can be attributed to political reasons (Chipangura 2015). In 2013, an exhumation was carried out at Butchers Site in Rusape by personnel from the NMMZ and the FHT. The latter organisation insisted on demarcating black humus as evidence of human remains without any anthropological evidence (Chipangura 2015) (Fig. 28.1). The application of forensic archaeological methods and anthropological techniques in the search, location, recovery, and identification process would make for a more professional, reliable, and ethical means of working with the dead. The presence of commingled remains from several sites, such as William Mine in Mount Darwin and Antelope Mine in Kezi, may require more advanced forms of analysis in the identification process, such as odontology, DNA, podiatry, and friction ridge skin analysis (Dupras et al. 2006).

28.6 Legislation

There is no legislation covering the handling of human remains in Zimbabwe. The legislation used by the NMMZ is the National Museum and Monuments Act (1972), which oversees the protection of archaeological monuments and predates 1890 (Eppel 2015). One of the aim's of this Act, specifically Section 2(b), is to care for monuments or buildings which are "known or believed to have been erected, constructed or used in Zimbabwe before the 1st January, 1890, but does not include an ancient working" (National Museum and Monuments Act 1972, Section 2(b)). Countries that have experienced conflict, which has consequently led to the loss of human life, need a comprehensive legislative framework in place that specifically addresses search, recovery, and identification protocols of deceased individuals (International Committee of the Red Cross 2015; Klinkner 2017). The implementation of such legislation in Zimbabwe should address the integrity of post-conflict processes, such as, ownership of human remains, accountability of atrocities, anthropological and archaeological procedures, and ethical approaches to investigations (Márquez-Grant and Fibiger 2013). This type of legislation has been successfully implemented elsewhere in the world. Following the fall of military juntas in Argentina and Chile, changes to pre-existing legislation have brought about legal liabilities to surviving offenders and restitution to victims (Amnesty International 1993). Under International Law, the Geneva Convention IV (1949) states that when an individual is deceased, they should, where possible, be buried in individual graves, which are marked and suitably maintained. Zimbabwe's neighbour, South Africa, which is still investigating the disappearance of over 2000 people who disappeared during apartheid (1948–1991), have introduced various pieces of legislation to cover the investigation, handling, and storage of human remains (Aronson 2011). The only piece of relevant legislation in Zimbabwe is the National Museum and Monuments Act (1972), which is inadequate in terms of scope, authority, issues associated with the missing, and mass graves (Eppel 2015). The lack of legislation in Zimbabwe makes the present and immediate future of exhuming remains void in law and ethics. Similarly, the new legislation signed into law, the National Peace and Reconciliation Act (2018), by President Munangagwa in January 2018 does not state any provision surrounding exhumation or reburial.

28.7 Politicisation of Human Remains

In Zimbabwe, and Southern Africa in general, human remains play a central role in shaping historical narratives, space, symbolism, and as a representative of the struggle from colonial rule (Muchemwa 2010; Eppel 2014). Politicisation is a process in which human remains are used to represent a certain historical narrative (Fontein 2010). Politicisation of human remains is not a new phenomenon and has occurred in other countries, such as Argentina and Chile (Robben 2010, 2014). In contemporary Zimbabwe, human remains are often used for political mileage and shaping ideologies (The Standard 2011; Fontein 2014). The emergence of the MDC in 1999 broke the hegemony that the ruling ZANU-PF had held in the country for two decades. Due to the support the party had garnered from white commercial farmers and its liberal policies, the party was often branded as puppets of the West (Sachikonye 2005; Mutsvairo 2016). When human remains were discovered in March 2011 at William Mine (Mount Darwin), state media and ZANU-PF aligned politicians went into overdrive, describing the remains as evidence of Rhodesian atrocities against local people (Fontein 2014). The local and only television broadcasting channel, the Zimbabwe Broadcasting Corporation (ZBC) made a special bulletin about the event. A selection of local community leaders and children were forced to attend the exhumation of the remains as they were being removed from the mineshafts (The Standard 2011). This coercion of people resulted in a well-attended event and acted as propaganda for the ZANU-PF against local opposition.

In 2014, Robert Mugabe delivered a speech during the Heroes Day celebration and initiated a campaign to return skulls allegedly being held by the National History Museum in London (England; Thorneycroft and Laing 2015). The skulls were taken as trophies during the first Shona and Ndebele uprisings of the late 1890s. The National History Museum admitted that they were in possession of the skulls and, at the time of writing this chapter, requested the Zimbabwe government to send their representatives to the museum so that the remains could be scientifically verified and repatriated back to Zimbabwe. What irked some of the victims of various atrocities at the time was the need to campaign for the return of remains that had been taken abroad in the past whilst ignoring the mass graves that are regularly discovered in the country.

On a similar line, the opposition is not immune from attempts to politicise human remains, as illustrated by the case of Christpower Maisiri, who was 12 years of age at the time of his death. Christpower was the son of a local aspiring councillor, Shepherd Maisiri, whose hut was set alight by suspected ZANU-PF supporters in February 2013, at the height of another violent election campaign (Chikukwa 2013). The crime scene pictures were used by the opposition (the MDC) at the time to highlight the atrocities being committed against their members (Nehanda Radio 2013). Since the matter was under investigation, and therefore sub judice, it brings into question ethical, cultural, and legal issues (Soderland and Lilley 2015). Was it ethical for the opposition to display the pictures of a deceased child whose investigation was still underway? Whilst it was important for the opposition to highlight the murder, this had to be balanced against the need for the investigation to be carried out expeditiously and with integrity to ensure the perpetrators were apprehended (Dutelle 2017). At the time of writing this chapter, the offenders of the crime, whilst known locally, have yet to be arrested (Nehanda Radio 2013). Politicisation of remains by both state and opposition is therefore not ethical as it affects the recovery of human remains and undoubtedly has an emotional impact on survivors and the kin of deceased individuals.

28.8 Memorialisation

Memorialisation of victims of the Liberation War is held annually on the 12th August at the National Heroes' Acre in Zimbabwe. The North Koreans built the monument in 1980 and, at the time of writing, 122 people are buried at the site (National Museum and Monuments 2017). In addition, each region has a provincial Heroes Acre where junior members of the Liberation War are buried (National Museum and Monuments 2017). What constitutes an individual to be declared a national or provincial hero is subject to debate (Ndlovu-Gatsheni and Willems 2009). The decision on a national level rests upon the President by the powers under the National Heroes Act (1984, Section 3) and, by extension, the ruling ZANU-PF politburo (Mpofu 2014). No individual deemed to be a member of the opposition has ever been buried at this acre. These selection criteria have been heavily criticised as it is seen as partisan and an attempt to reconstruct and redefine national concepts on the Liberation War narratives (Muchemwa 2010; Ndlovu-Gatsheni 2011). In contrast to the recognition and organisation that goes into memorialisation of victims of the Liberation War, events pertaining to other democides that have occurred, such as the Matabeleland massacres, political violence, and diamond deaths, are often curtailed or banned altogether (Mlotshwa 2016; Chiketo 2017).

28.9 Truth and Reconciliation

Most countries that have experienced internal and external conflicts have implemented mechanisms for memorialisation, truth, and reconciliation (Hayner 2001). Truth commissions are temporary state constituted bodies set up to investigate past human rights abuses, patterns of abuse, and are an important step in healing, accountability, ascertaining historical facts, and cohesion of various groups who have been affected by conflict in the past (Anthonissen and Blommaert 2007; Hirsch et al. 2012). These processes are yet to be fully established in Zimbabwe, almost four decades after independence. In 2018, the new President, Emerson Mnangagwa signed into law the National Peace and Reconciliation Act (2018), which facilitates the establishment of a National Peace and Reconciliation Commission. However, the National Peace and Reconciliation Bill failed to be ratified by the Zimbabwe parliament on two occasions due to political interests and contextual information, such as the atrocities covered by this Bill, the responsible authority, and powers of the minister (Heal Zimbabwe Trust 2016; Ndlovu 2017b). These provisions have been included in the new Act regardless of the aforementioned flaws. Some perpetrators of the atrocities are still members of parliament, and sit side by side with victims (New Zimbabwe 2017). Nonetheless, it is hoped that the implementation of a National Peace and Reconciliation Commission will lead to greater support for victims of these atrocities, and the enactment of sound scientific guidelines and standards that are to be followed upon the discovery, exhumation, and identification of human remains in Zimbabwe.

28.10 Conclusion

The aim of this chapter was to provide an overview of the ethical challenges associated with the exhumation and identification of human remains in Zimbabwe. From this chapter, it is clear that the situation in Zimbabwe is extremely complex, and investigators must take into account the survivors of past atrocities, plus a multitude of political, legal, ideological, and cultural factors when conducting mass grave investigations. Each of the ethical challenges, outlined in Table 28.2, need addressing by the government in future legislation. There is also an exigent need to initiate a missing person database and collect appropriate samples (i.e. DNA samples) from surviving kin. These will assist in the reconciliation and correlation of information about missing persons, while reference samples will facilitate in the positive identification of deceased individuals. Therefore, it is essential that there is

Table 28.2 Ethical dilemmas, issues, and recommendations regarding the treatment of human remains from conflicts in Zimbabwe

Dilemma	Issue	Recommendations
Acknowledgement of atrocities	Denial at State level	Public acknowledgment and apologies to the victims
Investigation of atrocities	Selective and not publicised. Chihambakwe Report on Gukurahundi has not been released 30 years on (CCJP 2007)	Investigations led by the Government and international agencies
Use of forensic archaeology and anthropology in exhumation	Members of the FHT are not trained. The Amani Trust are semi-trained but not allowed. Others are unknown	The implementation of a legal requirement for trained archaeologists and anthropologists to work on exhumations
Misidentification and overestimation	By the FHT	Legislation stating that only trained anthropologists analyse human remains
Politicisation	Mostly by the State and sometimes by opposition	International organisations should be involved during the exhumation process to ensure human remains are not politicised
Compensation	Only provided for Liberation War cadres; none for victims of the atrocities after 1980	Compensation given to all victims
Memorialisation	Only for victims of the Liberation War. Others are either banned or curtailed by the State	All victims should be memorialised
Issuing of 'death certificates'	By the State, in 2017 with no investigation	All suspicious deaths should be investigated
Victim participation	Only FHT. Other groups have been banned	All groups should be invited to assist in the search, recovery, and analysis of human remains
Enabling legislation	None that address exhumation or reburial	New legislation is needed that deals with the recovery and identification of victims involved in these conflicts
Cultural approaches to burial	Not observed for victims in mass graves, particularly in the Matabeleland provinces	All remains should be exhumed and offered an appropriate burial in line with local customs

open dialogue between politicians, victim groups, and scientists. A key issue in Zimbabwe is the lack of holistic approaches used when working with contemporary human remains. It may thus be appropriate to invite specialists from overseas that deal with mass graves following international standards and protocols (e.g. the International Committee of the Red Cross (ICRC) and International Commission on Missing Persons (ICMP)) to train willing members of the public. This would ensure that the highest scientific standards are being followed in the search, recovery, and identification of victims. The National Peace and Reconciliation Act (2018) does not make provision for the search, recovery, and identification of post conflict remains, which therefore makes it vapid in terms of exhumation processes. It therefore requires other subsidiary legislation to make the ethical recovery of remains possible.

Subsidiary legislation that could assist in future exhumations should take into account, and make provisions for, culture and social approaches to mourning and reburial, which is important for family members. Additional provisions should include the formation of peripheral organisations, such as a Human Tissue Authority (akin to the UK), and implementation of forensic techniques in the identification process. These methods would be carried out by trained Missing Person Teams that have received appropriate training, and adhere to professional standards. Additionally, the role of spirit mediums should be defined, and have frameworks that will ensure that their role does not interfere with forensic evidence.

In conclusion, holistic approaches to the search, recovery, and identification of human remains in Zimbabwe involving various stakeholders such as victim groups, National Peace and Reconcilation Commission (NPRC) commissioners, and relevant international organisations (for example the ICMP), is needed sooner rather than later. This approach will ensure that professional, ethical, and culturally suitable approaches to the recovery and identification of human remains satisfy all individuals that have been affected by the atrocities discussed in this chapter; indeed, this will assist in providing closure for all those touched by these events.

Acknowledgements The authors would like to thank the anonymous reviewer for their useful suggestions and comments in the preparation of this chapter.

References

Alexander, J., J. McGregor, and T. Ranger. 2000. *Violence and Memory: One Hundred Years in the 'Dark Forests' of Matabeleland.* Oxford: James Currey.

Amnesty International. 1993. *Disappearances and Political Killings: Human Rights Crisis of the 1990s—A Manual for Action.* https://www.amnesty.org.uk/cse/search/DisappearancesandPoliticalKillingsAHumanRightsCrisisofthe1990s. Accessed 21 September 2017.

Amnesty International. 2011. *Zimbabwe Mass Graves Must Be Exhumed by Forensic Experts.* https://www.amnesty.org/en/press-releases/2011/04/zimbabwe-mass-grave-bodies-ust-be-exhumed-forensic-experts/. Accessed 13 September 2017.

Anthonissen, C., and J. Blommaert. 2007. *Discourse and Human Rights Violations.* Amsterdam: John Benjamin Publishing Company.

Aronson, J.D. 2011. The Strengths and Limitations of South Africa's Search for Apartheid-Era Missing Persons. *International Journal of Transitional Justice* 5: 228–262.

Benyera, E. 2014. The Contribution of Mass Graves to Healing and Closure: The Case of Chibondo in Mt Darwin, Zimbabwe. *International Journal of Humanities and Social Sciences* 4 (1): 47–56.

Bhebe, N., and T.O. Ranger (eds.). 1995. *Soldiers in Zimbabwe's Liberation War*. London: James Currey.

Bird, E. 2014. *Special Branch War: Slaughter in the Rhodesian Bush: Southern Matabeleland, 1976–1980*. Solihull: Helion and Company.

Blau, S., and D.H. Ubelaker (eds.). 2016. *Handbook of Forensic Anthropology and Archaeology*. London: Routledge.

Buikstra, J., and D. Ubelaker (eds.). 1994. *Standards for Data Collection from Human Skeletal Remains*. Fayetteville: Arkansas Archaeological Survey.

Catholic Commission for Justice and Peace in Zimbabwe (CCJP). 2007. *Gukurahundi in Zimbabwe: A Report on the Disturbances in Matabeleland and the Midlands, 1980–1988*. New York: Columbia University Press.

Charamba, F.C. 2015. Heroes Acre, A Bastion of Patriotism, Tourist Attraction. *The Herald*. 15 July. http://www.herald.co.zw/heroes-acre-bastion-of-patriotism-tourist-attraction/. Accessed 21 September 2017.

Chiketo, B. 2017. Relief for Arrested Foreign Nationals. *The Daily News*. 12 November. https://www.dailynews.co.zw/articles/2017/11/12/relief-for-arrested-foreign-nationals. Accessed 23 November 2017.

Chikukwa, J.W. 2013. *Zimbabwe: The End of the First Republic*. Bloomington: Authorhouse.

Chipangura, N. 2015. *Archaeologists and Vernacular Exhumers in Zimbabwe*, Unpublished Report.

Church and Civil Society Forum. 2012. *Gukurahundi Victim Re-burial Stopped in Matobo*. http://www.ccsf.org.zw/areas-of-work/community-mobilization/articles/gukurahundi-victim-re-burial-stopped-matobo. Accessed 3 May 2018.

Cilliers, J. 2015. *Counter-Insurgency in Rhodesia*. New York: Routledge.

College of Policing. 2017. *Recovery of the Deceased and Human Remains*. https://www.app.college.police.uk/app-content/civil-emergencies/disaster-victim-identification/recovery-of-the-deceased-and-human-remains/. Accessed 21 September 2017.

Coltart, D. 2016. *The Struggle Continues: 50 years of Tyranny in Zimbabwe*. Auckland Park: Jacana Media.

Cox, J.L. 2016. *From Primitive to Indigenous: The Academic Study of Indigenous Religions*, 2nd ed. New York: Routledge.

Deng, F.M. 2011. Sovereignty as Responsibility for the Prevention of Genocide. In *Confronting Genocide*, ed. R. Provost and P. Akhavan, 57–79. Dordrecht: Springer.

Dengu-Zvogbo, K. 1996. *Inheritance in Zimbabwe: Law, Customs, and Practice*. Harare: SAPES Trust.

Dirkmaat, D. (ed.). 2015. *A Companion to Forensic Anthropology*. Chichester: Wiley-Blackwell.

Doran, S. 2017. *Kingdom, Power, Glory: Mugabe, Zanu and the Quest for Supremacy, 1960–1987*. Midrand: Sithatha.

Duday, H. 2009. *The Archaeology of the Dead: Lectures in Archaeothanatology*. Oxford: Oxbow Books.

Dupras, T.L., J.J. Schultz, S.M. Wheeler, et al. 2006. *Forensic Recovery of Human Remains: Archaeological Approaches*. Boca Raton: CRC Press.

Dutelle, A.W. 2017. *An Introduction to Crime Scene Investigation*. Burlington: Jones and Bartlett Learning.

Eppel, S. 2014. Bones in the Forest in Matabeleland, Zimbabwe: Exhumations as a Tool for Transformation. *International Journal of Transitional Justice* 8: 404–425.

Eppel, S. 2015. The Heroic and the Hidden Dead. In *Forensic Archaeology: A Global Perspective*, ed. W.J.M. Groen, N. Márquez-Grant, and R. Janaway, 359–368. Chichester: Wiley.

Eppel, S., and B. Raftopoulos. 2010. *Developing a Transformation Agenda for Zimbabwe*. Cape Town: The Institute for Democracy in South Africa.

Equipo Argentino de Anthropologia Forense (EAAF). 1999. *Zimbabwe*. http://www.eaaf.org/cr_zimbabwe/2005/12/country_report_.html. Accessed 9 March 2018.

Equipo Argentino de Anthropologia Forense (EAAF). 2000. *Zimbabwe*. http://www.eaaf.org/cr_zimbabwe/2005/12/country_report_.html. Accessed 9 March 2018.

Equipo Argentino de Anthropologia Forense (EAAF). 2001. *Zimbabwe*. http://www.eaaf.org/cr_zimbabwe/2005/12/country_report_.html. Accessed 9 March 2018.

Fontein, J. 2004. *Traditional Connoisseurs' of the Past: The Ambiguity of Spirit Mediums and the Performance of the Past in Southern Zimbabwe*. Edinburgh: University of Edinburgh, Centre of African Studies.

Fontein, J. 2010. Between Tortured Bodies and Resurfacing Bones: The Politics of the Dead in Zimbabwe. *Journal of Material Culture* 15 (4): 423–448.

Fontein, J. 2014. Remaking the Dead. In *Governing the Dead: Sovereignty and the Politics of Dead Bodies*, ed. F. Stepputat, 114–140. Manchester: Manchester University Press.

Geneva Convention (IV) Protection of Civilian Persons in Time of War (adopted 12 August 1949), 75 UNTS 288, Article 130.

Global Witness. 2017. *An Inside Job: Zimbabwe, The State, The Security Services and a Decade of Disappearing Diamonds*. London: Global Witness.

Gumbo, M. 1995. *Guerilla Snuff*. Harare: Baobab Books.

Hill, G. 2011. *Zimbabwe. Death by Silence. Unpublished Report*. Cambodia: International Association of Genocide Scholars.

Hayner, P.B. 2001. *Unspeakable Truths: Confronting State Terror and Atrocity*. New York: Routledge.

Heal Zimbabwe Trust. 2016. *Is Zimbabwe Ready for an Effective Truth Justice and Healing and Reconciliation Process*. Harare: Heal Zimbabwe Trust.

Hirsch, M.B., M. Mackenzie, and M. Sesay. 2012. Measuring the Impacts of Truth and Reconciliation Commissions: Placing the Global 'Success' of TRCs in Local Perspective. *Cooperation and Conflict* 47 (3): 386–403.

Human Rights Watch. 2009. *Diamonds in the Rough: Human Rights Abuses in the Marange Diamond Fields of Zimbabwe*. https://www.hrw.org/report/2009/06/26/diamonds-rough/human-rights-abuses-marange-diamond-fields-zimbabwe. Accessed 9 March 2018.

Human Rights Watch. 2011. *Zimbabwe Perpetual Fear: Impunity and Cycles of Violence in Zimbabwe*. New York: Human Rights Watch.

Hunter, J., and M. Cox. 2005. *Forensic Archaeology*. London: Routledge.

Hunter, J., B. Simpson, and C. Sturdy Colls. 2013. *Forensic Approaches to Buried Remains*. Chichester: Wiley Blackwell.

International Committee of the Red Cross. 2015. *Guiding Principles/Model Law on the Missing*. Geneva: International Committee of the Red Cross.

Interpol. 2013. *Disaster Victim Identification Form*. http://www.interpol.int/INTERPOL-expertise/Forensics/DVI-Pages/Disaster-victim-recovery-form. Accessed 21 Jan 2018.

Jones, A. 2016. *Genocide: A Comprehensive Introduction*. New York: Routledge.

Katongomara, A. 2017. VP Rules out Exhumations of Victims of Gukurahundi. *The Chronicle*. 3 March. http://www.chronicle.co.zw/vp-rules-out-exhumations-for-victims-of-gukurahundi/. Accessed 3 May 2018.

Klinkner, M. 2008. Forensic Science for Cambodian Justice. *International Journal of Transitional Justice* 2: 227–243.

Klinkner, M. 2017. Towards Mass-grave Protection Guidelines. *Human Remains and Violence* 3 (1): 52–70.

Kriger, N. 1995. The Politics of Creating National Heroes. In *Soldiers in Zimbabwe's Liberation War*, ed. N. Bhebe and T.O. Ranger, 148–162. London: James Currey.

Lan, D. 1985. *Guns and Rain: Guerrillas and Spirit Mediums in Zimbabwe*. London: James Currey.

Lemkin, R. 1944. *Axis Rule in Occupied Europe: Laws of Occupation—Analysis of Government—Proposals for Redress*. Washington, D.C.: Carnegie Endowment for International Peace.

Machenyuka, F. 2011. Chibondo Reburials in Progress. *The Herald*. 13 August. http://www.herald.co.zw/chibondo-reburials-in-progress/. Accessed 1 October 2017.

Magaisa, A. 2016. Presidential Amnesty and Impunity in Zimbabwe. *The Big Saturday Read*. 22 April. https://www.bigsr.co.uk/single-post/2016/04/22/The-Big-Saturday-Read-Presidential-Amnesty-A-short-history-of-impunity-and-political-violence-in-Zimbabwe. Accessed 10 April 2018.

Manayiti, O. 2016. Jonathan Moyo Reburies Gukurahundi Slain Father. *NewsDay*. 6 October. https://www.newsday.co.zw/2016/10/jonathan-moyo-reburies-gukurahundi-slain-father/. Accessed 17 September 2017.

Mapepa, L. 2015. Fallen Heroes Remains Reburied in Chipinge. *The Manica Post*. 11 September. http://manicapost.co.zw/fallen-heroes-remains-re-buried-in-chipinge/. Accessed 13 September 2017.

Márquez-Grant, N., and L. Fibiger (eds.). 2013. *The Routledge Handbook of Archaeological Human Remains and Legislation: An International Guide to Laws and Practice in the Excavation and Treatment of Archaeological Human Remains*. London: Routledge.

Mashaya, B. 2017. Three Illegal Diamond Miners Killed in Marange. *The Daily News*. 3 October. https://www.dailynews.co.zw/articles/2017/10/03/three-illegal-diamond-miners-killed-in-marange. Accessed 24 November 2017.

Mlotshwa, K. 2016. Police Ban Gukurahundi Commemorations. *Zimbabwe News*. 14 December. http://www.thezimbabwenewslive.com/politics-31721-police-ban-gukurahundi-commemorations.html. Accessed 21 September 2017.

Movement for Democratic Change. 2017. *Roll of Honour*. http://www.mdc.co.zw/. Accessed 12 December 2017.

Mpofu, S. 2014. Memory, National Identity and Freedom of Expression, Discussing the Taboo in the Zimbabwe Public Sphere Age. In *Handbook of Research on Political Activism in the Information Age*, ed. A.M.G. Solo, 114–128. Hershey: Information Science Reference.

Muchemwa, B. 2002. *Death and Burial Among the Shona: Christian Celebration of Death and Burial in the Context of Inculturation in Shona Culture*. Harare: Pastoral Center.

Muchemwa, K.Z. 2010. Galas, Biras, State Funerals and the Necropolitan Imagination in Re-constructions of the Zimbabwean Nation, 1980–2008. *Social Dynamics* 36 (3): 504–514.

Mudzungairi, W. 2011. Whose Interests are Exhumations Serving? *Newsday*. 22 March. https://www.newsday.co.zw/2011/03/2011-03-22-whose-interests-are-exhumations-serving/. Accessed 13 September 2017.

Mukonori, F. 2012. *The Genesis of Violence in Zimbabwe*. Harare: Centre for Peace Initiatives in Africa.

Mutsvairo, B. 2016. *Participatory Politics and Citizen Journalism in a Networked Africa: A Connected Continent*. Basingstoke: Palgrave Macmillan.

Mwandayi, C. 2011. *Death and After-Life Rituals in the Eyes of the Shona: Dialogue with Shona Customs in the Quest for Authentic Inculturation*. Bamberg: University of Bamberg.

National Heroes Act. 1984. Parliament of Zimbabwe, Harare.

National Museum and Monuments Act. 1972. Parliament of Zimbabwe. Harare.

National Museum and Monuments Zimbabwe. 2017. *About Us*. http://www.nmmz.co.zw/. Accessed 12 January 2018.

National Peace and Reconciliation Act. 2018. Parliament of Zimbabwe, Harare.

Ndebele, Z. 2007. *Gukurahundi: A Moment of Madness* [DVD]. Bulawayo: Ndebele Productions.

Ndlovu, N. 2017a. Pressure Groups Tours Gukurahundi Graves. *Zimbabwe Daily*. 11 September. https://www.thezimbabwedaily.com/news/156767-pressure-groups-tours-gukurahundi-graves.html. Accessed 1 October 2017.

Ndlovu, Q. 2017b. Human Rights Groups Hail Mphoko's NPRC Bill. *NewsDay*. 22 May. https://www.newsday.co.zw/2017/05/human-rights-groups-hail-mphokos-nprc-bill/. Accessed 17 September 2017.

Ndlovu-Gatsheni, S. 2003. The Post-colonial State and Matebeleland: Regional Perceptions of Civil-military Relations, 1980–2002. In *Ourselves to Know: Civil-military Relations and Defence Transformation in Southern Africa*, ed. R. Williams, G. Cawthra, and D. Abrahams, 17–38. Pretoria: Institute for Security Studies.

Ndlovu-Gatsheni, S.J. 2011. *The Construction and Decline of Chimurenga Monologue in Zimbabwe: A Study in Resilience of Ideology and Limits of Alternatives*. Pretoria: University of South Africa.

Ndlovu-Gatsheni, S.J., and W. Willems. 2009. Making Sense of Cultural Nationalism and the Politics of Commemoration Under the Third Chimurenga in Zimbabwe. *Journal of Southern African Studies* 35 (4): 945–965.

Nehanda Radio. 2013. Christpower Maisiri Murder Pictures. *Nehanda Radio*. 27 February. http://nehandaradio.com/2013/02/27/christpower-maisiri-murder-in-pictures/. Accessed 24 September 2017.

New Zimbabwe. 2017. MP Says Still Traumatized by Gukurahundi. *New Zimbabwe*. 8 October. http://newzimbabwe.com/news-39489-MP+says+heart+bleeds+over+Gukurahundi/news.aspx. Accessed 8 October 2017.

Nhambura, F. 2013a. Rusape Butchers Camp Relived. *The Herald*. 16 April. http://www.herald.co.zw/rusapes-butcher-camp-relived/. Accessed 13 September 2017.

Nhambura, F. 2013b. Man With Rare Calling. *The Herald*. 5 June. http://www.herald.co.zw/man-with-a-rare-calling/. Accessed 13 September 2017.

Nkala, S. 2017. Mphoko in Fresh Gukurahundi Storm. *NewsDay*. 6 July. https://www.newsday.co.zw/2017/07/mphoko-fresh-gukurahundi-storm/. Accessed 21 September 2017.

Pfukwa, C. 2008. The Female Nom De Guerre (War Names) in the Zimbabwean Liberation War 1. *Latin American Report* 24 (2): 50–64.

Pringle, J.K., A. Ruffell, J.R. Jervis, et al. 2012. The Use of Geoscience Methods for Terrestrial Forensic Searches. *Earth-Science Reviews* 114: 108–123.

Reeler, T. 2009. *Sublimal Terror, Human Rights Violations and Torture in Zimbabwe During 2008*. Braamfontein: Centre for the Study of Violence and Reconciliation.

Robben, A.C.G.M. 2010. Testimonies, Truths, and Transitions of Justice in Argentina and Chile. In *Transitional Justice: Global Mechanisms and Local Realities after Genocide and Mass Violence*, ed. A.L. Hinton, 179–205. New Brunswick: Rutgers University Press.

Robben, A.C.G.M. 2014. Governing the Disappeared-living and the Disappeared-dead: The Violent Pursuit of Cultural Sovereignty During Authoritarian Rule in Argentina. In *Governing the Dead: Sovereignty and the Politics of Dead Bodies*, ed. F. Stepputat, 143–162. Manchester: Manchester University Press.

Rosenblatt, A. 2015. *Digging the Disappeared: Forensic Science After Atrocity*. Stanford: Stanford University Press.

Ruffell, A., J.K. Pringle, and S. Forbes. 2014. Search Protocols for Hidden Forensic Objects Beneath Floors and Within Walls. *Forensic Science International* 237: 137–145.

Sachikonye, L.M. 2005. Political Parties and the 2005 Elections in Zimbabwe. *Journal of African Elections* 4: 63–73.

Sachikonye, L.M. 2011. *When a State Turns on its Citizens: 60 Years of Institutionalised Violence in Zimbabwe*. Harare: Weaver Press.

Share, F. 2017. Declare Rutanhire National Hero. *The Herald*. 21 August. http://www.herald.co.zw/declare-rutanhire-national-hero/. Accessed 1 October 2017.

Sithole, B. 2014. Nkomo, Thin Line Between Honour and Dishonour. *Bulawayo 24 News*. 10 January. https://bulawayo24.com/index-id-opinion-sc-columnist-byo-41168-article-joshua+nkomo:+thin+line+between+honour+and+dishonour.html. Accessed 20 May 2018.

Smith, D. 2011. Grave Containing up to 60 People Found at Zimbabwe School. *The Guardian*. 5 October. https://www.theguardian.com/world/2011/oct/05/mass-grave-found-zimbabwe-school. Accessed 21 January 2018.

Soderland, H.A., and I. Lilley. 2015. The Fusion of Law and Ethics in Cultural Heritage Management: The 21st Century Confronts Archaeology. *Journal of Field Archaeology* 40: 508–522.

Smolensky, T.K. 2009. Rights of the Dead. *Hofstra Law Review* 37 (3): 1–42.

Southern Eye. 2014. Gukurahundi Victim Reburied. *Southern Eye*. 21 October. https://www.southerneye.co.zw/2014/10/21/gukurahundi-victim-reburied/. Accessed 12 December 2017.

The Herald. 2013. Man with a Rare Calling. *The Herald*. 5 June. https://www.herald.co.zw/man-with-a-rare-calling. Accessed 21 April 2018.

The Standard. 2011. Row Over Fresh Mt Darwin Human Remains. *The Standard*. 20 March. https://www.thestandard.co.zw/2011/03/20/row-over-fresh-mt-darwin-human-remains/. Accessed 1 October 2017.

Thorneycroft, P., and A. Laing. 2015. Britain Confirms Robert Mugabe's Claim a London Museum Has Zimbabwean Heroes' Skulls. *The Telegraph*. 14 August. http://www.telegraph.co.uk/news/worldnews/africaandindianocean/zimbabwe/11802355/Britain-confirms-Robert-Mugabes-claim-a-London-museum-has-Zimbabwean-heroes-skulls.html. Accessed 21 September 2017.

Tshuma, A. 2017. Human Remains Found in Kezi. *The Chronicle*. 30 May. http://www.chronicle.co.zw/human-remains-found-in-kezi/. Accessed 13 September 2017.

Tuller, H., and M. Durić. 2005. Keeping the Pieces Together: Comparison of Mass Grave Excavation Methodology. *Forensic Science International* 156: 192–200.

United Nations. 1948. *Convention on the Prevention and Punishment of Genocide*. New York: United Nations.

United Nations. 2016. *The Minnesota Protocol. The Investigation of Potentially Unlawful Death*. New York: United Nations.

Vambe, M.T. 2012. Zimbabwe Genocide: Voices and Perceptions from Ordinary People in Matabeleland and the Midlands Provinces, 30 Years on. *African Identities* 10: 281–300.

Verdirame, G. 2000. The Genocide Definition in the Jurisprudence of the Ad Hoc Tribunals. *International and Comparative Law Quarterly* 49 (3): 578–598.

Werbner, R. 1991. *Tears of the Dead: The Social Biography of an African Family*. Harare: Baobab Books.

ZIPRA v. FHT Judgement 61/11 HC 880/11 (2011).

Chapter 29
The Mummy Autopsy: Some Ethical Considerations

Dario Piombino-Mascali and Heather Gill-Frerking

Abstract Mummies are the preserved or partially-preserved remains of human beings. When studying mummies, researchers must understand the many ethical issues that arise from working with ancient and historic human remains. One common debate is the use of autopsy versus minimally-invasive methods of analysis for the study of mummies. This chapter considers several ethical issues associated with the study of human mummies and, in particular, discusses two case studies to illustrate the particular issues associated with these two approaches in this field of research.

29.1 Introduction

29.1.1 Defining "Mummification"

While the definition of a mummy might seem quite obvious to many, the public perception of what a mummy is can be highly variable, and often focuses on Egyptian bandage-wrapped mummies. In general, a mummy is best described as "… a human or animal body in which soft tissue, such as skin, muscle, fat, ligaments, or organs, are preserved" (Gill-Frerking 2018, 295) (Figs. 29.1 and 29.2). Mummies are generally divided into three categories: spontaneous (or natural), anthropogenic (or artificial), or a combination of both. Spontaneous mummies are preserved solely as a result of the environmental conditions surrounding the dead body. Certain environmental conditions can prevent decay and conversely lead to mummification. Bodies require water and air to decompose, and the absence of one or both of these elements can lead to the preservation of soft tissue (Lynnerup 2007;

D. Piombino-Mascali (✉)
Department of Anatomy, Histology and Anthropology, Vilnius University, Vilnius, Lithuania
e-mail: dario.piombino@mf.vu.lt

H. Gill-Frerking
NTK Services, Frankford, ON, Canada

K. Squires et al. (eds.), *Ethical Approaches to Human Remains*,
https://doi.org/10.1007/978-3-030-32926-6_29

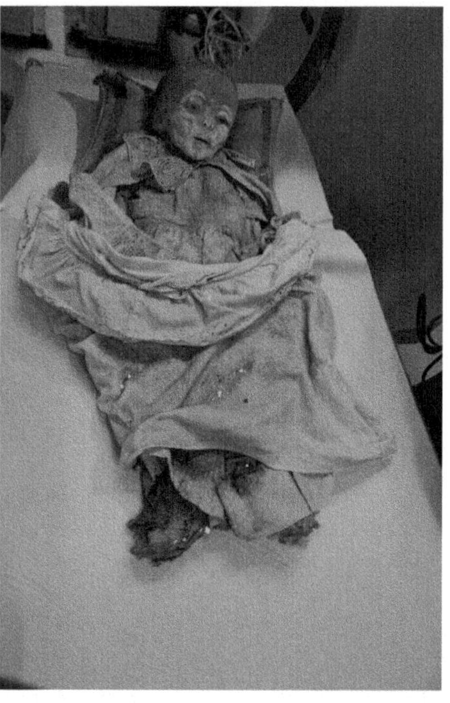

Fig. 29.1 A well-preserved mummy from Palermo (Italy). Since the mummy is essentially intact and the soft tissue is in excellent condition, invasive sampling is not recommended in this case. Photograph by Dario Piombino-Mascali

Piombino-Mascali et al. 2017). Anthropogenic mummies are the result of cultural practices. Many cultures used specific burial rituals that led to the preservation of the dead, all of which vary through time and geographical location. The best known of these mummies are inarguably from ancient Egypt, but other anthropogenic mummies can be found in Chile (Arriaza 1995) and Papua New Guinea (Beckett et al. 2011), for example. "Combination" mummies preserve as a result of both environmental and cultural processes. These are not common occurrences, but some of the best-known examples of such mummies come from the Altai region of Siberia. These bodies are partially-eviscerated, stuffed with grasses and buried in permafrost soil. The combination of removal of the gut material (which reduces the potential for abdominal decay), and the permafrost environment, has resulted in several well-preserved mummified individuals (Rudenko 1970).

Mummy studies is an important sub-discipline of bioarchaeology, providing data that are not normally available during the study of skeletonised remains alone (Aufderheide 2003). Although mummy studies have been employed in some form for over 200 years, there has been a considerable evolution in the approaches adopted, shifting from a pioneering phase of forensic dissection, to the employment of minimally-invasive and minimally-destructive technology, primarily radiological studies, that allow for historic and ancient human remains to be studied in a manner that aids their preservation (Aufderheide 2003). Cesarani et al. (2003) used computed tomography (CT) to study 13 wrapped Egyptian mummies. These authors

Fig. 29.2 A partially-mummified body from Vilnius (Lithuania). The soft tissue of this mummy is not well preserved, and areas where there is incomplete soft tissue are acceptable regions for tissue sampling, since there would be little further damage to the mummy. Photograph by Dario Piombino-Mascali

noted that it was possible to determine critical data such as sex, age-at-death, identification of disease or trauma, stature estimation and other skeletal measurements, and the presence of foreign objects, such as amulets and other jewellery—without the need to disturb any wrappings or otherwise undertake any invasive or destructive analyses. More recently, a study by Dedouit et al. (2010) compared virtual and macroscopic studies of an adult female Siberian mummy from the early eighteenth century, to determine whether equivalent data could be obtained through minimally-destructive means. Although autopsy allowed correction of the interpretation of a spinal lesion (post-infectious versus Schmorl's node) over multi-slice computed tomography (MSCT), a common method of radiological analysis in mummy studies, the minimally-destructive imaging and dissection otherwise produced the same results for the overall anthropological interpretation of the mummy (Dedouit et al. 2010), demonstrating that little was gained by destructive dissection. Thus, it must be carefully considered whether mummy dissection is necessary for a thorough and accurate analysis of human remains or whether alternative minimally-destructive methods will suffice. Where autopsy is undertaken, however, researchers must contemplate the physical, scientific, and ethical implications of this technique.

The choice of methodology in mummy studies should be part of the initial research plan. The most important aspect of methodology selection is dependent upon the intention of the study, that is, exactly what information does the researcher hope to learn from the analysis of the body. Once that decision is made, researchers choose the methods, which best suit the collection of the data sought. Since mummies are human beings, all decisions about methods of analysis must also consider the most ethical approach to analysis in each specific case, while still allowing the scientist to attempt to answer their primary research question. Mummies, like most material from archaeological sites, are irreplaceable resources. Researchers should cause as little harm as possible to the mummy during scientific investigations. While significant advances have been made in the methods used for the minimally-destructive analysis of mummies over the past few decades, constant technological developments suggest that improved methodologies will be developed in the future. It is impossible to guess exactly what new methodologies will develop, or what they may be able to uncover. It is very likely, however, that researchers will be able to determine even more biological information about individuals and populations with the application of new technological methods to test sound hypotheses.

This chapter presents two examples of current mummy research projects with different approaches to the study of human mummies. One research group, based in Italy, adopts the consistent use of autopsy, which causes extensive destruction to the specimen. The second group, in South Korea, employs destructive physical sampling only under highly-restrictive circumstances, limiting the damage caused to the mummy. These case studies will be used to highlight the need for researchers to move away from destructive analyses and, instead, consider greater application of minimally-invasive and minimally-destructive methods of analysis, such as medical imaging. The chapter will illustrate that destructive methods cause irreplaceable loss of palaeopathological data information pertaining to cultural practices in the past. It will also discuss ethical concerns related to the dissection and analysis of prehistoric and historic human mummies. Finally, this contribution serves as a plea to bioarchaeologists, palaeopathologists, and curators to avoid destruction of bio-cultural human heritage during the analysis and display of mummified human remains.

29.1.2 Sources of Mummies

There are two “sources” of mummies: those that are newly discovered accidentally or through archaeological excavation, and those held in the collections of museums, academic institutions, private individuals, or other locations. Since mummies are rarely discovered, researchers often examine whole or partial preserved human remains from institutional collections. Anyone working with these mummies, whether based at the institutions or accessing the collections for analysis, have professional and ethical obligations to ensure both the long-term conservation of the bodies, and the possibility of any potential future research. In the past, some mummies (e.g. Aleut mummies in Alaska) were skeletonised for investigation and storage (Aufderheide 2003, 79), possibly without any analysis of the soft tissue. The Windeby Child, a well-preserved Iron Age adolescent male bog body, dating to around 150 – 0 BC (van der Plicht et al. 2004), was excavated from peat in Northern Germany in 1952 (Gill-Frerking 2014). Following a thorough analysis of the mummy, the skeletal elements were separated from the soft tissue, and stored separately. The soft tissue was partially incorporated into a permanent museum display, replicating an approximation of the appearance of the body in the bog (Gill-Frerking 2014). Other mummies were conserved using methods that would never be considered in current museum practice, and which potentially impaired modern analyses. For example, several Iron Age bog bodies from Schleswig-Holstein, Northern Germany, were excavated from 1871 through 1960 and radiocarbon dating indicated they all dated to around 410 BC – AD 620 (Gill-Frerking 2014). The bodies were all conserved with various methods appropriate for the time, but detrimental to modern bioarchaeological analyses using medical imaging (Gill-Frerking 2014). In the case of an adult male, the Rendswühren Man, excavated in 1871, the head had been completely reconstructed with wire, metal, stuffing of an indeterminate material, and realistic-looking gutta-percha teeth (Gill-Frerking 2014). As part of a larger research project, the mummy underwent CT scanning in 2003, but the conservation methods used in 1871 affected the quality of the imaging. Furthermore, archive records noted specific injuries to the skull of the individual during the detailed autopsy in 1871, but these could not be confirmed, since the skull was no longer available for assessment, having been entirely replaced during conservation (Gill-Frerking 2014).

Visual inspection followed by medical imaging techniques are the two primary minimally-destructive stages employed to analyse mummies. The first step when examining any mummy should be a detailed visual inspection, noting, for example, visible evidence of trauma and pathology, sex, method of mummification, current state of preservation, and body modification, such as tattoos. The second step is to use advanced medical imaging techniques for internal analysis, including CT (Rühli and Chhem 2004; Conlogue et al. 2008; Friedrich et al. 2010; Öhrström et al. 2010; Panzer et al. 2010; Allam et al. 2011; Cavka et al. 2012; Panzer et al. 2013; Piombino-Mascali et al. 2014; Panzer et al. 2015; Davey and Drummer 2016) and microcomputed tomography (μCT) (Nelson et al. 2018). Minimally-invasive procedures such as endoscopy, using either a camera for visual inspection of internal cavities or tools for extracting small biopsy samples, can be used with mummies that may have naturally-occurring areas where the camera can be inserted (e.g. via nasal passages, or crevices created when the thorax collapses from desiccation). This minimises the potential damage to the mummy, provided the operator using the device employs extreme caution when manipulating the instrument to avoid damaging the inflexible, desiccated, fragile tissues.

As noted by Lynnerup (2007), the autopsy of mummified remains poses two major concerns. Firstly, working with a preserved body, which can be associated with archaeological artefacts, such as textiles and adornments, compromises its integrity and irreparably modifies valued cultural heritage. Secondly, ethical concerns arise. A dead body represents a once-living being and, therefore, must always be treated with dignity and respect. Cultural beliefs and burial practices should be considered, and the human remains must always be handled with care and deference (Kaufmann and Rühli 2010). Indeed, Kaufmann and Rühli (2010) go so far as to emphasise that if mummy researchers apply frameworks similar to those of biomedical ethics, ancient mummies are, of course, unable to give "informed consent" to any analyses. They further suggest that this may violate the deceased person's individualism and right of integrity, but are cautious to stress that there are philosophical questions as to whether it is possible to harm the bodily integrity of the dead (Kaufmann and Rühli 2010).

Additional ethical issues in mummy studies include the often-contentious issue of the display of mummies in exhibitions, the potential for repatriation, and the application of basic codes of ethics that are important for scholars to consider (Charlier 2014; Day 2014). According to some, it is inappropriate to display human remains, including mummies, in museum exhibitions, regardless of the scientific or cultural value of the exhibit (Day 2014). These opinions are often held by a small, but often somewhat vocal, minority. While it might seem logical to suggest that those that do not approve of displaying mummies could simply choose not to attend these types of exhibitions, this seldom satisfies such critics, who frequently demand that mummies and other human remains be completely hidden from public view, preferably locked away in museum storage areas. In some cases, there are requests for repatriation of the human remains (Charlier 2014). This means that the mummy or skeleton is returned to its country or culture of origin. Discussions of aspects of repatriation from a legal or cultural perspective are extremely complex and best discussed elsewhere. For the purposes of this chapter, however, it is important to note that some mummies have been repatriated via legal instruments. One example is an infant mummy taken from a cave in the Hanapeepee Valley region of Kauai (Hawaii) in 1893 (Preucel et al. 2003). After negotiations and arrangements made under the requirements of the Native American Graves Protection and Repatriation Act of 1990, more commonly known as "NAGPRA", the University of Pennsylvania Museum of Archaeology and Anthropology returned the mummy to Hui Malama I Na Kupuna O Hawai'I Nei in August 1991 (Preucel et al. 2003).

Mummies present particular challenges in terms of ethical analyses within international settings. Many mummies are removed from their original contexts, often not by archaeologists, but by looters or others, with little or no care for their surrounding context. Valuable historical and cultural contextual information is lost when the provenience of the mummy is unknown. Furthermore, many mummies are examined outside of their country of origin. This leads to a new set of ethical questions related to the rights to study a particular mummy, for instance, whether the mummy stays in its current location or is considered for repatriation to its home country, the legislation of handling ancient human remains in the country of origin, and in the country where the investigation is conducted. All of these matters must be addressed on a case-by-case basis, but researchers are strongly advised to create international, multidisciplinary teams that include members from the country of origin, whenever possible. At the very least, researchers should contact colleagues in the mummy's country of origin, to establish whether there are any other special permissions or requirements that must be met during analysis. One part of accepting an ethical research approach to mummy studies includes maintaining professional relationships with international colleagues and with representatives of mummy source nations.

One additional challenge faced by mummy researchers relates to the potential analysis of mummies held in private collections (e.g. Halcrow et al. 2018). Indeed, both human and animal mummies are of great interest to collectors. Mummies held in private collections are generally unknown: there may not be an available public inventory list and information about these mummies may be almost impossible to obtain. For the most part, it is not illegal to buy, sell, or trade human mummies (see Huffer and Charlton, this volume). None of the current existing international legal frameworks prevent the private ownership of human mummies, nor do these frameworks provide any protection of such prehistoric or historic remains in private collections (Frerking and Gill-Frerking 2017). It is, however, usually illegal to import or export a mummy from its home country without specific documentation from the appropriate government agency. One example is shrunken heads from South America. Several cultures in the Northern countries of South America produced shrunken heads, for a variety of cultural reasons. As recently as the early 2000s, genuine shrunken heads were purchased by collectors of Pre-Columbian art and antiquities in North America, Europe, and Asia (Verano 2003). The heads were illegally exported from their home countries, especially Peru, to the collector's country through black market channels (Verano 2003). In many cases, there is no doubt that a specific mummy must have been acquired illegally since it could not have been legally or legitimately exported from its country of origin (Frerking and Gill-Frerking 2017). A difficult ethical question arises for mummy researchers when asked to study one or more mummies held in a private collection. While the researcher could provide substantial new data about a mummy or group of mummies that were previously unknown, there are significant risks in providing professional analyses of these mummies for private collectors. First and foremost, the research provides additional information about the collector's mummy. This increases the mummy's monetary or trade value between collectors. Secondly, the research can establish the collector's mummy as "legitimate", especially if published as part of a museum catalogue or academic publication, making it easier for the collector to sell or trade that mummy in the future. For the purposes of this chapter, "legitimacy", refers to a general acceptance that the collector has a "right" to "own" the mummy, despite any prior nefarious history that may be associated with it, such as a potential illegal means of acquisition. Even loaning the mummy as part of a temporary museum exhibition provides the same legitimacy. Finally, the researcher must be prepared to understand that the collector may not be truthful about the date or manner of acquisition of the mummy. If a mummy researcher studies mummies in private collections, they must understand the ethical and professional implications that accompany such a decision.

Cultural property lawyers recommend that "the development and promotion of guidance at the professional and scientific level is critical" (Paradise and Andrews 2007, 236), recognising that national and international legislation to regulate the analysis of human remains is poor or non-existent. Limited legal protections exist, usually in the form of international treaties, which are partially- or fully-implemented in national law. The protection, however, may depend on how prehistoric and historic human remains are categorised for the purposes of legislation, which is a particularly complex issue (see Frerking and Gill-Frerking 2017). At present, there appears to be no efforts to modify international legislation regarding the protection of prehistoric and historic human remains. Whether this is due to a lack of interest in these protections, or a lack of awareness of the need for these protections is unclear. It is likely, however, that the greatest and most effective legislative change can occur at the local and national level. If communities, larger administrative regions (e.g. provinces and cantons), and nations develop, implement, and, most critically, stringently enforce legislation with significant penalties, then there may be a greater chance of protecting human remains.

29.2 Case Studies

29.2.1 Dissection in the West: Italian Mummies

Since the development of palaeopathology as a discipline, mummy studies have been popular in Italy, probably due to the large number of both spontaneous and anthropogenic preserved remains that are found throughout the country (see Aufderheide and Aufderheide 1991; Ciuffarella 1998; Baggieri et al. 2001; Ciranni and Fornaciari 2004; Panzer et al. 2010, 2013; Piombino-Mascali et al. 2011). It is worth noting that these mummies are primarily historic in date. Starting in the 1980s and through the early 2000s, research groups have carried out dissections of mummies in order to obtain bioanthropological and palaeopathological information, and to process samples for further biomedical investigation and storage (Fornaciari 1998). Several collections that have been subjected to this type of analysis, include the mummies of the Aragonese family and a large number of historic personages from 38 coffins located in the sacristy of the San Domenico Basilica of Naples, including King Alfonso I, Ferrante I, Ferrante II, Queen Giovanna IV, the Marquis Ferdinando d'Avalos, as well as the Marquise Maria of Aragon (e.g. Fornaciari 1998; Fornaciari et al. 1999, 2003, 2009, 2012; Ottini et al. 2011). The bodies, all richly dressed in precious clothes made of silk, brocade, and other fabrics, rest in wooden coffins, which are in two tiers. The smaller coffins of the lower row are generally of anonymous individuals, whereas the larger coffins of the upper row are identified by the coats-of-arms and the names of the persons buried inside. In this specific case, the mummies were stripped of their textiles, which are now on permanent exhibition in the church, and then autopsied. The 50 spontaneously-enhanced mummies from the Church of Santa Maria della Grazia in Comiso (Sicily), which belong to either friars or laymen (Fornaciari 1998), met the same fate as those from the San Domenico Basilica. All of the mummies were male and the names and dates of death were known for some individuals (Ciranni et al. 1999). The overall purpose for the research on this specific collection of mummies was not stated. Five mummies of the Convent of San Giorgio degli Osservanti in Goriano Valli, in the province of L'Aquila, Abruzzo (Ventura et al. 2006), were examined through autopsy. In this study, pathologies, such as pneumonia and other lung conditions, goiter, and arteriosclerosis, were identified (Ventura et al. 2006). Like the previous mummies, the overall purpose for the research was not specified. According to the researchers, a "posterior approach" was chosen in order not to compromise future display of the bodies, although in one case, due to poor preservation of the subject, a classic anterior forensic dissection was carried out (Ventura et al. 2006). The most recent dissection of which we are aware is the case of Cangrande della Scala (1291–1329), Lord of Verona (Fornaciari et al. 2015). Following Cangrande's death in 1329, his body was temporarily kept in the Church of Santa Maria Antiqua in Verona, before being moved to a marble tomb in the churchyard, and finally to a tomb over the church entrance (Fornaciari et al. 2015). In 2004, officials permitted the tomb to be opened for a multidisciplinary investigation of Cangrande, with more recent research conducted in an attempt to confirm Cangrande's reported cause of death (Fornaciari et al. 2015). In order to "avoid damage", the autopsy was performed using an unusual method. Here, scientists produced a circular opening of the abdomen, from the sternum to the pubis, which allowed sampling of the body cavities (Fornaciari et al. 2015).

In each of these cases, autopsy was the main method of examination, although techniques such as medical imaging were used to support the research. Interestingly, according to Italian cultural heritage law (Legge 1° giugno 1939), issued during the Fascist period (1922–1945) and still active at the time of the mummy investigations discussed, mummies fall within the "protected" category since they are deemed as "cultural assets" (Piombino-Mascali and Zink 2011). Nevertheless, in each case, permission was granted for each of these investigations by local governmental institutions, allowing dissection, sampling, and, as a consequence, the creation of tissue banks for the researchers involved. The tissue banks are still in existence today, but it is unclear how accessible these banks are by those not associated with original projects. Some tissue banks, such as the Ancient Egyptian Mummy Tissue Bank at Manchester Museum in the United Kingdom, are made accessible to researchers not associated with that specific project, through contact with the director of the tissue bank (Lambert-Zazulak et al. 2003). The authors have anecdotal knowledge of other researchers retaining tissue samples from various mummies for the creation of tissue banks of various sizes, but most of these tissue banks are project-specific and contain very limited samples. Larger tissue banks, such as those taken by the Italian projects discussed above, should be accessible to researchers not associated with the project, provided analysis of the tissue is necessary to address a specific research hypothesis that cannot be addressed by any other methodology. It is ethically irresponsible of mummy researchers to take extensive tissue samples from mummies and retain those samples for their exclusive use or long-term custody. Researchers who undertake such invasive sampling should also make lists of all tissue samples taken with the following information: date and location of the sample on the body, tissue type, approximate size of sample, quality of preservation (if this can be determined), method of sampling, method of preservation, method of storage, and storage location. Researchers should make these lists available to others in the field, and indicate possibilities for collaboration, where possible. It is absolutely critical for any researcher who takes tissue samples to remember that they are taking samples of human beings and samples must be taken carefully and respectfully.

In the Italian cases reviewed in this chapter, there was no clear indication of the specific type of permission that was secured to the researchers at the time of the projects, or the extent to which researchers were allowed to conduct invasive analyses. This suggests that, in most cases, the researchers self-governed the research activities, at best. At the time of these destructive examinations, no code of ethics existed at the national level for the investigation of this specific type of remains and there were no government objections to the research. However, since mummies are of historic, and not forensic, interest, the mummy research should have been subjected to the existing cultural heritage laws (Piombino-Mascali and Zink 2011). In this sense, the code of ethics issued by the National Council for Research Ethics Commission, which provides a useful framework for researchers to adopt, is a novelty (CNR 2016). Specifically, the code indicates that norms of professional standards and behaviour must be respected and that the destruction of cultural heritage should be prevented (CNR 2016). Destructive analyses, if necessary, must strictly intend to document the final status of the artefact after analysis. This means that any destructive sampling must be solely for the purpose of determining the state of preservation, planning methods of long-term conservation, or to provide information necessary for the documentation and protection of heritage, such as radiocarbon dating to confirm the period of a prehistoric mummy.

In some cases, oversight may be required by the institution responsible for the human remains, whether a museum, religious institution, or other organisation, but many institutions are happy to cooperate with researchers, especially those who have a long-standing reputation in the field. While well-known researchers may seem like the most logical people to work with rare specimens, such as mummies, not all researchers are committed to minimally-destructive mummy analyses. Longevity in the field should not be the primary criterion when choosing someone to work with a collection of mummies. Institutions should be prepared to question a researcher's preferred methodologies. Institutions can rarely afford to undertake research on mummies (or other objects in their collections), so the offer to study mummies may be of tremendous interest and benefit to the institution—so much so that they are not always aware of potential problems and may not ask enough questions prior to the start of a research project. For example, the institutions may not be aware that the researcher that has approached them is using out-dated methods or techniques that will cause substantial damage to the mummy, despite the availability of alternative methods of analysis. It is of the utmost importance that the institution ensures that the potential researcher intends to be respectful of the mummy throughout the entire analysis. Institutions that are responsible for care of mummies need to consider the long-term implications of any potential analyses. It is recommended that institutions do some background research into those requesting to undertake analyses, and ensure that the researchers have provided a detailed proposal of the purpose and methodologies of the intended research. They should question researchers about the need for any destructive sampling, to ensure that it is undertaken only as a last resort, i.e. when non-destructive methods are unavailable to answer specific essential questions (e.g. radiocarbon dating). Finally, the institutions should question researchers about their intentions regarding the data collected during the research. Will a copy be made for the institution's archive, if requested? Do researchers have plans for dissemination of the data through academic publications, conference presentations, or public means, such as museum exhibitions or community presentations? Communication between researchers and curating institutions is critical—before, during, and after any research is conducted. It is important for all affected parties to be involved in the planning, and, later, the dissemination and sharing of research results, both in academic and public fora. Ideally the research can be a collaboration between the institution and the researchers.

29.2.2 Dissection in the East: Korean Mummies

An interesting approach to the study of mummified remains comes from South Korea, where 38 mummies from the Joseon dynasty (late fourteenth to early twentieth centuries), have remarkable preservation of both soft tissues and precious fabrics (Song and Shin 2014). The bodies, recovered from several sites, were all spontaneously mummified, probably because of the presence of the so-called "lime-soil mixture barrier" (LSMB) (Song and Shin 2014). All of the mummies recovered from the Joseon dynasty were buried in wooden coffins that were placed in a tomb sealed with a mixture of lime and soil, known as *Hoegwakmyo* (Kim et al. 2008). This specific tomb structure was mandated by standardised "national or private neo-Confucianist rituals" (Kim et al. 2008, 615), and these tombs were used only by *Sadaebu*, the gentlemen or ruling class nobles of the dynasty (Kim et al. 2008). As with all spontaneous mummies, the burial environment was solely responsible for the preservation of these bodies. Not all LSMB tombs, however, have produced mummified bodies. Many of the tombs have no preserved remains at all. The preservation mechanism of LSMB tombs is not fully understood (Kim et al. 2008).

Since the early 2000s, Korean scientists investigating the Joseon mummies have yielded a significant amount of information about pre-modern Korean populations (Oh et al. 2017). A congenital hernia was identified in an adult male of around 45 years of age from the city of Andong, in Southeast Korea (Kim et al. 2014). A topknot was visible on the man's head, providing evidence that the man was married, since unmarried men were forbidden from wearing their hair in that manner (Kim et al. 2014). In another case, endoscopy was used to determine the presence and preservational status of internal organs in a child mummy from Yangju, as part of a wider study to determine the methodological effectiveness of endoscopy for examining Korean mummies (Kim et al. 2006a). The endoscopic imaging successfully identified remnants of the child's diaphragm, liver, intestines, lungs, ribs with attached intercostal muscles, shrunken heart, brain, and spinal cord in the vertebral canal (Kim et al. 2006a). In many of these studies, the mummies are later fully autopsied.

There are often detailed family records for long-established genealogical histories. In some cases, it is possible to identify living descendants of the mummies that are being studied. This allows the family to be involved in decision-making processes regarding the analysis of the mummy in question. The mummies of the Joseon tombs were discovered during the process of *Ijang*, a ritual process of "moving a tomb to a new cemetery" (Song and Shin 2014, 147), presumably because the original location was at risk from redevelopment. Descendants performing *Ijang* ceremonies might allow academic studies of any mummified ancestors, but could also refuse to allow any examination (Song and Shin 2014). Initially, clothing historians could only undertake examination of the tomb contents following the completion of the *Ijang* ritual processes, but over time, scientists were permitted to begin examinations during the *Ijang* (Song and Shin 2014). Clan documents and engraved tombstones enable the identification of specific individuals and their descendants (Kim et al. 2006b). Specific written documents, such as the *Jokbo* and the *Silrok*, can provide detailed, individualised personal histories, which assist with the interpretation of the mummies, in terms of such things as the health, lifestyle and status of the individual, kinship relationships, and funeral practices (Kim et al. 2006b).

Interestingly, while the study of such bodies might be permitted by the descendants of these mummies, their curation in scientific institutions or museums is not (Kim et al. 2017). Therefore, after thorough, responsible research, most of the bodies are cremated, in accordance with the wishes of the descendants (Kim et al. 2017). Prior to cremation, the mummies undergo CT scans, which creates a permanent, three-dimensional record of the remains. In fact, objections regarding the long-term storage of imaging data have yet to be raised. Subsequently, post-factum dissection is carried out to compare visual and virtual data, and to take samples for further biomedical investigation, if permission is granted by the families. Although these mummies usually undergo cremation, researchers still undertake a conservation-oriented approach towards the bodies. Researchers adopt strict protocols to treat the dead in a respectful manner. To successfully conduct studies on the mummies, it is essential for researchers to build, and maintain, a good relationship with family members (Oh et al. 2018). Researchers organise periodic briefing sessions to notify relatives of any progress in the research. Paying homage to the dead through religious rituals is also important for both families and researchers, to express respect for the mummified individuals. In South Korea, different religions coexist, so the memorial ceremony for each body follows the descendants' wishes. According to the most recent available census data (UNData 2015), the majority of South Koreans are listed as "no religious affiliation", but this may be because they do not see themselves associated with a "formal" religion, but with a form of Shamanism. Other religions identified by South Koreans include Buddhism, Catholicism, "Christian", Confucian, and Protestant (UNData 2015).

Finally, in South Korea, mummy research is subject to review at an academic level. Institutional review boards grant permission for ethically-sensitive aspects of the research, for example collecting samples for genetic testing, for the destructive analysis of human remains, and ensuring that dignity and respect are maintained (Kim et al. 2017). In circumstances where invasive samples, such as endoscopic-based biopsies, are planned by researchers, and the purpose of this type of invasive sampling is permitted by the institutional review boards, permission must first be obtained from living descendants. It is possible for invasive sampling and analyses to occur, but only under restricted conditions and with consent (Kim et al. 2017). This ensures that the purpose of the research is valid and justifies the indignity of damaging the human remains.

29.3 Discussion

In the early nineteenth century, a passion for all things Egyptian, known as "Egyptomania" arose, following Napoleon's military campaigns in Egypt. During that time, people bought mummies in Egypt as souvenirs and curiosities, and brought them back to Europe and North America. Many of these mummies became part of the collections in small and large museums, but others became objects of study in curious ways. Victorians held "mummy unwrapping" parties that sometimes involved the dissection of a mummy after the meal, both of which attracted large crowds during public events in London and other cities in the UK (British Archaeological Association 1848; Anonymous 1889).

Without modern technology, however, dissection was the only method available to permit gross anatomical observations and secure samples in the early days of mummy studies (Aufderheide 2003). In order to understand the health of the individual, for example, it was necessary to conduct an autopsy on the mummy, for the macroscopic examination of internal organs and other structures, and to extract samples for detailed histological analysis. In England, the noted German anthropologist Johann Friedrich Blumenbach, autopsied Egyptian mummy bundles as early as the late eighteenth century (Taylor 2014). This was followed by other mummy unwrapping examples spanning the early nineteenth century through to the early twentieth century (Aufderheide 2003). While later autopsies focused on understanding the health and disease of ancient populations, nineteenth century research mainly aimed at understanding the features of the embalming process. Scholars involved in such activities included Italian physician Agostino Bozzi Granville, British surgeon Thomas Pettigrew, author of "A History of Egyptian Mummies", as well as British Egyptologist Margaret Murray (Aufderheide and Rodríguez-Martin 1998). Beyond the study of anthropogenic mummification, new interests developed, for example in nineteenth century Italy, researchers became particularly fascinated by the process of spontaneous tissue preservation. For instance, the abundance of mummy remains from religious buildings is commonly attributed to environmental factors, including soil chemistry (Aufderheide 2003). This resulted in additional mummy autopsies, such as those carried out by Francesco Maria Marcolini, Carlo Maggiorani, and Gaetano Corrado, on remains from Venzone, Ferentillo, and Cagliari, respectively (Ventura et al. 2005; Cardin 2014).

These studies were subsequently published between 1831 and 1899. This approach continued throughout the twentieth century, for example, the autopsy of PUM II (Pennsylvania University Museum) carried out by the Paleopathology Club in Detroit in 1973 and the Manchester Mummy Project in 1975 (Aufderheide 2003). In the final decades of the twentieth century, however, with the development of minimally-invasive and minimally-destructive techniques, the debate about the exhibition and study of human remains has slowly led to a general consensus that mummies should no longer be dissected for research purposes (Moissidou et al. 2015). It is not clear exactly when or where this shift in thinking began. Although professional association and working group guidelines in human osteology produced statements and recommendations for excavating and analysing human skeletal material in the 1990s and early 2000s (e.g. McKinley and Roberts 1993; APABE 2005), these documents did not address mummies. Yet in the specialised sub-discipline of mummy studies discussions and debates about ethical issues were common at conferences since at least 1993 (Seipel 1996; Gill-Robinson 2007). Such discussions often relied upon the code of ethics issued by the International Council of Museums, which was first released in 1986 (ICOM 2006). According to the latter, "[r]esearch on human remains and materials of sacred significance must be accomplished in a manner consistent with professional standards and take into account the interests and beliefs of the community, ethnic or religious groups from whom the objects originated, where these are known" (ICOM 2006, Sect. 2.5). Nevertheless, the first publication discussing ethics of the analysis of human mummies was printed much later (Kaufmann and Rühli 2010). As part of this, the developments in technology meant that scientists could obtain information about the sex, health and disease status, and current state of preservation through minimally-destructive means. In order to answer certain research questions, it was no longer necessary to destroy a mummy through autopsy.

As noted above in the section on Italian mummies, some researchers continue to dissect mummies. Although considered a valid investigation technique by some, dissection of human mummies is conditioned by a variety of factors, including ethical and cultural concerns, curatorial considerations, and the specific scientific scope and intention of the research (Aufderheide 2003). These often result in conflicts between dissection and conservation. To minimise potential disagreements, researchers should actively address ethical issues prior to undertaking destructive analyses. These include, among others, the right to body integrity, which does not cease with death, the violation of a body, which results in acts against the deceased's personal beliefs, the absence of informed consent by the investigated subjects, and the absence of consent in terms of cultural heritage by any stakeholder related to the remains (Kreissl Lonfat et al. 2015). The concept of "bodily integrity" refers to the notion that a person can decide on the treatment of their own body; this right does not end after death (Kreissl Lonfat et al. 2015). The issue of consent crosscuts with this concept when considering prehistoric and historic human remains. For mummies being researched, living descendants rarely exist or can seldom be identified; the South Korean cases discussed above are rare exceptions. As noted by Kreissl Lonfat et al. (2015, 1177) "[N]obody else can give consent for the use and potential destruction of historical human remains in terms of bodily integrity… consent will always be in terms of the remains being a cultural heritage, in terms of kinship or possession". Contemporarily, the matter of consent may be sought from known kin or kinship groups, such as a related Indigenous group, but this is a complex issue that researchers should consider as part of their research development plan. One example of a strong relationship between an Indigenous group providing consent and mummy researchers undertaking analyses is the study of a young male found on an icefield in Northern British Columbia (Canada) in 1999 (Beattie et al. 2000). The partially-mummified body was approximately 550-years-old. While specific ancestors could not be determined for the man, he was found in the traditional geographic territory of the Champagne and Aishinik First Nations (CAFN). The man was named *Kwäday Dän Ts'ínchi*, meaning "long ago person found" (Beattie et al. 2000, 135), and the CAFN was given the final responsibility for the "final disposition of the human remains" (Beattie et al. 2000, 133). In terms of "personal identity" after death, it is rarely possible for researchers to know the identity of a specific mummy. While it might be possible to establish details about the cultural heritage of an individual alongside specific details about the individual based on the physical examination of their body, it is exceptional to know the name and personal identity of a specific individual. A good example of this is the mummies of ancient Egypt, where information about individuals, including aspects of their life histories, may be gleaned from coffin inscriptions (Budde 2010).

Another significant advancement towards an ethically-oriented approach to mummy studies is a focus on professional attitude. Scientists dealing with human remains must respect the interests and the beliefs of the community from which the remains originate. Studies must be planned with specific research goals, and should not offend human dignity, which remains even after death. Furthermore, researchers must consider that autopsy, by definition, causes a significant loss of data that reduces the information available to future researchers (e.g. if organs have been removed). When the destructive autopsy approach is compared to the descendant-driven approach taken by South Korean researchers, the latter approach appears to be more sensible because, despite cremating the mummy in most circumstances, all dissections require ethical behaviour and demand institutional approval (Kim et al. 2017).

While not specifically addressed by the case studies in this chapter, the ethical issues associated with the rights of a group to hold informed consent to a prehistoric individual may also be relevant in mummy studies. Groups may be related by "religious affiliation, tribe, or family line" (Paradise and Andrews 2007, 266). These matters may not only cross cultural and ethical lines, but also legal lines, particularly in the complex world that is cultural property law and cultural heritage law. While anthropologists and archaeologists consider a mummy to be a person, not an object, if skirmishes arise over matters of consent between the institution or other steward of the mummy and researchers (e.g. who has the ability to give consent for analyses), the law might consider the mummy to be an object and courts might consequently apply aspects of traditional property law and rights of ownership

(Paradise and Andrews 2007). Researchers within the discipline of mummy studies must attempt to determine exactly "who is affected, the proposed analysis, and what [is] the level of responsibility … to each person or group of people" (Paradise and Andrews 2007, 266). Although these issues have most often arisen in conjunction with skeletal remains, there will, no doubt, be occasions where mummified remains occur in contexts where groups must be consulted, and research conducted with the approval of the group members. Technological developments will provide a double-edged sword for mummy studies; certainly, improved methods for minimally-destructive analyses will be discovered, but new ethical challenges will continue to arise out of each new discovery. It is impossible to anticipate what some of these challenges will be, but bioarchaeologists will, no doubt, work to develop acceptable methods for the ethical analysis of human mummies.

29.4 Conclusion

The analysis of human mummies must be considered from many perspectives. Firstly, mummies are the remains of people, and must be treated accordingly—respectfully, and in a dignified manner. Secondly, mummies, as people, are members of a community, and, as such, the values of the community must be respected, as far as is possible. This applies whether mummy researchers are dealing with family members or members of another group, such as a tribe or one that is religiously-affiliated. Thirdly, mummies are unique repositories of human biological and cultural information. While it is important to collect data as part of the analytical process, it is also vital to preserve the maximum amount of data for future generations to study, through the use of new techniques, tools, and ideas (wherever possible). In order for each of these aspects of research to be respected during the analysis of a mummy, an ethical approach must be taken by researchers. This may include developing a comprehensive research plan that includes consultation with descendants or other group members or applying minimally-invasive or minimally-destructive techniques of analysis.

Certainly, mummy studies researchers must develop strong international collaborative networks, which can only strengthen the possibility of ethically responsible mummy research. Based on the work of the authors, and the information presented in this chapter, it is clear that greater efforts need to be made to formalise and standardise mummy research protocols and practices, prepare national and international codes of ethics related to mummy research, and ensure strict penalties for researchers who fail to follow the protocols. Finally, mummy researchers need to become actively involved, both nationally and internationally, in encouraging the development of enforceable legislation for the protection of prehistoric and historic human mummies. Researchers must proactively involve communities, institutions, and, when possible, family members, in decision-making processes at all stages of the research. The recommended changes and practices would help to protect mummies and guarantee that anyone working with mummies meets high ethical standards of professional behaviour.

Based on the suggested development of new codes of ethics, and their subsequent adoption by the scientific communities, the future of mummy autopsy appears unclear. This suggests that the few researchers still involved in such activities are far too optimistic about the possibility of carrying out dissections on historic remains (Gaeta et al. 2017; Fornaciari 2018). For example, sampling internal organs should be limited to bodies that show an extensive lack of soft tissue, allowing unimpeded access to the body cavities.

In summary, there are a substantial number of ethical considerations in the study of human mummies. Thus, the authors make the following recommendations to all researchers who work with mummified human remains:

- Always remember that mummies are human beings that *must* be treated respectfully;
- Base all research on hypothesis-driven research questions, and choose research methods that cause the least amount of physical damage possible to the mummy in order to answer the research question(s);
- Remember that the use of technology is to support the research question, not simply because it is possible for a particular technique to be used;
- Form strong collaborations with the institutions that are allowing the study of the mummy, descendant family members or cultural community members of the mummy, and multidisciplinary research teams, ideally including members of the mummy's source nation and, finally;
- Be cognisant of apparently peripheral, but still related, issues, such as the display of mummies in museum exhibitions, the illicit trafficking and sale of human mummies, and the repatriation of mummies to Indigenous communities.

References

Advisory Panel on Archaeology of Burials in England [APABE]. 2005. *Guidelines for Best Practice for the Treatment of Human Remains Excavated from Christian Burial Grounds in England*. Swindon: Advisory Panel on Archaeology of Burials in England.

Allam, A.H., R.C. Thompson, L.S. Wann, et al. 2011. Atherosclerosis in Ancient Egyptian Mummies: The Horus Study. *JACC Cardiovascular Imaging* 4 (4): 315–327.

Anonymous (1889) A Mummy Unrolled: Detaels [sic] of an Interesting Exhibition in London. *The New York Times*. 30 December.

Arriaza, B.T. 1995. Chinchorro Bioarchaelogy: Chronology and Mummy Seriation. *Latin American Antiquity* 6 (1): 35–55.

Aufderheide, A.C. 2003. *The Scientific Study of Mummies*. Cambridge: Cambridge University Press.

Aufderheide, A.C., and M.L. Aufderheide. 1991. Taphonomy of Spontaneous ("Natural") Mummification with Application to the Mummies of Venzone, Italy. In *Human Paleopathology: Current Syntheses and Future Options*, ed. D.J. Ortner and A.C. Aufderheide, 79–86. Washington, D.C.: Smithsonian Institution Press.

Aufderheide, A.C., and C. Rodríguez-Martín. 1998. *The Cambridge Encyclopedia of Human Paleopathology*. Cambridge: Cambridge University Press.

Baggieri, G., S. Dipilato, E. Dragoni, et al. 2001. Paleo-Images of Mummy A4, the Infant Mummy, and Other Bodies from the Basilica of St. Francesco in Arezzo. *Paleopathology Newsletter* 113: 8–12.

Beattie, O., B. Apland, E.W. Blake, et al. 2000. The Kwäday Dän Ts'ìnchi Discovery from a Glacier in British Columbia. *Canadian Journal of Archaeology* 24: 129–147.

Beckett, R.G., U. Lohmann, and J. Bernstein. 2011. A Field Report on the Mummification Practices of the Anga of Koke Village, Central Highlands, Papua New Guinea. *Yearbook of Mummy Studies* 1: 11–17.

British Archaeological Association (1848) Museum of Antiquities. *The Times*, 14 August.

Budde, D. 2010. The Mummy and Coffins of Nes-pa-kai-schuti. In *Mummies of the World*, ed. A. Wieczorek and W. Rosendahl, 329–333. New York: Prestel.

Cardin, M. 2014. *Mummies Around the World: An Encyclopedia of Mummies in History, Religion, and Popular Culture*. Santa Barbara: ABC Clio.

Cavka, M., A. Petaros, G. Ivanac, et al. 2012. A Probable Case of Hand-Schueller-Christian's Disease in an Egyptian Mummy Revealed by CT and MR Investigations of a Dry Mummy. *Collegium Antropologicum* 36: 281–286.

Cesarani, F., M.C. Martina, A. Ferraris, et al. 2003. Whole-Body Three-Dimensional Multidectector CT of 13 Egyptian Human Mummies. *American Journal of Roentgenology* 180: 597–606.

Charlier, P. 2014. Naming the Body (or the Bones): Human Remains, Anthropological/Medical Collections, Religious Beliefs, and Restitution. *Clinical Anatomy* 27 (3): 291–295.

Ciranni, R., M. Castagna, and G. Fornaciari. 1999. Goiter in An Eighteenth-Century Sicilian Mummy. *American Journal of Physical Anthropology* 108: 427–442.

Ciranni, R., and G. Fornaciari. 2004. Juvenile Cirrhosis in a 16th Century Italian Mummy. Current Technologies in Pathology and Ancient Human Tissues. *Virchows Archiv* 445: 647–650.

Ciuffarella, L. 1998. Palynological Analyses of Resinuous Materials from the Roman Mummy of Grottarossa, Second Century AD: A New Hypothesis About the Site of Mummification. *Review of Palaeobotany and Palynology* 103: 201–208.

Conlogue, G., R. Beckett, Y. Bailey, et al. 2008. Magnetic Resonance, and Endoscopy to Examine Mummified Remains. *Journal of Radiology Nursing* 27: 5–13.

Consiglio Nazionale delle Ricerche [CNR] (2016) Codice di etica e deontologia per i ricercatori che operano nel campo dei beni e delle attività culturali. Roma: Consiglio Nazionale delle Ricerche.

Davey, J., and O.H. Drummer. 2016. The Use of Forensic Radiology in Determination of Unexplained Head Injuries in Child Mummies—Cause of Death or Mummification Damage? *Journal of Forensic Radiology and Imaging* 5: 20–25.

Day, J. 2014. 'Thinking Makes It So': Reflections on the Ethics of Displaying Egyptian Mummies. *Papers on Anthropology* 23 (1): 29–44.

Dedouit, F., A. Géraut, V. Baranov, et al. 2010. Virtual and Macroscopical Studies of Mummies—Differences or Complementarity? Report of a Natural Frozen Siberian Mummy. *Forensic Science International* 200: e7–e13.

Fornaciari, G. 1998. Italian Mummies. In *Mummies, Disease and Ancient Cultures*, ed. A. Cockburn, E. Cockburn, and T. Reyman, 266–281. Cambridge: Cambridge University Press.

Fornaciari, G. 2018. Histology of Ancient Soft Tissue Tumors. *International Journal of Paleopathology* 21: 64–76.

Fornaciari, G., V. Giuffra, F. Bortolotti, et al. 2015. A Medieval Case of Digitalis Poisoning: The Sudden Death of Cangrande Della Scala, Lord of Verona (1291–1329). *Journal of Archaeological Science* 54: 162–167.

Fornaciari, G., V. Giuffra, S. Marinozzi, et al. 2009. "Royal" Pediculosis in Renaissance Italy: Lice in the Mmmy of the King of Naples Ferdinand II of Aragon (1467–1496). *Memórias do Instituto Oswaldo Cruz* 104 (4): 671–672.

Fornaciari, G., A. Marchetti, S. Pellegrini, et al. 1999. K-Ras Mutation in the Tumor of King Ferrante I of Aragon (1431–1494) and Environmental Mutagens at the Aragonese Court of Naples. *International Journal of Osteoarchaeology* 9: 302–306.

Fornaciari, G., S. Marinozzi, V. Gazzaniga, et al. 2012. The Use of Mercury Against Pediculosis in the Renaissance: The Case of Ferdinand II of Aragon, King of Naples, 1467–96. *Medical History* 55 (1): 109–115.

Fornaciari, G., G. Zavaglia, L. Giusti, et al. 2003. Human Papillomavirus in a 16th Century Mummy. *Lancet* 362: 1160.

Frerking, C., and H. Gill-Frerking. 2017. Human Remains as Heritage: Categorisation, Legislation and Protection. *Art, Antiquity and Law* 22 (1): 49–73.

Friedrich, K.M., S. Nemec, C. Czyrny, et al. 2010. The Story of 12 Chachapoyan Mummies Through Multidetector Computed Tomography. *European Journal of Radiology* 76: 143–150.

Gaeta, R., V. Giuffra, and G. Fornaciari. 2017. Cancer in the Renaissance Court of Naples. *Lancet Oncology* 18: e432.

Gill-Frerking, H. 2014. The Impact of Historical Post-excavation Modifications on the Re-examination of Human Mummies. *Papers on Anthropology* 33 (1): 45–57.

Gill-Frerking, H. 2018. Mummification. In *The Routledge Companion to Death and Dying*, ed. C. Moreman, 295–306. New York: Routledge.

Gill-Robinson, H.C. 2007. *Ethics and Responsible Communication as Part of Evidence-Based Methods in Mummy Studies*. Paper Presented at the 6th World Congress on Mummy Studies, Teguise, Lazarote, Canary Islands, Spain, 20–24 February 2007.

Halcrow, S.E., K. Killgrove, G.R. Shug, et al. 2018. On Engagement with Anthropology: A Critical Evaluation of Skeletal and Developmental Abnormalities in the Atacama Preterm Baby and Issues of Forensic and Bioarchaeological Research Ethics. *International Journal of Paleopathology* 22: 97–100.

International Council of Museums [ICOM]. 2006. Code of Ethics for Museums. *International Journal of Cultural Property* 13 (4): 393–408.

Kaufmann, I.M., and F.J. Rühli. 2010. Without "Informed Consent"? Ethics and Ancient Mummy Research. *Journal of Medical Ethics* 36 (10): 608–613.

Kim, Y.-S., M.J. Kim, H.A. Hong, et al. 2017. The Scientific and Ethical Background of the Invasive Studies on the Korean Mummies of the Joseon Ddynasty. *Asian Journal of Paleopathology* 1: 5–11.

Kim, Y.-S., I.S. Lee, G.-U. Jung, et al. 2014. Radiological Diagnosis of Congenital Diaphragmatic Hernia in a 17th Century Korean Mummy. *PLoS One* 9 (7): e99779.

Kim, M.J., C.S. Oh, I.S. Lee, et al. 2008. Human Mummified Brain from a Medieval Tomb with a Lime-soil Mixture Barrier of the Joseon Dynasty, Korea. *International Journal of Osteoarchaeology* 18: 614–623.

Kim, S.B., J.E. Shin, S.S. Park, et al. 2006a. Endoscopic Investigations of the Internal Organs of a 15th Century Child Mummy from Yangju, Korea. *Journal of Anatomy* 209: 681–688.

Kim, M.J., S.S. Park, G.D. Bock, et al. 2006b. Medieval Mummy from Yangju. *Archaeology, Ethnology, and Anthropology of Eurasia* 4 (28): 122–129.

Kreissl Lonfat, B.M., I.M. Kaufmann, and F.J. Rühli. 2015. A Code of Ethics for Evidence-Based Research with Ancient Human Remains. *The Anatomical Record* 298: 1175–1181.

Lambert-Zazulak, P., P. Rutherford, and A.R. David. 2003. The International Ancient Egyptian Mummy Tissue Bank at the Manchester Museum as a Resource for the Palaeoepidemiological Study of Schistosomiasis. *World Archaeology* 35 (2): 223–240.

Legge 1° giugno 1939-XVII, n. 1089. Gazzetta Ufficiale (1939) No. 184(80), 8721–8728. August 8.

Lynnerup, N. 2007. Mummies. *American Journal of Physical Anthropology* (Supplement) 50: 162–190.

McKinley, J.I. and Roberts, C. 1993. *Excavation and Post-excavation Treatment of Cremated and Inhumed Human Remains*. Institute of Field Archaeologists Technical Paper Number 13. Reading: Institute of Field Archaeologists.

Moissidou, D., J. Day, D.H. Shin, et al. 2015. Invasive Versus Non Invasive Methods Applied to Mummy Research: Will this Controversy Ever Be Solved? *BioMed Research International* 192829: 1–7.

Nelson, A.J., Harris, S., Saleem, S. et al. 2018. *Maidstone EA 493—A Mummified Anencephalic Fetus from Ancient Egypt*. Paper Presented at the Extraordinary World Congress on Mummy Studies, Athanatos, Santa Cruz de Tenerife, Tenerife, Canary Islands, Spain, 21–25 May 2018.

Oh, C.S., J.H. Hong, J.B. Park, et al. 2018. From Excavation Site to Reburial Ground: A Standard Protocol and Related Ethics of Mummy Studies in South Korea. *Asian Journal of Paleopathology* 2: 1–8.

Oh, C.S., I.U. Kang, J.H. Hong, et al. 2017. Tracing the Historical Origin of Joseon Mummies Considering the Structural Similarities Between the Burial Systems of Korean and Chinese Families. *Papers on Anthropology* 26 (2): 68–81.

Öhrström, L., A. Bitzer, M. Walther, et al. 2010. Terahertz Imaging of Ancient Bone and Mummies. *American Journal of Physical Anthropology* 142: 497–500.

Ottini, L., M. Falchetti, S. Marinozzi, et al. 2011. Gene-Environment Interactions in the Pre-industrial Era: The Cancer of King Ferrante I of Aragon (1431–1494). *Human Pathology* 42 (3): 332–339.

Panzer, S., H. Gill-Frerking, W. Rosendahl, et al. 2013. Multidetector CT Investigation of the Mummy of Rosalia Lombardo (1918–1920). *Annals of Anatomy* 195: 401–408.

Panzer, S., M.R. Mc Coy, W. Hitzl, et al. 2015. Checklist and Scoring System for the Assessment of Soft Tissue Preservation in CT Examinations of Human Mummies. *PLoS ONE* 10 (8): e0133364.

Panzer, S., A.R. Zink, and D. Piombino-Mascali. 2010. Radiologic Evidence of Anthropogenic Mummification in the Capuchin Catacombs of Palermo, Sicily. *RadioGraphics* 30 (4): 1123–1132.

Paradise, J., and L. Andrews. 2007. Tales from the Crypt: Scientific, Ethical, and Legal Considerations for Biohistorical Analysis of Deceased Historical Figures. *Temple Journal of Science, Technology and Environmental Law* 26: 223–299.

Piombino-Mascali, D., H.C. Gill-Frerking, and R. Beckett. 2017. The Taphonomy of Natural Mummies. In *Taphonomy of Human Remains: Forensic Analysis of the Dead and the Depositional Environment*, ed. Schotsmans, E.M.J., Márquez-Grant, N., and Forbes, S.L., 101–119. Hoboken: John Wiley and Sons.

Piombino-Mascali, D., R. Jankauskas, A. Tamošiunas, et al. 2014. Atherosclerosis in Mummified Human Remains from Vilnius, Lithuania (18th–19th centuries AD): A Computed Tomographic Investigation. *American Journal of Human Biology* 26: 676–681.

Piombino-Mascali, D., S. Panzer, and S. Marvelli. 2011. The "Sicily Mummy Project": First Results of the Scientific Campaigns (2007–2010). In *Geschichte und Tradition der Mumifizierung in Europa: Beiträge zu einer Tagung im Museum für Sepulkralkultur*, ed. Sörries, R., 25–31. Kassel: Die Arbeitsgemeinschaft Friedhof und Denkmal e.v.

Piombino-Mascali, D., and A.R. Zink. 2011. Italy/Italia. In *The Routledge Handbook of Archaeological Human Remains and Legislation*, ed. N. Márquez-Grant and L. Fibiger, 221–232. London: Routledge.

Preucel, R.W., L.F. Williams, S.O. Espenlaub, et al. 2003. Out of Heaviness, Enlightenment: NAGPRA and the University of Pennsylvania Museum of Archaeology and Anthropology. *Expedition* 45 (3): 21–27.

Rudenko, S.I. 1970. *Frozen Tombs of Siberia: The Pazyryk Burial of Iron Age Horsemen*. Berkeley: University of California Press.

Rühli, F.J., and R.K. Chhem. 2004. Diagnostic Paleoradiology of Mummified Tissue: Interpretation and Pitfalls. *Canadian Association of Radiologists Journal* 55 (4): 218–227.

Seipel, W. 1996. Mummies and Ethics in the Museum. In *Human Mummies. A Global Survey of Their Status and the Techniques of Conservation*, eds. Spindler, K., Wilfing, H., Rastbichler-Zissernig, E. et al., 3–7. Wien: Springer.

Song, M.K., and D.H. Shin. 2014. Joseon Mummies Before Mummy Studies Began in Korea. *Papers on Anthropology* 23 (1): 135–151.

Taylor, J.H. 2014. The Collection of Egyptian Mummies in the British Museum: Overview and Potential for Study. In *Regarding the Dead. Research Publication 197*, eds. Fletcher, A., Antoine, D., and Hill, J.D., 103–114. London: The British Museum Press.

UNData (2015) *Population by Religion, Sex and Rural/Urban Residence: Republic of Korea. United Nations Statistics Division*. http://data.un.org/. Accessed 30 July 2018.

van der Plicht, J., W.A.B. van der Sanden, A.T. Aerts, et al. 2004. Dating of Bog Bodies by Means of ^{14}C–AMS. *Journal of Archaeological Science* 31: 471–491.

Ventura, L., G. Miranda, C. Mercurio, et al. 2006. Paleopatologia Delle Mummie Naturali Dell'Abruzzo Interno (Secoli XVIII–XIX). *Medicina nei Secoli* 18 (3): 875–896.

Ventura, L., A. Ranieri, G. Miranda, et al. 2005. Gaetano Corrado: A Pioneer in Ophthalmology, Forensic Medicine and…Paleopathology. *Journal of Biological Research* 80 (1): 274–275.

Verano, J.W. 2003. Mummified Trophy Heads from Peru: Diagnostic Features and Medicolegal Significance. *Journal of Forensic Sciences* 48 (3): 525–530.

Chapter 30
Concluding Remarks

Kirsty Squires, David Errickson and Nicholas Márquez-Grant

30.1 Ethical Considerations When Working with Human Remains

Throughout this volume a multitude of ethical dilemmas concerning the exhumation, analysis, curation or retention, display, and publication of human remains have been explored from a wide variety of contexts around the world. These considerations take into account not only complete skeletons, but also body parts, fragments of bones, their associated personal effects and/or artefacts, and their virtual form. The dilemmas encountered are wide ranging and with their own set of challenges, yet many of the themes raised by bioarchaeologists, anatomists, forensic anthropologists, archaeologists, museum curators, philosophers, and Indigenous communities are intertwined and recur again and again. Indeed, many of the ethical conundrums raised in this publication have been acknowledged for many years and professionals have attempted to address these concerns through the publication of best practice (e.g. DCMS 2005; BABAO 2010a, 2019a; APABE 2013, 2017; ICRC 2017) and ethical guidelines (e.g. AAPA 2003; BABAO 2010b, 2019b; WAC 2018) in recent years.

This volume has demonstrated a wide range of ethical dilemmas that must be considered when dealing with human remains; as well as how different professions in a number of countries from various geographical and chronological contexts may

K. Squires (✉)
Staffordshire University, Science Centre, Leek Road, Stoke-on-Trent ST4 2DF, UK
e-mail: Kirsty.Squires@staffs.ac.uk

D. Errickson · N. Márquez-Grant
Defence Academy of the United Kingdom, Cranfield Forensic Institute, Cranfield University, Shrivenham SN6 8LA, UK

K. Squires et al. (eds.), *Ethical Approaches to Human Remains*,
https://doi.org/10.1007/978-3-030-32926-6_30

approach the ethical issues associated with working with human remains. However, it is clear that more needs to be done. This is particularly evident in the context of repatriation, display, and curation of human remains, the exhumation and identification of victims of genocide and war, and the rise of destructive or invasive sampling, trade in human remains, social media, and 3D data. Within the past decade, there have been examples of those working in archaeology, anthropology, and the medical sciences that develop tunnel vision and are solely focused on research outputs, the acquisition of research funding, and receiving promotions and coveted awards. This focus has therefore resulted in the beliefs and opinions of the living and the deceased being overlooked. Yet, simultaneously there have been increased efforts to liaise with families to create projects for social outreach and to consider the wider educational output and impact of research. The subject of working with the dead is highly emotive (Williams and Giles 2016; Bolchini 2019). If descendants, religious and non-religious groups, or other claimant individuals, are against the exhumation and analysis of human remains, specialists must consider these on a case by case basis while respecting these beliefs and encouraging discourse on the subject with all relevant stakeholders (DeWitte 2015; Balter 2017; Schleier 2019). Successful collaboration with descendants and local communities is possible, as demonstrated in Southeast Asia (see Halcrow and colleagues, this volume) and Spain (see Renshaw, this volume). Transparency and dialogue with the living will empower the public to remember and commemorate their dead in a way they deem to be appropriate. More importantly, managing family expectations within a forensic anthropology setting, especially in human rights cases, is also important (Márquez-Grant and colleagues, this volume). Above all, no matter the geographical or temporal context, is dignity and respect for the deceased and also the relatives left behind in recent cases (see Moon, this volume).

This volume has also raised ethical issues and recommendations that have, until now, received very little if any attention in the literature; for example the use of skeletal collections in universities (see Caffell and Jakob, this volume), the ethics of working with mummified remains (see Piombino-Mascali and Gill-Frerking, this volume), the curation and the trade of human remains online (see Huffer and Charlton, this volume), and regional specific cases (e.g. see Silika and Squires, this volume). Whilst these topics are not new, these chapters will raise further awareness of the issues encountered by professionals working in these spheres. These will thus act as a starting point for future discourse and the development of further ethical guidelines at both national and international level for those working with human remains in these areas. It goes without saying that the discussions and associated recommendations presented throughout this volume can undoubtedly be used to inform future practice within bioarchaeology and forensic anthropology.

To conclude, we have summarised a number of recommendations that we think derive from the work contained in this volume.

30.2 Recommendations

This volume highlights the need for greater transparency and collaboration, not only with other specialists, but also with the public. We cannot stress enough the importance of public engagement and social outreach, and this should not be ignored. As previously mentioned, great efforts have been made to involve the public with successful results. It is often difficult to accept the opinion of others, especially if it does not match our own. Nevertheless, we must listen to other views and be open with those who may be affected by the exhumation, analysis, retention, display, and repatriation of human remains. There will be ongoing debates and different interests, but of utmost importance are the human remains themselves. Sometimes they must be protected from further damage, (e.g. due to construction and infrastructure projects) resulting in the exhumation of the dead, whilst in other cases they will be returned to their loved ones for a dignified burial. There must be better communication between scientists, those whose work involves human remains, and the public, whilst never forgetting in some known cases, the wishes of the deceased. It is universally accepted that working with human remains is a privilege (WAC 1989; BABAO 2010b). Hence, this unique opportunity must never be taken for granted.

We believe, that several recommendations can be drawn from this volume, including:

- A need for greater awareness and incorporation of ethical issues surrounding human remains in relevant university degree programmes;
- Some deliberation of ethical concerns should be raised in publications, regardless of geographical location or temporal period. These ethical considerations should be included in all publications, even if to solely indicate that the 'remains were examined with dignity and respect';
- The need to work, be open, and objective with those affected by ethical issues associated with human remains regardless of the circumstances and controversies related to a case. After all, those working with human remains not only contribute to science, but can help to reunite the dead and the living;
- Greater collaboration and transparency with organisations and claimant groups, whether bioarchaeological or forensic anthropological, that have codes of practice and guidelines to ensure the recovery, identification, repatriation, and (re)burial of individuals is ethical and considers the cultural practices and ideological beliefs of the deceased and their descendants;
- Reaching out to the wider community and raising awareness of ethical concerns. By engaging with the public, there may be a better way of overcoming the ethical challenges we face in our work;

- It is not only the human remains themselves that create this dilemma, but also any associated information, such as photographs, digital data, and recording forms. This therefore requires further reflection regarding the ownership, security, and storage of these data;
- Ethical dilemmas change over time and we must keep up with new ethical concerns, such as developments in technology, as they arise.

We are sure that whilst we may have resolved, in part, how to address the dilemmas raised in this volume, with time there will be another list of ethical issues that emerge. This will provide a new challenge and, potentially, a new book.

References

Advisory Panel on Archaeology of Burials in England [APABE]. 2013. *Science and the Dead: A Guideline for the Destructive Sampling of Archaeological Remains for Scientific Analysis.* Swindon: English Heritage and the Advisory Panel on Archaeology of Burials in England.

Advisory Panel on Archaeology of Burials in England [APABE]. 2017. *Guidelines for Best Practice for the Treatment of Human Remains Excavated from Christian Burial Grounds in England.* 2nd ed. Swindon: Advisory Panel on Archaeology of Burials in England.

American Association of Physical Anthropologists [AAPA]. 2003. *Code of Ethics of the American Association of Physical Anthropologists.* http://physanth.org/about/committees/ethics/aapa-code-ethics-and-other-ethics-resources/. Accessed 13 May 2018.

Balter, M. 2017. The Ethical Battle Over Ancient DNA. *Sapiens.* 30 March. https://www.sapiens.org/archaeology/chaco-canyon-nagpra/. Accessed 17 May 2018.

Bolchini, C. 2019. Photographing the Dead: Images in Public Mortuary Archaeology. In *The Public Archaeology of Death*, ed. H. Williams, B. Wills-Eve, and J. Osborne, 85–94. Sheffield: Equinox eBooks Publishing.

British Association for Biological Anthropology and Osteoarchaeology [BABAO] (2010a) *Code of Practice: BABAO Working-Group for Ethics and Practice.* http://www.babao.org.uk/assets/Uploads/code-of-practice.pdf. Accessed 13 May 2018.

British Association for Biological Anthropology and Osteoarchaeology [BABAO] (2010b) *Code of Ethics: BABAO Working-Group for Ethics and Practice.* http://www.babao.org.uk/assets/Uploads/code-of-ethics.pdf. Accessed 13 May 2018.

British Association for Biological Anthropology and Osteoarchaeology [BABAO]. 2019a. *BABAO Code of Practice.* https://www.babao.org.uk/assets/Uploads/BABAO-Code-of-Practice-2019.pdf. Accessed 23 November 2019.

British Association for Biological Anthropology and Osteoarchaeology [BABAO]. 2019b. *BABAO Code of Ethics.* https://www.babao.org.uk/assets/Uploads/BABAO-Code-of-Ethics-2019.pdf. Accessed 23 November 2019.

Department for Culture, Media and Sport [DCMS]. 2005. *Guidance for the Care of Human Remains in Museums.* London: Department for Culture, Media and Sport.

DeWitte, S. 2015. Bioarchaeology and Ethics of Research Using Human Skeletal Remains. *History Compass* 13(1): 10–19.

International Committee of the Red Cross [ICRC]. 2017. *Management of Dead Bodies after Disasters: A Field Manual for First Responders.* Geneva: International Committee of the Red Cross.

Schleier, C. 2019. Smithsonian Channel Explores UK Concentration Camps in 'Adolf Island'. *The Times of Israel.* 21 June. https://www.timesofisrael.com/smithsonian-channel-explores-uk-concentration-camps-in-adolf-island/. Accessed 21 June 2019.

Williams, H., and M. Giles (eds.). 2016. *Archaeologists and the Dead: Mortuary Archaeology in Contemporary Society*. Oxford: Oxford University Press.

World Archaeological Congress [WAC]. 1989. *The Vermillion Accord, Archaeological Ethics and the Treatment of the Dead: A Statement of Principles Agreed by Archaeologists and Indigenous Peoples at the World Archaeological Congress, Vermillion, USA*. http://worldarch.org/code-of-ethics/. Accessed 12 August 2018.

World Archaeology Congress [WAC]. 2018. *Code of Ethics*. http://worldarch.org/code-of-ethics/. Accessed 13 May 2018.

Correction to: Ethical Approaches to Human Remains

Kirsty Squires, David Errickson and Nicholas Márquez-Grant

Correction to:
K. Squires et al. (eds.), *Ethical Approaches to Human Remains,* https://doi.org/10.1007/978-3-030-32926-6

The original version of the book was inadvertently published with incorrect citations in Chapters 2, 6, 18, 19, 23 and Backmatter. The erratum chapters and book have been updated with the changes.

The updated versions of these chapters can be found at
https://doi.org/10.1007/978-3-030-32926-6_2
https://doi.org/10.1007/978-3-030-32926-6_6
https://doi.org/10.1007/978-3-030-32926-6_18
https://doi.org/10.1007/978-3-030-32926-6_19
https://doi.org/10.1007/978-3-030-32926-6_23
https://doi.org/10.1007/978-3-030-32926-6

K. Squires et al. (eds.), *Ethical Approaches to Human Remains*,
https://doi.org/10.1007/978-3-030-32926-6_31

Index

K. Squires et al. (eds.), *Ethical Approaches to Human Remains*,
https://doi.org/10.1007/978-3-030-32926-6

Printed by Printforce, the Netherlands